ECONOMIC ANALYSIS
AND POLICY

PRENTICE-HALL INTERNATIONAL, INC., *London*
PRENTICE-HALL OF AUSTRALIA, PTY., LTD., *Sydney*
PRENTICE-HALL OF CANADA, LTD., *Toronto*
PRENTICE-HALL FRANCE, S.A.R.L., *Paris*
PRENTICE-HALL OF JAPAN, INC., *Tokyo*
PRENTICE-HALL DE MEXICO, S.A., *Mexico City*

MYRON L. JOSEPH
*Associate Professor of Economics
and Head, Department of Industrial Management
Carnegie Institute of Technology*

NORTON C. SEEBER
*Assistant Professor of Economics
Carnegie Institute of Technology*

GEORGE LELAND BACH
*Maurice Falk Professor of Economics and Social Science
Carnegie Institute of Technology*

ECONOMIC ANALYSIS AND POLICY

Background Readings for Current Issues

PRENTICE-HALL, INC.
Englewood Cliffs, New Jersey

PREFACE

Economics seems a lively science to students when they can see its relevance to important issues of concern to them. This volume of readings has been designed especially to broaden students' understanding of their economic evironment and to pose important controversial problems of public policy to which they can apply the tools of economic analysis. It is intended to supplement the usual coverage of elementary texts in these ways, rather than by repeating or advancing further the theory presented in the leading texts. It is focused on giving students the material for real, lively problem-solving experience on the big economic problems of our time. Above all, we have tried to help build a foundation that students will find useful as they do their own thinking on major economic issues five or ten years from now, long after they have escaped the threat of the final examination.

The selections included are not brief paragraphs or excerpts. Each is long enough to convey the substance and "feel" of the position being stated by the author, and really can be understood and analyzed by the student. Our purpose is to help students achieve thoroughness and depth of understanding—not to provide a superficial, passing brush with historical backgrounds and the issues at stake.

There are several good readings volumes already available. We believe this one differs significantly in the following respects.

(1) The selections are chosen especially to provide the basis for independent student problem-solving experience on such big, relatively unstructured problems as "automation," disarmament, inflation, the use of wage-price guideposts, and government control of business.

(2) There are several readings on the political, sociological, and organizational aspects of the environment, within which real-world solutions to economic problems must be reached. For example:

   (a) Selections on the plight of the unemployed worker and the aged poor.

   (b) President (then Senator) Kennedy's account of the pressures facing a legislator in his consideration of economic legislation.

   (c) Accounts by Alfred Hayes, President of the Federal Reserve Bank of New York, and by two economists of the actual process of monetary policy formation and of the considerations taken into account in this process.

v

(3) Several selections provide concrete historical background for current economic problems, enabling students to consider current issues against the background of events and attitudes that have produced them. For example:

(a) The sit-down strikes and picket lines of the 1930's still help explain the attitudes and behavior of many union leaders and members today.

(b) The Smoot-Hawley tariff issues of the 1920's illuminate the pro- and anti-free trade arguments of the 1960's.

(c) The unemployment and desperation of the great depression of the 1930's were crucial in shaping modern attitudes toward economic stabilization and social security policies.

(d) The financial panic and bank holiday of those depression days provide a vivid backdrop for current monetary and financial problems.

We have included historical readings on all of these subjects, covering both the economic and non-economic forces at work.

(4) To illuminate and clarify the big public policy issues of today, we have included directly conflicting statements by economists, political leaders, and other observers. These are intended not only to sharpen the economic issues, but also to help students understand the deep cross-currents often involved in economics, how economic analysis is used by different people, and the interactions of economic and non-economic forces in actual policy-making process. Examples are:

(a) The conflicting arguments of Secretary Ribicoff and the American Medical Association on "Medicare."

(b) The opposing views of J. K. Galbraith and of Ernest van den Haag, a strong conservative, on the expansion of the range of social services provided by government.

We believe this volume will be a significant aid to teachers who want to supplement a solid, analytically-oriented text with readings that provide rich background materials for a sample of big policy problems. These readings should help to crystallize the issues with which the student must grapple if, by applying economic analysis, he is to reach his own solutions on complex major real-world issues.

The complex task of integrating the activities of three authors working with hundreds of possible readings was deftly managed by our secretary, Frances Gibson. Sally Rowley and Ruth Corrigan, in the Carnegie Institute of Technology Library, were invaluable in helping to assemble the materials in the volume.

M. L. J.
N. C. S.
G. L. B.

CONTENTS

B.

PRICE INDEXES AND INFLATION

C.

DEPRESSION

D.

CONSUMPTION PATTERNS

E.

MONETARY POLICY

E.

FISCAL POLICY

G.

DEBT

P A R T   T H R E E

**MARKETS, THE PRICE SYSTEM, AND THE
ALLOCATION OF RESOURCES, 173**

A.

THE MARKET SYSTEM

B.

BUSINESS PRICE-SETTING AND PROFIT GOALS

C.

BIG BUSINESS AND GOVERNMENT POLICY

D.

THE FARM PROBLEM

P A R T   F O U R

THE DISTRIBUTION OF INCOME, 267

PART FIVE
THE PUBLIC ECONOMY, 317

PART SIX
THE INTERNATIONAL ECONOMY, 361

A.

INTERNATIONAL TRADE

ECONOMIC ANALYSIS
AND POLICY

PART ONE

THE FOUNDATIONS OF ECONOMIC ANALYSIS

1. Economic Generalizations or Laws

Alfred Marshall

What is economics about? How should it be studied? Is it a science in the same sense that the natural sciences are? The famous English economist Alfred Marshall presents the classical view that "economics is a study of mankind in the ordinary business of life," and discusses its relation to other scientific fields.

2. The Methodology of Positive Economics

Milton Friedman

In the previous selection Alfred Marshall gave one view on the nature and role of economics. Here a noted contemporary American economist argues that economics must be a "positive" science; it should be objective in the same sense other sciences are, and the real test of a good economic theory is its ability to predict actual economic behavior.

3. The Three Solutions to the Economic Problem

Robert Heilbroner

What to produce and how to divide up the goods and services produced—these are the key economic questions faced by all societies. Professor Heilbroner describes three broad approaches to the allocation of resources and distribution of products.

4. Can We Afford Our National Goals?

Leland Hazard

We Americans have many partially conflicting economic goals. Professor Hazard estimates the costs of attaining the well-publicized set of goals for America which were suggested by President Eisenhower's 1960 Commission on National Goals.

1 ECONOMIC GENERALIZATIONS OR LAWS

Alfred Marshall

Alfred Marshall was perhaps the most influential economist in the world during the last part of the nineteenth and early part of the twentieth century. He was Professor of Economics at Cambridge University.

Political Economy or Economics is a study of mankind in the ordinary business of life; it examines that part of individual and social action which is most closely connected with the attainment and with the use of the material requisites of wellbeing.

Thus it is on the one side a study of wealth; and on the other, and more important side, a part of the study of man. For man's character has been moulded by his every-day work, and the material resources which he thereby procures, more than by any other influence unless it be that of his religious ideals; and the two great forming agencies of the world's history have been the religious and the economic. Here and there the ardour of the military or the artistic spirit has been for a while predominant: but religious and economic influences have nowhere been displaced from the front rank even for a time; and they have nearly always been more important than all others put together. Religious motives are more intense than economic, but their direct action seldom extends over so large a part of life. For the business by which a person earns his livelihood generally fills his thoughts during by far the greater part of those hours in which his mind is at its best; during

them his character is being formed by the way in which he uses his faculties in his work, by the thoughts and the feelings which it suggests, and by his relations to his associates in work, his employers or his employees.

*   *   *

The advantage which economics has over other branches of social science appears then to arise from the fact that its special field of work gives rather larger opportunities for exact methods than any other branch. It concerns itself chiefly with those desires, aspirations and other affections of human nature, the outward manifestations of which appear as incentives to action in such a form that the force or quantity of the incentives can be estimated and measured with some approach to accuracy; and which therefore are in some degree amenable to treatment by scientific machinery. An opening is made for the methods and the tests of science as soon as the force of a person's motives—*not* the motives themselves—can be approximately measured by the sum of money, which he will just give up in order to secure a desired satisfac-

From *Principles of Economics,* 8th ed. (New York: The Macmillan Co., 1920), pp. 1–2, 15, 31–33, 36–37. Reprinted by permission.

tion; or again by the sum which is just required to induce him to undergo a certain fatigue.

It is essential to note that the economist does not claim to measure any affection of the mind in itself, or directly; but only indirectly through its effect. No one can compare and measure accurately against one another even his own mental states at different times: and no one can measure the mental states of another at all except indirectly and conjecturally by their effects.

*   *   *

It is the business of economics, as of almost every other science, to collect facts, to arrange and interpret them, and to draw inferences from them. "Observation and description, definition and classification are the preparatory activities. But what we desire to reach thereby is a knowledge of the interdependence of economic phenomena. . . . Induction and deduction are both needed for scientific thought as the right and left foot are both needed for walking." The methods required for this twofold work are not peculiar to economics; they are the common property of all sciences.

*   *   *

Let us then consider more closely the nature of economic laws, and their limitations. Every cause has a tendency to produce some definite result if nothing occurs to hinder it. Thus gravitation tends to make things fall to the ground: but when a balloon is full of gas lighter than air, the pressure of the air will make it rise in spite of the tendency of gravitation to make it fall. The law of gravitation states how any two things attract one another; how they tend to move towards one another, and will move towards one another if nothing interferes to prevent them. The law of gravitation is therefore a statement of tendencies.

It is a very exact statement—so exact that mathematicians can calculate a Nautical Almanac, which will show the moments at which each satellite of Jupiter will hide itself behind Jupiter. They make this calculation for many years beforehand; and navigators take it to sea, and use it in finding out where they are. Now there are no economic tendencies which act as steadily and can be measured as exactly as gravitation can: and consequently there are no laws of economics which can be compared for precision with the law of gravitation.

But let us look at a science less exact than astronomy. The science of the tides explains how the tide rises and falls twice a day under the action of the sun and the moon: how there are strong tides at new and full moon, and weak tides at the moon's first and third quarter; and how the tide running up into a closed channel, like that of the Severn, will be very high; and so on. Thus, having studied the lie of the land and the water all round the British isles, people can calculate beforehand when the tide will *probably* be at its highest on any day at London Bridge or at Gloucester; and how high it will be there. They have to use the word *probably,* which the astronomers do not need to use when talking about the eclipses of Jupiter's satellites. For, though many forces act upon Jupiter and his satellites, each one of them acts in a definite manner which can be predicted beforehand: but no one knows enough about the weather to be able to say beforehand how it will act. A heavy downpour of rain in the upper Thames valley, or a strong north-east wind in the German Ocean, may make the tides at London Bridge differ a good deal from what had been expected.

The laws of economics are to be compared with the laws of the tides, rather than with the simple and exact law of gravitation. For the actions of men are so various and uncertain, that the best statement of tendencies, which we can make in a science of human conduct, must needs be inexact and faulty. This might be urged as a reason against making any statements at all on the subject; but that would be almost to abandon life. Life is human conduct, and the thoughts and emotions that grow up around it. By the fundamental impulses of our nature we all—high and low, learned and unlearned—are in our several degrees constantly striving to understand the courses of human action, and to shape them for our purposes, whether selfish or unselfish, whether noble or ignoble. And since we *must* form to ourselves some notions of the tendencies of human action, our choice is between forming those notions carelessly and forming them carefully. The harder the task, the greater the need for steady patient inquiry; for turning to account the experience, that has been reaped by the more advanced physical sciences; and for framing as best we can well thought-out estimates, or provisional laws, of the tendencies of human action.

*   *   *

Economic laws, or statements of economic tendencies, are those social laws which relate to branches of conduct in which the strength of the motives chiefly concerned can be measured by a money price.

There is thus no hard and sharp line of division between those social laws which are, and those which are not, to be regarded also as economic laws. For there is a continuous gradation from social laws concerned almost exclusively with motives that can be measured by price, to social laws in which such motives have little place; and which are therefore generally as much less precise and exact than economic laws, as those are than the laws of the more exact physical sciences.

*   *   *

It is sometimes said that the laws of economics are "hypothetical." Of course, like every other science, it undertakes to study the effects which will be produced by certain causes, not absolutely, but subject to the condition that *other things are equal,* and that the causes are able to work out their effects undisturbed. Almost every scientific doctrine, when carefully and formally stated, will be found to contain some proviso to the effect that other things are equal: the action of the causes in question is supposed to be isolated; certain effects are attributed to them, but only *on the hypothesis* that no cause is permitted to enter except those distinctly allowed for. It is true however that the condition that time must be allowed for causes to produce their effects is a source of great difficulty in economics. For meanwhile the material on which they work, and perhaps even the causes themselves, may have changed; and the tendencies which are being described will not have a sufficiently "long run" in which to work themselves out fully.

*   *   *

Though economic analysis and general reasoning are of wide application, yet every age and every country has its own problems; and every change in social conditions is likely to require a new development of economic doctrines.

2 THE METHODOLOGY OF POSITIVE ECONOMICS

Milton Friedman

Milton Friedman is Professor of Economics at the University of Chicago.

In his admirable book on *The Scope and Method of Political Economy* John Neville Keynes distinguishes among "a *positive science* . . . [,] a body of systematized knowledge concerning what is; a *normative* or *regulative science* . . . [,] a body of systematized knowledge discussing criteria of what ought to be . . . ; an *art* . . . [,] a system of rules for the attainment of a given end"; comments that "confusion between them is common and has been the source of many mischievous errors"; and urges the importance of "recognizing a distinct positive science of political economy.

*　　*　　*

Positive economics is in principle independent of any particular ethical position or normative judgments. As Keynes says, it deals with "what is," not with "what ought to be." Its task is to provide a system of generalizations that can be used to make correct predictions about the consequences of any change in circumstances. Its performance is to be judged by the precision, scope, and conformity with experience of the predictions it yields. In short, positive economics is, or can be, an "objective" science, in precisely the same sense as any of the physical sciences. Of course, the fact that economics deals with the interrelations of human beings, and that the investigator is himself part of the subject matter being investigated in a more intimate sense than in the physical sciences, raises special difficulties in achieving objectivity at the same time that it provides the social scientist with a class of data not available to the physical scientist. But neither the one nor the other is, in my view, a fundamental distinction between the two groups of sciences.

Normative economics and the art of economics, on the other hand, cannot be independent of positive economics. Any policy conclusion necessarily rests on a prediction about the consequences of doing one thing rather than another, a prediction that must be based—implicitly or explicitly—on positive economics. There is not, of course, a one-to-one relation between policy conclusions and the conclusions of positive economics; if there were, there would be no separate normative science. Two individuals may agree on the consequences of a particular piece of legislation. One may regard them as desirable on balance and so favor the legislation; the other, as undesirable and so oppose the legislation.

*　　*　　*

The ultimate goal of a positive science is the development of a "theory" or "hypothesis" that yields valid and meaningful (i.e., not truistic) predictions about phenomena not yet observed. Such a theory is, in general, a complex intermixture of two elements. In part, it is a "language" designed to

Excerpts reprinted from *Essays in Positive Economics* by Milton Friedman, by permission of the University of Chicago Press; copyright 1953 by the University of Chicago.

promote "systematic and organized methods of reasoning." In part, it is a body of substantive hypotheses designed to abstract essential features of complex reality.

Viewed as a language, theory has no substantive content; it is a set of tautologies. Its function is to serve as a filing system for organizing empirical material and facilitating our understanding of it; and the criteria by which it is to be judged are those appropriate to a filing system. Are the categories clearly and precisely defined? Are they exhaustive? Do we know where to file each individual item, or is there considerable ambiguity? Is the system of headings and subheadings so designed that we can quickly find an item we want, or must we hunt from place to place? Are the items we shall want to consider jointly filed together? Does the filing system avoid elaborate cross-references?

*   *   *

Viewed as a body of substantive hypotheses, theory is to be judged by its predictive power for the class of phenomena which it is intended to "explain." Only factual evidence can show whether it is "right" or "wrong" or, better, tentatively "accepted" as valid or "rejected." As I shall argue at greater length below, the only relevant test of the *validity* of a hypothesis is comparison of its predictions with experience. The hypothesis is rejected if its predictions are contradicted ("frequently" or more often than predictions from an alternative hypothesis); it is accepted if its predictions are not contradicted; great confidence is attached to it if it has survived many opportunities for contradiction. Factual evidence can never "prove" a hypothesis; it can only fail to disprove it, which is what we generally mean when we say, somewhat inexactly, that the

hypothesis has been "confirmed" by experience.

To avoid confusion, it should perhaps be noted explicitly that the "predictions" by which the validity of a hypothesis is tested need not be about phenomena that have not yet occurred, that is, need not be forecasts of future events; they may be about phenomena that have occurred but observations on which have not yet been made or are not known to the person making the prediction. For example, a hypothesis may imply that such and such must have happened in 1906, given some other known circumstances. If a search of the records reveals that such and such did happen, the prediction is confirmed; if it reveals that such and such did not happen, the prediction is contradicted.

The validity of a hypothesis in this sense is not by itself a sufficient criterion for choosing among alternative hypotheses. Observed facts are necessarily finite in number; possible hypotheses, infinite. If there is one hypothesis that is consistent with the available evidence, there are always an infinite number that are. . . . The choice among alternative hypotheses equally consistent with the available evidence must to some extent be arbitrary, though there is general agreement that relevant considerations are suggested by the criteria "simplicity" and "fruitfulness," themselves notions that defy completely objective specification. A theory is "simpler" the less the initial knowledge needed to make a prediction within a given field of phenomena; it is more "fruitful" the more precise the resulting prediction, the wider the area within which the theory yields predictions, and the more additional lines for further research it suggests.

*   *   *

Unfortunately, we can seldom test particular predictions in the social sciences by experiments explicitly designed to eliminate what are judged to be the most important disturbing influences. Generally, we must rely on evidence cast up by the "experiments" that happen to occur. The inability to conduct so-called "controlled experiments" does not, in my view, reflect a basic difference between the social and physical sciences both because it is not peculiar to the social sciences—witness astronomy—and because the distinction between a controlled experiment and uncontrolled experience is at best one of degree. No experiment can be completely controlled, and every experience is partly controlled, in the sense that some disturbing influences are relatively constant in the course of it.

*   *   *

A [. . .] serious effect of the difficulty of testing economic hypotheses by their predictions is to foster misunderstanding of the role of empirical evidence in theoretical work. Empirical evidence is vital at two different, though closely related, stages: in constructing hypotheses and in testing their validity. Full and comprehensive evidence on the phenomena to be generalized or "explained" by a hypothesis, besides its obvious value in suggesting new hypotheses, is needed to assure that a hypothesis explains what it sets out to explain—that its implications for such phenomena are not contradicted in advance by experience that has already been observed. Given that the hypothesis is consistent with the evidence at hand, its further testing involves deducing from it new facts capable of being observed but not previously known and checking these deduced facts against additional empirical evidence. For this test to be relevant, the deduced facts must be about the class of phenomena the hypothesis is designed to explain; and they must be well enough defined so that observation can show them to be wrong.

*   *   *

Misunderstanding about this apparently straightforward process centers on the phrase "the class of phenomena the hypothesis is designed to explain." The difficulty in the social sciences of getting new evidence for this class of phenomena and of judging its conformity with the implications of the hypothesis makes it tempting to suppose that other, more readily available, evidence is equally relevant to the validity of the hypothesis—to suppose that hypotheses have not only "implications" but also "assumptions" and that the conformity of these "assumptions" to "reality" is a test of the validity of the hypothesis *different from* or *additional to* the test by implications. This widely held view is fundamentally wrong and productive of much mischief. Far from providing an easier means for sifting valid from invalid hypotheses, it only confuses the issue, promotes misunderstanding about the significance of empirical evidence for economic theory, produces a misdirection of much intellectual effort devoted to the development of positive economics, and impedes the attainment of consensus on tentative hypotheses in positive economics.

In so far as a theory can be said to have "assumptions" at all, and in so far as their "realism" can be judged independently of the validity of predictions, the relation between the significance of a theory and the "realism" of its "assumptions" is almost the opposite of that suggested by the view under criticism. Truly important and significant hypotheses will be found to have "assumptions" that are wildly inaccurate descriptive representations of reality, and, in general, the more significant the theory, the more unrealistic the assumptions (in this sense).[1] The reason is simple. A hypothesis is important if it "explains" much by little, that is, if it abstracts the common and crucial elements from the mass of complex and detailed circumstances surrounding the phenomena to be explained and permits valid predictions on the basis of them alone. To be important, therefore, a hypothesis must be descriptively false in its assumptions; it takes account of, and accounts for, none of the many other attendant circumstances, since its very success shows them to be irrelevant for the phenomena to be explained.

To put this point less paradoxically, the relevant question to ask about the "assumptions" of a theory is not whether they are descriptively "realistic," for they never are, but whether they are sufficiently good approximations for the purpose in hand. And this question can be answered only by seeing whether the theory works, which means whether it yields sufficiently accurate predictions. The two supposedly independent tests thus reduce to one test.

* * *

Economics as a positive science is a body of tentatively accepted generalizations about economic phenomena that can be used to predict the consequences of changes in circumstances. Progress in expanding this body of generalizations, strengthening our confidence in their validity, and improving the accuracy of the predictions they yield is hindered not only by the limitations of human ability that impede all search for knowledge but also by ob-

stacles that are especially important for the social sciences in general and economics in particular, though by no means peculiar to them. Familiarity with the subject matter of economics breeds contempt for special knowledge about it. The importance of its subject matter to everyday life and to major issues of public policy impedes objectivity and promotes confusion between scientific analysis and normative judgment. The necessity of relying on uncontrolled experience rather than on controlled experiment makes it difficult to produce dramatic and clear-cut evidence to justify the acceptance of tentative hypotheses. Reliance on uncontrolled experience does not affect the fundamental methodological principle that a hypothesis can be tested only by the conformity of its implications or predictions with observable phenomena; but it does render the task of testing hypotheses more difficult and gives greater scope for confusion about the methodological principles involved. More than other scientists, social scientists need to be self-conscious about their methodology.

One confusion that has been particularly rife and has done much damage is confusion about the role of "assumptions" in economic analysis. A meaningful scientific hypothesis or theory typically asserts that certain forces are, and other forces are not, important in understanding a particular class of phenomena. It is frequently convenient to present such a hypothesis by stating that the phenomena it is desired to predict behave in the world of observation *as if* they occurred in a hypothetical and highly simplified world containing only the forces that the hypothesis asserts to be important. In general, there is more than one way to formulate such a description—more than one set of "assumptions" in terms of which the theory can be presented. The

---

[1] The converse of the proposition does not of course hold: assumptions that are unrealistic (in this sense) do not guarantee a significant theory.

choice among such alternative assumptions is made on the grounds of the resulting economy, clarity, and precision in presenting the hypothesis; their capacity to bring indirect evidence to bear on the validity of the hypothesis by suggesting some of its implications that can be readily checked with observation or by bringing out its connection with other hypotheses dealing with related phenomena; and similar considerations.

Such a theory cannot be tested by comparing its "assumptions" directly with "reality." Indeed, there is no meaningful way in which this can be done. Complete "realism" is clearly un-

attainable, and the question whether a theory is realistic "enough" can be settled only by seeing whether it yields predictions that are good enough for the purpose in hand or that are better than predictions from alternative theories. Yet the belief that a theory can be tested by the realism of its assumptions independently of the accuracy of its predictions is widespread and the source of much of the perennial criticism of economic theory as unrealistic. Such criticism is largely irrelevant, and, in consequence, most attempts to reform economic theory that it has stimulated have been unsuccessful.

*   *   *

3   THE THREE SOLUTIONS TO THE ECONOMIC PROBLEM

Robert Heilbroner

Robert Heilbroner is a member of the faculty at the New School for Social Research and a well-known free lance writer.

THE THREE SOLUTIONS TO THE ECONOMIC PROBLEM

Thus to the economist, society presents itself in an unaccustomed aspect. He sees it essentially as an elaborate mechanism for survival, a mechanism for accomplishing the complicated tasks of production and distribution necessary for social continuity.

But the economist sees something else as well, something which at first seems quite astonishing. Looking not only over the diversity of contemporary societies, but back over the sweep of all history, he sees that man has succeeded in solving the production and distribution problems in but three ways. That is, within the enormous diversity of the actual social institutions which

guide and shape the economic process, the economist divines but three overarching *types* of systems which separately or in combination enable humankind to solve its economic challenge. These great systemic types can be called economies run by Tradition, economies run by Command, and economies run by the Market. Let us briefly see what is characteristic of each.

Tradition

Perhaps the oldest and, until a very few years ago, by far the most generally prevalent way of solving the eco-

From Robert L. Heilbroner, *The Making of Economic Society,* copyright 1962 by R. L. Heilbroner, pp. 9–17. Reprinted by permission of Prentice-Hall, Inc., publisher.

nomic challenge has been tradition. It has been a mode of social organization in which both production and distribution were based on procedures devised in the distant past and rigidified as the outcome of a long process of historic trial and error.

Societies based on tradition solve the economic problems very manageably. First, they deal with the production problem—the problem of assuring that the needful tasks will be done—by assigning the jobs of fathers to their sons. Thus a hereditary chain assures that skills will be passed along and that the on-going jobs will be staffed from generation to generation. In ancient Egypt, wrote Adam Smith, the first great economist, "every man was bound by a principle of religion to follow the occupation of his father and was supposed to commit the most horrible sacrilege if he changed it for another." [1] And it was not merely in antiquity that tradition preserved a productive orderliness within society. In our own Western culture, until the fifteenth or sixteenth centuries, the hereditary allocation of tasks was also the main stabilizing force within society. Although there was some movement from country to town and from occupation to occupation, birth usually determined one's role in life. One was born to the soil or to a trade; and on the soil or within the trade, one followed in the footsteps of one's forebears.

Thus tradition has been the stabilizing and impelling force behind a great repetitive cycle of society, assuring that society's work would be done each day very much as it had been done in the past. Even today, among the less industrialized nations of the world, tradition continues to play this immense organizing role. In India, until very recently at least, one was born to a caste which had its own occupation. "Better thine own work is, though done with fault," preached the Bhagavad-Gita, the great philosophic moral poem of India, "than doing other's work, even excellently."

Tradition not only provides a solution to the production problem of society, but it also regulates the distribution problem. Take, for example, the Bushmen of the Kalahari Desert in South Africa who depend for their livelihood on hunting prowess. Elizabeth Marshall Thomas, a sensitive observer of these peoples, reports on the manner in which tradition solves the problem of distributing their kill.

The gemsbok has vanished . . . Gai owned two hind legs and a front leg, Tsetchwe had meat from the back, Ukwane had the other front leg, his wife had one of the feet and the stomach, the young boys had lengths of intestine. Twikwe had received the head and Dasina the udder.

It seems very unequal when you watch Bushmen divide the kill, yet it is their system, and in the end no person eats more than any other. That day Ukwane gave Gai still another piece because Gai was his relation, Gai gave meat to Dasina because she was his wife's mother . . . No one, of course, contested Gai's large share, because he had been the hunter and by their law that much belonged to him. No one doubted that he would share his large amount with others, and they were not wrong, of course; he did. [2]

The manner in which tradition can divide a social product may be, as the illustration shows, very subtle and ingenious. It may also be very crude and, by our standards, harsh. Tradition has often allocated to women, in nonindustrial societies, the most meager portion of the social product. But however much tradition may accord with or de-

[1] *The Wealth of Nations* (New York: Modern Library, Inc., 1937), p. 62.

[2] *The Harmless People* (New York: Alfred A. Knopf, Inc., 1959), pp. 49–50.

part from our accustomed moral views, we must see that it is a workable method of dividing society's production.

Traditional solutions to the economic problems of production and distribution are most commonly encountered in primitive agrarian or nonindustrial societies, where in addition to serving an economic function, the unquestioning acceptance of the past provides the necessary perseverance and endurance to confront harsh destinies. Yet even in our own society, tradition continues to play a role in solving the economic problem. It plays its smallest role in determining the distribution of our own social output, although the persistence of such traditional payments as tips to waiters, allowances to minors, or bonuses based on length of service are all vestiges of old traditional ways of distributing goods, as is the differential between men's and women's pay for equal work.

More important is the place which tradition continues to hold, even in America, as a means of solving the production problem—that is, in allocating the performance of tasks. Much of the actual process of selecting an employment in our society is heavily influenced by tradition. We are all familiar with families in which sons follow their fathers into a profession or a business. On a somewhat broader scale, tradition also dissuades us from certain employments. Sons of American middle-class families, for example, do not usually seek factory work, even though factory jobs may pay better than office jobs, because "bluecollar employment" is not in the middle-class tradition.

Even in our society, which is clearly not a "traditional" one, custom provides an important mechanism for solving the economic problem. But now we must note one very impor-

tant consequence of the mechanism of tradition. *Its solution to production and distribution is a static one.* A society which follows the path of tradition in its regulation of economic affairs does so at the expense of large-scale rapid social and economic change.

Thus the economy of a Bedouin tribe or a Burmese village is in few essential respects changed today from what it was a hundred or even a thousand years ago. The bulk of the peoples living in tradition-bound societies repeat, in the daily patterns of their economic life, much of the routines which characterized them in the distant past. Such societies may rise and fall, wax and wane, but external events—war, climate, political adventures and misadventures—are mainly responsible for their changing fortunes. Internal, self-generated economic change is but a small factor in the history of most tradition-bound states. Tradition solves the economic problem, but it does so at the cost of economic progress.

Command

A second manner of solving the problem of economic continuity also displays an ancient lineage. This is the method of imposed authority, of economic command. It is a solution based not so much on the perpetuation of a viable system by the changeless reproduction of its ways, as on the organization of a system according to the orders of an economic commander-in-chief.

Not infrequently we find this authoritarian method of economic control superimposed upon a traditional social base. Thus the Pharaohs of Egypt exerted their economic dictates above the timeless cycle of traditional agricultural practice on which the Egyptian economy was based. By their orders, the supreme rulers of Egypt brought into being the enormous economic effort which built the pyramids, the temples, the roads. Herodotus, the Greek historian, tells us how the Pharaoh Cheops organized the task.

[He] ordered all Egyptians to work for himself. Some, accordingly, were appointed to draw stones from the quarries in the Arabian mountains down to the Nile, others he ordered to receive the stones when transported in vessels across the river. . . . And they worked to the number of a hundred thousand men at a time, each party during three months. The time during which the people were thus harrassed by toil lasted ten years on the road which they constructed, and along which they drew the stones; a work, in my opinion, not much less than the Pyramid.[3]

The mode of authoritarian economic organization was by no means confined to ancient Egypt. We encounter it in the despotisms of medieval and classical China which produced, among other things, the colossal Great Wall or in the slave labor by which many of the great public works of ancient Rome were built. Of course, we find it today in the dictates of the communist economic authorities. In less drastic form, we find it also in our own society, for example, in the form of *taxes*—that is, in the preemption of part of our income by the public authorities for public purposes.

Economic command, like tradition, offers solutions to the twin problems of production and distribution. In times of crises, such as war or famine, it may be the only way in which a society can organize its manpower or distribute its goods effectively. Even in America, we commonly declare martial law when an area has been devastated by a great natural disaster. On such occasions we may press people into service, requisition homes, impose curbs on the use of

private property such as cars, or even limit the amount of food a family may consume.

Quite aside from its obvious utility in meeting emergencies, command has a further usefulness in solving the economic problem. Unlike tradition, the exercise of command has no inherent effect of slowing down economic change. Indeed, the exercise of authority is the most powerful instrument society has for *enforcing economic change*. One example is, of course, the radical alterations in the systems of production and distribution which authority has effected in modern China or Russia. But again, even in our own society, it is sometimes necessary for economic authority to intervene into the normal flow of economic life to speed up or bring about change. The government may, for instance, utilize its tax receipts to lay down a network of roads which brings a backwater community into the flux of active economic life. It may undertake an irrigation system which will dramatically change the economic life of a vast region. It may very considerably affect the distribution of income among social classes.

To be sure, economic command which is exercised within the framework of a democratic political process is very different from that which is exercised by strong-arm methods: there is an immense social distance between a tax system controlled by Congress and outright expropriation or labor impressment by a supreme and unchallengeable ruler. Yet whilst the means may be much milder, the *mechanism* is the same. In both cases, command diverts economic effort toward goals chosen by a higher authority. In both cases it interferes with the existing order of production and distribution, to create a new order ordained from "above."

---

[3] *Histories,* trans. Cary (London: 1901), Book II, p. 124.

This does not in itself serve to commend or condemn the exercise of command. The new order imposed by the authorities may offend or please our sense of social justice, just as it may improve or lessen the economic efficiency of society. Clearly, command can be an instrument of a democratic as well as of a totalitarian will. There is no implicit moral judgment to be passed on this second of the great mechanisms of economic control. Rather, it is important to note that no society—certainly no modern society—is without its elements of command, just as none is devoid of the influence of tradition. If tradition is the great brake on social and economic change, so economic command can be the great spur to change. As mechanisms for assuring the successful solution to the economic problem, both serve their purposes, both have their uses and their drawbacks. Between them, tradition and command have accounted for most of the long history of man's economic efforts to cope with his environment and with himself. The fact that human society *has* survived is testimony to their effectiveness.

The Market

There is also a third solution to the economic problem—that is, a third solution to the problem of maintaining socially viable patterns of production and distribution. This is the *market organization of society,* an organization which, in truly remarkable fashion, allows society to insure its own provisioning with a minimum of recourse either to tradition or command.

Because we live in a market-run society, we are apt to take for granted the puzzling—indeed, almost paradoxical—nature of the market solution to the economic problem. But assume for a moment that we could act as economic

advisers to a society which had not yet decided on its mode of economic organization. Suppose, for instance, that we were called on to act as consultants to one of the new nations emerging from the continent of Africa.

We could imagine the leaders of such a nation saying, "We have always experienced a highly tradition-bound way of life. Our men hunt and cultivate the fields and perform their tasks as they are brought up to do by the force of example and the instruction of their elders. We know, too, something of what can be done by economic command. We are prepared, if necessary, to sign an edict making it compulsory for many of our men to work on community projects for our national development. Tell us, is there any other way we can organize our society so that it will function successfully—or better yet, more successfully?"

Suppose we answered, "Yes, there is another way. Organize your society along the lines of a market economy."

"Very well," say the leaders. "What do we then tell people to do? How do we assign them to their various tasks?"

"That's the very point," we would answer. "In a market economy no one is assigned to any task. The very idea of a market society is that each person is allowed to decide for himself what to do."

There is consternation among the leaders. "You mean there is *no* assignment of some men to mining and others to cattle raising? No manner of selecting some for transportation and others for cloth weaving? You leave this to people to decide for themselves? But what happens if they do not decide correctly? What happens if no one volunteers to go into the mines, or if no one offers himself as a railway engineer?"

"You may rest assured," we tell the leaders, "none of that will happen. In a market society, all the jobs will be filled because it will be to people's advantage to fill them."

Our respondents accept this with uncertain expressions. "Now look," one of them finally says, "let us suppose that we take your advice and let our people do as they please. Now let's talk about something important, like cloth production. Just how do we fix the right level of cloth output in this 'market society' of yours?"

"But you don't," we reply.

"We don't! Then how do we know there will be enough cloth produced?"

"There will be," we tell him. "The market will see to that."

"Then how do we know there won't be *too much* cloth produced?" he asks triumphantly.

"Ah, but the market will see to that too!"

"But what *is* this market that will do all these wonderful things? Who runs it?"

"Oh, nobody runs the market," we answer. "It runs itself. In fact there really isn't any such *thing* as 'the market.' It's just a word we use to describe the way people behave."

"But I thought people behaved the way they wanted to!"

"And so they do," we say. "But never fear. They will want to behave the way you want them to behave."

"I am afraid," says the chief of the delegation, "that we are wasting our time. We thought you had in mind a serious proposal. But what you suggest is madness. It is inconceivable. Good day, sir." And with great dignity the delegation takes its leave.

Could we seriously suggest to such an emergent nation that it entrust itself to a market solution of the economic problem? That will be a problem to which we shall return. But the very perplexity which the market idea would rouse in the mind of someone unacquainted with it may serve to increase our own wonderment at this most sophisticated and interesting of all economic mechanisms. How *does* the market system assure us that our mines will find miners, our factories workers? How does it take care of cloth production? How does it happen that in a market-run nation each person can indeed do as he wishes and, withal, fulfill the needs which society as a whole presents?

Economics and the Market System

Economics, as we commonly conceive it and as we shall study it in much of this book, is primarily concerned with these very problems. Societies which rely primarily on tradition to solve their economic problems are of less interest to the professional economist than to the cultural anthropologist or the sociologist. Societies which solve their economic problems primarily by the exercise of command present interesting economic questions, but here the study of economics is necessarily subservient to the study of politics and the exercise of power.

It is a society which solves its economic problems by the market process that presents an aspect especially interesting to the economist. For here, as we shall see, economics truly plays a unique role. Unlike the case with tradition and command, where we quickly grasp the nature of the economic mechanism of society, when we turn to a market society we are lost without a knowledge of economics. For in a market society it is not at all clear that the problems of production and distribution will be solved by the free interplay of individuals without guidance from tradition or command.

. . . But . . . there is a problem which has surely occurred to the reader. As our hypothetical interview with the leaders of an emergent nation must have suggested, the market solution appears very strange to someone brought up in the ways of tradition or command. Hence the question arises: how did the market solution itself evolve? Was it imposed, full-blown, on our society at some earlier date? Or did it arise spontaneously and without forethought? These are the questions to which we must first turn, as we retrace the evolution of our own market system out of the tradition- and authority-dominated societies of the past.

4 CAN WE AFFORD OUR NATIONAL GOALS?

Leland Hazard

Leland Hazard is Professor of Industrial Administration and Law at Carnegie Institute of Technology, and a former Vice-President and General Counsel for the Pittsburgh Plate Glass Company.

We Americans are having a new and disquieting experience. Like the man who at some time between the ages of 45 and 60 discovers that he must ration his strength, we find ourselves beginning to take inventory. Can we achieve all our goals at once? That is the question that now begins to nag us.

And it is a new feeling for us. Unlimited competence seems to have been indigenous to American folk thought. Our homely sayings attest to the feeling. "We do the possible at once; the impossible takes a little longer." And in the past we have done the impossible again and again.

The only mythology we have—Indian lore aside—has to do with prodigious labors and incredible accomplishments. The innumerable tales of Paul Bunyan depict an American superman type—in strength and in wit. Remember?

When Paul moved his lumbering camp to flat North Dakota, he got his blacksmith, Ole, to make him a cross-cut saw three miles long. Paul was so strong that he did not need help on the two-man saw. Sometimes the Little Chore Boy, who weighed 800 pounds, would ride the other end. Paul didn't mind much except when the little fellow dragged his feet on the ground. Paul's great blue ox, Babe, was so big that once when Paul's pet crow started to fly from the left horn to the right he got lost. This was in mid-winter, but the crow did not find its way back to the left horn until the spring thaw. Once when Paul was plowing with Babe in the western plains, the great ox broke loose and before Paul could bring him under control the Grand Canyon had been made.

Such—symbolized in our folk tales —is the strength of America. But now we begin to wonder. Have we grown weaker? Or is it simply that the work to be done now is greater than that of clearing forests and breaking plains?

*　*　*

It is not only that we Americans have attributed to ourselves boundless competence. We have also indulged ourselves in a belief in a benign future, a good future, a future guaranteed in some way by our system itself. This optimism, this faith in improvement,

From *Harvard Business Review*, May–June, 1962, p. 6 ff. Reprinted by permission.

progress, and growth, has been as real to the American as belief in hell was real to Dante or belief in a sensuous heaven is real to a Moslem.

We have even dared to consider heaven on earth as a reasonable goal. We would gain it by our strength—in a new era, friendly at long last to man's ancient hope for freedom from toil and want. To us the word future has been synonymous with the better life—in the end, the good life.

We have held our faith in an attainable heaven on earth despite the unpromising record of man's history. Throughout all recorded time most men have known only dreary drudgery at best, slavery at worst, hunger, hardship, and haunting fear. So evil have most eras been for the run of mankind that all mythologies and religions have glorified some dimly remembered past, some Illyria, or have lived for a heaven of green pastures after death, the present invariably being too insufferable to be extolled.

But these dour facts of history belonged, we thought, exclusively to an ancient past, a past to which for several reasons we fancied ourselves unrelated. We had had no Middle Ages, no feudalism, no religious oppression. We had inherited the best of the Industrial Revolution; we came to the United States for religious freedom; our founding fathers wrote democracy into the cleverest Constitution of all time; we determined upon universal education. We were free men, and Adam Smith told us—in the very year in which our Revolution severed what ties we had with the Old World—that if each person avidly pursued his own individual, selfish interest, the "hidden hand" of the market place would bear in its palm a good society.

Who am I to say that America has been dreaming? We have come, in fact, a long way toward abolishing poverty.

In 1929, 32% of families in the United States had incomes of less than $2,000. In 1960, after adjustment to the 1960 dollar purchasing power, only 13% have incomes that similarly fall below the minimal standard for health and well-being.

And for many of those families we have relief. A few years ago Madame Pandit Nehru was shown one of our conventional Christmas lists of the 100 neediest families. She remarked, after examining the case histories, "I am unimpressed. The worst of these cases is opulence by Indian standards."

But lowering across our skies are clouds, their size and color depending on whether one is an optimist, a pessimist, or just indifferent. It is not only that communism is dividing the world between the free and the unfree, as we choose to put it. There is something more subtle and baffling: hatred of the United States in the Asian and African worlds—not to mention in our own hemisphere.

A distinguished Indian demographer, who spent the winter of 1958–1959 inside People's (we call it Red) China, told me that, despite British colonialism in pre-Communist China and despite the truly significant American missionary contributions to Chinese health and education, it is the United States more than Great Britain which is branded with the ugly epithet, colonialism. "Unreasonable," he added, "but a fact." A psychiatrist once put the case better even than Shakespeare's "Blow, blow, thou winter wind" with "Why does that man hate me so? I never did anything for him."

In the short 16 years from Hiroshima to now, our historical position of security behind our two oceans has shifted to one of open vulnerability to nuclear attack. So many of us would be destroyed that large numbers of us are declaring in advance a disinterest in survival. In any case we have come in a very short time from a sense of omnipotence to an ominous doubt about our very survival.

And finally we are half-baffled by a dilemma. If we do gird ourselves for the garrison state—determined at all costs to survive—will we lose so much in the process that survival will be worthless? And if we do gamble everything on survival, when shall we know the outcome? It is not so simple a case as to risk all on one toss of the coin. For it may be that in the lifetime of the youngest of us neither heads nor tails will come up.

* * *

In this setting, President Eisenhower's Commission on National Goals in 1960 presented us with a 15-point program which ran the gamut from "The Individual" (whose status "must remain our primary concern") to "The United Nations" (which "remains the chief instrument available for building a genuine community of nations").[1] In 1961 President Kennedy added a sixteenth goal: "to put men on the moon and bring them back."

President Eisenhower's distinguished Commission, headed by Henry M. Wriston (former President of Brown University, and currently President of the American Assembly), made no attempt to estimate the cost of the announced goals—either individually or in total. Declaring that "resources are a crucial test of a nation's ability to attain its goals" and that "costs must always be carefully weighed," it was "this Commission's conclusion that the levels of public spending we would need to realize the recommendations of this Report are attainable." The conclusion is predicated upon "an annual growth rate of 3.4 per cent or

---

[1] *Goals for Americans* (Englewood Cliffs, N. J.: Prentice-Hall, Inc., 1960).

higher," tax reforms, economies, "savings in the federal agricultural program," and greater efficiency throughout government. But the report ends with this question: If the goals "should require a somewhat higher level of taxation, can we bear this level without consequences which themselves would make the goals more difficult to reach?"

The Commission presented no analysis of costs or estimate of resources. No balance between costs and resources was attempted; no suggestion was given about priorities among goals if resources should prove inadequate. As philosophers, the Commission produced a moving document; as accountants and budget makers they simply did not grasp the nettle. This should not, however, be taken as a disparagement of the Commission's laudable attempt to make specific the aspirations of our democratic economy.

The Commission writes off its default with such platitudes as: "The increase in defense expenditures is difficult to predict," and "Domestic expenditures are also hard to estimate." Difficult, yes; impossible, no!

Twenty-five years ago it might well have been impossible to cost America's goals. But today we possess the measurement and projection techniques with which to appraise a balance between our aspirations and our resources. It is remarkable that in practical America no agency—governmental or private—has performed this obviously sensible and necessary function.

We Americans suffer a mental block about financial analysis on the macrocosmic scale. We pretend that big figures are beyond us. "When it gets to be over $14.25, I get lost" is a sample homespun Americanism, symptomatic of the kind of intellectual isolationism that is reflected in our ambivalence about the global involvement of our nation. If our resources were estimated as $100 and the total cost of our goals $200, we would have no difficulty in seeing that some goals simply could not be afforded right now. Some would have to be postponed. But when the ratio is expressed in billions (even if the billions add up to the same ratio as did the $100 and the $200), we indulge ourselves in the delusion that the figures are too big to be meaningful.

I propose an exercise for readers of this article. I shall take the goals which the Eisenhower Commission has articulated, and price them very tentatively. The analytical work necessary for more accurate pricing has not yet been done, but even a rough beginning such as mine should prove useful. Then, after adding the price for President Kennedy's moon goal, I shall strike a balance against estimated resources. The time span for the analysis will be the decade ending 1970.

I am conscious of considerable temerity in this effort. There is the possibility of apparent double-counting as among the 16 goal categories. The price I shall place on each goal will be the discretionary expenditure (over and above the treadmill expenditure) necessary to achieve the goal. To avoid unduly prolonging this article, I must say simply that the possibility of double-counting has been considered more than once. Every effort has been made to avoid significant duplications.

I am aware also of the risks in casting the analysis in dollars rather than in terms of specific resources. Resource analysis may be the only dependable method of allocation in the emergency conditions of national crisis—war, for example. In such emergencies dollar analysis may very well be illusory. But when a substantial time period is involved, as in our case, and the question is one of estimating the amount of future GNP (over and above the treadmill expenditures) available to buy the

goals, then the dollar analysis would seem to be justified. At least one may make a start by the dollar route and so avoid the dilemma of the man who never wore shoes because he could never decide which one to put on first. One should not hesitate merely because of difficulty or because there may be some imperfections in analytical innovations.

Readers who are interested in assessing the methods used to arrive at these estimates will find them spelled out in the Appendix. Also included for examination is a statement of the sources of my projections, supplied by Dr. Gerhard Colm and the staff of the National Planning Association of which I have held various offices during the past 15 years.[2]

During the period between 1961 and 1970, our strength—that is, our ability to spend money for any purpose—will increase from $520 billion per year to $800 billion per year. At first blush it would seem that the amount of the increase, $280 billion per year, would be available for enhanced expenditures toward our goals. But the case is not that simple.

In order to reach the $800-billion gross figure by 1970 we must make input capital and consumption expenditures for plant, equipment, transportation, housing, and living—all just to keep ourselves where we are, and to take into account the increased population of 1970. (The $800-billion figure assumes a growth rate of about 4.2% per year after unemployment has declined to not more than 4%. If these assumptions are too optimistic, then the deficiency of total resources for total goals will be even greater than the amount with which this article concludes.)

---

[2] This appendix has not been reproduced (ed.).

These input expenditures (or we might say "these treadmill expenditures") required to reach the figure of $800 billion are estimated at $130 billion per year as of 1970. This figure reduces the $280 billion so that by 1970 we shall have an estimated $150 billion per year to expend toward achieving our goals at the higher levels proposed by the President's Commission.

How far will this $150-billion figure go toward achieving these goals? Obviously, the answer requires that we cost the goals one by one and see what total they come to.

Here are the goals as they are listed in the Commission's report, the reasons given for them having been *summarized from the Commission's own language*. Each goal that lends itself to pricing will have a price tag appended. These prices—given in 1961 dollars—will be the amounts (above treadmill expenditures) which the United States must expend to achieve the goals set by the Commission. Let me underscore this point by repeating that all figures in this analysis are for expenditures *above the level of current expenditures* for the several categories.

I. GOALS AT HOME

1. The Individual. The status of the individual must remain our primary concern. All our political, social, and economic institutions must further enhance the dignity of the citizen, promote the maximum development of his capacities, stimulate the responsible exercise of these capacities, and widen the range and effectiveness of opportunities for individual choice.

Price: none. Yet we should realize that our concern with the individual probably acts as a short-range drag on the economy. The Red Chinese economy, which sacrifices individuality to regimentation of citizens in the blue-ant communes, is growing at a rate faster than ours. In the long range, we believe that our emphasis on the individual will pay off.

2. Equality. In this decade we must sharply lower those last stubborn barriers of religious prejudice, employment handicaps for women, and racial discrimination.

Price: none, despite the fact that these discriminations are both a long- and short-range drag on the economy.

3. The Democratic Process. The degree of effective liberty available to its people should be the ultimate test for any nation. Democracy is the only means so far devised by which a nation can meet this test.

Price: none. Comments similar to those given for Goal 1 apply.

4. Education. The development of the individual and the nation demands that education at every level and in every discipline be strengthened and its effectiveness enhanced. The increase in population and the growing complexity of the world add urgency.

The Commission says:

Every state should have a high-level board of education.
Teachers' salaries at all levels must be improved.
Two-year colleges should be within commuting distance of most high school graduates.
Graduate school capacity must be approximately doubled.

Price: private expenditures, $4 billion per year; public expenditures, $13 billion per year. These estimates take into account (a) the higher standards proposed by the Commission and (b) the growing percentage of the population seeking higher education. To cover these factors, expenditures for private education would increase at the rate of approximately 6% per year over tread-mill expenditures. For public education, the increase per student outlay would make a weighted average of about 5% per year above treadmill expenditures.

5. *The Arts and Sciences.* Information and knowledge must be advanced on every front. In science we should allot a greater proportion of our total effort to basic research, (a) to realize fully the rapidly unfolding opportunities to extend still further our understanding of the world, and (b) to enrich applied science and technology so essential to the improvement of physical health, economic growth, and military power.

The Commission believes the arts to be a vital part of human experience. In the eyes of posterity, the success of the United States as a civilized society will be largely judged by the creative activities of its citizens in art, architecture, literature, music, and the sciences. Our theater must be revitalized; it must have the kind of support in universities, colleges, and communities that will give it greater strength at the roots. Professional artists require rigorous discipline; provisions should be made for the long years of training which are required. We should raise our critical standards and widen the area and depth of public appreciation.

Price: culture, $1 billion per year; research and private expenditures, $10 billion per year; public expenditures (defense and nondefense), $10 billion per year. The estimate of $1 billion per year for culture is obviously minimal if the U.S. government is even to begin doing what other governments do for culture. As for research, the estimates are an extrapolation from projections made by the National Science Foundation. For details, see the Appendix to this article.

6. *The Democratic Economy.* The economic system must be compatible with the political system. The centers of economic power should be as diffused and as balanced as possible. Too great concentrations of economic power in corporations, unions, or other organizations can lead to abuses and a loss of the productive results of fair competition. Individuals should have maximum freedom in their choice of jobs, goods, and services.

Price: see Goal 7.

7. *Economic Growth.* The economy should grow at the maximum rate consistent with (a) primary dependence on free enterprise and (b) the avoidance of marked inflation. Increased investment in the public sector is compatible with this goal.

Such growth is essential in order for our nation to achieve its goals of full employment (i.e., to provide jobs for the approximately 13,500,000 net new additions to the work force during the next ten years), an improved standard of living, and an assured international competitive strength.

Price (for both Goals 6 and 7): $115 billion per year for increased standard of living at the rate of 3% per year until 1970; additional capital investment at the rate of $18 billion per year by 1970.

The figure of $115 billion for increased standard of living includes (a) basic consumer needs: food, clothing, shelter, household operation; (b) other consumer requirements: household furnishings, personal and business services, personal care; (c) transportation: purchases of new and used cars, expenditures for upkeep and operation, fares for local and inter-city transportation; (d) consumer luxuries and semiluxuries: tobacco, alcoholic beverages, communications, toys, sports equipment, spectator amusements, other recreational activities, foreign travel and personal remittances abroad, jewelry and watches.

The figure of $18 billion per year is the estimated necessary additional capital expenditure (above treadmill capital expenditures) if, as of 1970, a rate of growth of approximately 5% is found essential to attain the level of economic well-being postulated by the Commission—a not improbable necessity.

8. Technological Change. Technological change should be promoted and encouraged as a powerful force for advancing our economy. It should be planned for and introduced with sensitive regard for any adverse impact on individuals. Where re-employment within the industry is not possible, retraining must be carried out through vocational programs managed locally and financed through state and federal funds.

The Commission observes that public and private leadership is required where whole areas are economically distressed. Measures to encourage industries to move to such communities and relocation programs for individuals are justified, says the Commission, and consideration should be given, where necessary, to state and federal government participation in loans and grants to aid community efforts and to underwrite support for programs of retraining.

Price: included as part of Goals 5 and 7.

9. Agriculture. The Commission recognizes that the relative financial return to agriculture in the economy has deteriorated and that the ultimate goal must be a supply-demand equilibrium to permit the market ("while offering a fair return to farmers") to determine the manpower and capital committed to this sector of the economy.

The Commission notes that a separate problem concerns the 50% of all farmers who operate at subsistence levels and produce only 10% of the farm product. For them, new opportunities must be found through training and location of new industries in farm areas. During this decade, nonfarm jobs must be found (locally wherever possible) for about 1.5 million farm operators who now earn less than $1,500 a year.

Price: no additional expenditures are estimated. The Commission strongly suggests that some economies in existing farm programs are possible.

10. Living Conditions. According to the Commission, we must remedy slum conditions, reverse the process of decay in the larger cities, and relieve the necessity for low-income and minority groups to concentrate in debilitated areas.

We should also seek solutions for haphazard suburban growth. In many parts of the country, the goal should be a regional pattern which provides for a number of urban centers, each with its own industries, its own educational, cultural, and recreational institutions, and a balanced population of various income levels and backgrounds. The needs of a growing population for parks and recreation must be met.

The Commission concludes that private and civic initiative are vital to such programs and that the attainment of these goals will involve massive investment—but that in the long run they will pay handsome social and economic dividends.

Price: urban development and residential construction including streets and transit, $32 billion per year (private) and $12 billion per year (public);

road construction and allied facilities, $4 billion per year; increase in the general government services (significantly related to Goal 10 and also related to Goals 7 and 11) including civilian safety (fire, police, and prisons), natural resources (including water resources), and public utilities other than transit, $10 billion per year.

The figures for urban development and residential construction are predicated on the assumption that the Commission's goal for urban renewal will be attained by the year 1970. For more details see the Appendix.

11. Health and Welfare. The Commission reports an enormously increased demand for medical care. To meet this demand we must have more doctors, nurses, and related medical personnel, as well as more hospitals, clinics, and nursing homes. Federal grants for the construction of hospitals should be continued and extended to other medical facilities.

Price: for health, welfare, and charitable contributions, $20 billion per year (private) and $16 billion per year (public). These estimates reflect the Commission's assumption that we must raise the standards of the poorest segment of our society.

II. GOALS ABROAD

12. To Build an Open and Peaceful World. The Commission advises that our principles and ideals impel us to aid new nations. The preservation and strengthening of free institutions of underdeveloped countries, as well as the defense of the Free World, require a substantial increase in the amount of foreign aid, to be equitably shared by the major free nations.

We must encourage far larger numbers of qualified Americans to live and work abroad. While half a million American civilians now live abroad, their number and ability to represent the United States creditably must rise rapidly in the next decade if we are to attain an adequate level of exports and foreign investment and carry out programs for training and technical assistance. To meet this need, universities, businesses, and the federal government should each in the appropriate fields greatly increase language and other specialized training for such work.

Price: for foreign aid and private foreign investment, $5 billion per year (private), $5 billion per year (public).

13. To Defend the Free World. Communist aggression and subversion threaten all that we seek to accomplish at home and abroad. The power and opportunities of the Sino-Soviet nations are such that it will be a major task to prevent their expansion in the coming decade. Nevertheless, warns the Commission, we must never lose sight of our ultimate goal: to extend the opportunities for free choice and for self-determination throughout the world.

For the common defense, we must maintain and strengthen our military alliances elsewhere. Specifically, the Organization of American States must continue to have our unstinting support, and our commitment to NATO must remain firm. Our other military alliances and relations in the Middle East and Asia must likewise be reaffirmed and strengthened. Communist China's blatant hostility to the United States makes it especially urgent to strengthen our Pacific defenses and our ties with our Pacific allies.

Price: military defense, $8 billion per year; civil defense, $5 billion per year.

14. Disarmament. Since a major nuclear war would be a world catastrophe, the limitation and control of nuclear armament are imperative. Disarmament should be our ultimate goal. It cannot be attained without eliminating the sources of distrust and fear among nations.

In view of the complex interaction of arms control and national security, we must organize a major government effort for the study and analysis of political, military, and technical issues in order to provide a sounder basis for policy formulation and negotiation.

Price: see Goal 15.

15. The United Nations. A key goal in the pursuit of a vigorous and effective U.S. foreign policy is the preservation and strengthening of the United Nations. Over the next decade it will be under tremendous strain. However, the United States must continue to recognize the UN as the chief instrument available for building a genuine community of nations and must remain its major financial provider.

Price: $5 billion per year, which includes UN bond issues and contributions to support an international army and a police force. If these expenditures should not materialize, by reason of collapse of the United Nations, then an equivalent $5 billion per year, at least, would have to be added to the U.S. defense cost given as the price of Goal 13.

16. Space, Including the Moon. President Kennedy and other top officials in Washington have been very frank about the high expense of the moon-shot program while stressing its political and scientific importance.

Price: $7 billion per year.

    *   *   *

The total of the prices given for these 16 goals is *$300 billion per year.* How close can we come to affording the price?

Earlier, we established that our gross national product is estimated to reach $800 billion by 1970, or $280 billion above the 1960 GNP figure. But the built-in expenditures and investments necessary to reach this $800-billion figure will be $130 billion. Hence there is only a surplus of $150 billion which by 1970 we can apply toward the $300 billion estimated to be the price of the goals established by the Commission. The amount of the deficit is obvious—$150 billion, or exactly 50% of the capital needed.

The reader may think that I am taking our goals too seriously. But if he thinks so he will be consciously or unconsciously saying to himself that I take too seriously all the goals except those which *he* happens to consider important, forgetting that other citizens will be arguing with equal fervor the supremacy of other goals.

This is the exact reason why we must use the knowledge and techniques we now possess to measure much more precisely than ever before the cost of our goals and the magnitude of our resources. The rough figures I have provided will be criticized. But my answer is to let the critics come up with their own figures. If our resources are in fact adequate, that will be good news, but I would like to see the figures and the analyses.

Some will say that the cost of goals in a dynamic society such as ours will always exceed resources and that the market place and the political process or both will properly allocate the available (scarce) resources. But must the market place and the political process always be uninformed and left to muddle through? Is there a virtue in uninformed decisions just because they are multiple? I think not.

Our democracy must face up to a degree of discipline beyond our past custom. If resources are in fact inadequate to meet our goals, then there are two courses open simultaneously: (1) to analyze goals for priorities and (2) to analyze resource potentials for enhancement. Once we have taken these steps, we then face the job of disseminating the findings widely, effectively, and forcefully. This done, we may then rely with more confidence on the political process and the market place.

The function of costing goals with analytical precision and of determining priorities among goals, should resources indeed prove inadequate, is not now being performed by any governmental or private agency. The initiative should come from some competent private agency. Time is of the essence. The emergency is great. As Shakespeare warned:

"There is a tide in the affairs of men,
Which, taken at the flood, leads on to
fortune;
Omitted, all the voyage of their life
Is bound in shallows and in miseries."

This can apply to nations also. If we are to take the tide at the flood, we must support hope with thought, resolutions with techniques, goals with resources—all in measured balance and more tightly disciplined than ever before in America.

NATIONAL INCOME, EMPLOYMENT, AND ECONOMIC GROWTH

A.
ECONOMIC GROWTH

5. **How to Raise the High-Employment Growth Rate by One Percentage Point**

   Edward F. Denison

   The rate of economic growth depends on many factors. A noted economist offers a program for raising our growth rate, including estimates of how much might be achieved through different concrete measures—and he suggests that speeding up the long-term growth rate by even one per cent is a tough job.

6. **The Process of Technical Change**

   Edwin Mansfield

   Recent research suggests increasingly that technological advance is a crucial factor in American economic growth, perhaps the most important factor of all. Professor Mansfield outlines a sweeping set of research findings which trace the process of technical change from research and development expenditures, through invention, to innovation and its spread in different types of industries.

7. **Investment in Human Capital**

   Theodore W. Schultz

   Investment in "human capital" through education and training has clearly been a major factor in our persistent, rapid economic growth. In this selection one of America's leading economists argues that we ought to do more to encourage such investment, and examines some of the issues involved.

8. Economic Growth: Investment in Technological Progress and Plant and Equipment

Economic Report of the President

Economic growth has become a major issue of national economic policy. In this report the President's Council of Economic Advisers advances a program of government action to speed technological progress and the rate of capital investment. It includes some controversial proposals.

B.
PRICE INDEXES AND INFLATION

9. The Consumer Price Index—Technical Questions and Practical Answers

Sidney A. Jaffe

The following four articles deal with the recurring problem of inflation, its measurement and its effects. Dr. Jaffe provides an authoritative description of the widely-used Bureau of Labor Statistics consumer price index and how it is constructed.

10. Measuring the Cost of Quality

Richard Ruggles

Is the B.L.S. consumer price index an accurate barometer of changes in the cost of living? Many economists believe that the index overstates the actual rise in prices because it fails to take into account adequately improvements in the quality of the products included. Professor Ruggles examines this important problem.

11. The German Nightmare

Donald B. Woodward and Marc A. Rose

The German experience following World War I provides a vivid picture of what happens when a great inflation breaks loose and runs wild. This account emphasizes the close ties of most such inflations to major wars and their aftermath.

12. Inflation in Perspective

G. L. Bach

The problem of inflation in the United States today differs widely from the post-war hyper-inflation in Germany. Professor Bach examines the nature of modern "creeping" inflation and the ways it affects the behavior of the economy.

C.
DEPRESSION

13. Black Depression

Frederick Lewis Allen

Words are inadequate to convey the human misery, the despair, the baffled uncertainty and hopelessness in the great depression of the 1930's. The long bread lines, the silent factories, the wandering "Okies," the "dust bowl," the evicted hungry families huddled in cardboard shacks—these were the desperate reality of the depression behind the statistics. These pages should convey a little of this reality to a generation for whom the great depression is increasingly far away and unreal.

14. Job Hunters

E. Wight Bakke

What it means to look for a job when there aren't any jobs is the picture conveyed by this diary of a few weeks in the life of an unemployed job hunter in 1933. The creeping, deadening impact of week after week of such job hunting was the human side of unemployment for millions of men.

15. When All the Banks Closed

Arthur A. Ballantine

The banking crisis and nationwide financial collapse were central parts of the national economic breakdown of the 1930's. One-third of our money supply was wiped out. For a time in 1933 every bank in the United States was closed. This report tells a story that may never be repeated, if we have learned our lessons well —a story of financial panic and inadequate liquidity for the banking system. The next selection tells the same story from the point of view of an individual banker.

16. The Pit

Marriner S. Eccles

> Our banking system rests on the confidence of
> the people. Marriner Eccles, later head of the
> Federal Reserve System, tells what the bank
> panic of 1932–33 meant to an individual
> banker, and how he tried to deal with it.

D.
CONSUMPTION PATTERNS

17. Consumption Expenditures in Recovery Phase

Anne N. Probst

> Since the 1930's we have learned much about
> the behavior of the economy. This article re-
> ports recent findings on the behavior of con-
> sumption spending in recoveries, and illustrates
> how economists use the detailed statistics reg-
> ularly collected by federal governmental agen-
> cies.

E.
MONETARY POLICY

18. Money Supply and Stable Economic Growth

Edward S. Shaw

> A leading economist reviews our monetary his-
> tory and concludes that a simple policy of in-
> creasing the money stock at a stable rate an-
> nually, without trying to counter each business
> fluctuation, would make the greatest contribu-
> tion to stable economic growth.

19. The Operation of the Open Market Committee

Alfred Hayes

> The President of the Federal Reserve Bank of
> New York presents an authoritative statement
> on the way monetary policy is formulated in
> the Federal Open Market Committee, stressing
> the continuous consultative process used by the
> substantial number of Federal Reserve officials
> involved. Compare this with the following selec-
> tion.

20. The Mysterious World of the Fed

Delbert C. Hastings and Ross M. Robertson

These observers, one a former economist for the Federal Reserve, argue that the elaborate board and committee arrangements of the Federal Reserve in actual operation contribute little to arriving at sound economic policy, and that we would be better off with a simpler organizational structure and more focused responsibility.

F.
FISCAL POLICY

21. Budget Balancing for Economic Stabilization

Joint Economic Committee

The Joint Economic Committee of Congress presents concisely the argument that the federal budget exercises a strong repressive effect on economic recovery if it swings from deficit to surplus too early as national income rises. The Committee stresses the need to look behind the "administrative" budget to the budget transactions as they actually affect the economy, and recommends some changes to make budget policy more effective. A minority member dissents vigorously.

22. The New Look in Tax and Fiscal Policy

Paul A. Samuelson

Conflicting policy goals confront the government's economic policy makers at every turn. A leading economist suggests how we may be able to achieve apparently conflicting ends by using a proper "mix" of fiscal and monetary policies.

23. United States and Western Europe Differ on Budget Deficits

Edwin L. Dale, Jr.

Although many observers criticize the large budget deficits in the United States since the 1920's, European economists and businessmen increasingly suggest that undue concern for a balanced federal budget may account for the United States' lagging growth rate in recent years. In fact, the western European nations have used much more expansionary budget policies than we have.

24. Is the Food Stamp Plan Working?

Julius Duscha

Huge farm surpluses together with hungry unemployed people have long posed a contradiction that seems unreasonable to most people.
The food stamp plan represents one way of
meshing the goals of providing enough to eat
for the unemployed and of keeping farm prices
high.

G.
DEBT

25. Changes in Debt Levels

Joint Economic Committee

The Joint Economic Committee stresses that
borrowing and debt can be expected to rise as
the economy grows bigger, and that the share
of government debt in the total has declined
steadily and rapidly over the last decade.

26. The Debt Problem and Economic Growth

Paul W. McCracken

As saving grows in an expanding economy,
someone must borrow the funds and put them
to work. Here a prominent economist argues
that continued growth in the federal debt may
be necessary if private borrowing doesn't do
the job, and (by implication) that paying off
the national debt might be a major step in the
wrong direction.

A.

ECONOMIC GROWTH

5 HOW TO RAISE THE HIGH-EMPLOYMENT GROWTH RATE BY ONE PERCENTAGE POINT

Edward F. Denison

Edward Denison is a senior member of the research staff of The Brookings Institute in Washington.

My assignment is to devise a package of proposals that can raise the growth rate over the next twenty years by one percentage point. The package was put together for this session, but my estimate of the contribution each ingredient of the package would make to growth rests upon a study which is about to be published by the Committee for Economic Development.

I was asked to talk about ways of altering the growth of the economy's productive potential, when success in maintaining fairly full utilization of labor and other resources is assumed. We must also find ways to validate the high-employment assumption, but that is outside the present discussion.

Next, I shall be concerned with ways to raise the growth rate of real national income or product as defined and measured by the Department of Commerce. Certain characteristics of these output measures somewhat limit the ways available to raise their growth rate. They preclude raising the growth rate by shifting resources so as to produce things that are more urgently wanted; for example, by eliminating distortions in the pattern of output introduced by

excise taxes, monopoly or farm programs. Again, the treatment of quality change in the price indexes bars raising the future high-employment growth rate of measured output by developing new or better final products more rapidly.

I omit from my discussion steps that would increase the satisfactions derived from output without changing its amount as measured. However, I shall not consider shifts of resources that would increase measured output while leaving unchanged or reducing a "truer" output measure. Real national income or product may be thought of as an index with certain biases that may be fairly uniform over time so long as steps are not taken deliberately to "rig" the index.

The specific series I shall use to measure economic growth is the index of real national income, which is the same thing as the index of real net national product except that components are weighted by factor cost rather than market price. It is *net* income or product, not GNP, that economic policy

From the *American Economic Review,* May, 1962, pp. 67–75. Reprinted by permission.

properly seeks to maximize. Factor cost valuation is more appropriate and convenient than market price valuation for examination of changes in productivity or inputs. However, the conclusions I shall reach would be little changed if reference were to net or even gross national product.

Next, the assigned topic concerns means of changing the growth rate over a twenty-year period. This is a reasonable period to consider, but it should be understood that the length of the period greatly affects my results. Because most ways of changing output, and hence affecting the growth rate, are in the one-shot category, it is easier to raise the growth rate by a given amount for twenty years than for a hundred. Suppose, for example, some obstacle to efficient production costs us 1 per cent of the national income. If the obstacle were eliminated, which could be done only once, the level of national income thereafter would be 1 per cent higher than if the obstacle remained. The effect on the growth rate is approximately 1 per cent divided by the number of years over which the growth rate is computed. Thus elimination of the obstacle would raise the growth rate computed over a twenty-year period by one-twentieth of a percentage point, and the growth rate computed over a hundred-year period by one-hundredth of a percentage point. Some measures, on the other hand, would not have their maximum effect in a period as short as twenty years. Provision of additional education to the young and an increase in the saving rate are examples.

I shall use 1960 to 1980 as my twenty-year period, as if it were now 1960, because the calculations I draw on were based on those twenty years. But nothing would be changed materially by substituting 1961 to 1981, or 1962 to 1982.

Next, this paper is not directed to the question of how we can raise the growth rate from what it was in the past. The question posed for this session by Edward Mason is how the growth rate can be raised by one percentage point from "whatever the speaker thinks it will be" if unemployment is low, and in other respects we continue existing policies. I project a 1960–80 growth rate of 3⅓ per cent in potential national income, starting from a 1960 high-employment level. The amount by which this projected rate exceeds the actual rate in the past is not part of the one percentage point increment my prescription must provide. My task is to indicate how to raise the high-employment growth rate from 3⅓ per cent to 4⅓ per cent. Let me also stress that the topic is not whether 3⅓ per cent is a correct projection given existing policies, but how the rate can be raised one percentage point from whatever it would be if we do nothing special to affect it.

So much for ground rules. Now for some general observations. First, the difference between a 3⅓ per cent rate and a 4⅓ per cent rate is big. One implies an increase in per capita income from 1960 to 1980 of 33 per cent, the other of 61 per cent. Thus, a prescription to raise the growth rate of total income by one percentage point must be powerful enough to nearly double the anticipated increase in per capita real income. This conclusion must be modified insofar as the growth rate is to be stimulated by more immigration.

Second, I can hardly stress enough that, as I use the term, economic growth refers only to output. Quite aside from defects in measures of output, aggregate output is anything but a complete measure of economic welfare or economic progress, even less of total welfare or progress. To talk about changing even economic welfare, we would have also to consider, at the very least, real costs of production and the distribution of income and output.

In the present context this is no small caveat. It is the heart of the matter. The output we get, aside from involuntary underuse of resources, is determined by individual and collective decisions as to what is or is not worth doing.

I stress that to accelerate growth requires that someone act differently than he would otherwise, that this action usually means higher costs as well as higher output, and that more output is never the only effect of any action we might take. To decide whether steps to accelerate growth are sensible requires comparison of costs, the size of the effect on growth, and side effects.

This leads to the first of two conditions I deem essential for any program to stimulate growth a great deal beyond what it will be if we have no such objective. It is that the public be persuaded that acceleration of growth must be made an overriding national goal. Moreover, it must probably be persuaded of this for reasons other than the increase in individual welfare— probably reasons related to the external situation facing the country. This is necessary because there is a presumption that the more important steps required impose costs that exceed the income benefits and thus reduce welfare. Otherwise they presumably would be taken anyway. Even where the benefits may exceed the costs for the country as a whole, we are usually dealing with some deep-seated condition, often of long standing, that is likely to be changed only for some new and overpowering reason.

The presumption that the costs of a proposed change exceed the benefits may be refuted in specific instances. We need not suppose that we now act rationally on the basis of full information in reaching all of our individual and collective decisions, so we need not assume that every step that would increase growth would reduce individual welfare. In putting together my own package of proposals, I try to stress those where I think the possibility is greatest—I do not mean that it is necessarily great— that present practices derive from ignorance and would be changed by greater knowledge and understanding. This may imply a certain arrogance on my part, but without some such approach this paper could not be written.

The second condition necessary for any large effort to stimulate growth is full utilization of resources. It will hardly be possible to obtain support for a broad program to increase our productive potential unless we use rather fully the potential that we do have. Indeed, if unemployment is persistently high, we can look forward to actions that will reduce growth, including greater public and private restrictions on efficient production, and reduction of hours intended to spread employment rather than to increase leisure.

To add one percentage point to the growth rate I shall suggest a thirteen-part program that seems to me to combine feasibility, in the sense of avoiding things no one knows how to do, with minimization of sacrifice. The expected contribution from each proposal to the growth rate over twenty years will be stated in hundredths of a percentage point. Thus we need means of adding 100 hundredths of a percentage point to the growth rate.

Let me now indicate the general approach I use to assess the effect of each proposal on the growth rate. To raise the growth rate over twenty years by one hundredth of a percentage point requires some action not now in prospect that would make the 1980 national income .2 per cent, or nearly 2 billion dollars, larger than it would be in the absence of that action. The action must serve either to increase the quantity or quality of labor, land, or capital going into the productive system, or else to increase their productivity.

Because of the presence of economies of scale, an increment of slightly less than .2 per cent to total factor input in 1980 would probably suffice to raise the 1980 national income .2 per cent. I assume the addition to output would exceed that in total input by one-eleventh. Hence an increase in total input of slightly over .18 per cent would raise output by .2 per cent. This could, in principle, be accomplished by increasing all kinds of input by .18 per cent or only one kind of input by a larger percentage. From national income data I estimate that labor comprises 77 per cent of total input, capital 20 per cent, and land 3 per cent. Hence we could raise total input by slightly over .18 per cent in 1980 if we could raise labor input alone by .24 per cent over what it would otherwise be, or capital input alone by .93 per cent, or land input alone by 6.10 per cent. My proposals would not change the ratio of capital to labor input very much, so the problem of diminishing returns is not acute.

I shall first suggest some ways to increase inputs, indicating the contribution expected from each and sketching the basis of the estimate, and then turn to ways of raising productivity.

1. Yearly net immigration currently equals .2 per cent of our population. As recently as 1911–15 it averaged .6 per cent. Immigration could be increased simply by changing the law. I assume the additional immigrants would make a per capita contribution of labor two-thirds as large, after adjustment for quality differences, as does the existing population. On this assumption, doubling the present immigration rate would raise labor input in 1980 by about 2½ per cent, enough to add .10 to the growth rate of national income.

Extra immigration probably would not lower the per capita income of the existing population, but it would impose some other costs. It would also benefit our international relations. More immigration seems to me among the most sensible means of stimulating growth.

2. By working three hours a week, or about 8½ per cent, longer than we otherwise would in 1980, we could add .28 to the growth rate.

My projection of a 3⅓ per cent growth rate assumed that normal annual working hours will drop the equivalent of four hours a week from 1960 to 1980. This is about the rate at which they dropped during the fifties and much less than they dropped during the thirties and forties. Had I assumed a drop of only one hour instead of four, my projected growth rate would have been .28 higher. The calculation that we could add .28 to the growth rate by working three hours a week longer assumes that, in the range within which we will then be operating, more than three-fourths of the impact of shorter hours falls on output rather than being offset in labor efficiency. A decline of only one hour a week in twenty years would allow some leveling down where hours are especially long and some additional holidays, vacations, or coffee breaks, but no change in the standard forty-hour week.

Longer hours are in my list partly because it would be hard to obtain the desired total effect on the growth rate without them. But it is at least possible that we tend to arrive at a level of hours too short to maximize welfare. I say this partly because so little is known about the amount of income that actually is sacrificed for more leisure, and partly because hours have sometimes been shortened in order to spread employment.

Acceptance of this proposal requires employment opportunities so abundant that work spreading disappears as a reason for shortening standard hours, no reduction in legal standards for hours, and probably general acceptance by labor and employers of the need to maintain present hours. Since the AFL-CIO has already established the thirty-five hour week as an objective, this means a change in the present policy of labor.

3. I call upon additional education to raise the quality of labor enough to add .07 to the growth rate. I estimate that this requires addition of one year to the average amount of schooling that would otherwise be received by everyone leaving school between now and 1980. This estimate is derived from existing income differentials among groups with different amounts of education, and the assumption that three-fifths of these differentials result from more education rather than reflect associated variables such as natural ability. It allows for the loss of work by those who will be in school in 1980 rather than working, on the assumption that if they were working their labor would be of half the average quality. Provision of the extra schooling would absorb .3 or .4 per cent of the national income.

My national income projection already assumes a considerable increase from the present age at which young people leave school. This trend can be confidently anticipated. To add still another year, without adversely affecting the quality of education, would place great strain on educational resources and require a major effort to secure teachers and facilities. Noneconomic benefits of extra schooling seem to me large, and this is another case where we might do more than we will be doing if the public had complete information on which to base decisions.

4. I estimate that we could add .03 to the twenty-year growth rate if we could cut in half structural unemployment and underemployment that results from long-term declines in labor requirements in individual areas and industries, including agriculture.

To contribute to growth in any real sense this must be done by speeding reemployment in expanding industries and areas, not by curtailing the displacement of workers that results from demand shifts or technological progress. If we have a buoyant economy in which unfilled jobs at least match the number unemployed, there ought to be ways to cut these types of structural unemployment in half. Swedish experience can be drawn upon in devising means.

5. I look to increased capital input for a contribution of .20 to the growth rate. This requires capital input in 1980 to be 19 per cent larger than it would be otherwise. Whereas my projection assumes a 64 per cent increase in capital input from 1960 to 1980, capital input must nearly double in the same period to provide this additional contribution to growth.

I look for this to be made possible by the other measures proposed to raise growth. I assume here that the crucial difficulty in accelerating growth by increasing the rate of capital formation concerns the possibility of providing attractive investment opportunities rather than of changing saving propensities. Hopefully, the other means of accelerating growth that I am suggesting would bring about the required broadening of investment opportunities. The capital-output ratio will be the same in 1980 if real national income increases 4⅓ per cent a year and capital input doubles or if national income increases 3⅓ per cent a year and capital input increases 64 per cent.

To raise capital formation this much requires a higher fraction of national income to be saved during the next twenty years, even though income would itself be larger with a higher growth rate. Hence it would require the sacrifice of consumption that could otherwise be made. If net private saving proves inadequate for so high a rate of net investment, as it may, additional saving could be provided by a surplus in the federal budget.

These five ways of increasing labor and capital input would provide 68 of the required 100 hundredths of a point in the growth rate. For the remaining 32 hundredths, I turn to ways of increasing output per unit of input.

6. From estimates by Gary S. Becker, it can be inferred that employment discrimination against Negroes, taking their qualifications as given, costs us .8 per cent of the national income. If discrimination could be abolished within twenty years by a concerted national effort, this would add .04 to the growth rate. To the extent that progress will be made anyway the economic costs of discrimination twenty years hence will be less than now, and the opportunity for further growth stimulation is overstated.

7. For nearly two centuries most economists have held that restrictions on international trade reduce output and living standards while most [of] the public has believed the exact opposite to be true. The economists are right, but I am not sure how they can become more persuasive in the future than in the past. The cost to us of misallocation of resources resulting from barriers to international trade is not easy to estimate, but I have put it at about 1½ per cent of the national income. My projection assumes this percentage will not change. A serious program to stimulate growth would sweep away all barriers to imports and use our willingness to do so as leverage to get foreign nations to eliminate barriers to our exports. If we could eliminate all barriers far enough in advance of our twenty-year deadline to allow basic readjustments in production and trading pat-

terns to be made throughout the world, this would add .07 to the growth rate.

8. Resale price maintenance laws result in the use of more resources in trade than are required to perform the function. Their cost is very hard to estimate, but I believe it to be large. If, as I have guessed, fair trade costs us 1 per cent of the national income, repeal of fair-trade laws could add .05 to the growth rate.

9. Formal obstacles imposed by labor unions in some industries against the most efficient use of resources costs us output, although again it is very difficult to say how much. My guess is that the cost here might also be 1 per cent of the national income. It seems to me possible that a determined program to adopt better ways of meeting labor's needs might cut this cost in half. This would add .02 to the growth rate.

10. The effectiveness of labor incentives is important to productivity. Close correspondence between each employee's individual contribution to production and his individual reward, and employee awareness of the correspondence, are crucial. Shifts from time rates to piecework have sometimes been accompanied by large increases in productivity. Greater use of incentive pay systems where they are or can be made feasible is the obvious way to obtain substantial improvement. Better evaluation of individual performance for use in setting pay differentials among salaried employees and others paid by time, and in promotion, and more honest letters of recommendation, would be helpful. Certain changes in the tax laws might also help. It strikes me as possible that an intensive effort to improve incentives along these lines could contribute .05 to the growth rate. This could be done, for example, if the efficiency of one-tenth of the work force could be raised 11 per cent.

11. We could add to output by per-

mitting consolidation in the regulated industries where this would mean greater efficiency. If claims that as many as 200,000 employees could be eliminated by railroad consolidation are correct and some minor economies are possible in other regulated industries, consolidation could add about .02 to the growth rate.

12. We could increase output by shortening the lag of average business practice behind the best known. My projection assumes that knowledge will be advancing fast enough to contribute .8 percentage points to the growth rate of real product, as measured, in the next twenty years. This exceeds my estimate of its rate of advance in the past. If we could shorten the lag of average practice behind the best known by nine months, which I consider a large reduction for the whole economy, output in 1980 would therefore be .6 per cent larger than otherwise and the twenty-year growth rate .03 higher. My projection of national product already assumes a reduction of nine months in the lag; thus I am calling for an additional nine-months reduction.

Sweeping away all barriers to international trade, aside from the benefits previously taken into account, would put pressure for modernization upon protected industries that are not now highly competitive, and some of the other steps I have suggested would be slightly helpful in this respect. For the rest, we should have to look to better means of disseminating information and alertness in adopting it. I may note in passing that there is nothing to be added on this account to the contribution of additional investment to growth that I have already computed.

13. For the final .04 required to reach my goal of a full point in the growth rate I look to the advance of knowledge itself. This requires that the state of knowledge in 1980 be where it would otherwise be in 1981. I would be uncomfortable in looking for a large contribution because we know too little about how to alter the rate at which knowledge relevant to production advances to feel sure we know how to get much more out of this source of growth. There is little evidence that the big postwar increase in research and development expenditures has had much effect on the rate of increase in measured productivity. Moreover, present prospects are that we shall absorb into research and development all the qualified personnel that will be available and be expanding these human resources as fast as is likely to be fruitful. But something can probably be done about the distribution of effort. There is extreme concentration of research expenditures in a few product lines and industries. In 1956, industries accounting for only 31 per cent of the national income made 96 per cent of research and development expenditures. Moreover, most of the effort, by far, is devoted to development of new and better products rather than cost reduction. It seems likely that greater dispersion of research effort might get us ahead faster, and it is to steps to bring this about that I would look for the additional contribution to growth.

I suspect there are important possibilities of raising productivity in research. But in the absence of agreement even on whether we should move toward more or less organization and planning of research, I cannot very well recommend what should be done that would not otherwise be done.

This completes my prescription for raising the growth rate by one percentage point. The contributions to be obtained from the individual elements obviously are crude estimates, but with any luck overestimates will be offset by underestimates and the package should achieve the assigned target.

Many alternative packages of proposals could be put together to arrive at the same effect on the growth rate. The study from which this list is drawn tries to provide a rather complete menu of the choices available to stimulate growth. From that list anyone can make his own combination. This particular package is fairly concrete and practical in the sense that the principal steps required do not exceed our knowledge. I have tried to put together as attractive a package as I could. In my view it would not impose intolerable burdens. But this does not mean I am advocating it or think the country would necessarily be better off for adopting it. This depends mainly on a judgment as to how important it is to raise the rate at which output grows, and why.

6   THE PROCESS OF TECHNICAL CHANGE

Edwin Mansfield

Edwin Mansfield is Professor of Economics at Carnegie Institute of Technology.

1. Introduction

In recent years, there has been an enormous increase in the amount of attention devoted by social scientists, government officials, businessmen, and labor leaders to the subject of technical change. At least four factors account for this. First, there has been a growing conviction in government and elsewhere that the American economy is not growing as rapidly as it should, and a growing awareness that our rate of economic growth depends very heavily on our rate of technical change. Second, the advent and continuation of the cold war has made it painfully obvious that our national security depends on the output of our military research and development effort. Third, economists and others are coming to realize the full importance in various markets of competition through new products and processes rather than direct price competition. Fourth, unemployment created or aggravated by technical change has become increasingly acute, the problem reaching such dimensions that the President recently labeled it one of the foremost problems of the Sixties.

Despite the considerable amount of space devoted in newspapers and professional journals to the various problems associated with technical change, we know surprisingly little about the process by which new processes and products are invented, developed, commercialized, and accepted. The purpose of this paper is to summarize some of the findings of a continuing study of this process that I have been conducting. These findings pertain to a number of aspects of the process of technical change. Rather than try to integrate the results into a single, all-inclusive theoretical structure, we shall consider a number of important questions regarding this process and summarize very briefly the results to date which bear on them. Because of limitations of space, it is impossible for the paper to include all of the qualifications and limitations of the results. Those interested in more detailed discussion are referred to my others papers.

From *Economics of Research and Development,* ed. Richard Tybout (Ohio University Press, 1963). Reprinted by permission.

2. The Expenditures of the Firm on Research and Development

Most of the nation's R and D is financed by the federal government, principally for defense and space activities. The amount spent for such purposes is, of course, dictated very largely by military and political considerations. Besides these expenditures, there is also an enormous amount of R and D being financed by private industry; and an important question is: What determines the amount spent on R and D by a firm in an industry where government financing plays a small role—like chemicals, petroleum, drugs, glass, and steel?

According to the simple model that I propose, a firm sets its expenditures so as to move part way from the previous year's level toward a desired level that depends on the firm's expectation regarding the average profitability of the R and D projects at hand, the profitability of alternative uses of its funds, and its size. The firm's speed of adjustment toward the desired level depends on the extent to which the desired level differs from the previous year's level and on the per cent of its profits spent during the previous year on R and D.

This model was formulated in part on the basis of interviews with research directors and other executives of a number of firms in the chemical and petroleum industries. For eight firms where the necessary data could be obtained, this model, in more specific and operational form, could fit historical data regarding these firms' expenditures quite well. Moreover, when supplemented with additional assumptions, it could fit the 1945–58 data for 35 firms in five industries (petroleum, chemicals, drugs, glass, and steel) quite well, and it could do a reasonably good job of "forecasting" their 1959 expenditures. Of course, the model is a more apt de-

scription of decision-making regarding applied research and development than basic research, but the latter is quite small in this context.

Because of the small number of observations and the roughness of the basic data, the results are obviously tentative. But if reasonably trustworthy, they have at least three significant implications. First, they allow us to make rough estimates of the effect of certain kinds of government policies on the amount a firm spends, in money terms, on research and development. For example, what would be the effect on a firm's expenditures of a change in tax policy that increased the prospective profitability of each of its R and D projects by one per cent? Assuming that the model holds and that the firm's actual and desired expenditures would be approximately equal, the effect in 1958 would have been to increase the expenditures of the petroleum firms for which we have data by about one per cent. Among the chemical firms, the effect would have been to increase expenditures by about two per cent. Given current data, estimates of this sort could be made on a current basis.

Second, the fact that the model fits the data so well seems to imply that the process by which a firm's R and D expenditures are determined is not so divorced from profit considerations as some observers have claimed. If firms "establish research laboratories without any clearly defined idea of what the laboratories could perform," and blindly devote some arbitrarily determined percentage of sales to R and D, it is difficult to see why the model fits so well.

Third, the results provide new evidence regarding the effects of a firm's size on the amount spent on R and D. They indicate that, among large and medium-sized firms in the petroleum, chemical, and drug industries, there was no tendency in 1959 for the per cent of a firm's sales devoted to R and D to increase with the size of the firm. If anything, the opposite was the case.

3. Research and Development and Inventive Output

The second subject I wish to consider here is the productivity of industrial research and development, an area where measurement problems are extremely acute. On the basis of the crude measurements that could be made, does it seem that a firm's output of significant inventions is closely related to the amount it spends on R and D? Is there any evidence that the productivity of a firm's R and D activities increases with the amount spent on R and D? Is there any evidence that productivity is greater in large firms than in small ones?

To help answer these questions, detailed studies were made of the chemical, petroleum, and steel industries. To measure the inventive output of firms in the chemical industry, we used Langenhagen's data on the number of significant inventions (weighted roughly by a measure of their importance) carried out by various large chemical firms. In the petroleum and steel industries, we used Schmookler's list of important inventions in petroleum refining and my list of important petrochemical and steel innovations. Results were obtained for about ten large firms in each industry.

Calculations based on these crude data suggest the following three conclusions. First, holding size of firm constant, the number of significant inventions carried out by a firm seems to be highly correlated with the size of its R and D expenditures. Thus, although the payout from an individual R and D project is obviously very uncertain, it seems that there is a close relationship over the long run between the amount a firm spends on R and D and the total

number of important inventions it produces.

Second, the evidence from this cross-section analysis seems to suggest that increases in R and D expenditures, in the relevant range and holding size of firm constant, results in more than proportional increases in inventive output in chemicals. But in petroleum and steel, there is no real indication of either economies or diseconomies of scale within the relevant range. Thus, except for chemicals, the results do not indicate any marked advantage of very large scale research activities over medium-sized and large ones.

Third, when a firm's expenditures on R and D are held constant, increases in size of firm seem to be associated in most industries with decreases in inventive output. Thus, the evidence suggests that the productivity of an R and D effort of given scale is lower in the largest firms than in the medium-sized and large ones.

4. The Size of Innovators

The significance of the innovator has been stressed repeatedly by Schumpeter and others. One of the most important questions regarding the innovator is concerned with its size. Is it true that the largest firms have been the first to introduce a disproportionately large proportion of the important new processes and products that have been developed in recent years? Is it true that they dominate the picture to a larger extent now than in the past?

To help answer these questions, studies were made of the iron and steel, petroleum, and bituminous coal industries. Using lists obtained from trade journals and engineering associations of the important processes and products first introduced in these industries since 1918, we determined whether in each case the largest four firms seemed to introduce a disproportionately large share of these innovations. Then a simple model was constructed to explain why the giant firms accounted for a disproportionately large share of the innovations in some cases, but not in others; and an attempt was made to estimate whether innovations would have been introduced more slowly if these large firms had been broken up.

The principal results are as follows: First, although it is often alleged that the largest firms do more than their share of the pioneering, this is not always the case. For example, in petroleum refining and bituminous coal, the largest firms accounted for a larger share of the innovations than they did of the market. But in iron and steel, they accounted for less.

Second, the evidence seems quite consistent with a simple model (which is designed to explain these differences), which predicts that the largest four firms will do a disproportionately large share of the innovating in cases where (1) the investment required to innovate is large relative to the size of the firms that could use the innovation, (2) the minimum size of firm required to use the innovation is large relative to the average size of firm in the industry, and (3) the average size of the largest four firms is much greater than the average size of all potential users of the innovation.

Third, some very rough estimates suggest that, if the larger firms in the petroleum and bituminous coal industries had been broken up, it would have had a detrimental effect on the rate of innovation. On the other hand, in the steel industry, their dissolution might have had positive effects. However, before relaying the news to the Attorney General, two things must be considered. (1) The underlying theory and data are extremely rough. (2) The results are based on the past behavior of the steel companies, which may be different in important respects from their more recent and future behavior.

Fourth, there is evidence that the smallest steel, bituminous coal, and oil firms did less innovating during 1939–58—relative to large and medium-sized firms—than in 1919–38. With the rising costs of development and the greater complexity of technology, this is not surprising.

5. Innovation and the Growth of Firms

Having considered the size of the innovators, another important question is: How large has been the payoff for a successful innovation? Perhaps the best single measure of a firm's rewards is the rate of return on its investment; but because of data limitations, I investigated the effect of a successful innovation on a firm's growth rate, another interesting, if incomplete, measure of its success. First, I determined which firms were first to introduce about 100 new processes and products regarded by trade journals and engineering associations as being the most important that occurred in the iron and steel and petroleum industries since World War I. A comparison of the growth rates of these innovators—during the period in which the innovation occurred—with those of other firms of comparable initial size helps to indicate how great the payoff was, in terms of growth, for a successful innovation.

The results show that, in every time interval and in both industries, the successful innovators grew much more rapidly (during a 5–10 year period after the innovation occurred) than the other firms, their average growth rate often being more than twice that of the others. According to my best estimates, the average effect of a successful innovation was to raise a firm's percentage annual growth rate by 4–13 percentage points, depending on the time interval and the industry. Taking each innovator separately, the difference between its growth rate and the average growth rate of other comparable firms seems to have been inversely related to its size. As one would expect, a successful innovation had a much greater impact on a small firm's growth rate than on a large firm's.

6. The Timing of Innovation

Another study in this series is concerned with the timing of innovation and its effects on the timing of expenditures on plant and equipment. The dates of first commercial introduction were determined for the 150 processes and products regarded by trade associations and trade journals as being the most important introduced during 1919–58 in the iron and steel, petroleum refining, and bituminous coal industries. Using these data, we see whether the rate of innovation in these industries seems to have increased in accord with the spectacular rise in R and D expenditures and whether the rate of occurrence of innovations has varied appreciably over the business cycle. In addition, we formulate and test an investment function that includes the effects of the timing of innovation on the timing of an industry's expenditures on plant and equipment.

The principal conclusions of this study are as follows: First, there was some apparent, but statistically nonsignificant, tendency for the rate of occurrence of innovations to increase over time in these industries. However, the rate of increase was significantly less than the rate of increase in R and D expenditures, indicating perhaps that the expenditures on R and D required to produce a significant innovation have increased considerably. If this is true in most other industries too, the much-publicized increase in total R and D expenditures greatly exaggerates the increase in the rate of innovation.

Second, it appears that process innovations were most likely to be introduced during periods when the industries were operating at about 75 per cent of capacity. Contrary to the opinion of many economists, there was no tendency for process innovations to cluster during the periods when operating rates were extremely high or extremely low. Apparently, innovation at the trough was discouraged by the meagerness of profits and uncertainty regarding the future. At the peak, some executives in the industries claim that it was discouraged by the lack of unutilized capacity where alterations could be made cheaply and without interfering with production schedules.

Third, a simple investment function combining the flexible capacity accelerator with a simple model of innovation-induced investment can explain the behavior of the level of investment in steel and petroleum more adequately than the accelerator alone. The timing of innovation is shown to have had a statistically significant and quantitatively important effect on the level and timing of expenditures on plant and equipment.

7. The Diffusion of Innovations

Finally, having considered the origin and initial introduction of an innovation, it is necessary to look at the subsequent diffusion process as well. Once an innovation has been introduced by one firm, what factors determine the rate at which other firms follow the innovator? What factors seem to determine whether one firm will be quicker than another to begin using a particular technique? Do the same members of an industry tend to lag behind in introducing innovations, or are the leaders in one case likely to be the followers in another?

An intensive study of the diffusion of more than a dozen major process innovations in the railroad, brewing, steel, and bituminous coal industries seems to indicate the following answers to these questions. First, there seems to be a definite "bandwagon" or "contagion" effect. As the number of firms in an industry using an innovation increases, the probability of its adoption by a non-user increases. This is because, as experience and information regarding an innovation accumulates, the risks associated with its introduction grow less and competitive pressures mount. Moreover, in cases where the profitability of an innovation is difficult to assess, the mere fact that a large proportion of a firm's competitors have adopted the innovation may prompt the firm to consider it more seriously.

Second, the rate of diffusion tends to be higher for more profitable innovations and for those requiring relatively small investments. The rate of diffusion also differs among industries, there being some slight indication that it is higher in less concentrated industrial categories. The relationship between these variables and the rate of diffusion is in accord with a simple model of the imitation process, and is surprisingly close. It may be useful for forecasting purposes, although one should note that in none of the cases considered were patents a relevant factor, since they were held by the equipment producers.

Third, there may be some tendency for the rate of diffusion to be higher when the innovation does not replace very durable equipment, when an industry's output is growing rapidly, and when the innovation's introduction into an industry is relatively recent.

Fourth, the speed with which a particular firm begins using a new technique is directly related to the firm's size and the profitability of its investment in the technique. But a firm's rate of growth, its profit level, its liquidity, its profit trend, or the age of its management seem to have no consistent or close relationship with how soon a firm adopts an innovation.

Fifth, in most industries, only a relatively weak tendency exists for the same firms to be consistently the earliest to introduce different innovations. The leaders for one innovation are quite often followers for another, especially if the innovations become available at widely different periods of time.

*   *   *

7   INVESTMENT IN HUMAN CAPITAL

Theodore W. Schultz

Theodore W. Schultz is Professor of Economics and Chairman of the Department of Economics at the University of Chicago.

. . . One proceeds at his own peril in discussing social implications and policy. The conventional hedge is to camouflage one's values and to wear the mantle of academic innocence. Let me proceed unprotected!

1. Our tax laws everywhere discriminate against human capital. Although

Excerpted from "Investment in Human Capital," *American Economic Review,* March, 1961, pp. 13–16. Reprinted by permission.

the stock of such capital has become large and even though it is obvious that human capital, like other forms of reproducible capital, depreciates, becomes obsolete, and entails maintenance, our tax laws are all but blind on these matters.

2. Human capital deteriorates when it is idle because unemployment impairs the skills that workers have acquired. Losses in earnings can be cushioned by appropriate payments but these do not keep idleness from taking its toll from human capital.

3. There are many hindrances to the free choice of professions. Racial discrimination and religious discrimination are still widespread. Professional associations and governmental bodies also hinder entry; for example, into medicine. Such purposeful interference keeps the investment in this form of human capital substantially below its optimum.

4. It is indeed elementary to stress the greater imperfections of the capital market in providing funds for investment in human beings than for investment in physical goods. Much could be done to reduce these imperfections by reforms in tax and banking laws and by changes in banking practices. Long-term private and public loans to students are warranted.

5. Internal migration, notably the movement of farm people into industry, made necessary by the dynamics of our economic progress, requires substantial investments. In general, families in which the husbands and wives are already in the late thirties cannot afford to make these investments because the remaining payoff period for them is too short. Yet society would gain if more of them would pull stakes and move because, in addition to the increase in productivity currently, the children of these families would be better located for employment when they were ready to enter the labor market. The case for

making some of these investments on public account is by no means weak. Our farm programs have failed miserably these many years in not coming to grips with the costs and returns from off-farm migration.

6. The low earnings of particular people have long been a matter of public concern. Policy all too frequently concentrates only on the effects, ignoring the causes. No small part of the low earnings of many Negroes, Puerto Ricans, Mexican nationals, indigenous migratory farm workers, poor farm people and some of our older workers, reflects the failure to have invested in their health and education. Past mistakes are, of course, bygones, but for the sake of the next generation we can ill afford to continue making the same mistakes over again.

7. Is there a substantial underinvestment in human beings other than in these depressed groups? This is an important question for economists. The evidence at hand is fragmentary. Nor will the answer be easily won. There undoubtedly have been overinvestments in some skills, for example, too many locomotive firemen and engineers, too many people trained to be farmers, and too many agricultural economists! Our schools are not free of loafers and some students lack the necessary talents. Nevertheless, underinvestment in knowledge and skill, relative to the amounts invested in nonhuman capital would appear to be the rule and not the exception for a number of reasons. The strong and increasing demands for this knowledge and skill in laborers are of fairly recent origin and it takes time to respond to them. In responding to these demands, we are heavily dependent upon cultural and political processes, and these are slow and the lags are long compared to the behavior of markets serving the formation of nonhuman capital. Where the capital market does

serve human investments, it is subject to more imperfections than in financing physical capital. I have already stressed the fact that our tax laws discriminate in favor of nonhuman capital. Then, too, many individuals face serious uncertainty in assessing their innate talents when it comes to investing in themselves, especially through higher education. Nor is it easy either for public decisions or private behavior to untangle and properly assess the consumption and the investment components. The fact that the return to high school and to higher education has been about as large as the return to conventional forms of capital when all of the costs of such education including income foregone by students are allocated to the investment component, creates a strong presumption that there has been underinvestment since, surely, much education is cultural and in that sense it is consumption. It is no wonder, in view of these circumstances, that there should be substantial underinvestment in human beings, even though we take pride, and properly so, in the support that we have given to education and to other activities that contribute to such investments.

8. Should the returns from public investment in human capital accrue to the individuals in whom it is made? The policy issues implicit in this question run deep and they are full of perplexities pertaining both to resource allocation and to welfare. Physical capital that is formed by public investment is not transferred as a rule to particular individuals as a gift. It would greatly simplify the allocative process if public investment in human capital were placed on the same footing. What then is the logical basis for treating public investment in human capital differently? Presumably it turns on ideas about welfare. A strong welfare goal of our community is to reduce the unequal distribution of personal income among individuals and families. Our community has relied heavily on progressive income and inheritance taxation. Given public revenue from these sources, it may well be true that public investment in human capital, notably that entering into general education, is an effective and efficient set of expenditures for attaining this goal. Let me stress, however, that the state of knowledge about these issues is woefully meager.

9. My last policy comment is on assistance to underdeveloped countries Here, even more than in domestic affairs, investment in human beings is likely to be underrated and neglected. It is inherent in the intellectual climate in which leaders and spokesmen of many of these countries find themselves. Our export of growth doctrines has contributed. These typically assign the stellar role to the formation of nonhuman capital, and take as an obvious fact the superabundance of human resources. Steel mills are the real symbol of industrialization. After all, the early industrialization of England did not depend on investments in the labor force. New funds and agencies are being authorized to transfer capital for physical goods to these countries. The World Bank and our Export-Import Bank have already had much experience. Then, too, measures have been taken to pave the way for the investment of more private (nonhuman) capital abroad. This one-sided effort is under way in spite of the fact that the knowledge and skills required to take on and use efficiently the superior techniques of production, the most valuable resource that we could make available to them, is in very short supply in these underdeveloped countries. Some growth of course can be had from the increase in more conventional capital even though the labor that is available is lacking both in skill and knowledge. But the

rate of growth will be seriously limited. It simply is not possible to have the fruits of a modern agriculture and the abundance of modern industry without making large investments in human beings.

Truly, the most distinctive feature of our economic system is the growth in human capital. Without it there would be only hard, manual work and poverty except for those who have income from property. There is an early morning scene in Faulkner's *Intruder in the Dust,* of a poor, solitary cultivator at work in a field. Let me paraphrase that line, "The man without skills and knowledge leaning terrifically against nothing."

8   INVESTMENT IN TECHNOLOGICAL PROGRESS AND PLANT AND EQUIPMENT

Economic Report of the President

INVESTMENT IN TECHNOLOGICAL PROGRESS

Technological knowledge sets limits on the productivity of labor and capital. As the frontiers of technology are pushed ahead, industrial practice and productivity follow, sometimes pressing close on the best that is known, sometimes lagging behind, with the gap varying from industry to industry and from firm to firm. A stimulus to economic growth can come either from increasing the rate at which the frontiers are advancing or from bringing the technology actually in use closer to the frontiers.

Research and Development

The advance of technological knowledge depends on the amount and effectiveness of the human and material resources devoted to research and development. The limited data available suggest that within industries and between industries there is a positive correlation between research effort and productivity growth. However, some of the most important developments affecting the productivity of a firm or industry may originate from research done by equipment and material suppliers, or from basic research done by government and the universities. The benefits of research activity are often widely shared.

Expenditures on research and development in 1960 totaled about $14 billion, as shown in Table 13. In 1961 the total was probably in the neighborhood of $15 billion, nearly three times the expenditures in 1953, and almost a third as large as business expenditures on fixed capital. After rough allowance for rising costs, the volume of research and development performed has approximately doubled since 1953. Between 1953 and 1960, research and development as a percentage of GNP in current prices doubled from 1.4 percent to 2.8 percent.

Research and development cover a wide range of activities aimed at increasing the stock of scientific and

From the *Economic Report of the President,* January, 1962, pp. 123–133.

Table 13

RESEARCH AND DEVELOPMENT EXPENDITURES, 1953 AND 1957–60
[Billions of Dollars]

Type of research, financing, and performance	1953	1957	1958	1959	1960
Total expenditures	5.15	10.03	11.07	12.62	14.04
By type of research:					
Basic research	.43	.83	1.02	1.15	1.30
Applied research and development	4.72	9.20	10.05	11.47	12.74
By source of funds: [1]					
Federal Government	2.74	6.38	7.17	8.29	9.22
Industry	2.24	3.39	3.62	4.03	4.49
Universities and other nonprofit institutions ...	.17	.26	.28	.30	.33
By performer:					
Federal Government	.97	1.44	1.73	1.83	2.06
Industry [2]	3.63	7.66	8.30	9.55	10.50
Universities and other nonprofit institutions [2]..	.55	.93	1.04	1.24	1.48

[1] Based on reports by performers.
[2] Includes research centers administered by organizations in this sector under contract with Federal agencies.
Source: National Science Foundation.

technical knowledge. As we move from basic research to applied research and to development, the goals become more closely defined in terms of specific practical objectives, the predictability of the results increases, and the benefits become less diffuse. More than 90 percent of research and development spending is for applied research and development—most of it for development. Slightly less than 10 percent is for basic research.

Approximately three-fourths of the Nation's total research and development effort is performed by industry, and over half of this is financed by the Federal Government. Profit considerations naturally lead private firms to concentrate on developing and improving marketable products. Even here, supplementary government support can pay off handsomely. Estimates suggest that hybrid corn research, of which perhaps one-third was publicly supported, yielded a substantial return to society over and above the returns to farmers and seed producers.

Less than one-third of all basic research is done by industry. Government, the universities, and other nonprofit institutions, although doing only one-fourth of total research, do most of the Nation's basic research. Such research seldom results directly or immediately in new products and processes. But in the long run, basic research is the key to important advances in technology. Fundamental inventions like the transistor—an outgrowth of basic research in solid-state physics—may revolutionize large sectors of industry and have a tremendous ultimate effect on productivity.

Although research and development spending is increasing rapidly in most industries, more than 55 percent of industrial research is performed by two industry groups, the aircraft and parts industry, and the electrical equipment and communications industry, as shown in Table 14. This heavy concentration of industrial research reflects primarily the concentration of defense contracts.

Industrial research is also heavily concentrated in large firms. In 1958, firms employing more than 5,000 persons accounted for 84 percent of total industrial research spending, significantly more than the share of these firms in manufacturing employment.

The Federal Government plays a much larger role in financing than in performing research. It is estimated that in 1961 the Government paid for about two-thirds of the total national research effort including, in addition to work done in government laboratories,

Table 14

FUNDS FOR INDUSTRIAL RESEARCH AND DEVELOPMENT, BY SOURCE AND INDUSTRY, 1960

| Industry | Funds for research and development, 1960 | | | | | | Research and development funds as percent of net sales, 1959 [1] |
| | Amount (millions of dollars) | | | Percentage change from 1959 | | | |
	Total	Federal Government	Company	Total	Federal Government	Company	
Total	10,497	6,125	4,372	10	9	11	4.2
Food and kindred products	106	9	97	19	([2])	15	.3
Paper and allied products	66	1	65	12	([2])	12	.8
Chemicals and allied products	1,047	303	744	10	7	12	4.3
Petroleum refining and extraction	289	25	264	6	4	6	1.0
Rubber products	115	35	80	4	—5	8	2.0
Stone, clay, and glass products	82	4	78	14	([2])	11	1.4
Primary metals	164	18	146	19	20	19	.7
Fabricated metal products	126	54	72	2	—7	9	1.7
Machinery	993	384	609	5	—5	12	4.2
Electrical equipment and communication	2,405	1,634	771	7	4	16	11.3
Motor vehicles and other transportation equipment	849	216	633	—2	—13	3	3.4
Aircraft and parts	3,482	3,027	455	15	16	9	20.8
Professional and scientific instruments .	416	211	205	18	21	15	8.3
Other industries	358	205	153	18	19	17	([3])

[1] Data apply to all manufacturing industries and to the communication and crude petroleum and extraction nonmanufacturing industries.

[2] Percent change not computed for an industry where the amount in the base period was less than $15 million.

[3] Not available.

NOTE.—Detail will not necessarily add to totals because of rounding.

Source: National Science Foundation.

almost 60 percent of the research undertaken in industry-run laboratories and over 70 percent of the research done by universities. About 70 percent of government research and development spending is accounted for by the Department of Defense. The Atomic Energy Commission and National Aeronautics and Space Administration together account for nearly 20 percent.

In addition to its direct contributions to research and development spending, the Federal Government has stimulated private research and development activity. The science information services of the National Science Foundation, the Atomic Energy Commission, the Office of Technical Services of the Department of Commerce, and other government agencies contribute to the over-all efficiency of national research and development. Federal tax law encourages research and development by making such costs fully deductible in the year they are incurred. The Small Business Act encourages spending on research and development, including cooperative research, by small companies. Moreover, the Federal Government makes an important contribution to the training of future research scientists and engineers through its support of education and basic research in the universities.

Strengthening research and devolopment. During the 1950's, the number of professional scientists and engineers in the United States increased at an annual rate of approximately 6 percent. Total resources allocated to research and development grew at an even faster rate because a rising proportion of all scientists and engineers were engaged in research, and because supporting personnel, equipment, and material per research scientist increased. During the 1960's, these trends will continue, but one limit to growth will be the supply of scientists and engineers in certain fields. Future investment in research will be limited largely by the quantity and quality of earlier investment in education.

Overemphasis on current research and development activity should not be permitted to erode the underlying educational base. Just as research is investment for the economy, education is investment for research. The needs for educational expansion stressed earlier in this chapter include urgent requirements for laboratories, laboratory equipment, and other science teaching facilities.

A greater share of research and development resources and talent should be devoted to basic research and to prototype development and experimentation in fields which promise major advances in civilian technology. Military research helped to create such important discoveries as isotope medicine, the computer, and the jet engine. The important impact on civilian technology of these offspring of military research suggests that high returns might be achieved if sights were set higher in nonmilitary research. Since the risks of basic research and experimental development are very great, and since the rewards for success are not confined to single firms or even industries, there is a case for public support to attract additional resources into this work.

In a number of industries, firms which are highly efficient in production and marketing may be too small to undertake an efficient research and development program. In others, a research tradition is lacking, or research is discouraged because the benefits tend to diffuse beyond the market grasp of individual firms. In agriculture, all these conditions are present, and the high returns to society from government support of research suggest that comparable programs, to increase research in certain manufacturing industries, might be highly desirable.

*   *   *

More Effective Use of Existing Technology

(1) In some industries there are legal obstacles to technical change. The housing construction codes of many localities provide a prominent example. In principle, these codes protect the public from shoddy construction; in practice, they often prevent the use of new materials, designs, and techniques which are superior to the old, and a lack of uniformity among codes in different localities discourages mass production of certain prefabricated housing components. With respect to construction codes in partic-

ular, the Housing and Home Finance Agency should continue to encourage the adoption of performance standards for codes and should strengthen its programs of testing and evaluation.

(2) American labor has a remarkable record of acceptance of new technology; but understandable resistance to the displacement of labor by new equipment has occasionally developed when opportunities for retraining and re-employment were not clearly visible. The Federal Government can help considerably, first, by pursuing effective policies to maintain full employment, and second, by expanding and improving its programs in job training and retraining.

(3) The process of technological change would be smoother if society knew better how to reap the rewards and reduce the costs. Research in the social, behavioral, and managerial sciences can lead to more efficient use of resources and to quicker grasp of the opportunities afforded by technological progress. Improved understanding may, in time, yield ways to ease the burdens of adjustment. Strengthening of research in these auxiliary fields is needed to gain maximum benefit from research which creates new technology.

(4) Innovation is facilitated by a flow of information about new technical developments. Since many firms, especially small ones, are not in a position to follow new technological developments closely, the Government can play a useful role by providing business with relevant information and analysis. These service functions of the Department of Commerce and the Small Business Administration should be substantially strengthened. The success of the Federal-State Extension Service in speeding the diffusion of agricultural technology serves to illustrate how effective such programs can be.

(5) The Panel on Civilian Technology, composed of a group of distinguished scientists, engineers, businessmen, and economists, has been brought together under the joint auspices of the office of the President's Special Assistant for Science and Technology, the Department of Commerce, and the Council of Economic Advisers. The panel is examining opportunities for stimulating civilian research and development as well as for more effective use of existing technology. It has begun to address itself particularly to those sectors of our economy where major social and economic benefits could be expected to accrue from technological advances.

(6) By eliminating monopolistic and collusive barriers to the entry of new business and by maintaining the spur of competition to innovation and the utilization of technology, antitrust enforcement tends to create conditions which encourage economic growth.

INVESTMENT IN PLANT AND EQUIPMENT

Between the resourcefulness of the labor force and the ideas of the laboratory on one side and the satisfaction of consumption needs on the other, the indissoluble link is the economy's stock of plant and machinery. Our own history and the experience of other industrial countries alike demonstrate the connection between physical investment and growth of productive capacity. Without investment in new and renewed plant and equipment, skills and inventions remain preconditions of growth; with it, they become ingredients.

Investment as a Source of Growth

Investment in fixed capital leads to increased capacity both by equipping new members of the labor force with capital up to existing standards and by providing greater amounts for all workers. Since 1929, the stock of privately owned plant and equipment (in constant prices) has grown relative to private man-hours worked by nearly 80 percent (Chart 10) and by nearly 50 percent relative to the private labor force. Nearly all of the latter increase has taken place during the postwar period. Between 1929 and 1947, the rate of investment was sufficient only to provide enough capital—although more modern capital—to keep pace with a growing labor supply. No increase in capital per worker occurred. Since 1947, the rate of growth in the ratio of capital stock to labor supply has been approximately 2.7 percent a year, but there is a perceptible difference between the growth records of the first and second halves of the postwar period. From 1947 to 1954, the amount of capital per worker increased by 3.5 percent a year; in contrast, the annual increase from 1954 to 1960 averaged only 1.9 percent.

The importance of investment in the

INDEXES OF BUSINESS OUTPUT, CAPITAL STOCK, AND MAN-HOURS.

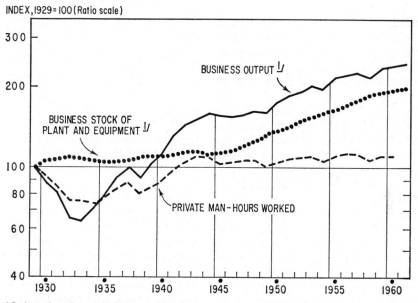

INDEX, 1929 = 100 (Ratio scale)

[1] Indexes based on data in constants prices.
Source: Council of Economic Advisers (based on data from various government and private sources).

growth process is suggested by the parallel movement of the growth of potential output per man and the growth of capital per man (Table 15). Both ratios grew more rapidly after 1947 than before, and more rapidly between 1947 and 1954 than subsequently. In general, the experience since 1929 supports the belief that the more rapidly the capital stock grows relative to the labor force, the greater will be the growth in potential output per worker, provided that other necessary conditions are met.

Though there was no increase in capital per worker between 1929 and

Table 15

GROWTH IN BUSINESS POTENTIAL CAPITAL-LABOR AND
OUTPUT-LABOR RATIOS, 1929–60

[Percent per year]

Item	1929 to 1947	1947 to 1960	1947 to 1954	1954 to 1960
Capital stock per worker [1]	0.0	2.7	3.5	1.9
Output per worker [2]	1.5	2.8	3.3	2.1

[1] Business capital stock is built up from private purchases of plant and equipment, with allowance for retirements; excludes religious, educational, hospital, other institutional, and farm residential construction.

[2] Business output is gross national product minus product originating in general government, government enterprises, households and institutions, the rest of the world, and services of existing houses.

NOTE.—Details of series are available upon request.

Source: Council of Economic Advisers.

1947, there was a slow increase in productivity which must be attributed to technical progress and to improvement in the quality of both labor and capital. When, as in subsequent years, investment was more rapid, there was an accompanying acceleration of productivity gains. These gains were not simply the result of the separate contributions of the advance of knowledge, the improved skills of the working population, and the rise in capital per worker, but came in large part from the interaction of all three.

Investment in new equipment serves as a vehicle for technological improvements and is perhaps the most important way in which laboratory discoveries become incorporated, in the production process. Without their embodiment in new equipment, many new ideas would lie fallow. Conversely, the impact of a dollar's investment on the quality of the capital stock depends on how rapidly increases in knowledge have taken place. This interaction between investment and technological change permits each worker to have not only more tools, but better tools as well.

The slower rate of growth of the capital stock in recent years provides one explanation for the accompanying slower growth of labor productivity and potential output. The proportion of output devoted to investment, and the rate of growth of the capital stock itself, are measures of the diversion of current resources to the creation of future capacity. During the period 1947–54, expenditures on business fixed investment averaged 11.0 percent of GNP and the stock grew at an annual rate of 4.2 percent (valued in 1961 prices). In the period 1955–60, 9.8 percent of GNP was invested and the capital stock grew at an annual rate of 3.2 percent. The ratio of investment to potential GNP is even more relevant; in this case, the ratios are 10.9 percent and 9.4 percent for the two periods. This difference of 1.5 percent in the fraction of potential GNP invested represents nearly $45 billion of additional capital.

Policies to Encourage Investment

(1) *Adequate levels of demand.* The single most important stimulant to investment is the maintenance of full utilization of capacity. The historical record shows that when output falls below its potential the rate of growth

of the capital stock declines. Expected profit from investment is strongly influenced by the expected demand for the output that the new capital will help produce, even if the investment is meant largely for cost reduction rather than capacity expansion. Estimates of future demand are colored by the experience of the present and the recent past. During periods of economic slack, estimates of future demand are relatively pessimistic, and many projects are foregone which would appear profitable under conditions of high demand.

There is a tendency to think of profitable investment opportunities for the whole economy as exhaustible: the more of them that are used up in any one year, the fewer remain. There may be some validity to this view for a single industry, which can mistakenly expand its capacity beyond the possibilities of future market demand. But for the entire economy, what appears as unavoidable excess capacity is in fact avoidable deficiency of demand. There are, and always will be, unsatisfied wants for a higher standard of living, though the demand for any particular product may perhaps be satiated. The investment boom of 1955–57 did not make inevitable the excess capacity that has ruled since then. Instead, it created an opportunity for higher levels of production in later years, had the demand been forthcoming. The opportunity was lost; even before the cyclical peak in the third quarter of 1957, the growth of demand slowed down and excess capacity began to emerge.

It is true that, with any given level of technology, a higher rate of investment can occur only through the acceptance of investment opportunities of lower profitability. But appropriate tax and monetary measures can make even these investments sufficiently attractive. And technical progress can

have the same effect. To equip a more rapidly growing labor force also demands a larger volume of investment relative to potential GNP. Fortunately, if actual output is held close to a rising potential output, faster labor force growth will open opportunities for additions to plant and equipment which would be economically unattractive if the labor supply situation were tighter. Thus a higher ratio of investment to output can be more easily maintained. When excess capacity already exists, however, profitability is low for that reason alone, and the growing labor force appears as a threat, instead af the stimulus to investment it really is.

In addition to serving as an indicator of future profits, the level of aggregate demand, through its impact on current profits, plays an important role in providing finance for investment. The importance of the level of economic activity in determining profits is indicated in Chart 3, which shows that net and gross profits as a percentage of GNP fluctuate very closely with the rate of capacity utilization. A policy that sustains near-capacity operations goes beyond strengthening the profitability of investment; it insures an ample supply of low-cost internal funds, which itself encourages investment.

(2) *Monetary and credit policy.* The open market operations of the Federal Reserve and the debt-management operations of the Treasury exert a powerful influence on supply conditions in credit markets. If economic growth were the only end to be served, the sole object of monetary and credit policy would be to assure an adequate flow of funds to finance the needed capital formation at interest rates appropriate to the basic profitability of investment. This was pointed out by the Chairman of the Board of Governors of the Federal Reserve System in March 1961, in a statement to the Joint Economic

Committee: "As I have said many times in the past, before this Committee and others, I am in favor of interest rates being as low as possible without stimulating inflation, because low rates can help to foster capital expenditures that, in turn, promote economic growth."

Use of monetary techniques for growth purposes must, of course, be limited by the demands placed on them by other national objectives. In the present situation, for example, monetary policy has a role to play in the attainment of recovery from recession and in the restoration of balance of payments equilibrium. Policies for growth and recovery are complementary, since any policy that stimulates investment will simultaneously stimulate aggregate demand. This situation, however, will not always prevail. When excessive demand threatens inflation, stability and growth goals will tend to push monetary policy in opposite directions. At such times, the importance of economic growth would suggest the major use of other measures—principally budgetary surpluses—to achieve stability. For when demand is strong enough to generate pressure on existing capacity, and only then, rapid growth requires that enough resources be withheld from other uses to make a sustained high rate of investment possible without inflation. Under these circumstances, a surplus in the Federal budget plays the constructive role of adding to national saving and making resources available for investment. The role of a policy of monetary ease at full employment is then to insure that the resources freed by a tight fiscal policy are indeed used for investment and not wasted in unemployment.

The current balance of payments problem puts additional constraints on the use of monetary policy to promote recovery and growth. The techniques developed by the Federal Reserve to meet the new situation have already been discussed in Chapter 1, Part II.

(3) *Tax policy.* Every tax system is the product of particular needs and economic conditions; no tax system can be neutral in its effects on the ways in which households and business firms earn and spend their incomes. If faster economic growth is desired, revision of the tax structure is called for, to permit a higher rate of investment once full use of resources is achieved.

The Administration's program encompasses two complementary approaches to this objective. The first is an investment tax credit equal to 8 percent of investment in eligible machinery and equipment; the second is revision of the guidelines for the tax lives of properties subject to depreciation.

The investment credit will stimulate investment by reducing the net cost of acquiring depreciable assets, thus increasing expected profitability. The increase will vary inversely with the expected life of the asset. For an asset with a service life of 10 years and an after-tax yield of 10 percent before the credit, the investment credit will increase the expected rate of return by about one-third. The increase in net yield will be greater for less durable equipment and smaller for more durable equipment.

Investment decisions are also influenced by the availability of funds. The investment tax credit will increase by some $1.5 billion the flow of cash available for investment under conditions anticipated for 1962.

Since the credit applies only to newly acquired assets, the entire incentive effect is concentrated on the profitability of new capital and no revenue is lost in raising the profitability of assets already held by business firms. It is an efficient way of encouraging re-equipment and modernization of productive facilities, as well as the expansion of capacity. The credit will thus help to accelerate economic growth and improve our competitive position. It will also increase the attractiveness of investment at home relative to direct investment abroad. In both ways the credit will help to ease our balance of payments problem.

Revision of tax lives for depreciable property is desirable as a matter of equity to reflect more accurately the influence of obsolescence on economic lives of capital assets. Present guidelines were established 20 years ago on the basis of replacement practices of the depressed prewar years. Depreciation, designed to reflect the loss in value of plant and equipment over time, is a function not alone of "wear and tear," but also of technological progress, changes in the relative costs of economic inputs, competitive conditions, and consumer tastes and demand. Through its favorable effects on cash flows, expected rates of return, and risk, liberalized depreciation will tend to stimulate investment.

The investment tax credit, coupled with liberalized depreciation, will provide a strong and lasting stimulus to the high rate of investment that is a major requirement for accelerated economic growth. Together, they will provide incentives to invest comparable to those available in the rapidly growing industrial nations of the free world.

Attention to Federal income tax ad-

justments to stimulate investment must not be allowed to obscure the role of State and local tax policies and practices in economic growth. The tax collections of these governments are nearly half as large as Federal collections. In fiscal year 1960, they increased by more than 10 percent, or $3.7 billion.

The power to tax under this governmental system is shared by thousands of separate jurisdictions. Improved coordination among them will improve economic efficiency. Identical tax sources are frequently utilized by two, three, and even four layers of government without appropriate cooperation. Taxing authorities occasionally use their powers in ways that capriciously affect decisions concerning the location of plants and disrupt normal competition. The result may be a misallocation of resources and economic loss.

The Congress has recognized the need for better intergovernmental coordination. It has provided for the creation of the Advisory Commission on Intergovernmental Relations to foster "the fullest cooperation and coordination of activities between the levels of governments." The Advisory Commission, composed of representatives of the executive and legislative branches of all levels of government, has already made important recommendations for the coordination of local taxes by the States and for improved tax coordination and cooperation between Federal and State governments.

B.
PRICE INDEXES AND INFLATION

9   THE CONSUMER PRICE INDEX

Sidney A. Jaffe

Sidney A. Jaffe, Bureau of Labor Statistics, U. S. Department of Labor.

INTRODUCTION

The daily flow of correspondence received by the Bureau asking for information on our procedures, criticizing the Consumer Price Index, demanding explanations of its movements and questioning its accuracy is a continual reminder of the public interest in our work and of the importance of the statistics we produce. When the index starts to rise, the retailers challenge us to prove it because, they insist, their prices have not gone up. When we report lower food prices and the index falls, the housewives scoff at us for not knowing the facts of family living.

At the same time, we are subjected to a continuous crossfire from the experts, the statisticians, economists, market researchers, and others who use the index in various ways for analytical purposes. One of the surprising aspects of our critical audience is that so many of them have no conception of what the CPI really is. And this misunderstanding is not confined to the statistically uninitiated—housewives, retired military officers, and retail store proprietors. Some members of our own statistical profession have revealed a remarkable lack of knowledge about the figures they criticize. Or when they do have that knowledge they sometimes criticize the index because they differ with us about what the index should measure.

In this paper I shall attempt to answer some of the questions, technical and otherwise, most frequently raised about the Consumer Price Index. My answers will of course be limited by the fact that we haven't found solutions to all the questions raised both within and outside the Bureau. Needless to say we welcome all the help we can get in finding practical answers to our problems.

It is a well-known principle in the index field that every index number is related to a specific question or problem. There is no index number that serves all purposes and answers all questions. The CPI is designed to measure only one thing—the change in prices of goods and services paid by families of urban wage earners and clerical workers to maintain their level of living. Many of the questions about the index arise from a misunderstanding of the index and an attempt to interpret it as something that it is not supposed to be. At the start, therefore, it might be well to explain what the CPI is and also explain what it is not.

_____

From _Hearings Before the Subcommittee on Economic Statistics of the Joint Economic Committee,_ Congress of the United States, May 1–5, 1961, pp. 603–611.

DEFINITION OF THE CONSUMER PRICE INDEX

The title, "Consumer Price Index" was adopted in 1945 as a substitute for the more popular term "The Cost of Living Index." This was done at the suggestion of a special committee of the American Statistical Association appointed at the request of the Bureau of Labor Statistics to review and evaluate the index. In testimony before a committee of Congress, Ewan Clague, Commissioner of Labor Statistics, explained the rationale of the name change and described the index in the following words:

"A cost-of-living index, as defined in contemporary economic thinking, is an index of the change in the cost of maintaining the same or an equivalent standard of living from one time to another, or from one place to another. The key to this concept is in the word 'equivalent.' Properly speaking, what distinguishes a cost-of-living index from the more narrowly defined price index is that in a cost-of-living index we would try to measure the changes in the cost of an equivalent market basket of goods and services whereas in a price index we try to measure the same market basket."

But the term "cost-of-living" is very commonly interpreted even more broadly to comprise what one newsman has called the cost of better living. At another point in his testimony Mr. Clague noted that the error in this reasoning "is the notion that either a price index or a cost-of-living index is intended to measure changes in costs of living that arise from changes in standards of living. Usually when people live better, when they buy more or better goods and services, it costs more. This kind of change would be reflected in an index of family expenditures, but not in a price index or a cost-of-living index." "Furthermore," Mr. Clague continued, "while it would be possible to make an index of family expenditures, the use of such an index to adjust wages would lead to the circular absurdity of saying, 'The more I spend the more the index will go up, and the more the index goes up, the more I'll have to spend.' "

It requires only a few additional sentences to describe the fundamental character of the Consumer Price Index. The population group to which the index refers is the aggregate of families of city wage earners and clerical workers. In structure the index is of the Laspeyres type with weights representing typical expenditures of the defined population group in a base period. The prices entering into the index calculation are transaction prices corresponding to types of transactions which actually take place in the markets patronized by the index population.

*   *   *

SAMPLING

Statisticians who ask how well the CPI measures the price movements of the wage-earner's basket of purchases often have in mind the precision of the index in terms of its sampling error. I must regretfully answer them that while we believe the CPI provides a measurement of price change sufficiently accurate for practical uses, we are unable to supply a statistical measure of its precision. Before going on with the reasons for this, I would like to state further that I don't consider this lack terribly important. The idiosyncrasies of the price data are far more significant in determining the character and accuracy of a price index. I am afraid that a measure of sampling error that ignored the problems of price measurement and comparison would, by giving a wrong impression of accuracy, defeat its own purpose.

The CPI is built upon a series of samples. The primary sampling units are the cities in which we sample households for determination of weights and measurement of rents, or outlets for collection of prices. The selection of items, and of varieties and qualities of items, is still another mode of sampling. Completing the index structure is a sampling in time, since we collect prices in different cities and for different items at different intervals. Aside from the selection of the cities there are few features of the index where the Bureau has been able to apply systematic sampling. The principal exception[s] where probability sampling is applied are in the selection of households for the consumer expenditure surveys which supply the index weights and in the sample of rents for which we use a probability cross section of households for our data.

The selection of outlets in which we price, in particular, presents difficulties to a probability approach. Except for foods we are able to obtain only a relatively few quotations per item. Yet we would like these to be representative of different kinds of stores in the various locations (central city, neighborhood, suburban) in which index families shop. We have had to achieve these objectives largely by a judgment selection.

Since the probability sampling is so generally accepted as desirable, its honoring in the breach calls for some explanation. Given unlimited resources it would probably be possible to establish probability sampling procedures for all components of the Consumer Price Index. However, because of the wide scope of the index, the diversity of elements that must be sampled, and the complexity of the marketing situations in which prices must be gathered, there is no practical probability sampling approach that can be applied with present resources. This does not mean that we at the Bureau ignore the statistical principles of sampling. They are applied to the extent that is practical and are alway held forth as guides to our day-to-day sampling decisions.

COVERAGE

Another question often raised is how much of what people buy is covered in the index and how the items for pricing are selected. The typical family may buy 3,000 or more items in the course of a year; we obtain prices on a sample of about 300 specific commodities and services. The selection of the item for pricing was made in two stages. First, all items which accounted for 1 per cent or more of consumer expenditures as determined in the BLS benchmark surveys were considered for pricing. Then, on the basis of the Consumer Expenditures Survey results and special price studies all expenditure items were grouped into families of related commodities or services which had similar price trend characteristics. The most important item in each price family was then included in the index sample. The value weights of the unpriced items were imputed to the items selected as representative. The weights and imputations have remained relatively unchanged since the latest revision of the CPI completed in 1952. Obviously changes in spending patterns, market practices, and products during the past 8 years have altered these relationships somewhat. A complete review of the sample and the imputation system will be made as part of the major revision program which we will undertake during the next four years.

In the meantime, how have changes in products and expenditures affected the validity of the index? Critics of the index often exaggerate the importance of items and weights because they forget that the index is a measure of change, not levels. Insertion of new products or shifts in weights does not necessarily affect the index to any marked extent. Currently, for example, we are being questioned about the new compact automobiles. If they are not included in the sample, it is argued, the index will fail to reflect the true price situation. They are lower in price, it is true, but they are a different item and we have no reason to believe that the price trends for the small cars will not conform to the trends shown by the standard models.

There is, of course, another aspect of this problem. If buyers generally shift from high-priced big cars to lower-priced small cars a change occurs in the basic structure of expenditures. But such changes in spending patterns are constantly occurring in some degree. Here we face a dilemma. If we revise the items and their weights frequently it is difficult to define what the index means. As a practical matter, therefore, we use what is essentially a fixed market basket over the period of years between the general index revisions. This provides a meaningful measure of price trends over relatively short periods of time, perhaps ten years or so. Over very long periods, however, the whole complex of products and services changes to such an extent that a fixed base price comparison is obviously impossible. There is nothing today comparable in all respects to the wheat, oil and wine which formed the basis for the first price index, and there's nothing we can do about it.

*   *   *

PROBLEMS OF QUALITY CHANGE

Quality can be defined in several ways. It may be described in physical terms: type of material, size, color, flavor, weight, calorie content, etc. Variations in quality may be indicated by performance: miles per gallon, speed, or length of life, ease and/or expense of repairs. In addition, buyers apply many purely subjective tests in judging quality, such as style, prestige value, etc. In a sense, of course, the ultimate measure of quality lies in the consumer's subjective evaluation. He assesses the value of the good in terms of the satisfaction it provides. And this is the crux of our problem.

Collection of data for the CPI is based upon the principles of specification pricing. In order to insure that we are pricing the comparable items from month to month and from city to city, a list of the significant characteristics of each item is set forth for the guidance of our pricing agents. The quality determining elements of the specification are established in discussions with manufacturers, merchandisers, and buyers. Generally the specifications include more information pertaining to the quality or intrinsic value of an item that our field agents can in practice apply in selecting items in the stores for pricing. Our experience has often been that the store owners and buyers are not sufficiently acquainted with their merchandise to answer our detailed questions on specifications. Nor can our agents, well trained though they are, uncover all the facts regarding quality and conformance to specification by a personal inspection of the merchandise; e.g., the "innards" of a TV set.

Our greatest difficulties with specification pricing arise primarily from product changes and the failure of our specification mechanism to provide a measurement of the dollar worth of new items as compared with the items they replace. This has led to criticisms somewhat along the lines of the following syllogism: (*a*) with technology on an upward trend, this year's products are better than last year's; (*b*) the BLS compares prices of this year's products against last year's; (*c*) therefore the BLS price index is biased upward. The missing link in this logic is the BLS price index mechanism.

There are varying practices employed in the Consumer Price Index for the comparison of prices when products change. For example, in the case of automobiles our practice has been to substitute the new model car for the previous model, assuming no quality change except for those features which affect some easily observed difference in operational characteristics and for which a value can be determined. Usually such changes involve the incorporation in the standard model of some feature which had formerly been offered as an extra. Thus, for example, if backup lights had been offered as an extra-cost feature at $25 on last year's model but are included in the quoted price for the new model, we would assume a quality improvement worth $25 in the new model. If last year's model was introduced at $2,500 retail, without the backup lights, and the new model with backup lights comes in at $2,600, we would show a price increase of $75, unless there were other added features similar to the backup lights. In such a comparison we would make no allowances for such changes as greater length or more wrap in the windshield, because we have no objective standard by which to determine the relationship between quality and price for such features.

The practice of making direct price comparison between new items and their counterpart old items would seem to lead to some bias, as in the automobile component of the index. Among the many changes in automobiles, however, not all, certainly, can be considered unqualified improvements. Some "improvements" have been abandoned because they were found to be unworkable, too costly to maintain or not of sufficient appeal to the car buyer.

Where information on the effect of quality changes on prices or costs is available the Bureau attempts to adjust the prices being compared to an equivalent quality basis. The use of cost information in this context is considered an expedient of not much more than minimum acceptability for approximating the market value of a quality change. In the absence of information on price and cost differences due to quality, the BLS uses either direct comparison procedures, as in the automobile example, or linking procedures. The first procedure, on the assumption of higher quality, introduces an upward bias in the index. The linking procedure, on the other hand, by introducing a new item at the index level of the old item which it replaces can be presumed to cause a downward bias when the price trend is upward.

*   *   *

My remarks may have implied that quality is conceptually measurable, even if in practice measurement is difficult or impossible. This is not the case. Quality is often something subjective or personal, as in the case of women's hats, or taste in foods and drinks. No objective standards are available, for example, to determine just what constitutes a premium beer, unless one wished perhaps to use advertising outlays as a criterion. Are the differences between the various cola drinks a matter of quality or a matter of taste? Since the formulas are kept secret, the objective criterion of manufacturing cost is not available, and would it be appropriate even if it were? What the BLS generally does in these cases is to price by brand name and not make price comparisons across brands. This is all right until there is a switch of brands; then, in the absence of a basis for price comparison, the new brand price is linked in at the former index level. When prices are on the upgrade such a procedure has a downward bias, but no other available method seems preferable.

10   MEASURING THE COST OF QUALITY

Richard Ruggles

Richard Ruggles is Professor of Economics at Yale University.

The bogy of inflation is with us again. This cry, which was chronic during the Fifties, has been a major factor in determining our monetary and fiscal policies. Since these policies are based on the movements in the price indexes, it is time to consider whether our confidence in these indexes is justified.

In 1948 the Consumer Price Index has increased by approximately 25 per cent. A large part of this increase—about one-third of it—occurred in the brief space of one year, at the beginning of the Korean war. The other two-thirds was spread more or less evenly over the other 12 years —an average increase of about one and a half per cent a year.

In view of these statistics, policy makers might have concluded that we had relative price stability in the Fifties, except at the beginning of the Korean war when scare buying forced prices up. Instead, we hear much about a continual and insidious price creep. When price indexes continued to rise during periods of recession, such as in 1958, many policy makers concluded that rising prices stemmed from increasing costs due to excessive wage demands and administered prices of monopolies.

To understand what has *really* been happening to prices, we must first examine the factors responsible for the rises in the index. For this purpose let us take a look at the 12 per cent increase in the Consumer Price Index that has occurred since the Korean war. There are major segments of consumer purchases for which prices have not risen at all since that time. The price index for consumer durables, for example, shows a decline of approximately three per cent. On the other hand, the index for medical care rose by more than 30 per cent. On the average, the prices of services rose a substantial 23 per cent, while those of commodities rose only six per cent.

This difference in behavior largely reflects the fact that the price of a service is generally the rate of compensation of those performing it. And these wages naturally rise as per capita income rises. In the last 50 years the prices of services relative to those of commodities have risen continually as a consequence of such general rises in living standards. Commodity prices, on the other hand, can sometimes reflect increased productivity. If the increase

From *Challenge*, Vol. X, No. 2, November, 1961, pp. 6–9. Reprinted by permission.

in output per man-hour is greater than the increase in the wage rate, the cost of production may actually fall, thus permitting lower commodity prices despite higher wages.

The identification of price indexes with rates of pay in the service industries involves the implicit assumption that the productivity of the service industries has remained unchanged. In some instances, this assumption may be correct, but in others quite wide of the mark.

In the case of medical care, for example, the apparent 30 per cent price increase of the last eight years must be qualified by considering the increase in medical knowledge, better drugs and the new preventive medicines. Certainly the Salk vaccine was a tremendous medical advance which, in addition to sparing many lives, will save consumer dollars that would have gone for the treatment of polio.

Basically, then, the measurement of price changes comes down to a question of whether one gets more or less for his money. In the field of medical care it can be argued that most people would rather pay today's prices for today's medical care than yesterday's prices for yesterday's medical care. The fact that diseases were treated more cheaply in yesterday's world is more than offset by the increased knowledge and new drugs available for curing disease today. Although it is difficult to measure improvement in the *quality* of medicine in quantitative terms, there is no justification for ignoring it— which is what our present method of computing price indexes does.

The problem of measuring changes in quality also arises in the commodity components of the Consumer Price Index. In the Congressional hearings on government price statistics conducted early this year, Prof. Zvi Griliches of the University of Chicago

reported on the effect that changes in specifications had upon automobile prices. Dr. Griliches computed the value of specifications such as size, automatic transmission, horsepower, etc., by taking the price differences for a given year among cars with these varying specifications. Automobile prices were then adjusted to take into account the different features included as standard equipment in each year.

On this basis, using the value of specifications given by the 1954 price schedule, the prices of the "low-priced three" dropped 27 per cent from 1954 to 1960, although their unadjusted list price rose 34 per cent, and the Consumer Price Index for these automobiles reported a rise of 11 per cent. The significance of this study is not that the Consumer Price Index for automobiles needs some minor adjustment to reflect the true price situation, but rather that the overemphasis on price change is itself in question. Instead of an 11 per cent price increase over this period, there may have been a price reduction of as much as 27 per cent.

This same kind of analysis could, of course, be applied to other major kinds of consumer durables, such as home laundry equipment, refrigerators and freezers, portable radios, cameras and hi-fi equipment. Almost all of these have shown considerable change in recent years. If the change in *quality* were taken into account the price index for consumer durables would have fallen far more than the three per cent now reported.

Besides the quality change in existing goods, we should also take into account the effect of the introduction of totally new commodities upon the consumer's purchasing power. The index of consumer prices is purposely designed so that the introduction of new goods or the dropping of old ones will have no effect. Thus the introduction of such things as television, synthetic fibers and plastic products has had no effect upon the index.

But the introduction of new products obviously *does* have an influence upon consumers' standards of living, just as do quality improvements in existing products. It is quite possible to imagine an economic system which obtains its higher standard of living through the introduction of new products which are superior to the old ones they replace. In such a system, the consumer might continuously get more value for his dollar, even though the prices of the old products rose steadily due to rising wage and material costs. Yet conventional price indexes would show this situation as one in which prices are rising and consumers are getting less for their dollars. Although, of course, in our economy not all of the improvement in the standard of living comes about through the substitution of new products for old, it does seem clear that much of it has been achieved in this way, despite the systematic exclusion of this factor from price indexes.

Innovations and new products are not restricted to the durable goods field. They have, for instance, been highly significant in the food industry over the last decade. Meals are much easier to get and the choice available to the housewife is much greater. There will be those who claim that the additional packaging and processing now common is an undesirable element of cost, and that the personal contact between the individual proprietor and the customer has been lost. Conversely, it can be argued that increased attention to packaging not only standardizes the merchandise, but it raises the level of sanitation and grading. In addition, the freedom to examine goods allows the customer to make comparisons before buying in a way that would not have been possible before.

It is, of course, not possible to measure accurately the dimensions of quality and product change. Nevertheless, one can safely suggest that, given the size of the average yearly increase in the Consumer Price Index since Korea, quality and product improvements may well have been much greater, so that

MAKE-UP OF THE CONSUMER'S MARKET BASKET *

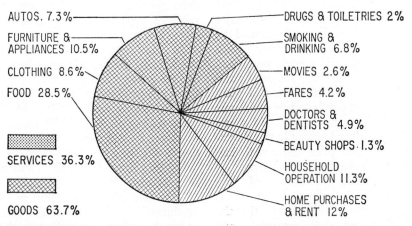

AUTOS. 7.3%
FURNITURE & APPLIANCES 10.5%
CLOTHING 8.6%
FOOD 28.5%
SERVICES 36.3%
GOODS 63.7%

DRUGS & TOILETRIES 2%
SMOKING & DRINKING 6.8%
MOVIES 2.6%
FARES 4.2%
DOCTORS & DENTISTS 4.9%
BEAUTY SHOPS 1.3%
HOUSEHOLD OPERATION 11.3%
HOME PURCHASES & RENT 12%

* Relative weights of goods and services used by Bureau of Labor Statistics to Prepare the Consumer Price Index.

we may actually have had declining rather than rising prices.

This does not mean that price indexes are completely invalid. Price indexes are useful in that they can show the relative differences in price behavior over time or between countries. For example, the eight per cent increase in the price index at the beginning of the Korean war indicates that prices were rising more rapidly in this period than at any other time in the decade of the Fifties.

In periods of hyperinflation, such as have been experienced by some Latin American countries in recent years, where the price index may rise by as much as 80 per cent in a single year, the indexes give a good indication of what is happening since such large increases cannot be offset by quality change. It is only in periods when price changes are relativly small that it becomes a serious error to use the indexes as an exact measure of what is taking place in the economy. In such periods the systematic biases of the price index may well be greater than the reported price change.

The defects of the Consumer Price Index are also inherent in the other price indexes which are used to deflate the gross national product to measure the change in real output. Two major categories of goods are produced by the economy besides consumer goods. These are goods and services purchased by the government, ranging from school teaching to missiles, and plant and equipment purchased by producers for use in later production. To measure the quantity of output in these categories, we need price indexes to calculate it in noninflationary terms.

In measuring the output of government, it is assumed—as it is throughout the service sector—that the productivity of civil servants never changes. The price indexes for this area are merely based on the changes in pay of government employees. While one may be tempted to agree with this evaluation of civil servants, the fact is that the introduction of computers, office machines and other automatic equipment has greatly increased the effectiveness of the individual worker. For example, the 1960 census data were processed by microfilming the original schedules and automatically producing magnetic tape for the electronic computers. Automatic equipment performed jobs which took thousands of clerks in previous censuses. Not only was the payroll reduced, but far more information was made available in a much shorter space of time. Output per census employee thus rose very considerably.

Similar examples of the increased output of government employees can be cited at the local level. For example, policemen have been provided with radio-equipped patrol cars and, more recently, transistorized walkie-talkies. Street cleaners have been given mechanized equipment. In some areas—education, for instance—progress is more difficult to measure. Yet most of us would be unwilling to have our children given the same education as we received, especially in the areas of sciences and mathematics.

In producers' durable equipment, once again, the price indexes leave out quality change and new products. But there are probably very few industries in which producers in 1960 would have been willing to buy 1950 models of machines even if they could get them at the 1950 prices. According to the Wholesale Price Index the 1960 price of producers' durable equipment was 23 per cent above the 1950 price; if producers' durable equipment showed as much quality change as was shown in the study referred to above for automobiles, it seems probable that in fact prices actually fell.

For construction, both industrial and residential, the index is computed on the basis of wage rates and material cost. Thus again it is assumed that productivity does not change. While the construction industry is notorious for its lack of progressiveness, if we consider the new methods of off-the-site fabrication of components it is obvious that this assumption is not entirely valid. Once again, it seems that price indexes have greatly exaggerated the actual price rise.

Thus, we see that for almost every category of goods, whether purchased by consumers for household consumption, by government for public services or by producers for plant and equipment, the conventional price indexes do not reflect the effects of the introduction of new products and the improvement of existing products, or the increased productivity of those performing services. These omissions mean that the price indexes are higher than they should be. And since the indexes are used to deflate the value of current output and calculate its worth in noninflationary terms, our rate of growth is thus considerably understated.

The fact that our growth rate has probably been higher than we thought does not mean, however, that we should be any happier vis-à-vis the Russians. These elements would also have at least as much effect upon the Russian figures. As we well know, the Soviet rate of technological progress in some areas has exceeded ours, but even in the areas where they are still well behind us, the *rate* at which they introduce new technology might be faster than ours.

A half-century ago many more industries were producing the kind of output that could be measured quite satisfactorily in quantity terms. Today new major industries such as electronics, chemicals, machinery and household appliances account for an increasingly important share of our output. In all these industries the changes in prices and output are very difficult to measure, since the nature of the products is continually changing. It may mean, therefore, that the national concern over a sagging economic growth rate is really not warranted. The problem may be our inability to measure growth represented by product changes and increased productivity in the service industries. The inadequacy of the price indexes will become even more glaring in the years ahead.

It is interesting to speculate on what will happen to our measurement of output when further growth does not take the form of additional consumption of identical items, but rather of the consumption of goods of improved quality, the substitution of new products for old and the consumption of higher quality services. In such a world, our conventional price indexes would fail to catch the quality improvement; they would not recognize that the substitution of new products for old was any increase in the standard of living; and they would report the continued increase in the use of services solely in terms of the rates of remuneration. Thus they might show an economy with constant output and rising prices, even though the standard of living was increasing rapidly. What is perhaps more serious, the conventional price and output indexes would fail completely to distinguish between a dynamic economy and one that was truly stagnant.

The single-minded pursuit of price stability, coupled with the false soundings given by our present price indicators, is likely to lead our economy policy makers astray. The tragedy of the postwar period is not so much the low rate of growth (which we cannot measure anyway), but rather the underutilization of our resources and the low level of investment to which the continuous existence of excess capacity leads.

At the quiver of a decimal point in the Consumer Price Index, the government has instituted restrictive monetary and fiscal policies. Its objective has been to restrain demand so that producers would find themselves with excess capacity and thus would not raise prices; and labor unions would be deterred by the existence of unemployment from seeking wage increases. The economy has been either in a depressed state or under restraining monetary and fiscal policies throughout almost the entire period since Korea. It is small wonder that in such an environment the rate of investment is low. In an economy where a false fear of inflation continually holds demand in check, even a low level of investment creates capacity which cannot be fully utilized.

With this in mind, it is appropriate to inquire what a faster rate of growth and better utilization of our capacity would do to our price indexes. Historically, if we look at any period of upward change in the general level of activity, we find that the price indexes rise. Thus, for example, in the recovery from the depression of the 1930s, prices in certain sectors responded sharply to the increase in demand. Farm prices rose by about 85 per cent in the five years from 1932 to 1937. Even in the metals industry, prices went up about 30 per cent. At the same time, unemployment dropped from 25 per cent to about 14 per cent. It cannot very well be argued that these price rises were the result of excess demand pressing on fully employed resources.

In other words, growth and the increase in real income tend to produce price increases in certain sectors irrespective of the pressure on resources. If the price index is to remain stable, the increases in such sectors would have to be balanced by lower prices in other sectors, where productivity increases would permit prices to fall. Given the imperfections of our price indexes, however, economic growth will almost inevitably result in an upward movement of the price index irrespective of the pressure of demand.

Despite the relatively high unemployment rate of close to seven per cent, there is a tendency to minimize the underutilization of our resources which has resulted from too much concern with small movements in the price index. It is argued that at least four per cent of this is frictional unemployment, and thus that we are operating at 97 per cent of full employment—a high level in anybody's vocabulary. Such a computation, however, is very misleading. The unemployment rate is not very closely related to the economy's excess capacity. The spread of automation and the increase in the number of white-collar employees means that many industries can expand their output considerably without hiring many more workers. Thus, a steel company operating at 50 per cent capacity might be able to double its output by adding 10 or 20 per cent more employees. This is even more true in such sectors of the economy as electric power, communications, finance, insurance and retail trade—all sectors whose activity (and thus output) increases with an increase in the general level of activity of the economy without requiring any substantial increase in manpower.

This relationship between the increase in man-hours employed and the increase in output shows up clearly in the over-all statistics. In the recoveries from all of our past recessions output has risen much faster than man-hours employed. On average, output tends to rise during economic recoveries about three times as fast as the man-hours required to produce it. In the first six months of the present recovery, if we are to believe the figures, an increase in output of approximately five per cent has been accompanied by an increase in man-hours of less than one per cent.

Much of the increase in manpower that is needed, furthermore, does not come from the reservoir of the unemployed. Unutilized manpower within firms is drawn upon, and cuts in the workweek which may have been put into effect during the recession are restored. With increasing employment opportunities, the labor force itself tends to expand, thus providing additional resources. Even allowing for frictional unemployment, it seems reasonable that there could be an increase of 10 or 12 per cent in man-hours.

The Council of Economic Advisers has estimated that in early 1961 the economy was operating at a level some 10 per cent below full capacity. This figure seems far too conservative when one takes into account the additional man-hours available and their relation to potential output. If past performance is a guide, it would not seem unreasonable to suppose that the 10 or 12 per cent additional man-hours which were available in the spring of 1961 could have been utilized to produce 25 per cent more output. This seems all the more likely since, by late summer of 1961, output had risen by about five per cent and unemployment had not fallen at all.

It is true, of course, that an increase in real output of 25 per cent, even though it created no pressure on resources, would cause our price indexes to rise. Under present anti-inflation policy we would then move quickly to prevent such real output increases from occurring. In fact, that is exactly what we are doing, even though the increase in real output has been far less than this. The price indexes have quivered, and there is talk of putting the brakes on. Those wishing to restrict demand have labeled the unemployment "structural," and thereby have succeeded in removing it from their own consciences. This rationalization may satisfy them, but it is not much help for the unemployed—since it is obvious that the only cure for unemployment, whether structural or any other kind, is more jobs, and you don't get more jobs by restricting demand, no matter how much retraining you do.

The loss in potential output may not seem to be very impressive when expressed in percentage of total output, but, in fact, we waste through under-utilization an amount equal in size to two or three times what we now spend on defense, or 20 to 25 times as much as we now are giving in foreign aid. These wasted resources could rebuild our cities and automate our factories within a few short years; they could raise our rate of growth to equal or surpass that of any other nation.

This then is the cost of taking our price indexes too seriously. We inhibit real growth, because growth by its very nature must lead to increases in the price indexes. And because this inhibited growth in output does not keep up with the growth in our capacity to produce, we have ever-present excess capacity. The excess in machines is self-limiting; producers soon learn when investment is unprofitable. But the excess in manpower is harder to dispose of—the unemployed are there, and you can't really make the problem go away by saying that they don't exist.

11   THE GERMAN NIGHTMARE

Donald B. Woodward and
Marc A. Rose

Donald B. Woodward is an economist with wide experience in Government.
Marc A. Rose was a newspaper and magazine editor, and served as a senior editor of *Reader's Digest*.

Wildest of all the inflations the world ever has seen, the German orgy after the war is the horrible example held up in solemn warning before the eyes of anyone who ventures to suggest that money might be managed to avert, or at least to soften, the impact of violent price upheavals.

Indeed, it was a nightmare. Large classes of the population paid bitterly for it. But the candid historian must record that there were some compensations to the nation at large. At least it wiped out internal debt, albeit by the brutality of complete repudiation.

Before the war, the German mark was firmly based on gold, with a parity of 23 cents. Germany, in fact, was the nation which broke up bimetallism in Europe. Demanding a $1,000,000,000 gold indemnity from France at the close of the Franco-Prussian war, she seized the opportunity to use the gold as a base for a single-standard currency.

The war put a severe strain on the German economy, but the depreciation of the mark was not beyond recovery; after the armistice, the mark was quoted at about 12 cents.

Then came the peace negotiations. When the full weight of the terms imposed under the Treaty of Versailles became apparent, the Germans felt their situation hopeless—and so did financiers in other countries. The new government's financial difficulties kept increasing. The nation's debt was heavy, and much of it was not funded. It was necessary to resort to the expedient of printing marks, mere fiat money, to pay the government's expenses. By early 1920, the mark was worth about 1 cent, gold. The decline was checked at that point, and there was even some improvement; but late in 1921, the mark began to sink again in terms of foreign exchange. Reparations had been fixed at 132,000,000,000 gold marks, or some $33,000,000,000. More and more, Germany was completely discouraged at the outlook; financial recovery looked impossible, and the occupation of the Ruhr in January, 1923, seemed to show that the harder the Germans tried to beat their way upward the more the demands that would be made upon them.

The Treasury proceeded to issue bills to the Reichsbank at an accelerating rate, discounting them for paper money. The printing presses ran more and more rapidly; pieces of currency were issued in denominations of millions of marks. Prices, of course, kept rising, which steadily increased the government's expenses and made it necessary to print more currency. The spiral was started; nothing, it seemed, could break it. Under the conditions, there was little incentive to try.

The banks, which had participated

Reprinted with permission of the McGraw-Hill Book Company, Inc., from *Inflation* by Donald B. Woodward and Marc A. Rose; copyright 1932, 1933, 1935 by the McGraw-Hill Book Company, Inc.

very little at the outset, began to discount bills at the Reichsbank and to increase their loans and deposits. Ultimately, the municipalities began to issue money, also the railroads, and many other institutions. Metal coins previously used for small change disappeared into hoarding or were converted into paper, the bullion content being worth vastly more than the stamped value of the coins.

Before the war, the total money in circulation in Germany had averaged about 6,000,000,000 marks. At the end of 1923, the authorized circulation was 518,000,000,000,000,000,000—518 billions of billions. No estimate ever has been attempted of the amount of other currencies in circulation. Conditions were utterly chaotic.

In November, 1923, the situation was taken in hand. A new currency unit, the rentenmark, was established, its value put at 1,000,000,000,000 —a million million—of the marks it was to supersede. The new rentenmark was fixed at parity with the prewar mark—that is, at 23 cents. Incidentally, it was pure fiat money, but its value was successfully controlled in terms of gold.

The Dawes plan was made effective in 1924, fixing Germany's obligations to the outside world at a point more nearly within reason. With that encouragement, the reichsmark was established on a gold basis, also at 23 cents.

That was the end of inflation. Behind this bare story of the course of events are a million human comedies and tragedies. No one ever will record even a small part of them. But some of the most fantastic and absurd incidents are remembered.

As this one: the total German mortgage debt before the war was about 40,000,000,000 marks. At the peak of the inflation, 40,000,000,000 marks were worth less than a cent. All the mortgages in Germany could have been paid off for 1 cent, American. A box of matches sold for more than 6,000,-000,000 marks, which it will be remembered was the total amount of money in circulation in Germany in prewar years.

Things happened as in a fever-ridden dream. Prices changed by the hour. Before the summit was reached, a ham sandwich was quoted at 14,000 marks one day and 24,000 marks the next. An article in a retail store priced at 5,000,000,000 marks in the morning had increased to 12,000,000,000 by afternoon. A sheet of writing paper cost 120 marks—$30 at prewar exchange—while yet the inflation was young. Interest rates rose to 900 per cent, and even then lenders at times were not protected, because by the time they were paid—even tenfold—the sum they received was worth less than the sum they lent.

What this meant in terms of human hardship can easily be imagined. Savings patiently built up by a lifetime of thrift might buy as much as a package of cigarettes. Life insurance policies matured—and the proceeds would not buy a handkerchief. It might be cheaper to light a cigar with a bond than to buy a match. The thrifty were penalized; the only wise folk were the spendthrifts. The nation became a spendthrift one, of course; everyone who received money rushed madly to convert it into goods. Things would be worth more tomorrow, perhaps this very afternoon. Money would be worth less. Debts were wiped out; farm mortgages were paid off with a sack of potatoes.

Translated into economic jargon, the creditor class was ruined; debtors were freed. People who had lived on investments were paupers.

The government tried to protect its citizens but could not do much. Prices of necessities were fixed from time to time to assure people of food and a roof over their heads, but fixing prices at a reasonable level one day did not solve the problem the next. Wages were moved up frequently—in the early stages, every month, then every ten days, but they always lagged behind the cost of living. The principle of fixing wages on a sliding scale geared to the cost of living was adopted, but it never was very popular with labor, because most workingmen did not understand its complexities, and those who did protested that the scale was inadequate. Labor troubles were widespread.

While great classes were being pauperized, other skillful manipulators were becoming fabulously wealthy. The speculators' method was to borrow money, buy goods or real estate or factories, then pay off the debt in worthless money. Then they could either keep the tangibles or sell them and repeat the operation.

Business of course boomed, for everyone was buying goods. A great boom developed in the stock market, from the scramble to buy shares in tangible properties.

Toward the close of the era, many localities began to quote prices of foreign currencies, usually dollars. Various institutions issued scrip redeemable in goods—rye, barley, coal, wood, and even kilowatt hours.

It was impossible, obviously to plan ahead in terms of paper money. Construction and similar industries languished.

After monetary stabilization, there was a brief depression, but business did not for long stay inordinately dull, since there had been an accumulation of demands for goods and services that could not be supplied during the inflation—demands for new homes and improved factories, for example. So recovery progressed with reasonable rapidity.

But profound changes had been made in the social structure. There were new rich and new poor. The middle class, by and large, suffered most. The very poor had had little to lose; many of the wealthy had known how to protect themselves. Businesses emerged with most of their debts wiped out.

12 INFLATION IN PERSPECTIVE

G. L. Bach

G. L. Bach is Maurice Falk Professor of Economics at Carnegie Institute of Technology.

Recently many economists and businessmen have argued that we face a new type of "cost-push" and "administered-price" inflation substantially unlike the traditional "excess-demand" or "demand-pull" inflation. From this argument they draw major new public policy implications that cast serious doubt on the efficacy of traditional monetary and fiscal policies against inflation. At the same time, and for many of the same reasons, they argue that

From the *Harvard Business Review,* January–February, 1958, pp. 99–110. Reprinted by permission.

we have entered a new period of long-run secular inflationary drift that will be difficult if not impossible to avoid. But for every claim there is a counter-claim—that the new inflation is no different, that long-run inflation is not inevitable.

In the midst of all this controversy, almost everyone is against inflation, at least in principle. Even Sumner H. Slichter now states that he is not for inflation but just accepts it as the lesser of two evils. Recent debate has begun to clarify the issues and to probe under the earlier superficial diatribes against "inflation"—which is often undefined. Yet little attention has been given to spelling out carefully and systematically just what the results of "creeping" (i.e., moderate) long-range inflation are, and which of these results we should try to prevent or encourage. In this article I propose:

1. To argue that the distinction between the new "cost-push, administered-price" inflation and the traditional "excess-demand" inflation, although real, is less substantial than is often argued, and is of much less significance for the conduct of governmental monetary-fiscal policy against inflation than is commonly supposed.

2. To summarize briefly the major economic effects of recent "moderate" American inflation, together with some comments on comparable recent inflations abroad, in the hope of throwing some light on the effects of continuing inflation.

3. To suggest, in the light of these facts, some of the public policy implications for the present and foreseeable future.

WHAT IS IT?

One reason why so many arguments about inflation get nowhere is that the disputants too often fail to define the term. This is especially unfortunate because there is no one "best" definition of inflation on which all the experts agree. Some speak of rising prices themselves as inflation. Others think of inflation in terms of the cause, often cited as excess monetary demand, and describe rising prices as merely a symptom. Still others, combining these definitions, define inflation as a situation of excess monetary demand which forces up prices after full employment has been reached.

By inflation I shall mean a rise in the price level or, what is the same thing, a fall in the purchasing power of the monetary unit. To measure changes in the price level, I shall generally use the well-known United States Bureau of Labor Statistics Index of Consumer Prices or Index of Wholesale Prices. But for most of what I say the precise index used is not of crucial importance, so long as it is a broadly based one and represents many prices in the economy.

*   *   *

Under the proposed definition, rising prices are inflation whether they rise rapidly or slowly (a small rise in prices is a little inflation, and a big rise a large inflation), and whether there is full employment or not. The likelihood of rising prices is, of course, greater after full employment has been reached, but history shows us that prices may rise substantially before resources are fully employed. And there is some reason to suppose this phenomenon of rising prices together with some unemployment may become increasingly common. It occurred last year, and it may well occur again this year if present moderate recession tendencies persist.

THE NEW INFLATION

In the new inflation, it is argued, powerful labor unions push wages upward faster than productivity increases. Then the leading firms in oligopolistic industries (where one or a few firms dominate the field and substantially establish prices, as in the automobile industry) raise their prices at least enough to cover the increase in costs, and often more. When total demand is strong, this wage-price spiral may rise rapidly. Even when the aggregate demand is relatively weak, some economists argue, union wages and administered prices will continue their upward push. Appreciable unemployment is no sure check to this "sellers' inflation."

The new inflation, according to this view, does not necessarily depend upon excess total monetary demand for its existence. Though wages and prices in highly competitive sectors of the economy may not rise rapidly or at all, unionized wages and administered prices—both widespread in our economy—mean persistent secular inflation.

By contrast, the traditional view of inflation is that prices in the aggregate rise when there is too much money chasing too few goods—that is, when there is excess total demand for goods and services offered for sale at prevailing prices. This is "demand-pull" inflation. Such a view looks on markets as competitive to a substantial degree. Prices rise when demand runs ahead of supply, and only then to any significant degree. Where individual firms or unions set wages or prices, they cannot get far out of line with what the demand side of the market will bear. If they do, surplus labor and surplus goods will exert a heavy drag on further price advances or even bring price reductions. Persistent long-run inflation will occur only if for some reason excess total demand prevails. And the traditional view suggests that excess demand can prevail for long only if the money supply (demand deposits and currency) increases more rapidly than total output of goods and services.

How Different?

In extreme cases the new and the old inflations may be quite different. If inflation is generated by a large increase in the money supply (say by huge government expenditures financed by bank borrowing), it is clear that we have traditional excess-demand inflation. Whether the wage-price structure is highly competitive or not, both wages and prices will be bid up rapidly as the new money is spent.

In most cases, however, the difference between the new and the old is plainly one of degree. The economy has never been perfectly competitive with prices and wages responding only to impersonal market forces of supply and demand. Both wages and prices have long been administered to varying degrees in different markets. And with nearly all administered wages and prices there is a margin, large or small, within which the price is set mainly according to the judgment of the price setter. If competitive pressures are strong, this discretionary margin is small; but if the seller has a substantial monopoly position, it may be quite large.

But no seller, no matter how administered his prices, can long escape the test of the market. He can raise his wage or price; but if his price moves far beyond customers' willingness or ability to buy, he will lose sales. If many prices are moving up at the same time, widespread sales losses may occur as prices across the board begin to outrun consumer incomes.

How Far?

The important thing is that a cost-push, administered-price inflation can-

not continue long unless there is growing total demand in the economy. Costs may "push" upward on prices, but, unless total demand is growing, the resultant price increases will not go very far. Thus there is a limit—the cold hand of lack of demand—which every seller must ultimately face unless the demand side of the market is rising too.

If the new and the old inflations are different only in degree, what of the argument that a long-run inflationary drift is inevitable because of the union wage push and the administered-price structure of our economy? The answer is: it is inevitable only if excess demand is provided to support the inflation. Organized labor is much stronger now than over past decades; moreover, there are many administrative price setters. But this is clearly not enough to guarantee long-run inflation. Indeed, we may have intermittent periods of some deflation.

As Peter L. Bernstein pointed out in the July 1957 issue of this magazine, the past decade has seen several circumstances especially conducive to inflation (shortage of labor, strong postwar demand, and high postwar liquidity), and these may well vanish in the near future. But, to argue, as Bernstein does, that because these special forces vanish the likelihood of long-range inflation also vanishes, seems to me to miss the main point: whether there will be excess demand. Neither do the arguments of Jacoby or Slichter really emphasize this key condition of continuing inflation.

There will be persistent excess total demand if governmental policy, as made by the Federal Reserve Board, Congress, and the executive branch in budget making, assures the excess total demand—whether in response to excessive wage-price policies or to more traditional pressures like defense

spending needs. If the policy of the Federal Reserve Board and of the rest of the government denies excess total demand, then there will not be any substantial amount of long-range inflation.

This brings us squarely to the issue of governmental monetary-fiscal policy in assessing the likelihood of long-range inflation. But first let us consider what some of the major economic effects of inflation have been in America over the past two decades.

WHAT ARE ITS EFFECTS?

What are the major economic effects of moderate inflation? From a casual reading of the daily papers and a sampling of the history books and campaign speeches of recent years:

It bleeds the little fellow and the laborer.

It increases profits at the expense of wages—or it transfers profits to the wage earner.

It lowers the national standard of living.

It leads inevitably to boom and bust.

It transfers income and wealth from the poor to the rich—or from the rich to the poor.

It wipes out the value of savings.

It induces waste and dissolution.

Clearly, not all of these allegations can be true, at least not of any one inflation at any one time. What are the real effects? To get an answer, we must break the question down into two more specific parts: (1) What effect does inflation have on the *total volume* of goods and services being produced—that is, on the "real gross national product" or "real national income"? (2) What effect does it have on the *distribution* of those goods and services among the various individuals and groups in society?

The logical approach would seem to

be to look at the American inflation of the past two decades, supplemented by experience in other countries. Helpful as this information may be, though, it does not provide a thoroughly satisfactory basis for predicting the future. One trouble is that we can never be sure in the complex interplay of forces just what conditions inflation actually *caused* during the past two decades. Even though changes occured together with or just after inflation, we cannot be sure that other forces were not the causes. Secondly, even if we could identify precisely cause and effect in the past, we could never be sure that the future would be just like the past.

Accordingly, in analyzing the effects of inflation, we need to supplement historical observation by economic theory. The problems of accurate interpretation and evaluation are difficult, but, by combining history and theory, we can get some idea of the main lessons to be drawn from the welter of evidence, argument, and counterargument.

Remember throughout that we are considering moderate, relatively slow inflations like that in America recently, not the great hyperinflations of postwar Central Europe.

Total Economic Output

Consider first the effect of inflation on the economy's total output. Imagine this total output, the real gross national product, as a huge pie of real goods and services. The question is: Does inflation either increase or decrease significantly the total size of the pie? Of course, the money value of any year's pie can be raised by bidding up prices, but this would merely raise the *money* gross national product, not the nation's *real* output and income.

Inflation may increase or decrease the nation's total output now or in the future, or it may have no effect at all. For simplicity, let us consider the *current* effects of inflation as being those which occur within, say, the next year or so, and the *future* effect as being those which show up over a longer period.

Does inflation reduce current real output? There is little a priori reason to suppose that moderate inflation reduces the size of the current national output. The evidence of history is flatly against this claim, *except* in cases of runaway, or hyper-, inflation. The common belief that inflation disrupts the economy and reduces its total output apparently goes back largely to the massive hyperinflations of Central Europe following World War I. At that time the currency became substantially worthless; a wheelbarrow full of money was needed to buy one meal; and speculative activity became more rewarding than productive work. By 1923 in Germany, for example, shortly before the collapse, this diversion of energy from normal productive work had become a vast drag on the output of real goods and services.

But in milder inflations history shows output generally rising. In the United States since 1937, for example, prices have roughly doubled, but the money value of our national output has risen to over 400% of 1937. Total real output has more than doubled. A similar picture has prevailed in most other countries over this same period—for example, in almost all of non-Communist Europe, where the inflation has far exceeded ours in some cases.

To be sure, it was easy to increase real output in the late 1930's, since there was so much unemployment. But the growth in total output, paralleling inflation, has been a persistent one both here and abroad, even in full-employment conditions. Conversely, cases of appreciable inflation accompanied by an appreciable drop in total real output have been rare indeed.

Output, of course, reflects managerial decision making. Jacoby and Slichter have argued vigorously as to whether the recent American inflation has disrupted managerial decision making and lowered the quality of managerial performance. But, boiled down, their argument is largely of a " 'tis, 'taint" variety. The answer seems to me clear: we just do not know, and cannot tell unambiguously from the limited evidence. But, as Slichter points out, the economy has, over-all, done very well indeed over these inflation decades; managerial decision making cannot have been too greatly upset.

These historical facts do not prove that inflation has not exerted a downward pressure on output. It is possible, of course, that other expansive forces have overcome any downward pressure that inflation has exerted. The evidence indicates, however, that if this has been the case, the depressive impact of inflation has generally been a weak one.

Does inflation increase current real output? Some scholars have claimed that inflation stimulates output and employment, especially in periods of widespread unemployment. There is no doubt that output has generally risen in periods of inflation. But this does not necessarily mean that inflation has generally, or ever, *caused* the rising output, or has even been *necessary* to it. It should be borne in mind that output has also risen in periods of stable, or even slightly declining, prices; the 1920's in the United States provide a leading example. Thus, to see inflation and increased output together by no means automatically indicates that rising prices are the cause.

We are thrown back, then, to a considerable extent on theory. The main arguments are that inflation increases current output by:

1. Pushing up prices faster than costs (especially wages) rise, thereby increasing profits and stimulating investment and output.

2. Inducing lagging income groups to work harder and longer.

3. Stimulating buying and output now because the expectation of continued inflation puts a premium on early purchases.

It is generally agreed that arguments #1 and #3 hold only when substantial unemployment exists; the second argument may apply even in high-employment periods. Let us see.

Price-cost differentials. The wage lag has apparently played a major role in many past inflations. But, as is shown below, wages have not lagged appreciably behind prices. Indeed, wages throughout the western industrialized world seem to be increasingly mobile in an upward direction, in many instances linked to rising prices through built-in escalator clauses.

Some other costs may lag in inflation, even though wages do not. Interest charges, rents, many salaries, and other costs are temporarily fixed in dollar terms as selling prices of business products rise. But these lags can easily be overcome by only a modest wage lead.

Inflation does lead to substantial overstatement of profits under prevailing accounting practices, because depreciation and inventory replacement costs are understated. This overstatement of profits may induce businesses to invest and to produce more than they otherwise would. Partial estimates suggest that this understatement of replacement costs approached one-third of corporate profits during the decade of the 1940's. While most businessmen surely recognize the phantom nature of part of their inflation-period profits, it may be that the figures nevertheless stimulate them to increase their investment spending beyond what the "real" profit figures warrant.

Lagging income groups. How valid is the argument that inflation drives lagging income groups, especially non-workers, to work more and harder in order to protect their real incomes? Casual observation turns up numerous cases where this effect seems to apply —retired men driven back to part-time work, wives of college professors working to supplement their husbands' lagging salaries, school teachers driving taxis or working in industry during summer vacations. But it is doubtful that the effect is a major one, at least for creeping inflation, for two reasons.

(a) The largest groups whose incomes are pinched by inflation are old folks and employees of nonprofit organizations, neither likely sources of major increases in productive power. (b) The ratio of the labor force (i.e., people in and looking for jobs) to the number of people of labor-force age has shown no significant growth tendency during inflation, except during the war period. While the proportion of women holding jobs has risen steadily over the past 25 years, outside of the war period there has been no significant relationship between the rate of increase and the rate of inflation. So it seems doubtful that inflation has had much to do with the *number* of people working today.

Speculation. Will the expectation of continuing inflation lead to increased current real output? This is an obviously short-run argument. Inflation fears may temporarily stimulate buying, but people and businesses cannot pile up inventories indefinitely on speculation that prices tomorrow will be higher than today. Except as a "shot in the arm," this can hardly be a major effect.

Slichter has properly emphasized one other factor. When prices are rising generally, resources are bid into growing industries from mature or declining industries by higher wages and prices. Without inflation, prices in declining industries would have to fall. This would be painful, and resources might be reluctant to leave. But the real difficulty is the need to move, either way. Chalk up a small credit to inflation as a social lubricant, therefore. Whether it significantly increases total output is a more dubious matter.

Does inflation reduce future real output? There are two major arguments that inflation reduces future real output: (a) the boom-and-bust argument that inflation causes a speculative situation that is necessarily followed by a bust and depression; and (b) the much longer-run argument that inflation discourages saving and thus decreases the rate of capital accumulation, which holds down the economy's long-run growth rate.

What is the evidence for the boom-and-bust argument? History both supports the argument and contradicts it. Thus it is clearly wrong to say that inflation *must* be followed directly by collapse and depression. For example, in the United States, the United Kingdom, France, and most of Western Europe substantial inflation more or less continuously over the past two decades has been paralleled by a persistent growth in real national output. In Brazil inflation averaging over 10% per year has continued since the 1930's with rising real output. In Japan the postwar picture is similar.

On the other hand, examples of inflation-induced collapse do exist. The post-World War I slump of the early 1920's in the United States may be an example. Certainly the massive hyper-inflations have led to major economic collapse. Conclusion: a Scotch verdict, neither case proven. Rapid inflation

Table 1

INFLATION, PRODUCTION, AND EMPLOYMENT FROM 1952 TO 1955
(1952 = 100)

	United States	Belgium	France	Germany	Italy	Nether-lands	Sweden	United Kingdom
Cost of living:								
1953	101	100	99	98	102	100	101	103
1954	101	102	99	98	105	104	102	105
1955	101	101	100	100	108	106	105	110
Industrial production:								
1953	108	100	97	109	110	110	100	106
1954	100	106	106	122	120	120	104	114
1955	112	114	117	141	130	128	110	119
Employment:								
1953	103	99	98	104	100	103	97	101
1954	100	99	99	109	101	107	98	104
1955	102	101	100	118	103	109	100	107

SOURCE: Data are from J. Herbert Furth, "Indicators of Inflation in Western Europe, 1952–1955," *Review of Economics and Statistics,* August 1956, pp. 336–337.

may lead to economic collapse, but milder inflation certainly may not.

How about the argument that inflation discourages saving and retards capital accumulation? Proponents claim that inflation erodes the value of accumulated saving and thus encourages current consumption. This theory sounds convincing, but here again there is a counterargument—that inflation shifts income to the rich and to corporate profits and thereby increases saving relative to consumption.

The historical evidence is mixed. Everyone knows of individual cases where friends have said they might as well spend their money now as to save it and lose its value through inflation. In hyperinflation this effect is obviously dominant. But counterexamples are easy to find, too; for instance, in almost all the post-World War II inflations of the western world, capital accumulation has proceeded rapidly. In the recent American inflation, to complicate matters, the traditional pattern of income redistribution toward profits and the rich has been shaken.

Until recently, it seemed clear that moderate inflation increased saving and capital goods accumulation relative to consumption, and thus increased long-run total output. This occurred as inflation shifted income from the poor to the rich and from workers to businessmen. But certainly recent American experience does not support this interpretation. On balance, the wage share has risen appreciably relative to property income during the past two decades, and the share of the rich has declined a little.

In summary, there is no very strong case that inflation of *modest* proportions either increases or decreases substantially the rate of capital accumulation. Inflation militates against saving in most forms, but the motives for saving are many and mixed, and modern society provides some effective investment channels to escape the erosion of inflation.

Some Recent Evidence

Table 1, outlining the experience of European countries plus the United States over the mild inflationary period of 1952 through 1955, shows no consistent relationship at all between inflation and changes in production:

The largest increase in output and employment occurred in West Germany, which had no inflation at all; the smallest in Sweden, which had an intermediate amount of inflation.

Italy, with a slightly smaller price increase than Sweden and the United Kingdom, had a much larger increase in output than either.

The United States and Belgium, with almost no inflation, had a bigger increase in output than inflationary Sweden but less than noninflationary Germany and the mildly inflationary Netherlands.

The figures cannot be explained away by such differences between countries as varying increases in the supply of money, varying money wage rates relative to prices, or varying positions on international trade account.

Distribution of Output

We have found that the effect of moderate inflation on total real output appears to be slight under most circumstances and not a priori predictable. But what effect does it have on the relative size of the pieces of the national income pie going to different individuals and economic groups? If we can judge from the American inflation of the past two decades, it does have an impact, but not as much as is often claimed. And the redistribution that does take place does not correspond very well to some of the common preconceptions about inflation.

How are different income groups affected? Since 1939 every broad functional economic group in the United States has gained substantially in real income. Within the rapidly growing total, however, wages and salaries did *not* lag behind profits as a share of the national income. On the contrary, the wage share grew appreciably over the period. Moreover:

Farmers, who are commonly supposed to gain most from inflation, saw their share of the national income decline persistently, perhaps in spite of inflation, but decline nevertheless.

The share represented by corporation profits held stable or declined slightly.

Unincorporated businesses, usually thought to be gainers from inflation, also took a cut in their share of the total.

The interest share dropped drastically during World War II, as interest rates were held down by government policy, but has since grown moderately back toward its earlier level.

The rent share has changed little.

There is no evidence that inflation has shifted income from the poor to the rich; if anything, the effect may have been the other way.

The most significant thing about Figure 1, which shows these changes, is the lack of dramatic functional income shifts over two decades of inflation. Thus, it is not to the effect on major income groups, but rather to the effect on particular segments and individuals within these major groupings, that we must look for the major redistributional effects of inflation, although the basic shift to the wage and salary share is pronounced.

Because inflation penalizes primarily those whose incomes rise more slowly than the incomes of their fellows, it has been those with fixed incomes who lost relatively, whether rich or poor, young or old, farmer or city dweller. Above all, it appears that older people's piece of the national income pie suffered most. Their share of the national income dropped substantially as inflation ate away at their largely fixed incomes.

Here it appears that inflation has discriminated against the middle incomes and the poor. Well-to-do retired individuals can afford to diversify the investments which underlie their retirement incomes and to include substantial amounts of such variable income assets as common stocks and real estate, whose dollar yields increase with inflation. But to the lower income families and widows this alternative is hardly open. To be sure, Slichter has properly emphasized that there are some offsets; for instance, Social Security payments have increased greatly, and many older people have jobs. But this does not eliminate the basic fact that inflation is a major blow to this group, which lives considerably on past savings.

The other most important lagging income group appears to have been employees of nonprofit organizations—of governments and of other nonprofit institutions, especially teachers. In some cases, teachers' salaries have lagged so greatly that their real incomes have actually declined during the greatest boom of our history.

More generally, it is the "passive" economic groups—those who sell no products on which they can raise the price or who work under arrangements where their output cannot readily be raised in price—who have suffered at the expense of the "active" groups in society. The major economic groups, on the other hand, especially wage and salary earners, appear to be increasingly effective in protecting their own income shares during slow inflation.

Fig. 1
Shares of National Income in Inflation, 1939–1956.

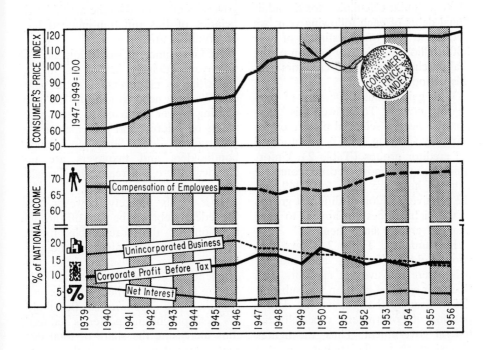

Debtors and Creditors

It is well recognized that inflation transfers wealth (future purchasing power) from creditors to debtors. This is because the debtor who borrows $100 and repays the same $100 later when prices are twice as high repays only half as much real purchasing power.

The American inflation since 1939 has wiped out in this way over half a trillion dollars of creditors' claims on debtors (in 1957 prices). All fixed-dollar-value intangible assets (such as bank deposits, currency, mortgages, government and corporation bonds, life insurance reserves, and pension and retirement funds) are debts owed to creditors and are susceptible to this erosion by inflation. In 1939 all such assets totaled about $320 billion. If we calculate the loss of purchasing power on these debts up to the present and make a similar calculation for the additional debts of each following year, we obtain the very rough estimate of over $500 billion inflationary erosion of the real purchasing power of creditors over this period.

Who gained this huge sum of purchasing power? To answer this question, we need a sectorial picture of the economy showing main net debtor and net creditor groups (Table 2). Unfortunately, the most recent complete data we have are those for 1949, but the relative position of different groups in the picture does not appear to have changed greatly since then.

In summary, Table 2 shows that "households" (families and individuals) were massive net creditors, and that their creditor position was substantially offset by the massive net debtor position of government, especially the federal government. Thus, the figures also show that inflation has caused a

Table 2

NET DEBTORS AND CREDITORS IN THE AMERICAN ECONOMY FROM 1939 TO 1949

(In billions of dollars)

	1939	1949
Households	+$87	+$249
Unincorporated businesses	+ 3	+ 16
Nonfinancial corporations	−25	− 17
Financial corporations	− 3	+ 17
Governments	−68	−263

SOURCE: Data are computed from Raymond Goldsmith, *A Study of Saving in the United States* (Princeton, Princeton University Press, 1955), Vol. III, Tables W-14, 15, and 16. Plus figures show net creditor status; minus figures show net debtor status.

huge transfer of purchasing power from households to the federal government. But this is clearly not the end of the matter, since the government is not some separate entity but is an agency for all of us. We must look *through* the government to see who the actual beneficiaries of this inflation-induced levy on creditors are.

At first glance, it would appear that taxpayers (that is, all of us in our capacities as taxpayers) are the gainers. We now need to give up less purchasing power in taxes to meet payments on interest and principal on the government debt. Since government bondholders and taxpayers are not identical, there is a real shift of wealth from creditors to taxpayers.

It is highly unlikely, however, that the federal debt will be paid off through taxation in the foreseeable future. Who, then, is the gainer of the purchasing power confiscated from government creditors by inflation? The buying public as a whole gains *in proportion to its expenditures*. Bondholders' real purchasing power is reduced, thus increasing the share of total current output that the rest of the buying public can command as their incomes rise with inflation.

Put in common-sense language, government bondholders and moneyholders are partially expropriated by inflation, and the benefit is distributed over the whole population, with the biggest benefits to those who buy the most. Although government creditors and spenders are the same people to some extent, on balance savers *in fixed dollar value assets* subsidize spenders. There is no clear evidence that in moderate inflation this effect transfers real income from the poor to the rich or, in a fully employed economy, from rich to poor.

How are different creditor groups affected? Since all of us are parts of households, more information on particular types of households is needed if we are to see clearly the impact of inflation on us as creditors. Some relevant information is summarized in Table 3.

All households combined hold about 3% of their total wealth in the form of fixed dollar value assets. By contrast, they are in debt up to only a little over 10% of their total wealth. The difference is a measure of their net creditor position. Nearly every major group of households is a substantial net creditor.

Table 3

ASSETS AND DEBTS OF HOUSEHOLDS IN EARLY 1950

Per cent Total	Per cent of all households	Total assets (in billions)	Per cent of total assets: Monetary assets	Variable price assets	Debts
All households	100%	$613	24%	76%	11%
By 1949 money income before taxes:					
Under $1,000	14%	$ 39	19%	81%	12%
1,000–2,999	40	119	26	74	13
3,000–4,999	29	150	27	73	16
5,000–7,499	11	107	25	75	12
75,000 and over	5	188	19	81	5
By occupation:					
Professional and semiprofessional	7%	$ 61	32%	68%	10%
Managerial	4	40	27	73	12
Self-employed	8	155	16	84	6
Clerical and skilled	41	136	29	71	18
Unskilled	12	23	31	69	14
Farm operators	9	97	13	87	12
Retired	5	55	31	69	2
All other	14	46	28	72	8
By net worth in 1950:					
Negative net worth	5%	$ 2	30%	70%	490%
$0– 1,999	33	17	46	54	33
2,000– 9,999	34	117	29	71	20
10,000–24,999	18	162	24	76	9
25,000–59,999	7	135	22	78	6
60,000 and over	3	180	17	83	3
By age of head of household:					
18–24	10%	$ 9	23%	77%	20%
25–34	23	69	22	78	27
35–54	40	285	24	76	12
55 and over	26	244	23	77	4

SOURCE: Data are from Raymond Goldsmith, op. cit., Tables W-46, 47, 48, 49, based in turn primarily on Federal Reserve–Michigan Survey Research Center survey of consumer finances for early 1950. Columns may not add to totals because of minor unascertained items and rounding.

The extent to which different groups are net creditors varies a good deal, however. Thus:

The heaviest net creditors, relative to their incomes, are older people, especially those who are retired. They hold a larger proportion of their wealth in fixed dollar value assets than any other major group, largely because of the importance to them of insurance and pension and other retirement funds. It is they who, relative to their total wealth, stand to lose most as creditors when inflation comes. Moreover, they are least in debt and do not reap offsetting benefits on that score.

At the other extreme, the very penurious or injudicious who are so heavily in debt as to have a negative net worth and younger families in the 25–34 age range are the least susceptible to "creditor" loss from inflation. They are substantially in debt, which is, other things being equal, a good state to be in during inflation.

The very well-to-do families are slightly higher net creditors than the average, relative to their total wealth, and their debts are small. Thus, they appear quite vulnerable to inflation. On the other hand, they hold an exceptionally large proportion of their total assets in "variable price" form (common stock, real estate, and so on), which serves as a partial offset to their exposure as net creditors.

Interestingly, most American households appear to have made comparatively little effort during the long period of persistent inflation to switch from their position as heavy net creditors. While the data are inadequate, they suggest only a mild attempt by most households to shift to more "inflation-proof" assets, even in periods of rapidly rising prices.

COPING WITH IT

The real danger of creeping inflation is that it will pick up steam and grow beyond a creep. While there is little evidence that creeping inflation is disastrous, there is overwhelming evidence that a hyperinflation is. Just where the costs of inflation mount to major proportions is hard to specify. It is clear, though, that the more rapid the rise in prices is, the more inequitable and disruptive shifts in income and wealth may become, and also the greater the danger that productive activity may be shifted into unproductive lines to "beat the inflation."

Creep or Gallop?

Is the danger that creeping inflation will turn into galloping inflation a real one for the United States if we do not check it in the creeping stage? I believe that real hyperinflation is extremely unlikely. On the other hand, I am concerned that the creep may become a little faster during the next five years, even though it may possibly be interrupted by a business recession.

My prediction is that excess income claims of labor, business, and agriculture will persist—and probably mount. Our democratic government, essentially committed to maintaining high-level employment, will find it extremely difficult not to provide the additional purchasing power needed to support employment at higher cost and price levels as wages and prices of strong income groups are pushed up. This it can do either through deficit financing or by providing additional bank reserves to finance private loans.

Once people understand this process and trust government underwriting of high-level employment, there is logically no limit to the rate of inflation which might develop. But, as a practical matter, the inflation is not likely to be a rapid one (outside of war periods) because income groups are not yet confident enough of government policy to put aside caution in their income claims, because widespread competition slows price increases, and because public fear of inflation is strong enough to restrain private and public action that conspicuously produces rapid price increases.

This is the long-run peacetime inflation danger. It arises from the fact that we are a society of powerful economic and political groups, and that, as such, we place top priority on the maintenance of a high level of employment and are willing to use federal monetary and fiscal policies to achieve this. Without these two interacting factors of powerful excess income claims and governmental high-employment policy, there is little reason to expect persistent secular inflation in America—in the absence of war.

Accordingly, a fundamental approach to limit inflation must either blunt the excess income claims or prevent the provision of additional purchasing power through the banking system.

Checks on Income Claims

The first approach does not seem promising. President Eisenhower has repeatedly exhorted labor and management to moderate their wage and price claims, but with little success. A few economists have suggested drastic action to break up the monopolistic powers of large unions and large corporations, but action sufficiently strong to eliminate the problem this way seems unrealistic on the modern scene. Others have suggested countervailing power—making businesses and other groups even stronger to resist the pressures of the unions. But it will still be tempting for management to give in to the unions and merely pass the cost along in the form of higher prices, which is by all odds the easier solution when two powerful giants meet.

A more sophisticated suggestion is that we improve the inducements to businesses to hold down costs, perhaps by lowering the corporation income tax rate and thereby reducing the extent to which the government itself indirectly bears the cost of any wage increase granted. Some have suggested imposition of direct governmental controls over wages and prices. Still other writers have emphasized that the ultimate solution must lie in an increased sense of responsibility on the part both of unions and of management in moderating their claims for higher wages and prices.

Each of these ideas has merit. But none of them provides a very reliable basis for giving up a search for effective inflation hedges.

Monetary-Fiscal Policy

In the last analysis, almost everyone comes back to federal monetary-fiscal policy—if the job is to be done. Monetary-fiscal policy has a harder time in an economy of administered prices and wages since its impact may be slower and less predictable in any short period. The credit squeeze of tight money falls unequally on different firms and different industries; in general, the least credit-worthy (often the smaller, highly competitive firms) feel the pinch of monetary restriction first. Slower though the check may be, however, shortage of total monetary demand is one sure way of checking inflation.

But if, as Slichter has argued, it is extremely difficult in times of moderate inflation to generate large federal surpluses to fight inflation, and if a really tight money policy can work only by generating unemployment, is this approach a *realistic* solution? My answer is that monetary policy against inflation is workable if it has the support of the public—and only if it does!

By limiting the supply of money the Federal Reserve Board can check inflation. Without more money, total expenditures will not long continue to grow.

No seller, no matter how powerful, will continue to raise prices if the consumer cannot continue to buy at the higher prices; and, with a fixed money supply, consumers can continue to buy at higher prices only if they spend the existing money supply faster—only if there is an increase for V in the old textbook equation $MV = PT$ (where M represents money, V, the velocity of turnover of money, P, the price, T, the number of units sold). It is true that V may increase to a moderate extent. For example, over the past two years the money supply has increased by only 1% per year while total expenditures have risen 5% per year. History shows, though, that no *major* inflation will occur without an increase in the money supply. While a federal policy that holds the money supply constant may not work precisely and completely, it will certainly shut off any substantial inflationary sweep within a moderate amount of time. Perhaps selective controls, like consumer credit, can help to pinpoint monetary restraint where inflationary rises are strongest, but they can do only a small part of the job.

The real issue, thus, is whether the Federal Reserve Board (and the federal government) will stand firm and refuse to increase the money supply when the pressure for higher prices and wages necessitates more total spending power to prevent falling sales and unemployment.

Pressure To Be Resisted

Tight money that checks inflation may cause unemployment, and the Federal Reserve authorities do not want that particular result. Slichter and Jacoby have argued vigorously about just how much unemployment would be required to hold down inflationary wage demands if tight money pressure were applied. Argument of this sort is helpful in exposing the issues, but it seems to me quite illusory to suppose that we can answer this question accurately now.

Critics of tight money argue that only large-scale unemployment can be counted on to check inflationary wage and price policies. This seems overly pessimistic to me, and I suspect we may be seeing now a rather effective demonstration of the way tight money can slow down inflation without inducing a major recession. Our post-World War II experience has provided encouraging evidence, as has that of other countries. Whatever the weight of these arguments, the crucial point is that, to avoid inflation in an economy of major power groups, the government must convince the public and the major economic groups within the public, by temporary unemployment or otherwise, that we *will* act to check inflation, even at the cost of some temporary unemployment and unsold goods.

If we do not convince them, we will have inflation and probably as much unemployment too in the long run. For, however fast a government pumps in money, the wage and price demands of the powerful groups can readily be raised more rapidly. The 1958 wage demands of the major unions may well be eye openers on this score. *Thus, we face the same temporary unemployment issue whether we draw the line against power-group inflation at the creeping or at some more advanced stage.*

The basic issue is not, then, whether we shall have inflation with full employment, or stable prices with unemployment. It is likelier to be whether we shall have stable prices or inflation, with some temporary unemployment in either case. Viewed in this way, the case for creeping inflation becomes a good deal less appealing than Slichter has made it seem.

Where shall we take our stand against ever-rising income claims? A stable price level policy is not necessarily better than others, such as a slowly rising price level policy, but it seems to me to present by all odds the strongest rallying point for public support. It is the most equitable position, given the general presumption in our habits and economic mores that the value of the monetary unit is roughly stable. We can all agree that high-level employment is our first objective, but we must still face the fact that inflation is not necessarily, or even probably, the road to maintaining high-level employment.

*   *   *

C.
DEPRESSION

13   BLACK DEPRESSION

Frederick Lewis Allen

Frederick Lewis Allen has been editor of *Harper's* magazine, and has written several popular books describing different periods of American history.

*   *   *

Statistics are bloodless things.

To say that during the year 1932, the cruelist year of the Depression, the average number of unemployed people in the country was 12½ million by the estimates of the National Industrial Conference Board, a little over 13 million by the estimates of the American Federation of Labor, and by other estimates (differently arrived at, and defining unemployment in various ways) anywhere from 8½ to 17 million—to say this is to give no living impression of the jobless men going from office to office or from factory gate to factory gate; of the disheartening inevitability of the phrase, "We'll let you know if anything shows up"; of men thumbing the want ads in cold tenements, spending fruitless hours, day after day and week after week, in the sidewalk crowds before the employment offices; using up the money in the savings bank, borrowing on their life insurance, selling whatever possessions could be sold, borrowing from relatives less and less able to lend, tasting the bitterness of inadequacy, and at last swallowing their pride and going to apply for relief—if there was any to be got. (Relief money was scarce, for charitable organizations were hard beset and cities and towns had either used up their available funds or were on the point of doing so.)

A few statistical facts and estimates are necessary, however, to an understanding of the scope and impact of the Depression. For example:—

Although the amount of money paid out in interest during the year 1932 was only 3.5 per cent less than in 1929, according to the computations of Dr. Simon Kuznets for the National Bureau of Economic Research, on the other hand the amount of money paid out in salaries had dropped 40 per cent, dividends had dropped 56.6 per cent, and wages had dropped 60 per cent. (Thus had the debt structure remained comparatively rigid while other elements in the economy were subjected to fierce deflation.)

Do not imagine, however, that the continuation of interest payments and the partial continuation of dividend payments meant that business as a whole was making money. Business as a whole lost between five and six billion dollars in 1932. (The government figure for all the corporations in the country—451,800 of them—was a net deficit of $5,640,000,000.) To be sure, most of the larger and better-managed companies did much better than that. E. D. Kennedy's figures for the 960 concerns whose earnings were tabulated by Standard Statistics—mostly big ones whose stock was active on the Stock Exchange—show that these 960 leaders had a collective profit of over a third of a billion. Yet one must add that "better managed" is here used in a special sense. Not only had labor-saving devices and speed-ups increased the output per man-hour in manufacturing industries by an estimated 18 per cent since 1929, but employees had been laid off in quantity. Every time one of the giants of industry, to keep its financial head above water, threw off a new group of workers, many little corporations roundabout sank further into the red.

While existing businesses shrank, new ones were not being undertaken. The total of domestic corporate issues —issues of securities floated to provide capital for American corporations— had dropped in 1932 to just about *one twenty-fourth* of the 1929 figure.

But these cold statistics give us little sense of the human realities of the economic paralysis of 1932. Let us try another approach.

Walking through an American city, you might find few signs of the Depression visible—or at least conspicuous—to the casual eye. You might notice that a great many shops were untenanted, with dusty plate-glass windows and signs indicating that they were ready to lease; that few factory chimneys were smoking; that the streets were not so crowded with trucks as in earlier years, that there was no uproar of riveters to assail the ear, that beggars and panhandlers were on the sidewalks in unprecedented numbers (in the Park Avenue district of New York a man might be asked for money four or five times in a ten-block walk). Traveling by railroad, you might notice that the trains were shorter, the Pullman cars fewer—and that fewer freight trains were on the line. Traveling overnight, you might find only two or three other passengers in your sleeping car. (By contrast, there were more filling stations by the motor highways than ever before, and of all the retail businesses in "Middletown" only the filling stations showed no large drop in business during the black years; for although few new automobiles were being bought, those which would still stand up were being used more than ever—to the dismay of the railroads.)

Otherwise things might seem to you to be going on much as usual. The major phenomena of the Depression were mostly negative and did not assail the eye.

But if you knew where to look, some of them would begin to appear. First, the breadlines in the poorer districts. Second, those bleak settlements ironically known as "Hoovervilles" in the outskirts of the cities and on vacant lots—groups of makeshift shacks constructed out of packing boxes, scrap iron, anything that could be picked up free in a diligent combing of the city dumps: shacks in which men and sometimes whole families of evicted people were sleeping on automobile seats carried from auto-graveyards, warming themselves before fires of rubbish in grease drums. Third, the homeless people sleeping in doorways or on park benches, and going the rounds of the restaurants for leftover half-eaten biscuits, piecrusts, anything to keep the fires of life burning. Fourth, the vastly increased number of thumbers on the highways, and particularly of freight-car transients on the railroads: a huge army of drifters ever on the move, searching half-aimlessly for a place where there might be a job. According to Jonathan Norton Leonard, the Missouri Pacific Railroad in 1929 had "taken official cognizance" of 13,745 migrants; by 1931 the figure had already jumped to 186,028. It was estimated that by the beginning of 1933, the country over, there were a million of these transients on the move. Forty-five thousand had passed through El Paso in the space of six months; 1,500 were passing through Kansas City every day. Among them were large numbers of young boys, and girls disguised as boys. According to the Children's Bureau, there were 200,000 children thus drifting about the United States. So huge was the number of freight-car hoppers in the Southwest that in a number of places the railroad

police simply had to give up trying to remove them from the trains: there were far too many of them.

Among the comparatively well-to-do people of the country (those, let us say, whose pre-Depression incomes had been over $5,000 a year) the great majority were living on a reduced scale, for salary cuts had been extensive, especially since 1931, and dividends were dwindling. These people were discharging servants, or cutting servants' wages to a minimum, or in some cases "letting" a servant stay on without other compensation than board and lodging. In many pretty houses, wives who had never before—in the revealing current phrase—"done their own work" were cooking and scrubbing. Husbands were wearing the old suit longer, resigning from the golf club, deciding, perhaps, that this year the family couldn't afford to go to the beach for the summer, paying seventy-five cents for lunch instead of a dollar at the restaurant or thirty-five instead of fifty at the lunch counter. When those who had flown high with the stock market in 1929 looked at the stock-market page of the newspapers nowadays their only consoling thought (if they still had any stock left) was that a judicious sale or two would result in such a capital loss that they need pay no income tax at all this year.

Alongside these men and women of the well-to-do classes whose fortunes had been merely reduced by the Depression were others whose fortunes had been shattered. The crowd of men waiting for the 8:14 train at the prosperous suburb included many who had lost their jobs, and were going to town as usual not merely to look stubbornly and almost hopelessly for other work but also to keep up a bold front of activity. (In this latter effort they usually succeeded: one would never have guessed, seeing them chatting with their friends as train-time approached, how close to desperation some of them had come.) There were architects and engineers bound for offices to which no clients had come in weeks. There were doctors who thought themselves lucky when a patient paid a bill. Mrs. Jones, who went daily to her stenographic job, was now the economic mainstay of her family, for Mr. Jones was jobless and was doing the cooking and looking after the children (with singular distaste and inefficiency). Next door to the Joneses lived Mrs. Smith, the widow of a successful lawyer: she had always had a comfortable income, she prided herself on her "nice things," she was pathetically unfitted to earn a dollar even if jobs were to be had; her capital had been invested in South American bonds and United Founders stock and other similarly misnamed "securities," and now she was completely dependent upon hand-outs from her relatives, and didn't even have carfare in her imported pocketbook.

The Browns had retreated to their "farmhouse" in the country and were trying to raise crops on its stony acres; they talked warmly about primal simplicities but couldn't help longing sometimes for electric light and running hot water, and couldn't cope with the potato bugs. (Large numbers of city dwellers thus moved to the country, but not enough of them engaged in real farming to do more than partially check the long-term movement from the farms of America to the cities and towns.) It was being whispered about the community that the Robinson family, though they lived in a $40,000 house and had always spent money freely, were in desperate straights: Mr. Robinson had lost his job, the house could not be sold, they had realized on every asset at their command, and now they were actually going hungry—

though their house still looked like the abode of affluence.

Further down in the economic scale, particularly in those industrial communities in which the factories were running at twenty per cent of capacity or had closed down altogether, conditions were infinitely worse. Frederick E. Croxton's figures, taken in Buffalo, show what was happening in such communities: out of 14,909 persons of both sexes willing and able to work, his house-to-house canvassers found in November, 1932, that 46.3 per cent were fully employed, 22.5 per cent were working part time, and as many as 31.2 per cent were unable to find jobs. In every American city, quantities of families were being evicted from their inadequate apartments; moving in with other families till ten or twelve people would be sharing three or four rooms; or shivering through the winter in heatless houses because they could afford no coal, eating meat once a week or not at all. If employers sometimes found that former employees who had been discharged did not seem eager for re-employment ("They won't take a job if you offer them one!"), often the reason was panic: a dreadful fear of inadequacy which was one of the Depression's commonest psycho-pathological results. A woman clerk, offered piecework after being jobless for a year, confessed that she almost had not dared to come to the office, she had been in such terror lest she wouldn't know where to hang her coat, wouldn't know how to find the washroom, wouldn't understand the boss's directions for her job.

For perhaps the worst thing about this Depression was its inexorable continuance year after year. Men who have been sturdy and self-respecting workers can take unemployment without flinching for a few weeks, a few months, even if they have to see their families suffer; but it is different after a year . . . two years . . . three years. . . . Among the miserable creatures curled up on park benches or standing in dreary lines before the soup kitchens in 1932 were men who had been jobless since the end of 1929.

At the very bottom of the economic scale the conditions may perhaps best be suggested by two brief quotations. The first, from Jonathan Norton Leonard's *Three Years Down,* describes the plight of Pennsylvania miners who had been put out of company villages after a blind and hopeless strike in 1931: "Reporters from the more liberal metropolitan papers found thousands of them huddled on the mountainsides, crowded three or four families together in one-room shacks, living on dandelions and wild weed-roots. Half of them were sick, but no local doctor would care for the evicted strikers. All of them were hungry and many were dying of those providential diseases which enable welfare authorities to claim that no one has starved." The other quotation is from Louise V. Armstrong's *We Too Are the People,* and the scene is Chicago in the late spring of 1932:—

"One vivid, gruesome moment of those dark days we shall never forget. We saw a crowd of some fifty men fighting over a barrel of garbage which had been set outside the back door of a restaurant. American citizens fighting for scraps of food like animals!"

Human behavior under unaccustomed conditions is always various. One thinks of the corporation executive to whom was delegated the job of discharging several hundred men: he insisted on seeing every one of them personally and taking an interest in each man's predicament, and at the end of a few months his hair had turned prematurely gray. . . . The

Junior League girl who reported with pride a Depression economy: she had cut a piece out of an old fur coat in the attic and bound it to serve as a bathmat. . . . The banker who had been plunged deeply into debt by the collapse of his bank: he got a $30,000 job with another bank, lived on $3,000 a year, and honorably paid $27,000 a year to his creditors. . . . The wealthy family who lost most of their money but announced bravely that they had "solved their Depression problem" by discharging fifteen of their twenty servants, and showed no signs of curiosity as to what would happen to these fifteen. . . . The little knot of corporation officials in a magnificent skyscraper office doctoring the books of the company to dodge bankruptcy. . . . The crowd of Chicago Negroes standing tight-packed before a tenement-house door to prevent the landlord's agents from evicting a neighbor family: as they stood there, hour by hour, they sang hymns. . . . The one-time clerk carefully cutting out pieces of cardboard to put inside his shoes before setting out on his endless job-hunting round, and telling his wife the shoes were now better than ever. . . . The man in the little apartment next door who had given up hunting for jobs, given up all interest, all activity, and sat hour by hour in staring apathy. . . .

*   *   *

Not only were ideas boiling; the country was losing patience with adversity. That instinct of desperate men to rebel which was swelling the radical parties in a dozen Depression-hit countries and was gathering stormily behind Hitler in Germany was working in the United States also. It was anything but unified, it was as yet little organized, and only in scattered places did it assume the customary European shape of communism. It had been slow to develop—partly because Americans had been used to prosperity and had expected it to return automatically, partly because when jobs were vanishing those men who were still employed were too scared to be rebellious, and simply hung on to what they had and waited and hoped. (It is not usually during a collapse that men rebel, but after it.) There had been riots and hunger-marches here and there but on the whole the orderliness of the country had been striking, all things considered. Yet men could not be expected to sit still forever in the expectation that an economic system which they did not understand would right itself. The ferment of dissatisfaction was working in many places and taking many forms, and here and there it was beginning to break sharply through the orderly surface of society.

In the summer of 1932 the city of Washington was to see an exciting example of this ferment—and a spectacular demonstration of how not to deal with it.

All through June thousands of war veterans had been streaming into Washington, coming from all over the country by boxcar and by truck. These veterans wanted the government to pay them now the "adjusted compensation" which Congress had already voted to pay them in 1945. They set up a camp —a shanty-town, a sort of big-scale "Hooverville"—on the Anacostia flats near the city, and they occupied some vacant land with disused buildings on it on Pennsylvania Avenue just below the Capitol. More and more of them straggled to Washington until their number had reached fifteen or twenty thousand.

Among such a great crowd there were inevitably men of many sorts. The Hoover Administration later charged that many had had criminal records, or were communists. But unquestionably the great majority of them were genuine veterans; though there was one small communist group, it was regarded with hostility by the rest; in the main this "Bonus Expeditionary Force" consisted of ordinary Americans out of luck. They were under at least a semblance of military discipline and were on the whole well-behaved. Many brought their wives and children along, and as time went on the Anacostia camp took on an air half military and half domestic, with the family wash hanging on the line outside the miserable shacks, and entertainers getting up impromptu vaudeville shows.

General Pelham D. Glassford, the Washington superintendent of police, sensibly regarded these invaders as citizens who had every right to petition the government for a redress of grievances. He helped them to get equipment for their camp and treated them with unfailing consideration. But to some Washingtonians their presence was ominous. A group of the veterans—under a leader who wore a steel neck-brace and a helmet with straps under the chin, to support a broken back— picketed the Capitol for days while the Bonus bill was being considered; and on the evening when the bill was to come to a vote, the great plaza before the Capitol was packed with veterans. The Senate voted No. What would the men do? There were people looking out the windows of the brightly lighted Senate wing who wondered breathlessly if those thousands of ragged men would try to rush the building. But when their leader announced the news, a band struck up "America" and the men dispersed quietly. So far, so good.

Some of them left Washington during the next few days, but several thousand stayed on, hopelessly, obstinately. (Where had they to go?) Officialdom became more and more uneasy. The White House was put under guard, its gates closed and chained, the streets about it cleared, as if the man there did not dare face the unrest among the least fortunate of the citizenry. It was decided to clear the veterans out of the disused buildings below the Capitol (to make way for the government's building program); and on the morning of July 28, 1932, General Glassford was told that the evacuation must be immediate. He set about his task.

It began peacefully, but at noon somebody threw a brick and there was a scuffle between the veterans and the police, which quickly subsided. Two hours later there was more serious trouble as a policeman at whom the veterans had thrown stones pulled his gun; two veterans were killed before Glassford could get the police to stop shooting. Even this battle subsided. All Glassford wanted was time to complete the evacuation peacefully and without needless affront. But he was not to get it.

Earlier in the day he had told the District Commissioners that if the evacuation was to be carried out speedily, troops would be required. This statement had been needlessly interpreted as a request for military aid, which Glassford did not want at all. President Hoover had ordered the United States Army to the rescue.

Down Pennsylvania Avenue, late that hot afternoon, came an impressive parade—four troops of cavalry, four companies of infantry, a machine-gun squadron, and several tanks. As they approached the disputed area they were met with cheers from the veterans sitting on the curb and from the large crowd which had assembled. Then suddenly there was chaos: cavalrymen were riding into the crowd, infantrymen were throwing tear-gas bombs, women and children were being trampled and were choking from the gas; a crowd of three thousand or more spectators who had gathered in a vacant lot across the way were being pursued by the cavalry and were running wildly, pell-mell across the uneven ground, screaming as they stumbled and fell.

The troops moved slowly on, scattering before them veterans and home-going government clerks alike. When they reached the other end of the Anacostia bridge and met a crowd of spectators who booed them and were slow to "move on," they threw more gas bombs. They began burning the shacks of the Anacostia camp—a task which the veterans themselves helped them accomplish. That evening the Washington sky glowed with fire. Even after midnight the troops were still on their way with bayonets and tear-gas bombs, driving people ahead of them into the streets of Anacostia.

The Bonus Expeditionary Force had been dispersed, to merge itself with that greater army of homeless people who were drifting about the country in search of an ever-retreating fortune. The United States Army had completed its operation "successfully" without killing anybody—though the list of injured was long. The incident was over. But it had left a bitter taste in the mouth. Bayonets drawn in Washington to rout the dispossessed—was this the best that American statesmanship could offer hungry citizens?

The farmers were rebellious—and no wonder. For the gross income of American agriculture had declined from nearly 12 billion dollars in 1929 —when it had already for years been suffering from a decline in export sales —to only 5¼ billions in 1932. While most manufacturing businesses dropped their prices only a little and met slackened demand with slackened production, the farmer could not do this, and the prices he got went right down to the cellar. Men who found themselves utterly unable to meet their costs of production could not all be expected to be philosophical about it.

Angry Iowans, organized by Milo Reno into a Farmers' Holiday Association, were refusing to bring food into Sioux City for thirty days or "until the cost of production had been obtained"; they blockaded the highways with spiked telegraph poles and logs, stopped milk trucks and emptied the milk into roadside ditches. Said an elderly Iowa farmer with a white mustache to Mary Heaton Vorse, "They say blockading the highway's illegal. I says, 'Seems to me there was a Tea Party in Boston that was illegal too.' "

Elsewhere farmers were taking the obvious direct means to stop the tidal wave of mortgage foreclosure sales. All through the prairie country there were quantities of farmers who not only had heavy mortgages on their property but had gone deeply into debt for the purchase of farm machinery or to meet the emergencies of years of falling prices; when their corn and wheat brought to even the most industrious of them not enough money to meet their obligations, they lost patience with the laws of bankruptcy. If a man sees a neighbor of his, a formerly successful farmer, a substantial, hard-working citizen with a family, coming out of the office of the referee in bankruptcy stripped of everything but an old team of horses, a wagon, a few dogs and hogs, and a few sticks of furniture, he is likely to see red. Marching to the scene of the next foreclosure sale, these farmers would drive off prospective bidders, gather densely about the auctioneer, bid in horses at 25 cents apiece, cows at 10 cents, fat hogs at a nickel—and the next morning would return their purchases to the former owner.

In a quiet county seat, handbills would appear: "Farmers and workers! Help protect your neighbors from being driven off their property. Now is the time to act. For the past three and a half years we have waited for our masters, who are responsible for the situation, to find a way out. . . . On Friday the property of ———— is to be sold at a forced auction at the courthouse. . . . The Farmers Committee has called a mass protest meeting to stop the above-mentioned sale." And on Friday the trucks would drive up to the courthouse and men by the hundreds, quiet, grim-faced, would fill the corridors outside the sheriff's office while their leaders demanded that the sale be not held.

They threatened judges in bankruptcy cases; in one case a mob dragged a judge from his courtroom, beat him, hanged him by the neck till he fainted—and all because he was carrying out the law.

These farmers were not revolutionists. On the contrary, most of them were by habit conservative men. They were simply striking back in rage at the impersonal forces which had brought them to their present pass.

*   *   *

But it was during 1934 and 1935— the years when Roosevelt was pushing through his financial reforms, and Huey Long was a national portent, and the languishing NRA was put out of its misery by the Supreme Court—that the thermometer in Kansas stayed week after week at 108 or above and the black storms raged again and again. The drought continued acute during much of 1936. Oklahoma farms became great dunes of shifting sand (so like seashore dunes, said one observer, that one almost expected to smell the salt). Housewives in the drought belt kept oiled cloths on the window sills and between the upper and lower sashes of the windows, and some of them tried to seal up every aperture in their houses with the gummed paper strips used in wrapping parcels, yet still the choking dust filtered in and lay in ripples on the kitchen floor, while outside it blew blindingly across a No Man's Land; roads and farm buildings and once green thickets half-buried in the sand. It was in those days that a farmer, sitting at his window during a dust storm, remarked that he was counting the Kansas farms as they came by.

Retribution for the very human error of breaking the sod of the Plains had come in full measure. And, as often happens, it was visited upon the innocent as well as upon the guilty—if indeed one could single out any individuals as guilty of so pervasive an error as social shortsightedness.

Westward fled the refugees from this new Sahara, as if obedient to the old American tradition that westward lies the land of promise. In 1934 and 1935 Californians became aware of an increasing influx into their state of families and groups of families of "Okies," traveling in ancient family jalopies; but for years the streams of humanity continued to run. They came along U. S. Highway 30 through the Idaho hills, along Highway 66 across New Mexico and Arizona, along the Old Spanish Trail through El Paso, along all the other westward trails. They came in decrepit, square-shouldered 1925 Dodges and 1927 La Salles; in battered 1923 Model-T Fords that looked like relics of some antique culture; in trucks piled high with mattresses and cooking utensils and children, with suitcases, jugs, and sacks strapped to the running boards. "They roll westward like a parade," wrote Richard L. Neuberger. "In a single hour from a grassy meadow near an Idaho road I counted 34 automobiles with the license plates of states between Chicago and the mountains."

They left behind them a half-depopulated countryside. A survey of the farmhouses in seven counties of southeastern Colorado, made in 1936, showed 2878 houses still occupied, 2811 abandoned; and there were also, in that area, 1522 abandoned homesites. The total number of drought refugees who took the westward trek over the mountains was variously estimated in 1939 at from 200,000 upwards—with more coming all the time.

As these wanderers moved along the highways they became a part of a vast and confused migratory movement. When they camped by the wayside they might find themselves next to a family of evicted white Alabama sharecroppers who had been on the move for four years, snatching seasonal farm-labor jobs wherever they could through the Southwest; or next to tenant families from the Arkansas Delta who had been "tractored off" their land—expelled in order that the owner might consolidate two or three farms and operate them with tractors and day labor; or next to lone wanderers who had once held industrial jobs and had now for years been on relief or on the road—jumping freights, hitchhiking, panhandling, shunting back and forth across the countryside in the faint hope of a durable job. And when these varied streams of migrants reached the Coast they found themselves in desperate competition for jobs with individuals or families who for years had been "fruit tramps," moving northward each year with the harvests from the Imperial Valley in southern California to the Sacramento Valley or even to the apple-picking in the Yakima Valley in Washington.

Here in the land of promise, agriculture had long been partly industrialized. Huge farms were in the control of absentee owners or banks or corporations, and were accustomed to depend upon the labor of migratory "fruit tramps," who had formerly been mostly Mexicans, Japanese, and other foreigners, but now were increasingly Americans. Those laborers who were lucky enough to get jobs picking cotton or peas or fruit would be sheltered temporarily in camps consisting typically of frame cabins in rows, with a water line between every two rows; they were very likely to find in their cabin no stove, no cots, no water pail. Even the best of the camps offered a way of life strikingly different from that of the ruggedly individualist farmer of the American tradition, who owned his farm or else was preparing, by working as a resident "hired man," or by renting a farm, for the chance of ultimate ownership. These pickers were homeless, voteless nomads, unwanted anywhere save at the harvest season.

When wave after wave of the new migrants reached California, the labor market became glutted, earnings were low, and jobs became so scarce that groups of poverty-stricken families would be found squatting in makeshift Hoovervilles or bunking miserably in their awkward old Fords by the roadside. Being Americans of native stock and accustomed to independence, they took the meager wages and the humili-

ation bitterly, sought to organize, talked of striking, sometimes struck. At every such threat, something like panic seized the growers. If this new proletariat were permitted to organize, and were to strike at picking time, they might ruin the whole season's output of a perishable crop. There followed anti-picketing ordinances; the spectacle of armed deputies dislodging the migrants from their pitiful camps; violence by bands of vigilantes, to whom these ragged families were not fellow-citizens who had suffered in a great American disaster but dirty, ignorant, superstitious outlanders, failures at life, easy dupes for "red" agitators. This engulfing tide of discontent must be kept moving.

Farther north the refugees were likely to be received with more sympathy, especially in regions where the farms were small and not industrialized; here and there one heard of instances of real hospitality, such as that of the Oregon town which held a canning festival for the benefit of the drought victims in the neighborhood. The well-managed camps set up by the Farm Security Administration were havens of human decency. But to the vast majority of the refugees the promised land proved to be a place of new and cruel tragedy.

* * *

14 JOB HUNTERS

E. Wight Bakke

E. Wight Bakke is Sterling Professor of Economics, and Director of the Labor and Management Center, Yale University.

The foreman tapped Joseph Torrio on the shoulder as he pulled the switch on his machine. "Clapham wants to see you, Joe."

Reprinted from *The Unemployed Worker*, by E. Wight Bakke (Yale University Press, 1940), by permission of the publisher.

"You mean—I'm getting my time, Jim?"

"Just temporary, I hope, and you know what I think of your work, old man. It won't be long—unless—but why worry about it? Clapham will give you the dope."

With a slow step Joe headed for the front office where Clapham, the company's personnel department, was already telling some of his mates what Joe knew to be "the bad news." He sat down on a bench in the outer office. His turn had come! Here he was an eighteen-year man. Others had been laid off one by one, but he had thought his job was safe. Why, he had been a foreman in the night shift during the War, and now Clapham was going to tell him the bad news! It wouldn't be easy for Clapham, for in spite of the fact that the workers dubbed the personnel department, "the worse-n-hell department," Clapham was a good egg. He knew most of the men by sight if not by name.

"Torrio," called the office boy.

As he walked out the front gate he could hardly remember what Clapham had said. He had been thinking his own thoughts. A phrase or two penetrated his preoccupation. "Tough break . . . no new orders . . . maybe only a short time . . . but better look around, no telling when . . . call you if things pick up."

This was not the first time he had been laid off, but this time the ugly rumors that "the company was slipping," that "the whole damned country is on the rocks," had created a fear he had not felt before. He'd lay off a couple of weeks—he deserved a vacation after eight years of steady work. But if he didn't get called back in that time, he'd start hunting another job.

Joseph Torrio in 1933 had about 18,000 companions in the city who joined him in this search for work. What kind of job is looking for a job, and how did these workers who had been "told the bad news" go about that task? They came to unemployment with an economic equipment which we have attempted to describe in some detail. We have suggested that they are motivated in their economic activity by the desire: to play one or more socially respected roles, to obtain the measure of economic security deemed possible by their associates, to gain an increasing degree of control over their own affairs, to understand the casual forces in their problems of self-maintenance. We have surveyed the essential controlling conditions of their economic environment and the effect of these in furthering or frustrating their progress toward these goals. We have recorded the normal adjustments made in the face of these conditions, which adjustments provide them with a stock of habitual practices available as suggestive alternatives in meeting the problem of unemployment.

How did they use this equipment in effecting the new economic adjustments made necessary by the loss of their jobs? In the following chapters we shall try to share the experience of Torrio and his mates as they set about bridging the gap between jobs.

THE JOB OF JOB HUNTING

In a factory town the great majority of workers are accustomed to assume that factory employment is the major, if not the only, possibility of making a living. Joseph Torrio after his two weeks' vacation "pounded pavements" for an additional four weeks. We need not go with him to every gate, but a sample of his experiences taken from his diary kept for us during that time will help us to understand why he left off searching for that kind of job six weeks after his layoff.

April 19, 1934.

Decided to have a go at the State Employment Office. Got there at eight. Fellow I knew sitting on steps. Big sign there "No loitering in the doorway." Janitor or someone came down and asked him to move.

"Are you going upstairs?" he asked. "If you are, go, but don't sit here." The fellow jumped; not looking at the janitor, he began a loud bluster about his father paying taxes to support the place and he could sit on the steps if he wanted to. When the janitor left, he returned to the steps for a moment. Meanwhile a group of people had gathered to see what was going on.

Asked the janitor when the manager would be in. He said, "Nine o'clock." Decided to come back. When I got back, a line had formed clear out into the street. I took my place. Officials and clerks kept coming and had a good cheery word for us as they passed. But after they had gone, many sarcastic remarks followed them like, "Gives you a nice smile, but that's all."

The manager himself drove up before the office a little past nine—appeared sore that there was no parking space in front of the office. The fellows standing outside purposely raised their voices so he could hear and made remarks such as, "Not much use coming here, they never do anything but tell you to come back in sixty days"; "What'd they ever do for me?—Nothing"; "First it was April 1st, then it was the 15th, and now it will be God knows when."

One of the young fellows asked an official of the Bureau as he entered the building if there was anything in his line available—stated he was a soda jerker or plumber's helper—or

he'd "take anything." The official smiled and wanted to know if the fellow was following the ads in the newspaper. The fellow returned to the group, swore a moment, and asked, "Who ever got a job from the ads in a paper?"

Fellow next to me was apparently an electrician. He was sore because he couldn't get a P.W.A. job. He said, "All these contractors have their own men and when this Employment Office tries to do the hiring for the P.W.A. jobs, it doesn't know where to get off. The P.W.A. provision reads that the contractor must take men from the State Employment Bureau where they are able to do the work. Well, the Bureau sends its men out. They work for a day, and then they are let go as not fit for the job; then the contractor has fulfilled the specifications and hires his own men."

I register, but they say not much chance today; maybe a week from today. I go out. Tony grabs my arm. He says, "Work?—there is no work. I go to the Employment Office. I stand and wait. Soon—my turn. I give the girl my card. She takes it, turns it over and over in her hand. Bluff—just to take up time. By and by, she gives it back. 'Sorry, nothing today.' I say, 'But I no work in three years, with seven children, what do I eat?' She reply, 'Come back again, maybe soon there will be something.' It is the big bluff."

Jim joins us at the foot of the stairs. He's mad too. "God, I'm disgusted with this place, and everybody else is that I know. Some fine day a mob's going to drop down on this place and tear it apart. I'm telling you, these fellows from down around Wooster Street aren't going to take this tomorrow business forever."

Looks as though I'd be better off to depend on the grapevine. Word gets around plenty fast if they're taking men on any place.

April 27.

Up at seven, cup of coffee, and off to Sargent's. Like to be there when the gang comes to work, the lucky devils. Employment manager not in. Waited in his outer office fitted with six benches and about thirty nearly worn out chairs. Took a bench—looked more likely to stay up. Three others waiting, two reporting for compensation. Other one laid off two weeks ago and said he called at office every day. He inquired what I was doing and when I said "looking for work" he laughed. "You never work here? No? What chance you think you got when 400 like me who belong here out?" Employment manager showed up at 9:30. I had waited two hours. My time has no value. A pleasant fellow; told me in a kind but snappy way business was very bad. What about the future, would he take my name? Said he referred only to the present. Nothing more for me to say, so left. Two more had drifted into office. Suppose they got the same story. Must be a lot of men in New Haven that have heard it by now.

Down Chestnut Street to Peck Brothers. Thought something might be going there. Since beer bill they have been calling back old employees, might have use for another hand. No real employment office here. From street into a long hall with two offices both with clerks on each side of hall. Picked the wrong one. Smart flapper didn't even speak just tossed her head and thumb in the direction of across the hall. Went across and another girl at an information desk asked if I had ever worked there before. Told her "No." She said no immediate chance then, but I could file an application; but added, "It won't do you no good as there is plenty of our own men to fill the jobs for some time to come." Guess I won't get a job till they've skimmed the cream from their own men. That's proper of course and a good break for them. But if it's like this all over, what's the point in applying for jobs? Filled out application anyway—might as well, didn't have any better way to spend my time. No one else here looking for work.

No heart for any more so dropped into Jake's for a doughnut and a glass of milk and then went home.

April 28.

To New Haven Clock Company. Met a company "dick" who said plant was shut down till Monday. Gave me an application blank and said, "You look all right, fill this out in ink. Do it neatly, and they may give you a break. Do you know anybody inside?" I said, "No." Then he shrugs his shoulders and says, "Well, I don't know if there is much use you sending this in then, but you might try."

In the afternoon went to the park and talked with men trying to find out what luck they had had. No good news.

May 2.

Started out at seven for New Haven Clock Shop. No one in employment office. Lady at information desk asked, "What do you want?" I told her. She wanted to know if I had worked there before and when I said "No," she didn't even ask if I had any experience in clockmaking (which I have). And when I started to tell her so, she cut me off with, "No use—sorry." Suppose she gets tired too.

From Clock Shop to E. Cowells and Co. who make auto equipment. If they want to have old men, well, I worked here in 1916 and 1917. Didn't get to see anyone here because just as you get to the hall there is a big sign "No Help Wanted." You can't miss it, and

I find it kind of hard to disregard a sign of that type. I assume it means what it says or they wouldn't have gone to the trouble and expense to have it painted. I'll have to see a fellow I know who works there. He may know some way to get me on the call list, seeing how I once worked there.

Having heard Seamless Rubber was working quite steady I went down there. Regular employment office furnished with one bench. Another chap, a foreigner, waiting also. In about ten minutes a fellow asked us our business and told us very politely they had no jobs even for skilled men, let alone laborers. No use to tell him I wasn't always a laborer for I never had done the skilled jobs on rubber.

Saw a sign hanging out of one place in gilt letters, "No Help Wanted." In guilt, mind you, as if to make it more permanent.

Then to Bradley-Smith candymakers, where I had also worked before. The first few days I hadn't had the heart for more than a couple of tries a morning. I'm getting hardened to the word "No" now, though, and can stick it out most of the morning. Brad-ley-Smith has no employment office. The telephone switchboard operator is apparently instructed to switch off anyone looking for work, as she made quick work of my question. I notice no one seems to be instructed to find out if we know anything about the business or work. Firms might be passing up some good bets for their force. But apparently that isn't important now.

Walking away, met two friends out going the rounds too. They said it was useless and that they were only looking through force of habit. That's going to be me before long. Even if they hadn't said so. I'm thinking it is useless to run around like this; you just appear ridiculous, and that gets your goat— or would if you kept it up too long. Wish I had some drag with someone on the inside of one of those gates. I expect it's that everyone knows they have to know someone that keeps me from having more company at the employment offices. This is what a former pal of mine who is up at Yale calls "competition in the labor market," I guess. Well, it's a funny competition and with guys you never see.

*   *   *

15   WHEN ALL THE BANKS CLOSED

Arthur A. Ballentine

Arthur A. Ballentine, Undersecretary of the Treasury when the banks closed in 1933, was subsequently a well known corporation and tax lawyer.

*   *   *

Officially the bank closing, with its threatened business paralysis, was called a "holiday." A more suitable term would have been "holocaust." But terminology, like much that entered into the extraordinary event, was largely a matter of public psychology.

What was at work was of course the great depression in its impact upon banks and also upon the currency. At critical times it becomes apparent that

From "When All the Banks Closed," by Arthur A. Ballentine, *Harvard Business Review,* March, 1948, pp. 129, 134–138. Reprinted by permission.

banking and currency are by no means matters of abstract theory or mere mathematics; much else enters in.

* * *

During January, and strikingly in February, came gold withdrawals, not for normal purposes but as a means of hoarding or flight from the dollar. Earlier the trouble had been with the panic desire to turn bank deposits into cash; at this time the idea was the more disastrous one of turning cash into gold, in the belief that more gold could be obtained for the dollar then than later.

Withdrawals of gold owned outside the United States had been withstood by the banking structure in 1931 and 1932. Such withdrawals had a natural limit. Withdrawals of gold by domestic depositors, worried or astute about the future of the paper dollar, were a drain on the very basis of our currency and had almost no limit.

Crisis in Michigan

The renewed drains upon the banks came to a head in February, 1933, in Michigan. In that state most of the larger banks had been grouped together into two holding companies. The failure of one member of such a group was likely to cause loss of confidence in other members, and quite possibly in the other group as well. The assets of important Michigan banks depended in large measure upon the underlying values of Michigan low real estate, which had greatly increased in the years before the depression.

In February the Guardian Detroit Union Group, the smaller of the two groups, requested the Reconstruction Finance Corporation for a loan of $50 million in addition to loans aggregating upwards of $13 million which had already been received. Mr. Edsel Ford was the largest stockholder in this group, and the Ford interests had already backed the group to the amount of some $16 million. This critical loan came under discussion at the White House. There Senator James Couzens of Michigan took the position that if a loan were made for more than what was strictly the value of the collateral, he "would denounce the loan from the housetops." Senator Couzens had strongly favored publicity for all RFC loans, but why he took this exacting position about the proposed Detroit loan was not ascertained. (This and subsequent developments may have had some relation to the personal hostility between Senator Couzens and Henry Ford.)

Examiners of the Reconstruction Finance Corporation, working with examiners for the banks, did their utmost to support as large a loan as possible. It was thought that a total loan of $41 million might meet the situation, but the highest total the examiners felt they could place on the collateral offered was $37 million.

Although in normal times determination of the value of securities on loans held by banks is not difficult, in panic times such valuation calls for very real judgment. In the RFC, as in the Treasury, the view prevailed that normal times would come again and that good securities should be valued in the light of such expectation, and in the later stages that view made some progress with the bank examiners. Particularly in the early days of the great depression, however, banking difficulties were unnecessarily aggravated by insistence of bank examiners on using market transactions, even though clearly panic-induced, as the sole guide in appraisals. In such a disturbed time, with a forceful Senator standing by ready if not eager to criticize, appraisal was indeed very difficult.

On February 11 Secretary of Commerce Roy D. Chapin and I went to

Detroit as representatives of the Reconstruction Finance Corporation and the Administration, to see whether some plan could not be put through to avoid the impending disaster of the closing of the Detroit banks.

Negotiations with Ford. The plan worked out for the Guardian Trust Company required the subordination by the Ford Company of more than $7.5 million of claims on the Guardian Trust Company, in favor of small creditors, as well as the subordination of certain other larger claims. It also involved the raising of about $4 million of new capital for the group and $2 million of new capital for a company to handle mortgages.

It was believed that these steps, together with the maximum RFC loan, would keep open the Guardian group and protect the larger First National group. Mr. Chapin and I found that local interests were entirely willing to come in on what was required of them but that their cooperation depended on the suggested subordination of the Ford claims and reasonable participation by Mr. Edsel Ford in the furnishing of the new capital.

On the morning of February 13 Mr. Chapin and I had a long talk with Henry Ford, who had present his son Edsel Ford and Mr. E. G. Leibold. Mr. Ford, who had been informed about the plan, stated at once that he would not participate in any way either by further subordination of Ford deposits or by furnishing part of the necessary additional capital required. He further stated that if the Guardian Trust Company did not open on the next day, he would withdraw the $25 million which his company had on deposit with the First National, the largest Detroit bank.

Mr. Ford expressed the belief that the urgent request for further support of the Guardian Trust Company by him was due to some plot against him, which Mr. Chapin and I did not understand. Mr. Ford also said that he could not believe that the government would let the banks of Detroit close for lack of the aid asked of him. Mr. Chapin and I explained very carefully that the government could not legally provide loans beyond the appraised value of the collateral, or supply new capital; that the saving of the Guardian Trust Company therefore required the Ford participation; that its closing, and that of the First National group which would surely follow, would paralyze business in Michigan; and that this paralysis would probably extend throughout the country.

In spite of all that Mr. Chapin and I could say Mr. Ford remained of the opinion which he originally expressed, stating that in the event of such disaster he would start a new business again if necessary, as he still felt young.

The failure of the plan for keeping open the Guardian Trust Company left to the governor of the state no course except to exercise his authority under a Michigan statute and to declare on February 13 a holiday for all the banks in Michigan. Under the original proclamation the holiday was to be for four days only. It was still hoped in Washington that a plan could be promptly devised for reopening the Michigan banks, but interests were conflicting and these efforts were fruitless.

Roosevelt's Refusal to Make a Statement. President Hoover believed throughout that the destructive drain on the banks could be stopped by a declaration of policy by President-elect Roosevelt. On February 17 the President sent to the President-elect a letter setting forth the underlying factors as he saw them, stating that "the major difficulty is the state of the public mind . . . which has reached the height of general alarm"; that necessary credit agencies had been created to meet the needs of the banks; but that "confidence must run parallel with expanding credits." President Hoover urged that the President-elect, being in the position, by reason of the support of Congress, to make effective whatever policies he endorsed, give prompt assurance "that there will be no tampering or inflation of the currency, that the budget will unquestionably be balanced, and that the Government credit will be maintained by refusal to exhaust it in the issue of securities." President Hoover added that it would be a help if Congressional leaders could be advised to cease publication of the RFC loans. All these measures he had urged upon Congress in his messages.

Reply to President Hoover's letter was received on March 1. The President-elect in that reply stated that he was dismayed to find that the letter which he had written a week earlier had not gone to President Hoover. That earlier letter, which was enclosed, stated:

I am equally concerned with you in regard to the gravity of the present banking situation, but my thought is that it is so very deep-seated that the fire is bound to spread in spite of anything that can be done by way of mere statement.

That "fire" had been spreading, and it kept on spreading.

The Crisis. Holidays were declared in other states. The destructive forces at work were closing in upon the New York City banks. Those banks lost nearly $1,420 million in deposits in the five weeks immediately preceding the national holiday.

No measure adequate to meet the destructive forces were available to the Administration, acting without Congressional support. Provisions for Clearing House certificates were carefully considered; however, the device of a negotiable certificate of ownership in bank assets, which had served to relieve currency shortage in some prior crises, was utterly inadequate to meet what was an asset and gold crisis rather than a currency crisis.

Most careful consideration was given in the Treasury to possibilities of helpful action under Section 5(b) of the Trading With the Enemy Act of October 6, 1917, as amended September 24, 1918. That provision gave authority to the President to "investigate, regulate, or prohibit, under such rules and regulations as he may prescribe, by means of licenses, or otherwise, any transactions in foreign exchange and the export, hoarding, melting or earmarkings of gold or silver coin or bullion or currency." The thought was that under this section the President might, by proclamation, at least stop the destructive withdrawals of gold. The Attorney General advised, however, that continuing authority under that war-emergency act was too doubtful to sustain action unless full sanction by Congress would assuredly and promptly follow.

By March 3 it was apparent that further ravages of the panic would be likely to impair the Federal Reserve Banks themselves. The gold reserves of the Federal Reserve Bank of New York had been reduced to very close to the permitted minimum of 40% against note liabilities. Suspension by the Federal Reserve Board of the gold requirements, although permitted by law, was likely to intensify the panic. The Federal Reserve Board reluctantly agreed that a closing of the banks had become necessary in fairness to depositors who stood firm and in order to retain a better basis for restoring the banking structure.

Currency in circulation had then mounted to a record total reported at over $7.5 billion and gold holdings of the Federal Reserve Banks had fallen over $575 million, more than half for hoarding. The number of banks that had suspended operations since 1929 had mounted to 5,500, or about 1 in 5, involving deposits aggregating some $3½ billion.

The National Bank Holiday

The night before inauguration we spent at the Treasury in intensive communications by telephone with state executives of the principal states not yet on the holiday basis. In the early hours of the morning, the governors of New York and Illinois had acted. March 4 saw substantially all banks in the country, including the Federal Reserve Banks, closed by state action. At the Treasury momentary relief at not having to hear about further inroads on the banks was replaced by anxiousness for prompt ending of the banking paralysis.

The first step was to present to President Roosevelt the proclamation, prepared at the Treasury, of the "bank holiday" which would operate uniformly throughout the nation. The proclamation bore the date of March 6 and provided that during the period of the holiday no banking operations should be carried on except to the extent permitted by the Secretary of the Treasury with the approval of the President. The proclamation was made under the authority of Section 5(b) of the Trading With the Enemy Act, mentioned previously, and cited "heavy and unwarranted withdrawals of gold and currency from our banking institutions for the purpose of hoarding—creating conditions of national emergency."

The President's proclamation was accompanied by a call for a special session of Congress to convene March 9, and was issued with assurance that constructive Congressional action so needed would then be taken.

*   *   *

16   THE PIT

Marriner S. Eccles

Marriner S. Eccles has been Chairman of the Board of Governors of the Federal Reserve System. He is now President of the First Security Corp., President of the Eccles Investment Co., and director of a number of corporations.

During 1930 I awoke to find myself at the bottom of a pit without any known means of scaling its sheer sides.

Since the crash of 1929, men I respected assured me that the economic crisis was only temporary and that soon all the things that had pulled the country out of previous depressions would operate to that same end once again. But the weeks turned to months. The months turned to a year or more. Instead of easing, the economic crisis worsened. The pit grew deeper and I found myself in it.

On the morning of the awakening, I saw for the first time that though I'd been active in the world of finance and production for seventeen years and

Reprinted from *Beckoning Frontiers* by Marriner S. Eccles, by permission of Alfred A. Knopf, Inc.; copyright 1951.

knew its techniques, I knew less than nothing about its economic and social effects. Yet, by itself a confession of ignorance led nowhere. Friends whose estates I managed, my family, whose interests I represented, and the community at large, in whose economic life I played a sensitive role, all expected me to find the way out of the pit. Yet all I could find within myself was despair. Having been reared by my father to accept the responsibilities of wealth and having been placed by circumstances at the helm of many enterprises, there were times when I felt the whole depression was a personal affront.

Wherein had I been at fault?

Night after night following that head-splitting awakening I would return home exhausted by the pretensions of knowledge I was forced to wear in a daytime masquerade. I would slump forward on a table and pray that by a supreme act of will the answers would somehow be revealed. As an individual I felt myself helpless to do anything. I heard grass-roots talk that "the government ought to do something." But why the government? Wherein is the government different from the individual? Is it not just a sum of all individuals? Or, granting there is a difference, what specifically should the government do?

For instance:

What should be done in a situation where the dollar was so painfully sound when measured by its power to buy goods and services that when prices fell and unemployment increased, the dollar somehow got "sounder"?

What was to be done in a siutation such as I faced in our lumber mills, where we would operate at a loss even if men worked without pay?

What was to be done by our banks when loans on homes, farms, livestock, and securities or to business and industrial enterprises could not be paid because values had drastically declined?

What was to be done when the pressure on the banks to "get liquid" so as to meet depositor claims caused a situation where the liquidation of debts made it impossible to pay off debts?

What was to be done when men on the farms and in the cities, who needed each other's goods, were stranded on opposite river banks without the consumer purchasing power by which they could navigate a crossing for trading?

These were not academic questions. They were intimately connected with day-to-day dangers, and particularly the danger of a sudden run on the banks. It didn't matter where the run started. A weak bank that closed its doors could create community tensions of a sort that could close the doors of sound banks as well.

Fortunately, the banks of the First Security Corporation kept their doors open throughout the depression. No depositor lost one penny. But time after time the life of our organization was imperiled by failures or imminent failures in neighboring banks. Physical nearness alone tended to involve all banks in the fate of any one of them. I still grow weak when I think of the runs or threatened runs with which we had to deal.

The first one occurred in 1931 in Ogden. Here one of the most highly regarded and oldest banks in the entire state was the Ogden State Bank. Under the management of the Bigelow family it had served the community well for over forty years. In size it was only slightly smaller than our Ogden banks. But the officers of our banks were, like myself, young men or men relatively new to the community. We didn't have the sort of public confidence enjoyed by the Ogden State Bank. If it got into trouble, what could the community expect of a bank managed by much younger and less experienced men?

I had advance warning of trouble when Archie Bigelow, the president of the Ogden State Bank, revealed to Bennett and me that his bank was facing great losses on its loans due to the deflation, that its capital and surplus were impaired, and that it was losing deposits. But Bigelow felt his bank could be saved if it was merged with our Ogden banks.

Examination of the imperiled bank showed that it was so far gone it would pull down our banks if they were linked to it as a lifesaver. Came the week-end in the late summer of 1931 when doom could no longer be staved off. Word reached us that the Ogden State Bank would not open its doors on the coming Monday.

We knew we could expect a severe run on our Ogden banks; we also knew that when word of it got around, the effect would extend to other areas where the First Security Corporation owned banks. These others had to be alerted and prepared for imminent developments, and because our Ogden banks were the central institutions in our banking complex, it was imperative that they break the run as quickly as possible and stay open at all costs.

The Sunday preceding the Monday when the Ogden State Bank did not open, I called together all the officers and directors of the First National and the First Savings banks. Having a list of all the important commercial accounts held by the Ogden State Bank, I pointed out to the directors and officers of our banks that the firms represented on the list would be without banking facilities on Monday morning when the Ogden State Bank remained closed. Yet they would need to make deposits, get currency, borrow money, and issue checks. The directors of our banks were to pick out the firms on

the list with whom they had close personal or business dealings. Then on Monday morning they were to call the heads of these firms, invite them to deposit their funds on hand with our banks, and say that if they needed a loan or currency we would be glad to take care of their pressing needs. I wanted not only to gain an inflow of deposits but to develop confidence among the employees of those firms. They would be paid in checks drawn on our banks, and the combined incoming traffic would help reverse the current of the outgoing traffic we knew was to be expected on the next day.

The officers and directors went at this job with zeal and set in motion what it was hoped would happen.

While this plan was formed to stabilize our commercial accounts held locally, we had cause to fear a concealed run on our commercial and bank accounts that could start at distant points. Specifically, like other city banks, we held balances of many outside corporations as well as of independent country banks in the area. We knew that if the officials of these outside concerns heard of a run on our banks, they would take precautionary measures to avoid getting caught short. They would either ask for a direct transfer of funds or they would make a draft or checks on our banks and deposit them with other banks.

I'd seen this happen many times. I'd also seen its aftermath. The process by which large corporations, for instance, withdrew funds from the hinterland and concentrated them in New York and other large cities hastened the collapse of countless country banks. Having this danger in mind, we felt we had a fighting chance to overcome it if, first, our outside accounts were warned in advance of an imminent run, and, second, if they heard the news directly from us and not from press reports or from some other source. That Sunday night a telegram was drafted for delivery the first thing Monday morning to each of our outside accounts.

The telegram read:

THE OGDEN STATE BANK WILL NOT OPEN ITS DOORS THIS MONDAY MORNING. THIS WILL CAUSE SOME DEMANDS FOR WITHDRAWAL OF FUNDS ON OUR OWN BANKS. WE HAVE ANTICIPATED THIS FOR SOME TIME AND ARE FULLY PREPARED TO MEET ANY AND ALL DEMANDS WHICH ARE MADE UPON US. WE FELT IT DESIRABLE THAT YOU SHOULD GET THIS INFORMATION FIRST HAND.

Fortunately, there was not a single transfer of funds from among the accounts that received these telegrams.

While we made this bid to shore up the confidence of our commercial accounts, we realized that the greatest potential danger lay with the savings group. If they were thrown into panic by a run on our savings bank, the effect would not be self-limiting. Our national bank shared the same premises with our savings bank; a run on the latter would certainly be duplicated in a run on the former. In view of this, all officers and employees of the national and savings banks were contacted that Sunday and asked to be at work the next morning at eight o'clock.

When they assembled the next morning, I told them what they would have to face in a few hours. "If you want to keep this bank open," I said, "you must do your part. Go about your business as though nothing unusual was happening. Smile, be pleasant, talk about the weather, show no signs of panic. The main burden is going to fall on you boys in the savings department. Instead of the three windows we normally use, we are going to use all four of them today. They must be manned at all times because if any teller's or clerk's window in this bank closes for even a short time, that will stir up more panic. We'll have sandwiches brought in; no one can go out to lunch. We can't break this run today. The best we can do is slow it down. People are going to come here to close out their savings accounts. You are going to pay them. But you are going to pay them very slowly. It's the only chance we have to deal with the panic. You know a lot of depositors by sight, and in the past you did not have to look up their signatures, but today when they come here with their deposit books to close out their accounts, you are going to look up every signature card. And take your time about it. And one other thing: when you pay out, don't use any big bills. Pay out in fives and tens, and count slowly. Our object is to pay out a minimum today."

The tellers and clerks ably carried out their part of the act despite the crowd that surged through the doors of the bank the moment they were opened. Someone with an objective turn of mind could have learned much that day about the degree to which banking is understood by the community at large. I recall one depositor, for instance, who in great anxiety closed his savings account and with the currency given him promptly bought a cashier's check. He did not know that if the bank closed, his check would be worth no more than his deposit. But amidst the pushing and shoving inside the bank there was little time to reflect on matters of this sort.

At two o'clock that afternoon Bennett, my brother George, and I met to decide what should be done when the regular three-o'clock closing hour was reached. The crowd in the bank was as taut as it was dense. Some people had been waiting for hours to draw out their money. If we tried to close at three, there was no telling what might happen. But, as in all other things, a poverty of alternatives made us adopt the boldest one. We decided to make an exception of this one day and to remain open so long as there were people who wanted to get their money.

In the meantime a call had been put through to the Federal Reserve Bank in Salt Lake City to send currency to our Ogden banks as well as to all others in the Frist Security Corporation. The armored car that brought funds to us in Ogden arrived on the scene as in the movies when the Union cavalry charges in to save all from the Indians. The guards strode through the crush inside the bank, and all made way before them.

Of equal importance in the events of the day, Morgan Craft, the deputy manager of the Federal Reserve Bank in Salt Lake City, had been a passenger in the armored car that raced to Ogden. When he entered our bank, I grabbed his arm and led him through the crowd to a black and gold marble counter in the officers' section of the savings bank. Mounting the counter, I raised my hand and called for attention:

"Just a minute!"

There was instant silence.

"Just a minute!" I repeated. "I want to make an announcement. It appears that we are having some difficulty handling our depositors with the speed to which you are accustomed. Many of you have been in line for a considerable time. I notice a lot of pushing and shoving and irritation. I just wanted to tell you that instead of closing at the usual hour of three o'clock, we have decided to stay open just as long as there is anyone who desires to withdraw his deposit or make one. Therefore, you people who have just come in can return later this afternoon or evening if you wish. There is no justification for the excitement or the apparent panicky attitude on the part of some depositors. As all of you have seen, we have just had brought up from Salt Lake City a large amount of currency that will take care of all your requirements. There is plenty more where that came from." (This was true enough—but I didn't say we could get it.)

"And if you don't believe me," I continued, "I have here Mr. Morgan Craft, one of the officers of the Federal Reserve Bank, who has just come up in an armored car. Mr. Craft, say a few words to the folks."

I pulled him up to the top of the counter. He not only said a few words, but threw in one or two for extra measure.

"I just want to verify what Mr. Eccles has told you," he said. "I want to assure you that we have brought up a lot of currency and there is plenty more where that came from."

This, again, was perfectly true. But he didn't say the currency belonged to us. Nevertheless, the mood of the day was so unreasoning that men were heartened by words as meaningless as those which caused them fright. In a split instant the faces before me relaxed in relief. The edge in all voices seemed to vanish. Some people stepped out of line and left the bank. And a happy buzz replaced the waspish one heard earlier. The word was passed to the crowd outside the bank: "They are going to stay open. They are going to stay open."

*   *   *

D.
CONSUMPTION PATTERNS

17 CONSUMPTION EXPENDITURES IN RECOVERY PHASE

Anne N. Probst

Anne N. Probst is an economist in the U.S. Department of Commerce.

Consumption expenditures have moved up since early this year, and [as pointed out in the opening business summary] are now an important factor in current trends. The decline from the late 1960 peak was moderate, and the 3 percent rise from the first quarter 1961 low brought third quarter outlays to a new high. Early indications for the final quarter suggest a further gain, paced by a rebound in auto purchasing from the relatively low summer volume. There has been considerable variation of demand in particular lines of business, and durable goods sales have on the whole been low relative to the current level of income.

Consumer Purchasing Over the Cycle

It is the purpose of this article to analyze the current tendencies and the longer-term structural changes in consumer purchasing of goods and services. The chart clearly shows that fluctuations in total consumer spending have been of limited amplitude around a growth tendency, though the durable goods segment shows a much more sensitive pattern than the other two major segments. This volatility in total consumption is one of the major characteristics of its cyclical pattern, and its declining relative size in recent years is an important factor in the longer-run pattern.

Outlays for durable goods have not been showing the buoyancy of the earlier postwar period. Unsatisfied demand for durables remaining after World War II and the effects of the Korean hostilities no doubt had a lifting effect on these purchases, although the cyclical swings have been pronounced in each of the postwar recessions. In these same years consumer expenditures for nondurable goods continued upward, although at a somewhat less rapid pace than in the earlier period. The high growth rate of outlays for services has been maintained but, as may be seen from the chart, the proportion of consumer expenditures for services is now back to the 1929 proportion of 40 percent, after two decades of war and reconstruction distortions during which it has been much lower.

Buying and Income

Examination of the relationships of the relative changes in consumption expenditures and its major components to disposable personal income in the post-

From the *Survey of Current Business*, November, 1961, pp. 11–14.

war period suggests that changes in disposable personal income account for nearly all the variation in total consumer purchases of goods and services. Indeed, the relationship is one of direct proportionality—i.e., on the average for the postwar period each 1 percent change in income has been associated with a 1 percent change in expenditures. The relationship is quite stable, with only minor deviations during cyclical turns, although wider fluctuations occurred during the Korean hostilities.

Nondurable goods demand has shown a high degree of constancy in its relationship to income in the period since Korea. The slope suggested by this relationship is 0.75, with those for food and clothing somewhat lower, and those for other major nondurable goods slightly higher.

Fluctuations around a logarithmic regression covering the postwar period are appreciable in the case of durable goods purchasing. Substantial deviations are apparent in cyclical periods and in response to Korean developments and the special factors in the 1955 automobile market. The slope for the 1948–61 period as a whole is slightly under one; the instability of the relationship is such, however, that the average is not typical of any particular set of years in the postwar period. The slope has been well below unity in more recent years, with the flattening noticeable in both autos and the furniture-appliance group.

Outlays for services do not respond much to cyclical influences and relations to incomes are highly unsatisfactory since the correlations really are with trends—the average growth rate has been 7 percent per year.

* * *

Consumers' demand for services in recent years of "catching up" has been relatively stronger than the demand for goods. Growth has not merely been confined to those consumption items which are classified as services. Among goods, growth has been above average for processed foods, new types of fabrics, and other items which economize on such household services as cooking and laundering.

The recovery of the service component of personal consumption expenditure—from the abnormally low warend position—is measured on the charts. From 1948 through 1960 dollar expenditures for services were up 133 percent compared to 95 percent for durables and 54 percent for nondurables; the rise in disposable personal income was 86 percent.

Part of the explanation for this is the more rapid price advance for services in the postwar period, about twice as much as the rise in prices of either durable or nondurable goods. Here again, one must keep in mind the influence of price controls, their relative incidence, and the different time periods over which they were lifted. Thus, this represents in some measure a catching up of service prices from the war restraints. After adjusting to constant dollars, the expansion of service expenditures from 1948 to 1960 while substantially in excess of nondurable goods, was not quite so large as the growth in durable goods purchasing from its still abnormally low level in 1948.

Table 1 presents these changes in consumption and compares them with the prewar period. In addition, the period 1953 to 1960 is shown to avoid the distortions of the early postwar years. Again the greater rise in service prices was present—twice as much as the increase in goods prices—but even after adjustment for price changes, service expenditures advanced half again as much as either durables or nondurables.

Table 1

CHANGES IN PERSONAL CONSUMPTION EXPENDITURES, 1929–60

	Current dollars			Constant (1954) dollars		
	1929–48	*1948–60*	*1953–60*	*1929–48*	*1948–60*	*1953–60*
	Percent change					
Total	126	84	41	56	50	27
Durable goods	147	95	35	66	70	26
Nondurable goods ...	162	54	29	61	35	20
Services	77	133	62	45	65	37

SOURCE: U.S. Department of Commerce, Office of Business Economics.

Allocation of Consumer Dollar

The result of this differential movement in consumption expenditures for the various goods and services in the most recent period has been a change in the proportion of the consumer dollar expended for such items. Compared with 1953, the consumer today is spending 7 cents more on services, and this has been offset by a decline of 2 cents on durable goods and 5 cents on nondurables.

Changing Distribution of Consumer Spending

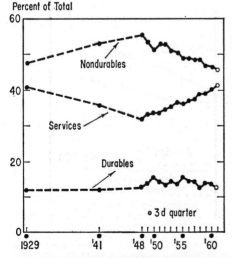

Percent of Total

U.S. Department of Commerce, Office of Business Economics 61-11-14.

As shown in the chart, this shift from goods to services has been quite pervasive; the over-all result is only to a small extent the result of diverse and offsetting trends.

Among the nondurables, the portion of the dollar spent for food has shown the largest decline in the last 7 years, falling by nearly 4 cents. It must be noted, however, that the largest share still goes for food—almost 21 cents. Clothing and semidurable housefurnishings also have declined in relative importance—the former by about 1 cent. Increases in the shares spent for gasoline and oil, and for drugs, cosmetics, and nondurable toys and games were not enough to offset the declines in the other more heavily weighted types of nondurables. After a sharp rise in the early postwar years, the proportion allotted to gasoline and oil has tended to level off—i.e., dollar expenditures for these products are now moving in line with total spending.

The over-all durables pattern is somewhat clouded because of the part played by automobiles. As is shown in the chart, the proportion of expenditure going to autos and parts has shown considerable volatility and very little trend, though perhaps slightly downward, in the last 7 years. Furni-

SHIFTS IN SPENDING PATTERNS

With Only Few Exceptions, Services Take Increasingly More, and Goods Less, of the Consumer Expenditure Dollar

Cents per Consumer Dollar

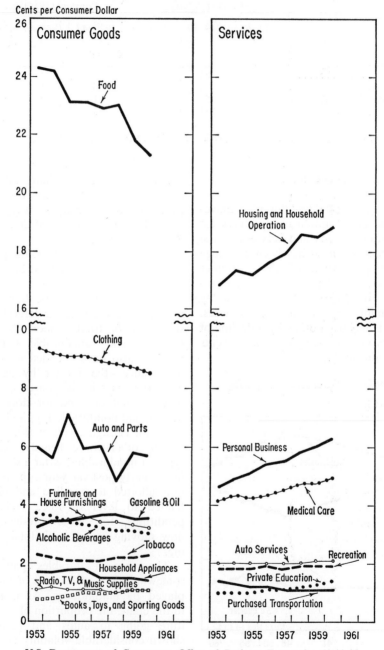

U.S. Department of Commerce, Office of Business Economics 61-11-15.

ture and household equipment outlays have had a downward drift, but this has been offset by an advance in other durables which include such items as jewelry, toys, and ophthalmic products. Thus, the share going to all durables is currently slightly below the average in the postwar years.

Among the services, all of the major groups except personal services and transportation show rising proportions. Interest payments and medical care have shown larger-than-average growth. Over the longer term, however, it may be noted that the consumer in 1960 spent about the same proportion of his consumption dollar on services as he spent in 1929 (see chart). The services proportion rose in the early depression years of the thirties, then gen-erally fell until the end of World War II, and has risen since.

The distribution of the service dollar, however, has changed significantly in the three decades since 1929. Among the more important shifts was the declining relative importance in rent paid by tenants, and the increasing proportion of imputed rent as home ownership grew. In aggregate, however, housing in current dollars takes almost two cents less of the current consumer dollar than it did in 1929. This reduc-tion has been offset by increases of one cent each for medical care and household operation (more particularly for the enormously increased services provided by gas, electricity, and tele-phone facilities).

*   *   *

E.
MONETARY POLICY

18   MONEY SUPPLY AND STABLE ECONOMIC GROWTH

Edward S. Shaw

Edward S. Shaw is Professor of Economics at Stanford University.

DEFINITIONS OF MONEY

Everyone Rolls His Own

It is almost true that everyone rolls his own definition of money and has his own rules for measurement of the money supply. Federal Reserve people are noncommittal, and in the representative *Federal Reserve Bulletin* offer no tabulations headed *Money* or *Supply of Money*. Their essays about money coat the term with a film of adjectives—"active" money, "relatively active" money, "inactive" money. Our central bank cultivates uncertainty even in monetary semantics.

The rest of us have been no more incisive. Here is a list of items from which we concoct now one, now another definition of money with measurements to match. The figures apply to a date chosen at random, February 26, 1958.

From *United States Monetary Policy;* The American Assembly, 1958, pp. 49–71. Reprinted by permission.

MONEY OR NOT?

Item	Amount ($ billions)
Currency outside banks	$ 27.3
Demand deposits adjusted	105.5
United States Government balances in banks	4.2
Treasury cash holdings	.7
Time deposits of commercial banks	57.5
Other time deposits	33.4

"Money," as the composite of some items above, increased in amount over the year before the date of measurement. "Money" comprising a different combination of these items decreased over the year. If you suspect that there was monetary expansion, you can tailor a definition to your suspicion. If you prefer to think that there was monetary contraction, you can be right again—with a different definition.

There is good fundamentalist authority for counting as money only the hard core of legal tender, the first item in our Table. There is equally reputable reformist authority for counting items that are not mentioned in the Table, for counting anything called a "deposit" in any institution called a "bank." I can cite no authority for including "shares" of savings and loan associations or credit unions, though authority may not be lacking when and if the associations win their battle of nomenclature and become "banks" owing "deposits."

A Personal Preference

The definition that strikes the writer's fancy begins with the dictum *A dollar is a dollar.* A unit of money bearing the price, or face value, of $1 today bears the same price tomorrow and next year. It discharges a debt for $1 anytime, and it always buys something else with a price tag of $1. No one haggles over money's price.

This definition is not quite as rigorous as it may seem, because one would count in money not merely legal-tender pocket money but checking balances as well. The latter do depreciate a little in price, subject as they are to service charges. And they would appreciate a little, if Congress once again permitted interest credits on demand accounts. This definition is flexible enough to admit anything that people use as money—as a means of payment: money is as money does!

Modern money is a debt, differing from other forms of debt in that its price does not vary. It is a debt of the monetary system—the commercial banks, the Federal Reserve Banks, and the Treasury monetary accounts. It is issued to other sectors of the economy in payment by the monetary system for purchases principally of nonmonetary securities and monetary metals. Textbooks classify our money as "token" money, to distinguish it from fragments of one commodity or another that people have used, in other times and places, as fixed-price means of payment.

THE SUPPLY OF MONEY

At any moment the supply or quantity of money is the monetary system's dollar aggregate of fixed-price debt. It is the sum of all legal tender in pockets and tills together with the sum of all unused credits to checking accounts. The "quantity of money" that economists talk about is this simple statistic doctored in various ways.

An observation at a moment of time does not give as accurate a "fix" as is necessary for precision in relating the supply of money to, say, national income for a year. Instead of a momentary measurement, one needs an average figure for money outstanding.

An average supply or quantity of

money may be outrageously inflation-ary if it is spread over a small commu-nity, grossly deflationary if the com-munity is much larger. Especially in a growth context, it is often the money supply *per capita* that one needs for analytical purposes. This is not a datum regularly accessible in official tabula-tions or elsewhere, possibly because most of us are preoccupied with the behavior or misbehavior of money in the short run, too few of us with mone-tary phenomena in periods long enough for significant change in the population of money-users.

The money we are discussing is *nominal* money—the face value of the monetary system's debt. Economists usually suppose that it is *real* money, rather than nominal money, that affects levels and patterns of economic activity and economic welfare. Real money is the purchasing power of nominal money. The supply of real money is the supply of nominal money deflated by some one or other index of prices for things that money buys. Old hands at monetary analysis are ruefully aware that no price index is quite right for measurement of the real money supply and of changes in it.

As one puts the quantity of money into one statistical disguise after an-other, he can get very different im-pressions of its behavior. The sum of currency outside banks and demand deposits adjusted, without statistical frills, was nearly $140 billions on De-cember 31, 1956, and nearly $138 billions on December 25, 1957. Obvi-ously the supply of money was reduced about 1.4 per cent. But was it? In real terms, *per capita* of our noninstitu-tional population, the supply of money fell from $1,177 to $1,103. This is a decline of 6.3 per cent. In its policy of restraint for 1957, was the Federal Reserve aiming at the target of 1.4 per cent or at the target of 6.3 per cent?

The "supply of money" that central banks manipulate, that people hold most of the time and spend once in a while, that economists investigate, is not, then, a simple concept. It is a fig-ure so transformed by its visit to the statistical beauty parlor as hardly to be recognizable by its closest friends. Lay-men take warning; there may be more than meets the eye in any measurement of the supply or quantity of money!

GROWTH IN THE SUPPLY OF MONEY: FIRST THE THROTTLE, THEN THE BRAKES

It was a common complaint, be-fore passage of the Federal Reserve Act in late 1913, that our monetary system was inelastic. The Federal Re-serve Act and its amendments, and ad-ministration of the Act, have quashed that complaint. Partly out of conviction and partly to arouse discussion, we are going to argue that the Act and its ad-ministrators have put far too much elasticity into our monetary system. Switching metaphors, our point will be that it was a mistake to demolish the old Model T monetary system of the pre-1914 era. The juggernaut that has replaced it is not designed, nor is it driven, on principles that are com-patible with monetary stability in a growing economy. These are fighting words that call for adequate documen-tation.

The Statistical Record (Stop and Go in Monetary Policy)

The Table which follows is a rough tracery of our monetary experience during 1896–1957. It measures growth in nominal money over the entire period and during seven sub-periods. The sub-periods begin with 1896–1914, when the old monetary system was running out its last miles under critical inspection by a bevy of monetary commissions, public and private. In four of the remaining six sub-periods, policies of the new monetary system were stipulated primarily by the Treasury Department. In the other two sub-periods, monetary policy was stipulated by the Federal Reserve Board, *alias* the Board of Governors of the Federal Reserve System.

The four "Treasury" intervals were:

1914–1919
1933–1941
1941–1945
1945–1951

In two of these intervals the monetary system was conscripted for war finance. For the greater part of 1933–1941 any "independent" monetary policy was subordinated to the broad objective of restoring liquidity to an economic system that had been parched and seared by deflation. The Treasury's parental concern with the viability of its debt distinguishes the years 1945–1951.

The two interludes of "Board" tenure were:

1919–1933
1951–1957

Both interludes opened with a palace revolution, within the federal executive, against the Treasury's excessive concern with its debt. The first closed in the disaster of a monetary moratorium. The second continues, but once again—as in the two decades before 1914—the vigilantes are gathering into monetary commissions.

In 1896 the nominal supply of money was at the near-microscopic level of $3.8 billions. At the close of 1957, the nominal supply of money was thirty-six times larger, or $137.7 billions. The average annual compound rate of growth was approximately 6

STOP AND GO IN MONETARY POLICY

Period	Change in Nominal Money ($ billions)	Annual Rate of Change (%)
1896–1914	$ 7.5	6
1914–1919	11.4	15
1919–1933	−3.5	−1
1933–1941	27.7	14
1941–1945	55.5	21
1945–1951	22.2	3
1951–1957	13.2	2
(1896–1957)	134.0	6

Six Decades in Review

per cent. One had no need for a microscope to see the money supply at the end of last year.

For perspective, the growth rate of 6 per cent in nominal money may be compared with the more modest growth rate of about 3.75 per cent in real value of money. Evidently prices rose at the average annual rate of 2.25 per cent. It may come as a mild surprise that this degree of price inflation has been our method of repudiating about $100 billions of growth in nominal money: nominal money increased by $134 billions; real money by perhaps $30–35 billions in 1896–1957. Our textiles may have been shrink-proof, but our dollar has not. (See accompanying table and chart, which show annual values of real output, money supply, price level and real money in the United States over the period 1900–1957.)

The Model-T Period

Consider the pre-Federal Reserve years 1896–1914 a little more closely. In correspondence with accelerating growth in physical production and in the nation's real income, the money stock grew at the average rate of 9 per cent in 1896–1906. From year to year there was relatively little variation in the rate of growth. After 1906 the tempo of growth slackened throughout the economy, the annual rate of growth in money falling to a little less than 3 per cent. The money supply declined in one year (1907); and it rose in each year of depression, including the dismal year of 1908. During 1906–1914 variation in annual rates of growth was narrow.

Waving aside the seasonal stresses of the old monetary system, which were amenable to treatment on the principle of the Aldrich-Vreeland Act, one is tempted to shed a nostalgic tear for our monetary experience in the two decades prior to the Federal Reserve Act. The monetary system was Model T, but it was not too much for us to handle.

Drag-racing the Monetary System

The Federal Reserve Act multiplied both horsepower and brakepower in the monetary system. Since 1914 effective control of the system has alternated between Treasury and Reserve Board. The Treasury takes out its aggressions on the throttle of the new machine. The Board reaches for the brakes. And the money supply lurches along a sawtooth course of growth.

In 1914–1919 the annual rate of growth in nominal money was accelerated from 3 to 15 per cent. Then the brakes! Over the next fourteen years, there was a net decline in the money supply. To be sure, there was growth in money balances of 1 per cent annually to 1929; but then deceleration set in at the average annual rate of 6 per cent. This is not a profile of monetary stability.

Twice during its tenure of control in 1919–1933, the Reserve Board presided over a decline of nearly 10 per cent in nominal money. In both years,

1921 and 1930, the monetary brakes were applied to an economic system that was already on the skids of deflation. In eight of the fourteen years there was net monetary contraction, and in six of these eight years monetary contraction was superimposed on other depressing circumstances. In two years of cyclic recession, 1924 and 1927, it is true that the Reserve Board followed the precedent of the old monetary system in increasing liquidity. But these were years when such a stimulus was less necessary than in four of the six years in which the Board departed from pre-1914 tradition.

The Board's license to drive the monetary system was, in effect, suspended in 1933, when the Treasury took over the controls. Probation was granted in 1936–1937, but once more the Board applied the brakes too hard. The United States economy slid into the recession of 1937–1938, and again the Board's license to drive was lifted.

Over fourteen years, 1919–1933, the Board had subjected the economy to a negligible rate of growth in money. In the next eight years, apart from the interlude of 1936–1937, the Treasury chauffeur reversed monetary policy and subjected the economic system to an absurdly high rate of monetary expansion. By 1941 the prestige of monetary policy was, properly, very low indeed.

In reaction to the monetary experience of 1919–1933, the Congress added to the monetary system's capacity for both acceleration and deceleration in the series of reforms that appeared during 1933–1945. Retrospectively, it seems that the rational thing to do was to put the system on automatic pilot after 1914–1933 and disengage manual controls. Important statutory restraints on monetary expansion were eased or eliminated, and powerful new discretionary restraints were added. This is the kind of reform

GROSS NATIONAL PRODUCT, MONEY SUPPLY and PRICE LEVEL of the UNITED STATES, 1900-1957.

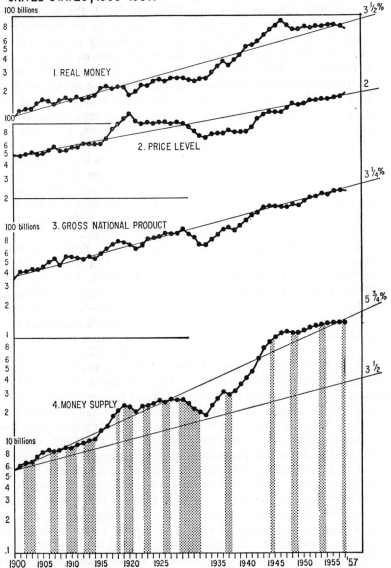

The shaded areas are periods of economic recession. Dates at the base of the chart are at year-ends. The straight trend lines joining the initial and terminal points on the four curves give the average annual rate of growth in each series, compounded annually.

1.
$$\frac{M}{P} \text{ (Real Money)}$$

2. Price Level (implicit deflator for gross national product).
1929 = 100 (= P)
1900–1949: Raymond W. Goldsmith, A Study of Saving in the United States, I, p. 377.
1949–1957: Survey of Current Business, June, 1957, adjusted from 1947 base to 1929 base.

3. Gross national product, 1929 prices (= T)
1900–1949: Raymond W. Goldsmith, A Study of Saving in the United States, III, p. 429.
1949–1957: Survey of Current Business. Deflator adjusted to 1929 base.

4. Adjusted demand deposits plus currency outside banks, year end figures (= M).
1900–1949: Raymond W. Goldsmith, A Study of Saving in the United States, pp. 382-3.
1949–1957: Federal Reserve Bulletin.

GROSS NATIONAL PRODUCT, MONEY SUPPLY AND PRICE LEVEL OF THE UNITED STATES, 1900–1957

	M *	P **	M/P ***	T ****
1900	$ 5,934	50	$11,868	$37,442
1901	6,536	50	13,072	40,901
1902	6,994,	51	13,714	41,495
1903	7,167	52	13,783	43,641
1904	7,827	51	15,347	43,190
1905	8,730	52	16,790	45,869
1906	9,159	56	16,356	50,940
1907	8,889	59	15,066	52,353
1908	9,086	55	16,520	48,700
1909	9,576	56	17,100	56,279
1910	9,674	59	16,400	56,158
1911	10,371	60	17,285	55,161
1912	10,665	64	16,664	55,468
1913	11,105	64	17,351	57,815
1914	11,565	64	18,070	55,532
1915	13,812	65	21,250	60,635
1916	16,015	72	22,243	67,300
1917	18,408	87	21,159	74,187
1918	21,171	98	21,603	78,875
1919	23,799	110	21,635	77,418
1920	22,812	125	18,248	73,298
1921	20,601	105	19,620	68,700
1922	22,804	99	23,034	72,775
1923	23,284	102	22,824	83,980
1924	24,797	101	24,551	85,427
1925	26,096	102	25,584	87,970
1926	25,510	103	24,748	93,833
1927	26,447	100	26,447	95,092
1928	26,784	101	26,519	96,136
1929	26,518	100	26,518	103,800
1930	24,669	96	25,697	94,400
1931	21,780	87	25,034	87,400
1932	20,343	78	26,081	74,800
1933	19,771	75	26,361	74,300
1934	23,178	79	29,340	82,000
1935	27,043	81	33,383	89,300
1936	31,010	81	38,284	101,400
1937	29,625	85	34,853	106,200
1938	31,739	83	38,240	101,500
1939	36,181	83	43,592	110,300
1940	42,274	84	50,326	120,800
1941	48,607	91	53,414	139,600
1942	62,865	110	57,150	146,866
1943	79,619	121	65,801	160,601

SOURCES:
 * Adjusted demand deposits *plus* currency outside banks for end-year dates.
1900–1949, Raymond W. Goldsmith, *A Study of Saving in the United States,* I, pp. 382–3.
1950–1957, *Federal Reserve Bulletin.*
 ** Deflator of gross national product.
1900–1949, Goldsmith, *ibid.,* I, p. 377. 1929 = 100.
1950–1957, based on series by U.S. Department of Commerce, *Survey of Current Business* as adjusted from 1947 base to 1929 base.
 *** Column 1 divided by column 2.
 **** Gross national product in 1929 prices.
1900–1949, Goldsmith, *ibid.,* III, p. 429.
1950–1957, current figures in *Survey of Current Business,* divided by column 2.

GROSS NATIONAL PRODUCT, MONEY SUPPLY AND PRICE LEVEL OF THE
UNITED STATES, 1900–1957—(Continued)

	M *	*P* **	*M/P* ***	*T* ****
1944	90,455	127	71,224	168,258
1945	102,341	128	79,953	169,144
1946	110,044	126	87,336	167,558
1947	113,597	139	81,725	167,500
1948	111,599	150	74,399	172,900
1949	111,165	149	74,608	172,000
1950	117,670	151	77,927	189,000
1951	124,549	162	76,882	203,000
1952	129,002	165	78,183	209,000
1953	130,542	167	78,169	218,000
1954	134,402	168	80,001	215,000
1955	137,900	170	81,118	230,000
1956	139,726	175	79,840	236,000
1957	137,700	184	74,837	236,000

one might have expected if the post-1914 monetary mechanism had been driven skillfully. Yet bad driving was rewarded by placing a new and still more powerful machine in the driver's hands!

This is not the occasion to debate wartime economic controls. One may simply offer the opinion that the rate of growth in money during 1941–1945, on the order of 21 per cent annually, is a blemish on our record that no amount of rationalization can erase. We expanded the money supply at a rate surpassing by a wide margin even the requirements for rapid real growth in wartime; then deputized thousands of price policemen in OPA and WPB to patrol the channels of moneyflow. The money accelerator was pushed to the floorboard, and policemen were deployed in droves to keep the public out of the way of the money juggernaut. The new monetary system was not the cause but the instrument of our folly.

The Board's fight for repossession of the monetary system was not won until 1951. The foot, shackled since 1936–1937, was freed and instinctively stepped on the monetary brakes again. The ensuing screech of complaint in the security markets, in the Spring of 1953, still echoes in our ears.

Since the Reserve Board settled back on the brakeman's seat in 1951, real national income has grown at approximately 4 per cent annually, real money a little over 1 per cent annually, nominal money 2 per cent. After five years of reckless acceleration in 1914–1919, fourteen years of excessive deceleration in 1919–1933, eighteen years of reckless acceleration in 1933–1951, we are again in the deceleration phase of our monetary drag-race. The economy's spinal column has not snapped as it has been whipped back and forth by alternating pressure on throttle and brake; but no credit is due to our "elastic" monetary system for our survival. Safety belts, sometimes known as built-in stabilizers, take up some of the strain, as OPA and WPB did in wartime. It is a pity that some of the ingenuity spent in contriving nonmonetary stabilizers has not been spent instead on stabilizing growth of the money supply.

In its twenty years of brakesmanship, the Board has permitted an average annual increase in the money supply of $440 millions. This rate of nominal growth is almost identical with the rate of nominal growth in 1896–1914, but in real terms it can hardly be half as rapid. It is a small fraction of the economy's rate of growth in real income. In its twenty-three years the Treasury has permitted an average annual increase in the money supply of $4,880 millions. It has added $11 to the money supply for every $1 permitted by the Board. Neither rate of expansion is close to an appropriate target rate.

In its twenty years of control, the Board has presided over an absolute decrease in nominal money during nine years. There has been price deflation in eleven of its twenty years. There have been no more than six years in which the Board has permitted nominal money to increase at a rate comparable with growth in the nation's productive capacity. The Treasury team that took over monetary control when the Board moved out has inflated money in all but three of its twenty-three years, a record that may be saluted at least for its consistency.

Neither driver of the monetary system has demonstrated sensitive reflexes to cyclical turning points along our road of growth. The old Model T was more maneuverable on the curves. With its predilection for restraint, the Board has characteristically punished a cyclical boom past its prime, aggravating ensuing depression. The notorious instances are 1919–1921 and 1929–1933, but the cyclical turning points of 1953 and 1957 are not exceptions to the rule.

A Robot at the Wheel

There are numerous alternative designs for a monetary system. The design that this country has hit upon builds into the monetary system an enormous capacity for both inflation and deflation. In successive trips back to the Congressional fix-it shop, the system's elasticity has been increased. As it is now put together, the United States monetary system is a brilliant solution for short-period instability in some security markets. But it has financed long-period inflation on the commodity markets, interrupted by painful episodes of excessive deceleration in monetary growth and declines in price levels. In its first half-century, the system has not created the temperate monetary environment that is most congenial to stable growth in real terms.

Now that the monetary system is undergoing revaluation, fundamental changes in its design should at least be discussed. The writer's own feeling is that, on balance, there would be improvement in its performance if the monetary system were put on automatic pilot. This suggestion is not a new one. The Reserve Board had to contend thirty years ago with proposals for automatized monetary control and turned them down in favor of "judgment in matters of credit administration."

What instructions are to be fed into an automatic monetary pilot? From the long list of alternatives that have been proposed in the history of monetary thought, one of the simplest appears most feasible. It is that, year in and year out, the nominal supply of money should increase by the *average* rate of growth in demand for nominal money at a stable level of commodity prices. According to usual estimates, which should be refined, the appropriate annual growth rate would be on the order of 3–4 per cent.

For any good other than money, no eyebrows would rise over the premise that it is right to balance supply with demand. But "demand for money" is not a concept in popular use. There is no mention of it in the Federal Reserve Act. Only one small tabulation remotely akin to it is published in the *Federal Reserve Bulletin*. If the demand for money is to be considered as the standard for regulation for money supply, a moment spent in probing demand may not be amiss.

THE "DEMAND STANDARD" FOR MONETARY CONTROL

The pure gold standard is an automatic rule of monetary control. And so is pure bimetallism. The automatic rule that I am reviving for consideration may be termed the "demand standard" of monetary control. What it means can be worked out very simply with the help of a familiar expression:

$$MV = PT$$

The Money Equation

All symbol-scarred veterans of Elementary Economics will recall that M is the average nominal supply of money during a period of time. V stands for the average frequency in turnover for a unit of money against the flow of goods and services from the community's productive facilities. P is the price level of goods and services, and T is their physical quantity—the national real income.

The money equation is a better tool for our use if it is twisted a little:

$$M = (1/V) \ (P) \ (T)$$

A second twist replaces the inconvenient expression $1/V$ with k and changes the order of terms:

$$M = P \ (kT)$$

Now we have the nominal supply of money M counterpoised against the community's demand for nominal money $P(kT)$. The community's demand for money in real measure—for money balances in terms of their purchasing power—is kT alone. And k is simply a proportion, a desired proportion, between the community's real balances in money and the community's real income.

With its seasonal and cyclical wrinkles ironed out, k is a remarkably stable relationship. In this country, k increased through the nineteenth century and apparently changed very little after 1900 in trend measurements. For present purposes, it may be stipulated that real money is a commodity, demand for which now grows at the same rate as real national income. Demand for money, of course, is motivated both by the utility of money as a means of payment and by the safety of money as a fixed-price asset.

Equality between M and $P(kT)$ is probably rare and fleeting. When it happens, there is monetary equilibrium. At all other times there is monetary disequilibrium. During most of the Treasury's tenure in monetary control, disequilibrium has been in the inflationary direction. Then M has exceeded $P(kT)$ at a stable level of prices P, so that money has been in excess supply. During approximately one-half of the Board's tenure, disequilibrium has been in the deflationary direction. Then M has been depressed below $P(kT)$ at a stable level of prices, so that money has been in excess demand.

Under the Demand Standard of monetary control, the automatic pilot would be instructed to increase M in step with the long-run growth rate of T. On the evidence that k is disposed to stability and on the judgment that a constant P is optimal for our economy and our social structure, the automatic pilot would link growth in money to growth in output of goods and services. Better evidence may turn up that k rises a little as we produce more goods *per capita,* and the view may win out that a little price inflation is good for us. Then the automatic pilot would be instructed to be a little more generous with the supply of nominal money. In effect, the pilot would be told to aim for the spot where monetary equilibrium should be, and not to worry about missing its target in the short run.

Missing the Turns in Monetary Control

Responsibility for monetary control other than by a fixed and simple rule, is too heavy a cross to thrust upon Treasury officials or upon a small group of men in an independent agency. A quick glance over possible disturbances to monetary equilibrium may indicate why some monetary technicians do conclude that automation is overdue in monetary control.

Economic systems must grow—in effective labor force, in productive capital, in output T. According to the money equation, growth in output increases demand for money. Other things equal, it creates excess demand for money. But other things do not long remain equal. If the community has less money than it wants, it reduces demand for goods. Then growth in output implies unwanted growth in inventories. Inventories full to overflowing may be cleared by price reductions, but prices reduced in an unbalanced way cannot be relied upon to dispel excess supply of goods and excess demand for money. Price deflation is painful, and it can cumulate out of all proportion to its initial cause.

Excess demand for money is not cured by economy in demand for money k. Instead k may rise, as deflation threatens, and accentuate excess demand for money. The sensible solution for a shortage in money balances is simply creation of more money balances, in nominal amount, by the monetary system.

Consider a second source of monetary instability. The k in the money equation is stable in longer periods, not seasonally and not cyclically. Business recession is initiated by an increase in k that precedes the cyclical turning point apparently by a variable interval. Demand for money rises at the expense of demand for goods. Excess demand for money eventually is satisfied, but its costs mount up in the forms of falling prices, falling output, and falling employment.

In every recession popular attention focuses on a villain. The latest villain is the "cost-price push," the rise in price that imperfectly competitive sellers force upon their markets not in response to current demand but in anticipation of demand. The cost-price push is characteristic of endemic inflation, but its first consequence is deflationary. It generates excess demand for money so that there is pressure brought to bear upon a monetary authority to underwrite advancing prices with increasing supplies of nominal money. If the monetary authority accedes to pressure, the cost-price push intensifies. If the monetary authority defies pressure, excess demand for money at inflated prices punishes output and employment.

Awkward manipulation of nominal money is the final source of monetary instability. Any monetary authority makes its decisions on the basis of information that is incomplete and not altogether accurate or timely. The authority in our monetary system is handicapped by technically imperfect controls. The authority cannot see clearly the road that the monetary system should travel and, in comparison with ideal designs, the steering devices are primitive. We do not have fingertip control of money, with the result that the best-laid plans for management of M can miscarry, and widen the supply-demand gap of monetary disequilibrium.

In the light of monetary experience, it appears that many of us have romanticized monetary control. It is an illusion that the money supply can be manipulated, according to the daily flux of economic statistics and their translation by men of refined intuition, into continuous equilibrium. The limit of feasibility is to ascertain the trend rate of growth in demand for money at a given price level and to set the money supply automatically on the same course. Some may ask: In a serious economic recession, should not the monetary authorities be required to augment the money supply even *more* than this rule would call for? The answer is "no." When the *nominal* supply of money is growing at a stable rate, a serious recession would itself generate a very large increase in *real* money. If the door is opened even slightly to discretionary monetary management, there is no point at which it can be closed.

Money vs. Credit

The essential characteristic of a monetary system is that it produces money: it creates the money supply. The essential function of a monetary system is to adapt the money supply to the community's demand for money. The adaptation is most felicitious for real economic growth when nominal money expands along the same trend line as demand for money at a stable level of commodity prices.

Money has purchasing power. When the monetary system creates money for the rest of us to hold in money balances, the monetary system can obtain something of value in exchange. That something may be gold or silver. According to some students, that some-thing should be composite bundles of raw materials, or foreign bills of exchange, or even bricks. The monetary authority need not be instructed to buy something with the money it creates. It could give away the purchasing power its money-creation commands, perhaps in remission of taxes.

How the monetary system does dispose of this purchasing power is incidental to the primary job of creating money. Any social benefits that result from its disposal of purchasing power are a by-product of the money industry. Any monetary system must have a technique for getting rid of the money that it produces, but there are innumerable techniques, and their relative merits should be a matter of secondary concern.

Our monetary system takes gold and silver from the community, but these purchases exhaust only a fraction of the purchasing power that creation of money puts at the system's disposal. A much larger fraction is spent on securities—in "making loans" and "granting credits." The by-product of our monetary system is credit.

I cannot emphasize too strongly that "credit" is a by-product. I cannot emphasize too strongly that it is an optional by-product. Congress willing, our monetary system need not be an investor in consumer credit, business loans, mortgages, and Treasury debt. It need not be staffed with loan and investment committees. It could be staffed with commodity specialists who would fill warehouses with goods rather than portfolios with bonds and notes.

The Congress, the Federal Reserve Board, and the Treasury have been preoccupied with the by-product of our monetary system. Their correct course would have been to prescribe and administer rules of growth in the amount of money balances, then to tackle the lesser issue of what to do with the fallout of purchasing power. The course they have chosen, and still pursue, is to prescribe and administer rules for disposition of purchasing power on securities. As they see it, the money supply is the by-product of their operations, and the monetary system should create as much or as little as is necessary for "accommodating commerce and business" with credit and for maintaining "sound credit conditions." Our monetary management has been credit-minded, not money-minded.

The Federal Reserve Act bristles with injunctions upon the monetary system to grant this kind of credit and not that kind. Be open-handed with agriculture and starve the stock market. The Board concerns itself with proliferating details of *credit* granted to government, business, and consumers. Quality and quantity of credit are its operating criteria. During its tenure in monetary management, the Treasury falls in line with the same tradition, fitting policy to the alleged requirements of government as borrower rather than to the requirements of the community as holders and users of money. When Board and Treasury disagree, the points of contention are the quantity, quality, and terms of credit.

The Federal Reserve Act is not the constitution of a monetary system. A new Act should be prepared, in two sections. Section I would declare the rule of growth in money balances. Section II would specify disposition of the purchasing power that growth in money balances provides to the monetary system, and its preamble would state unambiguously that Section II is subsidiary to Section I.

Laymen often suspect some perversity in monetary affairs, and rightly so. The goal of a monetary system should be literally to create the right amount of money balances. What the system does with the money is second-ary. For the rest of us, coming into possession of purchasing power is presumably a means, and the end we work for is the intelligent use of purchasing power. The monetary system is on the other side of the Looking Glass.

The Demand Standard in Action

By the rule of the Demand Standard, the nominal supply of money would be increased at a constant rate compounded annually. The rate would be adjusted only with Congressional assent, since full and free debate on the matter of long-run price inflation or deflation is no less important than full and debate on such issues as tax burdens or labor policy or foreign aid.

The technical procedures of adding to the stock of money should be no more difficult to establish than the procedures of extracting tax payments from the community for subsequent spending under the government budget. Monetary expansion could be a daily, weekly, or monthly "spending" by the monetary system. It could be adapted to seasonal instabilities in demand for money balances.

Demand for money would grow parallel with the money supply in the long run, but its growth line would rise and fall in shorter periods. In each recession, the combination of an increasing money supply and a decreasing demand for money would generate excess supply of money. In each cyclic boom, the combination of increasing money supply and still more rapidly increasing demand for money would generate a shortage in money. Both recession and boom would call forth automatically the kind of imbalance between supply of and demand for money that is cyclically corrective. No one has a principle for doing any better by discretionary means.

On various pretexts, each important user of "credit" would be able to make an eloquent case for some expansion of the money supply in his behalf. The Treasury would request support of new issues. Agriculture would expect credit accommodation for crop movements. Business, large or small, would cry out its need for "capital," and consumers would remember when banks courted their demands for loan funds to spend on cars, houses, and appliances. No sympathy should be wasted on any of these complaints, because giving in to it would mean a demonstrably inflationary acceleration in the growth rate of money.

It is no more difficult to administer orderly growth in money than disorderly growth. Every banker is more than a little proud of his ability to turn down credit applications. The automaton of the Demand Standard can be taught to say "no" to any demand upon the monetary system that would violate the basic rule of growth in means of payment.

ANOTHER BUILT-IN STABILIZER

This country takes pride in its built-in stabilizers, the economic balance-wheels that automatically limit our deviations from normal growth. The stabilizers are automatically sensitized to economic instability and go into action against it without forethought, plan, or discretion. It is not a radical proposal that monetary control should be added to the list of self-activating countermeasures against disturbances in the growth process. Two lines of argument favor the proposal. One is that discretionary control of money supply has done badly. The other is that stable growth in money contributes to stable growth in other economic dimensions.

Discretionary Monetary Management Has Had Its Day

On the evidence of our monetary experience since 1914, American money management has not been a success. Over the long period, the money supply M has been inefficiently balanced against money demand $P(kT)$ at relatively stable prices. The long run casts its shadow over shorter periods. In the 1930's the long run had been deflationary, and the mood of deflation restrained short-run recoveries. As we see it now, the long run has been inflationary, and the mood of inflation permeates short-run expectations. There is an hypothesis that chronic inflation is partly to blame for one paradox of the 1957–1958 recession. The paradox is that prices have run uphill against the gravity of deflation. Perhaps the gravity of long-run inflation has exerted the stronger pull.

Our monetary managers have not succeeded in the cyclical short run. Students of business cycles fail to find convincing evidence that business cycles have shortened in duration since 1914. They find considerable evidence that cycles have become more violent, with amplitude of movement increased. I indicated earlier that monetary management has not been delicately attuned to cyclical turning points. It has missed the turns when monetary policy might have been most effective in damping instability.

Our monetary managers have not sensed the need of a growing economy for stability of monetary expectations. The deeds of management have cultivated alternately expectations of inflation and expectations of deflation. As for words, the notion has developed somehow that the monetary authority is privileged to behave as a benevolent despot; that the authority may mask its plans and policies and neglect to advise the community of its plans and intentions; that the community's prospect concerning the balance of supply and demand for money should be confused and uncertain.

If any form of policy should be explicit, out in the open for all to see, it is monetary policy. There should be certainty of price inflation or certainty of price deflation rather than doubt concerning the monetary atmosphere in which economic plans will materialize. Uncertainty is an impediment to growth. It depresses rational investment, defers gains in productivity, and contributes to the scarcities that policy is supposed to remedy.

The Positive Case for Automatic Monetary Control

The case for automatic control does not rest solely on disillusionment with discretionary control. There are six principal ways in which continuous and stable growth in money can increase the probability of growth in real output at a relatively high rate with minimal perturbations.

1. Stable growth in money lays the foundation for a solvent and efficient payments mechanism. In recurrent inflation, bank capital is sharply reduced relative to bank assets and deposits. Each deflation undermines bank capital through deterioration in asset quality. Our own banking system is propped upright, at public expense, by various devices that are presumed to be adequate substitutes for private investment in banking. Each of these devices has originated during violent movements in the money supply.

2. Stable growth in money supplied and demanded removes one hazard of private or governmental economic planning. That is uncertainty about the length of the monetary yardstick that planners use to measure prospective costs and revenues. Our own monetary system provides us with a yardstick, the value of the dollar, that has been shrinking for sixty years. Steady shrinkage at a constant rate is tolerable and certainly not as damaging to the planning process as shrinkage by fits and starts. Our yardstick has been rubberized, stretching out in each deflation and snapping back in each bout we have with inflation.

3. Stable growth in money avoids the inflations that distort the form of real capital accumulation, and it relieves the economic system of the interruptions in capital formation that result when deflation is applied as the remedy for inflation. Deflation does not undo damage done by inflation: it compounds the damage. During inflation savings are used wastefully on capital projects that are made to seem worthwhile by advancing prices. During deflation savings are destroyed by underemployment of men and resources. Savings misapplied or lost are never recoverable.

4. Stable growth in money and stability in the price level create a favorable environment for flexible indivdual prices and price relationships. General price deflation results in specific price rigidities, usually in the form of price floors. It invites combination in restraint of price adjustments downward. General price inflation produces its own crop of controlled or administered prices. The controls may be ceilings imposed by buyers or escalators dictated by sellers. Flexibility of the price level promotes rigidity of price relationships. Since a private-enterprise society relies upon flexible price relationships to allocate resources and guide demands, flexible price levels reduce its growth potential.

5. Stable growth of money and stability in the price level diminish social

conflict. Deflation in the last century was politically and socially divisive. Inflation in this century has helped to cleave the population into pressure groups. Any pronounced swing in the price level incites an organized March on Washington and concessions to noisy claimants for special advantage. When price levels are on the move, rational competition of the market place loses out to passionate competition for political leverage.

6. Steady growth in money contributes to development of orderly financial arrangements throughout the community. Deflation creates its distinctive pattern of debt, financial assets, and financial institutions. Inflation gives rise to a different pattern. Debtors are affected by a consideration that should not occur to them—the chance of windfall gain by inflation, of windfall loss by deflation. Creditors pick and choose their financial assets not solely according to debtors' real productivity but also according to debtors' vulnerability to unstable price levels. Loanable funds are allocated inefficiently among borrowers through a financial mechanism that is unduly intricate and expensive.

Stable growth in money minimizes financial distractions in the growth process. Stop-and-go growth in money, dignified as "monetary management," is a nervous tic in the economic system that diverts to finance attention and resources that should be spent on real aspects of development. Money is at its best when it is unobtrusive, its supply increasing according to a firm rule that is known to everyone.

AN INNING FOR THE OPPOSITION

It is not too partisan to say much less about the con's of automatic money than about the pro's. The principle of

"look-Ma-no-hands" in money management has been debated so often that the critics have their brief well in hand. I shall tip off a few of their points simply to warn readers that there are two sides of the issue.

Objection 1

There is no one infallible rule of monetary growth. Since any single standard will not do, we must entrust our monetary fate to authority. It will deduce, in frequent conclave of its experts, the community's need for money and turn the money tap to just the right volume. Money is a mystery, and the layman should delegate its management to the expert.

Rejoinder

There is no expert in money management. Neither of our money-management teams, the Treasury or the Board, has earned the accolade of public confidence. Both teams have *expertise* in credit-management, but that is a different matter.

No one can measure the community's "need for money"—the quantity demanded at a stable price level in a growing economy—on a day-to-day or even month-to-month basis. There is no clear channel of communication from public to monetary authority that reports growth in demand for money $P(kT)$ so that growth in supply can be in continuous balance with it. The balance of supply with demand for *money* is not improved when it is the practice of the authority to study demand for the wrong thing—for *credit*.

Objection 2

The first half-century of our experiences with discretionary management has not been a fair test. It has been distorted by two world wars and their aftermath of crisis and disaster. The Treasury and the Board have done remarkably well under the circumstances. In a tranquil world the Federal Reserve Act would be an effective charter for sound money.

Rejoinder

Peace and tranquility are not on the horizon of the next half-century. It is just as well to take the pessimistic stand that temptations to misuse the monetary system will not diminish. There will be occasions when the Treasury will want to borrow cheaply in disregard of monetary stability. There will be occasions when the Board will think it wise to disillusion the inflationary expectations that Treasury policy has generated.

If there were clear sailing ahead, discretionary management would be good enough. With trouble in prospect, it is more important to put monetary control on automatic pilot so that mistakes in policy will not aggravate our misfortunes. When inflationary forces are rampant, we will not want them intensified by monetary expansion in behalf of cheap credit for the Treasury. When deflation is the hazard, we will not want it accelerated by the Board's precautions against the next inflation. In rough weather the wheel of the monetary system should be lashed down.

Objection 3

A growing economy has a changing pattern of credit requirements. Legitimate demands for credit rise and fall, and they come from different sectors of the community in an unpredictable rotation. There must be a flexible program of credit control, and a central management of credit that is alert to satisfy legitimate demands while discouraging speculation, to segregate credit of high quality from credit of low quality, to smooth out discontinuities on credit markets, and to encourage development of credit facilities.

Rejoinder

Granted that credit management by the banking system is an important resource-allocation function in the United States economy, the linkage of money with credit is an historical accident. Credit is one of various possible uses for the purchasing power that the monetary system commands as it increases the money supply. Whatever the use may be, disposing of the monetary system's purchasing power is incidental to the process of creating money.

The Credit Standard of money management, written into the Federal Reserve Act and administered by Treasury and Board, is a built-in destabilizer of economic activity. The community's demands upon the monetary system for credit grow quantitatively and improve qualitatively in each cyclic boom. They shrink in volume and deteriorate in quality during each cyclic relapse. The effect of linking the money supply to the cyclic yo-yo of credit demand is to intensify cycles.

Real growth is measured in terms of goods. It is not measured in terms of credit. In guiding real growth, monetary expansion should have the direct impact on markets for goods that fiscal policy has. Monetary policy is not committed by any Law of Nature to work its effects upon goods only after a detour through the markets for credit. Monetary policy yields perverse results on markets for goods when the impression develops, as it has in this country, that the credit detour is the end of the line for monetary policy.

In earlier phases of American economic growth, credit markets were embryonic. Then the banking system necessarily wore two hats, as supplier of money and as supplier of credit. Now the credit markets have matured, and there are efficient channels outside of the banking system for the flow of funds from saving to investment in real capital. Now the monetary system can attend to its essential function of supplying money.

Objection 4

The Demand Standard is provincial. It would isolate the American economy from world markets, raising a domestic rule of monetary growth to a pedestal above the principle of international economic cooperation. In view of this country's responsibility for stable growth internationally, self-interest in monetary policy is a luxury we cannot afford.

Rejoinder

American monetary policy has not abided by the rules of an international standard since 1914. The national gold stock has been a buffer between money here and money abroad. On the record the Credit Standard has been autarchic.

Sawtooth growth in the money supply of this country indicates our immaturity as London's successor to the role of international central bank. If a stable dollar is to be the anchor of a stable pound, peso, franc, yen, or piastre, rates of growth in the supply of dollars must vary no more between such extremes as *plus* 20 per cent and *minus* 10 per cent. Under our present rules of monetary management, we are announcing that we do not choose to run for the job that was London's for a century. Under an automatic rule, there would be less incentive for our allies to work out their own regional monetary coalitions.

IN CONCLUSION

Monetary economics has been dormant for two decades. Other aspects of economic analysis have left it far behind. It is so becalmed in an intellectual doldrum that no gentle breeze of inquiry can stir it. A lively storm of controversy may raise the prestige of monetary economics as an intellectual discipline, and it can do no harm to the prestige of the Federal Reserve as an instrument of social welfare if its prestige is deserved. The present paper is a bid for the active interchange of views that may restore vitality to thinking about money.

19   THE OPERATION OF THE OPEN MARKET COMMITTEE

Alfred Hayes

Alfred Hayes is President of the Federal Reserve Bank of New York.

*   *   *

It goes without saying that the Federal Reserve Bank of New York, of which I have the privilege of being the chief executive officer, undertakes a great variety of important activities, most of which are related in some degree to the operations of the Federal Open Market Committee. I am thinking of such things as handling the reserve and borrowing accounts of the member banks, the provision of currency, the processing and crediting of checks received for collection, the expediting of wire transfers of deposit balances among banks and of Government securities among investors, the calling and disbursement of funds for the United States Treasury, the handling of transactions for foreign central bank and government accounts representing settlement of the United States balance of payments with other countries, and the supervision of member banks. These activities, most of which we undertake in common with the 11 other Federal Reserve Banks, have a great deal to do with the System's major responsibility of contributing to an efficient and adequate money and credit mechanism for the Nation. But they are sometimes referred to as "defensive" or "passive" operations, in contrast with the three "dynamic" or "active" instruments—reserve requirements, discount rates, and open market operations—which are employed in our efforts to minimize both inflation and deflation and to facilitate sturdy economic growth.

To discuss the Federal Open Market Committee's activities without referring to all three of these instruments would be quite misleading. For while it is true that the Board of Governors alone has the responsibility for determining reserve requirements, and while discount rates are established by the individual Reserve banks—subject to review and determination by the Board of Governors—in practice the Federal Open Market Committee has become the principal forum in which these two instruments, as well as that of open market operations, are discussed and weighed by representatives of the entire System in arriving at a systemwide consensus as to what should be done at any given time in the field of general credit control. The emergence of the Federal Open Market Committee as the meeting place where representatives of all parts of the System's complex structure can be brought together, for joint discussion of interrelated responsibilities, is one of the most interesting, and also probably one of the most constructive developments in Federal Reserve history.

Meetings of the Federal Open Market Committee are generally held every 2 or 3 weeks in Washington, so that I have been privileged to attend some 6 or 7 times since I became associated with the New York Reserve Bank. As

Statement by Alfred Hayes, reprinted from *Hearings Before the Subcommittee on Economic Stabilization of the Joint Economic Committee,* Congress of the United States, December 10 and 11, 1956, pp. 142–150.

you know, the Committee consists of 12 members, including the 7 members of the Board of Governors and 5 of the Reserve bank presidents. The president of the New York Reserve Bank is continuously a member, while the other four presidents are appointed in rotation. The 12 members of the Committee which was established by statute, sit and reach decisions as responsible individuals, not as representatives of any constituency. Each must find the answer, in the light of all the facts and his own conscience, to the question: "What policy of credit control would be the best policy under present conditions for the economy of the United States?" Naturally each member brings to the Committee the full benefit of any special information available to him, including —in the case of the Reserve bank presidents—information concerning economic conditions in the various districts and the views concerning them held by businessmen and others; but each member also gives careful consideration to nationwide conditions and makes his final judgment on that basis.

The 7 presidents who are not, at the time, members of the Federal Open Market Committee nevertheless attend these meetings regularly by invitation and participate in the discussions on the same basis as the 12 Committee members, with the sole exception that they have no vote on matters requiring a vote. Thus the Committee obtains a firsthand report on conditions in each of the 12 Federal Reserve districts. During the periods between meetings, the 7 Governors and the 12 Presidents are of course pursuing their various other duties, but they are also preparing for the coming deliberations of the Federal Open Market Committee by observing the results of policies established at previous meetings, gathering new economic data, and continually reviewing their judgments of past decisions and current events. In New York, for example, our senior officers gather at least once each week to review important developments, and we have another special meeting of officers a few days in advance of each Federal Open Market Committee meeting for the special purpose of discussing the current state of business and credit conditions, Treasury finance, and related matters, and what type of credit policy seems best suited to this state of affairs.

At each Federal Open Market Committee meeting the procedure is to have the Manager of the System Account, who is also vice-president in charge of the securities function at the New York Reserve Bank, lead off with any observations he may wish to make on what has actually happened in the Account and in financial markets in general since the last meeting. He will already have furnished each member of the Board of Governors and each president with special written reports that are complete through the close of business on the preceding day. Thereafter two of the senior staff members of the Board of Governors present a comprehensive and detailed summary of current business and credit conditions in the country as a whole. After this the Chairman, following such introductory remarks as he considers appropriate on domestic or foreign developments, calls on each president and each governor, in turn, to give his appraisal of the current situation and to state his views concerning appropriate policy in the circumstances. Customarily the president of the New York Reserve Bank is called on first, and, because of the location of the bank in the country's money center, I usually talk of business and credit developments and expectations in national terms, and of the open market and other Federal Reserve policies I would consider appropriate in the light of those developments. The other presidents usually start off with comments on conditions in their particular districts and they, too, give their views as to credit policy. Likewise each member of the Board of Governors states his opinion concerning the appropriate policy after discussing any particular developments in the country's economy which appear to him pertinent. Generally the last man to comment is the Chairman of the Federal Open Market Committee, who is of course also Chairman of the Board of Governors. He summarizes his own appraisal of the situation and then undertakes the difficult task of pulling together the threads of all the preceding discussion and expressing the consensus of the meeting in terms of, first, how the directive to the New York Reserve Bank should be worded and, second, what specific actions are called for in the way of open market purchases or sales or other credit control measures—perhaps mentioning, for example, the possibility that consideration may be given to discount rate changes by the various Reserve banks, or to changes in reserve requirements by the Board of Governors. The Chairman then gives all present a chance to state whether they agree with his understanding of the consensus. The Manager of the System Account is asked whether the instructions are sufficiently explicit to enable him to carry out the Committee's wishes effcetively, and at this point the Committee has an opportunity to convey to the Manager any nuances of policy which they think should be kept in mind.

I have been greatly impressed by the effectiveness of this whole procedure in bringing together a variety of disinterested and objective views on our country's economic conditions and problems, and then in deriving from these a reasoned consensus as to monetary and credit policy. Often the opinion of any one member is not yet crystallized when he arrives at the meeting, and it may well be modified during the meeting by this process of give-and-take. On the other hand, I think it is pretty clear that with 19 well-informed people having a full opportunity to present their views, on the basis of data assembled by able staffs throughout the System, it would be quite impossible for any one man holding an extreme position to dominate the Committee and dictate the Committee's conclusions. Indeed, the thinking of any one man may not be fully in accord with the consensus; the consensus is acceptable because it is a fusing of all the views, and it provides a workable basis for operations. Over time, such a consensus is bound to be far more reliable than the occasional flash of insight that a single individual might produce.

I have been struck by the degree of harmony which has been achieved in this whole procedure. It has almost always been possible, without even the formality of a vote, to reach a consensus through the give-and-take of reasoned discussions.

As I have already indicated, the general conclusions of the Committee as to credit policy are set forth in the directive issued to the Federal Reserve Bank of New York. The directive is amplified by the statement of the consensus and by the full discussion, all of which are of course noted in the Committee's minutes. From this point on, and until the next Federal Open Market Committee meeting, the primary responsibility for conducting open market operations is in the hands of the Federal Reserve Bank of New York, acting in accordance with the instructions of the Committee. With the country's money market and securities markets centered in New York, most open market operations must necessarily be executed there, but I would like to stress that the New York bank is acting at all times for the System as a whole on the instructions of the Committee and is at all times responsive to the Committee's wishes. In my capacity as a member and Vice Chairman of the Federal Open Market Committee, I am in a position to help interpret the Committee's wishes to the Manager, and he himself has of course been present at the last meeting when he was specifically instructed on the varied detailed considerations which the Committee wishes him to keep in mind. He knows, for example, approximately what member bank reserve position the Committee believes appropriate, or he may have been told to give only secondary consideration to this factor and for a time to be guided primarily by such factors as the tightness of the banking structure in the money centers, the degree of market pressure suggested by United States Treasury bill rates and other money market rates, the impact of a large Treasury borrowing operation, and even more broadly by that on-the-spot appraisal of current attitudes and actions which is described as the "feel" of the market.

A comprehensive procedure has been worked out for keeping the Board of Governors and the other members of the Federal Open Market Committee promptly and fully informed on market conditions and all actual transactions for the System account, as well as on contemplated transactions. One of the most effective tools to this end is the so-called daily conference call at 11 a.m., each business day, when the manager of the account or his assistant talks by telephone with the economic adviser and a senior economist of the Board of Governors. The presidents of those Federal Reserve banks outside of New York who are currently serving

on the Committee also participate by long-distance telephone in these discussions on a rotating basis, 1 President sharing in the call for a period of 2 or 3 weeks. At the New York Reserve Bank, the first vice president or I often "sit in" on the telephone call and many times both of us are present. (The first vice-president is, in conformity with the statute, my alternate as a member of the Federal Open Market Committee.) The manager of the account summarizes conditions in the money and capital markets, the various reports or comments received from the dealers in United States Government securities, the reserve position of the principal New York banks, and the reserve position of the country's member banks as a whole—together with the New York Reserve Bank's expectations as to changes in this national reserve position day by day for the next few weeks. The manager then indicates whether these available data and expected developments point to a need for open market operations in order to fulfill the Federal Open Market Committee's instructions, i. e., whether Treasury bills should be purchased or sold, whether repurchase agreements should be made with dealers, whether holdings of acceptances should be increased or run down, and in approximately what amount any or all of these might be considered. Participation in the call provides the economic adviser to the Board of Governors and the other president who is taking part in the call, the opportunity and responsibility of contributing their views as to existing conditions and the proposed course of action, particularly as these relate to the policy set at the most recent Federal Open Market Committee meeting. Usually there is immediate agreement, but suggestions may be made which result in some modification of the manager's program. Immediately following this conversation, a full summary is prepared at the Board and distributed to all of the Governors in Washington; the same summary is sent by wire to the various Reserve bank presidents.

The staff of the Board of Governors is advised periodically during the day by telephone on all details concerning actual operations and market developments. In addition, a written report is submitted daily to the Board of Governors by the New York Reserve Bank with copies to the interested officers of the other Federal Reserve banks and branches. At the end of each statement week a full written report is submitted by the manager to the members of the Federal Open Market Committee and to the other presidents. These reports not only provide a complete statement of all actions taken but they also give a full running record of conditions in the money and capital markets, with emphasis on interest rate changes and on the behavior of United States Government and other security prices. Prior to each Federal Open Market Committee meeting, as I have mentioned earlier, a detailed recapitulation of all major market developments and all transactions since the last previous meeting is prepared for submission to all Committee members and the other presidents.

Questions may occur to the account manager between Federal Open Market Committee meetings, perhaps as a result of some unforeseen development at home or abroad, which appear to call for an interpretation of some policy decision reached at the last meeting. If it is a minor matter, the question may be settled by discussion with the president or first vice-president of the New York bank, but if it involves a major policy consideration, we may decide to consult by telephone with the Chairman, or, in his absence, with the Vice Chairman of the Board of Governors or some other member of the Committee. Or the initiative may come from Washington; i. e., Chairman Martin or Vice Chairman Balderston may telephone me and raise some question or make some suggestion having to do with interpretation of the current Federal Open Market Committee policy. If very urgent questions arise, it is possible to arrange on short notice for a telephone meeting of the Federal Open Market Committee to deal with whatever emergency may exist.

We in the New York Reserve Bank encourage the governors and the other Reserve bank presidents, as well as senior members of the staffs of the Board of Governors and of the other Reserve banks, to spend as much time as they can spare visiting our trading desk, observing the manager and his assistants carry out open-market operations, and familiarizing themselves with the actual market atmosphere in which these operations are conducted. I am happy to say that we have had fine visits of this kind recently from the chairman and several of the governors and presidents.

The chief point which I would like to emphasize is the high degree of close contact and close cooperation existing between the Federal Open Market Committee as the originator of all open-market policy and the Federal Reserve Bank of New York as the executor of this policy. In my brief experience with the System I have felt that this whole mechanism works very effectively in the public interest.

*   *   *

20 THE MYSTERIOUS WORLD OF THE FED

Delbert C. Hastings and
Ross M. Robertson

Delbert C. Hastings is Professor of Statistics, University of Minnesota; Ross M. Robertson is Professor of Business Economics at the University of Indiana and was formerly an economist for the Federal Reserve Board.

First-time visitors to the lovely Washington building that houses the Board of Governors of the Federal Reserve System are invariably struck by its lofty tone. Federal Reserve personnel and guests alike move decorously through marble halls and amber-lit, carpeted rooms that epitomize the vast dignity of the monetary authority. Highly placed staff members approach the offices of Board members with deference; lesser functionaries enter with an obsequious respect that makes onlookers uncomfortable. Indeed, an almost religious aura pervades the place, and the uninitiated expect momentarily to catch a whiff of incense or the chant of choirboys not far off.

The physical atmosphere is simply an extension of a carefully nurtured public image of trustworthiness and high morality. Because of the technicality of its operations and the obscurity of its statements of purpose, the Federal Reserve has avoided evaluation and criticism of its actions by the public at large. Instead, explicit comment has been left to academicians, highly placed financial managers, and a few members of Congress. Thus, the public trusts the Fed without fully understanding it; with the possible exception of the Federal Bureau of Investigation, no other government agency enjoys such high repute and splendid public relations.

To be sure, much of the System's prestige is merited. It performs its vast service roles—collectors of checks, fiscal agent for the U. S. government, and issuer of currency—with accuracy and dispatch. At both board and bank levels, the Federal Reserve can boast a research organization second to none. Yet it is by no means certain that the Fed has managed the money supply better than the money supply would have managed itself, nor is it clear that Federal Reserve influence on growth, stability, and price levels has been as beneficial as the Fed's reputation would suggest.

In a word, the Federal Reserve System has nobly performed its service functions. On the other hand, it is by no means certain that the control functions have been discharged with the imagination and vigor that modern central-bank action requires. Painfully sensitive to criticism, which invariably evokes defense reactions, the monetary authority gives continual evidence of an eroding self-consciousness. Indeed, System acceptance of responsibility for stability of prices and output seems to vary from time to time. The Fed certainly wants no competitors; whenever it has been suggested that an Administration economic policy group be

From *Business Horizons,* Spring, 1962, pp. 97–104. Reprinted by permission of the authors, *Business Horizons,* and the University of Indiana.

formed, there is immediate central-bank resistance to the proposal. Yet System authorities occasionally come close to admitting their inability to stabilize the economy, and, whenever the Congressional heat is on, central-bank spokesmen are at pains to explain that they can only nudge the economy in one direction or another, that there are too many variables to be controlled by any one institution. System attitude seems to be, "We will use the tools we choose in the way we choose, and if they don't do the job, we deny responsibility in the matter. But we don't want anyone else interfering." To understand the Fed, we must apprehend this deep-rooted instinct for self-preservation that manifests itself in insistence upon insulation from "political" interference.

The mysterious world of the Fed is really known only to its employees and its alumni—the insiders, as it were. No amount of examination, no amount of Congressional testimony, no amount of study by scholars temporarily connected with the System can reveal the inner workings of Fed mentality. Only years of participation in the charismatic effort of central-bank policy provide the sense of System motivation so essential to an interpretation of Fed dogma, facetiously referred to, internally, as the "party line." As alumni, now a decent interval away from System activity, we herewith set forth our observations about (1) the nodes of power in the System and (2) the tenuous lines of communication that carry power impulses from one node to another.

THE NODES OF POWER

Although its major structural outlines were laid down by the original Federal Reserve Act, the Federal Reserve System has evolved in a way clearly not foreseen by its founders. As in every organization that must act, there are important nodes of power within the System; the relative standing of these power centers depends somewhat on law, somewhat on custom, and somewhat on the economic facts of life, such as the size and wealth of the different Federal Reserve districts. In roughly descending order of power, the major nodes are as follows: 1. the chairman of the Board of Governors; 2. the other governors; 3. the staff of the board, in particular the senior advisers; 4. the Federal Open Market Committee; 5. the trading desk of the New York Federal Reserve Bank; 6. the president of the New York Federal Reserve Bank; 7. other Federal Reserve bank presidents; 8. boards of directors of the twelve banks; 9. System-wide committees, standing and ad hoc; and 10. the Federal Advisory Council.

This listing will doubtless raise eyebrows both inside and outside the System, but we consider it, nonetheless, a fair appraisal of the current order of power loci in the System. It is impossible to understand the operations of today's central bank without knowing the relative importance of these power centers.

It is common knowledge, of course, that the Banking Act of 1935 made a drastic switch in the seat of System power. Under the aegis of Benjamin Strong, fair-haired boy of J. Pierpont Morgan and the 1913 New York banking community, real authority in the System lodged in the hands of the chief executive officers of the several Reserve banks. Indeed, the quick seizure of the term "governor" by the executive heads of the twelve banks revealed their own assessment of their authority. Until Strong's death in 1928, the Federal Reserve Board made nearly futile efforts to seize the power it never had, and the terrible failure of the Federal Reserve to arrest the deflation of 1929–32 gave positive proof, if proof were needed, that board authority had been emasculated in practice. The designation in the Banking Act of 1935 of the "Board of Governors" signified the intent of Congress to make it the "board of bosses."

Even so, no one could have foreseen a generation ago the gradual settling of vast power in the person of the chairman of the board. The tradition of chairman domination was, of course, started during the reign of Marriner S. Eccles, but it has reached a new high under Chairman William McChesney Martin, Jr., able son of one-time Governor Martin of the St. Louis Reserve bank.

This is not to say that other board members are without authority. Yet the position of each one depends upon his intellectual quality and personal force. A board member not deemed a contributor to the welfare of the System is likely to be shunted aside and given assignments that keep him away from inner councils. On the other hand, a particularly knowledgeable governor may be given heavy responsibilities, especially if he has a bent for economic or legal analysis.

The fact remains that the chairman of the board is in a position to exercise a great measure of control over the board and thus over the entire System. His is the final word on appointments at both board and bank levels. He is the System spokesman in its relationships with Congress, other executive branches of the government, the President, and even with foreign governments. Within the law, his powers are circumscribed only by the personal qualities of the other governors and by the five-year term of his appointment to the chair. When, as in the case of Martin, the chairman possesses an uncommon singleness of purpose and great political ability, he will work by persuasion rather than by ukase. He nevertheless operates as a dominant political figure in the best and highest sense of the word.

The staff of the Board of Governors, particularly the senior advisers, are a frequently overlooked power center. To be sure, their influence is derived from that of the governors. But their proximity to the governors, their long service, and their familiarity with Fed history give them a more than considerable influence on policy matters. Old pros like Woodlief Thomas and Ralph A. Young command enormous prestige. Younger men like Guy E. Noyes, Director of Research and Statistics, exert their influence through control of research activities at both board and bank levels; all publications of the several banks as well as reports of System-wide committees must receive the approval of the board staff before release, and directives sent by staff members to the banks are accepted as bearing the authority of the Board of Governors.

Because it nominally determines the magnitude and direction of the most important monetary weapon—purchases and sales of government securities—the Federal Open Market Committee is the next most powerful organization within the System. Since it is the official forum as well as the administrative body for monetary policy actions, the FOMC has a key place in System councils. As late as 1953, the Open Market Committee met only quarterly, with an executive committee meeting more frequently to perform the significant policy-making functions. Since that time, however, the full committee has met at intervals of approximately three weeks. Although the official membership consists of the seven governors and five of the twelve bank presidents, all the presidents try to attend regularly.[1]

Resisting the inexorable erosion of authority at the bank level, the Federal Reserve Bank of New York always poses something of a threat to board authority in Washington. The trading desk, which administers the open market account upon receipt of FOMC directives, is the very nerve center of the System. Since, as we shall see, orders of the Open Market Committee are always ambiguous and often nebulous, the account manager, a vice-president of the New York Reserve bank, must have great latitude in making judgments. And though he may have many masters, not excluding the senior staff member of the board who advises with him each day, it goes without saying that the account manager's immediate boss, the president of the New York Reserve bank, will not be without influence. Indeed, a strong New York president can be a source of great annoyance and even friction in Federal Reserve councils. It is no secret that many officers in the System heaved a collective sigh of relief when Allan Sproul, one-time chief officer of the New York bank and in some respects the most artistic of all American central bankers, went into retirement. But no matter what the attitude of a New York president toward Washington may be, the counsels of that officer are bound to have weight as they reflect the opinions of the New York financial community.

It is no deprecation of the abilities and prestige of the other eleven bank presidents to say that they rank well down the list of System power centers. The presidents are in general gifted and articulate men, and their views will always be weighed by the board and its chairman. Nevertheless, the last remaining power of the banks vanished when the original tool of monetary management—changes in the discount rate—lost its money-market effectiveness. And since the appointments of presidents and first vice-presidents are subject to board approval, really serious resistance to board decisions is not to be expected at bank, to say nothing of branch, levels. It is probably not unfair to say that the boards of directors of the twelve banks have had their power reduced to that of nominating committees, which on occasion submit to the Board of Governors the names of possible president and first vice-president candidates. Like the boards of directors of the Reserve bank branches, their positions are largely honorific; and though the board expresses public gratitude for the "economic intelligence" furnished by bank and branch directors, the plain fact is that their monthly meetings are simply genteel bull sessions.[2]

Indeed, it is probably a fair generalization that the Reserve banks, at least outside New York City, exert their remaining vestiges of influence by placing their talented officers and economists on System committees. Thus, a System Committee to Study Consumer

---

[1] The president of the Federal Reserve Bank of New York is a permanent member and vice-chairman of the committee. Membership rotates among the other bank presidents as follows: Boston, Philadelphia, and Richmond; Chicago and Cleveland; St. Louis, Atlanta, Dallas; and Minneapolis, Kansas City, and San Francisco.

[2] Branches of Federal Reserve banks are a historic anomaly, originally established to salve the feelings of citizens disappointed at their failure to get a Reserve bank in their city. For this story see Ross M. Robertson, "Branches of Federal Reserve Banks," *Monthly Review*, Federal Reserve Bank of St. Louis, XXXVIII (August, 1956), 90–97.

Credit unquestionably affected board and Administration thinking with its multivolume 1957 report; more recently, a System committee has produced an influential report on the Federal Funds market. Furthermore, articulate individuals like Robert V. Roosa and George Garvy of New York, Clay J. Anderson of Philadelphia, and Homer Jones of St. Louis, through their writings and oral presentations, are likely to have an earnest and respectful hearing by the policy makers in Washington. They are nevertheless a long way from the seat of power.

The Conference of Presidents, once the vehicle of dominance over System policy, is now regarded largely as a forum for administrative and operating problems of the several banks. The presidents advise with each other on such matters as check collection, currency and coin issue, agency functions for the Treasury, and personnel classifications. The Federal Advisory Council, never even ostensibly a part of the formal power structure, is clearly an honorific group. Although their advice is presumably weighed by the Board of Governors, council members, like directors of banks and branches, bring personal prestige and orthodox witness as their chief contribution.

TRANSMISSION LINES OF POWER

Few Federal Reserve insiders would make a major rearrangement of the order in which we have listed the nodes of power, but many would express the honest conviction that we have underestimated the democratic processes by which System decisions are made. A look at these procedures may be helpful to a clear comprehension of them.

As a prerequisite to understanding, we must divest ourselves of a good bit of textbook foolishness about how monetary policy is effected. Although it is customary to speak of the instruments of monetary control, there is really only one—the extension and absorption of central-bank credit. The *means* by which central-bank credit is manipulated are irrelevant. Changes in reserve requirements, though still employed, are an anachronistic inheritance from the excess-reserve problem of the 1930's; any sensible person knows that required reserve ratios can be set at any level with consequent central-bank and commercial-bank adjustment to them. Changing the discount rate, though originally conceived to be the *only* weapon of monetary control, has long since lost its effectiveness; the discount rate is no longer a true money-market rate but serves simply as a Fed signal of reaffirmation of a policy in being or a change in monetary policy. In practice, the only demonstrable effect of the discount rate is to set an upper limit to the Federal Funds rate —that is, the rate charged one bank by another for the short-term loan of deposits with a Reserve bank. So we are left with one important instrument of monetary control—open market operations. System intervention in the government securities market is a day-to-day, hour-to-hour, minute-to-minute activity that intimately affects the lives of us all.

We have suggested that the chairman of the Board of Governors is by all odds the most powerful person in the System. But power is synonymous with substantial control over Federal Reserve credit. How, then, does the chairman exercise his great influence? Largely by being the mouthpiece and deciding vote of the Federal Open Market Committee.

In the conduct of FOMC meetings, a formality is observed that requires each governor and president in attendance, whether currently a member of the committee or not, to give a brief economic analysis and state his policy recommendations. By custom each member, together with the board secretary, the senior advisers, and the manager of the Open Market Account, occupies a fixed position around the great oval table in the committee room. After a brief business and financial analysis by the senior staff members, the account manager reports on his activities since the last meeting. Next, the governors and presidents take turns in order of their seating at the table, the circuit being made in one direction at one meeting and in the opposite direction at the next. The chairman speaks last, customarily framing his closing remarks in the form of a consensus of the preceding recommendations. Often, however, there is less than complete agreement among committee members; less often, but not infrequently, the chairman may wish to give stronger than usual direction to current policy. In such circumstances, the "Martin consensus" has emerged, this consensus being largely the view of the chairman himself, whether or not it coincides with that of the majority. Rarely—if then—are policy recommendations put into a motion and voted upon.

The account manager listens to the discussion and at its conclusion is asked by the chairman if he comprehends the wishes of the committee. He almost always answers in the affirmative. But though the account manager listens with great care, even tabulating the recommendations of each speaker, FOMC members frequently complain that they cannot communicate precisely with the manager. This problem has several dimensions. First, each committee member, being a rugged individualist, would probably be satisfied with little less than complete direction of

current policy. Second, because the FOMC does not make a precise statement of its wishes, the account manager must consider nineteen sets of recommendations, some of them rambling discourses on the state of the Union. Third, the three-week interval between meetings is long enough to require adaptations on the part of the manager, and these cannot possibly coincide with all nineteen committee opinions. Fourth, policy recommendations of FOMC members are stated in terms that are at best ambiguous—"a little tighter," or "about the same degree of ease," or "shoot for net free reserves between $500 million and $600 million." Committee members frequently disavow the free reserves target, pointing out that it lacks sufficient connection with the complex of economic variables to be useful as a measure of the effectiveness of policy. It is little wonder then that communication between the FOMC and the trading desk is poor. Nor is it any wonder that Chairman Martin, for better or worse, must determine a consensus that would lead only to endless argument if it were brought to a vote.

A more basic difficulty of communication arises from the unwillingness of the committee to state its economic outlook in precise terms. There exists in the Federal Reserve System an unwritten rule against explicit forecasting of business conditions; even modest attempts at prognosis are blue-penciled if written and ignored if expressed verbally. Members of the FOMC often remark that "we are making policy only for the next three weeks," the implication being that inaction or wrong action can be reviewed or corrected at the next meeting. Now it is manifestly impossible to frame an intelligent monetary policy without at least implicit forecasting; and since a major objective of monetary policy is cyclical amelioration, the forecast period must be a major portion of a cycle. Fortunately, many FOMC members have their own unstated projections. But the emphasis on the short term, the avoidance of a solid, common forecast, and the frequency of FOMC meetings all lead to erratic action, lagged responses, and policy more often than not based on correction of past errors rather than on anticipation of future events.

But whatever the difficulties and ambiguities of communicating with the trading desk, transmissions *are* made and received. However, the man in charge of the desk, no matter how dedicated, has a rough, tough job. If, as is frequently true, the FOMC has set some range of free reserves as its most precise measure of policy direction, the account manager ideally tries to achieve this goal in his day-to-day operations. But the goal is elusive, simply because some of the money-market factors affecting reserves cannot be predicted at all and others can be estimated only with difficulty. (Actual figures may become available only two or three weeks later.) Actions taken by the desk on the basis of the daily predictions of the money-market factors frequently turn out to have been perverse—in the wrong direction. The chief upsetting factor, of course, is Federal Reserve float, which is extremely volatile and almost completely unpredictable on a daily basis. Float could be safely ignored on a daily basis and dealt with only on a weekly average basis, Federal Reserve studies having shown that commercial banks do not alter their short-term investment positions on the basis of changing float levels. Yet fear of commercial-bank response ostensibly forms the basis for the frequency of a Fed's float-offsetting action, with consequent uncertainty in the money markets when desk action is in the wrong direction.

Another major influence on the administration of the trading desk is the solicitude of the Fed for the government security dealers, particularly for the nonbank dealers. The basic premises of this solicitude are that a "broad, deep, and resilient" market for government securities is necessary for successful Federal Reserve action and that such a market can be made only by financially impregnable dealers who can obtain financing on favorable terms. A "negative carry"—that is, a yield on any security held in inventory smaller than the rate paid on funds borrowed by the dealer—is taken as conclusive evidence that financing terms for the dealers are not favorable. The same concern is not felt for bank dealers, since they are assumed to have a ready internal source of funds to finance their positions.

Solicitude for the dealers is expressed in several ways. For example, the FOMC has approved and the desk has made frequent use of the repurchase agreement. Although this instrument is a means by which the desk can make bank reserves available for a short time with automatic withdrawal, it is also a means by which short-term credit is extended to a dealer. The timing is usually to the advantage of the dealer, because the desk makes the privilege available when there is a real pinch in the money market. The repurchase agreement is in reality a fully secured loan; the desk purchases securities (bills) from the dealer, who agrees to repurchase them within a definite period (maximum, fifteen days). Interest is computed on the basis of amount and term of loan rather than by reckoning the difference between purchase and sale price of the bills, as would be true in the case of a true purchase and repurchase.

Fed concern for the government securities dealer is further demonstrated by the expressed opinion that the money-market banks ought to favor the securities dealers in financing arrangements, particularly during tight-money periods. The money-market banks have protested that no group ought to be favored merely because of its function. Although the interest of the Fed authorities in maintaining a facilitating market organization is understandable, it is doubtful that financing favoritism is essential to a strong dealer organization. A hands-off attitude, requiring dealers to stand the market test of services rendered, charges made, and competition for custom, seems more likely to achieve ultimate Federal Reserve aims.

Nor is arranging Fed intervention in the government securities market to suit the convenience of nonbank dealers likely to inspire public confidence. Federal Reserve acceptance of the notion that System entry into the government securities market should be in short issues, preferably bills, had its philosophical basis in a weird principle of "minimum effective interference," a mystical idea that the limitless authority of the central bank could somehow be softened by dealing in securities "closest to money" in the spectrum of financial assets. But a careful reading of the famed *Ad Hoc Subcommittee Report* of 1952 makes it clear that strong support for the "bills only" dogma came from the dealers, who would avoid, for obvious reasons, "capricious" System purchases and sales throughout the maturity range of the Treasury list. Dealers with positions in bonds naturally want to be warned of fluctuations in bond prices by preliminary changes in the prices of bills.

RETURN TO REGIONALISM?

Knowledgeable men know perfectly well that the informal power structure of an institution—whether a Christian denomination, a great corporation, or a university—may well be more important than its formal one. So long as the distinction is clear, so long as people are aware of what is really going on, it makes little difference whether the formal or informal power centers are operative. But it makes a great deal of difference if the people in a democracy, unaware of the arbitrary nature of the actual decision making, go on believing that the money power, like all other sovereign power, is responsive to democratic processes. For plainly it is not.

We do not for one moment question either the integrity or the sincerity of the money managers. If government at all levels were staffed by men of the competence and dedication of those found in the Federal Reserve System, the American political system would be upgraded tremendously.

We do believe, however, that a realistic appraisal of System structure in terms of its genuine power centers leads to only one conclusion—that the regional structure, adopted by the framers of the Federal Reserve Act two generations ago, is presently outmoded and has become an expensive anachronism. We may as well face up to the fact that Federal Reserve banks have become only operating offices with responsibility for service functions and not, in any real sense, for monetary policy.

In our view a workable regional system *could* be devised. A return to regional structure would require, as a very minimum, restoration of the discount rate as an instrument of monetary control. Such a restoration implies the rescinding of Regulation A, the complex and meddlesome set of rules by which the twelve discount windows are presently administered. It further implies free access to discount windows at whatever rates the regional banks prescribe.

Ostensibly, the discount rates of the several banks are set by their boards of directors. In practice, they are raised and lowered at the wish of the board. When Chairman Martin senses the strategic moment has arrived for a discount-rate change, he initiates action via a discreet telephone call to one or more bank presidents out in the provinces. Once a Reserve bank president (at St. Louis, Kansas City, Atlanta, or Dallas, for example) has the word, it is up to him to get his board of directors, or the executive committee of his board, to do what the Reserve board wants. When the change is made, the business press ordinarily announces it as the simultaneous decision of two or more banks. Within ten days or so, all the other banks fall in line—not by mere chance, you may be sure.

There is much to be said for operating the discount window on a rate basis rather than on an administered basis. To be sure, Federal Reserve credit must be injected partly with regard to grand strategic considerations, as determined by the board and the New York bank. But much of the hour-to-hour and day-to-day intervention by the trading desk could be avoided by letting the commercial banks tell the Fed when they need reserves. It sounds a little old-fashioned to suggest that the private banking community may on occasion know what's best for it, but we'd like to return some of the reserve-injection initiative to the commercial banks.

There are reasons why it may be impossible to go back to a regional system. For one thing, the American economy has lost most of the provincial characteristics that marked it as late as the eve of World War II. For another, our understanding of monetary (stabilization) theory has changed since the formation of a geographically decentralized central bank, placing emphasis on unified control of the economy rather than on patchwork assistance to parts of it.

Yet there would be a demonstrable gain from making central-bank control less authoritarian. Moreover, continued centralization of the money power leads logically to the ultimate in a centralized power structure—combination of the central bank and the Treasury under a single head. Those who feel that such an arrangement bodes no good would do well to reflect on the possibility of greater reliance on markets in the implementation of central-bank policy.

F.

FISCAL POLICY

21 BUDGET BALANCING FOR ECONOMIC STABILIZATION

Joint Economic Committee

The effect of economic fluctuations on Federal tax receipts has long been recognized, but the significant influence that Federal budgetary policy has on the economy has been given serious attention only in the past few decades. Before World War I and even in the 1920's and into the 1930's, when the costs of past wars and national defense were slight, Federal activities were a small part of the total economy, and their economic impact was not viewed as a matter of great concern. In that environment, the budget was viewed largely as a measure of the Government's performance in handling its own affairs with prudence and efficiency. The primary test was the ability of policymakers to perform the necessary public services and tasks of the state without spending more than tax receipts. In the case of a general decline in activity, this test required that expenditures be trimmed to match falling receipts.

STABILIZING EFFECTS OF THE FEDERAL BUDGET

With better economic knowledge and the large growth of Government activities necessitated by national security and public welfare considerations, the perversity of such a policy became evident. Any reduction in Federal out-lays during recession diminishes the flow of incomes to the private sector and intensifies the decline in activity. Unless they are accompanied by tax cuts, reductions in expenditures result in a loss of jobs and a shrinking of incomes and tax revenues—all combining to make an endless chain of vain efforts to keep the budget in balance. Similarly, greater outlays, or lower tax rates, in prosperous periods can add to inflationary pressures.

Such accentuation of cyclical fluctuations through the activities of the Federal Government has become clearly recognized as imprudent and unsound policy. It is now generally recognized that the automatic fluctuations in Government receipts in response to changing levels of economic activity have beneficial stabilizing effects on the general economy. Tax receipts are closely related to private income. Therefore, tax receipts will tend to fall during periods of relatively slack activity in the economy and will tend to rise in periods when private incomes are high. In essence, proportionately lighter tax burdens are imposed upon individuals and businesses in times when private incomes are low. If tax burdens are re-

Excerpted from the *Annual Report of the Joint Economic Committee on the January, 1962 Economic Report of the President,* March 7, 1962, pp. 33–38, 91–117.

143

duced in these slack periods, relatively more income is left with individuals and businesses. Therefore, individuals and firms do not need to restrict their own purchases of goods and services as much as would be necessary if tax liabilities were maintained. Similarly, in inflationary periods tax receipts will tend to rise as incomes rise and thereby drain off purchasing power that might otherwise be used to accentuate inflationary pressures.

A Business View

One of our witnesses, representing a business research organization (the Committee for Economic Development), which has been at the forefront in encouraging fiscal policies to promote high employment and economic stability, stated his organization's agreement with these principles:

(*a*) Looking at the budget surplus as it would be under conditions of high employment, as a guide to budget policy;

(*b*) Setting expenditure programs and tax rates so they would yield a moderate surplus at high employment;

(*c*) Accepting actual departures from this target surplus, below in recession and above in boom, that result from automatic responses of tax yields and expenditures, as beneficial stabilizing influences on the economy;

(*d*) Accompanying this budget policy with a strong, flexible use of monetary policy;

(*e*) Being prepared, in some circumstances, to take further discretionary action in the budget, notably temporary tax reduction in recessions.

Also we have recommended, as the Economic Report does, that the national income budget, rather than the cash or the administrative budget, should be used in measuring overall budget policy. . . .

SIGNIFICANCE OF THE THREE FEDERAL BUDGETS

One of the most useful innovations in the analysis of Government budgets has been the development of procedures for estimating Government receipts and expenditures so that it is possible to set up a budget to represent the receipts and expenditures as they would work out if the economy were working continuously throughout the budget period at full employment. For the first time, the concept of the full employment receipts, expenditures, and surplus or deficit has found its way into the President's economic messages to the Congress, particularly into the Economic Report. These developments represent significant progress, for which the administration is to be commended.

This newer method of estimating the impact of Government fiscal operations on the general economy relates, moreover, not to the usual "administrative" or "cash" budgets but to what is now called the income-and-product-accounts budget. This latter is not constructed just to show how much funds need to be appropriated, or the total cash which Federal fiscal operations will take in or pay out. Rather, the income-and-product-accounts budget seeks to measure the direct effect on the economy of all Federal fiscal operations, and at the time when these effects occur, not just when bills are submitted and paid.

Since it is important to make a clear distinction among these three forms of budgets, a brief review may be in order.

Administrative Budget

The administrative budget has been developed in the form most useful to the appropriations committees of Congress. Expenditures are included in this budget because they are made from funds which have been considered by the Congress to be Government owned. Receipts are shown on a net basis, after refunds, to indicate only the amounts that will be available to meet expenditures. Many items, such as the receipts and expenditures of the Post Office Department and other public enterprises, are shown in the administrative budget only as net expenditures. These enterprises generally have the authority to spend against the receipts they collect, and Congress provides Government-owned money solely to meet any net deficits. Many other operations of the Government, such as trust funds and Government-sponsored enterprises, are largely ignored in the administrative budget because virtually no Government funds (technically defined) are required in these operations.

Cash Budget

The cash budget is designed primarily to show the cash flows between the Federal Government and the private economy (including State and local governments). It differs from the administrative budget in two principal ways: (1) The cash budget excludes transactions between agencies of the Government; for example, interest and other payments between the Treasury Department and the social security and other trust funds; and (2) the cash budget includes various transactions between the Federal Government and the private economy which involves the U.S. Treasury, though the amounts do not technically qualify as "Government-owned funds" and therefore are not reflected in the administrative budget. The principal amounts included in the cash budget, but not in the administrative budget, are the

transactions between Federal trust funds and the public. For example, the cash budget includes as receipts all employment taxes which enter social security trust funds and includes as expenditures all payments of social security benefits.

Income-and-Product-Account Budget

The income-and-product-account budget is provided in the national income and product accounts developed by the Commerce Department. Like the cash budget, it includes both the transactions of trust funds and some Government enterprises as well as administrative budget receipts and expenditures. It excludes financial items and exchanges of existing assets— transactions which affect liquidity in the private economy but have no direct effect on production or national income. It also excludes loans and guarantee programs of the Government, which do have an impact on the economy.

While both the cash budget and the administrative budget generally reflect receipts and expenditures in the year when cash changes hands, the income and product budget attempts to show receipts at the time when tax liabilities accrue, and expenditures for purchases of goods and services are shown as of the time the goods and services are produced and delivered.

CHANGES IN THE THREE BUDGETS COMPARED

Table 1 compares anticipated receipts and expenditures for the three different budgets for fiscal 1963, giving also the indicated changes from fiscal 1962. In addition, the table also shows the Council's estimates of what receipts and expenditures in the national income budget would be at an average rate of unemployment of 4 percent during each of the 2 fiscal years, instead of the unemployment rates actually prevailing and expected to prevail.

Thus it may be noted that the administrative budget for fiscal 1963 anticipates expenditures of $92.5 billion. This is an increase of $3.4 billion over fiscal 1962, of which $2.6 billion is for defense and space affairs, $0.4 billion for increased interest charges on the Federal debt, and $0.4 billion for all of the other functions of the Government combined.

Whereas the administrative budget for fiscal 1962 ran a deficit of $7 billion, the administrative budget for fiscal 1963 is, as has been widely reported, in balance. More precisely, it is expected to run a small surplus of approximately $0.5 billion.

The cash budget, on the other hand,

Table 1

VARIOUS FEDERAL BUDGET TOTALS FOR THE FISCAL YEARS 1962 AND 1963

[*In billions of dollars*]

	1962 estimate	1963 estimate	Change from 1962 to 1963
Administrative budget:			
Expenditures:			
National defense	51.2	52.7	1.5
International affairs and finance	2.9	3.0	.1
Space research and technology	1.3	2.4	1.1
Subtotal	55.4	58.1	2.7
Interest	9.0	9.4	.4
Other expenditures, net	24.7	25.1	.4
Total budget expenditures	89.1	92.5	3.4
Receipts	82.1	93.0	10.9
Cash budget:			
Expenditures	111.1	114.8	3.7
Receipts	102.6	116.6	14.0
National income budget:			
Expenditures	106.1	111.9	5.8
Receipts	105.6	116.3	10.7
National income budget at 4-percent unemployment levels:			
Expenditures	105.3 [1]	111.6 [1]	6.3 [1]
Receipts	113.1 [1]	120.3 [1]	7.2 [1]
Gross national product	547.5	592.5	45.0

[1] Estimates are shown computed to the nearest tenth of a billion to maintain internal consistency and the proper proportional change from year to year. This does not imply, however, that the estimates are believed to be accurate to $\frac{1}{10}$ of a billion dollars.

SOURCE: "The Budget in Brief," fiscal year ending June 30, 1963 (pp. 6 and 8), Council estimates of high employment budget, and gross national product estimates compiled by the committee staff.

anticipates receipts of $116.6 billion in fiscal 1963 and expenditures of $114.8 billion. The cash budget was also in deficit in fiscal 1962. The substantial surplus position ($1.6 billion) expected in 1963 is due largely to (*a*) net increases in payments into the trust accounts because of increased employment, and (*b*) higher unemployment compensation and social security tax rates.

As previously discussed, however, for purposes of judging the influence of the budget on the general economy, we are most interested in the national income budget. Here we may note that whereas this budget was almost in balance in fiscal 1962 ($0.5 billion deficit), for fiscal 1963 it is expected to run a sizable surplus ($4.4 billion). Thus, if the estimates are correct, Federal budget operations in fiscal 1963 will have a somewhat repressive effect on the general economy, even though the administrative budget is in balance.

Finally, coming to the national income budget as it would appear at a 4-percent rate of unemployment, we may note that for fiscal 1962 the surplus would have been $7.8 billion, whereas in fiscal 1963 it would be $8.7 billion. In addition to the absolute size of this surplus, it is also important to note that receipts will be increasing in fiscal 1963 a great deal more rapidly than expenditures. Elsewhere we point out that other estimates suggest that the 4-percent unemployment surplus in the national income budget may be substantially higher than the Council has estimated, because of even more rapid increases in receipts than the Council estimates.

REPRESSIVE EFFECT OF 1963 BUDGET

It is now anticipated that GNP will reach an annual rate of about $600 billion (in 1961 prices) by the end of fiscal 1963 and that at this annual rate unemployment will fall to approximately 4 percent of the work force by the end of that fiscal year. If GNP could be increased more rapidly to levels that would reduce unemployment to 4 percent of the work force throughout the entire fiscal year 1963, what amount of "full employment" budget surplus would occur? Federal expenditures, on an income-and-product-account basis, would apparently amount to about $111 billion, approximately 18.6 percent of the GNP at the 4-percent unemployment level, according to the projec-

tions made by the Council of Economic Advisers. The comparable figures were about 18.3 percent in fiscal 1961 and about 17.3 percent in fiscal 1957—the latter just prior to the contraction, from which the economy has not yet fully recovered. Hence, as a result of various national and social needs, expenditures have increased somewhat as a percentage of the 4 percent unemployment GNP.

The High Employment "Surplus"

At the same time, however, if 4-percent unemployment existed throughout fiscal 1963, the Council has estimated that Federal revenues in the national income accounts would amount to approximately $120 billion, about 20 percent of the high employment GNP. This is the same as in fiscal 1961 and compares with about 17.2 percent in fiscal 1957.

Hence, if the Nation were at a 4-percent unemployment level throughout fiscal 1963, the income-and-product budget would show a surplus of about $9 billion, approximately 1.5 percent of the 4 percent unemployment GNP. (As previously stated, the "surplus" in the first half of calendar 1963 will be running at the rate of $10 billion a year.) The comparable figures were 1.8 percent in fiscal 1961, and 1.4 percent in fiscal 1957. The actual projected surplus in the national income and product account is only 0.7 percent of the anticipated GNP. Other estimates suggest that the high employment surplus in fiscal 1963 might be as large as 2.5 percent of the high employment GNP.

A high employment surplus amounting to 1.5 to 2.5 percent of high employment GNP would, under present noninflationary conditions, raise significantly the proportion of the total flow of incomes through the economy that is set aside for savings, without necessarily insuring a parallel rise in investment. In fact, it seems possible that the additional flow of funds to the Federal Government would—either by adding to the Treasury cash balance or by returning funds to private savers via debt retirement—choke off recovery short of 96-percent employment by reason of holding the total of consumption and investment expenditures below 96-percent employment levels.

Obviously this does not mean that the Federal Government cannot, under any circumstances, run a high employment surplus as large as 1½ percent or more of the GNP. Indeed, under the inflationary conditions of 1947–48 and 1950–51 the Federal Government surplus ran to about 5 percent of the GNP, helping to reduce inflationary pressures. As we have repeatedly pointed out, the Government should set its budget policies so as to produce an excess of revenues over expenditures at high employment and make retirements of the public debt under high employment conditions.

But even a good policy can be carried too far. As we pointed out a year ago, we are seriously concerned lest our revenue system be capable of generating too large a Federal surplus at high employment, in which case employment high enough to produce any surplus will likely not be achieved.

*   *   *

THE COMMITTEE'S RECOMMENDATIONS

We live in a challenging age—and a dangerous one. All over the world, ideas and social institutions are in ferment; and, happily, all of this is not pointless unrest and conflict. New nations, those only now emerging from industrial prehistory, are busying themselves with ways of acquiring industrial tools, higher levels of literacy, and forms of economic organization by which they may attain the more abundant life. The older industrial nations are no less preoccupied with pushing forward the frontiers of science and technology, with gaining still higher levels of education and technical knowhow, and with better organizing their economic efforts. Indeed, so universal are these aspirations for better economic organization that the contest between East and West has become, in one of its forms, a race to determine which of the contestants is better organizing its economic efforts.

We think that the United States can do no less than make a maximum effort to provide a climate in which the great potential of our free enterprise system can be achieved. We cannot afford a continuation of the large gap between our economic performance and our economic potential, involving as it does tremendous losses in production, business profits, and workers' incomes.

We believe that public and private policies should be aimed at—

(1) completing the task of full recovery and restoring full employment;

(2) increasing the effectiveness of our stabilization policies, to help maintain the recovery achieved; and

(3) increasing efforts to improve our growth potential, including, principally a healthier and better educated population, more research and technological development, an increased rate of capital modernization, and a better diffusion of individual opportunities.

INCREASING THE STABILIZING EFFECTS OF FEDERAL PROGRAMS

The President has recommended several important steps to improve

Federal programs, particularly to strengthen their influences against cyclical recessions and inflationary tendencies in the economy. His principal recommendations and our comments follow.

Unemployment Compensation

The President has recommended legislation to strengthen the unemployment insurance system by providing for an extended benefit period for experienced workers at all times, and for all workers in times of high unemployment, by providing incentives to States to increase benefits, by extending coverage to 3 million additional workers, and other measures.

We favor this proposal. When the unemployment compensation legislation was enacted, Congress expected that compensation rates would provide workers with at least half their normal weekly earnings. Instead, compensation rates have not kept pace with average weekly earnings. We favor also extending the unemployment compensation system, insofar as it is practicable, to workers not now privileged to participate in the system. The President's proposal, if enacted, will provide better protection for workers and their families against the extreme hardships and stresses that can come with periods of joblessness. There can be no doubt that the unemployment compensation system has provided a powerful stabilizing influence on the whole economy and has thus benefited the employed as well as the unemployed. This stabilizing influence would be strengthened by enactment of the proposed legislation.

Standby Public Works

The President has recommended legislation to—

Provide standby authority for the President to accelerate and initiate up to $2 billion of capital improvements —Federal, State, and local—which authority may be used within 2 months after the unemployment rate (seasonally adjusted) has risen (1) in at least 3 out of 4 (or 4 out of 6) previous months and (2) has risen to a level at least 1 percentage point higher than its level 4 (or 6) months earlier.

We have previously recommended such a limited standby authority for projects which can be initiated and completed within a short time. We favor such authority, not for indiscriminate use, but for use in areas where heavy unemployment occurs. The proposal would add an important supplement to the arsenal of weapons for fighting recessions. This does not mean that we favor reliance on massive or long-term public works as an effective countercyclical program. On the contrary, our studies have led us to share the general view that such programs are likely to be too slow in starting and too late in ending.

Temporary Tax Cut Authority

The President has recommended legislation to—

Provide standby authority for the President to make temporary (6 months) reductions of up to a maximum of 5 percentage points in all individual income tax rates subject to congressional veto:

At the conclusion of the committee's intensive Study of Employment, Growth, and Price Levels 2 years ago, we strongly endorsed the principle of limited discretionary tax flexibility, and we are pleased to find the proposal in a Presidential recommendation. The present tax structure provides a very large degree of automatic flexibility, tending to counteract both recessionary developments and those of overemployment and inflation. We feel, furthermore, that the long-term goal should be to improve these automatic features. But since experience has provided no clear guidelines to perfection of automaticity, we favor making prompt, limited changes in tax rates from time to time as economic events warrant. We believe that had such actions been taken early in past recessions, large downswings and tremendous losses in production and incomes (and tax revenues) could have been avoided.

Witnesses before the committee have posed objections to the exact form of the present proposal—though not related to the economic substance of the proposal—and have suggested alternative approaches that might be equally effective. The practical objection to the proposal is that it involves a transfer of legislative function to the Executive, and a transfer of the Executive (veto) function to the Legislature —an arrangement involving doubtful consequences. Recognizing the urgency of prompt action, however, these witnesses have suggested that Congress enact legislation setting out the terms of the kind of temporary tax cut it will make, when asked to act quickly; with the "ground rules" thus established, Congress should be able to act quickly on a request for a temporary tax change and, indeed, to initiate such an action if need be. We believe that such an alternative procedure would be practicable.

In considering what legislation it will be willing to enact quickly, the Congress might consider alternatives to the President's proposal for an across-the-board tax reduction of 5 percentage points. The Commission on Money and Credit, in its recommendation on the matter, proposed that the cut be in the first income tax bracket only. Another recommendation frequently considered

is that the first income tax bracket ($2,000 for a single taxpayer) be split in half to create a new bracket for incomes up to $1,000.

Under the President's proposal, 40 percent of the tax reduction would go to individuals having incomes of $10,000 or more; under the CMC proposal 19 percent of the tax cut would go to individuals with incomes of $10,000 or more; the same amount of tax reduction, if applied to the first half of the first income tax bracket would distribute only 15 percent of the total amount to individuals having more than $10,000 income.

We also believe that the tax structure needs adjustment. As we have emphasized before, since tax rates are progressive and average incomes are continually rising, the budget tends to balance at ever-higher rates of unemployment—or, to put it another way, the "full employment" budget tends to generate larger and larger surpluses. Thus, we recommended in our annual report last year that the Treasury—

review the tax structure with a view to recommending a downward revision of taxes—not a temporary "tax cut"—and that it make further periodic reviews for the same purpose, say every 5 years.

Since the Treasury is now examining the revenue system, with an announced view of making other tax proposals later in this session of the Congress, we hope that it will seriously consider whether such an adjustment in tax rates is not now appropriate.

*   *   *

**INDIVIDUAL VIEWS OF
SENATOR WILLIAM PROXMIRE
TO THE MAJORITY REPORT OF
THE JOINT ECONOMIC
COMMITTEE**

While I find much to applaud both in the President's Economic Report and the report of the majority of the Joint Economic Committee to which these views are attached, I find it necessary to write these individual views for three main reasons.

Oppose Majority Criticism of Budget as Too Restrictive

First I must express vigorous disagreement with the shocking conclusion of the majority that the proposed budget may be too restrictive, that the relatively small surplus projected by the Treasury for the coming fiscal year on highly optimistic assumptions may be too large for the good of the economy.

The majority conclusion is an extreme reliance on what has become the new economic orthodoxy, the now predominantly accepted economic theory that the Nation must run a deficit as long as there are substantial unused economic resources.

Relying on this theory, the majority by implication counsels our Government—in the coming fiscal year—to run a deficit in the administrative budget, a deficit that would increase the national debt even if the coming fiscal year turns out to be a record-smashing boom year. If this advice had been followed in the past, this Nation would have run deficits in virtually every peacetime year of this century. Since deficits are all but certain in wartime—such a course would have given this country a truly astronomical national debt by today. Service costs on the national debt, already the second heaviest cost of the Federal Government, would have rivaled the immense defense costs as a burden on the taxpayer.

The position of the majority in objecting to the administration's small surplus as "too restrictive" is also wrong because it overlooks the fact that the principal economic impact of a budget is in the swing from deficit to surplus. The swing in the coming fiscal year is moderate.

All this is not to say that there is not a solid and proper case for compensatory fiscal policy. Certainly in the event of a serious depression or even a prolonged recession, a very strong case can be made against a surplus, and for following an expansionary fiscal policy in Government taxing and spending.

But the policy of deliberately planning a deficit in a predicted boom year in our economy is unconscionable.

This policy is not only wrong because of the immense national debt burden it would assure. It is also wrong because it would destroy whatever basis there now is for discipline and efficiency in Federal spending. Under this doctrine proponents of additional Government spending cannot only contend for the benefits of the service their spending would provide, they can almost always argue that the spending should involve no taxing because the resulting deficit will be a healthy thing for the economy and put idle resources to work.

The policy is also wrong because there is little evidence that it will work. There is no empirical evidence that the heavy spending and the immense and steady deficits—in relation to gross national product—in the thirties were a significant factor in pulling the Nation out of that depression.

The policy is wrong because its proponents assume that a relatively moderate shift on the order of $2 or $3 billion in the balance between Government spending and taxing can have a major effect on a $550 billion economy.

The policy is wrong because it over-

looks other more promising alternatives.

*　　*　　*

Temporary Income Tax Cut

The President has recommended
that Congress delegate to him the authority to reduce the personal income
tax temporarily. I emphatically oppose
this request. While the majority report
does not wholeheartedly support this
Presidential request, it does not directly
oppose it. I do.

In the event of a serious economic
setback, a tax cut might be desirable.
Under such circumstances I am confident that the Congress would promptly
respond to a Presidential request to
reduce taxes. Indeed, no witness at the
Joint Economic Committee's hearings
was able to adduce a single instance
when a Presidentially requested tax
cut was not granted.

It might be good public policy for
the Congress to agree with the administration on the type of tax cut that
would be most useful to combat a serious economic setback. It might be desirable for Congress to agree to give
congressional priority to any such request.

But for the Congress to surrender
even part of this prime congressional
power over taxes on such scanty justification would be very unwise. The balance of power between the Legislature
and the Executive has shifted significantly and perhaps necessarily in recent
years to the advantage of the Executive. For Congress to surrender its good
right arm—its taxing power—would
mark a very harmful and unnecessary
weakening of congressional power.

Presidential Public Works Discretion

For many similar reasons I am opposed to the President's request to the
Congress to grant him authority to
initiate $2 billion of public works
spending whenever unemployment has
been rising for 3 out of 4 or 4 out of 6
months and has risen by more than 1
percent above its level 4 or 6 months
earlier.

Such a formula, of course, provides
immense discretion for the President
to spend money without specific congressional approval.

It appears to be based on the theory
that there is some spending that ordinarily cannot be justified on its merits;
but might be justified in a period of
economic adversity as a method of recovery. I disagree that spending which
cannot be justified on its merits is likely
to be justified in terms of good public
policy except in times of very serious
economic adversity. While the argument for such spending might have solid
merit in the event of a depression, once
again—on the record—it is doubtful
if any President would have difficulty
under these circumstances persuading
the Congress to support a constructive
program.

What is more this proposal has the
serious demerit of authorizing grants
in aid to State and local governments
for projects which are peculiarly local
in their nature—police and fire stations
are an example—and should—if any
expenditure should—be left to local
discretion and local responsibility.

*　　*　　*

22   THE NEW LOOK IN TAX AND FISCAL POLICY

Paul A. Samuelson

Paul A. Samuelson is Professor of Economics at Massachusetts Institute of Technology.

I

There is much talk about taxes. When I flick on the dial of my radio in the morning, I hear a Congressman quoted on how our high level of taxes is ruining the Nation or a Senator's tape-recorded alarm over the unfair burden the poor man has to carry because the administration has been favoring big business. My morning paper at breakfast brings me the view of its editor that the United States has been pursuing unsound fiscal policy for the last 25 years. Scratch the barber who cuts my hair and you find a philosopher ready to prescribe for the Nation's monetary ills.

This is as it should be. We expect sweeping statements in a democracy. We hope that out of the conflict of extreme views there will somehow emerge a desirable compromise. Yet such sweeping statements have almost no validity from a scientific, or even from a leisurely commonsense point of view: spend as little as a year going over the factual experience of American history and of other economies, devote as little as a month to calm analysis of probable cause and effect, or even spend a weekend in a good economics library —and what will you find? Will you find that there breathes anywhere in the world an expert so wise that he can tell you which of a dozen major directions of policy is unquestionably the best? You will not. Campaign oratory aside, the more assuredly a man asserts the direction along which salvation is alone to be found, the more patently he advertises himself as an incompetent or a charlatan.

The plain truth is this, and it is known to anyone who has looked into the matter: The science of economics does not provide simple answers to complex social problems. It does not validate the view of the man who thinks the world is going to hell, nor the view of his fellow idiot that ours is the best of all possible tax systems.

I do not wish to be misunderstood. When I assert that economic science cannot give unequivocal answers to the big questions of policy, I do not for a moment imply that economists are useless citizens. Quite the contrary. They would indeed be useless if any sensible man could quickly infer for himself simple answers to the big policy questions of fiscal policy. No need then to feed economists while they make learned studies of the obvious. It is precisely because public policy in the tax and expenditure area is so complex that we find it absolutely indispensable to invest thousands of man-years of scholarly time in scholarly economic research in these areas.

Make no mistake about it. The arguments that we all hear every day of

From *Federal Tax Policy for Economic Growth and Stability:* Papers submitted by Panelists Appearing Before the Subcommittee on Tax Policy, Joint Economic Committee on the Economic Report, November 9, 1955, pp. 229–234.

our lives on the burning partisan issues have in every case been shaped by economists—by economists in universities, in business, in Government, and by that rarest of all birds, the shrewd self-made economist. What economists do not know about fiscal policy turns out, on simple examination, not to be known by anyone.

II

With this necessary preamble out of the way, let me record the general views that studies have led me to, about the current state of our fiscal system. This will clear the way for a more detailed analysis of taxes and growth, taxes and stable full employment, taxes and equity, taxes and the level of public expenditure programs.

Here then are the major facts about our system as I see them.

(1) The postwar American economy is in good shape. There is nothing artificial or unsound about its underpinnings. For more than a decade we have had generally high employment opportunities. Our production efficiency has been growing at a steady rate that compares well with anything in our history or in the history of countries abroad. For all this we must, in our present-day mixed economy, be grateful to both public and private institutions.

(2) The existing structure of Federal, State, and local taxes is in its broad features highly satisfactory. Repeatedly at the polls and through all the legitimate processes of government, the citizens of this Republic have indicated that they want our present type of fiscal structure—its substantial dependence at the Federal level on personal and corporate income taxes, its eclectic dependence on selective excises, on payroll levies for social security, on property and sales taxes at the local levels. If the consensus of citizens in our democracy were to be other than it is—toward less or more equalitarianism, toward less or more local autonomy—there is no reason that the careful analytic economist can see why our fiscal system is not capable of being altered in the desired direction. In other words, there is nothing in the mechanics of a modern economy which makes it impossible or difficult for the citizenry to get the kind of a tax system that they want; our tax system has plenty of give, plenty of room for adaptation and change.

All the above does not imply that we are living in a new era of perfection. The American economy now faces, and will continue to face, many tough problems, many hard decisions. And, to be sure, there are numerous imperfections, inconsistencies, and loopholes in the present tax structure; these do need improving.

What the optimistic diagnosis of the modern-day economist does contradict is the following:

(1) The view that America has long since departed from an orthodox fiscal policy and that it is only a matter of time until a grim Mother Nature exacts retribution from us for our folly in departing from the narrow line of fiscal rectitude. (This is a philosophical position that any dissenter from current trends is free to assume; but it is not a factually verifiable view about reality that dispassionate study of statistics and facts can substantiate.)

(2) The view, shared in by the extremes of both left and right wings, that our economy generally is moving in unsound directions so that we must ultimately end up in some unnamed disaster or convulsion. (In terms of business-cycle stability and efficient growth, the United States has in the

last dozen years dramatically refuted the sour expectations both of those who look back on a fictitious past golden age and of collectivists who look forward to a golden age that only a revolution can usher in.)

III

Turning now to the goals of any tax system, we can ask: What tax structure will give us the most rapid rate of growth? What tax system will give us the highest current standard of living? What tax structure will make our system most immune to the ups and downs in employment and prices that make American families insecure? What tax structure will realize most closely the community's sense of fairness and equity? What tax structure will have the least distorting effects on our use of economic resources, instead of maximizing the efficiency with which we produce what our citizens most want?

Upon careful thought it will be obvious that there cannot exist a tax system which will simultaneously maximize these five quite different goals of social life.

It is easy to see that high current living standards and rapid growth of our ability to produce are conflicting ends: you have only to look at a collectivized society like the Soviet Union, which decides to sacrifice consumption levels of the current generation in favor of a crash program of industrialization; you have only to reflect that historically in the slums of Manchester working families might have lived longer in the 19th century if England and the other nations had during the industrial revolution slowed down their rates of material progress; you have only to consider the problem of conserving scarce exhaustible natural resources to realize that every society must all the time be giving

up higher future resource potentials in favor of keeping current generation consumption as high as it is.

You can imagine a society that decides to devote its income in excess of the bare physiological existence level 100 percent to capital formation. You can imagine it—but there never has been such a society. Nor would any of us want to live in such a one. It should be obvious, therefore, that no sane person would ever seek a tax program which literally maximized our rate of economic growth. (Yet how many times over the chicken a la king have we all heard speakers reiterate this nonsensical goal.) It is just as obvious that no sane person would want to maximize present living levels if this meant eating up all our capital on a consumption bender that would leave us an impoverished Nation.

There is no need to go through all the other pairs of the five listed goals to show their partial incompatibility. If we are willing to frame a tax system that strongly favors thrifty men of wealth, we may thereby be able to add to our rate of current growth; if we encourage a gentle rate of inflation, we may be able to increase the profits in the hands of the quick-reacting businessman, perhaps thereby stepping up our rate of growth. So it goes, and one could easily work through the other permutations and combinations.

But not all of our five goals are necessarily competing. Some, when you realize them, help you to realize the others. If we succeed in doing away with the great depressions that have dogged the economic record, we may thereby add to our rate of growth. If we shape a graduated-tax system that enables lower income groups to maintain minimum standards of life, we may ease the task of stabilizing business activity. If we replace distorting taxes by less distorting alternatives, the fruits of the resulting more efficient production can add to our current consumption and to our rate of progress in capital formation.

I shall not prolong the discussion of the degree to which the diverse goals of tax policy are competing or complementary. For it will turn out that we can formulate proper policies without having to measure these important, but complicated, relationships.

IV

Upon being told by the economist that it is absurd for Congress to aim at the most rapid rate of growth possible and that it is equally absurd for Congress to aim at the highest possible current level of consumption, the policymaker may be tempted to say: "I understand that. Won't you therefore as an economist advise us as to just what is the best possible compromise between these extremes?"

A good question but, unfortunately, not one that the expert economist can pretend to give a unique answer to. If he is honest, he must reply: "The American people must look into their own hearts and decide on what they consider to be the best compromise rate of growth."

Just because I have advanced degrees in economics and have written numerous esoteric works in the field, I am not thereby enpowered to let my personal feelings, as to how much the present generation ought to sacrifice in favor of generations to come, become a prescription for society. It would be as presumptuous for me to offer such specific advice as to let my family's notions about dental care determine how much the typical American family ought to spend on toothpaste. But it is legitimate for me as an economist to say this: "Whatever rate of capital for-

mation the American people want to have, the American system can, by proper choice of fiscal and monetary programs, contrive to do." This can be shown by an example.

Suppose the vast majority of the American people look into the future or across the Iron Curtain at the rate of progress of others. Suppose they decide that we ought to have a more rapid rate of capital formation and technological development than we have been having recently. Then the economist knows this can be brought into being (*a*) by means of an expansionary monetary policy that makes investment funds cheaper and easier to get. Admittedly, such an expanded investment program will tend, if it impinges on an employment situation that is already full and on a price level that is already stationary, to create inflationary price pressures and overfull employment—unless something is done about it. What would have to be done about this inflationary pressure? Clearly (*b*) a tight fiscal policy would be needed to offset the expansionary monetary policy: By raising taxes relative to expenditure, we would reduce the share of consumption out of our full employment income, releasing in this way the real resources needed for investment. (It should be unnecessary to go through the reverse programs which would be called for if the national decision were to slow down the rate of capital formation as compared to that of recent years.)

From these remarks it will be clear that economic science is not only neutral as to the question of the desired rate of capital accumulation—it is also neutral as to the ability of the economy to realize any decided-on rate of capital formation.

I repeat: With proper fiscal and monetary policies, our economy can have full employment and whatever rate of capital formation and growth it wants.

V

The optimistic doctrine that our economy can have stability and the rate of growth it wants may seem rather novel. Perhaps even a little shocking. But there are worse surprises yet to come.

The reader may think that my argument rests on something like the following reasoning:

Suppose that political party R is more concerned with progress than political party D, which shows a greater concern for the little man, with security, and with current consumption. Then if the Nation gives its approval to the general policy goals of R, the Government will have to change its emphasis away from reducing taxes on individuals—particularly rapid-spending lower-income people; and it will have to change its emphasis toward reducing taxes on business, in an attempt to bolster the incentives toward investment. In short, it is by changing the qualitative pattern of taxation, by sacrificing equity to incentive, that the community succeeds in getting higher levels of capital formation when it desires such higher levels.

I predict that much of the testimony before this subcommittee will proceed along these lines. Certainly much of the political discussion of the last 3 years, when it has had the courage to be frank, has been along these lines.

But this is not at all the train of thought that I wish to emphasize in my testimony. I want to cap the daring doctrine that an economy can have the rate of capital information it wants with a doctrine that may seem even more shocking. Naturally, I cannot here develop all of the underlying rea-soning, nor give all the needed qualifications. But I do in advance want to stress the earnestness with which I put it forward, and to underline that it does spring from careful use of the best modern analyses of economics that scholars here and abroad have over the years been able to attain. The doctrine goes as follows:

A community can have full employment, can at the same time have the rate of capital formation it wants, and can accomplish all this compatibly with the degree of income-redistributing taxation it ethically desires.

This is not the place to give a detailed proof of the correctness of this general proposition. It will suffice to illustrate it with two extreme examples.

In the first, suppose that we desire a much higher rate of capital formation but stipulate that it is to be achieved by a tax structure that favors low-income families rather than high-income. How can this be accomplished? It requires us to have an active expansionary policy (open-market operations, lowering of reserve requirements, lowered rediscount rates, governmental credit agencies of the FHA and RFC type if desired) which will stimulate investment spending. However, with our taxes bearing relatively lightly on the ready-spending poor, consumption will tend to be high at the same time that investment is high. To obviate the resulting inflationary pressure, an increase in the overall tax take with an overly balanced budget would be needed.

Alternatively, suppose the community wants a higher level of current consumption and has no wish to make significant redistributions away from the relatively well-to-do and toward the lower income groups. Then a tighter money policy that holds down investment would have to be combined with a fiscal policy of light taxation relative to expenditure. But note that in this case, as in the one just above, any qualitative mix of the tax structure can be offset in its effects by appropriate changes in the overall budget level and in the accompanying monetary policy.

23   UNITED STATES AND WESTERN EUROPE DIFFER ON BUDGET DEFICITS

Edwin L. Dale, Jr.

Edwin L. Dale, Jr. is a specialist on economic affairs for *The New York Times*.

Paris, May 10. The remarkably successful performances of Western Europe in recent years, contrasted with chronic unemployment and slow growth in the United States, has prompted a profound examination on both sides of the Atlantic.

With the evidence of five or six years of contrasting performance in hand, conclusions are being reached by Government officials, economists, and others. Some of the conclusions clash with widely held beliefs in the United States on such matters as the budget. However, the conclusions arrived at by various analysts appear to show a wide amount of agreement.

By every generally accepted test of economic performance except one, it is agreed, Western Europe as a whole has done better than the United States since about 1956. Economic growth has been twice as rapid in Europe as in the United States. This means total production has risen twice as fast.

Europe has had almost uninterrupted full employment and now has a labor shortage. Unemployment in the United States has mounted with each successive business cycle and is now just under 4,000,000. The standard of living, as measured by the income of the average citizen, has been rising faster in Western Europe, though the United States remains well ahead.

Investment in new plant and equipment and other assets, in relation to the total output of the economy, has been nearly half again higher in Western Europe than in the United States, most of it financed by rising business profits.

Europe's international balance of payments, the relationship between total payments to foreigners and total receipts from foreigners, has shown consistent surpluses. That of the United States has been in chronic deficit, with a consequent loss of gold.

The one exception—the one economic test by which the United States has had a better record—is in the effort to check the slow rise in prices that has afflicted all nations. Prices have risen slightly less in the United States in the last four or five years than in most European countries, though the rise has been small on both sides of the Atlantic.

Governments in Europe do a number of things differently from what is normal practice in the United States, ranging from different tax systems to tariff-cutting in European Economic Community, or Common Market. Thus few students of the recent economic record attribute the differing performances on the two sides entirely to one cause.

However, one cause is receiving the heaviest stress in analyses and comments. This is the contrast between American and European financial policies: government budget policy (spending and taxation) and monetary policy. These are the policies that strongly influence the total level of demand, or spending power in the economy. Demand has been consistently stronger in Europe, which means simply that business has been better most of the time.

In the United States the financial actions of the Government, for varying reasons, have normally been designed to check demand—mainly through budget decisions aimed at a surplus and frequent use of "tight money." (High interest rates.)

Budget deficits have often occurred, despite original decisions aiming at a surplus, because tax receipts failed to come up to expectations as the economy lagged. But, according to most current analyses, this has not altered the restrictive effects of the original decisions.

In Europe, Governments have almost never aimed at budget surpluses, by United States budget definitions. With demand already strong and tending to perpetuate itself, budget policy has normally been approximately "neutral," with most countries regularly running small deficits. When demand in the economy weakened, deficits were quickly increased on purpose, but this was seldom necessary.

An economist describes the contrast in these terms:

"The rule in Europe has been never to restrict demand by budget surpluses or tight money unless the economy reached the stage of being badly overheated, with a serious labor shortage and full-capacity operation by business. Even then, the restrictive policy has been maintained for as brief a period as possible. This is true of all countries.

"In the United States, partly because of a certain mythology about balanced budgets and partly for more plausible reasons, the rule has been to restrict demand, mainly by aiming at a budget surplus, each time the economy showed the slightest sign of rising, long before there was full employment or overheating.

"This fundamental difference has been at work since the middle of the last decade. In my opinion and that of many others, it accounts for most of the difference on the two sides."

A Government official expresses a common viewpoint:

"Quite frankly, I fear you will continue to do rather badly in the United States until you become more modern in the matter of the Federal budget and its use as an economic weapon. We have all learned the lesson in Europe some years ago. You never hear anyone talking about the 'national debt,' for example. We approve of deficits and they don't have to be inflationary.

"If your Government had aimed at one or two sizeable deficits at the right times over the past six years, instead of always trying to balance the budget and getting deficits by mistake, I will warrant you there wouldn't be half as many people out of work in West Virginia today. We have coal trouble, too, but we have no unemployment."

A businessman adds:

"Do not blame your troubles on automation. We have been investing in new machines in Europe faster than you have. The difference here is that Governments have pursued a policy of expansion, which means that demand has risen so fast and production with it that few people have been put out of work by mechanization. Those that have were able to find other jobs almost at once.

"Demand is natural. It has risen here without interruption because our Government helped it to do so. You could follow a policy of expansion too."

Western European Governments have averted budget surpluses mainly by compensating for a rapid rise in tax revenues. The compensation has been a rapid rise in spending—on schools, roads, agriculture, civil service pay and other things. Although spending has not been allowed to "run away," the increase in expenditures in nearly all countries has been considerably faster than in the United States. In addition, Government spending of all kinds in Europe represents a higher portion of the national income.

A few countries, notably Britain, have used tax cuts as an alternative to a rapid rise in spending. The net effect of European Government financial policies has not been inflationary, but,

more important, neither has it been restrictive.

A major reason for restrictive budget and monetary policy in Washington has been the unsatisfactory state of the United States' balance of international payments. Checking demand and spending has the aim of killing inflation and thus making a nation more competitive.

Economists and others in the United States and Europe differ on whether the balance of payments situation in the United States warranted a restrictive policy and whether the policy helped.

However, there is agreement, based on European experience, that a policy of expansion need not hold back exports. Western Europe's export performance has been outstanding.

There is also increasing agreement that modern "creeping inflation" is often the result, not of excess demand but of other causes, such as overly large wage increases. In such conditions, Western European Governments appear to believe, holding back demand brings on unemployment without helping much to reduce prices.

24   IS THE FOOD STAMP PLAN WORKING?

Julius Duscha

Julius Duscha is with the national news staff of the *Washington Post* and *Times Herald*.

Six million Americans get surplus food free each month because they claim that they do not have enough money to feed themselves. But experience with the recently revived New Deal food stamp plan indicates that the number of hungry Americans is probably far less.

Last summer the stamp plan replaced the free food program in Detroit and

seven other areas where unemployment is high. Immediately the number of people claiming to be short of food in these areas dropped by half, though there was no comparable reduction in relief rolls or improvement in employment.

From *The Reporter*, March 1, 1962, pp. 38–41; copyright 1962 by The Reporter Magazine Company. Reprinted by permission.

What, then, happened to these hungry people? The harsh fact seems to be that most of them were willing to pick up a free box of groceries but unwilling to spend a modest part of their small income for food in order to get free additional items that they badly need for an adequate diet.

Under the free food program now in effect in almost fifteen hundred counties, few questions are asked of applicants for the commodities. City and county welfare agencies get the food in carload lots from the U.S. Department of Agriculture. All that the local officials now do is hand it out. Whatever repackaging is necessary can be done cheaply, generally by persons on the relief rolls. In many depressed areas people get the food (usually flour, corn meal, and powdered milk) if they show up on distribution day. Welfare officials candidly admit that many families try to get along on the government free food and spend whatever money comes their way—money that they ought to be using on food to supplement the frugal surplus diet—on less essential products.

Under the food stamp plan a family of four with a monthly income of one hundred dollars, for example, would have to agree to spend at least eighteen dollars on food to get sixteen dollars' worth of additional food free. To put it another way, they buy thirty-four dollars' worth of food coupons from the government for eighteen dollars. The stamp plan thus seeks to make certain that needy families spend what they can afford for food, and the total purchasing power of the coupon makes it possible for them at least to approach a balanced diet.

Families participating in the plan, which is open to any low-income person whether or not he is on relief, may buy practically any food that they want simply by presenting the coupons at any grocery store that participates in the program. Only food from foreign countries is not included in the program. The free surplus food program, on the other hand, distributes starchy foods for the most part because those are the kind that are in oversupply. But the gray one-dollar coupons and the red twenty-five-cent coupons that the stamp plan participants receive each month are as good as legal tender both to the needy and to the grocers, who deposit them in banks like money. Federal Reserve banks then reimburse the local bankers. The coupons are slightly smaller than a dollar bill and can be sorted and counted by the same banking machines that handle paper money.

The food stamp plan was first tried out in the United States from 1939 to 1943. It was one of the latter-day New Deal innovations and was generally regarded as a successful way to help raise farmers' incomes by increasing food consumption among the needy. Orange and blue stamps were issued, the former good for the purchase of any food, and the latter valid only for surplus foods.

The plan was revived by Congress in the mid-1950's but was never put into effect because former Secretary of Agriculture Ezra Taft Benson vehemently opposed the idea. Instead, Benson commissioned a study designed to show that the national plan would cost at least $600 million annually. (The experimental program is actually costing less than three million dollars a month.) During the 1960 Democratic primary in West Virginia, President Kennedy promised to revive the plan if he were elected. Soon after Inauguration Day the President ordered Secretary of Agriculture Orville L. Freeman to put the plan on trial in eight areas. Although the program is primarily a welfare measure, it has remained an Agriculture Department responsibility because Congress usually will appropriate funds to help farmers, even if indirectly, far more readily than it will vote money to aid the needy.

FEEDING DETROIT'S HUNGRY

In Detroit not long ago I talked with welfare officials who are administering the food stamp plan and with many of the needy who are benefiting from it. Detroit, the only large city where the plan has been tested, itself accounts for eighty thousand of the 140,000 people benefiting from the program. The other areas where the plan has been in operation since last summer are McDowell County in West Virginia, Fayette County in the anthracite fields of Pennsylvania, Floyd County in eastern Kentucky, Franklin County in southern Illinois, the cities of Virginia and Hibbing and surrounding areas on the Northern Minnesota iron range, Silver Bow County in Montana, and San Miguel County in New Mexico. In all of these depressed areas the cost of the program is paid for by the Federal government but state and local welfare officials administer the plan. A total of 280,000 persons in the eight areas were getting free food before the stamp plan was substituted for the surplus direct distribution program. The stamp plan will be expanded this year to include additional depressed areas.

Welfare officials in the eight areas like the plan because it gets them out of the wholesale food business and because it can provide balanced diets for people in need. And in these days when spiraling welfare expenditures are often questioned, the stamp plan enables officials to show taxpayers that some of the money, at least, is being used for the unexceptionable purpose of feeding the hungry.

Before the food stamp plan was put into effect, the Detroit Welfare Department was the biggest food distributor in the city. Last spring it was handing out food each month to 190,000 persons—twelve per cent of the city's population. The lines at the surplus distribution centers got longer last winter after the Kennedy administration added butter and canned pork and gravy to the list of such surplus staples as rice, rolled oats, beans, peanut butter, dried eggs, and the familiar flour, corn meal, and powdered milk.

"When we had butter," Robert J. Temple, the assistant superintendent of the Detroit Welfare Department told me, "we always had more people applying for surplus food."

To unemployed Detroit automobile workers like M. C. Edwards, a forty-six-year-old widower who has been out of work for two years, the stamp plan means meat, potatoes, and milk. He is on relief and tries to live on $120 a month. He has a thirteen-year-old daughter to support. His rent is $50 a month and his heating bills sometimes run $25 a month in winter. Edwards gets $16 in free food coupons for the $32 he pays. (The size of a family and its income determine the ratio of bonus to purchased coupons.) Under the free surplus food program Edwards got only $8 worth of the limited number of surplus commodities. Edwards's case comes close to the average in Detroit, where for every dollar spent on food coupons fifty-two cents in bonus coupons are given away. The average for all eight food stamp areas works out to a thirty-seven per cent bonus. "If it weren't for the food stamps," said Edwards, an Alabama Negro who first came to Detroit in 1943, "I don't know what I'd do."

Agriculture Department studies of the stamp plan in Detroit and the other seven areas where it has been operating indicate that the program has substantially increased food consumption among the participating families. Purchases of meat, milk, fruits, and vegetables have accounted for eighty per cent of the increase. It is estimated that half of the low-income families using the plan now get enough food to meet adequate nutrition standards, while only one-fourth of all low-income families generally have a balanced diet.

"We like to think," said Temple, "that every time a few more families get into the plan it will mean another steer on the line back in Iowa." Up to now, however, the stamp plan has had no noticeable effect on the nation's ever-mounting farm surpluses or on farmers' income. Only a vastly expanded program would begin to make a dent in either of these perplexing farm problems.

After more than six months' experience with the food stamp plan, Detroit's welfare superintendent, Daniel J. Ryan, sees both its shortcomings and successes. Although the program is doing all that Ryan, an early supporter of the plan, had hoped it would do to improve the diets of the participants, he concedes that the plan is not reaching nearly as many people as could be helped by it. Ryan is a tough administrator who has long held that a welfare program ought not to dole out money to the needy without making certain that the funds are spent for essentials. Everyone who is on the City of Detroit relief rolls, which are financed with state and local funds, must use the food stamp plan. Relief recipients constitute half of the persons participating in the food stamp plan in the city.

PERSUASION OR COMPULSION?

But the Federal government cannot compel anyone to use food stamps. Thus, although the plan would seem to be ideally suited to the needs of families with small children, only about a third of the more than thirty-five thou-

sand people receiving Federal aid-to-dependent-children (ADC) grants in Detroit are taking advantage of the plan, despite intensive campaigns by relief officials to get them into the program. This is the story in the other food stamp areas, too.

Yet every one of these families would benefit from the food stamp plan, and Ryan thinks they all should be required to use it. Such a requirement may be written into the Federal relief laws Congress is being asked to revise this year. The amount of bonus coupons given to participants ranges from thirty-five to 150 per cent, and families with no income get all their coupons free. In addition to persons on relief, participants include families whose only income is from unemployment compensation benefits, retired persons who receive inadequate Social Security payments, elderly people with meager private means, and even a Detroit policeman with eight children who discovered that despite his $75 a week income he was still eligible because of his large family. The $30 that he receives each month in bonus coupons takes care of his milk bill. In Detroit a family of four with a monthly income of no more than $265 is eligible to participate in the plan.

Welfare officials believe that most of the people who were getting free surplus food but who have stayed out of the stamp plan are among low-income families who are not on relief, families getting unemployment benefits, ADC cases, and the aged. Some people with extremely low incomes do not understand that they qualify for the plan even though they are not on relief. Some of the aged do not eat as much as nutritionists say they should and therefore do not see how they could benefit from the program. It is also probable that people who didn't mind waiting in line for free food at an official agency of the government are embarrassed about the idea of showing up in a local grocery store with a form of money that calls attention to their poverty.

But welfare officials say that the vast majority of the missing simply do not want to commit any part of their small income for food. They have learned from hard experience that the rent, heat, and utility bills must be paid each month but that they can skimp on food if necessary to meet their other commitments and have a little money left over to spend as they wish. In many cases people would rather keep up payments on a television set or a car than exchange the cost of either or both for an adequate diet.

In the revived food stamp plan, however, are the seeds of a program that could make certain that every American family has enough of the proper kind of food. And welfare officials are convinced that the time may come when the providing of adequate amounts of food will be considered as necessary in an industrial society as pensions and unemployment-compensation benefits. But to be more than a modest success the stamp plan would need more compulsory features. There are good grounds for requiring everyone who receives relief to participate.

Ever since the extensive farm price support programs began in the early 1930's there has been an element of government subsidy in most food purchased by Americans, but some of the Federal farm programs have raised food prices and thus made it more rather than less difficult for many persons to eat adequately. It doesn't make sense for Americans to go hungry while their government is storing surplus food at a cost of nearly a million dollars a day. The food stamp plan offers at least one way to get more food sold over the counter in an open market.

G.

DEBT

25   CHANGES IN DEBT LEVELS

Joint Economic Committee

*   *   *

One of the concomitants of economic growth in this country has been a continuous addition to financial investment —and hence, a continuous addition to debt. The Nation has lent more—and hence borrowed more—as the Nation has grown wealthier. At the same time our economy has become more specialized, the needs to obtain money and put it to active use have increased.

Total Debt and GNP Have Risen Together

Total debt in the society has tended to remain relatively constant as a percentage of GNP. In other words, total debt has tended to rise, step by step,

From the *Annual Report of the Joint Economic Committee on the January, 1962 Economic Report of the President,* March 7, 1962, pp. 38–40.

with increases in GNP. Table 12, which groups years since 1922 in rough correspondence with the business cycles that have occurred since that date, indicates that total debt as a percentage of GNP has varied within about 5 percentage points, plus or minus, from the 41-year average, with the notable exception of the 1930 decade. This is not surprising, of course, in view of the fact that as GNP has tended to rise, savings levels have also risen and made more funds available for borrowing and for productive use in the economy. In

RATIO OF TOTAL PUBLIC AND PRIVATE DEBT TO GROSS NATIONAL PRODUCT

[Dollar amount in billions]

	Average debt	Average GNP	Ratio— percent
1916–21	$117.8	$ 73.3	162
1922–24	150.2	81.3	185
1925–27	173.6	94.2	184
1928–33	186.4	80.6	231
1934–38	183.9	79.8	231
1939–46	309.8	162.9	190
1947–49	472.1	248.9	190
1950–54	602.0	336.5	179
1955–57	757.0	413.3	183
Average ratio, 1916–57	—	—	190
Average ratio, 1916–57 (excluding 1930–34)	—	—	184

SOURCE: Marshall A. Robinson, "Debt and Economic Growth," in *Money and Economic Activity, Readings in Money and Banking,* Lawrence S. Ritter (ed.), Houghton, Mifflin Co. (1961), p. 41.

the period of the great depression, production and incomes fell so drastically that, despite widespread bankruptcies, the debt ratio increased to unusually high levels.

Federal Debt Declining Relative to GNP

The composition of total debt over time has changed. While public debt (Federal, State, and local) has risen in the postwar period, the percentage increases have been less than the percentage increases either in private debt or in GNP. Chart 9 indicates these relationships. In effect, the public sector has been financing its current and capital outlays more out of current income than has the private sector. Moreover, since the economy is growing more rapidly than public net borrowing, the significance of the public debt relative to total economic activity is actually declining. (See chart 1.)

CHART 1

Net Public and Private Debt as a Percent of Gross National Product
1946-1961

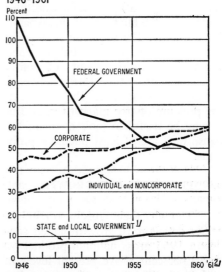

[1] For June 30.
[2] Estimated by Council of Economic Advisors.
SOURCE: *1962 Economic Report of the President,*

26 THE DEBT PROBLEM AND ECONOMIC GROWTH

Paul W. McCracken

Paul W. McCracken is Professor of Business Economics at the University of Michigan.

After a decade or so devoted to the matter, we have learned that 2½ per cent compounded doubles every 28 years. With this lesson learned, we are now very properly giving more attention to the conditions which are necessary to maintain the expanding economy. This is a sensible next-step. A look around the world certainly suggests that doubling living standards every generation is not automatic. It is, in fact, a most unusual performance, happening to only a small proportion of the world's population. Consequently the increasing emphasis on why it happens and what problems and roadblocks may be faced is all to the good —in order to be more certain that this historical trend will continue.

My comments will be confined to a tentative exploration of some questions concerning the financing of the expanding economy. The problems may never arise. Future gaps and imbalances and disequilibria arising out of fairly mechanical projections fortunately have a way of melting under the equilibrating pressure of free market forces. But it may be useful to look at them, because they are at least potential problems.

PROSPECTS FOR GROWTH

Though their results differ in minor details most growth models suggest a 1965 gross national product 40 to 50 per cent above present levels in real terms. This allows for somewhat more than a one per cent per year rise in the labor force, a slight decline in the length of the work week, and productivity improving at the rate of two to three per cent per year. Experience has, no doubt, taught us considerable humility about predicting long-run trends for even the more stable, slow-moving, and "forecastable" variables. Nevertheless a review of the projections whose target years have already been reached suggests that long-run GNP projections can be sufficiently accurate to serve as useful guides for public and private planning purposes. Indeed this is fortunate since for better or for worse, they are being so used.

An increase to a $565 billion GNP (in present prices) by 1965 ought to be quite feasible. It would actually require an improvement in productivity only moderately better than in the pre-war decade. Higher capital outlays, more research, technological development, greater attention to behavioral and motivational human relations problems —these ought to permit a growth rate substantially better than the pre-war decade, which included the lost weekend of the great depression. Whether the precise figure of a $565 billion GNP turns up in 1965, or a year or two earlier or later, is not a matter of great importance here.

_____

From the *Michigan Business Review*, November, 1956, pp. 11–15. Reprinted by permission.

RELATIONSHIPS BETWEEN DEBT AND GNP

Now for at least as long as regular data on total debt have been published, there has been a fairly close relationship between the volume of total net debt (public and private) outstanding and gross national product. This is, of course, perfectly understandable and to be expected. The size of the savings and deficits in the economy from which debts arise is related to the level of national income (and incidentally to its direction of change).

In the post-war period the ratio of the change in total net debt to gross national product fluctuated over a substantial range but averaged just over nine per cent. If the savings and deficits in the economy continue at about the same relative size, by 1965 we should have accumulated about $430 billion of additional debt, pushing the total to somewhat over $1,000 billion.

GNP AND INCREASE IN DEBT

(Dollar amounts in billions)

Year	GNP	Debt Change	Debt Change as Per Cent of GNP
1948	$257.3	$16.1	6.3
1949	257.3	14.2	5.5
1950	285.1	42.5	14.9
1951	328.2	33.9	10.3
1952	345.2	30.9	9.0
1953	364.5	30.4	8.3
1954	360.5	20.6	5.7
1955	387.2	51.3	13.2

SOURCE: Basic data from U.S. Department of Commerce.

One can, of course, look at this whole matter from another point of view. The ratio of the volume of total debt outstanding to GNP in years of reasonably good business conditions has ranged between 1.7 and 1.8. If this ratio continues, by the time we reach a $565 billion GNP, total debt outstand-

ing should range between $960 to $1,-020 billion. This compares with the actual figure of $658 billion at the end of 1955.

GROSS NATIONAL PRODUCT AND TOTAL NET DEBT

(in billions)

Year	GNP	Debt	Debt GNP
(1)	(2)	(3)	(4)
1916	$ 49	$ 82	1.67
1925	91	163	1.79
1929	104	191	1.84
1940	101	190	1.88
1945	214	406	1.90
1950	285	491	1.72
1955	387	658	1.70

SOURCE: Col. 2—U. S. Department of Commerce, except 1916 and 1925 from Paul W. McCracken, "Cyclical Implications of War-time Liquid Asset Accumulations," (Harvard, Doctoral Thesis, 1948); Col. 3—U. S. Department of Commerce.

Whether we look at the probable annual increases in debt or at the volume of debt outstanding which would be appropriate to 1965's GNP, we reach the conclusion that a $1,000 billion debt level will almost certainly be reached in the decade ahead.

HOW DEBT GROWS

The process by which these additional debts will come into being is obvious. Most of the country's annual net savings flow into savings deposits of banks, insurance companies, mutual savings banks, savings and loan associations, and into our great thrift institutions generally. With minor exceptions these institutions can invest these new savings only in assets which are the debts of others—mortgages, bonds, short-term loans, etc. If the economy is not to bog down, these saved dollars must be acquired by others and spent. And that is the process by which total public and private debts have doubled every quarter of a century or so. And our great financial institutions exist to facilitate this process.

Will we have any trouble reaching this $1,000 billion debt level? Probably not. Indeed our enthusiasm about taking on more debt in 1955 makes the whole question seem at least pointless and quite possibly absurd. Nevertheless there may quite possibly be some problems here, and it may be useful to explore them further. They illustrate, I think, the kinds of questions which are just under the surface of the projected GNP totals for some target year in the future.

At the end of 1955, total net debt was $658 billion. This consisted of $388 billion of private debt; $38 billion of state and local government debt; and $232 billion of net Federal debt (excluding securities held by trust funds, etc.).

Now who is going to account for the roughly $400 billion of new debts (net) to be created in the next 10 years? Obviously either government units or private borrowers, and in all probability the result will be some combination of the two. Let us assume for illustrative purposes that for the decade as a whole the Federal government's administrative budget is balanced. In the accompanying table, trust fund holdings of Federal obligations are assumed to increase by $22 billion, correspondingly reducing the net debt of the Federal government. State and local debt is assumed to rise in line with the increase in national income, or about 50 per cent. For the total to rise by the indicated or "needed" amount, net private debt must almost double in the next decade, rising to $733 billion.

This is not, of course, an extreme case. The figures could have been made to show much more startling results if substantial progress toward paying off the debt had been assumed.

Let us alternatively assume that pri-

TOTAL NET DEBT IN THE U. S., 1965

(First Estimate)
(Dollar amounts in billions)

Type	1955	1965	Per cent Change
Net private debt	$388	$ 733	+89%
State & local government debt	38	57	+50%
Federal government ..	232	210	— 9%
TOTAL	$658	$1,000	—52%

vate borrowers are prudent and increase their debts only in proportion to the increase in their income. In this case private debt could rise only to $590 billion, and Federal debt would need to increase $120 billion in the decade to give us a $1,000 billion debt total.

TOTAL NET DEBT IN THE U. S., 1965

(Second Estimate)
(Dollar amounts in billions)

Type	1955	1965	Per cent Change
Net private debt	$388	$ 590	+52%
State & local government debt	38	58	+52%
Federal government ..	232	352	+52%
TOTAL	$658	$1,000	+52%

NEEDED EXPANSION OF MONEY SUPPLY

We see this same problem in a somewhat different light by looking at it from the point of view of the money supply needed by 1965. There has, of course, been a fairly close long-run relationship between the money supply and gross national product. There is some evidence that secularly the money supply has been growing more rapidly than gross national product, but suppose we assume that the current ratio of about .53 continues. This suggests that we shall need about a $100 billion addition to the money supply by 1965. And all but 10–15 per cent of this must presumably be accounted for by an expansion of bank deposits.

MONEY SUPPLY AND GNP

(Dollar amounts in billions)

June 30	Money Supply	GNP	Money Supply / GNP
1929	$ 54.8	$104.4	.525
1941	73.4	125.8	.583
1951	174.7	328.2	.532
1953	192.6	364.5	.528
1955	207.7	387.2	.536
1965 p	300.0	565.0	.531

p—projected.

Let us explore some of the implications of this need for a 50 per cent increase in bank deposits by 1965. It will be useful to assume that the ratio of bank holdings of Federal obligations to the total Federal debt in the hands of the public will be the same in 1965 as in 1955. If the administrative budget is balanced over the next decade, and the Federal debt in the hands of the public declines about 10 per cent, bank loans will need to be almost exactly doubled for bank deposits to show the "needed" expansion. (Column A in the following table.) This assumes that bank holdings of "other investments" (mostly municipals) and cash resources will rise in proportion to the size of the economy.

ASSETS AND LIABILITIES, ALL U. S. BANKS

(Dollar amounts in billions)

Assets	6/55	6/65 (A)	6/65 (B)
Cash	$ 42	$ 63	$ 63
Loans	91	180	137
Federal securities	72	65	108
Other investments	21	31	31
Miscellaneous	4	6	6
TOTAL	$230	$345	

Liabilities	6/55	6/65 A & B
Deposits	$209	$314
Misc. Liabilities	3	4
Capital	18	27
TOTAL	$230	$345

For bank loans outstanding to rise only in proportion to the rise in incomes and sales (as measured by GNP), bank holdings of Federal government securities must increase $36 billion by 1965. (Column B in the table.) This, of course, might reflect simply a shift in ownership of the debt, with banks holding more and others holding less. But this merely transfers the problem since then the demand for private obligations by the nonbank public will be equal to the rise in their total assets *plus* the liquidation of their holdings of Federal obligations (required to meet the increased bank demand).

The dilemma remains: We must either accept the fact that private debts can for the indefinite future rise more rapidly than private incomes and sales, or we must have a Federal budget sufficiently unbalanced in the years ahead to provide the required additional government securities.

THE FINANCIAL REQUIREMENTS OF AN INCREASING NATIONAL INCOME

1. Is our growth potential possibly jeopardized by a sort of ideological double-mindedness about financial policy? There is a possibility that it is. The view that the public debt is too large and ought to be reduced substantially is still a very prevalent one and receives support in very high places. Secretary Humphrey, before the National Press Club last month, opposed any tax reduction because "it is high time to start reducing our huge debt."

Now this is a perfectly defensible view, and it may be that the public debt should be reduced in the years ahead. But it is fair to say that many of those who hold this view have also been disturbed by the current tendency for private debts to rise more rapidly than incomes. If economic growth is not to be placed in financial jeopardy, we must recognize that these twin tenets of fiscal orthodoxy are mutually inconsistent for the period ahead. We must have either unbalanced Federal budgets or unbalanced private budgets in the decade ahead, with private debts rising substantially more rapidly than incomes and sales in the latter case. But between now and 1965 we cannot have both.

There is, I think, the possibility that this will be a particularly interesting problem in the decade ahead. In the immediate postwar period private debts were so low that a rise relative to incomes constituted no worrisome problem. And during much of our history private debt has been virtually equal to total debt, so the question never really arose. But we are starting into the next decade with many persons already uncomfortable about the large volume of private debt. Yet because the Federal debt is still relatively quite large, private debts for several years must grow about 50 per cent more rapidly than incomes and sales if private debt is to account for the expansion of total debt.

A WAY OUT OF THE DILEMMA

There is, of course, one way out of this dilemma. If a substantially larger proportion of our savings were to go into equities, the proportion going into assets which are the debts of others could be correspondingly reduced. Measures which might facilitate such a shift would be all to the good. The greater tendency of pension funds to go into equities and the substantial growth of investment companies are among the evidences that we are moving in this direction.

Yet it does not seem probable that these changes will be of major proportion in the years ahead. For one thing, tax considerations make debt financing attractive for industry. And it is difficult to see a major shift into equities by insurance companies, banks, savings and loan associations, and the other major thrift institutions. For the decade ahead most of the savings flowing through these institutions (and this is most of *total* savings) will continue to be invested in bonds, mortgages, shorter term loans, and assets which generally are the debt of others.

THE BANKING SITUATION

2. Will we face institutional problems in expanding bank deposits and the money supply by the needed amount? Obviously there will be no problem in the mechanical sense. The Federal Reserve has enough elbow room through its own excess gold reserves and power to reduce member bank reserve requirements so that the primary reserve position of member banks will impose no limitation.

The question is more apt to arise from internal bank management policies. One already hears occasional comments that some banks feel their loans are as high as they should go relative to deposits. And many apparently feel that certain types of loans are as high relative to deposits as is wise.

The academic economist is not competent to question the wisdom of these policies. But if we are to get the required increase in bank deposits and the money supply, and the Federal debt is not to enlarge, bank loans will almost certainly continue to grow relative to deposits.

There will apparently be no impediment because of an inadequate growth of capital resources. The total capital accounts of commercial banks since 1950 have been growing at the rate of 5.7 per cent per year. If this rate continues, the 1965 capital-to-deposit ratio should be considerably larger than at the present time.

3. Will these developments create some upward pressure on interest rates? This is possible. If government securities become relatively less important in portfolios, private obligations may require higher interest rates to compensate for the increased risk exposure. Or, to put the matter in another way, the financing of more risky operations may become more difficult.

It is doubtful if in practice this pressure on interest rates will be very subtantial. Indeed, to the extent that the public debt does continue to enlarge, interest rates should be higher than if the Federal budget is balanced. A "tighter" monetary policy would be required (though also more difficult to execute) to compensate for an "easier" fiscal policy.

4. Does this have implications for monetary policy? I think it does. The Federal Reserve should be more than ever relieved from concern about debt management operations, and therefore more free to make policy decisions according to the needs of the economy. But with the economy more and more sustained by the expansion of private bank credit, the economic situation may well become even more sensitive to changes in Federal Reserve policy. Federal Reserve policy should become a more important and more sensitive instrument of control.

CONCLUSIONS

This all leads to two not very spectacular conclusions. First, having learned that 2½ per cent per year compounded doubles every 28 years, we must now devote more attention to the requirements for and problems which need to be faced if this rate of improvement in our standard of living is to be realized.

Second, unlike fiscal policy certainly and monetary policy possibly, our thinking about debt policy is in a most primitive stage relative to its probable importance for the economy in the decade ahead.

PART THREE

MARKETS, THE PRICE SYSTEM, AND THE ALLOCATION OF RESOURCES

A.

THE MARKET SYSTEM

27. The Wonderful World of Adam Smith

Robert Heilbroner

In 1776 Adam Smith described an economic world in which individual self interest, balanced by the competitive self interest of others, brought order out of economic chaos, and directed the society as if by an "invisible hand." Adam Smith's ideas have influenced economists and statesmen for almost two centuries, and still have tremendous appeal.

28. Who Gives Free Enterprise Its Sense of Direction?

Clarence B. Randall

Who gives direction to the marvelously intricate and efficient economic machine that is the American free enterprise system? Mr. Randall argues cogently that businessmen, motivated by financial gain, but tempered with a high sense of social responsibility, perform this function, and perform it well.

29. On the Principle of Consumers' Sovereignty

Tibor Scitovsky

In a competitive world, the economy's production is guided by the "dollar votes" of consumers. Professor Scitovsky argues that in our modern economic society, consumer choices are so complex and influenced so much by advertising that the simple "consumers' sovereignty" principle needs drastic modification.

B.
BUSINESS PRICE-SETTING AND PROFIT GOALS

30. Pricing in Steel and Consumer Appliances

A. D. H. Kaplan, Joel B. Dirlam,
and Robert F. Lanzilotti

Different firms set prices in different ways.
Three economists describe in detail how the
prices of steel and consumer appliances were
established by some leading firms.

31. The Price of Gasoline

Highway Highlights

In most places the retail price of gasoline is
about the same at all service stations. Does this
demonstrate that the retail gasoline business
is highly competitive, or does it suggest collusion? This article gives the industry's point of
view on how prices are set.

32. The Revenue Maximization Hypothesis

William Baumol

Economists traditionally explain that businessmen try to maximize profits. Professor Baumol
believes that although profits are important,
most businesses are more concerned with expanding their total sales.

C.
BIG BUSINESS AND GOVERNMENT POLICY

33. Economic Power and the Free Society

A. A. Berle, Jr.

In a society where giant corporations are commonplace, the question of who controls business enterprise—and for what ends—is paramount. Professor Berle points out that the
separation of ownership from control in the
modern corporation can lead to managerial
power without commensurate responsibility.

34. The Electric Conspiracy Case

Wall Street Journal

Agreements among producers to fix prices and market shares are illegal and inconsistent with the principles of a competitive society. This article discusses the development of an industrial conspiracy in the electrical equipment industry, and provides some insight into the problems and attitudes of the executives who were involved.

35. The Dilemma of Antitrust Aims

Theodore Levitt; reply by Walter Adams

Our antitrust laws are designed to eliminate monopoly and to ensure free competition among business firms. Professor Levitt argues that the competitive race will lead to the survival of large and powerful firms. In a reply, Professor Adams asserts that efficiency and huge size do not always go together in our economy, and that the antitrust laws are probably necessary to protect private rights and the public welfare.

36. The Antimerger Act, 1950–60

M. A. Adelman

In 1950 Congress passed a law prohibiting business mergers which would substantially lessen competition in the relevant market areas. Professor Adelman argues that some court interpretations of this law have in essence protected monopoly positions and impeded moves toward more competition.

D.

THE FARM PROBLEM

37. A Program for Agricultural Adjustment

Committee for Economic Development

Part of the thorny farm problem lies in the very efficiency of American agriculture. We can produce more than the nation will buy at currently supported prices. To alleviate these problems, the Committee for Economic Development proposes a long-range program to move resources—people and land—out of agriculture, while cushioning the short-run impact of the changes on farm families.

38. Statement in Reply to the CED

Orville L. Freeman

> Secretary of Agriculture Freeman argues that the CED proposals (see the previous article) would hurt farmers and would seriously disrupt the rest of the economy. The proposals would also, he argues, threaten the family farm.

A.

THE MARKET SYSTEM

27   THE WONDERFUL WORLD OF ADAM SMITH

Robert L. Heilbroner

Robert L. Heilbroner is a member of the faculty at the New School for Social Research and a well-known free lance writer.

A visitor to England in the 1760's would quite probably have learned of a certain Dr. Smith of the University of Glasgow. Dr. Smith was a well-known, if not a famous, man; Voltaire had heard of him, David Hume was his intimate, students had traveled all the way from Russia to hear his labored but enthusiastic discourse. In addition to his scholastic accomplishments, Dr. Smith was known as a rather remarkable personality. He was, for example, notoriously absent-minded: once he had fallen into a tanning pit walking along in earnest disquisition with a friend, and it was said that he had brewed himself a beverage of bread and butter and pronounced it the worst cup of tea he had ever tasted. But his personal quirks, which were many, did not interfere with his intellectual abilities. Dr. Smith was among the foremost philosophers of his age.

At Glasgow Dr. Smith lectured on problems of Moral Philosophy, a dis-cipline a great deal more broadly conceived in that day than in ours. Moral Philosophy covered Natural Theology, Ethics, Jurisprudence, and Political Economy: it thus ranged all the way from man's sublimest impulses toward order and harmony to his somewhat less orderly and harmonious activities in the grimmer business of gouging out a living for himself.

Natural theology—the search for design in the confusion of the cosmos—has been an object of the human rationalizing impulse from earliest times; our traveler would have felt quite at ease as Dr. Smith expounded the natural laws that underlay the seeming chaos of the universe. But when it came to the other end of the spectrum—the search for a grand architecture beneath the hurly-burly of daily life—our traveler

From *The Worldly Philosophers,* by Robert L. Heilbroner, pp. 28–57; copyright 1953, 1961 by Robert L. Heilbroner. Reprinted by permission of Simon and Schuster, Inc.

might have felt that Dr. Smith was really stretching philosophy beyond its proper limits.

For if the English social scene of the late eighteenth century suggested anything, it was most emphatically not rational order nor moral purpose. As soon as one looked away from the elegant lives of the leisure classes, society presented itself as a brute struggle for existence in its meanest form. Outside the drawing rooms of London or the pleasant rich estates of the counties, all that one saw was rapacity, cruelty, and degradation mingled with the most irrational and bewildering customs and traditions of some still earlier and already anachronistic day. Rather than a carefully engineered machine where each part could be seen to contribute to the whole, the body social resembled one of James Watt's strange steam machines: black, noisy, inefficient, dangerous. How curious that Dr. Smith should have professed to see order, design, and purpose in all of this.

Suppose, for example, our visitor had gone to see the tin mines of Cornwall. There he would have watched miners lower themselves down the black shafts, and on reaching bottom draw a candle from their belts and stretch out for a sleep until the candle guttered. Then for two or three hours they would work the ore until the next traditional break, this time for as long as it took to smoke a pipe. A full half day was spent in lounging, half in picking at the seams. But had our visitor traveled up north and nerved himself against a descent into the pits of Durham or Northumberland, he would have seen something quite different. Here men and women worked together, stripped to the waist, and sometimes reduced from pure fatigue to a whimpering half-human state. The wildest and most brutish customs were practiced; sexual appetites aroused at a glance were gratified down some deserted shaftway; children of seven or ten who never saw daylight during the winter months were used and abused and paid a pittance by the miners to help drag away their tubs of coal; pregnant women drew coal cars like horses and even gave birth in the dark black caverns.

But it was not just in the mines that life appeared colorful, traditional, or ferocious. On the land, too, an observant traveler would have seen sights hardly more suggestive of order, harmony, and design. In many parts of the country bands of agricultural poor roamed in search of work. From the Welsh highlands, Companies of Ancient Britons (as they styled themselves) would come trooping down at harvest time; sometimes they had one horse, unsaddled and unbridled, for the entire company; sometimes they all simply walked. Not infrequently there would be only one of the lot who spoke English and so could serve as intermediary between the band and the gentlemen-farmers whose lands they asked permission to aid in harvesting. It is not surprising that wages were as low as sixpence a day.

And finally, had our visitor stopped at a manufacturing town, he would have seen still other remarkable sights —but again, not such as to betoken order to the uneducated eye. He might have marveled at the factory built by the brothers Lombe in 1742. It was a huge building (for those days), five hundred feet long and six stories high, and inside were machines described by Daniel Defoe as consisting of "26,586 Wheels and 97,746 Movements, which work 73,726 Yards of Silk-Thread every time the Water-Wheel goes round, which is three times in one minute." Equally worthy of note were the children who tended the machines round the clock for twelve or fourteen hours at a turn, cooked their meals on the grimly black boilers, and were boarded in shifts in barracks where, it was said, the beds were always warm.

A strange, cruel, haphazard world this must have appeared to eighteenth-century as well as to our modern eyes. All the more remarkable, then, to find that it could be reconciled with a scheme of Moral Philosophy envisioned by Dr. Smith, and that that learned man actually claimed to fathom within it the clear-cut outlines of great purposeful laws fitting an overarching and meaningful whole.

What sort of man was this urbane philosopher?

"I am a beau in nothing but my books," was the way Adam Smith once described himself, proudly showing off his treasured library to a friend. He was certainly not a handsome man. A medallion profile shows us a protruding lower lip thrust up to meet a large aquiline nose and heavy bulging eyes looking out from heavy lids. All his life Smith was troubled with a nervous affliction; his head shook, and he had an odd and stumbling manner of speech.

In addition, there was his notorious absent-mindedness. In the 1780's when Smith was in his late fifties, the inhabitants of Edinburgh were regularly treated to the amusing spectacle of their most illustrious citizen, attired in a light-colored coat, knee breeches, white silk stockings, buckle shoes, flat broad-brimmed beaver hat, and cane, walking down the cobbled streets with his eyes fixed on infinity and his lips moving in silent discourse. Every pace or two he would hesitate as if to change his direction or even reverse it; his gait was described by a friend as "vermicular."

Accounts of his absence of mind were common. On one occasion he de-

scended into his garden clad only in a dressing gown and, falling into a reverie, walked fifteen miles before coming to. Another time while walking with an eminent friend in Edinburgh, a guard presented his pike in salute. Smith, who had been thus honored on countless occasions, was suddenly hypnotized by the saluting soldier. He returned the honor with his cane and then further astonished his guest by following exactly in the guard's footsteps, duplicating with his cane every motion of the pike. When the spell was broken, Smith was standing at the head of a long flight of steps, cane held at the ready. Having no idea that he had done anything out of the ordinary, he grounded his stick and took up his conversation where he had left off.

This absent-minded professor was born in 1723 in the town of Kirkcaldy, County Fife, Scotland. Kirkcaldy boasted a population of fifteen hundred; at the time of Smith's birth, nails were still used as money by some of the local townspeople. When he was four years old, a most curious incident took place. Smith was kidnaped by a band of passing gypsies. Through the efforts of his uncle (his father had died before his birth), the gypsies were traced and pursued, and in their flight they abandoned young Adam by the roadside. "He would have made, I fear, a poor gypsy," says one of his biographers.

From his earliest days, Smith was an apt pupil, although even as a child given to fits of abstraction. He was obviously destined for teaching and so at seventeen he went to Oxford on a scholarship—making the journey on horseback—and there he remained for six years. But Oxford was not then the citadel of learning which it later became. Most of the public professors had long ago given up even a pretense of teaching. A foreign traveler recounts his astonishment over a public debate there in 1788. All four participants passed the allotted time in profound silence, each absorbed in reading a popular novel of the day. Since instruction was the exception rather than the rule, Smith spent the years largely untutored and untaught, reading as he saw fit. In fact he was once nearly expelled from the university because a copy of David Hume's *A Treatise of Human Nature* was found in his rooms —Hume was no fit reading matter, even for a would-be philosopher.

In 1751—he was then twenty-eight —Smith was offered the Chair of Logic at the University of Glasgow, and shortly thereafter he was given the Chair of Moral Philosophy. Unlike Oxford, Glasgow was a serious center of study, and boasted a galaxy of talent. But it still differed considerably from the modern conception of a university. The prim professional group did not entirely appreciate a certain levity and enthusiasm in Smith's manner. He was accused of sometimes smiling during religious services (no doubt during a reverie), of being a firm friend of that outrageous Hume, of not holding Sunday classes on Christian Evidences, of petitioning the Senatus Academicus for permission to dispense with prayers on the opening of class, and of delivering prayers that smacked of a certain "natural religion." Perhaps this all fits into better perspective if we remember that Smith's own teacher, Hutcheson, broke new ground at Glasgow by refusing to lecture to his students in Latin!

But for all the inevitable academic rivalry, Smith was happy at Glasgow. In the evenings he played whist—his absent-mindedness made him a somewhat undependable player—attended learned societies, and lived a quiet and sheltered life. He was beloved of his students, noted as a lecturer—even Boswell came to hear him—and his odd gait and manner of speech gained the homage of imitation. Little busts of himself even appeared in booksellers' windows.

It was not merely his eccentric personality that gave him prestige. In 1759 he published a book which made an immediate sensation. It was entitled *The Theory of Moral Sentiments,* and it catapulted Smith immediately into the forefront of English philosophers. The *Theory* was an inquiry into the origin of moral approbation and disapproval. How does it happen that man, who is a creature of self-interest, can form moral judgments in which self-interest seems to be held in abeyance or transmuted to a higher plane? Smith held that the answer lay in our ability to put ourselves in the position of a third person, an impartial observer, and in this way to form a sympathetic notion of the moral (as opposed to the selfish) merits of a case.

The book and its problems attracted immediate interest. In Germany *das Adam Smith Problem* became a favorite subject for debate. More importantly, from our point of view, the treatise met with the favor of a brillant and intriguing man named Charles Townshend.

Townshend is one of those wonderful figures with which the eighteenth century seems to abound. A witty and even learned man, Townshend was, in the words of Horace Walpole, "a man endowed with every great talent, who must have been the greatest man of his age, if only he had common sincerity, common steadiness, and common sense." Townshend's fickleness was notorious; a quip of the times put it that Mr. Townshend was ill of a pain in his side, but declined to specify which side. As evidence of his lack of common sense, it was Townshend, as Chancellor of the Exchequer, who helped precipitate the American Revolution, first by refusing the colonists the right to elect their own judges and then by imposing a heavy duty on American tea.

But his political shortsightedness notwithstanding, Townshend was a sincere student of philosophy and politics, and as such a devotee of Adam Smith. What is more important, he was in a position to make him an unusual offer. In 1754 Townshend had made a brilliant and lucrative marriage to the Countess of Dalkeith, the widow of the Duke of Buccleuch, and he now found himself casting about for a tutor for his wife's son. Education for a young man of the upper classes consisted largely of the Grand Tour, a stay in Europe where one might acquire that polished finish so highly praised by Lord Chesterfield. Dr. Adam Smith would be an ideal companion for the young duke, thought Townshend, and accordingly he offered him three hundred pounds a year plus expenses and a pension of three hundred pounds a year for life. It was too good an offer to be declined. At best Smith never realized more than one hundred seventy pounds from the fees which, in those days, professors collected directly from their students. It is pleasant to note that his pupils refused to accept a refund from Dr. Smith when he left, saying that they had already been more than recompensed.

The tutor and His young Grace left for France in 1764. For eighteen months they stayed in Toulouse where a combination of abominably boring company and Smith's execrable French made his sedate life at Glasgow look like dissipation. Then they moved on to the south of France (where he met and worshiped Voltaire and repulsed the attentions of an amorous marquise), thence to Geneva, and finally to Paris. To relieve the tedium of the provinces, Smith began work on a treatise of political economy, a subject on which he had lectured at Glasgow, debated many evenings at the Select Society in Edinburgh, and discussed at length with his beloved friend David Hume. The book was to be the *Wealth of Nations,* but it would be twelve years before it was finished.

Paris was better going. By this time Smith's French, although dreadful, was good enough to enable him to talk at length with the foremost economic thinker in France. This was a M. Quesnay, a physician in the court of Louis XV and personal doctor to Mme. Pompadour. Quesnay had propounded a school of economics known as Physiocracy and devised a chart of the economy called a *tableau économique.* The *tableau* was truly a physician's insight: in contradistinction to the ideas of the day which still held that wealth was the solid stuff of gold and silver, Quesnay insisted that wealth sprang from production and that it flowed through the nation, from hand to hand, replenishing the body social like the circulation of blood. The *tableau* made a vast impression—Mirabeau the elder characterized it as an invention deserving of equal rank with writing and money. But the trouble with Physiocracy was that it insisted that only the agricultural classes produced true "wealth" and that the manufacturing and commercial classes merely manipulated it in a sterile way. Hence Quesnay's system had but limited usefulness for practical policy. True, it advocated a policy of *laissez faire*—a radical departure for the times. But in denigrating the industrial side of life it flew against the sense of history, for the whole development of capitalism unmistakably pointed to the emergence of the industrial classes to a position of superiority over the landed classes.

This was not a congenial philosophy to Adam Smith. The notion of the circulation of wealth he gladly accepted and acknowledged, but the idea that industry was somehow sterile and barren struck him as a peculiar construction of the world. After all, had he not grown up in Kirkcaldy and Glasgow where one could see wealth being created at every hand in the workshops and factories of craftsmen? But despite his rejection of the agricultural orientation of the Physiocrat cult (M. Quesnay's followers, like Mirabeau, were nothing if not adulatory), Smith had a profound personal admiration for the French doctor. Had it not been for Quesnay's death, the *Wealth of Nations* would have been dedicated to him.

In 1766 the tour was brought to an abrupt halt when the duke's younger brother, who had joined them, was murdered in the streets of Paris. His Grace returned to his estates at Dalkeith, and Smith went first to London, and then to Kirkcaldy. Despite Hume's entreaties, there he stayed, for the better part of the next ten years, while the great treatise took shape. Most of it he dictated, standing against his fireplace and nervously rubbing his head against the wall until his pomade had made a dark streak on the paneling. Occasionally he would visit his former charge on his estates at Dalkeith, and once in a while he would go to London to discuss his ideas with the literati of the day. One of them was Dr. Samuel Johnson, to whose select club Smith belonged, although he and the venerable lexicographer had hardly met under the most amiable of circumstances. Sir Walter Scott tells us that Johnson, on first seeing Smith, attacked him for some statement he had made. Smith vindicated the truth of his contention. "What did Johnson say?" was the universal inquiry. "Why, he said," said Smith, with the deepest impression of resentment, "he said, 'You lie!' " "And

what did you reply?" "I said, 'You are a son of a —!' " On such terms, says Scott, did these two great moralists first meet and part and such was the classical dialogue between two great teachers of philosophy.

Smith met as well a charming and intelligent American, one Benjamin Franklin, who provided him with a wealth of facts about the American colonies and a deep appreciation of the role which they might someday play. It is undoubtedly due to Franklin's influence that Smith subsequently wrote of the colonies that they constituted a nation "which, indeed, seems very likely to become one of the greatest and most formidable that ever was in the world."

In 1776, *Wealth of Nations* was published. Two years later Smith was appointed Commissioner of Customs for Edinburgh, a sinecure worth six hundred pounds a year. With his mother, who lived until she was ninety, Smith lived out his bachelor's life in peace and quiet; serene, content, and absent-minded to the end.

And the book?

It has been called "the outpouring not only of a great mind, but of a whole epoch." Yet it is not, in the strict sense of the word, an "original" book. There is a long line of observers before Smith who have approached his understanding of the world: Locke, Stewart, Law, Mandeville, Petty, Cantillon, not to mention Quesnay and Hume again. Smith took from all of them: there are over a hundred authors mentioned by name in his treatise. But where others had fished here and there, Smith spread his net wide; where others had clarified this and that issue, Smith illuminated the entire landscape. The *Wealth of Nations* may not be an original book, but it is unqestionably a masterpiece.

It is, first of all, a huge panorama.

It opens with a famous passage describing the minute specialization of labor in the manufacture of pins, and covers, before it is done, such a variety of subjects as "the late disturbances in the American colonies" (evidently Smith thought the Revolutionary War would be over by the time his book reached the press), the wastefulness of the student's life at Oxford, and the statistics on the herring catch since 1771.

A glance at the index compiled for a later edition by Cannan shows the range of Smith's references and thoughts. Here are a dozen entries from the letter A:

Abassides, opulence of Saracen empire under
Abraham, weighed shekels
Abyssinia, salt money
Actors, public, paid for the contempt attending their profession
Africa, powerful king much worse off than European peasant
Alehouses, the number of, not the efficient cause of drunkenness
Ambassadors, the first motive of their appointment
America [a solid page of references follows]
Apprenticeship, the nature . . . of this bond servitude explained
Arabs, their manner of supporting war
Army, . . . no security to the sovereign against a disaffected clergy

In fine print the index goes on for sixty-three pages: before it ends it has touched on everything: "Riches, the chief enjoyment of, consists in the parade of; Poverty, sometimes urges nation to inhuman customs; Stomach, desire for food bounded by narrow capacity of the; Butcher, brutal and odious business." When we have finished the nine hundred pages of the book we have a living picture of England in the 1770's, of apprentices and journeymen and rising capitalists, of landlords and clergymen and kings, of factories and farms and foreign trade.

The book is heavy going. It moves with all the deliberation of an encyclopedic mind, but not with the precision of an orderly one. This was an age when authors did not stop to qualify their ideas with ifs, ands, and buts, and it was an era when it was quite possible for a man of Smith's intellectual stature virtually to embrace the great body of knowledge of his times. Hence the book ducks nothing, minimizes nothing, fears nothing. What an exasperating book! Again and again it refuses to wrap up in a concise sentence a conclusion it has laboriously arrived at over fifty pages. The argument is so full of detail and observation that one constantly has to chip away the ornamentation to find the steel structure which holds it together underneath. Coming to silver, Smith detours for seventy-five pages to write a "diversion" on it; coming to religion, he wanders off in a chapter on the sociology of morality. But for all its weightiness, the text is shot through with insights, observation, and well-turned phrases that imbue this great lecture with life. It was Smith who first called England "a nation of shopkeepers"; it was Smith who wrote, "By nature a philosopher is not in genius and disposition half so different from a street porter, as a mastiff is from a greyhound." And of the East India Company, which was then ravaging the East, he wrote: "It is a very singular government in which every member of the administration wishes to get out of the country . . . as soon as he can, and to whose interest, the day after he has left it and carried his whole fortune with him, it is perfectly indifferent though the whole country was swallowed up by an earthquake."

The *Wealth of Nations* is in no sense a textbook. Adam Smith is writing to his age, not to his classroom; he is expounding a doctrine which is meant to be of importance in running an empire, not an abstract treatise for scholastic distribution. The dragons which he slays (such as the Mercantile System, which takes over two hundred pages to die) were alive and panting, if a little tired, in his day.

And finally, the book is a revolutionary one. To be sure, Smith would hardly have countenanced an upheaval which disordered the gentlemanly classes and enthroned the common poor. But the import of the *Wealth of Nations* is revolutionary, nonetheless. Smith is not, as is commonly supposed, an apologist for the up-and-coming bourgeois; as we shall see, he is an admirer of their work but suspicious of their motives, and mindful of the needs of the great laboring mass. But it is not his aim to espouse the interests of any class. He is concerned with promoting the wealth of the entire nation. And wealth, to Adam Smith, consists of the goods which *all* the people of society consume; note *all*—this is a democratic, and hence radical, philosophy of wealth. Gone is the notion of gold, treasures, kingly hoards; gone the prerogatives of merchants or farmers or working guilds. We are in the modern world where the flow of goods and services consumed by everyone constitutes the ultimate aim and end of economic life.

And now, what of the lessons of the text?

Two great problems absorb Adam Smith's attention. First, he is interested in laying bare the mechanism by which society hangs together. How is it possible for a community in which everyone is busily following his self-interest not to fly apart from sheer centrifugal force? What is it which guides each individual's private business so that it conforms to the needs of the group?

With no central planning authority and no steadying influence of age-old tradition, how does society manage to get those tasks done which are necessary for survival?

These questions lead Smith to a formulation of the laws of the market. What he sought was "the invisible hand," as he called it, whereby "the private interests and passions of men" are led in the direction "which is most agreeable to the interest of the whole society."

But the laws of the market will be only a part of Smith's inquiry. There is another question which interests him: whither society? The laws of the market are like the laws which explain how a spinning top stays upright; but there is also the question of whether the top, by virtue of its spinning, will be moved along the table.

To Smith and the great economists who followed him, society is not conceived as a static achievement of mankind which will go on reproducing itself, unchanged and unchanging, from one generation to the next. On the contrary, society is seen as an organism which has its own life history. To discover the shape of things to come, to isolate the forces which impel society along its path—this is the grand objective of economic science.

But until we have followed Smith's unraveling of the laws of the market, we cannot rush to this larger and more fascinating problem. For the laws of the market themselves will be an integral part of the larger laws which cause society to prosper or decay. The mechanism by which the heedless individual is kept in line with everybody else will affect the mechanism by which society itself changes over the years.

Hence we begin with a look at the market mechanism. It is not the stuff that excites the imagination or stirs the pulse. Yet, for all its dryness, it has an immediacy which should lead us to consider it with a respectful eye. Not only are the laws of the market essential to an understanding of the world of Adam Smith, but these same laws will underlie the very different world of Karl Marx, and the still different world in which we live today. Since we are all, knowingly or otherwise, under their sovereignty, it behooves us to scrutinize them rather carefully.

Adam Smith's laws of the market are basically simple. They tell us that the outcome of a certain kind of behavior in a certain social framework will bring about perfectly definite and foreseeable results. Specifically they show us how the drive of individual self-interest in an environment of similarly motivated individuals will result in competition; and they further demonstrate how competition will result in the provision of those goods that society wants, in the quantities that society desires, and at the prices society is prepared to pay. Let us see how this comes about.

It comes about in the first place because self-interest acts as a driving power to guide men to whatever work society is willing to pay for. "It is not from the benevolence of the butcher, the brewer, or the baker that we expect our dinner," says Smith, "but from their regard to their self-interest. We address ourselves, not to their humanity, but to their self-love, and never talk to them of our necessities, but of their advantages."

But self-interest is only half the picture. It drives men to action. Something else must prevent the pushing of profit-hungry individuals from holding society up to exorbitant ransom: a community activated only by self-interest would be a community of ruthless profiteers. This regulator is competition, the socially beneficial consequence of the conflicting self-interests of all the members of society. For each man, out to do his

best for himself with no thought of social cost, is faced with a flock of similarly motivated individuals who are in exactly the same boat. Each is only too eager to take advantage of his neighbor's greed if it urges him to exceed a common denominator of acceptable behavior. A man who permits his self-interest to run away with him will find that competitors have slipped in to take his trade away; if he charges too much for his wares or if he refuses to pay as much as everybody else for his workers, he will find himself without buyers in the one case and without employees in the other. Thus very much as in the *Theory of Moral Sentiments,* the selfish motives of men are transmuted by interaction to yield the most unexpected of results: social harmony.

Consider, for example, the problem of high prices. Suppose we have one hundred manufacturers of gloves. The self-interest of each one will cause him to wish to raise his price above his cost of production and thereby to realize an extra profit. But he cannot. If he raises his price, his competitors will step in and take his market away from him by underselling him. Only if all glove manufacturers combine and agree to maintain a solid front will an unduly high price be charged. And in this case, the collusive coalition could be broken by an enterprising manufacturer from another field—say, shoemaking—who decided to move his capital into glove manufacture where he could steal away the market by shading his prices.

But the laws of the market not only impose a competitive price on products. They also see to it that the producers of society heed society's demands for the *quantities* of goods it wants. Let us suppose that consumers decide they want more gloves than are being turned out, and fewer shoes. Accordingly the public will scramble for the stock of gloves on the market, and the shoe business will be dull. As a result glove prices will tend to rise as consumers try to buy more of them than there are ready at hand, and shoe prices will tend to fall as the public passes the shoe stores by. But as glove prices rise, profits in the glove industry will rise, too; and as shoe prices fall, profits in shoe manufacturing will slump. Again self-interest will step in to right the balance. Workers will be released from the shoe business as shoe factories contract their output; they will move to the glove business where business is booming. The result is quite obvious: glove production will rise and shoe production fall.

And this is exactly what society wanted in the first place. As more gloves come on the market to meet demand, glove prices will fall back into line. As fewer shoes are produced, the surplus of shoes will soon disappear and shoe prices will again rise up to normal. Through the mechanism of the market, society will have changed the allocation of its elements of production to fit its new desires. Yet no one has issued a dictum, and no planning authority has established schedules of output. Self-interest and competition, acting one against the other, have accomplished the transition.

And one final accomplishment. Just as the market regulates both prices and quantities of *goods* according to the final arbiter of public demand, so it also regulates the *incomes* of those who cooperate to produce those goods. If profits in one line of business are unduly large, there will be a rush of other businessmen into that field until competition has lowered surpluses. If wages are out of line in one kind of work, there will be a rush of men into the favored occupation until it pays no more than comparable jobs of that de-

gree of skill and training. Conversely, if profits or wages are too low in one trade area, there will be an exodus of capital and labor until the supply is better adjusted to the demand.

All this may seem somewhat elementary. But consider what Adam Smith has done, with his impetus of self-interest and his regulator of competition. First, he has explained how prices are kept from ranging arbitrarily away from the actual cost of producing a good. Second, he has explained how society can induce its producers of commodities to provide it with what it wants. Third, he has pointed out why high prices are a self-curing disease, for they cause production in those lines to increase. And finally, he has accounted for a basic similarity of incomes at each level of the great producing strata of the nation. In a word, he has found in the mechanism of the market a self-regulating system for society's orderly provisioning.

Note "self-regulating." The beautiful consequence of the market is that it is its own guardian. If output or prices or certain kinds of remuneration stray away from their socially ordained levels, forces are set into motion to bring them back to the fold. It is a curious paradox which thus ensues: the market, which is the acme of individual economic freedom, is the strictest taskmaster of all. One may appeal the ruling of a planning board or win the dispensation of a minister; but there is no appeal, no dispensation, from the anonymous pressures of the market mechanism. Economic freedom is thus more illusory than at first appears. One can do as one pleases in the market. But if one pleases to do what the market disapproves, the price of individual freedom is economic ruination.

Does the world really work this way? To a very real degree it did in the days of Adam Smith. Even in his time, of course, there were already factors which acted as restraints against the free operation of the market system. There were combinations of manufacturers who rigged prices artificially high and associations of journeymen who resisted the pressures of competition when it acted to lower their wages. And already there were more disquieting signs to be read. The Lombe brothers' factory was more than a mere marvel of engineering and a source of wonderment to the visitor: it betokened the coming of large-scale industry and the emergence of employers who were immensely powerful individual actors in the market. The children in the cotton mills could surely not be considered market factors of equal power with the employers who bedded, boarded, and exploited them. But for all its ominous portents, eighteenth-century England approached, even if it did not wholly conform to, the model which Adam Smith had in mind. Business *was* competitive, the average factory *was* small, prices *did* rise and fall as demand ebbed and rose, and prices *did* invoke changes in output and occupation. The world of Adam Smith has been called a world of atomistic competition; a world in which no part of the productive mechanism, laborer or capitalist, was large enough to interfere with or to resist the pressures of competition. It was a world in which each agent was forced to scurry after his self-interest in a vast social free-for-all.

And today? Does the competitive market mechanism still operate?

This is not a question to which it is possible to give a simple answer. The nature of the market has changed vastly since the eighteenth century. We no longer live in a world of atomistic competition in which no man can afford to swim against the current. Today's market mechanism is characterized by the huge size of its participants: giant corporations and equally giant labor unions obviously do not behave as if they were individual proprietors and workers. Their very bulk enables them to stand out against the pressures of competition, to disregard price signals, and to consider what their self-interest shall be in the long run rather than in the immediate press of each day's buying and selling.

Then, in addition, the growth of government intervention has altered the scope of the market mechanism. Like a medieval lord, the government does not recognize its master in the market; more often than not it *sets* the market rather than abiding by it. That all these factors have weakened the primary guiding function of the market is apparent: later we will be concerned with what contemporary economists have to say about this problem. But it would seem, nonetheless, that for all the new quality of twentieth-century industrial society, the great principles of self-interest and competition, however watered down or hedged about, still provide basic rules of behavior which no economic participant can afford to disregard entirely. It is not the neat world of Adam Smith in which we live, but the laws of the market can still be discerned in it if we look beneath the surface.

But the laws of the market are only a description of the behavior which gives society its cohesiveness. Something else must make it go. Ninety years after the *Wealth of Nations,* Karl Marx was to make the portentous announcement that he had unearthed "laws of motion" which described how capitalism proceeded slowly, unwillingly, but ineluctably to its doom. But the *Wealth of Nations* already had its own laws of motion. However, quite unlike the Marxist prognosis, Adam Smith's world went slowly, quite willingly, and more or less inevitably to Valhalla.

Valhalla would have been the last destination that most observers would have predicted. Sir John Byng, touring the North Country in 1792, looked from his coach window and wrote: "Why, here now, is a great flaring mill . . . all the Vale is disturb'd. . . . Sir Richard Arkwright may have introduced Much Wealth into his Family and into his Country, but, as a Tourist, I execrate his Schemes, which having crept into every Pastoral Vale, have destroyed the course, and the Beauty of Nature." "Oh! What a dog's hole is Manchester," said Sir John on arriving there.

In truth, much of England was a dog's hole. The three centuries of turmoil which had prodded land, labor, and capital into existence seemed to have been only a preparation for still further upheaval, for the recently freed agents of production began to be combined in a new and ugly form: the factory. And with the factory came new problems. Twenty years before Sir John's tour, Richard Arkwright, who had gotten together a little capital peddling women's hair to make wigs, invented (or stole) the spinning throstle. But having constructed his machine, he found it was not so easy to staff it. Local labor could not keep up with the "regular celerity" of the process— wagework was still generally despised and many a capitalist found his new-built factory burned to the ground out of sheer blind malice. Arkwright was forced to turn to children—"their small fingers being active." Furthermore, since they were unused to the independent life of farming or crafts, children adapted themselves more readily to the discipline of factory life. The move

was hailed as a philanthropic gesture— would not the employment of children help to alleviate the condition of the "unprofitable poor"?

For if any problem absorbed the public mind, besides its mixed admiration of and horror at the factory, it was this omnipresent problem of the unprofitable poor. In 1720 England was crowded with a million and a half of them—a staggering figure when we realize that her total population was only twelve or thirteen million. Hence the air was full of schemes for their disposition. Despairing schemes, mostly. For the common complaint was the ineradicable sloth of the pauper, and this was mixed with consternation at the way in which the lower orders aped their betters. Workpeople were actually drinking tea! The common folk seemed to prefer wheaten bread to their traditional loaf of rye or barley! Where would all this lead to, asked the thinkers of the day; were not the wants of the poor ("which it would be prudence to relieve, but folly to cure," as a contemporary pamphlet expressed it) essential for the welfare of the state? What would happen to Society if the indispensable gradations of society were allowed to disappear?

But if consternation described the prevalent attitude of the day toward the great amorphous mass of working England, it certainly did not describe Adam Smith's philosophy. "No society can surely be flourishing and happy, of which by far the greater part of the numbers are poor and miserable," he said. And not only did he have the temerity to make so radical a statement, but he proceeded to demonstrate that society was in fact constantly improving; that it was being propelled, willy-nilly, toward a positive goal. It was not moving because anyone willed it to, or because Parliament might pass laws, or England win a battle. It moved because there was a concealed dynamic beneath the surface of things which powered the social whole like an enormous engine.

For one salient fact struck Adam Smith as he looked at the English scene. This was the tremendous gain in productivity which sprang from the minute division and specialization of labor. Going into a pin factory, this is what Smith saw: "One man draws out the wire, another straights it, a third cuts it, a fourth points it, a fifth grinds it at the top for receiving the head; to make the head requires two or three distinct operations; to put it on is a peculiar business; to whiten it is another; it is even a trade by itself to put them into paper. . . . I have seen a small manufactory of this kind where ten men only were employed and where some of them consequently performed two or three distinct operations. But though they were very poor, and therefore but indifferently accommodated with the necessary machinery, they could, when they exerted themselves, make among them about twelve pounds of pins in a day. There are in a pound upwards of four thousand pins of a middling size. Those ten persons, therefore, could make among them upwards of forty-eight thousand pins in a day. . . . But if they had all wrought separately and independently . . . they certainly could not each of them make twenty, perhaps not one pin in a day. . . ."

There is hardly any need to point out how infinitely more complex present-day production methods are from those of the eighteenth century. Smith, for all his disclaimers, was sufficiently impressed with a small factory of ten people to comment on it; what would he have thought of one employing ten thousand! But the great gift of the division of labor is not its com-

plexity—indeed it simplifies most toil. Its advantage lies in its capacity to increase what Smith calls "that universal opulence which extends itself to the lowest ranks of the people." That universal opulence of the eighteenth century looks like a grim existence from our modern vantage point. But if we view the matter in its historical perspective, if we compare the lot of the workingman in eighteenth-century England to his predecessor a century or two before, it is clear that mean as his existence was, it constituted a considerable advance. Smith makes the point vividly:

Observe the accommodation of the most common artificer or day labourer in a civilized and thriving country, and you will perceive that the number of people of whose industry a part, though but a small part, has been employed in procuring him this accommodation, exceeds all computation. The woolen coat, for example, which covers the day-labourer, as coarse and rough as it may seem, is the produce of the joint labour of a great multitude of workmen. The shepherd, the sorter of the wool, the wool-comber or carder, the dyer, the scribbler, the spinner, the weaver, the fuller, the dresser, with many others, must all join their different arts in order to complete even this homely production. How many merchants and carriers, besides, must have been employed . . . how much commerce and navigation . . . how many ship-builders, sailors, sail-makers, rope makers . . .

Were we to examine, in the same manner, all the different parts of his dress and household furniture, the coarse linen shirt which he wears next to his skin, the shoes which cover his feet, the bed which he lies on . . . the kitchen-grate at which he prepares his victuals, the coals which he makes use of for that purpose, dug from the bowels of the earth, and brought to him perhaps by a long sea and a long land carriage, all the other utensils of his kitchen, all the furniture of his table, the knives and forks, the earthen or pewter plates upon which he serves up and divides his victuals, the different hands employed in preparing his bread and his beer, the glass window which lets in the heat and the light, and keeps out the wind and the rain, with all the knowledge and art requisite for preparing that beautiful and happy invention . . . ; if we examine, I say, all those things . . . we shall be sensible that without the assistance and cooperation of many thousands, the very meanest person in a civilized country could not be provided, even according to what we very falsely imagine, the easy and simple manner in which he is commonly accommodated. Compared indeed with the more extravagant luxury of the great, his accommodation must no doubt appear extremely simple and easy; and yet it may be true, perhaps, that the accommodation of a European prince does not always so much exceed that of an industrious and frugal peasant, as the accommodation of the latter exceeds that of many an African king, the absolute master of the lives and liberties of ten thousand naked savages.

What is it that drives society to this wonderful multiplication of wealth and riches? Partly it is the market mechanism itself, for the market harnesses man's creative powers in a milieu which encourages him, even forces him, to invent, innovate, expand, take risks. But there are more fundamental pressures behind the restless activity of the market. In fact, Smith sees deep-seated laws of evolution which propel the market system in an ascending spiral of productivity.

The first of these is the Law of Accumulation.

Let us remember that Adam Smith lived at a time when the rising industrial capitalist could and did realize a fortune from his investments. Richard Arkwright, apprenticed to a barber as a young man, died in 1792 leaving an estate of £500,000. Samuel Walker, who started a forge going in an old nailshop in Rotherham, left a steel foundry on that site worth £200,000. Josiah Wedgwood, who stumped about his pottery factory on a wooden leg scrawling "This won't do for Jos. Wedgwood" wherever he saw evidence of careless work, left an estate of £240,000 and much landed property. The Industrial Revolution in its early stages provided a veritable grab bag of riches for whoever was quick enough, shrewd enough, industrious enough to ride with its current.

And the object of the great majority of the rising capitalists was first, last, and always, to accumulate their savings. At the beginning of the nineteenth century, £2,500 was collected in Manchester for the foundation of Sunday schools. The sum total contributed to this worthy cause by the single largest employers in the district, the cotton spinners, was £90. The young industrial aristocracy had better things to do with its money than contribute to unproductive charities—it had to accumulate, and Adam Smith approved wholeheartedly. Woe to him who did not accumulate. And as for one who encroached on his capital—"like him who perverts the revenues of some pious foundation to profane purposes, he pays the wages of idleness with those funds which the frugality of his forefathers had, as it were, consecrated to the maintenance of industry."

But Adam Smith did not approve of accumulation for accumulation's sake. He was, after all, a philosopher, with a philosopher's disdain for the vanity of riches. Rather, in the accumulation of capital Smith saw a vast benefit to society. For capital—if put to use in machinery—provided just that wonderful division of labor which multiplies man's productive energy. Hence accumulation becomes another of Smith's two-edged swords: the avarice of private greed again redounding to the welfare of the community. Smith is not worried over the problem which will face twentieth-century economists: will private accumulations actually find their way back into more employment? For him the world is capable of indefinite improvement and the size of the market is limited only by its geographical extent. Accumulate and the world will benefit, says Smith. And certainly in the lusty atmosphere of his time there was no evidence of any unwillingness to accumulate on the part of those who were in a position to do so.

But—and here is a difficulty—accumulation would soon lead to a situation where further accumulation would be impossible. For accumulation meant more machinery and more machinery meant more demand for workmen. And this in turn would sooner or later lead to higher and higher wages, until profits —the source of accumulation—were eaten away. How is this hurdle surmounted?

It is surmounted by the second great law of the system: the Law of Population.

To Adam Smith, laborers, like any other commodity, could be produced according to the demand. If wages were high, the number of workpeople would multiply; if wages fell, the numbers of the working class would decrease.

Nor is this quite so naïve a conception as it appears at first blush. In Smith's day infant mortality among the lower classes was shockingly high. "It is not uncommon," says Smith, ". . . in the Highlands of Scotland for a mother who has borne twenty children not to have two alive." In many places in England, half the children died before they were four, and almost everywhere half the children only lived to the age of nine or ten. Malnutrition, evil living conditions, cold, and disease took a horrendous toll among the poorer element. Hence al-

though higher wages may have affected the birth rate only slightly, it could be expected to have a considerable influence on the number of children who would grow to working age.

Hence if the first effect of accumulation would be to raise the wages of the working class, this in turn would bring about an increase in the number of workers. And now the market mechanism takes over. Just as higher prices on the market will bring about a larger production of gloves and the larger number of gloves in turn press down the higher prices of gloves, so higher wages will bring about a larger number of workers, and the increase in their numbers will set up a reverse pressure on the level of their wages. Population, like glove production, is a self-curing disease—as far as wages are concerned.

And this meant that accumulation might go safely on. The rise in wages which it caused and which threatened to make further accumulation unprofitable is tempered by the rise in population. Accumulation leads to its own undoing, and then is rescued in the nick of time. The obstacle of higher wages is undone by the growth in population which those very higher wages made feasible. There is something fascinating in this automatic process of aggravation and cure, stimulus and response, in which the very factor which seems to be leading the system to its doom is also slyly bringing about the conditions necessary for its further health.

And now observe that Smith has constructed for society a giant endless chain. As regularly and as inevitably as a series of interlocked mathematical propositions, society is started on an upward march. From any starting point the probing mechanism of the market first equalizes the returns to labor and capital in all its different uses, sees to it that those commodities demanded are produced in the right quantities, and further ensures that prices for commodities are constantly competed down to their costs of production. But further than this, society is dynamic. From its starting point accumulation of wealth will take place, and this accumulation will result in increased facilities for production and in a greater division of labor. So far, all to the good. But accumulation will also raise wages as capitalists bid for workers to man the new factories. As wages rise further accumulation begins to look unprofitable. The system threatens to level off. But meanwhile workmen will have used their higher wages to rear their children with fewer mortalities. Hence the supply of workmen will increase. As population swells, the competition between workmen will press down on wages again. And so accumulation will continue, and another spiral in the ascent of society will begin.

This is no business cycle which Smith describes. It is a long-term process, a secular evolution. And it is wonderfully certain. Provided only that the market mechanism is not tampered with, everything is inexorably determined by the preceding link. A vast reciprocating machinery is set up with all of society inside it: only the tastes of the public —to guide producers—and the actual physical geography of the nation are outside the chain of cause and effect.

And observe, furthermore, that what is foreseen is a constantly improving state of affairs. True, the rise in the working population will always force wages back toward a subsistence level. But *toward* is not *to;* as long as the accumulation process continues—and Smith sees no reason why it should cease—there is a virtually endless opportunity for society to improve its lot. Smith did not imply that this was the best of all possible worlds: he had read Voltaire's *Candide* and was no Dr.

Pangloss himself. But there was no reason why the world should not *move* in the direction of improvement and progress. Indeed, if one left the market mechanism alone and allowed it and the great social laws to work themselves out, it was inevitable that progress would result.

In the very long run, well beyond the horizon, one could just discern the final destination for society. By then the "natural" level of wages would have risen considerably (for Smith assumed that basic subsistence wages were a sociological phenomenon rather than a brute animal fact). The landlord would also have fared well, for population would be large and pressing on what was, after all, a God-given and fixed supply of land. The capitalist alone would have suffered a difficult fate; since riches would have multiplied almost beyond calculation, the capitalist would realize the wages of management, but precious little profit beyond that: he would be a hard-working, well-remunerated, but certainly not luxuriously rich person. A strange paradise of hard work, much real wealth, and little leisure this would be.

But the road to society's eventual resting place was long and there was too much to be done between the world of Adam Smith and that final campground to warrant spending much time on its detail. The *Wealth of Nations* is a program for action, not a blueprint for Utopia.

Oddly enough, the book did not immediately take hold. It was actually ridiculed by Charles James Fox, the most powerful man in Parliament, and it was to be eight years until the book was quoted in Commons. Then when recognition came—as it did—it was from an unexpected ally. The rising capitalists—and let us remember that this sturdy, upstart class of parvenus was not bothered with twentieth-century ideas about equality or economic justice—found in Smith's treatise the perfect theoretical justification for their own opposition to factory legislation. The fact that Smith had written of "the mean rapacity, the monopolizing spirit of the merchants and manufacturers" and that he had said they "neither are, nor ought to be, the rulers of mankind" —all this was ignored in favor of the great point which Smith drew from his inquiry: *let the market alone.*

What Smith had meant by this was one thing; what his proponents made him out to mean was another. Smith, as we have said, was not the proponent of any one class. He was a slave to his system. His whole economic philosophy stemmed from his unquestioning faith in the ability of the market to guide the system to its point of highest return. The market—that wonderful social machine—would take care of society's needs *if it was left alone,* so that the laws of evolution might take over to lift society toward its promised reward. Smith was neither antilabor nor anticapital; if he had any bias it was in favor of the consumer. "Consumption is the sole end and purpose of all production," he wrote, and then proceeded to castigate those systems which placed the interest of the producer over that of the consuming public.

But in Smith's panegyric of a free and unfettered market the rising industrialists found the theoretical justification they needed to block the first government attempts to remedy the scandalous conditions of the times. For Smith's theory does unquestionably lead to a doctrine of *laissez faire.* To Adam Smith the least government is certainly the best: governments are spendthrift, irresponsible, and unproductive. And yet Adam Smith is not necessarily opposed—as his posthumous admirers made him out to be—

to *all* government action which has as its end the promotion of the general welfare. He warns, for example, of the stultifying effect of mass production, which robs men of their creative natural powers, and prophesies a decline in the manly virtues of the laborer, "unless the government takes some pains to prevent it." Similarly he is in favor of public education to raise the citizenry above the level of mere uncomprehending cogs in a vast machine.

What Smith *is* against is the meddling of the government with the market mechanism. He is against restraints on imports and bounties on exports, against government laws which shelter industry from competition, and against government spending for unproductive ends. Notice that these activities of the government largely have the interest of the *merchant* class at heart. Smith never faced the problem—which was to cause such intellectual agony for later generations—of whether the government is weakening or strengthening the market mechanism when it steps in with welfare legislation. Aside from poor relief, there was virtually no welfare legislation in Smith's day—the government was the unabashed ally of the governing classes, and the great tussle within the government was whether it should be the landowning or the industrial classes who should most benefit. The question of whether the working class should have a voice in the direction of economic affairs simply did not enter any respectable person's mind.

The great enemy to Adam Smith's system is not so much government per se as monopoly—in any form. "People of the same trade seldom meet together," says Adam Smith, "but the conversation ends in a conspiracy against the public, or in some diversion to raise prices." And the trouble with such goings on is not so much that they are morally reprehensible in themselves

—they are, after all, only the inevitable consequence of man's self-interest— as that they impede the fluid working of the market. And of course Smith is right. If the working of the market is trusted to produce the greatest number of goods at the lowest possible prices, anything that interferes with the market necessarily lowers social welfare. If, as in Smith's time, no master hatter anywhere in England could employ more than two apprentices or no master cutler in Sheffield more than one, the market system cannot possibly yield its full benefits. If, as in Smith's time, paupers are tied to their local parishes and prevented from seeking work where work might be found, the market cannot attract labor where labor is wanted. If, as in Smith's time, great companies are given monopolies of foreign trade, the public cannot realize the full benefits of cheaper foreign produce.

Hence, says Smith, all these impediments must go. The market must be left free to find its own natural levels of prices and wages and profits and production; whatever interferes with the market does so only at the expense of the true wealth of the nation. But because any act of the government—even such laws as those requiring the whitewashing of factories or preventing the shackling of children to machines— could be interpreted as hampering the free operation of the market, the *Wealth of Nations* was liberally quoted to oppose the first humanitarian legislation. Thus by a strange injustice the man who warned that the grasping eighteenth-century industrialists "generally have an interest to deceive and even to oppress the public" came to be regarded as their economic patron saint. Even today—in blithe disregard of his actual philosophy—Smith is generally regarded as a *conservative* economist, whereas in fact, he was more avowedly hostile to the *motives* of businessmen than most New Deal economists.

In a sense the whole wonderful world of Adam Smith is a testimony to the eighteenth-century belief in the inevitable triumph of rationality and order over arbitrariness and chaos. Don't try to do good, says Smith. Let good emerge as the by-product of selfishness. How like the philosopher to place such faith in a vast social machinery and to rationalize selfish instincts into social virtues! There is nothing halfhearted about Smith's abiding trust in the consequences of his philosophical beliefs. He urges that judges should be paid by the litigants rather than by the state, since in that way their self-interest will lead them to expedite the cases brought before them. He sees little future for the newly emerging business organizations called corporations since it seems highly improbable that such impersonal bodies could muster the necessary self-interest to pursue complex and arduous undertakings. Even the greatest humanitarian movements, such as the abolition of slavery, are defended in his own terms; best abolish slavery, says Adam Smith, since to do so will probably be cheaper in the end.

The whole complex irrational world is reduced to a kind of rational scheme where human particles are nicely magnetized in a simple polarity toward profit and away from loss. The great system works, not because man directs it, but because self-interest and competition line up the filings in the proper way; the most that man can do is to help this natural social magnetism along, to remove whatever barriers stand before the free working out of this social physics, and to cease his misguided efforts to escape from its thralldom.

And yet for all its eighteenth-century flavor, its belief in rationality, natural law, and the mechanized chain of human action and reaction, the world of Adam Smith is not without its warmer values. Do not forget that the great beneficiary of the system was the consumer—not the producer. For the first time in the philosophy of everyday life, the consumer is king.

Of the whole, what has survived?

Not the great scheme of evolution. We shall see that profoundly altered by the great economists to follow. But let us not regard the world of Adam Smith as merely a primitive attempt to arrive at formulations which were beyond his grasp. Smith was the economist of preindustrial capitalism; he did not live to see the market system threatened by enormous enterprises or his laws of accumulation and population upset by sociological developments fifty years off. When Smith lived and wrote there had not yet been a recognizable phenomenon which might be called a "business cycle." The world he wrote about actually existed, and his systematization of it, mechanical though it was, provides as good an explanation as any.

Yet something must have been missing from Smith's conception. For although he saw an evolution for society, he did not see a revolution—the Industrial Revolution. Smith did not see in the ugly factory system, in the newly tried corporate form of business organization, or in the weak attempts of journeymen to form protective organizations, the first appearance of new and disruptively powerful social forces. In a sense his system presupposes that eighteenth-century England will remain unchanged forever. Only in quantity will it grow: more people, more goods, more wealth; its quality will remain unchanged. His are the dynamics of a static community; it grows but it never matures.

But although the system of evolu-tion has been discarded, the great panorama of the market remains as a major achievement. To be sure, Smith did not "discover" the market; others had preceded him in pointing out how the interaction of self-interest and competition brought about the provision of society. But Smith was the first to understand the full philosophy of action which such a conception demanded, the first to formulate the entire scheme in a wide and systematic fashion. He was the man who made England, and then the whole Western World, understand just how the market kept society together and the first to build an edifice of social order on the understanding he achieved. Later economists will embroider Smith's description of the market and will inquire anxiously into the defects which subsequently appeared in it. None will improve on the richness and life with which Smith imbued this aspect of the world.

For Smith's encyclopedic scope and knowledge there can be only admiration. It was only in the eighteenth century that so huge, all-embracing, secure, caustic, and profound a book could have been written. Smith anticipated Veblen by a hundred and fifty years when he wrote: "With the greater part of rich people, the chief enjoyment of riches consists in the parade of riches, which in their eye is never so complete as when they appear to possess those decisive marks of opulence which nobody can possess but themselves." He was a statesman ahead of his time when he wrote: "If any of the provinces of the British Empire cannot be made to contribute towards the support of the whole empire, it is surely time that Great Britain should free herself from the expense of defending those provinces in time of war, and of supporting any part of their civil or military establishments in time of peace, and endeavour to accommo-

date her future views and designs to
the real mediocrity of her circumstances."

And perhaps no economist will ever
again so utterly encompass his age as
Adam Smith. Certainly none was ever
so serene, so devoid of contumacy, so
penetratingly critical without rancor,
and so optimistic without being utopian. To be sure, he shared the beliefs
of his day, in fact he helped to forge
them. It was an age of humanism and
reason, and while both could be per-
verted for the cruelest and most violent
purposes, Smith was never chauvinist,
apologist, or compromiser. "For to what
purpose," he wrote in the *Theory of
Moral Sentiments,* "is all the toil and
bustle of this world? What is the end of
avarice and ambition, of the pursuit of
wealth, of power, and pre-eminence?"
The *Wealth of Nations* provides his answer: all the grubby scrabbling for
wealth and glory has its ultimate justification in the welfare of the common
man.

At the end of his life, Smith was ripe
with honors and respect. Burke trav-

eled to Edinburgh to see him; he was
elected Lord Rector at his old University of Glasgow; he saw the *Wealth of
Nations* translated into Danish, French,
German, Italian, Spanish. Only Oxford ignored him; it never deigned to
give him an honorary degree. At one
time Pitt The Younger, then Prime
Minister, was meeting with Addington,
Wilberforce, and Grenville, and Adam
Smith had been invited to attend. As
the old philosopher walked into the
room, everyone rose. "Be seated, gentlemen," he said. "No," replied Pitt,
"we will stand until you are first seated,
for we are all your scholars."

In 1790 Smith died; he was sixty-
seven. Curiously, his passing attracted
relatively little notice; perhaps people
were too busy worrying about the
French Revolution and the repercussions it might have on the English
countryside. He was buried in the Can-
ongate churchyard with an unpreten-
tious tombstone; it states that Adam
Smith, author of *Wealth of Nations,* lies
here. It would be hard to conceive of
a more durable monument.

28   WHO GIVES FREE ENTERPRISE
ITS SENSE OF DIRECTION?

Clarence B. Randall   Clarence B. Randall is a former President of
Inland Steel Company. He has also held several
high government posts.

American businessmen are being
driven these days to take a hard second
look at the philosophy and the practices of free enterprise.

This system of accumulating private
capital under single control—and risking it for gain simply because of individual initiative—has come to businessmen as instinctively as the act of

breathing. In fact, until recently, some
of them lacked even a rudimentary
awareness that there *are* in the world
other systems for the production and
distribution of goods.

Reprinted by permission from *Think* Magazine, February, 1962; copyright 1962 by
International Business Machines Corporation.

All this is changing, thanks to the Russians. Instead of concealing their strength until they could choose their time to strike, they rather naively rang the alarm bell by rocketing Sputnik into orbit, and by putting the first man into space. Now the American businessman knows that the way of life to which his entire effort is dedicated is under severe challenge nearly everywhere in the world, and that he must either justify it by his conduct, or face the grim prospect that his grandchildren may lose it. He is staggered by the sudden realization that free enterprise does not automatically export itself, and that new nations, when given an opportunity for a free choice, are apt to reject it, and to accept the Communist program. Vigorous person that he is, he resents this incredible phenomenon, and a highly creditable determination to do something about it is seizing him.

When he takes this hard second look at himself and his way of life, what does he find? What are the "truths" which he holds to be "self-evident"?

His first truth is that the principle of freedom, upon which our form of democracy must irrevocably be based, is indivisible. There are no separate freedoms that may be specifically allocated to particular groups or institutions. The right to make private decisions with respect to the production of goods is precisely the same right exercised by the professor at the university who insists upon teaching whatever economic doctrine he believes to be true. Each must fight to the death to protect the right of the other, or all will be betrayed together. Whatever restricts one restricts both, and all who believe in freedom must jointly resist limitation wherever it appears, without immediate thought of self. We need all hands on deck all of the time if "life, liberty, and the pursuit of happiness," the national goals proclaimed in our Declaration of Independence, are to be preserved.

Filled with Freedom

It is this freedom, applied in industry to the point of saturation, which has given the American economy its enormous vitality and resiliency, and which the businessman is determined to see preserved at all cost.

This is so because no other system of production has yet been conceived which so effectively releases the full creative effort of each individual involved. Our industrial way of life dignifies the worth of the individual, first, by preserving for him full choice as to what calling he will embark upon, and, second, by rewarding him in direct ratio to the contribution he makes to society.

We believe that the incentives created by monetary compensation are both effective and moral. We have proved by our long history that the sum total of all effort when given freely, and with enthusiasm, in our form of society, is greater than the resultant of total effort that is brought forth by compulsion under collectivism. And we see not the slightest wrong in doing well by those who try, and not so well by those who do not. We believe that in granting rewards that are proportionate to effort we are merely giving recognition to the fact that in a free society the goals of the individual and those of society are not in conflict, but parallel.

In support of these truths, powerful testimony is now coming from behind the Iron Curtain. Of all people, the Communists are the most thorough-going of pragmatists. A thing has to work or it will be discarded. They boastfully began the reorientation of their industry on the starry-eyed theory that society would take from every man according to his ability, and grant him his share of the total production in strict accordance to his need, regardless of his effort. Now they know better. Quietly, they have dropped that theory, and now employ a wide range of group bonuses, and of individual incentives accomplished through both salary and emoluments. In a land that has few automobiles, a limousine and chauffeur can create powerful motivation. Add a *dacha* on the Black Sea, and the upward surge of production can be pronounced. In fact, incredible as it seems, the spread between the compensation of the manager of a steel plant in Russia, and that of the lowest paid worker is unquestionably greater than the comparable difference in the United States.

We apply this principle of freedom that saturates not only to the production of goods, but to their sale and distribution as well. We have no lonely commissar pontificating by himself as to what quantities and qualities of merchandise we should turn out. We vote all day every day as to what they should be. Every time a housewife goes into a supermarket and buys a package, she casts a ballot, as does her husband when he makes the down payment on an automobile. By totaling the resultant from an infinite number of such free choices, we arrive at consensus as to our goals.

In fact, the basic concept that underlies everything we do is the idea that the wisdom of the many is at all times more to be trusted than the wisdom of the few. There is always the chance under communism that a commissar may display great genius, but there is a still greater chance that he may display colossal ignorance and stupidity, and only fools would knowingly take such risks.

We employ the same principle of freedom that saturates in the formulation and gathering of the capital required in building and equipping our industrial plan, and in financing our operations. We rely on no other force than the incentive of intelligent self-interest for providing our funds. No individual is required to save. He may eat today and starve tomorrow, if he so elects. No part of that share of the product of his toil which has been allocated to him will ever be taken from him against his will in order that capital may be accumulated. But as a rational being, he soon senses that there is a future, and that for him and his family it will be a better future if he withdraws a part of his earnings from immediate consumption, and risks it for further gain by buying common stock of his company, or of another if he prefers.

This broad diffusion of ownership does two things. First, it keeps management on its toes; unless industry fully measures up and gives full value in terms of return on investment, the flow of capital will stop; people will spend and not save. And, second, those who own want to understand, and a means of communication is established by which people everywhere acquire insight into the problems of the national economy.

The powerful magnetic force which keeps the compass of industry pointing true north, to the welfare of society as a whole, is competition. The rule of survival of the fittest, the counterpart of freedom of enterprise, sternly demands that each separate unit of production put forth its utmost effort at all times, and that is social gain of a high order. We speak of ours as a profit system, but actually it is a profit and loss system, and the two forces of hope and fear operate in parallel to eliminate those whom in America we call the "free riders."

Danger Signs

When one businessman enters into a secret agreement with another businessman to restrict competition, he is either guilty of moral turpitude or ignorant of the enterprise system. The pegging of prices, the arbitrary dividing of territories, the withholding for a fixed period of advances in technology, and all similar devices which evil minds can think up to fatten profits at the expense of the consumer are a denial of our heritage. And they will destroy the enterprise system if they are allowed to persist. Such power over society cannot be lodged in private hands, and an angry public, when fully roused, will punish us all by withdrawing the privileges which it has bestowed in the field of private endeavor.

This, of course, raises the whole question of the importance of moral attitudes in the preservation of the enterprise system. It is actually more important that we be right than that we be effective. The very highest standards of ethics must henceforth govern the conduct of industrial leaders if society is not to turn against us; and we in the United States now comprehend this clearly.

We still have areas of weakness, however. Take executive salaries, for example. It is urgent and right that men who bear great responsibility should be generously compensated, but when moderation yields to avarice, hostile social forces are swiftly set in motion.

Here are some of the danger signs. When the top man has the highest salary in his industry, he may be justified, for someone has to be the high man, but he should be put upon great caution to be sure he is right. And when the top man submits his proposed compensation to no one but an "inside board," namely a group of directors who

work for him, he is clearly vulnerable.

We have erred, too, with respect to expense accounts. Under our law, legitimate entertaining may be deducted as a cost for purposes of computing the corporate income tax. But when the company president gives a champagne party at a night club, or uses the company airplane to take his friends on a duck-hunting trip, he steps far over the line of propriety. His conduct poses a threat to the survival of the entire private enterprise regime. His subversion and the Communist's differ only in degree.

On the other hand, there have been great advances in general probity during the years of the present generation. In my day, for example, I have seen commercial bribery all but completely eliminated. Time was that one company would place an industrial spy in the research department of a competitor, or when a supplier would buy the favor of a purchasing agent, but those moral lapses have been cleaned up—and cleaned up by industry itself, without the necessity for new laws.

In fact, the outstanding characteristic of the entire business community in the United States today, and the one which holds the greatest promise for the future, is its high sense of social responsibility. We now see clearly that the welfare of a particular enterprise and of the area in which it is located are inseparably linked, and we see further that the welfare of industry as a whole and of our country are likewise indivisible. It has taken a long time for this full sense of social mission to become the dominant philosophy of our industrial leadership, but such is now the unquestionable fact.

New Role for Businessmen

And it is right that this should be so. It is merely the logical extrapolation of a principle which, once accepted, could lead to only one conclusion: for every privilege bestowed upon individuals in a democratic society there is a corresponding obligation. Such is the essence of freedom. In the past, we have heard too much about our rights, not enough about our responsibilities. All this is now undergoing revolutionary change, and the businessman is assuming an important role in this significant transformation as he takes his hard second look at the enterprise system.

Nearly all leading American firms, for example, now set aside a part of their profits for philanthropy. Most of them do this by establishing a charitable foundation, which is administered by a special staff, and not by the board of directors. Through this medium they give support to hospitals, homes for the aged, child welfare institutions, health programs, and a wide variety of social agencies. This is only the beginning, however, and in large corporations literally hundreds of worthy causes will be assisted. Education stands high on the list, and liberal arts colleges are supported in parity with those which turn out technically trained graduates. Above all, the motive behind the allocation of such funds is not to help the company, but solely to serve the community and the nation. That is industrial statesmanship of the highest sort. We had a little trouble with the lawyers on this at the start, but it is now entirely clear that under our law a corporation may use its funds for the common good, as, of course, it should.

Moreover, businessmen in the United States now give themselves in addition to their money. You will find them lending their management skills to community institutions by taking unpaid executive posts, or by serving on boards of trustees, and you will find them employing their promotional gifts in leading fund-raising campaigns for charitable purposes. They are establishing by their conduct the proposition that free enterprise not only receives from society, but gives full value in return.

You will find businessmen in our government these days, too, at every level, carrying heavy responsibility at substantial financial sacrifice, and doing so with distinction. When, unexpectedly, a corporation officer is asked to close his desk for a term of years and go to Washington, or to his state capital, he does so in a high spirit of dedication. He knows that in this world of crises the demand for talent in government has greatly exceeded the supply, and he answers the call in the spirit of his new philosophy of social mission. Actually, the combination of the mature executive from business, paired with a career officer, makes a strong team. The professional provides the indispensable familiarity with the subject matter and the knowledge of how government operates; the amateur brings awareness of the state of public opinion and the courage to take a fresh approach, inasmuch as his own future is never at stake in anything he does. His greatest desire is to get the job done worthily, and go home.

Leaders in American industry are thus in many ways rising magnificently to the challenge of a world in torment and distress. They believe fervently that the forces of private initiative as released into the field of production in a free and democratic society bring greater good to more human beings than is possible under communism. But they also know that freedom brings responsibility, and that production as such is not a goal in itself. They are fully aware of their social obligations, and are determined to fulfill them abundantly.

29 ON THE PRINCIPLE OF CONSUMERS' SOVEREIGNTY

Tibor Scitovsky

Tibor Scitovsky is professor of Economics at the University of California, Berkeley.

Many attacks from many quarters have been launched in recent years on the principle of consumers' sovereignty. They have questioned the economist's wisdom in putting too great and exclusive a trust in the consumer's wisdom; and it is regrettable that these attacks have shaken the public's faith in the economist but have not shaken the economist out of his established modes of thought. Indeed, American economists have largely ignored these attacks, following an old American tradition of keeping hands off welfare economics —applying its results but refusing to cast a critical look at the derivation of these results. I have been fighting this tradition for some time, because I believe that much of the criticism is valid and economists should take it to heart. I have much more to say on the subject than time to say it in, and have said much of it already, so I shall confine myself here to two issues: the choice between market and collective goods, and the problem of whether the market can cater to consumers' tastes truly and well.

The first issue stems from the realization that the sovereignty of the consumer is not at all the same thing as the sovereignty of the individual or citizen. The consumer is just one facet of the individual—the one that has to do with the consumption of goods sold through the market. The consumer's welfare therefore is only a part of man's welfare and only a part even of his economic welfare. Choosing between market and collective goods, deciding whether a given service is better provided through the market or by public spending, determining the best allocation of public funds among their various uses—all these are economic choices no different and no less important than the consumer's choice between two market goods; and yet, our society has failed to develop adequate machinery through which the public could express its preferences on these issues. For, as Galbraith pointed out, advertising, the American tradition of self-reliance, belief in the advantages of private enterprise, and the economist's excessive preoccupation with consumer's choice in the market, not only have biased the American public against collective goods but even prevent its forming and expressing rational preferences on the economic aspects of any choice involving them, so much are these issues befogged by ideological considerations. The more's the pity, because a variety of recent changes and developments are rendering these choices ever more important.

Historically, there is plenty of excuse for such bias. For many centuries, food, clothing and shelter symbolized market goods, while cathedrals, palaces, and armies were the symbols of collective spending; and most of us would favor absolute priority of the first over the second group. The tendency to think in these terms persists

From *The American Economic Review*, May, 1962, pp. 262–268. Reprinted by permission.

today, although in most developed countries the choice has long ceased to be so simple. On the margin, which is where choices are made, most expenditures in a developed economy have to do with leisure; and today, society's marginal choice between market and collective expenditures is no longer a choice between more bread and more palaces but more nearly that between TV sets and other gadgets and appliances on the market side and public services and recreational and educational facilities on the collective side. This is the kind of choice that the Planning Commission of France must have had in mind when they recommended a faster expansion of collective services than of the consumption sector and warned against the social malaise that might result from catering to the consumer's every whim.

Another explanation of our undue emphasis on the consumption of market goods may be the fact that our economic thinking was formulated at a time when many collective goods were free but which today are no longer free. The increase in population density and man's tendency to fill the countryside with factories, automobiles, and empty beer cans have created a world in which fresh air, clean water, and the enjoyment of nature are no longer free goods. Smog control and the decontamination of polluted rivers are expensive operations, and so is the creation and maintenance of "nature areas" in a world whose wide open spaces are rapidly being subdivided into quarter-acre lots. The external diseconomies of the production and consumption of market goods render such collective goods increasingly scarce and expensive; but economic theory, social accounting, and most public policy still proceed on the fiction that external diseconomies are small enough to be neglected.

Besides the rise in living standards and the crowding of space, increased life expectancy, secular inflation, and uneven progress and the resulting change in relative prices are all among the factors that call either for more provision of collective goods and services or at least for a reconsideration of the question which goods and services should be provided collectively and which through the market. Increased life expectancy demands of the individual more and more careful long-run budgeting at the very time when secular inflation and the uncertainty it creates are diminishing the market's ability to handle long-run budgeting. This, together with the changing nature of the family, which no longer provides a place for the aged, explains the rising demand and rising recognition of demand for the collective provision of social security. Increased life expectancy is also bringing about a situation in which the leisure classes are no longer the rich but the aged, who however are at the same time also the poor modern society. This too is causing many people to wish to do some reallocating of spending from market goods to collective services.

Changing relative prices are another factor relevant here, because they can change people's ideas on which services should be distributed free and paid out of public funds, which should be subsidized, and which sold at full cost through the market. This is so, because given the distribution of income and wealth, the inequality with which a particular good is distributed depends on its price in relation to other prices. The higher its relative price, the more unequally the market distributes it. It can happen, therefore, that the rise in the price of a good should increase the inequality of its distribution beyond the point tolerated by public opinion, which will then demand either its subsidization and sale below cost or its free provision out of public funds. In this age of fast and uneven technical progress there are many instances of this happening. An illustration is the increasing public demand in developed countries for national health insurance or free medical care.

In discussing some of the factors that in today's more complex world call for greater reliance on collective goods and services, I am not forgetting the arguments against the element of compulsion and the lesser safeguards against inefficiency and waste in the public sector. In the past, we have fought these troubles the easy way by trying to minimize the public sector itself. Its growth and the increasing need for it may compel us to fight the hard way for its more satisfactory performance.

We can now proceed to our other subject: the criticism of consumers' sovereignty in the narrow sense. The two main objections here are, first, that in this age, when man's control over his fellowmen's beliefs is almost as great as his control over nature, the economist should still continue to regard consumers' preferences as a datum and the standard by which to judge the performance of the economy; and, second, that even by the questionable standard of consumers' preferences, the market economy performs badly, and for reasons not even considered in traditional economic analysis.

In the days of the handicraft economy, every piece of clothing, every piece of furniture was made to the specifications of the person who bought it; but from this position of 100 per cent consumer sovereignty we have retreated long ago. Consumers yielded their dominance first to merchants, who had the initiative in placing orders and specifying the nature and design of products for a long period, and later

to manufacturers, who now decide themselves what to produce. The consumer's loss of initiative involves no great loss of sovereignty as long as he is given an adequate range of alternatives to choose from and is able to distinguish the good from the bad and to recognize solid construction, good design, and practical and imaginative ideas. These conditions, however, are the less fulfilled, the more the economy and technology progress.

Economies of scale not only cheapen large-scale production but by raising wages they also raise the cost and diminish the profitability of small-scale production. This in turn raises the minimum volume of sales necessary to render production profitable and thus leads to an ever increasing narrowing of the range of variants of products offered and neglect of minority needs and tastes in the nature and design of goods produced and marketed.

The increasing neglect of minority preferences is a bad thing, because it is illiberal, makes for uniformity, and destroys to some degree the principal merit of the market economy: its ability to cater separately and simultaneously to different people's differing needs and tastes. Also, the more the market loses this ability, the greater the extent to which majority preferences are imposed upon minorities and the more do the nature and formation of these majority preferences become matters of public concern.

Now the very failure of the market to cater to minority preferences may have undesirable effects upon the development of majority preferences as well. Even the most ardent believers in consumer sovereignty must realize that most tastes are acquired, that bad tastes are as easy to acquire as good ones, and that the best one can hope for is that by example and imitation the good will prevail over the bad if given an even chance. An additional advantage, therefore, of a market that caters to different people's differing tastes is that it gives those with informed tastes a chance to set an example to the rest of the community. Informed people, however, are always a minority; and when they are too small a minority—or economies of scale are too great—for producers to cater to their demand, then they are unable to set an example and fulfill their educative function.

Informed people are partly the experts who either as professionals or as amateurs have an intimate knowledge of a particular type of consumers' good—and it goes without saying that the expert public for music is generally a different group of people from the expert buyers of automobiles. A second part of the informed public is composed of generally educated people, who either are informed or if not know how to inform themselves.

I should like to see the tastes of experts catered to, because they know something about technical excellence. I should like to have the preferences of the generally educated public respected, because they have a wider perspective, apply a variety of criteria, and pay attention to the relation and connection between different criteria.

I admit, of course, that the preference for an educated taste is simply the subjective preference of educated people; but they, or most of them, have the tremendous advantage of having, at an earlier stage, been uneducated and uninformed themselves. In the early work on the theory of consumer satisfaction, the Greeks could never resolve the problem whether men or women enjoyed more the pleasures of love, because they could not draw on the experience of people who had tasted these pleasures in both capacities. In approaching our problem we have no such handicap. I cannot claim that an informed person's tastes are better by any test than an uninformed person's, or that they are more conducive to happiness or more appropriate to the atomic age; but I can claim that they are based on knowledge of a wider range of alternatives, which includes the alternatives available to the uninformed person.

Let me also recall that the issue is not whether uninformed tastes should or should not be suppressed and displaced by informed ones. I am merely deploring and criticizing the tendency of scale economies to keep the market more and more from catering to informed, or, if you wish, highbrow, tastes and thus to keep these tastes from competing on an equal basis with uninformed and lowbrow tastes in molding the preferences of the public at large.

Who then influences the majority's preferences and how? I can think of several channels through which is imposed what David Riesman called "other directedness," not so much the taste of the representative consumer as what public-opinion experts believe to be his taste. As already mentioned, the increasing importance of scale economies has greatly raised the penalty producers have to pay for making the wrong guesses about consumers' tastes and putting unpopular products on the market. Hence the tendency of producers in an increasing number of fields to play safe and not to risk imaginative innovations in the new products, services, and publications they put on the market but to rely instead on market research into the consumer's unfulfilled desires. At its best, this can slow down genuine progress and innovation in the design of products; at its worst, it can lead to a serious misreading of the public taste and the imposition of a mythical majority taste that in fact few people share. The automobile industry, with its hand on the consumer's pulse, has for many years diagnosed a chronic yearning for longer and wider and more powerful cars; and had it not been for foreign competition, we—and they—might never have found out how wrong they were. Similarly, Hollywood used to proclaim twelve as the median age of the American movie audiences; and if it had not been for the success of foreign films, we would still live under the shadow of this depressing thought.

One trouble with such misreadings of the majority's mind is the difficulty of finding out how wrong they are. Competition seems no adequate safeguard. The consumer is all too often in the position of the voter who has but one candidate to vote for or several candidates who all stand for the same thing. And to complete the simile, the consumer too is subjected to a barrage of advertising to persuade him that he really wants the product which is the designer's realization of what the market researcher believes to be the average consumer's wishdream.

Another factor responsible for the other-directedness of the consumer's taste has to do with the increasing importance of durable goods in the consumer's budget. The most important of these, cars and houses, are bought not only for consumption but also as an investment for their resale value; and buying for high resale value means buying not what one wants but what one believes other people want. The consumer buys extra trim on his car, not necessarily because he wants it, but because the salesman assures him that it will raise the blue-book value of his car in the secondhand market. He is forced to avoid all but the most conventional design and construction in his house, because to get a good mortgage, the house must conform to what the appraiser believes, perhaps wrongly, the majority taste to be. Accordingly, house construction is governed to quite

an extent not by what the consumer wants but what an unimaginative and not very expert middleman expects other consumers to want.

Luckily for the consumer, his writ still runs in many areas; but it is none too soon to start thinking about how to remedy the situation. Also, the above points were merely a sample of the things that are wrong with consumer's sovereignty but a sufficiently representative sample to raise the question of remedies and policies. Most economists seem reluctant to face up to these questions, presumably because they visualize the dictatorship of an economic planner as the only alternative to the present situation. Such an attitude, however, shows a misunderstanding of the issues involved. Most critics object not to the consumer's sovereignty but to the ignorance and restrictions to which his reign is subject and to the influence businessmen have over it. We cannot and do not want to turn the clock back and return to a handicraft economy; and some shortcomings we may choose to put up with. However, some of those discussed in this paper can be remedied; and we may be able to establish safeguards to assure the satisfaction of a wider range of consumers and to guard against the undue and undesirable influencing of consumer's tastes. The choice is not whether consumers or a central planner should exercise sovereignty but whether and how the producer's power to ignore some consumers and influence the preferences of others should be curbed and modified.

This is not the place to discuss in detail the nature of a constructive answer to any of these questions; but a few precedents may be mentioned. Public carriers are required to offer service in off-peak hours and on little-traveled routes; the Pure Food and Drug Administration does impose curbs on a highly competitive industry; and Britain's Independent Television Authority is an excellent and successful example of how the influencing of consumers' tastes by market-research and public-opinion experts can be curbed, modified and supplemented by the influence of Distinguished Citizens. In a slightly different area, the survival of opera and serious drama and the publication of scholarly books are assured by subsidies—from the state in Western Europe, from other sources here.

All these, of course, are examples of exceptional cases justified by special circumstances. To extend them into a general rule would be much harder and more momentous than their admission as exceptions. Also, the further such policies are extended and the more the unfettered operation of the market is encroached upon, the more value judgments are involved. And here I should like to end on a note I started out with: the economist could wash his hands of value judgments only if the public's preferences were really given and he could accept them as such. As soon as this ceases to be true and the public's preferences are influenced by economic agents and the economic environment, value judgments on whether this influence is good or bad, in need of restraint or reform, cannot be avoided. If the economist feels incompetent to make such judgments himself, he should at least admit their legitimacy and provide the analytical framework to help others to make these judgments.

B.

BUSINESS PRICE-SETTING AND PROFIT GOALS

30   PRICING IN STEEL AND CONSUMER APPLIANCES

A. D. H. Kaplan, Joel B. Dirlam, and Robert F. Lanzilotti

A. D. H. Kaplan is a senior staff member of The Brookings Institution, and Research Professor of Economics, George Washington University; Joel B. Dirlam is Professor of Economics at Connecticut College; and Robert F. Lanzilotti is Professor and Head of Economics Department, Michigan State University.

STEEL

The pricing process in steel reflects the industry's history of price leadership and the influence of vertical integration. Earlier studies of steel pricing have concentrated on such factors as the forward integration of the major steel producers, the method of

From *Pricing in Big Business* by A. D. H. Kaplan, Joel B. Dirlam, and Robert F. Lanzilotti. (The Brookings Institution, 1958), pp. 13–23, 55–65. Reprinted by permission.

price quotation, the heavy investment and overhead costs, and the peculiarities of demand.[1] In the present context, however, interest is focused on the determinants of policy as they appear to a leading firm. Hence, little purpose would be served by attempting a detailed summary of factors that may affect steel pricing. Nevertheless, certain aspects of the price history of steel that are directly relevant to an interpretation of the views of management require consideration.

The quoted base price for basic steel and steel products tends to be uniform among firms following the lead of United States Steel. Finished steel is sold mostly by specification—this being true not only of highly fabricated pieces like structural steel, but also of the general run of sheets, plates, bars, rods, etc. Extra charges, which are imposed for variations in alloy and other specifications, are important in the final delivered price. Up to the Second World War, the industry apparently agreed on uniform extras to tie in differences in specifications with a uniform base price; but in recent years, this practice seems to have become less prevalent.[2] Room is left for differentials among companies in the final price, despite the fact that most standard products are quoted at base prices

plus extras showing no appreciable spread from the quotations of U.S. Steel. There still remains the freight advantage or disadvantage of location in relation to particular market outlets.

Mechanics of Pricing

United States Steel states that it employs a "stable margin" price policy, that is, in general it aims at maintaining margins despite variations in sales volume. In so doing it uses standard costs,[3] computed on the basis of 80 per cent of capacity as normal, and including an assignment of overhead burden to every product. Although the company continuously watches actual costs, it follows standard cost logic for pricing purposes. Standard costs are revised annually to account for such factors as increased labor costs, rising

---

[1] *E.g.* Carroll R. Daugherty, Melvin G. deChazeau, and Samuel S. Stratton, *The Economics of the Iron and Steel Industry* (1937).

[2] Special prices are made for large contracts, and there is evidence that charges for extras are less uniform than they once were. In this connection, there is strong opinion among producers that discrimination and secret price cuts are not characteristic in the industry. The reason offered by one steel executive is that virtually everyone knows everyone else's costs; in effect, that the industry operates in a gold fish bowl. Also "the price cuts of the thirties taught everyone a lesson."

---

[3] Standard cost may be defined as "predetermined cost for each operation, or each unit of finished product . . . intended to represent the value of direct material, direct labor, and manufacturing burden normally required under efficient conditions at normal capacity to process a unit of product." E. A. Green, National Association of Cost Accountants Bulletin, Vol. 16, cited in *Accountants' Handbook* (1944), p. 225.

One of the main purposes of employing standard costs is to avoid the presumption of significant changes in profits or efficiency when these may be due in a particular instance to a temporary change in the cost or market situation respecting a specific item. To provide for these shifting situations, cost standards are used to make the stated costs of parts, assemblies, and finished products accord more closely with planned objectives. A common objective to which standard costs are frequently geared is a break-even point regarded as normal or optimum —e.g., 70 or 80 per cent of capacity. Another purpose of standard costs is to control plant operations by developing and analyzing variances or differences between standard and actual costs; or by developing cost ratios or trends which use the standard costs as measuring rods.

markets, new machines, new processes, new kinds of coal used, and similar factors affecting actual costs.[4]

Standard costs are determined for each mill, but these individual standards are used primarily for gauging efficiency and for stimulating incentive at the local level. For pricing purposes, the standard cost used is an average, weighted by the volumes at respective mills. This means that in addition to changes in the factors mentioned above, as occasioning revisions in standard cost, allowance is also made for higher capital costs of new facilities. Thus, high capital costs exert an upward push on company-wide weighted standard costs and prices.

The company stresses the distinction it makes between what it calls "price structure" and "price level." Price structure involves "a hard-boiled application of standard costs in pricing individual products"; price level is concerned with the general or average level of prices for the corporation, which in the final determination of prices involves much more than standard costs. The distinction can be seen more clearly by a discussion of the use of standard costs in connection with the mechanics of an actual price change, such as occurred following the wage settlement of 1956.

General Price Revision, August 1956

The average increase of $8.50 per ton in steel prices on August 7, 1956

was determined essentially as follows: With the wage negotiations as a backdrop, the Executive Vice-President, Commercial directed his Price Division to recommend price schedules on the basis of hypothetical wage settlements.[5] According to a tradition in the steel industry, each cent-per-hour increase in direct labor costs adds another cent to steelmakers' non-wage costs per ton of steel. This working figure has been derived from experience in earlier wage settlements. With this labor-to-total cost ratio, the anticipated wage settlement is roughly doubled and multiplied by a traditional figure of twenty man-hours (more recently a figure of fifteen has been used to reflect higher efficiency) to yield the expected cost of a new wage package per ton of steel. Since the new contract (July 1956) was estimated to add 24 cents to the company's hourly labor cost per ton, an increase of $9.60 per ton was indicated.[6]

The Price Division bases its recommendations on more than this rule of thumb. It also makes a product-by-product analysis in which it considers proposals of the various product departments regarding changes in individual products. Whenever a product section of the company feels a change in base price is needed, it makes such recommendations in writing to the

---

[4] The market against which U.S. Steel measures adequacy of its capacity and its hoped-for share of sales is the projected total national market (including imports), broken down by individual product groups, by regions and mills. On the basis of these figures and the amount of various products the company feels it can and wishes to sell, the company's "operating plan" for the year is determined.

[5] The Price Division consists of four or five price analysts charged with the responsibility of continuing examination of the price problem from many different angles (demand, costs, competition, market strategy, etc.).

[6] The custom of using this crude method of estimating price increases largely explains the expectation of the "trade" generally that prices would go up by at least $9.60 per ton. Some estimates ran as high as $12 per ton on the average, since in 1955 the industry used a 2.5 to 1 basis of estimating the total cost impact of the wage settlement. *Business Week* (Aug. 11, 1956), p. 25.

Commercial Department. The form used for this purpose calls for a detailed justification of the recommendation in terms of the pricing history and competitive information on the product and the expected impact of the proposed revision on specific company accounts or industries. The recommendation is accompanied by financial information prepared by the comptroller showing on a per-ton basis the present and proposed cost, together with the present and expected profit or loss.

These recommendations and attached supporting information are presented to the director of the Price Division for his evaluation and in turn are submitted to the Vice-President, Commercial for final action. It is important to note the kinds of information before the price makers at this level of management (which actually evaluates proposed price changes and determines the changes to be made, when, and by how much). The changes are considered in terms of profit return on *sales,* not investment. This illustrates, as in the case of other companies in the sample, the way in which pricing officials view their product pricing problems, in contrast to the top level management, which views price policy primarily in terms of return on investment, but which does not actually determine prices.

Although the 1956 general price revision increased the composite average 6.25 per cent ($8.50 per ton), the prices of different products were not raised uniformly. Many products were raised more than 6.25 per cent, some less. The items tabulated on page 18 taken from U.S. Steel quotations announced immediately after the wage settlement illustrate the variations in the price increases.

These differences show, among other considerations, such factors as: holding back on changes during the year, the post-wage settlement being regarded as the most propitious time for a complete revision of prices; the labor cost factor in the given product; the

	Aug. 7, 1956 Price (Per ton)	Previous Price (Per ton)	Per Cent Increase
Alloy steel			
Billets, blooms, slabs	$107	$ 96	11.5
Hot rolled strip and sheet	155	144	7.6
Wire—Premier spring, high carbon	168	152	10.5
Wire products			
Nails	167	152	9.9
Barbed wire	187	175	6.9
Carbon steel			
Cold finished bars	137	125	9.6
Light rails	120	113	6.2
Plates, high strength (Man-Ten S)	127	120	5.8

company's leadership position in the product; expectations of the trade (and the potential pressure from congressional committees and the public). With the 1956 three-year contract, management expected to make more selective price changes as it deemed appropriate, rather than follow its earlier practice of general annual changes.[7]

-----
[7] This selective policy apparently was not followed in the general price increase of $6 per ton announced by U.S. Steel on July 1, 1957.

Cost-Price Relationships

That standard-cost doctrine has not been rigidly followed by the company in pricing is suggested by price changes that do not seem to conform to the usual varieties of standard-cost plus target return pricing. Standard-cost pricing is designed to avoid the necessity for making short-run changes in burden that would result if adjustments were continuously made for temporary changes in volume. Actually, U.S. Steel has not been able to ignore short-term shrinkage of demand. Moreover, it has not been able to carry its "fair return" logic to the point of forcing price increases in depressions to offset higher unit costs at low volume, because its competitors would not follow. Nor has it cut prices in boom periods, which would be the corollary of price increases in depressions.

Differences in margins among products were not demonstrated by the corporation in terms of cost and price data on given product lines, but were assumed to be generally recognized in the industry. Mill prices cannot be directly related to costs for U.S. Steel or its competitors, whose prices, with certain exceptions noted below, are generally designed to meet the corporation's prices. United States Steel has the same prices at Pittsburgh and in Ohio, Illinois, Indiana, and Alabama, and apparently averages mill costs to get such equalization.[8]

The Competitive Impact on Pricing

The intensity of competition from other steel companies varies with the effectiveness of U.S. Steel's price leadership. With swings in the business cycle, there has been some modification of the "full-cost stable-margin" pricing philosophy of U.S. Steel and its leading competitors. Competitors of the corporation are more likely to take premiums in periods of prosperity, while U.S. Steel appears to demand no more than its published prices. In recession, however, the company has followed the trend toward concessions initiated by competitors. United States Steel has tended to be the laggard in recognizing the price cuts of its rivals. The ostensible regularity and comparative rigidity in steel prices have been appreciably modified by the policies of steel companies other than U.S. Steel. From 1946 to 1950 the prices of many steel producers were substantially higher than those of U.S. Steel.

When pricing through the basing point system was in effect, there were apparently fewer exceptions to the leader-follower pattern. Yet, even in 1936 U.S. Steel had to cut its base prices to reflect levels prevailing generally in the industry but not yet "official." With all mills on an f.o.b. basis, when demand is heavy, there is perhaps less of a disposition on the part of competitors to follow U.S. Steel. The corporation's public announcement of October 1953, reiterated in its *Annual Report* for 1953—that when necessary to get the business, it would meet the lower delivered price of a competitor—suggests that when rivals expect operation will be less than capacity, they are more disposed to undercut U.S. Steel.[9] There is no indica-

---

[8] According to one pricing official, "standard costs on most products are much closer among mills than is commonly supposed: the variations run about 5 per cent." The Fairless Works is evidently an exception.

[9] "Under the revised policy, U.S. Steel will continue to quote prices f.o.b. its mills, or, if the customer so desires, it will quote delivered prices which reflect full transportation charges from shipping mill to destination. The revised policy, however, permits the meeting of a lower delivered price of a

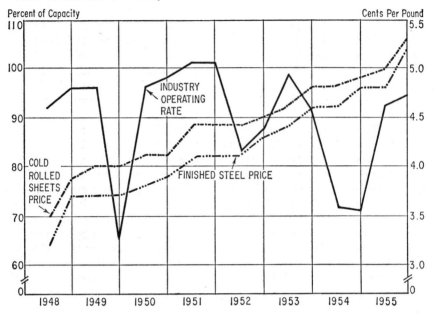

AVERAGE PRICES OF STEEL PRODUCTS AND
AVERAGE CAPACITY OPERATED, 1948–1955

tion that the October 1953 policy resulted in U.S. Steel's having to match price reductions that yielded its competitors a lower base price than U.S. Steel had set.

Opportunities to differentiate prices to take advantage of locations within a given natural market may vary with the particular products and sections of the country that are involved. In the East, for example, where Bethlehem Steel has four mills, the mill prices for semifinished steel plates, bars, and sheets are the same at all its mills and

competitor when necessary and commercially desirable in order to participate in the business of an individual customer. This change in policy is consistent with the stand long taken by U.S. Steel—that it has the right to compete in good faith in any market for the business of any consumer. This provision for meeting the lower delivered price of a competitor does not constitute a return to the so-called multiple basing point pricing method which was abandoned by the steel industry in 1948." U.S. Steel Corporation, *Annual Report, 1953*, p. 12.

identical with Pittsburgh prices. Structural prices are slightly higher than Pittsburgh, but are the same at all its mills, even Johnstown, which is near Pittsburgh. Yet, Sparrows Point prices are higher than Pittsburgh on wire rods, wire, and tin mill products. Some of these are made at the Johnstown mill, but for these products Pittsburgh prices are applied. Similarly, U.S. Steel's Fairless Works enjoys a $3.00 per ton price differential over other mills on standard bars, small shapes, and special quality and concrete reinforcing bars, and a $1.00 differential on hot- and cold-rolled sheets. Farther west, National Steel's Great Lakes plant near Detroit has enjoyed a differential over Pittsburgh of $2.00 (formerly $4.00) per ton on sheets. It is a moot question whether such differentials could be maintained in conditions of slack demand and underutilization of plant capacity by other steel producers, such as prevailed in 1953–54.

It also seems clear that firms will quote outside their natural territory and absorb freight. United States Steel management indicated in interviews that the 1953 announcement regarding its intention to meet the delivered prices of competitors should not be taken to mean that it will shade its base prices to meet individual situations. An officer explained that the company "is committed to a one-price policy; if it is deemed desirable to change price, it will be an across-the-board change." The management stated that it will do no more than equalize the freight disadvantage, even in those instances when U.S. Steel's base price is higher than a competitor's.[10] The company's determination to implement this policy strictly has been spelled out in a memorandum to all sales offices, with specific instructions respecting the conditions under which freight absorption cases would be considered by the Commercial Department.

Competitors, meanwhile, complain that prices on many steel products, even after the broad price readjustments carried through in 1956, have not been high enough to stimulate the desirable level of new investment in the industry. Generally, the assertion takes the form of the specific accusation that U.S. Steel is pricing as though new capacity cost $100 instead of the current $300 a ton. United States Steel has joined in complaints of an insufficient

return, yet apparently does not intend to relieve the pressure on its competitors.[11] A campaign by steel men to boost prices was dampened when U. S. Steel would not go along with a general price increase in the fall of 1955.

Although steel producers have complained, it is evident that the "art of followership" is still deeply embedded in the philosophy of pricing in the steel industry. National Steel has been a price follower in every line in which it engages, in two of which (tin plate and light sheet steel) it has been an important producer. Despite former President Weir's adoption of the position that steel prices should be based on full cost of the most efficient firm, the company nevertheless has rested profitably under the umbrella of U.S. Steel prices during a large part of its history.[12] National's price has generally followed the Pittsburgh price, with freight allowed when necessary. While the company unhesitatingly meets price cuts—and does so by reducing the base price rather than the extras—it makes no effort to lead in price reductions.

Thus, U.S. Steel's competitors, except to the extent that they produce specialities or otherwise tailor their services, feel forced to go along with the U.S. Steel base price plus trans-

---

[10] This would appear to be somewhat inconsistent with the earlier announcement about "meeting the delivered prices of competitors." Also, it is difficult to understand how customers could be gained or held (except in periods of steel shortage) if it meant that U.S. Steel's delivered price (with freight equalized) would still be higher than that of a rival steelmaker. It would appear that U.S. Steel will not *initiate any price shading*, but if threatened with loss of customers will retaliate as necessary to keep them—e.g., by freight absorption.

[11] Since 1940, according to a statement made by Mr. Fairless in 1953, U.S. Steel had not, in ten out of twelve years, recouped "a dime of added profit on the millions of extra tons of steel that [it] produced for the people of this nation," nor earned "one cent of increased return on the billion and a half of additional capital that has been poured into [its] business." *New York Times* (Apr. 26, 1953), p. 5.

[12] Recently the pinch of higher costs has led to industry criticism of prices under U.S. Steel's leadership as being inadequate to provide for depreciation and new capacity. National Steel Corporation, *Annual Report, 1955*, p. 6, and *1956*, p. 5.

portation cost in "normal" times when demand is heavy. By concentrating in those areas of steel making, particularly tin plate, where it can operate at low cost and raise technical standards, National appears to have been a successful operator. Indeed, one officer of U.S. Steel who has been with the corporation for many years has expressed the opinion that companies like National and Bethlehem, with more centrally located facilities, have been able to improve those facilities at the same location. United States Steel, by contrast, was disinclined to abandon its original locations and less adaptable steel capacity "because of long-continued obligations to community and to staff." Hence, it has had greater overhead burdens and lower margins in comparison with other steel companies. These disadvantages have been offset in part by the advantages accruing from "a very broad product line and also complete geographic coverage."

Patently U.S. Steel's policies pervade the pricing structure and price levels for all steel products. Even with products numbered in the thousands, and customers exceeding 100,000, the company has sought to apply a uniform, universally applicable pricing policy. Its price policy was characterized by one of the senior officials interviewed as follows: "U.S. Steel has never tried to price to maximum profit not only in the short run but even in the long run." It appears that U.S. Steel holds the philosophy of cost-plus pricing. Nonetheless, even such a company has difficulty in following a formula in pricing steel products—partly because of the differences in costs among plants and the heavy overhead factor, and partly from the desire to hold customers.

The corporation has given evidence of limiting profits and refraining from exploitation of shortages, which can be viewed as manifestations of awareness of its repsonsibilities and vulnerability as the largest and dominant firm in the industry. In the past, according to U.S. Steel, it has refrained from cutting off its semi-integrated customer-competitors in periods of shortage when it could make higher profits by sharply raising prices or by finishing the steel products itself—a problem that is not so important today with increased integration of smaller mills. President Fairless testified that the company has checked with its customers before raising prices and has held off in reducing published prices, in the interest of customers with heavy inventories. Moreover, on occasion it has accepted orders for certain items at a loss to keep its regular customers. Competitors, on the other hand, even when they believe that U.S. Steel's prices are not high enough, will not ordinarily go above them. The period following the Second World War was an exception. When U.S. Steel has suffered a decline in volume, as in 1954, its pricing philosophy has predisposed it to resist significant cuts. The relative regularity of steel prices through marked changes in operating levels occurring since 1947 seems to bear out the traditional tendency to resist price revisions in steel until action is unavoidable.

* * *

CONSUMER APPLIANCES

There are several stages in the pricing process of a major consumer appliance. During the early period of development of the new piece of equipment—automatic washing machine, refrigerator, TV set—prices differ widely as experience accumulates to determine the most wanted type. After the experimental years, when the consumer has come to know the general character of the product, the result of continuing surveys of dealers' experiences and consumers' reactions is to produce a consensus on what constitutes the "right" price for retail distribution. In the case of 1954 models of automatic washers, there was apparently a general understanding that $300 was the "right" figure to aim at in producing the standard model, for among twenty-four leading manufacturers' brands of automatic washing machines two out of three were priced at $299.95, or within a dollar of that figure. The list price being accepted as the starting point, the problem shifts to a consideration of what the manufacturer can profitably put into the product.

The information on consumer appliances (as with other electrical equipment) has for the most part been supplied by General Electric, the only electrical equipment company in the sample; but in the case of the automatic dishwasher, the cost and price breakdown given below was provided by a large appliance manufacturer not interviewed for this study. It will serve, nevertheless, to illuminate several aspects of pricing policy enunciated by General Electric representatives in respect to consumer appliances.

Starting from the retail list price of $299.95 the manufacturer deducts 40 per cent for the retailer's margin and about 7½ per cent for the wholesale distributors' margin, leaving roughly $156 out of which the manufacturer must get his cost plus profit. With all manufacturers having a similar target to work on, the competition appears to turn mainly on whether one manufacturer can put into the $156 more appeal value than another.

The competition can be shifted to greater emphasis on price by carrying in addition to the standard "de luxe" models more or less stripped models,

which eliminate certain automatic controls or trims featured in the former. At this lower level ($239.95 was a common figure), the manufacturers' standard brands encountered the private label brands of the mail order houses and the brands of various manufacturers catering to price-conscious buyers.

General Electric does not follow cost-plus pricing in the sense that it would determine the selling price from a calculation of its own costs. It prices for the market, actual or estimated. In pricing a new item, it prefers to go directly by market surveys to the consumer buyer where a controlled pricing experiment offers the same product with different prices in different areas and also, where feasible, through different channels of distribution.

In the opinion of a General Electric executive, the firm's experience shows that neither distributors and dealers nor the company's salesmen and executives are fully dependable in their guesses of what the consumer will pay for a product. Direct access to the consumers, confronting them with a real choice in a realistic selling environment, is the way to get answers to questions concerning the price-quantity relationship. Dealers can be more helpful in other aspects of marketing than pricing and determination of the features a product should have. This executive believes that in the future G.E. will pay more and more attention to the housewife in determining price and product features.

General Electric, like the other leading manufacturers, carried a $299.95 model among its 1954 automatic washers. But, unlike its competitors, G.E. featured its $349.95 model and treated its $299.95 as a partially stripped version of its standard model.

General Electric's approach to pricing a new consumer product can be illustrated directly by its development for the market in 1949 of a portable dishwasher. The dishwasher was tested in three markets, and the following three prices were set: $149.50; $169.50; $189.50. Each of these prices represented a different method of distribution, ranging from home demonstration at the top price to orthodox department store distribution without demonstration. (Several hundred dishwashers were made by essentially hand processes for this test.) The company thus learned about the relative effectiveness of various distribution methods and what needed to be improved in the product, particularly in styling, to make it more salable. General Electric price policy does not stress, indeed G.E. does not consider desirable, the use of low price in the early stages of development of a product as the means of tapping new markets and expanding uses. For example, when the new dishwasher was sold at $200 instead of $250, no more than 5 per cent of additional sales was believed to result. This was because the "service" idea of an automatic electric dishwasher was not yet so fully accepted as to make a price concession expand sales significantly. When the service idea caught on so that the sales reached about 15 per cent of the market potential, demand became very responsive to price. Similarly, in this early stage the stripped models of dishwashers were not particularly effective. The new portable dishwasher, for example, "looked too cheap." Another $5.00 spent on streamlining and in embellishment made it look like another $30 to the customer.

In its present policy on appliances, G.E. apparently exercises a degree of independence associated with maintenance of quality prestige for its products. Thus G.E. itself adheres to quoted prices. At the end of a year, when a new model is coming out, G.E. gives

notices to distributors and dealers and expects them to work off their inventory before the new model comes along.[13]

At the level of distributors, and more importantly at the level of dealers, it is recognized that quoted prices are as a rule not strictly adhered to. General Electric does not fair trade its major appliance lines. Executives explain that the techniques of indirect price concession on "big ticket" items have been so finely developed "that it would take a large staff of lawyers to police fair trading in 40 states." Evasions through trade-ins and wiring charges are hard to detect and harder to prevent. These General Electric products, however, have been fair traded in a few states where distributors make the decision. While G.E. has no right to tell distributors to whom to sell, and at what price, it does believe in maintenance of the margins considered necessary to perform adequate service. It is interested in seeing that service does not deteriorate.

Whether to advertise prices of major appliances nationally has been a moot question at G.E. During the immediate postwar inflation, the policy of advertising prices nationally was abandoned because of unsettled conditions, in which production of the advertising frequently lagged behind the rising cost level.[14]

------

[13] This was contrasted with the practice of some rivals of making early price cuts on the old model. One manufacturer has been known to make large additional quantities at the end of the model year and to dump the old model at low prices, while simultaneously selling the new. The general impression is given that large companies typically adhere to quoted prices of major appliances and that small companies with less well established brands are less punctilious on this score; but this was not explicitly stated to the interviewer.

[14] However, on small appliances under $25, which were fair-traded until 1958, prices have been nationally advertised.

The experience with television sets, which in 1948 and 1949 were selling at about a 20 per cent mark-up in New York City rather than the larger margin allowed for in the suggested list price, illustrated the difficulty of preventing price shading at the dealer level. The irregularities were related to the mortality rates of independent dealers in different areas. From the standpoint of General Electric, a fair estimate is that a dealer who carries major appliances and electronic items needs about 2,000 wired homes. This is probably a factor in its selection of dealers. The company likes to see dealers big enough to have at least two outside salesmen.

Although G.E. does not regard itself as operating on a cost-plus basis in the field of consumer appliances, its realizations nevertheless do not change drastically over time, partly due to the tendency noted above for manufacturers to settle through experience on a customary price and then adjust cost to price with a "normal" profit margin in mind. What changes there are would not be mainly attributable to departure of actual prices from quoted prices but rather to variations in the proportions of long and short margin products. This type of variation is not regarded as very important. However, there is a broad secular downward change in percentage of net profit to sales as well as cyclical fluctuation.

Small portable appliances, which are sold by G.E. to a great variety of dealers, were generally fair traded in the interest of maintaining profitable margins for the dealers. The small appliance fair trading unit of General Electric has pointed out that the number of small appliances it is possible to dispose of is largely dependent on ability to attract dealers. Up to a point, sales volume may be determined by consumer elasticity of demand, but as soon as the retail price is reduced to the point at which the dealer's profit margin begins to be undermined, there is a progressive decline in the number of dealers willing to carry the article and in the extent to which they will push its sale. The problem of the manufacturer, therefore, is to set the "optimum" price, which is the one that combines attractiveness to the consumer with a profit margin satisfactory to the dealer, and ensure it through fair trading. Since many of these items are supplied as gifts, their biggest sales occurring before Christmas and on other gift-giving occasions, the company may concentrate on building consumer prestige through attractiveness rather than on an effort to be the lowest priced producer in the line.

General Electric has supplied the following case history of a small specialty item that is not fair traded, as an example of the tests applied to determine the "right price" to be suggested to retailers.

Adjustable Night Light

The market for night lights has been well established in the American retail economy. Introduced more than twenty years ago, these small lights have increased in sales until today the annual sales volume is several million units. General Electric played a dominant role in introducing the original night lights and has enjoyed a satisfactory market position ever since. Several retail channels handle the sale of these lights. Variety chains were among the first actively to promote the item, but hardware stores, drug stores, and more recently food stores have all successfully merchandised night lights.

Recently General Electric looked for product innovations which would help:

1. Expand the market.
2. Add features to better suit the customer needs.
3. Secure larger share of available market.
4. Improve G.E.'s profit position.
5. Enhance the value of the entire G.E. Wiring Device Consumer Line.

General Electric recognized that if they were to find such a product it would be necessary to employ the "double profit" system, a profit for the manufacturer and a larger profit or benefit for the customer. The question arose as to what additional features, performance, or attractiveness could be added to the present product to increase the appeal to the customer. Actually, performance and attractiveness of the present night lights left little to be desired so it appeared that the solution must involve the matter of product features.

The Marketing Section had long realized that customers' comments concerning the present night lights were centered on two general areas:

1. *Quality of Light*—Some customers complained that there was too much light —others too little. There was no control of the intensity of the light in the present products. Light intensity control was particularly desirable in a sickroom.

2. *Position*—Two forms of night light were available. In one form the light was essentially parallel to the wall where it was out of the way and could not easily be disturbed in passing. However, since some outlets are mounted vertically and the remainder horizontally, some customers would find the night light in a vertical position and others in a horizontal position. Customers generally preferred the light to be vertical. In the second type, the light protruded straight out from the wall. This light was adjustable so that light always shone down but had the disadvantage that it was easily disturbed by persons passing by.

Product Planning Specifications. The Marketing Section decided that if they could have a "de luxe" item with the above two features at the "right price," they would have a product that would satisfy the requirements. But what was the "right price"? The earlier night lights had a retail price of about 59 cents. How much would the customers pay for the additional features? The Marketing Section concluded that since this was largely an impulse item, a top price of 98 cents was desirable. Further, since more and

more retail outlets were going to self-service, the package became more important since it must do the selling job to a large extent.

A preliminary investigation indicated that an attractive number of customers were willing to pay this premium for the "de luxe" item. A Product Planning specification was prepared describing the desired features, performance and attractiveness of the product. It was recognized that color was important since the item must attract attention on the counter. Conventional night light colors are brown, ivory, pink, and blue. Ivory was rejected because it was too translucent to achieve desired lighting effect (see below); brown was rejected because it was relatively unattractive; pink and blue were selected for their attractiveness on the counter as well as their nursery appeal. G.E. felt that the higher-priced item would be more attractive as a gift than the conventional 59 cent item. Further, it was hoped that the new item would not only appeal to the new customers but would also be sufficiently attractive to cause persons who had previously purchased night lights to purchase the new, more desirable one.

Engineering Problem. The major engineering problem consisted in finding a suitable means of dimming the light that would not be too costly. Conventional methods of dimming by the use of variable resistors or variable auto transformers were rejected because of cost and size. Finally, an ingenious means of dimming the light by a mechanical shutter was devised and this was designed into a light using the "Moon and Stars" as the motif. For full brightness the shutter was adjusted mechanically to "Full Moon" effect. For lowest brightness the shutter could be adjusted so that only the "Stars" gave off light. This design was found to be patentable.

The cost estimates, based upon this design, were somewhat disappointing. Since a lower than normal return would be realized at the previously considered retail price of 98 cents, the entire price question was re-opened.

Setting Selling Price. In the final determination of price it was necessary to review the objective of the development.

1. The new light was not intended to replace existing lights but rather to upgrade a portion of the market. Even though the total annual volume of night lights was several million units, the sale of anything over 100,000 units would be considered satisfactory for the new product. Costs were essentially constant after this volume was achieved.

2. This new light was originally conceived as a 98 cent item because this is the generally considered top price for "impulse" items. However, with price inflation, customers were conditioned to seeing items of this type move up beyond the dollar figure. Also, because this was conceived as being a gift item, the higher retail price might attract more customers. Since there was no competitive product, the customer had no direct method of establishing value and could only compare it to the then available but less desirable products selling at 59 cents. However, one difficulty with even the 98 cent price was that this item was designed to be sold on the electrical counter of the retail outlets previously mentioned. Since most items on this counter sold for a much lower price, there was the question of customer resistance to a product of this price being sold on this counter.

[It was noted that from the standpoint of the retailer the item must produce a profit compatible with the counter space required to display it. A higher priced item might produce for him more dollars of profit than one selling at a lower price with higher volume. Consequently a lower sales volume (with a higher price) could justify the necessary counter space as against a drive for volume through low margin pricing.]

3. A study was made of volume-selling price relationship required to achieve the same dollar profit to the Department. These data were calculated at 99 cents, $1.09, $1.19, and $1.29 selling prices. The study disclosed that it was necessary to sell twice as many at 99 cents as was necessary at $1.09 to achieve the same dollars of profit for the manufacturer. It was necessary to sell twice as many at $1.09 as at $1.29 to achieve the same dollar profit. Four times the volume was required at 99 cents as was required at $1.29 to produce the same dollar profit. Furthermore, since costs were estimated to vary only slightly with volume above 100,000, the higher selling price provided a better return on investment.

4. Items of this type often require special pricing for special promotions. The selling price was established high enough to allow for this type of promotion on a profitable basis.

5. The final question was the effect of pricing on volume in actual test situations. If the higher price reduced sales much below 100,000, it would not be considered despite the reasons cited above. Tests were conducted in various retail outlets in selected cities to test the effect of price on sales. These tests indicated that price was not a particular factor up to and including $1.29 but that sales fell off above this figure. Consequently, the item was introduced with a suggested retail of $1.29. However, since none of our wiring devices is fair traded and no effort is made to control or establish retail prices, we have no assurance that the price was followed in all instances.

* * *

31 THE PRICE OF GASOLINE

Highway Highlights

*   *   *

The charge that retail gasoline prices are identical within a community has led some consumers and legislators to conclude that gasoline suppliers must get together to fix prices. Otherwise, the reasoning goes, some service stations would be selling at much lower prices than others.

However, a careful investigation would probably show a significant variation in gasoline prices within a community of any size. Price similarities within a community may occur around what might be called clusters of competition. Service stations engaged in direct competition with each other generally charge identical or nearly identical prices for gasoline, except for such differences as may result from off-brand gasoline being sold at a lower price than well known brands.

Competitive Market

The fact is that similar or identical gasoline prices in an area actually reflect intense competition, rather than the opposite. When a product like gasoline is sold in a truly competitive market, no one can charge significantly higher prices than his competitors and keep his customers. Gasoline consumers are on wheels. They can look around and compare posted service station prices.

On the other hand, if one dealer charges prices substantially lower than the others in an area, business will gravitate to him. His competitors will either have to cut their prices to meet his or watch their volume decline to ruinously low levels.

Thus, competition in gasoline marketing acts as a brake on higher prices. Even in the more thinly-populated states many supplying companies compete for the market in addition to the private brands marketed by local suppliers. With the number of aggressive competitors in the field, it is impossible for any one company or group of companies to determine or control the price level. With a wide choice of competing brands the motorist is not at the seller's mercy. On the contrary, each seller must keep up with competition to survive. The oil business has become one of the most fiercely competitive in the country.

Gasoline prices—like the prices of other things—are not the same everywhere. But there is really no mystery about wide variations in prices—be they gasoline prices or prices of any other commodities. A number of economic factors have an important influence in determining the various price levels. Among these are transportation costs, which vary not only according to the distances involved but also according to the means of transportation available; storage expenses, wages and salaries, land values, taxes, local laws regulating the transportation or storage of gasoline, market conditions, and the intensity of competition. Further, in some areas of the country, climate and geography play an important role because gasoline consumption drops in the winter when climatic conditions discourage all but essential driving.

From *Highway Highlights,* April, 1962, pp. 8 ff. (Published by the National Highway Users Conference.) Reprinted by permission.

In sparsely-populated states the unit cost of transporting and marketing gasoline tends to be quite high.

Dealer's Problems

At the retail level the gasoline dealer has somewhat the same problem as the refiner. The dealer also has fixed costs to contend with—rent or property taxes, wages for his employees, the cost of his equipment and inventory. As in the case of the refiner, the dealer's unit costs go down as his sales volume rises, because his overhead costs remain more or less constant whether he is pumping 10,000 gallons of gasoline a month or 50,000.

But some dealers are situated in places where their gasoline sales volume is restricted by circumstances over which they have no control. That explains why, for example, a service station on a back road, serving neighborhood needs, often tends to charge somewhat more for gasoline than a service station on a heavily traveled main road—where competition is much more intense and the unit cost of selling gasoline is lessened by a big volume of sales.

The rural gasoline dealer in a state with low population and sharp seasonal changes is at a real disadvantage. He must provide the same services and maintain the same basic equipment as a dealer serving a busy main highway, but his sales volume is necessarily much lower and subject to a sharp decline when adverse weather sets in to discourage driving.

In New Hampshire, for instance, highway consumption of gasoline is 62 per cent lower during the month of February than in August. In Wisconsin, motor vehicles consume 71 per cent less gasoline in February than in June. In Montana, there is a 53 per cent decline in January over August. These seasonal setbacks for the gasoline dealer hurt because most of his fixed costs continue, and in the winter, when gasoline sales are slack, his overhead costs mount with the added cost of heating his service station.

Thus, dealers located off the beaten track must seek a bigger gross margin per sale than urban competitors.

Price Wars

Why do companies seem to raise and lower their prices simultaneously?

The key is in the two words "seem to." Neither wholesale or retail prices of different companies change "simultaneously"; they only *seem* to.

It has already been noted that gasoline prices tend to be similar within a given market area. Gasoline prices do change, however, and when they do it means that someone has taken the initiative. When a single seller lowers his price, he does so with the intention of gaining greater volume to make up the reduction in profit he suffers on each gallon he sells. Greater volume, however, can only come at the expense of the dealer's competitors. And these competitors must cut their prices or risk losing a large part of their sales to the lower priced station.

Price increases are even more hazardous. Unless based on a sound appraisal of the market in terms of supply, demand, and cost, the results of a price increase can be disastrous for the company which initiates it. If the market analysis is incorrect, and conditions do not convince other companies to follow, a severe drop in sales would be the immediate result for the initiating company. This company may thus be forced to revert to the price level of its competitors.

Sometimes the marketer who takes the initiative in a price adjustment is the one with the greatest share of the market; sometimes it is another company. Often in today's market place the leader in a price move is an independent marketer.

Detroit Example

In 1961 there was a widespread and long drawn-out price war in Detroit. When it finally ended and a uniform price prevailed, there were demands for investigation of "big," "simultaneous" price increases. However, *The Detroit News-Times,* after an investigation of its own, told its readers:

"The gasoline industry is highly competitive, at both retail and producer level. It was bristling competition which brought prices steadily down (with no political yelps about 'collusion') to the level from which they have not rebounded so sharply. It is that same competition which will prevent the current price from sticking if it is in fact too high."

In the final analysis under the competitive enterprise system, each competitor faces the challenge of making a profit, and if he fails to meet that challenge, his business will fail. In order to make a profit he must give the public what it wants at prices the public is willing to pay. The desires of the consuming public shape and give direction to all business activity.

As an exceptionally competitive industry, petroleum is particularly sensitive, and therefore responsive, to the public's preferences in product quality, service and price. Every company in every branch of the oil business must keep up with the pace of competition in order to hold its place in the market against the rival firms that are constantly pressing to capture some of its business.

32   THE REVENUE MAXIMIZATION HYPOTHESIS

William J. Baumol

William J. Baumol is Professor of Economics at Princeton University.

Before turning to the substantive material of this brief chapter, it is necessary to explain the limitations of the evidence on which its allegations, and some of those which occur later (particularly in Chapter 6), are based. Essentially, the assertions are no more than impressions gathered through casual observation of the operation of a number of business firms. In my work I have had occasion to examine in detail some of their decisions and the data on which they were based. Perhaps equally illuminating have been management's reactions to our own recommendations. These reactions certainly seemed indicative of the nature of management's objectives and, in particular, its attitude toward profit maximization. As we shall see, this will play an important part in the sequel.

It must be emphasized, then, that the empirical observations which are reported here were highly unsystematic and represent a sample which, as

Reprinted with permission of the Macmillan Company, from *Business Behavior, Value, and Growth* by William J. Baumol, pp. 27–32, 45–50; copyright 1959 by William J. Baumol.

statistical studies go, must be considered extremely small. Their only and peculiar virtue is that they can lay claim to having come, as it were, from the inside.

Let us turn now to the real matter of this chapter. I shall take the position that, *in day-to-day decision-making,* oligopolistic interdependence plays only a small role. Of course, plans for the launching of a really major advertising campaign, or for the introduction of a radically new line of products does usually involve some discussion of the probable competitive response. But often, even in fairly crucial decisions, and almost always in routine policy-making, only the most cursory attention is paid to competitive reactions. This apparently dangerous attitude does not usually lead the businessman into serious difficulty because, I believe, his more ordinary decisions are rarely met by prompt aggressive countermoves of the sort envisaged in many of our models. There are several reasons why this should be so.

1. Complexity of Internal Organization

The modern industrial giant is a mammoth organization which is almost always engaged in many activities —some of them highly diverse in character. Its great size and complexity have been accompanied by a correspondingly large and involved managerial organization. Proposals are characteristically inaugurated at points in the organization far removed from the makers of the final decisions. Moreover, because of the multiplicity of departments usually involved, and the uneasy truce between highly centralized control and departmental autonomy, responsibility is frequently divided and is rarely well defined. As a result decision-making is often a lengthy process whose outcome is fairly unpredictable.

This decision-making apparatus is too clumsy and slow-moving for effective interplay of strategy and counter-strategy among competing firms. A move by one of them, *provided it is not too radical,* may just be ignored by the others, simply because divided responsibility invites each decision-maker to shift the responsibility on to others. Even if some countermove is proposed the suggestion is likely to be watered down as it passes through various echelons and committee meetings. And what finally does come through is very likely to come only after a very considerable lapse of time.

2. The Use of Rules of Thumb

Top executives are usually too busy, and their computational skills are sometimes too limited for them to be able to probe very deeply into every business problem. Management's difficulty is that it must retain some measure of control over the operations of the firm without, at the same time, tying itself up in operational detail. This problem is solved by the frequent use of rules of thumb—prices are set by applying a standard markup to costs; advertising expenditures are determined by setting aside a fixed percentage of total revenues; and inventories are required to meet a preset turnover norm.

These rules of thumb do not work out too badly. They translate hopelessly involved problems into simple, orderly routines. They save executive time and permit a degree of centralized control over the firm's farflung operations. By and large, they probably contribute considerably to over-all operating efficiency. Most executives appear to recognize these rules for what they are— imperfect expedients designed to cope, in a rough and ready manner, with a difficult control and decision problem.

This is one reason frequently given for asking the advice of operations researchers.

But rules of thumb tend to reduce competitive give and take among oligopolistic enterprises. Because they must be relatively simple in order to be useful, these rules do not make provision for a variety of contingencies. For example, an average cost pricing rule takes no explicit account of recent trends in the decision patterns of other firms in the industry. It provides no elaborate directions for adaptation to each of the many possible moves of competitors.

In one rather typical case, the manufacturer of a fuel kept his price just slightly above that of the nearest competing fuel because his large overheads made his average cost rather high. When it was pointed out to him that a lower price could reduce his average costs substantially through an increase in his sales volume, he accepted the suggestion with apparently little concern for the possibility that his rival would retaliate by also cutting his price. Moreover, his confidence seems to have been justified by the results. It should be added that in this industry firms in many other cities seem to have had the same experience. Very likely, the manufacturers of the competing fuels failed to meet these price cuts because they too were using average cost pricing procedures.

3. Desire for the Quiet Life

In recent years the managers of large firms have displayed signs of a desire for respectability and security. To avoid difficulties with public regulatory authorities as well as with their own stockholders, managements have veered away from the rough and tumble. But firms who wish to live and let live are not likely to be anxious to make life unpredictable for one another. And it is my impression that business organizations have, to some extent, come to depend on each other to be well-behaved. In fact, they frequently seem to expect others to go along with their decisions and, if anything, to adjust their policies in a cooperative spirit. In some cases I have even seen the possibility of competitive countermoves considered as a sort of breach of etiquette—as a slightly shocking possibility.

4. Reservations

In making a case of this sort it is quite easy to exaggerate, and doubtlessly, I have somewhat overstated the point. It is not true that a reign of perfect and universal mutual inattention has descended upon our oligopolies. Among many firms there are unsettled border disputes which lead to occasional forays. For example, in one industry where pricing seems otherwise to be conducted on a gentlemanly basis, there is mutual suspicion of the discounts that are offered (for advertising purposes) for the use of their products by nonprofit organizations! One firm undertook a sort of cloak-and-dagger investigation to find out what rebates were really being offered, and indicated that it was prepared to do whatever was necessary to get its products displayed through this channel.

Moreover, it must be recognized that while it does not usually consist of a series of strategic moves and quick responses, vigorous competitive activity does take place. The oligopolist has a fiercely tender regard for his share of the market and, if ever he finds himself losing out, energetic steps may be expected. I will discuss some implications of this attitude later in the book. But for the moment it suffices to recognize its existence, and for me to reassert my belief that in its day-to-day pricing and output decisions, the oligopolistic firm takes only the most cursory glance at the probable reactions of its competitors in the confident expectation that their unresponsiveness (so long as there is no large change in market share) will continue very similar to its own.

It must be emphasized that there still remains a very important role to be played by the theory of oligopolistic interdependence and its analysis with the aid of tools like those provided by game theory. For decisions relating to radical changes in policy these are usually as relevant as our theory has always supposed. However, the ordinary problems of value theory, the routine pricing and advertising decisions are generally not beset by these complications. This has been the burden of the argument of this chapter. Since the remainder of Part I of this book is concerned with just such problems of value theory no more will be said about questions of interdependence until Part II.

5. The Logic of Oligopolistic Decision-making

If interdependence is demoted from its central role in the theory of oligopoly some alternative must be chosen to replace it. The obvious alternative is to assume that each firm tries to maximize its profits as though it were in isolation.

However, the consequences of such an assumption are not particularly satisfying. As I shall point out later, it leaves unexplained some frequently noted features of oligopolistic behaviour. Moreover, my experience, and apparently that of some others who have worked with business firms, is that profits do not constitute the prime objective of the large modern business enterprise. It must be made clear that I am not trying to reopen the tired and

tiresome argument against the economic man. Doubtlessly, he never existed and does not now, but he is still a very useful approximation. On the contrary, I believe the businessman can usefully be viewed as a calculating individual, but one whose calculations take account of profits in a manner which differs somewhat from the standard view.

I shall maintain that the size of the firm's operations shares with profits the role of prime objective. For the moment I shall say no more about this hypothesis, postponing my discussion until Chapter 6. But first, to lay the ground for some of my later discussion, and to help supply plausibility to my hypothesis, I shall argue in the next chapter that even to the profit maximizing firm the scale of its operation can become an important proximate objective.

*   *   *

THE REVENUE MAXIMIZATION HYPOTHESIS

Though businessmen are interested in the scale of their operations partly because they see some connection between scale and profits, I think management's concern with the level of sales goes considerably further. In my dealings with them I have been struck with the importance which the oligopolistic enterprises attach to the value of their sales. A small reversal in an upward sales trend which can quite reasonably be dismissed as a random movement sometimes leads to a major review of the concern's selling and production methods, its product lines, and even its internal organizational structure.

Before going on I must make an important terminological point. In ordinary business parlance the term "sales" refers not to the number of physical

units of one of its products which has
been sold but, rather, to the *total revenue* obtained by the firm from the purchases of its customers. In the near
universal multi-product firm any measure of over-all physical volume must
involve index number problems, and
the adoption of a value measure is
doubtless to be expected. In any event,
in the sequel I shall adhere to the businessman's practice and use the terms
"sales" and "total revenue" as syn-
onyms. As a reminder, however, I will
frequently employ "dollar sales" or
"sales revenue" or some other such expressions.

1. Disadvantages of Declining Sales

There are many reasons why the
businesman should show such concern
about the magnitude of his sales. Declining sales can bring with them all
sorts of disadvantages: there is reason
to fear that consumers will shun a product if they feel it is declining in popularity, though their information on
these matters is doubtless often spotty.
Banks and the money market will tend
to be less receptive to the desires of a
firm whose absolute or relative sales
volume is declining. Perhaps even more
important in this connection is the very
real danger that firms whose sales are
declining will lose distributors—a major marketing setback. Management
also is not unmoved by the fact that in
a declining firm personnel relations are
made much more difficult when firing
rather than hiring is the order of the
day. The firm which declines (or which
remains small when others expand) can
lose monopoly power and the power
to adopt an effective competitive
counter strategy when it is called for.
And it may become more vulnerable
to a general deterioration in business
conditions. For all these reasons the executive may reasonably conclude that

maintenance of as large a sales volume
as possible is the only way to succeed
in business.

Even if size did not promote profits,
personal self-interest could well induce
the managers of a firm to seek to maximize sales. Executive salaries appear
to be far more closely correlated with
the scale of operations of the firm than
with its profitability. And in the modern corporation, which is characterized
so often by separation of ownership
from management, many executives
find it politic to avoid an absolute or
relative decline in their operations.
Here, management's concern with the
volume of sales is compounded of its
very conscientious concern with the
responsibilities of its trusteeship and a
desire to play good stockholder politics.
In any event the effects are the same—
the volume of sales achieves the status
of a prime business objective.

2. Sales as an Ultimate Objective

Up to this point, I have, in essence,
been arguing that the firm may be expected to promote sales as a means to
further its other objectives—operational efficiency and, ultimately, profits.
So far, there is no necessary clash with
orthodox analysis.

But now I propose to take the next
step and suggest that the businessman
has gone still further in his regard for
sales volume. I believe that to him
sales have become an end in and of
themselves.

It must be made clear to begin with,
that this hypothesis in no way conflicts
with an assumption of rationality. People's objectives are whatever they are.
Irrationality surely must be defined to
consist in decision patterns which make
it more difficult to attain one's own
ends, and not in choosing ends that are,
for some reason, considered to be
wrong. Unless we are prepared to de-

termine other people's values, or unless they pursue incompatible objectives, we must class behaviour as rational if it efficiently pursues whatever goals happen to have been chosen.

The evidence for my hypothesis that sales volume ranks ahead of profits as the main object of the oligopolist's concern, is again highly impressionistic; but I believe it is quite strong. Surely it is common experience that, when one asks an executive, "How's business?", he will answer that his *sales* have been increasing (or decreasing), and talk about his profit only as an afterthought, if at all. And I am told the requirements for acceptance to membership in the Young Presidents Organization (an honorific society) are that the applicant be under 40 years of age and president of a company whose annual volume is over a million dollars. Presumably it makes no difference if this firm is in imminent danger of bankruptcy.

Nor is this failure to emphasize profits a pure rationalization or a mere matter of careless phrasing. Almost every time I have come across a case of conflict between profits and sales the businessmen with whom I worked left little doubt as to where their hearts lay. It is not unusual to find a profitable firm, in which some segment of its sales can be shown to be highly unprofitable. For example, I have encountered several firms who were losing money on their sales in markets quite distant from the plant where local competition forced the product price down to a level which did not cover transportation costs. Another case was that of a watch distributor whose sales to small retailers in sparsely settled districts were so few and far between that the salesmen's wages were not made up by the total revenues which they brought in. When such a case is pointed out to management, it is usually quite reluctant to abandon its unprofitable

markets. Businessmen may consider seriously proposals which promise to put these sales on a profitable basis. There may be some hope for the adoption of a suggestion that a new plant be built nearer the market to which current transportation costs are too high, or that watch salesmen be transferred to markets with greater sales potential and a mail order selling system be substituted for direct selling in little populated regions. But a program which explictly proposes any cut in sales volume, whatever the profit considerations, is likely to meet a cold reception. In many cases firms do finally perform the radical surgery involved in cutting out an unprofitable line or territory, but this usually occurs after much heart-searching and delay.

3. The Role of Profits

It is tempting to object that along this road lies bankruptcy; and so it would if management were prepared not only to subordinate profit considerations to sales, but to disregard profits altogether. After all, maximum sales might require prices so low that the costs would nowhere be covered. It is quite true that there is some conflict between the firm's sales goal and its profit objectives, and, as is to be expected, the matter is settled by compromise. The compromise is, of course, usually tacit, its terms ill-defined, and doubtless, it varies from case to case. But I think it is, nevertheless, possible to set up a formal relationship which is analytically useful and, at the same time, provides us with a reasonably close approximation to the facts.

The nature of this approximation is again best suggested by an illustrative experience. A manufacturer of a new synthetic yarn indicated that he was reluctant to promote sales by introducing his product at a price which would not cover the cost of his small initial outputs. The firm's usual rate of return on investment played an explicit and very fundamental role in these deliberations. It was made clear that management was not concerned to obtain profits higher than this. Once this minimum profit level was achieved, sales revenues rather than profits became the over-riding goal.

I suspect that the much publicized practice of average cost pricing is a crude attempt to achieve just this sort of goal. Prices are set at a fixed markup above average costs, not only because this is a convenient rule of thumb, but also because the practice appears to set a floor under the rate of return. Of course, it does not always work out in that way because volume can be mis-calculated and cost estimates may therefore turn out to be incorrect. But the objective of the procedure seems clear nevertheless.

I am prepared to generalize from these observations and assert that the typical oligopolist's objectives can usefully be characterized, approximately, as sales maximization subject to a minimum profit constraint. Doubtless this premise over-specifies a rather vague set of attitudes but I believe it is not too far from the truth. So long as profits are high enough to keep stockholders satisfied and contribute adequately to the financing of company growth, management will bend its efforts to the augmentation of sales revenues rather than to further increases in profits.

*   *   *

C.
BIG BUSINESS AND GOVERNMENT POLICY

33   ECONOMIC POWER AND THE FREE SOCIETY

A. A. Berle, Jr.

A. A. Berle, Jr. is Professor of Law at Columbia University. He was formerly Assistant Secretary of State, and has held several other high government positions.

The cycle of shift from individual possessory holdings into power systems, and from power systems back once more into possessory personal holdings, appears to be a kind of rhythm of history, especially in the West. As the feudal system merged into the king state, the revolutionary doctrine that there should be private property began to assert itself, reaching a high degree of philosophical justification in the middle of the Eighteenth Century when

From *Economic Power and the Free Society* (New York: Fund for the Republic, 1957). Reprinted by permission.

the French physiocrats declared that if a man was to be free, able to speak his own mind, depict his own thought and develop his own personality, he would have to have a base apart from one that was politically or ecclesiastically organized and controlled. The theory of private property as a part of freedom reached its culmination in the French Revolution and in the far slower and quieter industrial revolution in England.

No doubt the American system is the child of that revolution. Certainly the Jeffersonian ideal was a country in which everyone had private property, no one was very rich, no one was very poor. In order to make this system work, however, a companion theory was needed—that economics worked automatically. The self-interest of men levering against each other and controlling each other through competition resulted in a splendid ethical balance wheel, which was the open market. This leveled out inequalities, eliminated the inefficient and through competition prevented an undue concentration of power.

Adam Smith's *Wealth of Nations* consecrated the theory. Smith said that this strange animal "the corporation" could never be a major factor in economics because in it men worked for other men, and obviously no man would ever pay as much attention to other men's affairs as he would to his own. Therefore, such a collective enterprise could never play a major role in society. Its inefficiency would always be such that the workings of the market would eliminate it. Thus, the corporation was merely an agency of the state for specialized purposes, and those suspect.

At the convention which met to draw up the Constitution of the United States the proposal was made that the Federal government be given the power to incorporate. According to Madison's notes the answer was: No, a corporation prevented men from getting into action and this is a dangerous power. A corporation had not merely the privilege of existence but other privileges as well, or if it did not have them it could get them. As a result monopolies would arise and dominate the United States. This should not be allowed.

So the Federal government was specifically denied the power to create corporations. This was to be left to the states and it was assumed that they would not exercise this power or, if they did, would exercise it only as a means of carrying on government. This doctrine survived less than fifteen years. By 1791 the Federal government found it desirable to organize a corporation entitled the Bank of the United States, and in the 1819 Supreme Court case *McCulloch v. Maryland* Justice Marshall decided that the implied powers granted to the government of the United States included the power to form a corporation if it were apposite to the particular functions the government wished to perform. It is still true that the Federal government can create corporations only for governmental or quasi-governmental purposes; the states, on the other hand, have been allowed to create them as they would, and as our technology developed corporations began to proliferate to such an extent that by 1835 our great-grandfathers felt that the situation called for a close look.

As we look back on their findings now, they made a surprisingly accurate prediction of the probable effects of an unlimited corporate life. (They were not so sound, perhaps, in their estimate as to whether it was desirable or undesirable.) For the next fifty years they used every known legal means to keep a corporation to a single defined and manageable enterprise. The corporation lawyer of the period spent most of his time on the law of *ultra vires,* which dealt with corporations that tried to transcend the limits that had been set out for them. These limits ordinarily were:

First, that they could only own a limited amount of property, frequently and especially only a limited amount of real property. The fear was they would start absorbing huge quantities of land.

Second, that they could indulge in only one type of business. If a corporation was organized to run a flour-mill, it had to run a flour-mill and nothing more.

Third, that they should last only for a defined period of time, twenty or thirty years or whatever the statutory limitation was.

Not infrequently there was a fourth limitation. This was that the corporation should be subject to continuous inspection. The courts could appoint a "visitor"—today he would be called an auditor. He was authorized to inspect and analyze the workings of a corporation and report to the judge, who, in turn, had an undefined power to say what should or should not be done.

A variety of other limitations were imposed from time to time, all of them representing attempts to prevent exactly what happened:

First, that a corporation would grow so large that its economic strength would vastly outweigh the strength of any individual enterprise.

Second, that it would be able to rove the country, if not the world, at will and do what it wished in terms of economic enterprise.

And third, that it woud become a trust

for perpetual accumulation; that its assets, in so far as they were not distributed by way of dividends, would be permitted to pile up to unlimited amounts.

These three results have come about, of course. Corporations did do, have done and are doing exactly what our forefathers worried about. Part of their fear stemmed from the belief that the corporation was only an artificial personality and therefore did not have a soul or a conscience. Lacking a conscience, it had no morals and was *prima facie* dangerous. This is why throughout our history society has attempted to control and constrict the corporation.

The rise of the large contemporary corporation—the giant as we know it today, the true collectivism—began with the railroad systems. There were other large corporations, but the railroad systems were the ones that posed the real problems. They were the first to demonstrate the shift in the private property system that came about when we began to realize that there was no real way of constricting a corporation whose business the community needed. If its economic functions were necessary to the welfare of the community, the law somehow had to recognize that fact, however backhandedly. If a railroad needed to go through to the Pacific coast, the law had to find some way around the fact that the corporate power did not let it go that far.

A diagram of what was happening to private property while this was going on would look something like this:

"PP" or possessory property is where it all began in about 1810 or 1820. This is our great-great-grandfather's farm or forge, which he had not only created but owned and operated. This was the assumed unit of property at the beginning, and even today we still talk in those terms. This possessory property becomes incorporated as an enterprise and is immediately split into two functions. At the left is one function—"PR" or "passive receptive." This is the receptive side of property, the stockholder's share. The shareholder cannot manage. Every corporation statute in the country says that the business of the corporation shall be managed by its directors, and almost every court has agreed that the director is not an agent of the stockholder and does not have to follow his instructions. So the right-hand side of the diagram is "MC" or managing and creating.

The business of stockholders is primarily to receive; the business of management is primarily to manage and create. In the early days, when corporations were still small, the stockholder powerfully influenced the director but today they are so far apart that the stockholder can hardly communicate with management even by megaphone. We go through the ancient forms and it is good that we do so, but everyone knows that a stockholders' meeting is a kind of ancient, meaningless ritual like some of the ceremonies that go on with the mace in the House of Lords. The "passive receptive" side of the corporation, in short, is functionless.

The "MC" side looks better at first glance. But in any large corporation the management group is actually as striated as it is possible to be. The president and the chairman of the board probably work together as the theoretically responsible officers, but

they must operate through committees of officers—big officers, medium officers and little officers, all divided in as many different ways as the management experts can invent. While the top officers officially have the right to enter upon the property and do things, even though they are not able to own it, the fact is that they have had to sub-divide that right to such a degree that in practice the real possessor of a piece of property is the manager of the particular division or area of the property—and even he probably has to share his right with his plant manager if he's got one. This is possession without right, just as on the "passive receptive" side there is right without possession.

As things look now, this unbalance is about to be redressed. Whether it will be good redressing is another matter. Theoretically, management got its legitimacy by the fact that it represented the will of the shareholders. This was a kind of quasi-amateur democratic legitimacy. However, on examination, it was found that although the stockholders theoretically chose the management, in point of fact they were completely unable to do so. The management would send out a proxy naming three agents whom the stockholders appointed to cast their vote at a meeting. In older days the management often didn't even bother to say for what directors these proxies would cast their vote. Since the Securities and Exchange legislation, they have to do that, but the corporation secretary who sent out the proxies was the man who really determined what happened for all practical purposes in the power relationship. The president or the directors could fire him, of course, so he did what they told him to do. When the directors wished to renominate themselves or to add to their number or to fill a vacancy, they did it. This is still the method by which the directors in a great corporation are chosen. This is an automatic self-perpetuating oligarchy.

These are a string of bad words. There was at least one court case in which it was held that a self-perpetuating oligarchy was illegal. This was the famous case in which a life insurance company in New Jersey purchased control of a trust company by buying a majority of the shares. Thereafter it caused the trust company to purchase a majority of *its* shares. The result was an unbreakable ring. A New Jersey court said that this was illegal, created an oligarchy and was contrary to the theory of New Jersey corporation laws.

However, thereafter, somebody asked whether corporations really should be run democratically. Should this group or that group or the other group campaign against each other, offering inducements to shareholders to vote for them instead of the other group? Could corporations assimilate this kind of democratic government? There was no answer. In point of fact, the choice of management depends not on an assent of balanced interest but on expert judgment of technical ability with a companion judgment of honesty and character. As a result, for all practical purposes, management controls the corporation unless it is itself controlled by another oligarchy with enough shares to dominate the situation at all times.

There is a good deal of loose thinking about this. It is commonly believed that the holder of 20 per cent or 25 per cent of a corporation's stock can control that corporation. This was the inference in the recent du Pont-General Motors case. This is not true. It is true that with 20 per cent or 25 per cent of the stockholders' list of a large corporation *plus* control of the directors it can be done. But if the directors of General Motors decided not to vote with du Pont, it is very doubtful whether the du Pont interest is sufficient to be able to go out and get the other 30 per cent of General Motors stockholders which it would need. This is not pure theory. When a certain gentleman ran Standard Oil of Indiana he did various things that induced the so-called controlling group to want a change. They canvassed the board of directors and asked whether they would not fire the man. The directors said they would not. Thereupon the controlling group went to work to try to win the next election. Between their own and allied holdings they had slightly over 20 per cent of the stock. They did control in the end, and the man was fired. But they achieved it only by spending about $800,000 on a stockholders' campaign.

The control system in today's corporations, when it does not lie solely in the directors as in the American Telephone and Telegraph Company, lies in a combination of the directors of a so-called control bloc (a misnomer, incidentally) plus the directors themselves. For practical purposes, therefore, the control or power element in most large corporations rests in its group of directors and it is autonomous —or autonomous if taken together with a control bloc. And inheritance-tax distribution of stock being what it is, the trend is increasingly to management autonomy. This is a self-perpetuating oligarchy.

Meanwhile the next phase has been emerging. It will stay with us and it will be of some interest. This involves what are known as pension trusts— welfare funds and pension trust funds. A pension trust in most cases differs from an insurance trust in that it has an unlimited and indefinite obligation. It is there to pay pensions to X, Y and Z which shall be a fraction of the salaries X, Y and Z will have collected during the years of their tenure. The pension trust fund, if it is properly administered, has to think not merely of paying out a stated number of dollars in, say, 1980, as an insurance company does, but of having enough dollars to meet obligations later to be determined. No human being knows the future course of inflation of the dollar, prices, pay and so forth. Nevertheless, although the payment period may be twenty or thirty years away, the pension trusts must keep abreast of inflation at least as it affects pay.

This suggests, of course, that they must invest in equities, whereas, classically, trust funds invested in fixed obligations. This is the sharp difference between the kind of burden resting on an honorable pension trustee and on the directors of, say, the New York Life Insurance Company, whose business is to provide a stated number of dollars against stated contracts to pay those dollars with interest later on. The pension trust funds, therefore, belong among the stockholders in the "passive-receptive" column of our diagram because of their ownership of common stocks. The holdings of life insurance companies include less than 5 per cent in common-stock equities; in the pension trust funds equities are running close to 30 per cent of their assets and may be more. The total of pension trust funds at the moment is almost $31 billion. Roughly half of this is in the hands of insurance companies, which operate—perhaps erroneously—on the assumption that they have only another set of insurance policies. Ninety per cent of the remaining pension funds are in the hands of eight or nine New York banks, the largest single one being the pension trust fund of the American Telephone & Telegraph Company, which is about $2.2 billion so far and is operated by a com-

mittee through the Bankers Trust Company.

As a result of this broad-scale buying of equities the pension trusts are slowly "chewing up" control of those corporations which offer the best means of equity investment. These are voting equities. Thus far no attempt has been made to make use of this except in the case of the Sears Roebuck pension trust fund which undertook to buy Sears Roebuck stock and presumably now has a controlling interest in the company. As a result Sears Roebuck is socializing itself via its own pension trust fund, and is discovering that it is running into the same difficulty which a socialist or any other form of oligarchic government has—that it has self-contained control, and management is thus responsible to itself. Query: does it continue to have "legitimacy" when the only mandate it can refer to is its own?

The present $30 billion in the pension trusts of course is doomed to increase. These are compulsory savings and the funds must continue to accumulate. They now cover only about half of the non-farm labor force; they will undoubtedly soak up a considerable part of the balance before long, and must increase, particularly in view of the population rise. In addition, it will be another twenty or thirty years before this "levels off"; that is, before the payment from the funds begins to balance the incoming. The pension trust funds will perhaps level out at somewhere in the vicinity of $70 to $80 billion, probably increased by the coefficient of the increase in population or the increase in labor force within the population. This will mean that if the pension trusts continue to take the good equities as they have been doing, they may well have the prevailing control-stockholding position and the capacity to make it absolute. They will have, say, 20 per cent to 30 per cent of the good equity stocks and the capacity to increase that to 40 per cent or 50 per cent (45 per cent for practical purposes is a majority at any big stockholders' meeting).

With the rise of the pension trusts into the "passive-receptive" end of the corporation structure the old "passive-receptive" stockholder is gradually disappearing. At best he is, shall we say, a pensionnaire. The last vestige of his power to legitimate a management by a vote is in the hands of the pension trustees. He has an expectation arising out of the fact that he may have performed a certain number of years of acceptable work and fulfilled a certain number of other conditions. But does he have any property right in the pension trust? The courts say no. The power—what is left of it—lies in the trustees, or in those insurance companies which administer trusts.

When power is lodged in a particular group it has no choice except either to exercise it or to try to revolutionize the system. There is no way of avoiding power. If you take it and refuse to exercise it you suffer the fate of King Lear—the king who wanted to be king but did not want to be bothered. The trust funds admit they have it but they have thus far refused to use it. This situation cannot last very much longer. Somebody is bound to use that power, of necessity. Pension trusts are so concentrated that a relatively small amount in equities outbalances any number of scattered holdings.

The private property system in production, which began with our great-grandfather's farm and forge, has almost vanished in the vast area of American economy dominated by this system. Instead we have something which differs from the Russian or socialist system mainly in its philosophical content. Under a pure socialist or Communist system, in theory, every worker has an old-age pension at the end of his labors. We are developing the same thing by "socializing" property without a revolution. It is one of our more amazing achievements. Whether one likes it or not depends on one's philosophy.

Possessory private property in this area has been metamorphosed. In its place is a power pyramid. At the moment this is a management pyramid, but it is beginning to be balanced by a pyramid of men who have no possible property interest in the actual corpus but do have the power of choice—the pension trustees. These are naked power vehicles, with the "receptive" end so far dispersed that it cannot even be discerned. To make the joke complete, let us suppose that a pension trust liquidated itself tomorrow and satisfied its contract obligations. If it was a well-run trust, there would be a balance left over. That balance would very likely escheat to the state because there was no claimant to it left. In the most violently private-property-minded country in the world this is perhaps one of the most magnificent economic jests the world has seen.

None of this has come about as a result of the villainy of conspiring men. That might have been true in the free-wheeling corporation days of a hundred years ago, but it would be as ridiculous an assumption today as is the basic assumption of the Supreme Court decision in the recent du Pont case. This decision apparently assumed that because du Pont bought 23 per cent of General Motors forty years ago, perhaps hoping that it could control General Motors, du Pont still holds to the intention of exercising this control. Actually, there has been a kind of continual biological progression over the years. Change is part of the progression. Bigger enterprise was needed to satisfy the desires of the population. In addition, the techniques which made it possible to satisfy certain necessities made it *impossible* to rely only on the individual. Consequently, organization and power, not ownership, had to meet the resulting problems. The progression has been natural.

Today approximately 50 per cent of American manufacturing—that is everything other than financial and transportation—is held by about 150 corporations, reckoned, at least, by asset values. If finance and transportation are included, the total increases. If a rather larger group is taken, the statistics would probably show that about two-thirds of the economically productive assets of the United States, excluding agriculture, are owned by a group of not more than 500 corporations. This is actual asset ownership. (Some further statistical analysis is called for if financial corporations be included, for these, of course, double up. One of the largest and most plainly oligarchically controlled corporations in the United States, the Metropolitan Life Insurance Company, duplicates assets because it holds securities of other corporations.) But in terms of power, without regard to asset positions, not only do 500 corporations control two-thirds of the non-farm economy but within each of that 500 a still smaller group has the ultimate decision-making power. This is, I think, the highest concentration of economic power in recorded history. Since the United States carries on not quite half of the manufacturing production of the entire world today, these 500 groupings—each with its own little dominating pyramid within it—represent a concentration of power over economics which makes the medieval feudal system look like a Sunday School party. In sheer economic power this has gone far beyond anything we have yet seen.

We can talk about the various alleged legal controls which somehow or other, when the chips are down, neither control nor even seek to control. We can point out the fear of "monopoly" and "restraint of trade" and say that from time to time this fear has checked the process. True, our law has prevented any one of these power groups from becoming a monopoly, but it has not seriously prevented the concentration of power as power, though it has prevented certain ultimate results. The question is then: Why has concentrated economic power in America not got completely out of hand? Many of these corporations have budgets, and some of them have payrolls, which, with their customers, affect a greater number of people than most of the ninety-odd sovereign countries of the world. American Telephone & Telegraph, for example, based on combined population and wealth, would be somewhere around the thirteenth state of the union in terms of budget, and certainly larger than many of the countries of South America. Some of these corporations are units which can be thought of only in somewhat the way we have heretofore thought of nations.

Whether we like it or not, this is what has happened. As noted, it is not the product of evil-minded men. I believe that we must try to work with the system. The dangers are obvious. But history cannot usually be reversed. Until engineers and economic forces give us a way by which a man can manufacture an automobile in his back yard we will continue to have organizations the size of General Motors or Ford—as long as people want Chevrolets or Fords. We will have railroads the length of the Union Pacific as long as people want to go across the continent by railroad. In other words, until a combination of technique and organization can be invented permitting *individuals* to do the job, we are bound to try to make the best we can out of the situation. To my mind most of the results are rather surprisingly good.

This does not mean, however, that I am not afraid. I am. I believe it is the *content* of these systems rather than their *form* that matters. Their power can enslave us beyond present belief, or perhaps set us free beyond present imagination. The choice lies with the men who operate the pyramids, and with the men affected who can demand what they really want. Our Anglo-Saxon democratic liberties, after all, were beaten out, not against the framework of the personal possessory property regime, but against the background of two of the most brutal despotisms in Western history. Both the Angevin dynasty in Normandy and the Tudor dynasty in England were rank despotisms. The content of our democratic liberties from Magna Carta down was pumped in by extraneous moral processes. Our institutionalized liberties present the case of an institution conscripted into utility, rather than something that emerged full-armed from the head of Jove. It was probably better that way; the democracy of the Greeks did not work so very well.

We have to accept this power situation as, let us call it, a neutral mechanism subject to the control of the body politic as long as we *keep* it subject to that control. That control, I believe, will be essentially intellectual and philosophical, capable of being translated into legal rules when necessity arises. In that respect I make three points in summary:

I

The first is that whenever there is a question of power there is a question of legitimacy. As things stand now, these instrumentalities of tremendous power have the slenderest claim of legitimacy. This is probably a transitory period. They must find some claim of legitimacy, which also means finding a field of responsibility and a field of accountability. Legitimacy, responsibility and accountability are essential to any power system if it is to endure. They correspond to a deep human instinct. A man desires beyond anything else to have someone give him the accolade of "Well done, thou good and faithful servant," thereby risking the condemnation of "You have been no good—get out." If he has to say it to himself, or hear it from a string of people whom he himself has hired or controls, he is apt to die a cynical and embittered man.

The medieval feudal power system set the "lords spiritual" over and against the "lords temporal." These were the men of learning and of the church who in theory were able to say to the greatest power in the world: "You have committed a sin; therefore either you are excommunicate or you must mend your ways." The "lords temporal" could reply: "I can kill you." But the "lords spiritual" could retort: "Yes, that you can, but you cannot change the philosophical fact." In a sense this is the great lacuna in the economic power system today. In theory the stockholders can act as the "lords spiritual" through their vote. In fact they cannot, and they know they cannot. Are the pension trustees or their equivalent slowly emerging as the men who can? They had not thought so—nobody had thought so. They have been essentially a method of transmission of choice and not much else. We are looking for the kind of thing that C. Wright Mills in his recent book on the American power elite rightly said did not exist. He wrongly concluded, therefore, that the system was a mess, which it obviously is not. We are, if you choose, searching for the pyramid on the other side of our diagram. But every time we have had the chance to construct that kind of elite we seem to have abandoned it, and chucked in an administrator instead.

II

My second summary point is that the sheer power of invading personality is great and that a doctrine is already at work which plays a second joke on our constitutional system. The United States began by saying that its Federal government could not construct corporations and apparently by assuming that the states would not. Both have done so. It also said that corporations should be kept apart from governmental power. *De facto,* they have not been. We are now, in fact, beginning to converge on a doctrine which may well push right over the line when the next case comes up. This doctrine is that where a corporation has power to affect a great many lives (differing from the little enterprise which can be balanced out by the market) it should be subject to the same restraints under the Constitution that apply to an agency of the Federal or state government. In that case, the Bill of Rights and the Fourteenth and Fifteenth Amendments would apply. At the moment this is one jump ahead of current law. Yet it seems probable that this will be the next phase— just as we already have the constitutional doctrine that under the First Amendment you may not by private contract prohibit a Negro from buying land.

III

My third point is destined to be in infinitely greater controversy, and I do not know what the end of the con-

troversy will be. Great corporate power is exercised in relation to certain obligations:

1. It should supply the want in the area of its production. Where the community has come to rely on a corporation for steel, oil, automobiles or cigarettes, the corporation is obliged reasonably to meet that demand.

2. The price must not be considered extortionate. It must be "acceptable" —which doesn't necessarily mean fair or just.

3. It must provide at least some continuity of employment.

4. It must give a continuing attention to the technical progress of the art.

At every point in the individual history of large corporations there has been some moment of impact on the community when either the community felt the corporation was not fulfilling its obligations or, alternatively, the corporation realized it was up against a situation it could not handle. In every case the result has been either a friendly and orderly, or unfriendly and disorderly, hassle out of which a piece of planned economy emerged. Roughly two-thirds of American industry and much of American finance is now controlled by a formal or informal Federal industrial plan. Here are two illustrations at each end of the cycle.

The oil industry claims to be the most non-socialist, free-wheeling, private business that ever was. But the fact is that after many vicissitudes it sought control by, and is controlled by, various Acts of Congress. After orderly discussion certain laws were passed. Under these laws, first, the Bureau of Mines of the Department of Interior estimates the probable consumption month by month of gasoline and the chief oil products. Second, an interstate treaty exists among the oil-producing states, ratified by the Congress. Third, a Congressional Act makes it illegal to transport oil in interstate commerce which has been produced in excess of a state allowable. This legislation might break down if it were not for the fact that because there is a relatively concentrated system in the oil industry the refineries will not buy "non-certified" oil anyway. As a result, the big companies do not violate the Act; the little ones cannot; and the result is a planned oil economy by which supply is equated to demand and the oil industry from well to refinery to gas station is more or less geared to meet it.

Here is a disorderly example: Aluminum was manufactured by a monopoly which was ordered to be split up under an anti-trust decree. By a combination of administrative orders entirely without administrative rationale but all working toward the same end the Federal government used the aluminum plants it had itself created during World War II in order to set up two competitors to Alcoa. It likewise required Alcoa to sell its Aluminum of Canada shares. This was not enough by itself, so the government for a period of years handled its defense orders in such a way that the new companies had adequate assurance of a market until they could get properly under way. The policy still is to make certain that the new companies, which can stay in business only by being assured a reasonable market, will get the extent of market they need. There was a stockpiling arrangement at one time, followed later by the release of part of the stockpiled aluminum. In a wholly disorderly way which only the American system could ever conceive,

there arose the equivalent of a *de facto* planned economy in aluminum. At the moment this industry now sails away, free-wheeling. But there is not the slightest doubt that if conditions required transition back into a planned economy it would happen.

These two illustrations could be multiplied. The point is merely that (a) through constitutionalization of the corporation some attention is being paid to the protection of the individual; and (b) through a slowly emerging, industry-by-industry, flexibly-planned economy, some protection of the community is coming about.

Obviously a system like this is just as good as the ideas and strength of the body politic behind it. The same system in the hands, for example, of a Latin American dictator could produce terrible oppression.

There is a gradually growing feeling that pension trusts, for example, must be controlled. A pension trust ring could be something to bind a man beyond belief. It could bind him to his job. He could not change it without losing a substantial part of his life savings. He might be controlled in all sorts of ways. We are beginning to think even that the pension trust right which cannot be transferred to some other pension trust is suspect.

As men think, so they are. We are really seeking now a body of doctrine which will control power. I close by returning to my first point, which related to the desperate search for a field of responsibility and accountability referent to some point of view outside the system: that is, to some modern "lords spiritual." I suggest that the real purpose of the Fund for the Republic's basic issues program is to supply exactly that.

34 THE ELECTRIC CONSPIRACY CASE

Wall Street Journal

THE PROBLEMS OF PRICE FIXING

For a number of years various electrical companies and individuals successfully evaded the antitrust laws. They periodically met to fix prices, divide up markets and otherwise cartellize their industry.

But examination of court records of the cases indicates the conspiracy was not a very successful one. Prices were not fixed except temporarily—some one of the conspirators was forever evading the intent of conspiracy.

Markets were divided somewhat more successfully, but here again the planners of the market were always running afoul of new circumstances which did not fit into the master plan. Certainly the attempt to evade the give and take of the market place meant for the people and companies involved a good deal of unforeseen trouble—the law aside. Red tape flourished; bureaucracy, unofficial and perhaps illegal though it may have been, grew apace. The need for conspiratorial gatherings mounted, all as man-made rules were substituted for competition.

For example, the circuit breaker conspiracy involving General Electric, Westinghouse, Allis-Chalmers and Federal Pacific ran into this problem in 1958—what to do about the entrance onto the scene of a new company? While a new competitor is never an easy matter for an individual company, it was also quite complex for the conspirators.

What happened was that I-T-E Circuit Breaker Co., a factor in other aspects of the electrical equipment business, in 1958 bought out a small company and wanted to enter the circuit breaker field where prices were being fixed and markets allotted on a percentage basis.

"Now, room had to be made for I-T-E," Antitrust Chief Bicks noted in remarks at the arraignment of the defendants. "So a series of meetings began in January of 1958, at which I-T-E indicated its desire for some business. I-T-E had bought a company; it wanted to get into the business.

"The knowledge by I-T-E that it was entering into a pre-existing conspiracy is clear beyond doubt from the pattern of events in early 1958. I-T-E began meeting with the four conspirators that had been going, going more or less smoothly, it's true, with greater or less success, with greater or less mutual confidence that each of the conspirators was living up to his part of the deal, but, nonetheless, one constant conspiracy I-T-E sought to get in.

Over-all Policy

"In early 1958 I-T-E secured an agreement as to the over-all pricing policy leaving the allocation aside.

"The nature of that agreement arrived at in early 1958 at a series of meetings was roughly this, that general pricing would be tied to G.E.'s book price, that I-T-E in the southern part of California would be allowed 15% off, that I-T-E nationally would

From *The Wall Street Journal*, January 10, 12, 1962. Reprinted by permission.

be allowed 5% off . . . Remaining to be finalized was I-T-E's allocation share of the sealed bid business. This was discussed . . . I-T-E was cut in for a share of 4% following a series of conferences, and so from 1958 on everybody cut back a bit except Federal Pacific. . . .

The three big companies, G.E., Westinghouse, Allis-Chalmers . . . cut down their percentage. Federal Pacific came up from 10 to 15. I-T-E was cut in for 4. That was roughly the pattern of the conspiracy that kept on until the date of the indictment."

I-T-E, seeking to plead no contest in this case, said among other things that it was charged with being only a small factor in the industry for a short period of time. It has told its men to stay away from competitors, that if they're caught in such activities again they'll be fired.

It was one thing, as in the circuit breaker case, to agree that a certain company would get a specific piece of sealed-bid business. It was something else again to see that the designated company actually got the job. Here, again according to Mr. Bicks' statement to the court, is how that worked, amid burgeoning red tape.

"At a working level meeting where a particular big job was up for discussion the percentages initially would be reviewed in light of what was known as the ledger list, which had on it recent sealed-bid jobs given to the other defendants. In light of that ledger list it was decided which of the companies, to keep the percentages constant, would get the job. Now if that company was prepared to say the price at which it was going to bid, then the other companies could discuss among themselves what they would bid, add on for accessories, to make sure to give . . . the company . . . whose turn it was to get the job, the best shot at it.

Numbers Code

"If the company, whose job the particular rigged job was supposed to be did not know the price, there would be later communication, either by phone to homes with just the first names used, or by letter to homes with just first names of senders, with no return address, and this wonderful code . . . The numbers were 1, General Electric; 2, Westinghouse; 3, Allis-Chalmers; and 7, Federal Pacific. What happened to 4 or 5 and 6 until I-T-E, came in remains a mystery."

One of the great ironies of the conspiracies was that no matter how hard the participants schemed, no matter how friendly their meetings and communications might be, there was an innate tendency to compete. Someone was always violating the agreements to get more business and this continually called for new illegal plans. For example, price-cutting in sales of power switching equipment to Government agencies was getting out of hand in late 1958. This led to the "quadrant" system of dividing markets.

"So," declared Baddia Rashid, chief of the trial section of the antitrust division, "at a meeting in November of 1958 at Philadelphia . . . they decided that the best way to handle the sealed-bid market was to allocate the business; however, since there were sixteen companies involved in this particular conspiracy it would have been difficult to try to allocate the business as in other cases on a percentage basis, and therefore it was decided that it would be best to divide the country into four separate geographical areas which were called quadrants—the northwest quadrant, the southwest quadrant, the southeast quadrant, and the northeast quadrant.

"Four companies were assigned to

participate in each quadrant, and one of the company representatives in that quadrant was designated as a secretary for the purpose of handling the allocation within the particular quadrant." For example, ". . . in the northeast quadrant . . . meetings were held and it was decided that the business within that quadrant would be allocated in an alphabetical rotation . . ."

This plan did not work to everyone's satisfaction, but rather than fall back on the give and take of the market place which the law requires, the conspirators formulated another plan.

"In September of 1959, however, there were some complaints that had arisen because some companies felt they were not getting a sufficient share of the business . . . it appeared that certain of the quadrants were obtaining more sealed-bid business than other quadrants. Therefore, they held a meeting in Pittsburgh . . . in September, 1959 . . . and they discussed this situation . . . After some discussion it was finally decided that perhaps the best way to do it would be to go back to a national allocation scheme at which each company would be allotted a certain percentage of the business. They all agreed to that plan and each company was then asked to indicate what percentage of the sealed-bid market it felt it should obtain . . . An individual from one of the . . . companies was designated to act as secretary . . ."

But the basic problem, in this industry where price fluctuations were sometimes drastic, was "stabilizing" prices and efforts to bring this about spawned many a difficulty.

Reviewing the Books

In one case one conspirator sneaked in a bid on a product below the price level which had been agreed upon, the Government said. Discussions among the conspirators followed and the offending company was asked to bring in its books so they could be checked. The representatives of the other companies reviewed them and decided "that this company had deviated from the established prices. So the representative from this company indicated that henceforward he would try to control it a little better." Such meetings to keep the co-price-fixers in line were frequent in other cases.

In a case involving industrial controls these meetings became quite numerous. The Government characterizes this case as perhaps the most serious price fixing case encountered in the "past five or ten years." It counted 31 separate meetings from 1955 until the date of the indictment by the defendants, General Electric, Westinghouse, Square D Co., Cutler-Hammer Co., Clark Controller Co. and Allen-Bradley Co. Mr. Rashid spelled out some of the details for the court.

"The first (meeting) occurred in August of 1955, in Maine. At this meeting all of the defendants except a representative of General Electric were present . . . the individuals present agreed to increase the prices of industrial control equipment by 10% and to put this price increase into effect the following September. They mutually agreed that Cutler-Hammer would be the first to announce the price change and that the rest would follow thereafter.

"There was another meeting in November of 1955 at Atlantic City, New Jersey, in which again all the defendants except General Electric met to discuss the effect this recent price increase was having on the market.

"This was followed by a meeting in April of 1956 at Cleveland, Ohio. Between the November, 1955, meeting and the April, 1956, meeting, General

Electric had unilaterally put into effect a price increase. The rest of the companies therefore met in April of 1956 to decide what they would do . . . They had a discussion and decided that with respect to some products they would all follow G.E.'s prices; with respect to other products they would not follow it.

"When this was agreed upon General Electric thereafter retracted its price increase with respect to those products that the other companies did not agree to.

Mutual Complaints

"There was another meeting in May of 1956 at Hot Springs, Va., which was a so-called price-cutting-discussion meeting at which the companies got together to complain against each other when they were cutting prices from those that had been agreed upon."

In a frame-work of fixing prices, there arose also the problem of how to price a new product. In some cases the pricing problem evidently stymied introduction of the product.

At a meeting in May of 1957 at Hot Springs, Mr. Rashid declared, there was discussion of the Double O starter that Cutler-Hammer wanted to market. After general discussion there was a "consensus" reached "that it should sell for about two-thirds of the price of the starter then in existence. They tentatively agreed that this new product should be put on the market . . . on or about January 1, 1960."

The following November some of the conspirators met in the suite of Allen-Bradley at the Traymore Hotel in Atlantic City, the Government alleged.

"Cutler-Hammer at this meeting wanted to put on the market a low-quality starter; the other defendants (G.E. was not present) were complaining to Cutler-Hammer that that was a

bad practice, that what Cutler-Hammer should do should be to put on the market a high-quality standard and that the price of that product should be comparable to the price of existing starters, so that as Cutler-Hammer was contemplating reducing the price of this new starter by about 20% or 25%, that would have cut into the market of the starter that was then being marketed."

Then at a meeting on January 9, 1958, the Government said, ". . . they resumed a discussion of the Double O starter and they again criticized Cutler-Hammer for wanting a low-quality starter, and in the end the other companies won and it was agreed that Cutler-Hammer would put out a high-quality starter."

At the same meeting, "Square D Co. was criticized for having put out a new oil-type pushbutton enclosure . . . The reason they were criticized . . . was the price . . . was lower than the prices of comparable products then in existence."

These then are some of the unexpected tangles that developed from the electrical equipment conspiracies. No matter how diligently plans and schemes were laid, they somehow could not defeat the basic economic factors, which insisted on responding to the inherent forces of the free market.

*   *   *

Potentials for Trouble

Certainly the climate in which the individuals and companies in the heavy electrical equipment industry operated was loaded with potentials for trouble, and these may well have been the genesis of the legal difficulties which came to afflict a large segment.

The industry is a relatively compact one. Its members range from very large enterprises to relatively small ones. For example, among those indicted in the case were General Electric with $4 billion annual sales and Joslyn Manufacturing and Supply Co. of Chicago with annual sales of less than $2 million and only 45 production employees.

The industry is tightly-knit with many friendships among executives of competing firms; indeed, officials of smaller firms sometimes are former General Electric or Westinghouse Electric executives. The men involved oftentimes had similar educational backgrounds also—college graduates in engineering with a rise through technical ranks into the world of sales. There sometimes existed on the part of the men with the bigger companies an almost protective, big brother attitude toward the smaller companies; this was reciprocated.

And the friendships were not only professional but often quite personal. Trade association meetings fostered these. It was perhaps easy in the camaraderie of these meetings at upper-bracket hotels, amid speeches typical of any association lauding the industry's members and "mission," to draw even closer than business and background indicated. It was perhaps easy, with wives and children present, and acquainted from past conventions, to drift into the belief that nothing could be very wrong in such an atmosphere.

Darkening Grays

Indeed, many of the meetings took place at the conventions of the National Electrical Manufacturers Association and other trade groups. Rather typically, after a conventional and perfectly lawful meeting of some kind, certain members would adjourn for a rump session and a few drinks in someone's suite. It seemed natural enough that mutual business problems would be discussed—specifications, for example —and like as not prices would come up. In time it was easy enough to drift from general talk about prices into what should be done about them—and finally into separate meetings to fix them for everyone's mutual benefit.

Thus purely legal gatherings might have drifted into ones with increasingly dark shades of gray and finally into ones that were pretty black; more than one moralist has noted that it isn't the blacks and whites of situations that get initially law-abiding citizens into trouble; rather it is a progressive inability to distinguish between shades of gray.

It was especially easy in this industry to get into price discussions.

The economic position of the various companies has often been one of feast or famine—large orders or none at all for the gigantic pieces of equipment manufactured. Widespread overcapacity after World War II brought intermittent price warring. In 1955, for example, there occurred a price war, known throughout the industry as the "white sale," which saw some prices cut as much as 50%. Profit losses resulted and in some cases red ink. Again in 1957 there was a lesser wave of competitive cutting. At least during the "white sale" General Electric and Westinghouse wound up with most of the business. By reports then current some smaller companies were seeking Government intervention under the Sherman Act's anti-monopoly provisions.

The case has a number of ironic aspects but one of the great ones is that men in the large companies believed they had to protect the position of the smaller companies or run the risk of antitrust prosecution. Another is that much of the overcapacity underlying the "need" to fix prices was Government spurred. Fast tax write-offs, growing out of two wars in two decades, brought the greater capacity for defense that the Government wanted, but they also left the manufacturers with an embarrassing amount of plant.

As a result of this industry makeup, the friendships, and the price-capacity situation, there evidently developed in wide segments the philosophy that collusive activity was ethical, illegal though it might be.

Perhaps an extreme exponent of this view, though expressing a widespread one, is F. F. Loock, president, general manager and sales manager of Allen-Bradley Co. of Milwaukee, who has pleaded guilty.

Looking back on what happened, he says: "No one attending the gatherings (in the electrical controls industry) was so stupid he didn't know (the meetings) were in violation of the law. But it is the only way a business can be run. It is free enterprise."

Price fixing is not usually associated with the idea of free enterprise, with the idea that the market mechanism is to be the ultimate controlling factor, and that this mechanism must remain unimpaired either by individuals or governments. But there is a rationale for the cartel system which permits the general type of collusive activity the electrical men were engaged in. According to it, markets are divided and prices fixed so everyone involved can "get along." Even the consumer is supposed to benefit because stable markets aid stable production and supposedly costs can thus be stabilized.

"Protection Against Buyers"

Price competition is anathema to such a setup. Mr. Loock says one reason for the gatherings in his industry was "we also need protection against buyers" and the "illegal meetings gave us such protection."

Elaborating on the need for "protection," Mr. Loock cites one instance in which the purchasing agent of a major Detroit manufacturer told the electrical manufacturer another one had offered a lower price. "By discussing the matter, which was not true, among ourselves, we were able to iron out the problem." He concludes: "I believe that in an industry where money is necessary to continue research and development of products we should have some protection against the crookedness of some buyers."

There was also a feeling in the industry that the antitrust laws were unjust. With a rationale developed of friendly live and let live among competitors, laws designed to force competition seemed "Government interference." The question was also asked in the industry: If such getting together was all right under the old N.R.A. why isn't it all right now? Of course the N.R.A. of the 1930's was declared unconstitutional by the Supreme Court, but some say the industry's philosophy of "getting together" has roots in that era.

But if illegal "stabilization" was an industry way of life, it should not be assumed that relations were continually rosy among competitors, or that all authority in the industry was bent on collusive activity.

Getting together to fix prices did not alter the basically competitive situation prevailing in the industry's markets. Indeed, it often seems some attendance at the collusive meetings was with tongue in cheek as to stabilizing prices, with a real reason of finding out what the rest of the industry was up to in order to get the jump in the next price cutting wave. Too, some of the conspirators pretty much inherited their roles from predecessors, older men who may have felt more of a tug from the industry's "way of life" than they did. In fact there was personal dislike among some of the individual conspirators; perhaps an individual who did not

like himself for conspiring had little respect for others also so engaged.

*   *   *

35 THE DILEMMA OF ANTITRUST AIMS

Theodore Levitt; reply by
Walter Adams

Theodore Levitt is a member of the faculty at the Harvard University Graduate School of Business Administration; Walter Adams is Professor of Economics at Michigan State University.

Professor Adams' excellent paper on the antitrust case against the Aluminum Company of America suggests a few thoughts about the implications and significance of antitrust activities, and specifically about the idea of competition in our time.

He laments the fact that thirteen years of antitrust litigation failed to result in some sort of "dissolution, divorcement, or divestiture" of Alcoa, in short, in "the kind of physical reorganization of the industry necessary to bring about a competitive structure consistent with the objectives of the Sherman Act." Although they have refused to reorganize the industry—or specifically to atomize Alcoa—the federal courts have retained jurisdiction of the case until 1955, at which time the government may petition for additional relief if competition has by then not improved, or probably more accurately, if it has deteriorated. By this action, Adams quite rightly observes, the District Court has placed Alcoa on a five-year probation during which the latter will undoubtedly follow the policy so effectively employed by other monopolistic companies in the past of "live and let live," of "avoiding any aggressive or expansionary" activity which might give the government a basis on which

to press for dissolution, divorcement, or divestment in 1955. At the end of the probationary period the case will probably be closed, and Alcoa will remain intact, powerful, and domineering. A precedent sanctioning the aluminum type of integrated industry will have been established, with the "Big Three's" and the "Big Four's" cheerfully riding in on its tail to make a mockery out of our competitive system. This, Adams vigorously contends, is bad economics, bad public policy, and besides is not in keeping with the Sherman Act.

All this may be true, as far as the analysis goes. But it must go further. While business leaders may not do a good job of making the point, there *is* something to their charge that antitrust activities of the aluminum kind tend to punish efficiency, size, and success. As a matter of public policy we want business to compete, but we do not want any one producer (or any three in a given industry?) to win the competition. We want the kind of competition which does not lead to monopoly, and we behave as if there were

"The Dilemma of Antitrust Aims: Comment," by Theodore Levitt, and "Reply," by Walter Adams, from *The American Economic Review,* December, 1952, pp. 915–922. Reprinted by permission.

a benevolent natural law according to which it is not in the nature of things for someone to win the competition. As if to give this law a helping hand, we devise public policies to discourage anyone from winning the competition and to punish anyone who does win it. Yet at the same time we do not wish to discourage the enterprise, dynamism, and even scheming that make for getting competitive advantage—in short, for winning competition and creating monopolistic or tight oligopolistic situations. In a word, we wish to preserve competition but face the anomolous situation of punishing its most successful practitioners and of destroying those ingredients of competition that make competition possible and desirable.

One need not approve of the many iron-fist-in-velvet-glove techniques of big business in order to sympathize with its problems. Because of the increasing automaticity of the modern technology, because of the fantastically increased capital requirements, we should therefore not be surprised or alarmed at having more numerous three-producer, two-producer, or even one-producer industries. Electronics and atomic energy will hasten the necessity and inevitability of such industries, as the electrical revolution of the 1910's and 1920's so greatly helped increase industrial concentration then. The Sherman Act (as well as its patchwork progeny, the Clayton Act) was a reaction to the economic concentration that resulted from the leviathan of shady financial manipulations, immoral intrigue, and primitive aggrandizement of power. But today's concentration is the more-or-less inevitable consequence of a new and amoral leviathan—monster technology. Yet we continue to invoke the ethics of a horse and buggy antitrust law to the situation of a hot rod industrial society. The result is legalistic confusion and uncertainty and the possible eventual degeneration of the economic system.

Perhaps the "go-getting" component of the American business culture will survive antitrust attacks and provide a continuous stream of highly motivated business leaders, but it is not inconceivable that a series of successful prosecutions over a number of years of the type attempted in the aluminum case may throttle the dynamism of American capitalism, reducing competition to a sort of verbalistic remains of the real thing, to torpid manipulation of the symbols of competition in a system that is devoid of really dynamic creative activity.

We cannot have "old fashioned" intra-industry competition (or what appears for many to pass for the same thing, namely "workable competition") without reasonably expecting somebody to win or nearly win that competition. And we cannot have a policy designed to prevent such winning of competition that does not throttle the very thing the policy pretends to promote. This dilemma calls for a fresh approach to the antitrust problem. Two things may be said in that connection. First, the failure of a dominant producer to use his power to destroy his competitors is not, as Adams seems to suggest, a meaningless subterfuge designed to mollify the courts. Self-restraint is precisely what we expect the antitrust laws, and indeed all laws, to elicit. It does not follow that simply because an assailant is big and powerful his actions are therefore malicious. Perhaps what is needed is not to bring the assailant to trial, but to redefine our concepts of assault and competition in a way more nearly consistent with the necessary and inevitable structure of modern industry and society.

The second point that may be made in conection with the dilemma we face in trying to prevent someone's winning competition without destroying that which is a precondition to competition and which makes competition desirable, is that the Sherman Act should be replaced by a system of laws that recognizes the technological inevitability of monopoly and oligopoly in modern industry. It becomes increasingly more evident that the Sherman Act, with its implied suggestion of dissolution, divorcement, and divestiture, rigorously applied can destroy what is most precious about the system it naïvely tries to safeguard and preserve. The morality of the Sherman Act is anachronistic. We need to make a fresh start in our thinking about big business, competition, and business ethics and the kind of public policy we should have in connection with them. A profitable beginning might explore the wisdom and possibility of treating our "Big Three's" and "Big Four's" as new forms of modified public utilities, inevitable, desirable, but regulatable in a manner that preserves their dynamism, encourages their innovational drive, and makes them socially responsible. A public member or two sitting in on top-level strategy and policy meetings of the big producers and distributors may be able to do more by way of preserving and promoting enterprise, honesty, and efficiency in big business, and do more to preserve the kind of economy we seem to want than all the Victorian proscriptions of our present antitrust laws.

REPLY

(by Walter Adams)

In commenting on my study of antitrust action in the aluminum industry, Mr. Levitt once again raises the perennial question of the relationship between technology, size and efficiency. He contends that—given the "automa-

ticity of modern technology" and the "fantastically increased capital requirements" concomitant therewith—we should not be surprised or alarmed at having more numerous three-producer, two-producer, or even one-producer industries. On the basis of his belief that today's economic concentration "is the more-or-less inevitable consequence of a new and amoral leviathan—monster technology," he then concludes that "the Sherman Act should be replaced by a system of laws that recognizes the technological inevitability of monopoly and oligopoly in modern industry." Since Levitt's policy conclusion is merely derivative, I shall confine my remarks mainly to his basic assumption that giant industrial size is primarily the outgrowth of a 20th century technology which compels firms to be big in order to be efficient.

So far as I know, no scientific study has yet demonstrated that giant size is imperative for the optimum utilization of modern technology or the attainment of efficiency in mass production industries. Indeed, some of the recent evidence has tended to point in the opposite direction. Fragmentary as it is, this evidence may be summarized as follows:

1. *Wallace's Study of the Aluminum Industry.* In his monumental work on the aluminum industry, Wallace points out that vertical integration of alumina, power, and reduction stages is imperative in this industry, but that the size of the vertical combination should not approach monopoly proportions.

In the alumina stage, according to Wallace, a scale beyond an output of 15–18,000 tons per year brings no savings in cost of capital equipment per unit output, and offers very little chance to economize the use of labor. Considerations of plant efficiency at this stage have not required monopoly in the industry since 1909.

In the reduction stage, the Hall process for electrolytic reduction affords no opportunity for the use of large, specialized units of machinery or for extensive specialization of supervision. The process is a simple one, operated with simple equipment, and neither the process nor the equipment has undergone any fundamental change since the industry first began. The quantity of current which can feasibly be used in a single cell determines that the optimum size cell be relatively small. Requirements for electrical energy are unaffected by the scale of the reduction plant, since savings in power consumption and labor have been derived from improvements in electrical apparatus, design, and operation of cells, rather than from larger plants. According to Wallace, maximum effectiveness at the power and reduction stages has not required a monopolistic scale, in spite of the fact that the best structural firm will possess a hydro-electric development which is likely to be quite large and which will have favorable site characteristics and cheap transportation.

With respect to semi-fabrication and the finishing stages of the aluminum industry, Wallace shows that relatively small scale production in castings and utensils is quite economical, and that the most economical scale for a rolling mill need not be too large. Wallace feels that the experience of Alcoa, which has in the past operated a number of rolling mills, indicates that the optimum scale is not so large as to offset the advantage of having sheet mills located either at the reduction works or close to markets. He holds that maximum economy does not require monopolization of all fabricating operations by a single firm.

Wallace concludes that, all things considered, there was no economic reason for permitting the existence of a single-firm monopoly in the aluminum industry prior to 1936. If this conclusion is valid—if oligopoly would have been as efficient and feasible in 1936 as monopoly—the tremendous growth in demand since then, coupled with a substantially unchanged state of the arts, should—by present standards—justify the existence of a larger number of firms than today dominate the aluminum industry.

2. *Stocking's Testimony before the Celler Subcommittee on Monopoly Power.* In the course of his appearance before the Committee, Stocking presented some startling and highly significant facts on the efficiency of the nation's largest steel producer. Drawing on an unpublished report by the engineering firm of Ford, Bacon & Davis— a report prepared at the request of U. S. Steel itself—Stocking pictured the Corporation:

. . . as a big sprawling giant, whose production operations were improperly coordinated; suffering from a lack of a long-run planning agency; relying on an antiquated system of cost accounting; with an inadequate knowledge of the costs or of the relative profitability of the many thousands of items it sold; with production and cost standards generally below those considered everyday practice in other industries; with inadequate knowledge of its domestic markets and no clear appreciation of its opportunities in foreign markets; with less efficient production facilities than its rivals had; slow in introducing new processes and new products.

On the basis of the powerful indictment in this engineering report (as well as other equally devastating evidence), some of our foremost economists concluded that the dissolution of U. S. Steel into at least three separate integrated units would not violate the demands of modern technology. They assured the Committee that "one can be opposed to economic bigness and in favor of technological bigness in most basic industries without inconsistency."

3. *Findings of the President's Materials Policy Commission.* Although the Commission made no investigation of the relationship between size and efficiency *per se,* it did examine the implications of technological change in a number of important fields. Thus, in the case of the steel industry, the Commission believed that future technological developments would be of such nature as to reduce the optimum size of plant and, therefore, the amount of capital investment required for profitable operations. The Commission cited several specific innovations which would tend to render obsolete the more expansive and elaborate processes for steel production now in use. Said the Commission:

A significant consequence of recent advances in technology may conceivably be the emergence of enterprises conducting integrated operations on a much smaller scale. The utilization of local deposits of ore in the direct reduction of iron or in the production of pig iron in the electric furnace or in the low-shaft furnace, the utilization of local supplies of iron and local surpluses of scrap in the production of steel in the electric furnace or in the turbo-hearth, the continuous casting of semi-finished steel, and the finishing of steel in small mills—all of these operations are feasible. All of them can be undertaken with an investment much smaller than that required for production on a larger scale.

The Commission concluded, therefore, that the new developments in technology "may well provide the basis for a number of new establishments, turning out special products for local markets, each of them conducting continuously integrated operations on a small scale, and all of them contributing significantly to the supply of steel."

Such developments, if they do take place, would serve to demonstrate once again that the growth of the giant firm does not necessarily represent an inescapable, inevitable, and inexorable technological trend.

4. *Experience under the Public Utility Holding Company Act of 1935.* The evidence indicates that the dissolution proceedings under this Act did not preclude the optimum utilization of existing technology nor precipitate the fatal loss of efficiency which had been widely predicted prior to the law's passage. While the statistics are by no means conclusive, they do show that—in most cases—efficiency after dissolution was *increased,* and that this increase was reflected in the security values of those operating companies which were divorced from their parent organizations. That investors have benefited—primarily as a result of various dissolution proceedings—is perhaps most graphically demonstrated in the table at the top of the next page. [Omitted.] That consumers have simultaneously benefited from a decrease in ultility rates (which occurred despite constantly rising operating costs) is eloquent testimony to the wisdom and success of the dissolution program in the utility field. Here certainly is one industry where a substantial amount of deconcentration has not produced the decline in operating efficiency which management spokesmen had expected and feared.

In citing the foregoing fragmentary studies I do not mean to suggest that they provide a definitive answer to the problem of technology, size and efficiency, or a clear guide to public policy. As far as public policy is concerned, I would agree with Levitt that no firm should be punished for size or success achieved on the basis of efficiency and performance in the public interest. I would agree with Levitt that the goals of competition—the encouragement of efficiency, initiative, dynamism and enterprise—should be given a prominent place in our policy formulations. I have, therefore, drafted and advocated legislation which would permit a "monopolistic" firm to escape dissolution, divorcement and divestiture, if such firm can demonstrate that its size is necessary for the attainment of efficiency or that its business performance in the past has materially benefited the general public. Such a modification of the antitrust laws would, I believe, contribute substantially to a resolution of the dilemma raised in Levitt's comment.

However, while the incorporation of an efficiency standard into the antitrust laws can be justified on economic grounds, I do not believe that a more drastic revision of these laws is either necessary or desirable. Evidence to date certainly does not indicate the existence of an irreconcilable conflict between modern technological exigencies and a policy of enlightened and selective trust-busting. Neither does our experience with cartels, co-determination, public utility regulation (especially by the I.C.C. and C.A.B.), and the experiments with government ownership tend to demonstrate that these public control mechanisms are happy alternatives to a regime of competition. Doubtless, the antitrust laws are not perfect either in conception or enforcement. Doubtless, there is the danger that they may —under certain conditions—destroy the very things they seek to promote. This does not mean, however, that the antitrust laws are not worth the calculated risk we are taking. It does not mean that their replacement by alternative public policies, which have not proved too successful in the past, would be conducive to a greater protection of private rights or a more auspicious enhancement of the public good.

36   THE ANTIMERGER ACT, 1950–60

M. A. Adelman

M. A. Adelman is Professor of Economics at Massachusetts Institute of Technology.

This paper attempts to sum up one aspect of ten years' experience: what has been meant in practice by "competition" and "monopoly"? Such an appraisal must be tentative. Most complaints have only been issued in the last four years. The decided cases are few and none well established as precedents. The natural place to begin is with the standards of the other antitrust laws, for the Antimerger Act simply adds a new wing to the old structure.

The economic theory of antitrust is that the competitive process prevents firms from having substantial power to determine prices by limiting production. Hence there will be a better use of resources at any given time. To maintain or increase profit, firms must seek greater efficiency or innovation; hence more progress over time.

But better resource-use through effective competition was never more

Excerpted from *The American Economic Review,* May, 1961, pp. 236–244. Reprinted by permission.

than a minor object of the antitrust laws, though it has probably been an unintended major result. Legislators have never shown much interest in consumer welfare. Their chief concern has always been to protect some business firms against others, chiefly larger ones, and to prevent businessmen from being shut out of any particular market. The basic legal concept, as Mason pointed out twenty-three years ago, is not market control but exclusion. Now, a competitive system economizes scarce resources by excluding the less efficient firms and methods. A monopolized market excludes any who would enter it, efficient or not. To the business concern which suffers or fears exclusion and to its legislative supporters, the distinction is without a difference.

The history of the antitrust laws in this country, therefore, shows an ebb and flow of statutes and decisions, now emphasizing competition and now protectionism in the name of "fairness" or of opposition to "economic power"—a term which nicely confuses monopoly with economies of scale. But there has also been, over the long run, "a very real development of antitrust law toward increasing emphasis on market power at the expense of monopolizing and restraining practices in Sherman Act cases." The basic reason is that most transactions are between business concerns. Most attempts to fix prices or monopolize markets hurt businessmen and therefore invite antitrust attack. Were the whole business system vertically integrated, so that all sales were to final consumers, the antitrust laws would either be repealed or would become altogether protectionist. The consumer (not to mention the national income) has enjoyed a world he never made. The dissatisfaction with the Sherman Act, which has resulted in new legislation at various times, has stemmed both from the feeling that it

was not going far enough and that it was going the wrong way.

The antimerger law goes beyond the Sherman law, for it forbids certain acts where they may so much as tend to lessen competition; only the probability of the result must be shown. This distinction is real and important, but it is only one of degree. As early as 1904, Justice Holmes declared that the Sherman Act, "like many others, and like the common law in some cases, directs itself against the dangerous probability [monopoly] as well as against the completed result." Furthermore, the concept of antitrust "conspiracy" is in large measure based on probable results. The important point is that competition, or monopoly, is not a brute physical fact but rather a hypothesis confirmed by the available evidence. A high level of concentration, plus price behavior very different from competitive expectations, etc., indicates, let us say, chances of 9 to 1 of effective market control. A lesser level of concentration, weaker price evidence, etc., force us to put the odds lower. The simplest and, to my knowledge, the only meaningful, distinction between the standards of the Clayton and Sherman Acts is that the former requires a lesser weight of evidence, and is therefore more severe. But the tribunal in a merger case must analyze with the same tools exactly the same kinds and types of evidence as in a Sherman Act case. It is a pathetic illusion that the market is whatever the courts choose to call it. The market, like the weather, is simply there, whether we only talk about it or do something: apply to it the standards of Clayton, or of Sherman, or of any law, or none. This confusion between the legal standard and the economic fact is writ large in the Bethlehem Steel opinion, which designates as the geographic market in steel products the northeast quadrant of the United States, then also a three-state area within it, and then also each individual state: Ohio, Michigan, and Pennsylvania. This sinks below error into chaos. If the northeast quadrant is a market area—is the locus of the supply-demand forces that determine the price—then the other two areas are not. The evidence that sustains any one of the three market concepts necessarily condemns the others. Until there is a retreat from Bethlehem to reason, tribunals will be able to decide according to any visceral whim, by manipulating market definitions. But this undesirable randomizing of market definitions has also a definite protectionist bias, as will be seen.

Let us now consider the Antimerger Act criteria of competition and monopoly. The House Judiciary Committee, when reporting out the bill for passage, stated that "lessening of competition" might manifest itself, among other ways, in "an increase in relative size to the point where [the merging company's] advantage over its competitors threatens to be decisive." It had to follow, as the night the day, that complaints issued under the Act would allege simply that a merger would be a competitive advantage to the merging companies. By November, 1960, seventy-six complaints had been filed, thirty-nine by the Federal Trade Commission and thirty-seven by the Department of Justice. Of the seventy-six complaints, four may charitably be called doubtful, and fifty-two of seventy-two want the merger dissolved because the merging firms' "competitive position may be enhanced to the detriment of actual and potential competition"; or that the acquisitions have led or will lead to the diversion of trade, etc. There is a complete and unquestioning identification of competition with competitors. Of course, the active search for every possible advantage (or avoidance of any disadvantage) is both cause and effect of active competition, which thus comes under direct attack in the great bulk of the complaints.

Many may contain this language as mere "boiler plate." But the very fact that some do not shows that this explanation must not be pushed too far. But of course complaints begin cases rather than end them. Let us, therefore, look at the decisions. With only two exceptions (in the first of which the merger charge was really subordinate anyway), every decided case has been either a consent settlement or an order of divestiture.

The horizontal elements of mergers —i.e., involving markets in which both firms may be said to have been previously active—have been treated severely and—if maintaining competition is the object—rationally. (We assume for purposes of this paper that markets have been correctly found.) The key fact has been the degree of concentration, which may overlap considerably with the market share of the combination and the fewness of competitors. The combined market share need not be strikingly high. As a rule of thumb, one could say that 15 per cent and higher may be suspect.

Concentration is of course not to be equated with monopoly, but serious inquiry into concentration leads directly to the nature of the product, of substitution in demand and supply, and to entry, which has been given a properly heavy weight.

The tribunals have also paid attention to the character of competition in the market involved. In five cases they have held that competition is more than a little inhibited, so that the law should be particularly zealous to guard what is left and impose stricter standards for any merger. This use of marginal utility theory makes new law, for the holdings have *not* been that there was a monopoly or price-fixing agreement in sugar, steel, milk, or paper but only that there was a significant amount of control, not enough to violate the law against price fixing, yet a fact not to be ignored in interpreting the Antimerger Act. There is an obvious danger here of accepting too lightly superficial evidence of so-called "administered prices," a formal and meaningless category, and equating them to monopoly price. But then, every good rule can be abused. Half a dozen cases seem to have made it already clear that mergers with substantial horizontal elements, i.e., which significantly increase concentration in some markets, will not be permitted. This is a considerable achievement. The antitrust agencies are going to win and lose cases in this area, but the cases they lose will be those where the effect on concentration and competition will be adjudged insubstantial, so that the private economies need not be considered as social diseconomies.

The protectionist influence has not been needed or invoked as to horizontal elements. But it is being felt in the treatment of vertical and conglomerate elements, as must be expected. Vertical integration may reduce costs, thus yielding a competitive advantage. Vertical integration may also serve to extend market control into an adjacent stage or to increase the revenues from it. Let me state the problem in its most difficult form. Industry A sells a product to industry B at a price substantially above long-run marginal cost; output is restricted, as it must be, to keep the price up. There are now two good (if partly overlapping) profit incentives for a merger between a firm in A and a firm in B. The A company could operate at full capacity (higher level in the short run, larger scale in the long run); the B company would get its raw material at a competitive price and would not only earn a higher

profit on its existing output but could *ceteris paribus* expand output and get a bigger share of the market. Depending on the particular circumstances, vertical integration would be an extension of monopoly or the circumventing of monopoly by one firm or more. For if there is enough of this integration— and it may not take much—the additional output will collapse the monopoly at the earlier stage. If the law aims at competition, then whatever the severity or laxity of one's standards, one must for any sound decision see the market structure clearly and accept the basic principle that vertical integration is at most an extender or multiplier of pre-existent market control. Any multiplier times zero is still zero.

But if the policy is protection of business concerns against loss of sales or supply, then vertical integration becomes an offense either as a competitive advantage or as "foreclosing" or "forestalling"; i.e., if after merger A no longer supplies its old customers and B no longer buys from its old suppliers. Now, absent market control, A's old customers can contact B's old suppliers, or there can be a general multilateral shift. This is simply a trifling incident; and the law is not supposed to bother with trifles. This problem has long occupied Section 3 of the Clayton Act, which deals essentially with vertical integration by contract, and policy there has zigzagged. The basic dilemma obtrudes at every turn. A contract excludes other sellers from dealing with the buyer and other buyers from dealing with the seller. Lacking an analysis of the market, there is no way of saying whether the contract merely annoys competitors because it lowers costs or decreases competition by significantly narrowing the alternatives open to other buyers and sellers. Either situation confers a "power" upon the firms involved, but only occasionally and accidentally do the tribunals explain whether the "power" is monopoly or economy.

The easy way out has received the jaw-breaking name of "quantitative substantiality," and it means simply that when a substantial amount of dollars is involved, the contract or the merger is illegal. This is more than an error. It embodies protectionist policy in a definition by labeling a buyer or area as "a substantial market," or "a substantial segment of a market," from which it is illegal to exclude. This neatly avoids the inquiry into market structure, behavior, and results, while maintaining a deceptive appearance of it.

The attack on vertical integration per se is evident in six cases and decisive in two or three. (The General Motors-du Pont case has the most economic sense, once the market definition is granted.) Brown Shoe, which forbade the merger of a shoe manufacturer with a retailer, is the most clearly protectionist. Its first main doctrine is simple-minded extrapolation: since the baby grew six inches last year, in twenty more years he will be twelve feet tall. The metaphorical language about eating a whole apple one bite at a time is based on no more than that the merger raised Brown's share of national output from 5 to 5½ per cent. True, the court had previously defined the market other than nationally, but its neglect of its own definition, once it came to analyzing and predicting effects on the structure of the market, demonstrates that what purported to be market analysis was merely an ornament of discourse. Following the court's example, we should not take it seriously.

The second main thought is an alleged decrease in the number of shoe manufacturing plants, which if assumed true has no particular relation with concentration or fewness of sellers, but would indicate simply increasing economies of scale. If a decrease in the number of plants is a "bad thing" in itself, we are not told.

The real meat of the decision comes in repeated statements that "independent retailers are having a harder and harder time." The reason for this sad condition is that retailers affiliated with manufacturers have "advantages in buying, selling, insurance, business planning and practices, advertising and credit arrangements," etc.—in plain English, economies of scale and of integration. Whether or not these advantages really exist, what matters is that they are the explicit reason for stopping the merger. An alleged bow to "power to control price" is soon shown to be meaningless when the court says of an increase in Brown Shoe's sales: "Such increase, *regardless of percentage amount,* gives them power. Such power not only tends to create a monopoly but substantially lessens competition by eliminating the effectiveness of the independent retailer and the smaller manufacturer." It would be a wearisome task to comb out every other circumlocution. Translated into intelligible speech, it all means that the merging firms will gain economies which will make life harder for their competitors, and this must be forbidden.

*   *   *

["Conglomerate mergers" are still unsettled, and the F.T.C. chairman seems to look to decisions on vertical integration as pointing the way.]

The acquisition by a large and powerful diversified company of a small company in a discrete industry historically shared by a number of small companies competing on equal terms followed by drastic competitive injury to the smaller competitors might be a demonstration of anti-competitive effect sufficient to satisfy the statutory requisites even if the acquisition was truly conglomerate.

In the antitrust dictionary, "powerful" has no necessary connection with monopoly power or market control or even market share. It means "vast financial reserves," "overwhelming economic strength," "colossal corporate resources," or some other pompous polysyllabic combination meaning one four-letter word: size. And "drastic competitive injury" means simply loss of business. So a merger is illegal if (1) it involves a big company and (2) small business concerns afterward lose sales. Competition—pure, workable, effective, or whatever—has vanished, replaced by protectionism. Some small companies might have been losing business because they were inefficient or ill-adapted to new market conditions. Moreover, where firms are numerous, many must by chance alone be in difficulties as of any one moment. To blame their troubles, real or fancied, on the acquisition by the large company is clearly fallacious, *post hoc ergo propter hoc.*

The fallacy is, of course, logically distinct from the protectionist policy; either could exist without the other. Yet they are also parts of an antitrust mystique, according to which nothing ever happens by chance or because of economies of scale or general business conditions but always because of the big companies, unless this can be disproved beyond any reasonable or even unreasonable doubt. One does not really understand the antitrust process unless he has thumbed through pages on pages of testimony by businessmen, "a-weepin' and a-wailin' how they done him wrong," and then seen how seriously this "evidence" is regarded. This is why many cases last too long—this and a staff burdened with too many cases and too little economics and statistics. But that is another story.

In conclusion: The very existence of a separate legal standard for mergers is surely debatable and it was assumed here not proved. But Mason has suggested that, although "in Sherman cases, the existence of going concerns argues for the application of—at best —a relaxed standard of market power, there is every reason why, in Section 7 cases, the standard should be strict." It is going to be strict when market power is involved, and it may be even stricter against economies of scale and integration. The enforcement of the Antimerger Act shows the same three-sided conflict—among competition, protectionism, and laissez faire or business statesmanship—which has prevailed throughout the history of the antitrust laws.

D.

THE FARM PROBLEM

37   A PROGRAM FOR AGRICULTURAL ADJUSTMENT

Committee for Economic
Development

The Committee for Economic Development is a group of approximately 200 leading businessmen who are Presidents and Board Chairmen of large corporations.

**A PROGRAM FOR
AGRICULTURAL ADJUSTMENT**
**calls (a) for policies and programs
to attract excess resources
from use in farm production,
and (b) for measures to cushion
the effects of the adjustment
on property and people.**

First and fundamentally, we propose a set of measures assigned to bring about a condition in which:

1. A much smaller total quantity of resources will be used in agricultural production;
2. This smaller total of resources at use in farm production will be composed of a much smaller amount of labor, and, possibly, somewhat less capital;
3. Production per unit of resources used in agriculture will be higher;
4. Earnings per unit of resources used in agriculture will be higher, on the average, and these earnings will be obtained through sale of farm products without government subsidy or support.

Adjustment of farming to this condition is basic to solution of the farm problem.

Second, we propose a set of temporary, transitional measures designed to:

1. Prevent a sharp decline in farm incomes, and
2. Avoid further additions to stocks of farm goods, while the basic adjustment to the condition sketched above is being brought about.

It is an essential characteristic of these transitional programs that they should cushion the adjustment, but should do so in ways that do not prevent or retard the adjustment.

ATTRACTING EXCESS RESOURCES FROM USE IN FARM PRODUCTION

This is the heart of the matter in agricultural adjustment. Excess resources in use in the production of farm goods *is* the farm problem. Everything else suggested here is for the purpose of facilitating the fundamental transaction —withdrawal of excess resources from agricultural production—or serves to hold things steady while the basic transition is taking place.

From *An Adaptive Program for Agriculture* (New York: Committee for Economic Development, 1962), pp. 31–51. Reprinted by permission.

AN IMPROVED LABOR MARKET

Some of the measures we are suggesting here are broader than the program traditionally associated with agricultural policy, or lie outside what has been the usual farm policy scope. The fact is that the well-being of agriculture cannot be assured by programs having to do only with the production and marketing of farm goods: healthy agriculture requires a healthy economy as a whole and healthy relations between the farm and nonfarm sectors. It is obvious, therefore, that the Department of Agriculture would not be called upon to administer all the programs suggested here, but that, regardless of the fact that they are suggested in connection with solving the farm problem, they should be administered by agencies best able to do so.

1. High Employment

The maintenance of employment opportunities in non-agricultural industry and services is an essential condition for the most satisfactory agricultural adjustment.

In our diagnosis, the problem of getting excess resources out of agriculture is a nonfarm employment problem: resources, particularly labor, are engaged in farming when they could produce more, and earn more, outside agriculture. This implies that opportunities for their employment exist or can be created outside of agriculture. If this were not true, the problem of agriculture would be basically different.

We believe, of course, that high and growing employment can be maintained in the nonfarm economy. We have discussed the steps necessary to achieve this result in a recent statement that emphasized:

a) The potential contribution of monetary and fiscal policy to a steady rate of growth in total expenditures for goods and services, and

b) Moderation of the rate of increase of wages and other labor costs, so that the rise of total expenditures is not absorbed by higher prices, but takes effect in raising production and employment.

The importance of high employment for a resolution of the farm problem must be emphasized. The movement of labor from agriculture has shown itself to be responsive to the state of the non-agricultural labor market. A sustained period of high employment would itself make a major contribution to agricultural adjustment, and would contribute to the success of any other measures that may be undertaken.

While emphasizing the importance of high employment in the non-agricultural economy for the speed with which agricultural adjustment can be effected, we do not mean to suggest that the other parts of the program recommended here must await the achievement of high employment or should be suspended in the event of future departures from high employment. There has been significant movement of people from agriculture even in recent years when unemployment was unsatisfactorily high, and even in such circumstances measures to facilitate the outmovement will have constructive results.

2. Education

. . . 44 per cent of the farm population is presently below the age of 20.

Here, in our opinion, is a main key to agricultural adjustment: we have an opportunity to secure long-lasting relief from the overburden of people pressing upon farm income by getting a large number of people out of agriculture before they are committed to it as a career.

It is obvious that the extent to which we may be successful in using this key will depend upon the impression the farm youth gets when he looks at the nonfarm economy with an eye to uprooting himself permanently from farming. If employment prospects off the farm are high and growing, the attraction to farm youths of training for nonfarm careers will be strong; if the current prospects for employment off the farm are not attractive, young people deciding whether to commit them-

selves to a career on the farm or in the nonfarm economy can be expected to decide in large numbers that the long term prospects are best in farming. This tends to perpetuate the farm problem.

Recent studies have brought out that fewer farm youths than others (a) graduate from high school, (b) enter college, and (c) graduate from college.

Attendance of boys at school falls off sharply in countryside school districts, by comparison with the nation as a whole and with urban schools, beginning with the 16–17 year old age brackets (final years of high school):

PER CENT OF MALES ENROLLED IN SCHOOL [1]

| Age Groups | TOTAL | Place of Residence October, 1960 | | | Usual School Grade |
		URBAN	RURAL NONFARM	FARM	
5 years	64.1	74.1	58.0	33.7	Kindergarten
6 years	97.8	98.8	98.0	92.7	First
7 to 9 years	99.6	99.6	99.7	99.7	2–3–4
10 to 13 years	99.4	99.5	99.5	98.6	5–6–7–8
14 & 15 years	97.9	98.0	98.3	96.3	Fr & S, H.S.
16 & 17 years	84.5	85.1	85.4	79.7	Jr. & Sr, H.S.
18 & 19 years	47.8	51.4	46.8	33.5	Fr & S, Col.
20 & 21 years	27.1	31.1	20.8	18.8	Jr. & Sr, Col.

[1] Bureau of the Census, Current Population Report (school grades supplied).

. . . the United States as a whole derives 4.3 per cent of its personal income from farming, and no state derives more than 26.1 per cent; yet the nation devotes 44.5 per cent of its vocational education funds, exclusive of funds for home economics training, to training for agriculture. In the 20 states getting the highest percentage of personal income from farming (North Dakota, 26.1 per cent to Texas, 6.5 per cent), all but two—Arizona and Vermont—spend over half of their vocational education funds, excepting home economics, for training in the skills of farming.

This means that in many states where farming is strongest vocational education tends to perpetuate the farm

problem of too many people in agriculture by holding out extraordinary opportunities to train for farming as a vocation.

America's Resources of Specialized Talent,[1] a study published in 1954, gave the following summary of the relationship between the father's occupation and higher education:

The tendency for farm youths to have fewer years of schooling, and the emphasis on vocational education for farming, together with the above figures showing the relatively low proportion of farm youths in colleges, indicate that

[1] Report of the Commission on Human Resources and Advanced Training (Harper & Row, Publishers, New York), Dael Wolfle, Director.

Father's Occupation	Percentage of High School Graduates Entering College	Percentage of High School Graduates Graduating from College
Professional and semiprofessional	67%	40%
Managerial	50	28
White collar (clerical, sales, service)	48	27
Factory, craftsman, unskilled, etc.	26	15
Farmer	24	11

it is necessary to give attention to the amount and the kind of education farm youths get below the college level.

We have three recommendations on this vital aspect of the farm problem.

a) *This Committee has recommended a program for Federal aid to public education below the college level in the low income states.* If this program were put into effect, its preponderant effects in the improvement of educational attainments would be felt in lower income farm states. *We once again urge adoption of this program, and rejection of proposals for aid to all states.*

b) *Vocational education should be revamped to place its emphasis upon training in skills needed by expanding industries.* This means that vocational education in farming areas should be mainly for industrial, not agricultural, skills. There is need, as this Committee has pointed out elsewhere, for an expanded Federal effort to provide research and information to help guide state education departments and local school boards in what skills are in demand or coming into demand.

c) *Public and private policy should take dual account of the national needs (i) to reduce the number of people committed for their livelihood to farming, and (ii) to raise the national educational attainment, by measures to bring the participation of farm youths in higher*

education up to the national standard. Our recommendation (a) above tends in this direction, by increasing opportunities for youths in lower income farm states to qualify for college. There should also be a general increase in the availability on the basis of need and merit of loans and scholarship grants for college education. State and private funds for this purpose have been increasing and should continue to do so. Federal loan and scholarship funds for needy farm youths qualified for college study should be provided during the transition period in which a rapid migration from agriculture is needed. Here also, as in (a) above, major effects would be felt in lower income farm states.

It should be recognized by all agencies, public and private, that on the average the farm youth, more often than the nonfarm youth, will have to live away from home while he is at college, and that a college education therefore tends to be more "expensive" for farm youths than for others. This should be taken into account in judging need for financial help.

3. Mobility

Early in 1962, a Federal *Manpower Development and Training Act* was enacted. The objectives of the Act are to "appraise the manpower requirements and resources of the nation, and to develop and apply the information and methods needed to deal with the problems of unemployment resulting from automation and technological changes and other types of persistent unemployment."

In farming the counterpart of unemployment resulting from automation and technological changes is underemployment, or, as we have discussed it here, excess use of resources.

We are glad to see the problem of the excess use of resources *in farming,* particularly excess commitment of people, integrated with the *general* problem of the nation's manpower requirements, and the national, general need for policies to help the nation adapt to the ever changing skill requirements of the economy.

This coincides with our view, basic to the adaptive approach we are recommending for solution of the farm problem, that the farm problem is not unique, but is, rather, the leading case of a large class of problems where an industry is using too many resources, and, that solution of the farm problem lies in policies tending to improve, generally and overall, the efficient use of our resources, rather than in protectionist, specialized "farm policy."

The provisions of the new Manpower Act can be an important step in guiding and easing the movement out of farming of a large number of people in a short time, if the Act's purposes are interpreted as applying fully and specifically to the farm problem, and if they are vigorously pursued in that light. This includes:

Job Information

The Act requires the Secretary of Labor to promote, encourage or directly engage in programs of informa-

tion and communication concerning manpower requirements and improvement in the mobility of workers. We recommend additionally that:

The Federal-State Employment Service be expanded to rural areas, and its coverage made national and regional, rather than local only, and that:

The present farm labor service should expand its responsibility to include placement in off-farm work, instead of limiting its referrals to farm employment.

Careful attention should be given to the impact of the foreign worker program upon the wages of domestic migrant farm workers.

Retraining and Movement

The new Act establishes procedures for selecting and training workers for occupations requiring new skills. It specifies that workers in farm families with annual net income under $1,200 are eligible for retraining assistance under the Act. The Act provides allowances for training, subsistence and transportation, and for Federal assistance for state and private occupational training schools.

The adjustments required in agriculture will call for the movement of many people who would not be eligible for retraining under the provisions of the Act. It confines retraining allowances and other assistance to workers in farm families with net annual income below $1,200. Basically our objective should be to provide assistance for retraining where the individual will not get it without assistance and where the retraining will substantially increase his ability to produce and earn income. Some arbitrary definition of eligibility may be necessary for administration of the Act, but *we believe that the present definition is too restrictive so far as agriculture is concerned.*

The retraining of farm workers leaving farming should be considered one of the principal objectives of the new Act. Those responsible for the administration of the Act should have it clearly in mind that farming is the leading case of misuse of resources in the American economy, that over-commitment of people to farming for their livelihood is the special form of the use of excess resources in agriculture, and that the Manpower and Training Act should consequently be applied with all vigor to solution of the farm problem.

The provisions in the Act limiting and qualifying direct help programs to avoid abuse should be fully and carefully observed.

We recommend that retrained farm workers leaving farming should be assisted in moving to nonfarm work sites, by a program of loans to cover the cost of moving themselves and their families. Such assistance should be given once only for the purpose of leaving farming. It should be given only for movement from areas where there is excess labor supply and only for movements in excess of, say, 50 miles.

It should be emphasized that all such direct help programs should apply to farm tenants, hired hands and domestic migrant workers, as well as to farm proprietors and their families.

We regard direct help to farm people in finding better opportunities in the nonfarm labor force as necessary and desirable, because we believe that a small fraction of the funds now spent on agricultural subsidies would, if spent in ways that tended positively to induce the needed movement of human resources out of farming, result in higher national income and lower national outlays on subsidies.

ADJUSTMENT OF AGRICULTURAL PRICES

The basic adjustment required to solve the farm problem, adjustment of the resources used to produce farm goods, cannot be expected to take place unless the price system is permitted to signal to farmers how much is wanted, of what.[2]

Therefore, it is recommended that a Price Adjustment Program be instituted.

In order that the prices of our major farm products should give the correct signals for investment and production, *the prices of cotton, wheat, rice and feed grains and related products now supported should be allowed to reflect the estimated long run "adjustment price" of these products.*

The adjustment price would simultaneously satisfy two conditions. *First,* it is a price at which the total output of the commodity can be sold to domestic consumers or in commercial export markets without government subsidy. *Second,* it is a price at which resources efficiently employed in agriculture, after a period of maximum freedom to move out, could earn incomes equivalent to those earned in the nonfarm economy.

---

[2] The importance of the correct price signals for farm products was highlighted by recent developments in the dairy industry. During 1960, production and consumption of dairy products were about in balance and the government had to purchase only small amounts of surpluses. Then, in late 1960 and early 1961, the support price for dairy products was increased. This higher support price, together with lower feed grain prices, induced a sharp increase in the production of dairy products at a time when the demand for dairy products was not expanding. The result has been more resources in dairying, more output, and sharply increased expenditures for acquisition of surpluses to support prices of dairy products.

For most of these commodities the adjustment price is below the present support price and is likely to remain so even after a period of stimulated out-movement. This means that at prices below the present support prices sufficient resources would prefer to remain in agriculture, rather than move out under favorable conditions, to produce as large a volume of these commodities as would be bought by consumers, at home and abroad, at these lower prices. The willingness of labor to remain in agriculture after a period of maximum opportunity to move out, with the incomes they can earn at these lower prices, will be objective evidence that these incomes are "satisfactory." It will be possible for labor to earn satisfactory incomes at lower commodity prices because output per worker will be increased by two developments: a) the number of workers will be substantially reduced, which will increase the capital each worker has to work with, and b) restrictions on output per worker will be removed.

While the adjustment price for most of the major commodities is below the present support level, it is above the price that would result if the total output that the resources now in agriculture would produce were sold in an unsupported market. Such a purely free market price would be lower than the adjustment price we have in mind because it would result from marketing crops without previous adjustment of the resources used in their production. We propose below two measures, an expanded Soil Bank and a Cropland Adjustment Program, to keep production from exceeding demand at the adjustment prices during the transition period while the basic out-movement of resources is taking place.

The purpose of setting the adjustment price is to give farmers the best possible indication of the prices they may expect to receive during and at the end of the transition period, so that those farmers who do not think they can earn incomes they regard as satisfactory at those prices can take advantage of the transition period to move out. It is not proposed that the government should support prices at the adjustment price levels after the transition period. Neither should it be expected that market prices will remain permanently at the adjustment price levels after the transition period. The long-run course of agricultural prices will depend mainly upon the rate of growth of agricultural productivity and the rate of movement of resources into and out of agriculture.

We do not favor a gradual lowering of farm prices to the adjustment level, although we took a position in our statement on farm policy in 1956 favoring gradualism. Gradual price reductions in recent years have not affected the resources used in farming fast enough and have not allowed total production to flow into use. Therefore,

it is recommended that the price supports for wheat, cotton, rice, feed grains and related crops now under price supports be reduced immediately to the prices that could be expected to balance output and use, after the transition period, without new additions to government stocks. The undesirable effects on farm incomes during the transition period should be handled separately and simultaneously, as suggested later.

The importance of such price adjustments should not be underestimated. The lower price levels would discourage further commitment of new productive resources to those crops unless it appeared profitable at the lower prices. Also, the lower prices would induce some increased sales of these products both at home and abroad. Some of these crops are heavily dependent upon export markets. Finally, these price adjustments would put the United States into position to begin disentangling itself from export subsidies, import quotas, and other inconsistent policies which now surround our foreign trade in these farm products.

Specific adjustment prices to satisfy these principles will have to be estimated when the program is initiated, in terms of the facts and outlook at that time. It appears that at the present time (mid-1962) the adjustment price would be, for cotton about 22 cents a pound, for rice about $3 a hundredweight, for wheat about $1.35 a bushel, and for feed grains the equivalent of about $1 a bushel for corn.

These prices for wheat, rice and cotton are believed to approximate the prices at which these crops would be sold in the market without further accumulation of surpluses. The suggested price for feed grains is about the level that had been maintained for feed grains for two years prior to 1961.

To keep feed grain production from outrunning usage at the suggested adjustment price, we recommend below a Temporary Soil Bank, designed to hold output of feed grains below 155 million tons a year.

Consequently, although government supports of the crops designated above would continue at the adjustment price levels during the five year adjustment period, *it is not expected that the government would acquire surpluses except under exceptional and temporary circumstances.*

The effects of the adjustment prices would reach beyond our borders. The adjustment price suggested for cotton would permit our domestic cotton mills to compete on a more even basis with foreign mills, in our markets and in foreign markets. At present, foreign mills can buy United States cotton more cheaply than can our domestic cotton producers. The same would be true of our domestic flour millers and rice exporters.

An estimate of the market adjustment price for farm products will be partly a matter of judgment as long as markets are not free and earnings in farming are too low. However, this judgment must be made, and the preferable direction of error, if any, is clear in our present situation.

For several reasons it is important that price supports be moved to levels that, if wrong, will be low rather than high.

First, price supports on the low side will test the market demand for farm products. If this demand turns out to be higher than output at the support level we can meet the needs from our huge stocks.

Second, new resources (especially people) should be discouraged from entering agriculture, at least during the adjustment period, and the rate of entry in the longer run should not be excessive. Price supports set too high will tend to continue the errors of recent years.

Therefore, the costs of errors of setting supports too low initially are virtually zero as long as the income of farm people does not suffer as a result, whereas the errors of too high a level can only be corrected at considerable expense either to farmers or the public, or both.

If it is demonstrated over a period of time that the adjustment prices originally determined are too high or too low, the adjustment price should be corrected accordingly.

Where support prices are reduced to an adjustment level, production restrictions should be abolished.

In explanation:

Given two cushioning programs discussed later—a Cropland Adjustment Program and a Temporary Soil Bank— the output of the products for which we are suggesting reduction of supports to an adjustment price should be approximately in balance with domestic and export use at the recommended prices. Where it is exceptionally advantageous to produce these crops, producers would find it profitable to expand output at the adjustment price. Such would be the case for cotton in California and wheat in certain areas of the Plains.

On the other hand, in other areas farmers would find alternatives more attractive than continued production of the crops for which supports had been lowered. In some cases the alternative would be nonfarm employment. In other cases, the alternative would be the production of farm goods for which demand is rising fast (meat, for instance, as contrasted with wheat).

CUSHIONING THE PROCESS OF ADJUSTING THE RESOURCES USED IN FARM PRODUCTION— A CROPLAND ADJUSTMENT PROGRAM

What we are recommending with respect to land use is a program designed to turn land being misused in agriculture to better agricultural use. It is not a program to take land out of farming where there is no non-agricultural alternative use, since that would be wasteful. Our suggestions concern mainly the Western Plains and Mountain area. They are designed to convert land being used for the production of crops back to grassland. It is anticipated that if wheat is priced lower, farmers in this area will have better income raising livestock on this land, once it is returned to grass, than they have as arid country wheat farmers. The object of the program we are sug-

gesting is to assist them in converting their farms from plowland to livestock grasslands.

It is recommended that a Cropland Adjustment Program be instituted, to induce the reconversion of at least 20 million acres of Western Plains, and Mountain Region land from crop use to grass, as rapidly as possible.

To induce a farmer to convert from wheat production to grassland, the government would:

1. Pay an amount equal to the expected income from producing a crop, so that these conversion payments, together with the income protection payments mentioned later, would provide, over the adjustment period, an income equivalent to what the farmer would get if he produced a crop.
2. Make available technical assistance and planning in the conversion of cropland to grass, and share the costs of conservation practices, where applicable.
3. Require agreements on the part of the owner that, once converted, the land would not be returned to the production of wheat for some specified period.

This program is an extension and enlargement of the Great Plains Conservation Program started in 1956 and continued until the present time. What is proposed is an expansion and extension of its scope to induce greater participation.

The extraordinary demands of World War II and the immediate postwar period brought favorable wheat prices. These prices induced a substantial expansion in wheat acreage in the United States, from a low of 57 million acres in the early war period to over 77 million acres in the late 1940's. The increase in production was intensified by good weather. This expansion included a marked increase in the total acreage in the low rainfall areas of the Western Great Plains.

When wheat surpluses appeared,

acreage allotments were inaugurated and land was forced out of wheat. However, in this western region grain sorghums have been developed that are an alternative dry country crop to wheat—*as long as wheat and feed grain prices are maintained high enough to keep sorghum prices high.* In the Plains and Mountain region harvested wheat acreage declined by 9 million acres from 1952–53 (the last years before allotments) to 1957–58. Feed grain acreage meanwhile increased by over 12 million acres. This additional 12 million acres in feed grains can produce just about the amount of *surplus* feed grain produced annually in recent years before 1961. Moreover, total wheat production in this region still substantially exceeds prewar production despite the acreage allotments.

These basic facts point directly at what should be done:

1. Acreage converted to cropland in the dry areas must be returned to grass.

2. Wheat and feed grain prices should be allowed to tell farmers how much of each is wanted. That is, the price signals should be allowed to work.

As long as five years may be required to return this plowed land to grass. During this period farm operators would have to forego all or a major portion of their cash income and at the same time incur some out-of-pocket expenses. Even though the long run income prospects in the dry area would be higher from a grassland-livestock program than from wheat, if wheat were priced correctly, few farmers can afford to forego current income to make the change.

This is why we recommend a Cropland Adjustment Program. Payments under the plan should reflect the length of time required to establish grass. This will differ in various areas. Payments should end at the end of that time.

Payments under the Cropland Adjustment Program would be on a declining schedule, to mesh with the growth of new income from different use of the land.

A TEMPORARY INCOME PROTECTION PROGRAM

If price supports for wheat, rice, and cotton were reduced immediately to the level at which adjustment of resources would begin to take place, the income of the producers of these crops would decline sharply in the absence of any compensatory public policy. While such a quick and sharp decline in income might conceivably increase the rate at which needed adjustments took place, it would exact a high cost in terms of suffering of the farm people displaced.

Therefore:

We suggest that a *Temporary Income Protection Program be inaugurated,* to prevent the major impact of the required price adjustments from bearing excessively upon the farm community.

We recommend Temporary Income Protection payments only for wheat, rice and cotton because the price drop in other crops would be much less than for these three.

The Temporary Income Protection Program would have five controlling features:

1. Payments should be made only to farmers who now have acreage allotments for wheat, rice and cotton. The adjustment payments should be based upon a quantity of the product determined by the present acreage allotment and the normal yield of the farm for the previous two years prior to the beginning of the program.

2. The program would continue only five years.

3. Payments would be a declining per-

centage of the excess of the 1960 support prices over the adjustment price.

4. Payments would be independent of further production of these crops.

5. Payments would decline to zero within five years.

To illustrate the workings of the program in the case of wheat farming:

The farmer has a base period quantity of wheat, computed as above in Point 1. Let us assume that this quantity, for a particular farmer, is 1,000 bushels. The support price for wheat in 1960 was $1.78 a bushel. If the adjustment price, as described earlier, is $1.35 a bushel, this leaves a difference of 43 cents a bushel. In the first year of the program, the farmer would receive 1,000 times 43 cents, or $430. In the second year he would get 80 per cent of that amount, or $344. In the third year he would get 60 per cent of $430, or $258, and so on. In the sixth and succeeding years, there would be no income protection payments.

The farmer would get the income protection payments, based upon his former marketing quota, no matter how much wheat he grew, and even if he grew no wheat or grew something else. This provision is essential. The farmer should decide how much wheat to produce, if any, on the basis of what is profitable for him to do at $1.35 a bushel. It is essential that receipt of the supplemental payment should not be dependent upon the production of wheat. Otherwise the supplemental payment would simply be an additional price for wheat and an additional inducement to produce wheat, beyond what would be induced by the adjustment price.

The foregoing example has assumed that the adjustment price is constant during the five year period, but, as noted earlier, the adjustment price might be changed if circumstances indicated that it was too high or too low.

To put the above into the form of rules for the program, the income protection payments should:

1. be based upon (a) the acreage allotment held by the farmer and a marketing quota, converted to an income protection base derived from it, and (b) the difference between supports in 1960, and the new adjustment price;

2. decline to zero by the end of five years;

3. be made whether or not a crop was produced.

A TEMPORARY SOIL BANK

The third measure for cushioning adjustment should be a Temporary Soil Bank, to prevent feed grain production from exceeding demand in the next few years.

It is recommended that a Temporary Soil Bank should be established, to last not more than five years, and to hold feed grain output, during that time, to not over 150–155 million tons a year. The Temporary Soil Bank would extend, under conditions set fourth below, the existing Soil Bank.

If feed utilization per animal continued at the rate of recent years, it appears that by 1965 the domestic demand for livestock products will require the use of about 165 million tons of feed grains annually, at about 1960–61 prices. This would mean that feed grain and livestock prices should stabilize at about 1960–61 levels without the accumulation of feed grain stocks. Until such time as this balance is achieved, a Soil Bank program should be utilized in order to prevent low livestock prices or continued accumulation of feed grains.

The Temporary Soil Bank should be on a whole farm basis. First, the retirement of whole farms is less expensive in terms of the inducement needed to obtain the necessary land. *Second,* the whole farm retirement also retires both labor and capital from farming, thereby shrinking the total resource base in agriculture.

There has been much objection to the whole farm Soil Bank Program from the nonfarm people in rural communities. They have objected to the loss of sales and to the competition from farm people in the local labor market. However, the impact of the Soil Bank on adjacent communities will depend very much on the state of economic activity in the economy generally. Moreover, the program should be operated so that its impact will be minimized on individual communities or areas.

38   STATEMENT IN REPLY TO THE CED

Orville L. Freeman,
Secretary of Agriculture

The Secretary of Agriculture Comments on the CED Proposals

"The whole premise of the CED five-year plan is based on the stated goal of doubling the expected exodous from farming, pushing it up to a level of two million farm workers in the next five years, by means of an administered decline in farm income. This artificially accelerated dislocation of two million farmers seeking nonfarm jobs, together with the disruption of their families, plus the effects on the businessmen on Main Street and on those in rural towns and villages who provide professional and public services, all add up to a serious burden of adjustment and critically handicap the rest of the economy. A rate of economic growth sufficient to achieve satisfactory employment levels under normal conditions could be thrown out of balance by this additional load.

"Second, the CED five-year plan to end farm programs threatens to alter the basic character of American agriculture. If Government made good on its determination to stay out of the picture after five years, farmers would be faced with low and fluctuating farm prices. They would be left to deal with business firms in other sectors of the economy having monopolistic control over their markets. The result would be a disorganized agriculture where farmers were exploited by the large firms with whom they dealt in selling their products and buying farm supplies. Even the most efficient family farm would find it difficult to survive this type of economic pressure, and the control of agricultural resources would become increasingly concentrated into the hands of firms outside agriculture —firms which could and would begin to join together to raise prices to increase profits. . . .

"The real threat to the independent family is not, in most cases, the giant factory-scale corporation-owned farm employing labor in large crews. Rather, it is through the imposition of a pattern of controls by centralized private authority over the existing family-farming

Statement of Secretary of Agriculture Orville L. Freeman, July 18, 1962, as reported in *Current*, September, 1962. Reprinted by permission.

pattern." In the broiler industry, for example, which is dominated by large producers who process and market their own produce, "the independent farmer cannot compete with the integrated industry because he cannot gain access to improved breeds and strains of poultry stock, he cannot secure financing on equal terms, he cannot keep up with the rate of technological and managerial advance where research information is available only through private channels controlled by the integrators, or where access to markets is controlled by the integrators. . . .

"Moreover, the CED has apparently not been concerned with the class of farmers from which this out-migration would principally occur. If, for example, we were to move out of agriculture and into improved nonfarm job opportunities the least productive 44 per cent —grossing less than $2,500 a year— we would go a long way toward solving the problem of rural poverty for this group. But we would reduce total farm marketings by only 5 per cent, and the remaining 56 per cent of the farmers would have to face the disastrously low level of unsupported prices on high unrestrained production levels.

"If two million farmers were moved out of commercial agriculture (grossing over $2,500 per year) the decline in production would indeed be drastic, at least until science, technology and machinery could catch up.

"Probably there would be some out-migration from all income classes of farmers. If trends of the past few years were to continue most of it would come from the $2,500 to $5,000 gross income class. It is our best judgment that this out-migration could be forced and accelerated somewhat—although not to the extent of two million in five years —if we wish to pay the price in increased competition for nonfarm employment, increased social and economic problems in urban areas, and the drastic decline in business on Main Street in small towns of rural America.

"It is also our best judgment that, even if we were to pay this price, the out-migration would not be sufficient to leave adequate incomes, under 'free market' prices, to those who do remain."

Finally, the ultimate aim of the CED program—the abandonment of all farm programs—would "alter the nature of the nation's agriculture and seriously threaten the family farm system that has created the world's most successful agricultural productivity. The national economy and general welfare would suffer from the absence, in the CED program, of some of the major constructive aspects of the Administration's food and agriculture program, such as rural area development and the wise use of land resources to meet growing needs for conservation, wildlife and outdoor recreation."

THE DISTRIBUTION OF INCOME

43. Sit-Down at General Motors

Herbert Harris

It is easy to forget the frequently violent and emotional background of industrial unionism. This vignette of labor history describes the period when management had not yet recognized the right of employees to bargain through unions of their own choice. Unions defied companies, the courts, and police in their struggle for recognition.

44. Why They Cheer for Hoffa

A. H. Raskin

Jimmy Hoffa, President of the Teamsters' Union, is one of the most controversial figures in the labor movement. This perceptive article, written in 1958, explores the bases for Hoffa's strength, which has persisted in spite of the well-publicized exposures of the McClellan Committee and several attempts to send Hoffa to jail.

45. Union Democracy

Clark Kerr

In most cases, union government does not conform to the traditional two-party system of our democracy. Clark Kerr examines some of the pressures which help enforce leadership responsiveness to membership interests. He asserts that it is essential for this purpose that union constitutions guarantee effective competition for elective offices.

46. The Decline of the Labor Movement; Apathy of Workers

Solomon Barkin

Labor unions have not succeeded in arousing the interest of many unorganized workers. Writing from a strong trade union point of view, Mr. Barkin explains some of the major factors which have prevented the labor movement from increasing its membership.

39 GOOD PROFITS PROMOTE PROGRESS

Frederick R. Kappel

Frederick R. Kappel is Chairman of the Board of The American Telephone and Telegraph Company.

A few years ago, a group of Bell System managers made an intensive study of the relationship between profits and performance in American industry. They started with two questions: "Does profit do anything? Is it only a result or does it also cause things to happen that affect our economy?"

Their broad conclusion was that good profit, good business performance, and healthy economic progress all go together. But the men who made the study went further. Good profit, they suggested, does much more than parallel good performance. It is one of the essential factors in bringing good performance about. (The other essentials named were good management and a good product.) In other words, good profit is by no means merely a result; it is also causative, dynamic, and energizing.

These conclusions were based on the group's study of the actual case histories of companies in several industries. The weight of the evidence was that where profits have been relatively good, performance has also been relatively good, measured by several important criteria. Of the businesses analyzed, those that earned well had better growth records—with all that connotes of value delivered to consumers—than those that earned poorly. The more profitable companies put more investment (including more retained earnings) into new and improved equipment; they did more research and more innovating; they offered better job op-portunities; and they contributed more to community well-being.

Thus, the study group suggested that good profit should be regarded as a prime *cause* of economic and social progress. Profit, they felt is not merely an end result of the business process, but a lively functional element that does indeed "cause things to happen."

CONCEPTS OF PROFIT

The idea has had a mixed reception. Many people have said to me that they think it makes excellent sense; others have been critical. They have argued that, while good performance may indeed produce good profit, it is not demonstrable that good profit will generate good performance. Our study group, they contend, must have been putting its carts before its horses.

This critical reaction is not surprising. It is, after all, a new thought that profit can be causative in the sense suggested. For generations, profit has been regarded mainly as a result, a residue, a remainder, and this is still the popular notion. It is a notion derived, perhaps, from nothing more complicated than the classroom illustration that if a man grows an apple for 8 cents and sells it for 10, he is left with 2 cents profit. Or it may be that the classical economists of the last century are partly re-

From *Business Horizons,* Winter, 1961, pp. 21–28. Reprinted by permission of the author, *Business Horizons,* and the University of Indiana.

sponsible. As they saw the matter, according to the *Encyclopaedia of the Social Sciences,*

There was first a separation between rent and a kind of gross income of the capitalist, as the business man was then more or less correctly called; subsequently the latter fund was divided between the capitalist and the laboring classes. Wages were supposed to be determined independently, the final share of the capitalist being left as a residuum.

Residuum—there is something lifeless and inert about the very word. It gives linguistic support to the view that the figures on the bottom line belong also at the bottom of our scale of values; and perhaps the typical form of income statement, showing profit at the bottom, further encourages this view. This is too bad, for as I see it, the fact that profit is something left over does not in any sense define its character. Its appearance as a remainder merely reflects its place in time, which is necessarily after the transactions that produced it. But this is no clue to its nature or potential.

Thinking about this, I was interested when someone the other day called to my attention the views of Francis Amasa Walker, as discussed by John Chamberlain in his book *The Roots of Capitalism.* According to Chamberlain, Walker, a Civil War general, teacher at Yale, and later president of M.I.T., "isolated profit as the driving force of industrial progress." While Walker too saw profit as a result, he saw it also as something more. Profit, said Walker, is the special creation of the gifted enterpriser. He produces it "by his comprehension of the demands of the market; . . . by his organizing force and administrative ability; by his energy, economy, and prudence." Thus, profit is more than a result; it is the instrument of dynamic change.

The classical concept of profit as mere residue suggests that when profit has been gained, its vitality ends. It is not useful to society; rather, it is likely to serve only the convenience and comfort of those who have possession of it. All this fits in with many people's feeling that while a little bit of profit may do no harm, profits for the most part are bad. To what degree public distrust of business profits may be derived from the concept of profit as a residue or any other economic theory, I am not able to say. More important is the fact that there is at present little or no theory of the kind that might dispel distrust. So far as I can see, profits are distrusted largely because the public sees them as a manifestation of economic power; because there is evidence every now and then that certain profits have not been honestly earned; and because of the belief that profit is often a reflection of the ability of some people to gain at others' expense. But these are political, ethical, and emotional considerations. They have nothing to do with any principle of business profit as such. It will be a pity, therefore, if we cannot gain acceptance for some view of profit other than one that, implicitly at any rate, deprecates its social usefulness. From the concept of profit as mere residue it is only a step to the moral contention that paucity of profit is a demonstration of virtue, and only one more step to the proposition that if scant profit is a mark of high integrity, then no profit at all must be a mark of the highest.

The danger is that noneconomic considerations may in the end determine what is to be done about profit. We need, on the one hand, a clear understanding that aberrations in business practice, unwarranted exercise of power, and the like are in no sense indicators of the function of profit. On the other hand, we need a concept of profit so satisfying that it will be impossible to identify ethical failure with failure of the profit principle.

Let us go back a moment now to Walker, who found in profit the driving force of industrial progress. Today one hears countless voices that seem to be saying much the same thing. I have in mind all the economists and journalists who echo and re-echo the refrain that "the profit motive" is the dynamo of enterprise. But for some reason, at least in this country, it seems to me there is much more applause for the profit motive than there is for profits. It is almost as though there were two kinds of thought: One has something in common with Walker's views, except that the modern stress, as I have said, is on the motive alone, whereas Walker did not stop there; the other, which is strengthened by the residue theory, if not derived from it, appraises profit with a wary eye, as something acceptable only when it is scant.

THE PROFIT DILEMMA

In short, we are seriously at odds with ourselves about profits. Our attitude is: Hurrah for the profit motive and down with profits. Or as a Latin might put it, "Motive *si,* profit *no.*" We want people to work for profits, but we are not at all sure that we want them to be earned. This is economic schizophrenia. It is absurd to hold that profit is a desirable incentive but a poor achievement. Men cannot work on the basis that it is right and necessary for them to pursue a goal that, when they reach it, will prove a sterile thing at best, and at worst a harmful one.

The Russians, I may remark, are in no such dilemma. They want profits, the genuine article, and not just "the profit motive." Witness this statement from the draft program of the Soviet Communist party as translated by Tass and printed in *The New York Times* on Angust 1, 1961: "It is necessary to promote profitable operation of enterprises, to work for lower production costs and higher profitability."

Wouldn't it be interesting some day to see a platform of the Republican or Democratic party calling for higher profitability? I am sure we can count on both parties to continue advocating prosperity, but it would be a great thing for the country if we might also find included—say in 1964—a recommendation in favor of higher profitability, the necessary ingredient of that prosperity.

THE BENEFITS OF PROFIT

I have a good many reasons for believing that a plus in business profits fairly earned is a plus for everybody. *The profitable business has freedom to do what is right.* I did not say has freedom to throw money around. The business that is profitable can operate much more economically than the one that is not, for the profitable operation does not have to defer current expenditures that will improve long-run performance. The company that puts off doing what it ought to do, because it cannot afford it at the time, inevitably sacrifices long-run economies.

I could sum up much of what is in my mind by saying that good profits facilitate good management judgment, but since this statement needs particularizing, I shall try to illustrate.

Training

Let us look first at the training of people. This is essential to the vitality of any business enterprise and its ability to contribute to economic progress. The selection of able people is a crucial task requiring thought, time, and money, and it is but the start of a long-range development process that calls for more of all three. I am not thinking of formal training procedures alone, but of the whole complex of effort needed to bring about conditions that encourage personal growth, inspire quality performance, and enable the individual to realize deep satisfaction in his work. The business that has adequate means available is far more likely, I think, to make the conscious and continuous effort needed than the business that is hard up.

There is growing conviction that the best way to test managerial talent is to give young people from the start assignments that truly challenge their capacity—in preference to training routines that impose a minimum of responsibility, fail to offer the trainee any sense of having a real job, bore him unutterably, and give him sore feet from standing around. One of the good arguments in favor of testing men early in their careers is that they will learn from their mistakes. In saying this, I am not advocating mistakes at any time; we have, however, to be realistic. If we are going to give people responsibility in this way, there are bound to be some errors and they are bound to cost money (albeit less than the cost of bigger errors the same people might make in later years if they did not have the judgment gained from making little ones). But if we cannot stand the cost of the small errors, we are not going to assign the responsibility. In other words, we are not going to do what we know we ought to do to build the future.

It may be said that these examples hardly provide all the evidence needed to support the case for healthy profit. I agree. Before offering more illustrations, however, let me remind the reader that these I have mentioned lie in an area of special importance for the future. With the advance of technology, there is an ever-growing need for the training and retraining of men and women in almost every phase of industry. People must learn to use new arts effectively, find new markets for new products and services, and function to best advantage in new forms of organization. In short, industry in the years ahead faces a tremendous task in education, and if industry cannot earn the means, the task is simply not going to be done well. To put it another way, the country is well aware that the schools face a problem of unprecedented scope. But as we all know, education is not completed at school; it only begins there. This is the recurrent theme of every college commencement, and with good reason. Starting where the schools leave off, industry must shoulder a considerable part of the total responsibility for future education—quite apart from its financial contributions to the schools.

Physical Plant and Engineering

Another aspect of what I choose to call the vital or causative function of profit lies in the area of engineering and building plant facilities. Let us look at an example drawn from the telephone business, which must make heavy investment in physical plant in order to serve its customers.

A telephone engineer is called on to decide what size of telephone cable should be installed to serve a growing neighborhood. He knows it must serve perhaps 200 homes immediately. He is also reasonably confident that, in another couple of years, possibly 200 more homes will want service. Putting in a cable today that is big enough to serve all 400 homes will obviously cost more now than putting in one that will serve only 200. The carrying charges will be higher, too, of course. But if the engineer puts in the cable today that will serve only 200 homes, and another of equal size is needed two years later, the total cost and carrying charges will be considerably more in the long run.

So what will the engineer do?

If the company he is working for is hard up, he will have to put in the smaller cable because that is cheaper *now,* even though it is obvious that this course will be more expensive in the end. If, however, the company is in good financial shape, if it can readily get the capital needed for investment in the larger cable, and if the general level of earnings permits absorbing the higher carrying cost of the bigger cable until its full capacity is utilized, then the engineer will be encouraged to install the bigger cable. Again I point out that good profit favors doing what ought to be done.

It is a commonplace that profit or the prospect of profit is necessary to attract capital. Less emphasized, but no less important, is the fact that healthy profit in countless instances promotes capital's effective and efficient application. The example I have cited is not an isolated instance; telephone people, and no doubt others in many different lines of business, have to make thousands of decisions like the one mentioned above. In the making of all such decisions, reasonable present prosperity helps to promote long-run economy and progress.

In the last year or so, much public attention has centered on the fact that a large proportion of America's industrial plant is growing old. Surveys that have been made indicate that about a third of it is now so old and inefficient that it ought to be scrapped. The Secretary of the Treasury has said that the average age of the nation's plant is twenty-four years, and the President has observed that some two-thirds of

our machine tools are more than ten years old.

Aging plant is progressively more inefficient. We need to modernize our productive facilities to compete more effectively in world markets, help balance our international payments, and create job opportunities for our growing work force. Why then does industry retain so much old and inefficient plant? One important reason is that our tax laws do not allow industry enough depreciation expense, either in total or year by year. The result is understatement of true costs, corresponding overstatement of income, and, in consequence, a tax on capital. (Any levy on a proper expense that the law requires to be mislabeled as income must be a levy on capital; it cannot be anything else.) In any event, adequate depreciation plus adequate real profit has been made impossible.

I have been arguing my conviction that good profit works in favor of productive efficiency. It seems to me that the apprehensions about inadequate depreciation and the movement to find some remedy support this argument. In essence, what we have here is a growing concern that capable and effective businesses should be able to earn the real profits they need in order to become more productive. Maybe some people in government have not thought the matter through in this way; if they have not, I wish they would. Knowing the problem for what it really is might lead also to better understanding of the function of profit in other respects.

Lean Leavings Not Enough

The main effort in this article has been to suggest the meaning of a concept that says that profit is not something merely residual, but is causative and energizing. At this point, however, someone may well say, "Look here, this is all very well, but are you really talking about profit per se and how much of it there ought to be? It seems to me you are talking rather about some of the things a well-managed business needs to do *before* it makes a profit—before it is able to deposit that residue. There are other accomplishments that are also important: good wages and working conditions, for instance, safe working practices, research and development, the introduction of new products and services, alertness to consumer needs, and so on. So long as you accomplish these and still have something left over, this is what really counts, isn't it? And where is your proof that the residue, the profit, needs to be more than minimal?"

I can only answer that last question from actual experience as a manager, and this experience has convinced me that the quality of management performance is influenced in every aspect by the prospect of good earnings on the one hand, or of lean leavings on the other. For evidence, I have to turn again to events in the Bell System. This is not intended as special pleading, and I hope it will not be so interpreted. The fact is simply that to speak from experience, it is necessary to refer to it.

Our over-all earnings situation in the years soon after the war was poor. In the early 1950's, there was a slight improvement, and in the last few years there has been further improvement What one may trace rather easily, as earnings have risen, is an acceleration of projects that markedly increase the quality, dependability, and convenience of the service rendered.

For example, we measure the quality of telephone transmission in terms of how people might hear each other if they were conversing in a quiet open field. In 1950, transmission on the average long distance call was as though

the talkers were standing 15 feet apart. In the ten years following, this distance was reduced some 20 per cent—to about 12 feet. But with a better profit margin at hand, we are now working on a program to cut the distance down to less than 5 feet by 1970. This will make an enormous difference in the ease of conversation.

Perhaps it has been noticed also that as Bell System earnings improved in the later 1950's, there came a succession of new telephone instruments and systems for homes and offices. Direct distance dialing spread rapidly so that today about three-quarters of all our customers can dial their own calls to all parts of the nation. Ocean telephone cables to Europe, Alaska, and Hawaii have resulted in a great improvement in overseas services.

Today a program is under way to sharply reduce the occasions when people wanting to telephone in the busier periods of the day will find no circuits available. Another important project is construction of a bomb-resistant underground communications system across the continent. Our direct distance dialing program is proceeding on a schedule that will make such calling available to nearly every Bell System customer in the next four years. Means for automatically identifying the calling number are being installed under an accelerated program. Data-Phone services, which enable machines to communicate with other machines through the regular nation-wide telephone network, are being rapidly extended. Millions of dollars are being spent for the development of communications satellites that may permit global communications, including television and data as well as voice transmission, on a scale hitherto impossible.

Were the profits of the Bell System today no better than they were in the 1940's and well into the 1950's, it would be impossible for us to push ahead with anything like the same vigor. And if we could not maintain good earnings, we would necessarily have to put a checkrein on forward undertakings. Prudence would demand this.

Not that profit can or ever should be assured. It must be worked for and earned in every sense of the word. But if the ultimate end in sight is meager, few managers will bend extra effort to develop and proceed with new and useful long-range projects that increase current costs, or build additional excellence into their product, or take special pains with their maintenance, or spend either a million dollars or a hundred to make their plant and facilities more efficient. More likely, they will feel pressed to move in the reverse direction. They may compromise on quality; they may skimp on maintenance, or even do none for as long as possible. They may rely protractedly on the outmoded and outworn. Against his better judgment, against all his instincts to do the job well, the manager is pushed into ill-advised corner-cutting, into expedients and substitutes, into deletions and omissions that may not show immediately but will ultimately sap the long-run vigor and strength of the enterprise. In short, if he has no hope of prosperity by the means that will most benefit his customers and his company, which is to give real value and earn an equivalent reward, he is forced into the situation of trying to keep integrity in his financial statements by taking it away from his business.

THE BROADER VIEW

Earlier in this article I put some stress on the difficulties we get into if we admire profit as a goal but deplore it as an achievement. We cannot be half for profit and half against it. I wonder if the reason some of the critics of profit get into this situation may not be that they see business managers as dedicated *solely* to profit. Perhaps some managers are so dedicated. However, my observation is that most of them have a broader view. In a business like the one I am in, the question is ever present, "Which comes first, service or profits?" Our license, of course, is only to serve, nothing else. But to answer the question by separating the one from the other is difficult indeed. Years ago, the answer was given in these words, and I find it hard to improve them: "We must serve well to prosper. We must prosper to serve well."

I have omitted from this discussion such an obvious point as the fact that prosperity pays taxes. All it appears necessary to say is that if the government wants revenues, the government will do more than give lip service to the profit goal—it will really encourage the making of real profits, and rejoice in the result.

No discussion of business profits can be conclusive. But to refer again to the study mentioned at the start, where there is overwhelming evidence that profit, performance, and progress are intimately linked, may there not be wisdom in accepting the likelihood that profit is in fact an essential contributing factor? I realize that economics is not an exact science. By the same token, however, it seems necessary to say that no theory that denies a causative, creative role to business profits can be taken as definitive. From experience and observation, I am persuaded that good profits not only accompany and make manifest sound progress, but do in fact make important contributions to it, and must be regarded as essential to promote economic growth and the achievement of desirable economic goals. Only an economy in which industry and government see eye to eye on this, and work in harmony to nourish business profit, will realize its full potential in creating productive

efficiency, in delivering the greatest value to the consuming public, and in raising living standards.

40   PRICE BEHAVIOR IN A FREE AND GROWING ECONOMY: OBJECTIVES AND GUIDEPOSTS

The Economic Report of the President,
January, 1962

THE OBJECTIVES

Price behavior embraces both changes in the over-all *level* of prices throughout the economy and changes in price *structure*—the relation of particular prices to each other. Changes in either the level or the structure of prices have far-reaching influences which can affect for better or worse the performance of a free economy. Both aspects of price behavior are closely related to major problems which confront the U.S. economy today.

Our success in solving the international payments problem (discussed in the previous chapter) will depend to a major extent on our ability to avoid inflation. To recognize this compelling reason for price stability is not to say that stable prices are desirable only for their contribution to the achievement of equilibrium in our balance of payments. Even creeping inflation has effects on the distribution of income which are always capricious and often cruel, and it may generate perverse changes in the structure of prices. Galloping inflation is profoundly disruptive of economic efficiency and growth. But to these persisting arguments for avoiding inflation is now added the pressing and immediate need to strengthen the competitive-

ness of U.S. industry in world markets.

International competitiveness is affected by many considerations, including quality, variety, service, credit facilities, and promptness in delivery. But after full weight is given to these considerations, price remains at the heart of the matter. The effect of price developments on our international competitive position will not, of course, be determined by the behavior of U.S. prices alone; what counts is the change in the ratio of U.S. prices to the prices of those countries with which we compete in world markets. There is independent reason to expect in the next few years a moderate upward price trend in some competitive countries, but a decline in the ratio of our prices to theirs is obviously more likely if our own prices remain stable than if they rise.

Large potential gains in national economic welfare are at stake in the course of price developments over the next year or two. Stable prices—together with the many other measures to strengthen our payments position . . . —will move us toward equilibrium in our international payments. This, in

———
From *The Economic Report of the President,* January, 1962, pp. 167–168, 185–190.

turn, will remove a possible impediment to the vigorous pursuit of full employment.

It is always possible to strengthen the balance of payments, at least for a time, by weakening the economy. Checking and reversing the economic expansion would reduce our demand for imports by reducing our demand for all goods and services. Raising interest rates sharply would probably attract some foreign capital to the United States, but it would raise the cost and reduce the volume of domestic expenditures for new business plant and equipment and residential construction. This road to balance of payments equilibrium endangers the interests of the whole Nation and specifically the interests both of labor and of business; for the former it increases unemployment, while for the latter it lowers profits. Both groups stand to gain from price level stability, which lays the foundation for the harmonious coexistence of balance of payments equilibrium with full employment and rapid economic growth.

Price level stability does not, of course, require stability of all prices. On the contrary, the structure of relative prices constitutes the central nervous system of a decentralized economy. Changing relative prices are the signals and stimuli which foster the efficiency and guide the growth of such an economy.

Changing relative prices serve to ration scarce goods and services. They encourage consumers and business firms to economize on the use of things which have grown scarcer, and to use more freely those things which have become more abundant. They attract resources into the production of those things for which demand has increased, and encourage the outflow of resources from the production of things for which demand has declined. They provide

generous rewards to innovators, and then assure that the benefits arising from innovation are widely diffused throughout the economy. They direct economic activity into the most productive channels. A smoothly functioning price system, while it cannot solve all of the resource-use problems of our economy, is nevertheless an indispensable agent for reconciling decentralized private decision-making with national economic objectives.

In the context of current economic policy goals, flexible relative prices play an important role in encouraging maximum production and shaping the pattern of growth. As the economy approaches full utilization of productive resources, premature and stubborn bottlenecks may arise in some sectors while labor and capital are underutilized elsewhere. This danger is lessened if productive resources are sufficiently mobile to shift promptly into the sectors of the economy which are coming under pressure. Flexible price and wage relationships are not in themselves sufficient to assure that capital and labor will flow from relatively declining to relatively expanding sectors. But flexible price and wage relationships can smooth the process, both by signaling the directions in which resource movements should occur, and by providing incentives to encourage such shifts. Prices must fall as well as rise, however, if changing relative prices are to play their role in guiding resource movements without forcing a steady rise in the over-all level of prices.

*   *   *

GUIDEPOSTS FOR NONINFLATIONARY WAGE AND PRICE BEHAVIOR

There are important segments of the economy where firms are large or employees well-organized, or both. In these sectors, private parties may exercise considerable discretion over the terms of wage bargains and price decisions. Thus, at least in the short run, there is considerable room for the exercise of private power and a parallel need for the assumption of private responsibility.

Individual wage and price decisions assume national importance when they involve large numbers of workers and large amounts of output directly, or when they are regarded by large segments of the economy as setting a pattern. Because such decisions affect the progress of the whole economy, there is legitimate reason for public interest in their content and consequences. An informed public, aware of the significance of major wage bargains and price decisions, and equipped to judge for itself their compatibility with the national interest, can help to create an atmosphere in which the parties to such decisions will exercise their powers responsibly.

How is the public to judge whether a particular wage-price decision is in the national interest? No simple test exists, and it is not possible to set out systematically all of the many considerations which bear on such a judgment. However, since the question is of prime importance to the strength and progress of the American economy, it deserves widespread public discussion and clarification of the issues. What follows is intended as a contribution to such a discussion.

Mandatory controls in peacetime over the outcomes of wage negotiations and over individual price decisions are neither desirable in the American tradition nor practical in a diffuse and decentralized continental economy. Free collective bargaining is the vehicle for the achievement of contractual agreements on wages, fringes, and working conditions, as well as on the "web of

rules" by which a large segment of industry governs the performance of work and the distribtuion of rewards. Similarly, final price decisions lie—and should continue to lie—in the hands of individual firms. It is, however, both desirable and practical that discretionary decisions on wages and prices recognize the national interest in the results. The guideposts suggested here as aids to public understanding are not concerned primarily with the relation of employers and employees to each other, but rather with their joint relation to the rest of the economy.

Wages, prices, and productivity. If all prices remain stable, all hourly labor costs may increase as fast as economy-wide productivity without, for that reason alone, changing the relative share of labor and nonlabor incomes in total output. At the same time, each kind of income increases steadily in absolute amount. If hourly labor costs increase at a slower rate than productivity, the share of nonlabor incomes will grow or prices will fall, or both. Conversely, if hourly labor costs increase more rapidly than productivity, the share of labor incomes in the total product will increase or prices will rise, or both. It is this relationship among long-run economy-wide productivity, wages, and prices which makes the rate of productivity change an important benchmark for noninflationary wage and price behavior.

Productivity is a *guide* rather than a *rule* for appraising wage and price behavior for several reasons. First, there are a number of problems involved in measuring productivity change, and a number of alternative measures are available. Second, there is nothing immutable in fact or in justice about the distribution of the total product between labor and nonlabor incomes. Third, the pattern of wages and prices among industries is and should be responsive to forces other than changes in productivity.

Alternative measures of productivity. If the rate of growth of productivity over time is to serve as a useful benchmark for wage and price behavior, there must be some meeting of minds about the appropriate methods of measuring the trend rate of increase in productivity, both for industry as a whole and for individual industries. This is a large and complex subject and there is much still to be learned. The most that can be done at present is to give some indication of orders of magnitude, and of the range within which most plausible measures are likely to fall (Table 1).

Table 1

ANNUAL RATES OF GROWTH OF OUTPUT PER MAN-HOUR
1909 TO 1960

[*Based on establishment series*]

Industry series	Average annual percentage change			
	1909 to 1960	1947 to 1960	1947 to 1954	1954 to 1960
Total private economy	2.4	3.0	3.5	2.6
Nonagriculture	2.1	2.4	2.7	2.2
Nonmanufacturing	—	2.2	2.6	1.9
Manufacturing	—	2.8	2.9	2.9
Manufacturing corrected for varying rates of capacity utilization	—	2.8	2.8	3.1

There are a number of conceptual problems in conection with productivity measurement which can give rise to differences in estimates of its rate of growth. Three important conceptual problems are the following:

(1) Over what time interval should productivity trends be measured? Very short intervals may give excessive weight to business-cycle movements in productivity which are not the relevant standards for wage behavior. The erratic nature of year-to-year changes in productivity is shown in Chart 1. Very long intervals may hide significant breaks in trends; indeed in the United States—and in other countries as well—productivity appears to have risen more rapidly since the end of the second World War than before. It would be wholly inappropriate for wage behavior in the 1960's to be governed by events long in the past. On the other hand, productivity in the total private economy appears to have advanced less rapidly in the second half of the postwar period than in the first.

(2) Even for periods of intermediate length, it is desirable to segregate the trend movements in productivity from those that reflect business-cycle forces. Where the basic statistical materials are available, this problem can be handled by an analytical separation of trend effects and the effects of changes in the rate of capacity utilization.

(3) Even apart from such difficulties, there often exist alternative statistical measures of output and labor input. The alternatives may differ conceptually or may simply be derived from different statistical sources. A difficult problem of choice may emerge, unless the alternative measures happen to give similar results.

Selected measures of the rate of growth of productivity in different sec-

Indexes of Output per Man-Hour

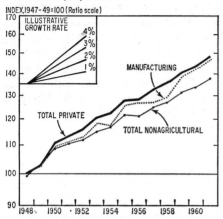

INDEX,1947-49=100 (Ratio scale)

Note: Man-hours estimates based primarily on establishment data.

Source: Department of Labor.

tors of the economy for different time periods are shown in Table 1. Several measures are given because none of the single figures is clearly superior for all purposes.

The share of labor income. The proportions in which labor and nonlabor incomes share the product of industry have not been immutable throughout American history, nor can they be expected to stand forever where they are today. It is desirable that labor and management should bargain explicitly about the distribution of the income of particular firms or industries. It is, however, undesirable that they should bargain implicitly about the general price level. Excessive wage settlements which are paid for through price increases in major industries put direct pressure on the general price level and produce spillover and imitative effects throughout the economy. Such settlements may fail to redistribute income within the industry involved; rather they redistribute income between that industry and other segments of the economy through the mechanism of inflation.

Prices and wages in individual industries. What are the guideposts which may be used in judging whether a particular price or wage decision may be inflationary? The desired objective is a stable price level, within which particular prices rise, fall, or remain stable in response to economic pressures. Hence, price stability within any particular industry is not necessarily a correct guide to price and wage decisions in that industry. It is possible, however, to describe in broad outline a set of guides which, if followed, would preserve over-all price stability while still allowing sufficient flexibility to accommodate objectives of efficiency and equity. These are not arbitrary guides. They describe—briefly and no doubt incompletely—how prices and wage rates would behave in a smoothly functioning competitive economy operating near full employment. Nor do they constitute a mechanical formula for determining whether a particular price or wage decision is inflationary. They will serve their purpose if they suggest to the interested public a useful way of approaching the appraisal of such a decision.

If, as a point of departure, we assume no change in the relative shares of labor and nonlabor incomes in a particular industry, then a general guide may be advanced for noninflationary wage behavior, and another for noninflationary price behavior. Both guides, as will be seen, are only first approximations.

The general guide for noninflationary wage behavior is that the rate of increase in wage rates (including fringe benefits) in each industry be equal to the trend rate of over-all productivity increase. General acceptance of this guide would maintain stability of labor cost per unit of output for the economy as a whole—though not of course for individual industries.

The general guide for noninflationary price behavior calls for price reduction if the industry's rate of productivity increase exceeds the over-all rate—for this would mean declining unit labor costs; it calls for an appropriate increase in price if the opposite relationship prevails; and it calls for stable prices if the two rates of productivity increase are equal.

These are advanced as general guideposts. To reconcile them with objectives of equity and efficiency, specific modifications must be made to adapt them to the circumstances of particular industries. If all of these modifications are made, each in the specific circumstances to which it applies, they are consistent with stability of the general price level. Public judgments about the effects on the price level of particular wage or price decisions should take into account the modifications as well as the general guides. The most important modifications are the following:

(1) Wage rate increases would exceed the general guide rate in an industry which would otherwise be unable to attract sufficient labor; or in which wage rates are exceptionally low compared with the range of wages earned elsewhere by similar labor, because the bargaining position of workers has been weak in particular local labor markets.

(2) Wage rate increases would fall short of the general guide rate in an industry which could not provide jobs for its entire labor force even in times of generally full employment; or in which wage rates are exceptionally high compared with the range of wages earned elsewhere by similar labor, because the bargaining position of workers has been especially strong.

(3) Prices would rise more rapidly, or fall more slowly, than indicated by the general guide rate in an industry in which the level of profits was insufficient to attract the capital required to finance a needed expansion in capacity; or in which costs other than labor costs had risen.

(4) Prices would rise more slowly, or fall more rapidly, than indicated by the general guide in an industry in which the relation of productive capacity to full employment demand shows the desirability of an outflow of capital from the industry; or in which costs other than labor costs have fallen; or in which excessive market power has resulted in rates of profit substantially higher than those earned elsewhere on investments of comparable risk.

It is a measure of the difficulty of the problem that even these complex guideposts leave out of account several important considerations. Although output per man-hour rises mainly in response to improvements in the quantity and quality of capital goods with which employees are equipped, employees are often able to improve their performance by means within their own control. It is obviously in the public interest that incentives be preserved which would reward employees for such efforts.

Also, in connection with the use of measures of over-all productivity gain as benchmarks for wage increases, it must be borne in mind that average hourly labor costs often change through the process of up- or down-grading, shifts between wage and salaried employment, and other forces. Such changes may either add to or subtract from the increment which is available for wage increases under the over-all productivity guide.

Finally, it must be reiterated that collective bargaining within an industry over the division of the proceeds between labor and nonlabor income is not necessarily disruptive of over-all price stability. The relative shares can change within the bounds of noninflationary price behavior. But when a disagreement between management and labor is resolved by passing the bill to the rest of the economy, the bill is paid in depreciated currency to the ultimate advantage of no one.

It is no accident that productivity is the central guidepost for wage settlements. Ultimately, it is rising output per man hour which must yield the ingredients of a rising standard of living. Growth in productivity makes it possible for real wages and real profits to rise side by side.

Rising productivity is the foundation of the country's leadership of the free world, enabling it to earn in world competition the means to discharge its commitments overseas. Rapid advance of productivity is the key to stability of the price level as money incomes rise, to fundamental improvement in the balance of international payments, and to growth in the Nation's capacity to meet the challenges of the 1960's at home and abroad. That is why policy to accelerate economic growth stresses investments in science and technology, plant and equipment, education and training—the basic sources of future gains in productivity.

41   THOSE PERPLEXING "GUIDEPOSTS"

Fortune

Among the difficulties encountered by governments seeking to guide the course of economic events in detail is that of making their directives intelligible, and then making them stick. The Kennedy Administration has been facing these difficulties in the field of wage policy. Last January its Council of Economic Advisers, under Chairman Walter W. Heller, staked out some "guideposts" for noninflationary wage and price behavior based on the general principle of productivity increase. After eight months there is mounting argument as to what the guides really mean and whether they are not, in fact, leading into a labyrinth.

As early as last February, Jules Backman, professor of economics at New York University, concluded that "the use of productivity as *the* guidepost for proper increases in wage and non-wage benefits should be rejected both on grounds of feasibility and economic desirability." More recently Professor Raymond J. Saulnier, who headed the Council of Economic Advisers in the Eisenhower Administration, has argued that the new guideposts are inadequate for an economy where profits and employment have been lagging. There has also been considerable skepticism about the guideposts in Washington among men who are close to labor matters.

H. M. Douty of the Bureau of Labor Statistics, for instance, has warned that government wage guides may encourage higher union demands. And William E. Simkin, director of the Federal Mediation and Conciliation Service, has discovered that this is just what has happened. The guides, he points out, have been misinterpreted to mean that wages should rise by 3 per cent per year no matter what the circumstances.

Reprinted from the September, 1962 issue of *Fortune* magazine by special permission; copyright 1962, Time, Inc.

So unions that might otherwise have settled for 2 per cent have held out for more. And, on the other side, employers have balked at realistic settlements above the 3 per cent line, and then have looked to Washington to back them up. In short, far from smoothing the path of collective bargaining, the guides may well have roughened it.

While this can scarcely be proved statistically, the guides have certainly not led to labor peace. In the first six months of this year work stoppages ran somewhat above the like period of 1961, and man-days lost rose to 9,800,-000 as against six million the year before. Wage increases averaged about 3 per cent, with fringe benefits piled on top of that. The Communications Workers used the guideposts to gain more this year than last. Other unions simply ignored the guides: West Coast construction workers' wages went up some 7 per cent in certain areas. One of the more curious foul-ups occurred in negotiations of the 500,000 non-operating railroad employees. The unions and the railroads were able to quote different aspects of the guideposts to support diametrically opposite views of what wages should be.

An Ambiguous "Contribution"

All this indicates that the council's prescription for wages and prices is a good deal more intricate and ambiguous than the term "guideposts" suggests. Its reflections as continued on pages 185–190 of its 1962 annual report might have stirred little comment if they had appeared in a learned economic journal. But coming from government officials in positions of power and responsibility, they were almost bound to cause discord. Many economists, including previous presidential advisers, have, of course, emphasized the truism that in the long run *real*

wages and incomes cannot advance faster than national productivity; we cannot consume more than we produce. But President Kennedy's council went beyond this negative rule. Its stated purpose was to make a "contribution" to greater public understanding of whether specific wage settlements and price movements would or would not be in the "public interest." And it proposed to do this by describing "how prices and wages would behave in a smoothly functioning competitive economy nearing full employment."

The council then laid down two general guides plus four major "modifications." The guide for *wages* is that "the rate of increase in wage rates (including fringe benefits) in each industry be equal to the trend rate of over-all productivity increase." The guide for *prices* is that they should fall in high-productivity industries and rise in low-productivity industries, with the over-all price level remaining stable. What the council has projected is an economy where wages advance on the long term but the public gets the benefit of at least some of the productivity increase through reduction of prices by the high-technology industries. This is a welcome emphasis as against the wholly unsound idea that wages should swallow up all productivity gains even in the most efficient industries, with the consumer left out entirely.

But the council's model is also highly theoretic. Reliable productivity figures are hard to come by or nonexistent in most industries, hence the council's admonitions on how prices should behave cannot be pinned down. With respect to "over-all" or national productivity there are of course some respectable though arguable statistics. And the council includes in its report a table showing that between 1909 and 1960 productivity in the U. S. private economy increased at an average annual rate of about 2.4 per cent, and that between 1947 and 1960 this rate rose to 3 per cent. But here it runs into a different kind of trouble. For it is apparently this figure that is used by labor leaders when they argue that all is well if wages go up by 3 per cent per annum.

Those "Modifications"

This argument, however, overlooks the modifications the council found it necessary to make in its general rules in order to relate them to the real world. One big modification is that wages would rise faster than the guide rate in an industry that would otherwise be unable to attract sufficient labor, or in which rates are exceptionally low compared with the range of wages earned elsewhere by similar labor. Per contra, wages are expected to rise more slowly than the guide rate in industries suffering from continuous unemployment or where wage rates have been exceptionally high.

Important modifications also apply to prices. Specifically, the council states that prices should rise faster than the guide rate "in an industry in which the level of profits was insufficient to attract capital required to finance needed expansion in capacity, or in which costs other than labor costs had risen." Prices would rise more slowly than the general guide rate in opposite circumstances.

All these modifications invite endless debate in application. In the wage negotiations for the nonoperating railway employees, the union argued for a substantial increase on the grounds that some rail wages had lagged behind those in the rest of the economy. But the employers countered with the argument that there was considerable unemployment in transportation, and so wages should actually be decreased.

Similar argument about the guide lines has beset negotiations in the aerospace industry. The United Automobile Workers was criticized by the New York *Times* for wanting a wage increase in excess of the national productivity increase. But Nat Weinberg of the U. A. W. retorted that wages of aerospace workers were "substandard" owing to the fact that they cannot use their full bargaining power in times of crisis. So under the wage modification of the council's guidelines, he argued, larger demands were justified.

What Bothers the Professor

But this is not all. The most important, if least noticed, qualification to the guides set forth by the council is that they describe a competitive economy at close to full employment. But the U. S. economy is not now at full employment (meaing 4 per cent unemployed), and one of the great tasks ahead is to create more job opportunities. In its 1962 report the President's council laid stress on the fact that employment depends on over-all demand, and that this in turn may be affected by government spending. But employment and unemployment also depend on the relation of wages and prices and profits. And this in turn means that a wage guide that might be appropriate to full-employment conditions would be quite inappropriate to conditions of underemployment. The council sees that this is true for particular industries. But it does not generalize the truth for the economy as a whole.

This is what bothers Professor Saulnier, who in a recent interview in *U. S. News & World Report* suggested that the council's productivity guideline was "inadequate in the present situation." Higher employment and investment, Saulnier pointed out, depend on a catch-up in profits. "And what would be best for our economy at this time would be wage advances that are actually less than the improvements in productivity. This would reverse the trend in cost-price relationships that has been suppressing business profits and stifling investment expenditures."

Professor Backman made this point in a somewhat broader connotation. In an exhaustive analysis of the whole productivity guide theory to wages, he says: "This proposal would perpetuate and aggravate the practice of granting annual (wage) increases without regard to underlying economic conditions. . . . Yet it is exactly such regular and inexorable increases which have characterized the postwar economy regardless of the factors which may have dictated against further increases in labor costs in some industries and local labor markets in some years. One result undoubtedly has been greater unemployment as workers have been priced out of some jobs or as the high cost of labor has intensified the search for satisfactory substitutes in the form of machinery or alternative means of achieving the production goal." And Backman sums up: "A proper national wage policy cannot be framed solely with the objective of preventing inflation. It also must consider the demand for labor and hence the impact on the volume of employment as well as other factors."

One Rule for Many

So the guideposts are not only highly ambiguous but also in one sense irrelevant to real conditions. There remains a final question bearing on any government attempt to influence specific wage and price decisions—namely, that of enforcement. The Administration has said repeatedly that it does not want to impose wage and price controls, and the council says in its 1962 report that all it wants to do is to contribute to public discussion. But sooner or later a government that takes a detailed position on wages and prices will be tempted to go further, as indeed the Kennedy Administration did in the case of steel. In this matter a study made by leading economists in 1961 for the Organization for European Economic Cooperation is much in point. The majority favored the idea that governments should adopt national wage policies. But the minority demurred and raised the enforcement point as follows: "Where wage-push inflation tends to develop, governments committed to a national wage policy would, in our opinion, have to become involved in rather extensive regulations relating to individual wages and prices. . . . We are opposed to moving in this direction."

The conclusion emerges that in an enterprise economy it is extremely difficult for the government to influence wages and prices directly and specifically without running into trouble. There is, however, one general rule that, if enforced, would make the setting up of guideposts largely unnecessary. This is the rule of competition and the maintenance of open markets both for industrial products and for labor. The Council of Economic Advisers recognized this in the case of industry, and its report is high in praise of the application of antitrust laws to business. Unfortunately, it does not follow through with this idea when it comes to wages and to labor unions, though on any objective analysis it is here that an unsolved monopoly problem lies. In the building trades there is restriction of freedom of entry; in steel there is power to close down an entire industry. In the view of a good many observers, the whittling down of union power is the true unfinished business of a government that wants to help achieve high levels of employment without inflation. And as economist Arthur Burns has put it: "If the powers of monopolies, whether of business or labor, were sufficiently curbed by law, there would be little or no need for the large intrusion of government into collective bargaining."

42 WHY WORKERS HATE TO CHANGE JOBS

Business Week

Sarah Williams is a laid-off auto worker with 13 years' seniority. If the auto industry prospers, she may be called back to her $2.40-an-hour job of running a sewing machine in the upholstery department at the Dodge plant in Detroit.

While she's waiting to be called back, she isn't trying to get a permanent job elsewhere. And temporary work is almost nonexistent. So she remains unemployed.

Sarah Williams is a living example of the immobility that seniority rights are building into the labor force. If it were not for the equity she has built up in 13 years at the Dodge plant, she could get a full-time job tomorow in the garment industry, where skilled operators are at a premium.

As it is, she doesn't want to lose her pension rights and other benefits, particularly not for lower pay than she was getting—and even if she did, employers in the garment trade would think twice about hiring a woman who would quit as soon as Dodge recalled her.

Vested Interest. There are many workers who have the same problem as Sarah Williams.

"Employees try to ride out layoffs and come back," says an executive of an auto company. "There's less tendency to have a 'float' in the labor market after employees have built up

equity in various benefit plans."

Seniority itself is not one of these benefits, but it is closely related to the package of rights that make up the employee's equity: supplementary unemployment benefits, pensions, holidays, paid vacations, health plans. The more seniority a worker has, the greater this equity and the greater his reluctance to change jobs. And this reluctance extends to workers who are nearing the point of gaining greater equity in these benefits.

This tends to leave only the youngest workers with any great freedom to change jobs without sacrifice of equity under seniority rights. And there are fewer of the youngest generation of workers, because of the low birth rate of the Depression years.

1. Employer's Attitude

The big factor is pension rights; most other benefits are so widespread that they have little effect on a worker's willingness to move from one job to another. They work two ways. They govern an employer's hiring policies about as much as they tend to freeze workers on their high-seniority jobs.

This shows up particularly in a key management decision: Do we hire more people or do we pay overtime to the present work force? The costs of "fringe" benefits are no longer marginal costs, from the employer's viewpoint, and management often decides it's cheaper to pay overtime at premium rates than to hire additional workers for what may be a short time.

Not Marginal Costs. According to the U. S. Chamber of Commerce, the costs of labor benefits, having doubled in 12 years, now average 22% of payroll.

A national food concern estimates its over-all costs for the so-called fringe benefits at 78¢ an hour for each employee. It figures retirement plans, social security, unemployment benefits, and workmen's compensation at 23.6¢ an hour; military leave, holidays, vacations, premiums, lunch and rest periods, and shift differentials at 54.4¢ an hour.

A farm equipment manufacturer estimates employee benefits at slightly more than 50¢ an hour. The American Iron & Steel Institute cites 70¢ an hour for such benefits in the steel industry, and the auto industry calculates 62¢ an hour. These costs depend more on the number of men at work than on the number of payroll hours. So up to a point it may cost no more to pay premium rates for overtime work than to add new people with a corresponding increase in fringe costs.

In weighing overtime against new hirings, management must also consider other costs that are hard to pin down, such as retraining of new people and the cost of additional foremen for the new work crews.

A Black Eye. For two other reasons, too, employers often elect to work people overtime, regardless of out-of-pocket costs, rather than hire new workers who may have to be laid off in a few months.

One reason is the touchy question of public relations. Layoffs give an employer a black eye among the company's total work force, in the plant's community, even in the financial world. "The bad publicity just isn't worth it," an auto executive says.

The other reason is the measurable effect on the company's rates for unemployment benefits. To hire a man and then lay him off after six months will hurt the employer's rated experience, which determines the premiums or taxes for these benefits. A bad employment experience rating in Michigan, for example, can cost the employer up to 4.5% of taxable payroll, or up to 12¢ an hour.

II. Holddown on Mobility

The ability and inclination of workers to move from job to job has been one of the great strengths of the American economy. Generations of historians have cited this factor as a major force in keeping the economy flexible and dynamic, nourishing the development of new frontier regions and new industries. That's why so many economists today are worrying about evidence that workers are less willing to move.

Most observers agree that the decline in mobility of labor is real and serious. They point to figures that the Bureau of Labor Statistics keeps on the number of "quits" in industry. Allowing for business ups and downs, this quit rate shows an apparent long-term tapering. In a report to the Fund for the Republic entitled Pension Funds and Economic Freedom, Robert Tilove says: "The conclusion seems inescapable that most private pension plans . . . exercise a restraining influence on labor mobility."

The Restless Young. Part of the change, however, must be attributed not to pensions but to a shrinkage in the number of the younger workers—the most mobile group, still searching for a permanent niche and not yet tied economically to any employer.

As early as 1913–14, a study showed that 81.3% of all workers "separated" had been on the payroll less than a year. Arthur M. Ross, a University of California economist, mentions a 1949 study of manual workers in New Haven, mostly nonunion labor. This survey found that 71% of the voluntary changers of jobs had less than three years' service, 80% less than five years, 94% less than 10 years.

It's an assumption among most experts that the lowest seniority is among the younger workers. That group is shrinking as a proportion of the total labor force. In 1940, the civilian labor force had 14.5% in the 20–24 age group; in 1956, only 8.8%. In 1940, the group between 45 and 64 years old made up 27.2% of the total; in 1956, a full 33%.

Problems in Manufacturing. The percentage shift has probably been even higher in manufacturing, which has more problems than employers as a whole must face. The actual number of production workers in manufacturing has not increased since 1951, while employment has boomed in wholesale and retail trades, finance, insurance, and government.

For one thing, manufacturing seems less attractive to the young, although its wage rates are high enough to hold onto the older workers. Mechanization has eliminated many jobs where a beginner might have gotten his start a generation ago.

Thus, manufacturing is more and more isolated from the rest of the labor market, in contrast to its former role as a vast pool with workers coming in and going out. With today's specialized technology, it is harder, for example, for a farm boy to become a machine operator, then to move out into retailing or banking.

III. More Mobility Ahead?

At any time, in any economy, some people should be shifting from job to job. If manpower should become inflexible and immobile, the U.S. would be confronted with a serious economic problem.

Some people think this problem is developing right now, but others see signs of a change. The current trend toward immobility contains the seeds of its own counter-trend, some experts say.

Pension Influence. For example, pension plans now act as a drag on job-changing, but they may prove eventually to have an equal and opposite effect.

Gerry E. Morse, industrial relations vice-president of Minneapolis-Honeywell Regulator Co., notes that a 10-year minimum for pension eligibility allows companies to hire over-age men (retired policemen as guards, for instance) without adding to pension costs.

Moreover, says Robert Tilove, "if a worker knows that pension plans—from the new job and perhaps from the old one as well—will still give him security in his years of retirement, he can feel a little freer to apply his personal savings to the risks of changing jobs."

"Money in the bank is an element of freedom," say Tilove. "And the ultimate right to a pension may offer some of the liberating influence of liquid assets."

Tilove adds that the vesting of pension rights (giving the worker an equity that he can take with him upon leaving a company) will also enlarge mobility, though fully vested plans will doubtless remain a rarity as far as blue-collar workers are concerned.

Early Retirement. More important to the mobility of the labor force, says Tilove, is the prospect that pensions can free workers from physically demanding jobs at an age early enough to let people take lighter jobs afterward.

Tilove cites the pension plan of United Parcel Service of New York, Inc., which has enabled some men in the 55 to 64 age bracket to retire. A high proportion of these men have gone into less demanding jobs, such as clerk, timekeeper, school bus driver, bank guard, messenger, dispatcher, and butter and eggs salesman.

This sort of development, Tilove points out, "may in time make a major contribution to labor mobility, to an extension of the working life, and therefore to national production."

Mobility within a given industry is already being aided by negotiation of industrywide pensions and by reciprocity between pension funds. A New York truck driver, for example, can switch to coverage in a New Jersey pension fund without sacrificing any

retirement benefits, and a ship's officer can move from an East Coast to a West Coast company under similar terms.

IV. Turning Point

In any case, the economists' worries about labor mobility will almost certainly end in the next half-dozen years.

The U.S. has reached a turning point in the composition of its labor force. The proportion of young people has in all probability hit bottom. The "hollow generation" born in the Depression years is already at work, and the input of young workers will increase rapidly as the wartime children come of age.

Entrance of large numbers of young people into the labor market is bound to boost the quit rate. Young people jump from job to job, exploring the possibilities open to them, with little regard for the fringe benefits they aren't yet entitled to. And their search for the "right" job can be expected to restore normal mobility to the labor force as a whole.

43   SIT-DOWN AT GENERAL MOTORS

Herbert Harris

*   *   *

The "sit-down" which between September 1, 1936, and June 1, 1937, involved 484,711 American workers not only in motors but in rubber, steel, textiles, shipbuilding, subways, oil-refining, shoes, newspaper publishing, baking, aircraft, and countless other manufacturing service and retailing spheres, is a strike of a very special kind. Whereas in the everyday variety employees leave mill or mine or store

or factory to picket outside their place of business, in the sit-down they remain inside at or near their usual posts but do no work. They just sit or stretch out on the floor or benches or loll around on their feet. And if a sit-down lasts long enough—dozens of them in mass-production plants last only a few min-

From *American Labor,* by Herbert Harris (New Haven: Yale University Press, 1938), pp. 288, 296–304. Reprinted by permission.

utes or a few hours—it becomes a stay-in, properly speaking, though the term sit-down is already a colloquialism used to describe this technique, per se, whatever its duration.

Its advantages are obvious. Police and militia can more easily disperse a picket line in the open than an "occupied" plant where windows may be barricaded and gates barred. "You can't ride a horse through a brick wall," remarked a grizzled old unionist in Detroit during the General Motors stay-ins. "With the sit-down today the boys don't have to put up with that, anyway."

*   *   *

From the mists and fogs of emotion-charged words marking the discussion of the sit-down one clear question emerges: Is purely legal title to a producing property the only right that should be recognized in the American democracy? The answer of the United Automobile Workers was put by its "in-and-out" vice-president, Wyndham Mortimer, when he inquired:

Is it wrong for a worker to stay at his job? The laws of state and nation, in a hundred ways, recognize that the worker has a definite claim upon his job; more fundamentally . . . every workman has a moral right to continue on his job unless some definite misconduct justifies his discharge. These sit-down strikers [i.e., in Flint and elsewhere] are staying at their work-places; no one has a better right to be there than these men themselves. . . . The sit-down strikers have performed valuable services in those factories; General Motors and the public alike have profited. . . . To call them trespassers now, and to deny their right as human beings to remain with their jobs . . . is manifestly unjust.

In Fint, Michigan, the power of General-Motors was arrayed against the implications of this view in a community where, out of 165,000 inhabitants,

50,000 depended directly upon the company for livelihoods gained from Buick, Chevrolet, and Fisher Body Plants. Anti-sit-down sentiment, after the first days of the strike, was crystallized by an organization called the Flint Alliance. It was in theory composed of "loyal employees" most of whom somehow contrived to resemble barflies and poolroom toughs from nearby Detroit. The Alliance also contained a sprinkling of General Motors executives and subadministrators and people from its technical and commercial divisions, some local businessmen, and almost all the vigilante-minded personalities in the vicinity, the kind of men, and there are many of them, who in their perpetual adolescence come fully alive only when they can have "adventure" by doing physical injury to others. The Alliance's propaganda was fabricated by the high-pressure, high-priced Floyd E. Williamson who, himself an "outsider" imported from Manhattan for his special purpose, amusingly enough based a large part of his anti-union blasts upon the "un-American activities" of "outside" organizers. The chairman of the Alliance was George E. Boysen, former paymaster in a Buick factory, and latterly himself the owner of a spark-plug concern. As the sit-down progressed, Alliance spokesmen grew daily more vociferous in their demands for violence, some of them promising that soon law and order committees of indignant citizenry would forcibly evict the sit-downers who by the thousand had "dug-in" for a long siege.

To oust the strikers, General Motors had secured from Judge Edward Black an injunction which commanded them to vacate company property and also forbade picketing. Although he owned nearly $200,000 worth of General Motors stock, Judge Black considered himself sufficiently impartial to issue his edict, a belief not entirely in accord with the more commendable traditions of the American bench. When Sheriff Wolcott delivered the Black document to the sit-downers he was jeered and good-naturedly told to go home. Meantime, company officials, both local and national, and U.A.W. and C.I.O. leaders were busy fencing, mustering all their skill for pary and riposte, all of them with an eye on the public gallery.

On January 12, the company shut off the heat in Fisher Body Plant No. 2 and its own gray-uniformed police, reinforced by regulars from the local Flint force, were instructed to prevent the shipment of food into the building. It was hoped that this "diet of cold and hunger" would break the morale of the sit-downers.

Inside the plant, the men missed their lunch, shivered, and grew restive at the prospect of being also deprived of their dinner. Shortly before seven o'clock that evening, a United Automobile Workers sound truck rolled up before the great rectangle of Fisher No. 2, with Victor Reuther, a top-notch organizer for the union, at the microphone. At first he politely asked the police, both public and private, for permission to have food sent in to the sit-downers from the union's kitchen. The metallic lungs of the amplifier lifted his voice high above the sounds of the street until everyone within a half-mile radius could hear his plea. The officers, both the gray and the blue, were mute. Reuther tried another tack. He appealed to them as workers, urging the necessity for coöperation among all kinds and degrees of labor. There was no response, save the cheers of the sit-downers. He then became more aggressive, assuring the officers that strikers outside the plant would get food to the sitters. Some fifteen minutes later a group of pickets carrying pails of coffee and cartons of buns, like an oversized

backfield, starting on an end run, bowled over the police guarding the door to the plant and brought food to their famished friends.

At 8:45 some sixty policemen set upon pickets stationed at plant entrances, clubbed them with night-sticks, and drove them inside the building. A sergeant smashed a glass pane in one of the doors and thrust the nozzle of a tear-gas gun through the jagged space, pumping shells into the vast interior. Other officers fired buckshot into pickets and men clustered near the door, wounding fourteen who were later removed to the hospital.

The sit-downers replied to this attack with literally everything they had: coffee-mugs, pop-bottles, and steel automobile hinges weighing two pounds each. At the beginning of the battle, a clarion voice from the sound truck cried: "We wanted peace. General Motors chose war. Give it to 'em!" In the road strikers formed a phalanx around the sound truck, repelled all efforts of police to dismantle it, and overturned three police cars and another belonging to the sheriff.

At midnight the policemen closed in their ranks and, with guns cracking, tried to rush the main entrance, only to be met by a devastating stream of water from a big fire hose which, along with the steel-hinge missiles, compelled them to retreat and finally to abandon their assault. This affair was promptly named "The Battle of the Running Bulls."

The bloodshed of that night, and the fears of more violence to come, resulted in the appearance of 1,500 of Michigan's National Guardsmen in Flint. Acting under instructions from the cool-headed, humanitarian Governor Murphy who was valiantly seeking to settle the strike by pacific means, they managed on the whole to preserve order almost impartially, though various commanders chafed at the restraints placed on them and would have preferred to try out their new machine guns, howitzers, and knowledge of the "how to quell" riots sections of military manuals on the sit-downers, in response to the beseechings of the Flint Alliance that the requirements of patriotism be fulfilled.[1]

Meantime—after the strikers by a ruse had captured the crucial Chevrolet motor assembly plant No. 4, and John L. Lewis had called on President Roosevelt to intercede for them against the "economic royalists represented by General Motors and the Du Ponts," who had opposed his reëlection with the same fervor that the auto workers had supported it; and also after Washington conferences between Secretary of Labor Frances Perkins and Alfred P. Sloan, president, and William S. Knudsen, vice-president of the company, had produced mutual recriminations—General Motors obtained from Circuit Judge Paul V. Gadola a significant and sweeping court order. It directed the sit-downers to evacuate company-owned plants under penalty of imprisonment for contempt of court and a fine of $15,000,000, the estimated value of the invested properties. Again Sheriff Wolcott served to mocking and derisive groups of determined men the order that set 3 P.M. on February 3 as the deadline for leaving the struck plants.

In reply the sit-downers sent telegrams to Governor Murphy, who was still exerting almost superhuman patience and persuasion to bring both sides into agreement. The message from Fisher Body Plant No. 1 read in part:

We the workers . . . have carried on a stay-in strike over a month in order to make General Motors Corporation obey the law [2] and engage in collective bargaining. . . . Unarmed as we are, the introduction of the militia, sheriffs, or police with murderous weapons will mean a blood-bath of unarmed workers. . . . We have decided to stay. . . . We have no illusions about the sacrifices which this decision will entail. We fully expect that if a violent effort to oust us is made many of us will be killed, and we take this means of making it known to our wives, our children, to the people of the state of Michigan and the country that if this result follows from the attempt to eject us, you are the one who must be held responsible for our deaths.

The night before the "zero hour" day of February 3, the sit-downers, pallid under blazing arc-lights, listened grimly to their radios, or played cards or parcheesi or checkers or dominoes, or tried to lose themselves in newspapers or magazines, or talked in subdued tones. Many were convinced that the morrow meant massacre. For defense against expected machine guns, inadequate clubs dangled from their belts. An air of almost Oriental passivity, as of men who wait in resignation for the beat of destiny's drum, hung over them. Their faces were stern and thoughtful, and few slept.

In the morning roads leading into Flint were filled with cars and trucks carrying union sympathizers from Akron, Lansing, Detroit, and Toledo who by the thousand swarmed over the town and had to take over the direction of traffic themselves, for no policemen were in sight. The visitors moved toward the various sit-down plants, and only the women's emergency brigades, with their red and green berets, brought color to a somber procession that for weapons held

---

[1] One major in particular confessed his bitter disappointment that he was unable to test the value of his pet idea, shooting vomiting gas into the sit-downers via the plants' ventilating systems.

[2] The National Labor Relations Act.

pokers, broom handles, and pieces of pipe.

While Flint's clocks ticked on toward the showdown hour of three in the afternoon, Governor Murphy in Detroit finally succeeded in arranging a conference between William S. Knudsen for the company and John L. Lewis for the United Automobile Workers. To Sheriff Wolcott, who had the duty of enforcing the Gadola eviction order, Governor Murphy wired that everything should be held in abeyance during the Knudsen-Lewis conversations; and the Sheriff, more than pleased to oblige, suddenly discovered that he lacked proper legal sanction, anyway, along with a sufficient force to carry out the Gadola edict, although the Flint Alliance and the company's legal staff in Flint assured him that they could together remedy both deficiencies.

When this turn of events was made known, sit-downers, pickets, and unionists from other cities made high holiday. Their violins, saxophones, banjos, cornets struck up hill-billy airs and square-dance tunes, and men and women swung partners joyously over the frozen lawns surrounding the various plants.

Next day the company complied with President Roosevelt's request that in the public interest its representatives should again meet with spokesmen of the strikers. A wearing week of conferences ensued between William S. Knudsen, G. Donaldson Brown, and John Thomas Smith for General Motors, and John L. Lewis, Lee Pressman (general counsel for the C.I.O.), Homer Martin, and Wyndham Mortimer for the strikers. Time after time only the moral strength and suasions of Governor Murphy, who presided over the negotiations, prevented their collapse, and cigarette and cigar ashes spilled over trays amid the temper-fraying clashes of strong wills and stronger wants.

Eight days later, the Governor, his face haggard with strain and lack of sleep, had the great personal triumph of seeing at long last a meeting of minds out of which came the agreement terminating one of the most important capital-labor disputes in recent times.

The contract signed by General Motors and the United Automobile Workers was a great step forward for unionism in motors and contained seven basic provisions: (1) recognition was to be granted to the U.A.W. for its members only, and not as sole collective bargaining agent; (2) straight seniority rules were to prevail after six months of service; (3) shop committees were to be set up to smooth out grievances on the job; (4) a survey of speed-up evils was to be made; (5) the forty-hour week was to continue in force; (6) time and a half for overtime was to prevail; (7) no discrimination was to be exercised against unionists, who could wear their union buttons and talk about their organization during lunch hours.

The union requests for a uniform minimum wage, affecting plants in all parts of the country, and for the thirty-hour week were both denied.

Primarily as the result of its sit-downers' forty-four-day defiance of General Motors, the United Automobile Workers (late in 1938) has some 370,000 dues-paying members out of an industry-wide maximum potential of 450,000. It is thus the third largest among the C.I.O. unions. It has collective bargaining agreements with all of the independents and with two of the Big Three, General Motors and Chrysler. Currently it is trying to unionize Ford against an opposition as stubborn as a peasant's prejudice and as strong as a billion dollars.

The U.A.W. is doubly young—both in its short time of existence as a union and in its membership, since the industry still places a premium upon speed and endurance in its workers, attributes most generally found in men and women under forty, even under thirty-five. The union's maverick sit-downs, condemned by motor magnates and (some of them) by Martin himself, have derived from a new sense of liberation from oppression; from flawed methods of adjusting "line" and departmental grievances; from foremen-worker antagonisms that had been piling up for years and were often aggravated by both the self-assertion of the new unionists and the desire of the straw boss to show them that he was still top-dog. Many of the pettier officials, indeed, still believe it their purpose in life to bring obloquy upon the union whenever possible; [3] and neither side has as yet been "educated up" to the patience and will to good will necessary for a harmonious management-union relationship.

---

[3] General Motors has discharged a superintendent who by "riding" unionists tried to provoke them into sit-down action.

44   WHY THEY CHEER FOR HOFFA

A. H. Raskin

A. H. Raskin is a writer on labor-management affairs for *The New York Times*.

The wail of a bagpipe cut through the shop steward's report that everything was O.K. at the barn of the Merchants Motor Freight. A chunky little man with the shoulders of a heavyweight boxer plowed past the six-footers in the overflow crowd at the rear of the union hall. Two truck drivers lifted him off his feet and bore him down the aisle. A thousand others leaped from their seats and cheered. Jimmy Hoffa was back with "the guys that made me."

Everyone wore a button with the slogan, "Hoffa—The Teamster's Teamster." Some wore two or three. This was the rank and file of Local 299 of the International Brotherhood of Teamsters—the local that started a tough, cheeky kid named James Riddle Hoffa on his climb from the loading platform of a grocery warehouse to the presidency of the country's biggest and strongest union.

And this was their answer to two years of effort by Senate rackets investigators to convince them that their union was being turned into a hoodlum empire by a faithless leader. Every instrument of mass communication—newspapers, magazines, television, radio and newsreels—had brought them the sordid record of union despoliation uncovered by the McClellan Committee.

They knew of the testimony that Hoffa had treated the union's money as his own, entered into subterranean relations with employers, suppressed the democratic rights of members by brute force and allied himself with the underworld. They knew of the Senators' charge that he had used his vast power in ways "tragic for the Teamsters Union

---

From *The New York Times*, November 9, 1958; copyright by *The New York Times*. Reprinted by permission.

and dangerous for the country at large." They knew of the merged labor federation's decision that their failure to cast out Hoffa made them pariahs unfit to live inside labor's house. All this they knew—and they let Hoffa know it made no difference. He was still their boy.

When he rose to speak, they were on their feet again, whistling, shouting, stomping. He waved them down with a quick gesture. He spoke in a flat tone —confident, insistent, bare of oratorical adornment. There was none of the platform magic of a John L. Lewis or a Walter Reuther.

Yet the sensation that came across was of relentless, elemental strength. The 45-year-old Hoffa exuded it, from the glossy hair that bristled away from his scalp like a porcupine's quills, past the chill, hooded eyes, to the rocklike hands. He teetered a little on the balls of his feet in the manner of a fighter about to throw a punch. His navy blue suit strained across his thick chest and heavily muscled arms. Here was no Dave Beck softened by easy living. For all his Cadillacs, his $50,000-a-year salary, his limitless expense account and his free hand with the union's millions, Beck's successor still looks, talks and acts like a truck driver.

No note of apology marked Hoffa's report on his stewardship. Everything was black or white, with all the black on the side of his critics. He had taunts for Senator McClellan ("He's back in Arkansas now trying to straighten out Faubus, I guess"); the newspapers ("they propagandize the teamsters for only one reason—because of the size and strength and militancy of the Teamsters Union"); college professors and other longhairs with proposals for laws to clean up labor ("they only talk that way after they have had four long glasses of booze").

That still left Hoffa with a few jibes to fling at the two union chiefs he con-

siders principally responsible for the Teamsters' expulsion from the A.F.L.-C.I.O.—George Meany ("he always hid in his office as a bookkeeper—he has yet to negotiate his first contract or meet his first scab on a picket line") and Walter Reuther ("here we talk a language the teamsters understand, not a language to change the United States into a socialistic country or to worry about what politician is elected").

He had a simple explanation for the charges that the union had become a homing ground for jailbirds: "All this hocus-pocus about racketeers and crooks is a smokescreen to carry you back to the days when they could drop you in the scrap heap like they do a worn-out truck." The teamsters applauded dutifully.

They kept applauding as he told them how much other unions owed them and how much they owed their union. He reminded them of the days when they worked seventy or eighty hours for $18 a week, without vacations, pensions, welfare, pay for breakdown time or seniority protection. "There are men here who used to pull Toledo for 75 cents or Chicago for $1.50; now the scale to Toledo is $17 and $34 or $36 to Chicago," he declared.

Always he was the teamster talking to teamsters: "You know me since I'm 17—the kid, you called me. They say I've got a police record. Sure, I've got a record and you know where I got it. It's no secret. There's not one thing there outside the labor movement. And I tell you Hoffa will have it again if they start kicking the truck driver around."

He warned them that the next five years would be "the five toughest years we ever saw in this union business," and this provided the jumping-off point for another slap at his detractors. "They even criticize me for calling this a business," he complained. "Well, what do you hire us for, if not to sell your labor at the highest buck we can get?"

There was much more, all designed to get across the point that "what we have had we can lose overnight, if we are foolish enough to become divided." And then it was time for the main business of the evening, a vote on whether Local 299 wanted to strip Hoffa and his executive board of their control over the union's finances and internal affairs.

"You are here for one purpose," Hoffa declaimed, "to show the solidarity and strength of this organization to those who think the teamster is a coward, that he can't find his way into his union hall or that he is the victim of a business agent who is a racketeer, a bum or a hoodlum. You and only you have established the rules of this organization, and only you—not the propaganda of the press and McClellan—will change the rules."

He waved a thick bundle of bills at the crowd. They represented all the local's obligations for the preceding month. He told the members they could insist on having each bill submitted to them for approval if they did not want to leave blanket authority in the officers' hands. "Send 'em to McClellan," was the bull-voiced suggestion of one rank-and-filer. The others shouted that they wanted the executive board to keep on using its judgment about how to spend the union's money.

The story was the same when Hoffa mentioned charges that the welfare and pension funds had been "stole blind" by investments he had made for his own profit or to help out his cronies. He lauded the funds' accomplishments, and he asked where his critics—"the great saviors of the workers"—had been when the union was battling to get the benefit programs set up. He contrasted the pension payments of $135

a month at age 60 with the lower standards in force in "many so-called progressive, clean unions."

When he got through and asked whether they wanted the union to change its way of doing business, there was a mass roar of "no, no, no." He was not satisfied with that. "Let's do this in an orderly way," he said, "so no one can charge I stole the vote." He called for a standing vote on whether the executive board should continue to have a blank check on the handling of union funds, the designation of convention delegates, the calling of strikes and all other matters of internal administration. Everybody stood up.

When the "nays" were called everybody sat down—except one brother, who had apparently had one beer too many on the way to the hall. When the crowd laughed, he slumped into his seat. That made it unanimous.

How significant was the whole performance? Should it be dismissed as the obeisance of cowed and servile men to a master armed with life-and-death power over their jobs? Did fear of physical violence against themselves or their families chain the members of Local 299 to the Hoffa truck? Was their vote an expression of insensate mass adoration akin to that extended to their fuehrers by the brain-washed populace of totalitarian lands?

None of these possible explanations seemed adequate for an observer who had spent three days before the meeting in individual contact with many of the drivers, talking to them privately in the terminals and on the loading docks.

Only two out of nearly 200 said they felt that the union was in a mess and that the membership was powerless to do anything about it. The others declared, with every indication of sincerity, that they felt Hoffa had done a standout job on wages, welfare, grievances and every other phase of union service. They brushed aside the accusations of gangsterism and racketeering as part of an attempt by outside forces to cut Hoffa down to size because he was doing too good a job in defense of the rank and file.

Their words added up to a hymn of contentment. Listen to Chad Virdin, an over-the-road driver, who shuttles the mail between Detroit and Jackson, Michigan, on a night run: "So far as I'm concerned, the union is 100 per cent. Every year that old raise is there and it has been ever since Hoffa took over." Or hear Robert E. Jones, a 345-pounder, who drives for the New York Central: "I think Jimmy Hoffa did more for the truck driver than anyone else who ever lived." Or these words from Clyde Miles, a loader on the dock at the Union Truck Company: "I'm only sorry there can't be more 299 locals and two Jimmy Hoffas. Where they get all that stuff in Washington, I don't know."

Some put their accent on the improvement in wages, from 65 cents an hour less than twenty years ago to $2.72 an hour now. Others enthuse about children delivered or operations performed at the expense of the welfare fund. Still others say that the thing they liked best was that Jimmy's office door was always open, that he was never too busy to listen to their gripes. Even now when he is in Washington, he will take a long-distance call collect if a member has an urgent problem.

He drives his staff harder than his members drive their trucks. A giant picture of Hoffa stares down, with the intensity of Big Brother, from the wall of the room in which the business agents have their desks. The headquarters contains a steam bath and massage table for their use, but they get little chance to luxuriate under the masseur's fingers. Hoffa's partner, Owen Bert Brennan, whose standing with the Mc-

Clellan Committee is no higher than Jimmy's own, laments that Hoffa never asks "how are you" or "how do you feel" when he telephones from the Capitol. His only query is, "What are you doing, and why the hell aren't you doing it right now?"

But even a casual visitor to the union offices is swiftly reminded that there is another side to the organization's affairs—the side that has caused the Senate investigators to bear down so heavily on underworld influence in the teamsters. The day that Hoffa was due back in town to attend the membership meeting, Philip Weiss, an industrialist with strong racket ties, strolled into the headquarters for a conference with Hoffa's aides.

Weiss was convicted two years ago of conspiring to steal $100,000 in auto parts, but his five-year jail sentence was set aside on a technicality. He is awaiting retrial in Detroit. When Hoffa was asked that night what Weiss was doing in the union, he shrugged indifferently. "He probably just dropped in to say hello; he does business with a lot of truck employers." And that was that.

The two union members who confided that they felt there was much that needed correcting in the local made it clear that they did not believe it would be healthy for them to try to do the correcting. "They have a way of eliminating you if you make trouble," said a car haulaway driver with twenty-two years in the organization. "What can one man do?" asked a platform loader. "Someone is going to have to clean it up."

And what of the top-heavy majority who do not rebel because they see nothing to rebel against, whose fealty to Hoffa is so great that they are prepared to disregard or disbelieve all the venality disclosed at the Washington hearings? An observer comes away with no sense that these are callous, calculating men, sunk in cynicism or allergic

298 THE DISTRIBUTION OF INCOME: *Part 4*

to considerations of conventional morality. Many are churchgoers, heads of families, war veterans. They seem to differ little from workers in auto plants or steel mills or other industries in the urges and satisfactions to which they respond.

If they lack polish, that is hardly a surprise. As Joseph McDonald, a moon-faced, barrel-bellied movie driver, who has been a member of the local since it was born, puts it: "We didn't build our union in this tough industry in a town this size with feather pillows."

It is precisely because the rank and file of Local 299 has so much resemblance to most teamsters and most workers that the enthusiasms with which they embrace the Hoffa brand of leadership is in many ways more disquieting than Hoffa's own long record of moral delinquency. For it tends to lend substance to the creed by which Hoffa lives, namely, that anything goes so long as the union keeps delivering fatter pay envelopes, bigger pensions and better conditions to its members. He summed up his prescription for keeping workers' loyalty in one of his wire-tapped conversations with extortionist Johnny Dio. It was: "Treat 'em right, and you don't have to worry."

This is the philosophy of the slot machine, with the gamble eliminated. The wheel is set for a payoff on every spin and while the dollar signs keep coming up no one is disposed to check too carefully on what is happening in the back room. The teamsters hold no monopoly on this attitude; it pervades much of our economic, social and political life. We admire the man who can deliver—how he delivers is much less important.

This is a concept that holds dismal implications for those who look to increased democracy in unions as the an-

swer to corruption. For it is distressingly apparent that Hoffa has emerged from all the attacks on him much more solidly entrenched than ever—not only in the allegiance of his home local but in every section of the 1,600,000-member brotherhood.

Votes of confidence have been piling up around him like confetti as he pilots his outcast teamsters uphill in wages and membership at a far faster clip than unions which proudly wear the Good Housekeeping seal of the A.F.L.-C.I.O. Against this backdrop of bread-and-butter gains, he has been mobilizing support for his fight to jettison his court-appointed monitors and win full control of the union at a new convention next March.

If the convention is held, the peppery little Detroiter seems sure to come out on top, and this time he will need none of the rigging tactics that cast so much shadow over his victory in Miami Beach a year ago. If Hoffa is stopped, it will be by the courts or other outside forces, not by any prohibitions from the rank and file.

No piling up of legislative safeguards for the exercise of democratic rights within the union seems likely to alter that fact in the near future. Unless Hoffa loses the energy and skill he has displayed as a delivery man for ever-expanding benefits for his members, there is every reason to believe he can count on their backing for an indefinite period.

That means that once again those who believe that unions should be something more than cash registers will have to rely on the long, slow road to reform. Public clamor and the multiplication of laws will not produce an overnight transformation, any more than they did when the State Crime Commission disclosed six years ago that underworld elements in the International Longshoremen's Association had hoisted the Jolly Roger over the Port of New York.

Only as we achieve loftier moral standards not only in labor but in business, politics and every other branch of our society can we hope for a real transformation. This is a road on which progress is sometimes agonizingly difficult, but it is an effort that must be made unless we are ready to concede that democracy itself is a failure.

45   UNION DEMOCRACY

Clark Kerr

Clark Kerr is President of the University of California, and formerly Professor of Economics at that University.

THE CENTRAL ISSUE—UNION IMPACT ON WORKER FREEDOM

Of the several issues involving labor today three are inherently simple issues. They are confined to specific segments of the labor movement but at the same time run into American life generally. These three issues are corruption, collusion, and violence.

Corruption exists and it is bad; but right and wrong are evident and hardly open to debate. Few unions are involved and other institutions in society have known and do know it also. Some remedies, including proper accounting procedures, are relatively easy to identify, although not always so easy to apply effectively.

Collusion also exists and it also is bad; but again the nature of virtue is not hard to define, although the line where it ends may be hard to draw in particular cases. (Virtue and the drawing of proper lines have met before on other stages.) Relatively few unions are affected and then nearly always jointly with their employers; and collusion, too, accompanies human nature almost throughout the span of social relationships.

Violence also is to be condemned. It has decreased greatly as a union tactic, however, and is subject to control by the many devices civilized man has created to insure law and order.

These are issues—they probably will be for a long time, and they deserve attention. But they are peripheral to the main controversy today.

The great current issue is the impact of the union on the freedom of the worker. This issue is not simple; it is most complex. It is one that runs through all or nearly all of the union movement and is central to its very existence. While not unknown as an issue in the spheres of government and the corporation, it is less intensely manifested there at the present time. Our nation has had a long, successful experience in creating a democratic framework for our government and protecting the liberties of individual citizens. Our corporations are not expected to be run on a democratic basis. They are founded on the model of the individual entrepreneur making his own

Excerpted from *Unions and Union Leaders of Their Own Choosing,* by Clark Kerr (New York: Center for the Study of Democratic Institutions, December, 1957), pp. 6–19. Reprinted by permission.

decisions; and corporations seldom have either a captive labor force or captive consumers (when they do have captive consumers they are usually subject to state control).

The unions are different. They have not had, like our government, a long and successful experience in developing a system of checks and balances, in limiting their sphere of endeavor, in defining and protecting the internal rights of their members. Unlike the corporation, they are founded on the assumption of internal democracy. They are associations of individuals, not collections of capital funds. Moreover, increasingly they have a captive membership. It is usually not possible for a union member just to withdraw in protest, without penalty, if he does not like the organization, its leaders, or its policy. We have here, most frequently, a more or less compulsory organization with substantial impact on the lives of its members.

American unions do make a major over-all contribution to a democratic industrial society—this is the first and most important observation to be made about their impact on worker freedom. They usually create a two-party legislative system governing the life of the work-place. In their absence, the rules would be set exclusively by the employer. Through the unions, the workers can have a direct influence on the nature of the rules under which they work. (Without a union they can also have an impact, by their choice of employers, but this is much less direct.) Also, unions usually insist on a grievance mechanism and this brings a judicial process into industrial life which is more impartial than when the employer sits as both prosecutor and judge. Beyond that, unions create a new power center which can, if it wishes, stand against the power centers of the state and the corporation, and these

latter power centers have gained greatly in recent years in their absolute strength. A rough balance among private and public power centers is the essence of a pluralistic society, and a pluralistic society is the only firm foundation for democracy in an economy based on industrial production.

Thus the unions have generally brought a better legislative and judicial process into industrial life and a better balance among the power groups of society. They have done this without the consequences that were so feared in times just past. It was believed that industrial conflict would tear society apart; the fact is that industrial peace is now the commonplace, and, except for the few unions still under Communist domination, American unions most certainly contribute to the social stability and security of our whole system. It was feared that unions would hamper productive efficiency and stifle progress; undoubtedly many union rules do retard production but there is no evidence that the over-all effect has been anything but relatively minor, and some new methods have been better received because of union consultation than they otherwise would have been in the light of the inherent conservatism of the work-place. It was feared that unions might distort inter-industry wage structures and that their actions would assure wild inflation; in fact, it is one of the wonders of the economic world that unions have had so little effect on wage structures; and their impact on price levels, while open to dispute, has certainly been no more than moderate. The fears of costly social conflict, of strangled production, of rampant inflation because of unions have proved largely without substance.

But a fear does remain that unions may take too much freedom from the worker, and this fear may not prove so groundless. If they do, they will not be the only institutions in our mass society which have conduced toward conformity. Big unions, big corporations, big government, and small individuals seem to be the order of the day.

If freedom is defined as the absence of external restraint, then unions reduce freedom, for they restrain the worker in many ways. They help to establish formal wage structures, seniority rosters, work schedules, pace of output, and the pattern of occupational opportunities, all of which limit his freedom of choice. They decide when he shall strike and not strike. They are —and this is one of the essentials to an understanding of unionism—disciplinary agents within society. They add to the total network of discipline already surrounding the workers through the practices and rules of the employer. They too insist upon order and obedience. It is inherent in their very existence. Two bosses now grow where only one grew before.[1]

Some loss of freedom, however, is inevitable in an effective industrial system. It will occur, more or less, whether the system is run by the employers alone, by the state alone, or even by the unions alone. Industrial society requires many rules and reasonable conformity to these rules. There must be a wage structure, a work schedule, and so forth, no matter who operates the system. This loss of freedom is one of the prices paid by man for the many benefits in income and leisure that can flow from industrial society. The challenge is that this price not be any higher than necessary. The issue lies in the

---

[1] This is not to suggest that it is not often and perhaps almost always better to have two bosses rather than one, for the union boss may help liberate the worker from the unilateral rule of the employer boss; but the worker is still subject to a web of rules and this web tends to be more thickly woven as a result of the presence of the union.

"more or less." The loss of freedom of the industrial worker will be substantial, as compared with the self-employed farmer or craftsman, but it may be less rather than more; and unions can make it either less or more.

UNION DEMOCRACY— DIFFICULTIES, DETRIMENTS, VIRTUES

Before we can determine how the reduction of freedom may be less rather than more, three introductory observations should be made:

1) Democracy in unions is inherently difficult to achieve. A union is variously expected to be at one and the same time —as Muste pointed out long ago—an army, a business, and a town meeting. Unions have usually ended up by being a business, serving the members but sometimes with those members having little more influence over the conduct of the business than stockholders have over a corporation. Unions have sometimes ended up as an army and have justified it, as Lloyd Fisher once remarked, in the terms the Communists have used to justify their "people's democracy," by reference to "capitalist encirclement." Unions have almost never ended up as a town meeting.

2) A good deal more democracy exists in unions than these comments and most outside observation would indicate. The national unions are the most visible entities and they are usually the least subject to democratic pressures. But at the local level, in many unions, there are contested elections, substantial turnover of officers, and face-to-face relations between members and leaders—here is the least entrenched bureaucracy. Particularly at the shop level, the relationship between shop stewards and workers is a responsive one. This local level is usually the most important to the workers. This is where

he lives and where his grievances are handled.

3) It is sometimes argued that unions need not or even should not be democratic. Different reasons are given for this conclusion. One line of argument is that unions have become largely functionless organizations and nobody really cares whether they are democratic or not. The state guarantees full employment and social security, and the employer has been seduced by human relations. Consequently, the worker has a job—often paid above the contract rate—a pension, and a friend, perhaps even a psychiatrist; and there is nothing for the union to do. Or, it is sometimes said, unions have become quasi-governmental bureaus. They help set minimum wages and schedules of hours, and they process grievances, as government bureaus sometimes do both here and abroad. Their work is largely routine and best handled in bureaucratic fashion; and so, again, why worry about democracy? Occasionally it is also said, unions function best if they are removed from the pressures of democratic life. They must respond to many pressures, not those of the membership alone but also the needs of the industry, the welfare of society, the concerns of other unions. They should take a longer view of events than the current membership is likely to take, for they are organizations with a continuing life. They will be more widely responsible to society and more businesslike in their operations if they are not subject to the demands and uncertainties of active democratic participation. The conclusion to this argument is that democracy causes internal and external strife and irresponsiblity.

Each of these reasons has some point to it. Unions perform less of a function than they did two decades ago; their work has become more routine as pattern-following and grievance precedents have become established; and internal democracy can cause external trouble, particularly for employers.

But the case for democracy can still be persuasive. If democracy is a superior form of government, as most of us would insist, it should be preferred in practice wherever it is possible.

Second, the workers can have a more effective voice in industry if they have an effective voice in their unions; and they are more likely to be satisfied with society if they have a sense of participation.

Third, if the unions lose their responsiveness to the interests of the workers, an opportunity is created for other organized elements, more politically motivated, to move in to represent these interests, as has happened in certain European countries.

ONE-PARTY GOVERNMENT— THE UNION CASE

The overwhelming majority of all the organizations of man throughout history have been ruled by one-party governments. Most of the time in most parts of the world all organizations have been under one-party rule. In certain parts of the world at certain times in history there have been a few two-party (or multi-party) organizations; but one-party rule is the standard and well-nigh universal case. The trade union is no exception. The International Typographical Union is the single deviant specimen on a national level in the United States.

Even in the democratic United States, the corporation, the political party, the fraternal order, the religious denomination, the farm organization, the welfare group, the student government, are all one-party organizations. Only in the public area, where it is by all odds the most essential, do we have two-party government.

The neglect of the one-party model of government, in view of its significance, is astounding. The rare instances of two-party and multi-party government have attracted most of the study. Certainly two-party government, as Lipset has persuasively argued, has much to recommend it. It provides criticism of the existing government, it makes ready an alternative government if the members want it, it reduces apathy, and does much else of value. But most men all of the time, and all men some of the time, function in one-party social organizations; and so do union members.

Why are unions one-party governments? There are several reasons. Partly, it is the requirement of unity in the face of external conflict. Partly, it is the control exercised by the leaders over the mechanism of the organization. But the answer lies much deeper than the fear of the enemy and the desires of the leaders. It is that there are no continuing conflicts except over ideology, and ideological conflicts tend to split unions rather than to create two-party systems within them. Witness the separate unions in several European countries and the split-off of Communist unions in the United States. Issues over wage increases, the handling of grievances, and so forth may lead to factions and leadership rivalry but not to two-party systems on a continuing basis.

Does one-party government mean that unions are inevitably "undemocratic"? If only two-party systems are really democratic, then the answer is obviously in the affirmative. But if organizations where the supreme power is retained by the members and which are reasonably responsive to membership desires may be called "democratic," even in the absence of a two-party system, then unions may be and many are "democratic."

There are dangers in any one-party government, but the system may serve its members well. It is most likely to do so, however, in the long run, if it is under the proper pressures. Traditionally, this pressure on trade-union government in the United States has come from four sources, all of them, unfortunately, now largely of historical importance only. In the passing of these four sources of pressure lies much of our current problem.

1) When union membership was more voluntary, leaders had to be responsive to the workers to get and retain members and this was an effective check on authority. As noted earlier, union membership is now, one way or another, often compulsory, the law notwithstanding; and it is likely to become more so. Union security, with all its other advantages, and leadership responsiveness tend to move in somewhat opposite directions; the voluntary sale and the forced sale lead to different behavior in any walk of life. This is not to support voluntary membership through the compulsion of the state for it seems neither possible in many situations nor, on balance, wise.

2) When dual unionism, now largely a relic, was an active force, it had somewhat the same impact as voluntary membership. Not individuals but groups could and did shift allegiance, and this acted as a check and balance. The idea of one union in one jurisdiction, however, is so firmly embedded in American union philosophy that dual unionism can exist only sporadically and temporarily.

3) The more or less permanent faction, stopping short of a second party but hovering in the wings ready to rush out on any inappropriate occasion, was a check on the leadership in many unions. The old-line Socialists served this function for many years, but the New Deal and time brought their

demise. The Catholic faction continues in a few unions, but usually only in those under left-wing control; otherwise there is little basis for a Catholic faction. There are few permanent factions today and fewer still in prospect. 4) The employer, particularly the recalcitrant employer, has historically been a check and balance on the union leadership. If the two organizations—the company and the union—appealing to the same constituency are in conflict, each will criticize the other and may even stand ready to try to destroy the other. But the day of fighting the unions is largely past, at least under conditions of full employment. The separation of interests between the leaders of the two organizations is decaying because industrial peace pays. Consequently, company pressure on most unions has been greatly reduced and in some instances has entirely disappeared.

UNION DEMOCRACY—THE POSSIBILITIES

With union membership increasingly compulsory, dual unionism declining, the permanent faction disappearing, and company opposition more rare, is there any hope for "democracy" or leadership responsiveness to membership interests in trade unions? There still is, for there are substitutes for these historical pressures. Six such possibilities will be suggested, with particular emphasis on the sixth.
1 *Membership interest.* Union memberships are traditionally apathetic except in some crisis, and very little can be done about it. Compulsory strike votes proved a farce in World War II and most bargaining issues cannot properly be put to membership vote. But some experiments might be undertaken with the polling of member-

ship opinion, with advisory referenda, and even with the use of television as a way for leaders to reach members, who will seldom come to meetings.
2 *"Professional" leaders.* Much is written about management as a profession. Perhaps union leaders might also become professional in the sense that they might be specifically trained for their jobs and might develop an "ethic" to guide their conduct—an ethic which sets boundaries to their behavior. They might, like city managers, be specifically trained for their jobs and responsible to an elected governing board.
3 *A new faith for the union movement.* Certain leaders today, in unions where the last vestiges of active democracy disappeared long ago, still serve their members well because of their adherence to the "old faith" of the union movement. But the "old faith" attracts few new followers. It was a fighting faith that grew out of evil conditions for the workers and union-busting by the employers. The conditions which gave rise to it no longer exist in the United States, although they continue to a degree in England and Germany, where the "old faith" still sets standards for union leaders. The social reformer holds himself—and is held by his environment—to a higher code of conduct than the business leader of the business union who quickly takes on the coloration of the industry with which he deals. If its ethics are high, his will be also; if they are low, so are his. The business union is a segment of the business.

What might this new faith be? It cannot be either "more, more, more and now." It cannot be a vision of class conflict. It might lie, as suggested later, in the development of unions as a liberating force in industrial society; and this might carry the union leader more into the intellectual and less into the business community.

4 *Local autonomy.* Local unions, by their inherent nature, clearly can provide more opportunities for democratic participation by the members than can national unions. Consequently, the more autonomy there is at the local level, the greater the democratic life of the union movement is likely to be. The big drop in democratic participation comes in the move from the one-plant to the multi-plant local or the district union. In the one-plant local, rival leaders can get known and be effective, issues can be discussed on a face-to-face basis, and democracy can be effective. In several European countries, for example, it is the local Works Council, with substantial powers, which arouses worker interest and participation. The multi-plant unit serves the interests of the entrenched leadership in a most emphatic way. The one-plant local with real authority is the most democratic entity in the trade-union movement. Considerable constitutional reform in most unions would be prerequisite to effective single-plant locals. Among other things, the institution of the "receivership" by regional and national officials would need to be curtailed.

5 *Union decertification.* It is certainly desirable to continue some mechanism through which members can exercise an option in favor of another union, or of no union at all. Such an option will rarely be employed but it should be available. If it is available and is used occasionally, it can act as a minor check and balance on union leadership.

6 *Discharge through rebellion.* The two-party system within unions, as we have seen, is an historical oddity. The regularly contested election is a rarity. Yet union officials do get changed other than as a result of death or retirement. Union officials are, in effect, "hired" by the membership for the duration of their good behavior, as tested imprecisely by the membership. The trouble comes when they need to be "fired." The mechanism then is a contested election in which the old leader is voted out of office. For such a contested election to take place two prerequisites are necessary: *1)* It must be possible for a faction to form and for its members to be reasonably free from retaliation through the operation of an impartial judicial process; and *2)* there must be secret elections at appropriate intervals. Other actors must be allowed to stand in the wings and be permitted to move on stage when the audience calls them. The dissatisfied individual and the antagonistic faction must be given an opportunity.

The term "competitive discharge" might be used in the sense that the leader is subject to constant evaluation by the members and is also subject to discharge through the process of electing a competitor who is free to appear when the conditions warrant. In the two-party system, the question is as to the better person; in the "competitive discharge" case, it is whether the incumbent should be fired or not. Deposed union leaders usually feel—and they are right—that they have been fired, not that they have been defeated. Among other things, they almost never seek election again once they have been discharged. They are like the old bull in the buffalo herd brought to his knees by the young challenger.

If trade-union democracy is defined as a system of government where the supreme power is largely retained by the members and can be exercised by them in an emergency at any and all levels, then the effective right of competitive discharge, by itself, is a sufficient basis for trade-union democracy. The essential feature of a trade-union constitution is whether it guarantees this right of competitive discharge.

This is the most we can reasonably expect, and it is also probably enough.

*   *   *

46   THE DECLINE OF THE LABOR MOVEMENT; APATHY OF WORKERS

Solomon Barkin

Solomon Barkin is Deputy Director of Manpower Division, OECD, and until recently Research Director of the Textile Workers Union of America, A.F.L.-C.I.O.

*   *   *

Beyond such deterrents as the opposition of employers and the structural deficiencies or disinterest on the part of the unions themselves, there are whole areas in the American economy where the apathy of employees to unionism is the primary obstacle—areas where workers have not responded in large numbers despite many efforts to arouse their interest and recruit them. Five groups are representative of these problems—employees of large corporations in which company and independent unionism has prevailed, as in the chemical and petroleum industries; women in manufacturing industries; non-manual workers; Negro workers; and low-wage service employees.

Among Chemical and Petroleum Employees

Unions represent about one third of the total work force in the large chemical and petroleum companies, but more than 40 per cent of this number are in independent plant or company unions. Within the chemical division the largest aggregate of company unions is in the du Pont Corporation, which embraces some 40,000 of the 70,000 employees in independent un-

ions. In petroleum about 100,000 workers belong to individual locals or federations of independent unions.

The three major national chemical unions, the Oil, Chemical and Atomic Workers International Union, the International Chemical Workers Union, and District 50 of the United Mine Workers Union, as well as the other unions with more specialized interests such as the Textile Workers Union of America in synthetic yarn and plastic plants, have tried to penetrate the unorganized areas and capture the local independent unions. They have carried on continual educational efforts to reach the employees and underscore the deficiencies of the independent unions. These efforts have succeeded from time to time. Some isolated gains have also been made in organization; production workers in five du Pont plants and craft workers in four more have been unionized and the OCAW was victorious at the Bayton, Texas, refinery of the Humble Oil and Refining Company, a Standard Oil Company of New Jersey subsidiary. But there has

From *The Decline of the Labor Movement*, by Solomon Barkin (New York: Center for the Study of Democratic Institutions, 1962), pp. 38–52. Reprinted by permission.

been no wholesale shift of independents to national unions such as occurred during the Thirties in the steel industry.

Organization of the workers in the giant corporations of these industries has been beset by many difficulties. The plants are generally small in number of employees, and they are isolated and scattered, thus depriving the workers of a close industrial identity. Moreover, many major companies have consistently fought unionism, even where they have acquiesced or have been forced to recognize unions. With few exceptions they have insisted upon individual plant bargaining units, resisting attempts at company-wide contracts. In the late Thirties several large companies, particularly in petroleum, encouraged employee representation plans which later became independent unions. They have not become serious challenges to employers because efforts to coordinate them into federations on a company or industry-wide basis have had little success. Recently these companies have bided their time even in promoting plant unions in new locations, believing this should be avoided as long as possible.

Resistance to unionism is strengthened by the selective hiring policies of the larger corporations, which tend to weed out potential union supporters. Long service, and in many instances continued recruitment of new employees from the families of current employees or on their recommendations build up a separate company identity which reenforces earlier rejection of unionism. Superior working conditions and benefits weaken the lure of unions. The management generally devotes much attention and spends considerable funds on communications and other personnel and human relations procedures to strengthen the company image. Supervisors are trained to contain

dissatisfaction. Individuals with union leanings are systematically eliminated. Wherever signs of union activity arise, the personnel departments try to correct the causes of discontent, discourage union support, and get rid of the sympathizers.

The independent unions have discouraged interest in genuine unions. While a substantial proportion of the workers realize they are company tools, they recognize and quite cynically admit that these "independents," either through their own power or through the threat of outside unionism, are able to bring them benefits approximately equal to those achieved by the national unions, without exposing them to the risks of strikes, outside direction, higher dues, and—most important of all— the active enmity of management. The differences in benefits or status have not seemed sufficiently large to persuade the majority to swing over to an outside union. Where there have been such movements, managements have invariably activated local community and corporate resources to dissuade workers, and generally they have succeeded.

The multiplicity of national unions has also weakened their individual ability to appeal to independents and to achieve adequate bargaining power with the large multi-plant companies. Two unions, the International Chemical Workers Union and the Oil, Chemical and Atomic Workers Union, have established joint company-wide councils which have promoted uniform standards on insurance and pension benefits. But these advances have not yet persuaded the independents to join them.

Among Women Employees

The weakness in organizing women workers stemmed originally from the prejudices of union members against recruiting women. As the number of women in industry multiplied, unions adopted liberalized admission policies and organization campaigns sought to enroll them. But before the Thirties measurable success was attained only in the needle trades. Later, in the upsurge of industrial unionism, thousands were embraced by the organization of entire plants. Union membership among women spread primarily in industrial establishments. Much progress was made in electrical goods manufacturing, textile products, retailing, and communications. But only the most limited advances were made in industries and occupations that employ women predominantly.

The challenge of organizing women is one shared with trade unions of other countries. In cultures where women have short-time employment expectations, their outlook tends to discourage easy recruitment. Unions in other countries have made special efforts at organizing and identifying women with the organization. Women representatives are chosen, and there are specific divisions to arrange activities for women workers. Only a few American unions make similar efforts.

The basic hurdle to easy acceptance of unionism by women in this country is their deep-seated disinclination to consider themselves permanent members of the work force, though some evidence exists that this attitude is changing. The individual woman seldom looks upon employment as her life-long destiny, even though women as a class constitute 32 per cent of the nation's labor force and many return to work after once leaving. Her principal preoccupations are courting, home-making, raising children, and the support of herself or her family. This emphasis on immediate personal concerns subordinates any interest in collective action. Personal discontent on the job is secondary. On the whole, she does not regard herself as the prime mover in the family's economic advance, even when she is. Personally ambitious women are likely to emphasize self-reliance as the best way to get ahead. Collective action is considered a channel of expression for men.

To overcome this image, unions appeal not only to immediate self-interest but also to the benefits of unionism for the family. Unions often send women organizers to contact women employees and arrange special educational activities for them. The accent in organizing shifts to the issues of equality of pay, rest periods, liberal sick leaves, and stricter rules for internal plant sanitation. Community support is sought to reenforce individual union appeals. The employers' call for personal loyalty has to be countered with an emphasis on independence and the rights of personal initiative.

Women who have become active trade unionists can be counted among its most ardent and devoted supporters, militant and vigorous. Many have achieved critically important positions in the leadership of strikes and other economic contests. Their group loyalties are most sharply projected on the work floor and in unions that tend to make them cohesive and important political units. While many are not interested in the routine work of local union administration, they are often very active in the social activities. Though not inclined to be joiners as are middle-class women, working women and workers' wives have been attracted to many union activities.

The conversion of women employees to unionism continues to be a major challenge. With the growing number of women workers, the job demands real attention.

Among Non-Manual Employees

The greatest weakness in the structure of the labor union movement is its slim representation in the predominantly non-manual industries and occupations. Its hold in the retail, wholesale, government, financial, insurance, real estate, and service employment sectors is narrow and tenuous. The ratio of union membership to total employment is well below 20 per cent, and in many types of jobs and in certain geographical areas unionism is practically non-existent. This is true despite the absolute and relative growth of employment in these sectors. From 39 per cent of the non-agricultural employment in 1919, the proportion of all non-manual employees rose to 48 per cent in 1930, 51 per cent in 1950, and 55 per cent in 1959.

The unionization of this vast body of American employees is essential to maintaining the strength of the trade union movement. As the numbers and the economic and political leverage provided by the older occupational and industrial sectors diminish, they need to be reenforced by expansion in the newer ones. No group except the white collar employees can adequately serve this end since their numbers are growing and already exceed the blue collar personnel. Moreover, they are now setting the pace for and coloring the outlook of the entire working population. Even automation and mechanization of clerical and selling functions will not stop these trends.

As industry is further automated, the mere maintenance of union bargaining strength will depend upon organizing non-manual personnel even in industries now considered predominantly organized. The ratio of non-production workers in manufacturing industry as a whole has already reached 25 per cent; and in some specific divisions such as ordnance it is 48 per cent; in others, like the more advanced chemical plants, it is even higher. The statistics revealed their practical application during recent public utilities strikes, when supervisors, technicians, and professional workers successfully maintained operation of the equipment. The bargaining strength of blue collar unions will be further limited unless they enlist the cooperation of the non-production workers.

Leaders of the American trade union movement have become aware of the challenge. They realize that the most optimistic figure of current union enrollment in white collar jobs is no more than 2,500,000, or less than 15 per cent of the total, with the organized highly concentrated in older employment areas. Organizational progress in newer fields has been sporadic, local, and slow. To wrestle with this problem the so-called white collar unions and the industrial unions in industries employing large numbers of clerical, technical, and professional employees are seeking new approaches. The achievements of European unions in organizing and bargaining for these employees provide an encouraging, if sometimes irritating, example.

The Industrial Union Department of the AFL-CIO called a meeting in 1957 to promote the need for action. This was followed up in 1959 with the formation of an inter-union Professional and Technical Workers Committee to help the affiliates analyze their difficulties, exchange ideas and experience, and learn from each other the methods that proved successful in promoting organizing drives. Seminars have been held since. One task is to substitute for the present relatively unfavorable image of unions among the unorganized a positive concept that suggests broader economic and social benefits, satisfaction of needs, and a desirable, practical alternative to the present anarchistic system of individual pursuit of immediate self-interest. Widespread acceptance will require a painstaking, persistent, and highly concentrated program of education designed to win over specific groups. These beachheads would then in all likelihood provide a practical demonstration of the value of unionism for all.

"Business unionism" will not in itself be able to break down the prejudices and distrust that permeate white collar attitudes toward unions. The individual clerk, draftsman, or accountant must come to realize that union membership means more than a mechanism for getting more money from the employer. A broader vision is essential to win over the white collar employee, just as it was to gain the support of the manual worker.

Clerical and kindred employees are found throughout American industry. They number well over 9,500,000, of whom some three quarters are possibly eligible for union membership. But union organization probably accounts for considerably less than 1,000,000 and is highly concentrated in railroads, communication, manufacturing, retail trade, and the federal postal service.

To reach such a diverse group, union appeals must necessarily be varied, but there are many common elements in the attitudes of clerical workers. They have enjoyed a degree of social status, job security, and collateral benefits that has set them apart from manual employees. Moreover, in the last decade the expanded demand for clerical help has generated a faith in their ability to wrest economic gains on the basis of personal merit. They have learned that their skills are highly transferable and that in periods of intense demand they could improve their positions by moving on to other employers. More than two thirds of these employees are women, and they have found that economic advances obtained in this manner or through other market pressures have been sufficient to satisfy their aspirations.

But there are offsetting forces such as the narrowing of wage and benefit differentials between clerical and manual workers. At best the benefits enjoyed by office employees are now often directly tied in with the gains made by the production workers. When the latter establish the pattern and their union signs an agreement, the former receive comparable improvements. The boast of many clerical employees is that their gains have kept abreast of advances in unionized industries. This practice is now sufficiently widespread that the tendency for narrowing the differences has been stopped.

Moreover, both groups of employees are now often huddled together in large organizations, pushed around by the same type of impersonal management, and subject to the whims and personal prejudices, the likes and dislikes, of supervision and the faceless pressures characteristic of large-scale operations. The insecurities induced by fluctuations of business, against which the salary worker was formerly insulated, are now increasingly part of his life. The possibility of displacement through technological change at least as real for him as they are for the factory employee.

Despite these vast changes, which have broken down the traditional image of clerical workers as being typically employed in small offices, maintaining close personal contacts with their bosses, and knowing the business intimately, unions have not made substantial progress. The white collar worker who functions in what is, for all practical purposes, a big factory has not yet proved any easier to approach. He has not been persuaded that further gains depend upon collective action. Unionism in his view is still primarily for manual workers. Individual self-reliance still strikes him as the primary channel for personal advancement.

Employers have gone to considerable lengths to harden and widen this antipathy toward unionism. Many have met the workers' economic expectations and provided personnel policies and procedures designed to implant a sense of security, freedom of communications, and individual status that might otherwise be sought through union membership and collective bargaining. Personnel men constantly use the threat of unionism to win management's approval for liberalized practices and policies. Addresses by personnel men at management meetings stress the success achieved in warding off unions by "beating them at their own game."

The greatest union gains among white collar workers have been in the retail and wholesale industries. Membership in this field has doubled in recent years, bringing the total to 10 per cent of the 11,000,000 potential. The latest organizational gains in retail trade have been in the mail order houses. Advances among store employees on a nationwide basis have been slow, but in some cities, such as New York, the penetration has been deep. Particular success has been achieved among units employing large numbers of manual workers with predominantly male employees or units with a favorable geographical location such as near or in unionized metropolitan centers.

However, the great gaps in unionization suggest the task ahead. Difficulties

arise from the predominance of women employees and of small, decentralized units, though they may be owned by large corporations. Part-time workers, employed for less than a full week or only for seasonal employment, constitute a vast segment of this work force. They may be permanently associated with the industry but seldom think of their jobs as permanent careers. In larger cities they shift from store to store depending upon opportunities and terms of employment. The young female employees view their occupational careers as of short duration, and are not likely union recruits in any case because they have been indoctrinated against unionism. To older women also employed in large numbers, the job is too essential to be endangered by protest.

Retail managements in recent years have systematically taken steps to head off unions by maintaining earnings and working conditions at better levels. Such steps have been more common in large cities where retail unions have already made some headway. Wage levels remain low in smaller towns and in areas untouched by unions.

The slow but persistent progress of unions in this field speaks forcefully of the inherent need for organization. Workers in many areas are seeking to raise wages and improve employment conditions to bring them up to the levels in unionized industries. Unions are learning to build upon the unrest among key workers and to utilize the core of leaders within the stores. The regular contact of retail and wholesale personnel with union members employed by the same management or by its contractors and suppliers has of course stimulated continued interest. But the gains have come only through diligent, persistent organizing campaigns. Spontaneous self-organization has been rare in recent years. Alliances between the Teamsters and retail unions, vital in many past successes, have disappeared or been strained by inter-union conflicts.

Professional and technical employees —with the exception of actors; airplane pilots, stewards, and stewardesses; musicians; movie-TV-radio writers, and newspaper reporters—have also resisted unionization. Most existing unions in this field arose with the sweep of unionism during the Thirties. Others were formed, but many have disappeared. The remaining nuclei are fragments of the potential for broader organization among such groups as teachers, social workers, scientists, engineers, and technicians.

Despite the expansion and probable continuing growth of these occupations, unions have only a small foothold—probably less than 10 per cent of the 1,000,000 potentially eligible. The collegiate or comparable training required for most professions has molded a keen identity among the occupational group, with specific responsibilities frequently formulated into codes of professional conduct. While these codes were designed primarily to fit the needs of the independent practitioner, they have also been considered binding on professional employees. This attitude gave greater weight to professional or public obligations than to personal self-interest. To the independent practitioner the client— whether patient, pupil, litigant, audience, or the general public—has highest priority, at least in theory. Economic self-interest must thus be advanced by raising qualifications and instituting systems of certification.

A favorable post-war climate for professional workers has reenforced their individualism. The persistent demand, often exceeding the supply; the

employers' fears of unionization; public discussion of the inadequate financial rewards for specific groups such as teachers, and public pressure on educational and other institutions have boosted wage and benefit standards. Individuals have been able to advance by moving from one employer to another. All these factors further discouraged a search for collective action. Interest in unionism tended to subside toward the end of the Fifties. Independent unions have weakened and many finally disintegrated. Several efforts to transfer their organizations to AFL-CIO affiliates failed.

Unfamiliar with unions, the professional employees have accepted the common unfriendly image of unionism propagated in the public prints, in schools, and by employers. At best they have tended to identify it with the needs of manual workers who would otherwise be individually helpless. Unions for professionals, many assumed, would follow policies adopted for other workers—policies that favored mediocrity, submerged the individual, and ruled out individual relations with superiors. Other rigid concepts persist even among some professional students of labor economies, who have rejected union membership for themselves despite the abundant evidence of flexibility demonstrated in the practices of existing professional unions.

The optimism about economic gains among professionals and technicians has of course not been universally justified. Employing agents have moved slowly and have had to be jarred along. Conditions are not generally satisfactory. But the discontent has not festered deeply enough to precipitate independent union organization except in restricted areas.

Professionals are searching for improvement, as witness the high rate of turnover among them. The causes are varied. Low salaries disturb many. Others deplore the narrowing of the differential between manual and professional workers and the dependence of the latter on wage movements among the former. Limited opportunities for advancement cause discontent. Experienced people in many professions lament that their earnings do not compensate them for their years, for newly hired college graduates are being paid generously in relation to their pay.

Perhaps the most striking example is the experience of young engineers, whose starting salaries since the end of World War II have startled their elders. Many have discovered that these salaries were contemplated for specific and professionally limited tasks with little scope for originality and little opportunity for either professional or financial advancement. Disenchantment has consequently been widespread.

Others fret at the non-professional and impersonal treatment meted out by management and the inclusion of non-professionals in their ranks. They are subjected to the same uniform policies and practices that govern the manual worker. This trend has proved irritating, as most professionals have been brought up to consider themselves as individuals to be dealt with as such and consulted on all matters affecting their performance. When their assignments are restricted and specialized, the use of their abilities is limited and their mobility is reduced. Instead of enjoying job security, they are as subject to the vagaries of the company's economic calculations as the ordinary manual worker. They have been taught that they are part of management and that advancement for many of them is possible only through promotions to administrative jobs. They want professional recognition, but it is often not

forthcoming. They want opportunities for professional study, but companies do not always provide them. Advances in income and status are channeled into classifications that are foreign to their own tests of performance.

Some professionals would have liked to see their associations undertake to secure redress for them and fight vigorously for their interest, but most of these groups have avoided the assignment. When the unrest became widespread and the threat of unionization real, several associations began an intensive anti-union battle. The National Society of Professional Engineers pronounced, "Professionalism and unionism are incompatible." A number of associations promulgated minimum employment standards and began providing information on wages and working conditions. Employment codes were adopted. The National Association of Social Workers organized a system of grievance hearings limited to issues involving violation of an agency's personnel policies, hoping that its members, who include supervisors, would be guided by its findings. But basically the professional associations, including as they do employer supervisors and non-supervisory professionals, are not equipped for adequate processing of complaints and are precluded from entering into collective bargaining arrangements.

In individual plants and companies "sounding board" committees, the counterpart of older employee representation plans, have been set up to provide a substitute for the union's grievance machinery. In addition, the agitation over professional unionism and the ensuing studies and investigations have led to improvements that have placated many professional employees to the point of diverting the drive for unionization. However, economic standards remain inadequate in a number of areas and the supply of personnel in them remains deficient.

Union organizations have been formed in various fields, mostly on a local basis. The American Nurses Association has undertaken collective bargaining on behalf of its members where it can get certification. Unions of engineers, social workers, and others have appeared here and there, but the rate of attrition has been high. Their handicaps include a lack of experienced leadership, insufficient resources, and an unwillingness to become part of the general trade union movement, which could give them both technical and economic assistance. Where there has been a close interrelationship between the production workers and the professionals, they have been able at times to use their joint economic power effectively to secure important gains for the professionals. But commitment to the concept of professionalism has deterred such free association in most cases. The myth persists that there is an essentially different status between other employees as a group and the professional employee.

Nevertheless, existing professional unions have made substantial contributions to the well-being and economic and professional status of their membership. Unions in the performing arts and for writers and newspapermen have made extraordinary advances, especially in dealing with the special economic problems of the professional employee. Their contracts speak eloquently of the flexibility of the collective bargaining process and the ability of each group to evolve programs and policies suited to its particular needs and the peculiar characteristics of the profession. The members of these unions have repeatedly demonstrated publicly their pride in their unions.

The prototypes for the professional union therefore exist. They deliberately try to integrate the promotion of the economic interests of their members and their status as creative individuals with the advancement of their competence and of public appreciation for the importance of the profession to society. These unions have not been adverse to and have in several instances worked closely with professional associations, either directly or through their overlapping memberships, to promote common professional interests.

But professional employees as a whole have not yet come to understand fully the need for collective action to promote their own interests along with those of their profession as a whole. The trade union movement has not vigorously pursued the task of organizing this key group of employees or sought to profit from successful experience. Nor has it established flexible enough approaches and adequate facilities for experimenting with new forms that could attract this special group and respond to its peculiar needs.

Among Negro Workers

The apathy of workers to unionization also shows up among the Negroes. The growing numbers entering the manual occupations make their organization vital to the maintenance of trade union power within established jurisdictions. As Negro membership has expanded to the current 1,500,000, it has become an increasingly higher proportion of total membership as well as the group with the highest rate of organization, probably close to 50 per cent of those eligible.

The recent accent in some Negro circles on the tardiness of certain unions in removing constitutional and practical bars to Negro membership has done much to dampen the Negroes' acceptance of unions that prevailed during the late Thirties and Forties.

The current coolness to unionism is derived in part from impatience with the conduct of individual unions and the reluctance of central labor bodies arbitrarily to impose solutions. Disillusionment among Negroes has spread and has increased the difficulties of appealing for their support.

The trade union movement in this country has been in the vanguard of the protagonists of Negro rights. Its principal leaders have advocated union organization of Negroes and sought to enforce desegregation and equality within the movement. But they have encountered regional prejudices and fears of economic competition, which in turn have led to exclusionary policies in some localities, particularly in craft unions. As a result, the emphasis is now upon eliminating all color lines in seniority, to open up jobs to colored workers on the railroads and in construction, and to gain broader rights of admittance to craft apprenticeships and to upgrading in all jobs and industries. The battles over these issues are being fought so vigorously and aggressively that the imputations of discrimination often tend to embrace the movement as a whole. Moreover, the debate identifies the unions as a major obstacle to the expansion of economic opportunities for Negroes. While there is no difference in principles and goals among the Negro leaders and the white trade unionists who are fighting discrimination on every front, the manner and content of the battle has done little to enhance the prestige of unionism among Negro workers.

Many unions have made significant contributions to facilitating the employment of Negroes as well as insuring them the fullest opportunities for advancement. Discrimination is being eliminated. Several national union leaders have enforced the principles of equal rights even upon reluctant locals and in difficult situations. Several national unions have supported governmental bodies that demanded the elimination of discriminatory practices by local unions. They have fought for contract clauses that assured equal rights and have been foremost in the battle for fair employment practice laws. The problem confronting the union movement is how to eradicate the last vestiges of prejudice and privilege among entrenched groups within a movement in which local autonomy and established rules limit the action of national officers.

While it is understandable that Negro union and civic leaders should continue to press their claims, the dilemma they face is how to achieve their goal without dampening the ardor for union membership itself among their followers. They are aware that unions are vital in their own battle for civil rights, as evidenced by their support of unions in the fight to defeat state right-to-work laws. But the enthusiasm for the cause of their own brethren has often tended to compromise their allegiance and support for trade unions.

Among Low-Wage Service Workers

No group demands more attention by the trade union movement than the 3,000,000 low-wage personal service employees. They are on the lowest rungs of the urban economic ladder and have standards only slightly better than those of the farm laborer. Conservative estimates place the earnings of at least half of the group at less than $1 per hour. Less than 10 per cent are currently covered by the federal Fair Labor Standards Act. Some employees have their earnings supplemented by public assistance to maintain themselves and their families. Occasional strikes momentarily disclose their dreary plight and shock the public conscience. But the result has been only local union organization or legislation. A national movement for correction of these conditions is necessary. The most significant move in this direction has been the proposal to amend the Fair Labor Standards Act to extend its coverage to these workers.

Trade unions have made some progress among employees of hotels, laundries, cleaning and dyeing establishments, and other personal service industries, but the total membership is very low. The problems of organization are a combination of those recited for employees in small shops in large cities, of low-income earners, of minority groups, and of employees in industries in which the employer enjoys small profit margins and in which business turnover is high. Where the economic setting is more stable and profitable, more progress has been made. Community-wide union support is often helpful in organizing these employees. The current efforts of the New York City Central Labor Council to assume part of the responsibility for organizing in these fields may provide a model for the rest of the country. This broad sponsorship will allow the campaign to be directed at the workers and also include educational activities to awaken community understanding and support.

The organizational program must also be broadly conceived to be truly constructive. Besides raising wage standards, it should seek to raise the educational and physical qualifications of the employees. It should also provide technical assistance to employers to enable them to run their businesses more efficiently at the same time they take on higher labor costs.

PART FIVE

THE PUBLIC ECONOMY

47. Extension of the Suffrage

John Stuart Mill

Our public economy allocates resources through taxation and government spending, following democratic election of representatives. J. S. Mill states the classic position that only those who pay the cost should have the voting franchise through which the expenditures and taxes are controlled.

48. The Theory of Social Balance

John Kenneth Galbraith

Professor Galbraith argues that we allocate too many of our productive resources to unimportant private purposes and to creating artificial wants, too few to such social purposes as slum clearance, education, and cultural activities. The result is a social imbalance which he argues should be remedied.

49. Private and Public Expenditures: A Reappraisal

Ernest van den Haag

This vigorous attack on Galbraith's "Affluent Society" alleges that there is no real meaning to "social imbalance," and denies that the public sector should be expanded at the expense of the private sector.

50. Courage and Politics

John F. Kennedy

Writing as the Senator from Massachusetts, President Kennedy describes the variety of pressures under which decisions are made by the Congress, and discusses the nature of the Congressman's responsibility to his constituents. This perceptive analysis of legislative behavior is a useful supplement to economic analysis in the examination of public policy issues.

51. For Fastest Growth—What Kind of Tax?

Henry C. Wallich

Professor Wallich argues that our present tax structure may inhibit economic growth because we depend heavily on high income taxes to finance public expenditures. He discusses some of the shortcomings of our present tax system and suggests a federal sales tax as a possible alternative.

52. The Effect of High Tax Rates on Executive Incentive

Crawford H. Greenewalt

A leading businesman argues that our high marginal income tax rates make it difficult to induce men with ability to enter the field of business, and that capable individuals are discouraged from exerting the effort necessary to make their greatest contribution.

53. Who Pays the Taxes?

Richard A. Musgrave

The data presented by Professor Musgrave permit a comparison of the rate of progression of various federal and local taxes. The author concludes that our tax structure is only slightly progressive over the range of middle incomes.

47   EXTENSION OF THE SUFFRAGE

John Stuart Mill

John Stuart Mill was a prominent economist during the middle of the last century who also wrote influential pieces on politics and ethics.

*   *   *

It is . . . important that the assembly which votes the taxes, either general or local, should be elected exclusively by those who pay something towards the taxes imposed. Those who pay no taxes, disposing by their votes of other people's money, have every

motive to be lavish and none to economise. As far as money matters are concerned, any power of voting possessed by them is a violation of the funda-

Excerpted from John Stuart Mill's *Considerations on Representative Government;* first published in 1861.

mental principle of free government; a severance of the power of control from the interest in its beneficial exercise. It amounts to allowing them to put their hands into other people's pockets for any purpose which they think fit to call a public one; which in some of the great towns of the United States is known to have produced a scale of local taxation onerous beyond example, and wholly borne by the wealthier classes. That representation should be co-extensive with taxation, not stopping short of it, but also not going beyond it, is in accordance with the theory of British institutions. But to reconcile this, as a condition annexed to the representation, with universality, it is essential, as it is on many other accounts desirable, that taxation, in a visible shape, should descend to the poorest class. In this country, and in most others, there is probably no labouring family which does not contribute to the indirect taxes, by the purchase of tea, coffee, sugar, not to mention narcotics or stimulants. But this mode of defraying a share of the public expenses is hardly felt: the payer, unless a person of education and reflection, does not identify his interest with a low scale of public expenditure as closely as when money for its support is demanded directly from himself; and even supposing him to do so, he would doubtless take care that, however lavish an expenditure he might, by his vote, assist in imposing upon the government, it should not be defrayed by any additional taxes on the articles which he himself consumes. It would be better that a direct tax in the simple form of a capitation, should be levied on every grown person in the community; or that every such person should be admitted an elector on allowing himself to be rated *extra ordinem* to the assessed taxes; or that a small annual payment, rising and falling with the

gross expenditure of the country, should be required from every registered elector; that so every one might feel that the money which he assisted in voting was partly his own, and that he was interested in keeping down its amount.

However this may be, I regard it as required by first principles, that the receipt of parish relief should be a peremptory disqualification for the franchise. He who cannot by his labour suffice for his own support has no claim to the privilege of helping himself to the money of others. By becoming dependent on the remaining members of the community for actual subsistence, he abdicates his claim to equal rights with them in other respects. Those to whom he is indebted for the continuance of his very existence may justly claim the exclusive management of those common concerns, to which he now brings nothing, or less than he takes away. As a condition of the franchise, a term should be fixed, say five years previous to the registry, during which the applicant's name has not been on the parish books as a recipient of relief. To be an uncertified bankrupt, or to have taken the benefit of the Insolvent Act, should disqualify for the franchise until the person has paid his debts, or at least proved that he is not now, and has not for some long period been, dependent on eleemosynary support. Non-payment of taxes, when so long persisted in that it cannot have arisen from inadvertence, should disqualify while it lasts. These exclusions are not in their nature permanent. They exact such conditions only as all are able, or ought to be able, to fulfil if they choose. They leave the suffrage accessible to all who are in the normal condition of a human being: and if any one has to forego it, he either does not care sufficiently for it to do for its sake what he is already bound to do, or he is in a general condition of depression and degradation in which this slight addition, necessary for the security of others, would be unfelt, and on emerg-

ing from which, this mark of inferiority would disappear with the rest.

*   *   *

48   THE THEORY OF SOCIAL BALANCE

John Kenneth Galbraith

John Kenneth Galbraith is United States Ambassador to India, on leave from his position as Professor of Economics at Harvard University.

It is not till it is discovered that high individual incomes will not purchase the mass of mankind immunity from cholera, typhus, and ignorance, still less secure them the positive advantages of educational opportunity and economic security, that slowly and reluctantly, amid prophecies of moral degeneration and economic disaster, society begins to make collective provision for needs which no ordinary individual, even if he works overtime all his life, can provide himself.

—R. H. TAWNEY [1]

The final problem of the productive society is what it produces. This manifests itself in an implacable tendency to provide an opulent supply of some things and a niggardly yield of others. This disparity carries to the point where it is a cause of social discomfort and social unhealth. The line which divides our area of wealth from our area of poverty is roughly that which divides privately produced and marketed goods and services from publicly rendered services. Our wealth in the first is not only in startling contrast with the meagerness of the latter, but our wealth in privately produced goods is, to a marked degree, the cause of crisis in the supply of public services. For we have failed to see the importance, indeed the urgent need, of maintaining a balance between the two.

[1] *Equality* (4th revised ed.), pp. 134–35.

This disparity between our flow of private and public goods and services is no matter of subjective judgment. On the contrary, it is the source of the most extensive comment which only stops short of the direct contrast being made here. In the years following World War II, the papers of any major city—those of New York were an excellent example—told daily of the shortages and shortcomings in the elementary municipal and metropolitan services. The schools were old and overcrowded. The police force was under strength and underpaid. The parks and playgrounds were insufficient. Streets and empty lots were filthy, and the sanitation staff was underequipped and in need of men. Access to the city by those who work there was uncertain and painful and becoming more so. Internal transportation was overcrowded, unhealthful, and dirty. So was the air. Parking on the streets had to be prohibited, and there was no space elsewhere. These deficiencies were not in new and novel services but in old and established ones. Cities have long swept their streets, helped their people move around, educated them, kept order, and

This selection from John Kenneth Galbraith's *The Affluent Society*, 1958, pp. 251–269, is reprinted by permission of an arrangement with Houghton Mifflin Company, the authorized publishers.

provided horse rails for vehicles which sought to pause. That their residents should have a nontoxic supply of air suggests no revolutionary dalliance with socialism.

The discussion of this public poverty competed, on the whole successfully, with the stories of ever-increasing opulence in privately produced goods. The Gross National Product was rising. So were retail sales. So was personal income. Labor productivity had also advanced. The automobiles that could not be parked were being produced at an expanded rate. The children, though without schools, subject in the playgrounds to the affectionate interest of adults with odd tastes, and disposed to increasingly imaginative forms of delinquency, were admirably equipped with television sets. We had difficulty finding storage space for the great surpluses of food despite a national disposition to obesity. Food was grown and packaged under private auspices. The care and refreshment of the mind, in contrast with the stomach, was principally in the public domain. Our colleges and universities were severely overcrowded and underprovided, and the same was true of the mental hospitals.

The contrast was and remains evident not alone to those who read. The family which takes its mauve and cerise, air-conditioned, power-steered, and power-braked automobile out for a tour passes through cities that are badly paved, made hideous by litter, blighted buildings, billboards, and posts for wires that should long since have been put underground. They pass on into a countryside that has been rendered largely invisible by commercial art. (The goods which the latter advertise have an absolute priority in our value system. Such aesthetic considerations as a view of the countryside accordingly come second. On such matters we are consistent.) They picnic on exquisitely packaged food from a portable icebox by a polluted stream and go on to spend the night at a park which is a menace to public health and morals. Just before dozing off on an air mattress, beneath a nylon tent, amid the stench of decaying refuse, they may reflect vaguely on the curious unevenness of their blessings. Is this, indeed, the American genius?

II

In the production of goods within the private economy it has long been recognized that a tolerably close relationship must be maintained between the production of various kinds of products. The output of steel and oil and machine tools is related to the production of automobiles. Investment in transportation must keep abreast of the output of goods to be transported. The supply of power must be abreast of the growth of industries requiring it. The existence of these relationships—coefficients to the economist—has made possible the construction of the input-output table which shows how changes in the production in one industry will increase or diminish the demands on other industries. To this table, and more especially to its ingenious author, Professor Wassily Leontief, the world is indebted for one of its most important of modern insights into economic relationships. If expansion in one part of the economy were not matched by the requisite expansion in other parts—were the need for balance not respected—then bottlenecks and shortages, speculative hoarding of scarce supplies, and sharply increasing costs would ensue. Fortunately in peacetime the market system operates easily and effectively to maintain this balance, and this together with the existence of stocks and some flexibility in the coefficients as a result of substitution, insures that no serious difficulties will arise. We are reminded of the existence of the problem only by noticing how serious it is for those countries—Poland or, in a somewhat different form, India—which seek to solve the problem by planned measures and with a much smaller supply of resources.

Just as there must be balance in what a community produces, so there must also be balance in what the community consumes. An increase in the use of one product creates, ineluctably, a requirement for others. If we are to consume more automobiles, we must have more gasoline. There must be more insurance as well as more space on which to operate them. Beyond a certain point more and better food appears to mean increased need for medical services. This is the certain result of the increased consumption of tobacco and alcohol. More vacations require more hotels and more fishing rods. And so forth. With rare exceptions—shortages of doctors are an exception which suggests the rule—this balance is also maintained quite effortlessly so far as goods for private sale and consumption are concerned. The price system plus a rounded condition of opulence is again the agency.

However, the relationships we are here discussing are not confined to the private economy. They operate comprehensively over the whole span of private and public services. As surely as an increase in the output of automobiles puts new demands on the steel industry so, also, it places new demands on public services. Similarly, every increase in the consumption of private goods will normally mean some facilitating or protective step by the state. In all cases if these services are not forthcoming, the consequences will be in some degree ill. It will be convenient to have a term which suggests a satisfactory relationship between the supply of privately produced goods and services and those of the state, and we may call it social balance.

The problem of social balance is ubiquitous, and frequently it is obtrusive. As noted, an increase in the consumption of automobiles requires a facilitating supply of streets, highways, traffic control, and parking space. The protective services of the police and the highway patrols must also be available, as must those of the hospitals. Although the need for balance here is extraordinarily clear, our use of privately produced vehicles has, on occasion, got far out of line with the supply of the related public services. The result has been hideous road congestion, an annual massacre of impressive proportions, and chronic colitis in the cities. As on the ground, so also in the air. Planes collide with disquieting consequences for those within when the public provision for air traffic control fails to keep pace with private use of the airways.

But the auto and the airplane, versus the space to use them, are merely an exceptionally visible example of a requirement that is pervasive. The more goods people procure, the more packages they discard and the more trash that must be carried away. If the appropriate sanitation services are not provided, the counterpart of increasing opulence will be deepening filth. The greater the wealth the thicker will be the dirt. This indubitably describes a tendency of our time. As more goods are produced and owned, the greater are the opportunities for fraud and the more property that must be protected. If the provision of public law enforcement services does not keep pace, the counterpart of increased well-being will, we may be certain, be increased crime.

The city of Los Angeles, in modern

times, is a near-classic study in the problem of social balance. Magnificently efficient factories and oil refineries, a lavish supply of automobiles, a vast consumption of handsomely packaged products, coupled with the absence of a municipal trash collection service which forced the use of home incinerators, made the air nearly unbreathable for an appreciable part of each year. Air pollution could be controlled only by a complex and highly developed set of public services—by better knowledge stemming from more research, better policing, a municipal trash collection service, and possibly the assertion of the priority of clean air over the production of goods. These were long in coming. The agony of a city without usable air was the result.

The issue of social balance can be identified in many other current problems. Thus an aspect of increasing private production is the appearance of an extraordinary number of things which lay claim to the interest of the young. Motion pictures, television, automobiles, and the vast opportunities which go with the mobility, together with such less enchanting merchandise as narcotics, comic books, and pornographia, are all included in an advancing gross national product. The child of a less opulent as well as a technologically more primitive age had far fewer such diversions. The red schoolhouse is remembered mainly because it had a paramount position in the lives of those who attended it that no modern school can hope to attain.

In a well-run and well-regulated community, with a sound school system, good recreational opportunities, and a good police force—in short a community where public services have kept pace with private production—the diversionary forces operating on the modern juvenile may do no great damage. Television and the violent mores of Hollywood and Madison Avenue must contend with the intellectual discipline of the school. The social, athletic, dramatic, and like attractions of the school also claim the attention of the child. These, together with the other recreational opportunities of the community, minimize the tendency to delinquency. Experiments with violence and immorality are checked by an effective law enforcement system before they become epidemic.

In a community where public services have failed to keep abreast of private consumption things are very different. Here, in an atmosphere of private opulence and public squalor, the private goods have full sway. Schools do not compete with television and the movies. The dubious heroes of the latter, not Miss Jones, become the idols of the young. The hot rod and the wild ride take the place of more sedentary sports for which there are inadequate facilities or provision. Comic books, alcohol, narcotics, and switchblade knives are, as noted, part of the increased flow of goods, and there is nothing to dispute their enjoyment. There is an ample supply of private wealth to be appropriated and not much to be feared from the police. An austere community is free from temptation. It can be austere in its public services. Not so a rich one.

Moreover, in a society which sets large store by production, and which has highly effective machinery for synthesizing private wants, there are strong pressures to have as many wage earners in the family as possible. As always all social behavior is part of a piece. If both parents are engaged in private production, the burden on the public services is further increased. Children, in effect, become the charge of the community for an appreciable part of the time. If the services of the community do not keep pace, this will be another source of disorder.

Residential housing also illustrates the problem of the social balance, although in a somewhat complex form. Few would wish to contend that, in the lower or even the middle income brackets, Americans are munificently supplied with housing. A great many families would like better located or merely more houseroom, and no advertising is necessary to persuade them of their wish. And the provision of housing is in the private domain. At first glance at least, the line we draw between private and public seems not to be preventing a satisfactory allocation of resources to housing.

On closer examination, however, the problem turns out to be not greatly different from that of education. It is improbable that the housing industry is greatly more incompetent or inefficient in the United States than in those countries—Scandinavia, Holland, or (for the most part) England—where slums have been largely eliminated and where *minimum* standards of cleanliness and comfort are well above our own. As the experience of these countries shows, and as we have also been learning, the housing industry functions well only in combination with a large, complex, and costly array of public services. These include land purchase and clearance for redevelopment; good neighborhood and city planning, and effective and well-enforced zoning; a variety of financing and other aids to the housebuilder and owner; publicly supported research and architectural services for an industry which, by its nature, is equipped to do little on its own; and a considerable amount of direct or assisted public construction for families in the lowest income brackets. The quality of the housing depends not on the industry, which is given, but on

what is invested in these supplements and supports.

III

The case for social balance has, so far, been put negatively. Failure to keep public services in minimal relation to private production and use of goods is a cause of social disorder or impairs economic performance. The matter may now be put affirmatively. By failing to exploit the opportunity to expand public production we are missing opportunities for enjoyment which otherwise we might have had. Presumably a community can be as well rewarded by buying better schools or better parks as by buying bigger automobiles. By concentrating on the latter rather than the former it is failing to maximize its satisfactions. As with schools in the community, so with public services over the country at large. It is scarcely sensible that we should satisfy our wants in private goods with reckless abundance, while in the case of public goods, on the evidence of the eye, we practice extreme self-denial. So, far from systematically exploiting the opportunities to derive use and pleasure from these services, we do not supply what would keep us out of trouble.

The conventional wisdom holds that the community, large or small, makes a decision as to how much it will devote to its public services. This decision is arrived at by democratic process. Subject to the imperfections and uncertainties of democracy, people decide how much of their private income and goods they will surrender in order to have public services of which they are in greater need. Thus there is a balance, however rough, in the enjoyments to be had from private goods and services and those rendered by public authority.

It will be obvious, however, that this

view depends on the notion of independently determined consumer wants. In such a world one could with some reason defend the doctrine that the consumer, as a voter, makes an independent choice between public and private goods. But given the dependence effect—given that consumer wants are created by the process by which they are satisfied—the consumer makes no such choice. He is subject to the forces of advertising and emulation by which production creates its own demand. Advertising operates exclusively, and emulation mainly, on behalf of privately produced goods and services.[2] Since management and emulative effects operate on behalf of private production, public services will have an inherent tendency to lag behind. Automobile demand which is expensively synthesized will inevitably have a much larger claim on income than parks or public health or even roads where no such influence operates. The engines of mass communication, in their highest state of development, assail the eyes and ears of the community on behalf of more beer but not of more schools. Even in the conventional wisdom it will scarcely be contended that this leads to an equal choice between the two.

The competition is especially unequal for new products and services. Every corner of the public psyche is canvassed by some of the nation's most talented citizens to see if the desire for some merchantable product can be cultivated. No similar process operates on

behalf of the nonmerchantable services of the state. Indeed, while we take the cultivation of new private wants for granted we would be measurably shocked to see it applied to public services. The scientist or engineer or advertising man who devotes himself to developing a new carburetor, cleanser, or depilatory for which the public recognizes no need and will feel none until an advertising campaign arouses it, is one of the valued members of our society. A politician or a public servant who dreams up a new public service is a wastrel. Few public offenses are more reprehensible.

So much for the influences which operate on the decision between public and private production. The calm decision between public and private consumption pictured by the conventional wisdom is, in fact, a remarkable example of the error which arises from viewing social behavior out of context. The inherent tendency will always be for public services to fall behind private production. We have here the first of the causes of social imbalance.

IV

Social balance is also the victim of two further features of our society—the truce on inequality and the tendency to inflation. Since these are now part of our context, their effect comes quickly into view.

With rare exceptions such as the post office, public services do not carry a price ticket to be paid for by the individual user. By their nature they must, ordinarily, be available to all. As a result, when they are improved or new services are initiated, there is the ancient and troublesome question of who is to pay. This, in turn, provokes to life the collateral but irrelevant debate over inequality. As with the use of taxation as an instrument of fiscal policy, the

---

[2] Emulation does operate between communities. A new school or a new highway in one community does exert pressure on others to remain abreast. However, as compared with the pervasive effects of emulation in extending the demand for privately produced consumer's goods there will be agreement, I think, that this intercommunity effect is probably small.

truce on inequality is broken. Liberals are obliged to argue that the services be paid for by progressive taxation which will reduce inequality. Committed as they are to the urgency of goods (and also, as we shall see in a later chapter, to a somewhat mechanical view of the way in which the level of output can be kept most secure) they must oppose sales and excise taxes. Conservatives rally to the defense of inequality—although without ever quite committing themselves in such uncouth terms—and oppose the use of income taxes. They, in effect, oppose the expenditure not on the merits of the service but on the demerits of the tax system. Since the debate over inequality cannot be resolved, the money is frequently not appropriated and the service not performed. It is a casualty of the economic goals of both liberals and conservatives for both of whom the questions of social balance are subordinate to those of production and, when it is evoked, of inequality.

In practice matters are better as well as worse than this statement of the basic forces suggests. Given the tax structure, the revenues of all levels of government grow with the growth of the economy. Services can be maintained and sometimes even improved out of this automatic accretion.

However, this effect is highly unequal. The revenues of the federal government, because of its heavy reliance on income taxes, increase more than proportionately with private economic growth. In addition, although the conventional wisdom greatly deplores the fact, federal appropriations have only an indirect bearing on taxation. Public services are considered and voted on in accordance with their seeming urgency. Initiation or improvement of a particular service is rarely, except for purposes of oratory, set against the specific effect on taxes. Tax policy, in turn, is

decided on the basis of the level of economic activity, the resulting revenues, expediency, and other considerations. Among these the total of the thousands of individually considered appropriations is but one factor. In this process the ultimate tax consequence of any individual appropriation is *de minimus,* and the tendency to ignore it reflects the simple mathematics of the situation. Thus it is possible for the Congress to make decisions affecting the social balance without invoking the question of inequality.

Things are made worse, however, by the fact that a large proportion of the federal revenues are pre-empted by defense. The increase in defense costs has also tended to absorb a large share of the normal increase in tax revenues. The position of the federal government for improving the social balance has also been weakened since World War II by the strong, although receding, conviction that its taxes were at artificial wartime levels and that a tacit commitment exists to reduce taxes at the earliest opportunity.

In the states and localities the problem of social balance is much more severe. Here tax revenues—this is especially true of the General Property Tax—increase less than proportionately with increased private production. Budgeting too is far more closely circumscribed than in the case of the federal government—only the monetary authority enjoys the pleasant privilege of underwriting its own loans. Because of this, increased services for states and localities regularly pose the question of more revenues and more taxes. And here, with great regularity, the question of social balance is lost in the debate over equality and social equity.

Thus we currently find by far the most serious social imbalance in the services performed by local governments. The F.B.I. comes much more easily by funds than the city police force. The Department of Agriculture can more easily keep its pest control abreast of expanding agricultural output than the average city health service can keep up with the needs of an expanding industrial population. One consequence is that the federal government remains under constant pressure to use its superior revenue position to help redress the balance at the lower levels of government.

V

Finally, social imbalance is the natural offspring of persistent inflation. Inflation by its nature strikes different individuals and groups with highly discriminatory effect. The most nearly unrelieved victims, apart from those living on pensions or other fixed provision for personal security, are those who work for the state. In the private economy the firm which sells goods has, in general, an immediate accommodation to the inflationary movement. Its price increases are the inflation. The incomes of its owners and proprietors are automatically accommodated to the upward movement. To the extent that wage increases are part of the inflationary process, this is also true of organized industrial workers. Even unorganized white collar workers are in a milieu where prices and incomes are moving up. The adaption of their incomes, if less rapid than that of the industrial workers, is still reasonably prompt.

The position of the public employee is at the other extreme. His pay scales are highly formalized, and traditionally they have been subject to revision only at lengthy interval. In states and localities inflation does not automatically bring added revenues to pay higher salaries and incomes. Pay revision for all public workers is subject to the temptation to wait and see if the inflation isn't

coming to an end. There will be some fear—this seems to have been more of a factor in England than in the United States—that advances in public wages will set a bad example for private employers and unions.

Inflation means that employment is pressing on the labor supply and that private wage and salary incomes are rising. Thus the opportunities for moving from public to private employment are especially favorable. Public employment, moreover, once had as a principal attraction a high measure of social security. Industrial workers were subject to the formidable threat of unemployment during depression. Public employees were comparatively secure, and this security was worth an adverse salary differential. But with improving economic security in general this advantage his diminished. Private employment thus has come to provide better protection against inflation and little worse protection against other hazards. Though the dedicated may stay in public posts, the alert go.

The deterioration of the public services in the years of inflation has not gone unremarked. However, there has been a strong tendency to regard it as an adventitious misfortune—something which, like a nasty shower at a picnic, happened to blight a generally good time. Salaries were allowed to lag, which was a pity. This is a very inadequate view. Discrimination against the public services is an organic feature of inflation. Nothing so weakens government as persistent inflation. The public administration of France for many years, of Italy until recent times, and of other European and numerous South American countries have been deeply sapped and eroded by the effects of long-continued inflation. Social imbalance reflects itself in inability to enforce laws, including signficantly those which protect and advance basic social justice, and in failure to maintain and improve essential services. One outgrowth of the resulting imbalance has been frustration and pervasive discontent. Over much of the world there is a rough and not entirely accidental correlation between the strength of indigenous communist parties or the frequency of revolutions and the persistence of inflation.

VI

A feature of the years immediately following World War II was a remarkable attack on the notion of expanding and improving public services. During the depression years such services had been elaborated and improved partly in order to fill some small part of the vacuum left by the shrinkage of private production. During the war years the role of government was vastly expanded. After that came the reaction. Much of it, unquestionably, was motivated by a desire to rehabilitate the prestige of private production and therewith of producers. No doubt some who joined the attack hoped, at least tacitly, that it might be possible to sidestep the truce on taxation vis-à-vis equality by having less taxation of all kinds. For a time the notion that our public services had somehow become inflated and excessive was all but axiomatic. Even liberal politicians did not seriously protest. They found it necessary to aver that they were in favor of public economy too.

In this discusion a certain mystique was attributed to the satisfaction of privately supplied wants. A community decision to have a new school means that the individual surrenders the necessary amount, willy-nilly, in his taxes. But if he is left with that income, he is a free man. He can decide between a better car or a television set. This was advanced with some solemnity as an argument for the TV set. The difficulty is that this argument leaves the community with no way of preferring the school. All private wants, where the individual can choose, are inherently superior to all public desires which must be paid for by taxation and with an inevitable component of compulsion.

The cost of public services was also held to be a desolating burden on private production, although this was at a time when the private production was burgeoning. Urgent warnings were issued of the unfavorable effects of taxation on investment—"I don't know of a surer way of killing off the incentive to invest than by imposing taxes which are regarded by people as punitive." [3] This was at a time when the inflationary effect of a very high level of investment was causing concern. The same individuals who were warning about the inimical effects of taxes were strongly advocating a monetary policy designed to reduce investment. However, an understanding of our economic discourse requires an appreciation of one of its basic rules: men of high position are allowed, by a special act of grace, to accommodate their reasoning to the answer they need. Logic is only required in those of lesser rank.

Finally it was argued, with no little vigor, that expanding government posed a grave threat to individual liberties. "Where distinction and rank is achieved almost exclusively by becoming a civil servant of the state . . . it is too much to expect that many will long prefer freedom to security." [4]

With time this attack on public services has somewhat subsided. The dis-

---

[3] Arthur F. Burns, Chairman of the President's Council of Economic Advisers, *U. S. News & World Report,* May 6, 1955.

[4] F. A. Hayek, *The Road to Serfdom* (London: Routledge & Kegan Paul, Ltd., 1944), p. 98.

order associated with social imbalance has become visible even if the need for balance between private and public services is still imperfectly appreciated.

Freedom also seemed to be surviving. Perhaps it was realized that all organized activity requires concessions by the individual to the group. This is true of the policeman who joins the police force, the teacher who gets a job at the high school, and the executive who makes his way up the hierarchy of Du Pont. If there are differences between public and private organization, they are of kind rather than of degree. As this is written the pendulum has in fact swung back. Our liberties are now menaced by the conformity exacted by the large corporation and its impulse to create, for its own purposes, the organization man. This danger we may also survive.

Nonetheless, the postwar onslaught on the public services left a lasting imprint. To suggest that we canvass our public wants to see where happiness can be improved by more and better services has a sharply radical tone. Even public services to avoid disorder must be defended. By contrast the man who devises a nostrum for a non-existent need and then successfully promotes both remains one of nature's noblemen.

49 PRIVATE AND PUBLIC EXPENDITURES: A REAPPRAISAL

Ernest van den Haag

Ernest van den Haag is Professor of Social Philosophy at New York University and a practicing psychoanalyst.

In *The Affluent Society,* John Kenneth Galbraith persuasively refurbishes the arguments in favor of widening the public and narrowing the private sector of our economy. Let me examine some of his major ideas.[1]

I

Galbraith argues foremost that there is an "imbalance" between the public and the private sector. Economists have overlooked that "imbalance" because their obsolete "conventional wisdom" leads them to focus on "scarcity," whereas we have "affluence."

Galbraith's argument here rests on his confusion or equivocation between the technical meaning of "scarcity"—i.e., need for allocation—and the colloquial meaning—i.e., insufficiency, or poverty. If the two meanings of scarcity are separated, his argument is seen to be without merit. Economists are aware that our affluence has increased (colloquial meaning): but affluence does not make rational allocation obsolete (technical meaning). Allocation, the subject matter of economics—the problem: how can we make the best use of our resources?—becomes "obsolete" only with the millenium. For, though we can and do produce a lot in tem-

[1] Most of Galbraith's arguments, were they correct, would not be necessary, and altogether they are not sufficient, for the conclusions he draws. I have discussed *The Affluent Society* as a whole in *Commentary* (September, 1960, and January, 1961).

From *Modern Age,* Spring, 1962, pp. 145–153. Reprinted by permission.

poral society, we cannot produce enough to satisfy all desires; thus it remains rational to allocate, *i.e.,* to choose between alternative satisfactions, and to economize, *i.e.,* to satisfy desires with the least expenditure of resources. Indeed, Galbraith himself advocates forcible reallocation of resources from the private to the public sector, thus implying that the scarcity, which makes allocation (choice) necessary, and which he is at pains to deny, is still with us. In his equivocation between the technical and colloquial meanings of scarcity, Galbraith is not altogether original. He follows the "conventional wisdom" of millenarians, Utopians, and Marxians. However, the chiliastic sects realized that there is scarcity in temporal society, and the Marxists realized that there is scarcity in non-communist society. The discovery that scarcity is "obsolete" in *our* society is original with Galbraith but no improvement on "conventional wisdom." [2]

Galbraith's "imbalance" itself turns out to be a rhetorical device disguised as an argument. No indication is given —let alone substantiated—as to where a "balance" could be found, or by what means one might locate it. Hence the word "imbalance" does no more than denote Galbraith's dissatisfaction with the present allocation of resources between the public and the private sector; his conclusion merely restates that premise, and his reasoning but asseverates what it is supposed to prove, namely, that the public sector should be expanded. [3]

Economists took the idea of balance from mechanics to describe a state without endogenous tendency to change (equilibrium). Galbraith gives it a laudatory sense—balance becomes an unspecified but ideal distribution between public and private sector—and proceeds to use the descriptive term prescriptively. By this device, he retains the authority the term derived from its objective reference, though he has surreptitiously cut it adrift. This public relations strategem has worked well; in defense of reason, I suggest that from now on, unless an author tells us how he determines "imbalance" in the economy, we ought to grant only that it exists in his mind.

Colin Clark has tried to prove that we suffer from the opposite imbalance, that the public sector is over-expanded whenever it uses (or, better, attempts to use) more than 25% of the national income. When that happens, he thinks, the ostensive welfare goals are defeated, and the economy generally suffers. At least Clark tells us how to locate his imbalance and its effects. He tries to prove a meaningful proposition. I do not think he succeeds; but Galbraith does not even try—and for good reason: he does not have a genuine proposition to which evidence could be relevant.

In Galbraith's defense, one may argue that some public expenditures are directly complementary to private ones. Without roads, cars are of no use. But even here, "imbalance" is misleading. The proper quantitative relationship between road and car expenditures has not been worked out with any precision; and it may be impossible to do

---

[2] The supposed disappearance of scarcity leads Galbraith to conclude that we need no longer emphasize productivity. A consistent conclusion, as dangerous as it is wrong.

[3] Galbraith suggests, often with striking illustrations, that specific public services are lagging. He takes it for granted that the lag is caused by insufficient financing. The term "imbalance" evades analysis of distribution

and of effectiveness of money within the public sector, which are the actual problems causing most of the deficiencies Galbraith mentions. More money is not likely to improve matters and may make them worse. Reorganization is called for.

so in any way that would permit us to speak of a general "balance."

Here Galbraith follows convention, but would have done better to abandon it: we usually treat public expenditures as a dependent variable and the private expenditures to be complemented by them as an independent one. Yet this is certainly wrong. Both must be treated as dependent variables. They are functionally interdependent. The problem is not how much road space is needed for automobile traffic growing at a given rate, but, how much automobile traffic should be supported, induced or balked, in view of public costs and various alternative expenditures and means of transportation. Roads invite automobile traffic as much as they accommodate it. (The underdeveloped countries illustrate very well that automobile traffic is as much a function of road building as *vice versa*.) Other factors—taxation, public transport, etc.—also influence automobile traffic.[4] When roads are built with public funds, surely we must base decisions on the comparative desirability of fostering and accommodating automobile traffic, and not exclusively on the desires of actual and prospective automobile users. (In the case of tollroads, this problem differs—although tollroads do cause costs in addition to those paid for by users.)

To treat public expenditures as a dependent variable complementing independent private expenditures is about as reasonable as it would be to say, 'since many people want to drive at a speed of 100 m.p.h. injuring more pedestrians than we now can take care of, we must multiply hospitals and cemeteries.' Shouldn't we instead, or as well, discourage speed, and other hazards, and perhaps traffic?

Whenever possible, the cost of the public complement to private expenditure should be defrayed by the most direct and main beneficiaries. A fuller application of this ancient rule of fiscal equity might, apart from its intrinsic merit, greatly reduce public expenditures: the private expenditures which are now subsidized by complementary public ones might be reduced if the complementary public costs were borne by the direct private beneficiaries through taxes.[5]

Though easily abused, the attempt to determine theoretically complementarities between specific public and private expenditures can be fruitful when the relationship between the interdependent variables is treated as independent, and *both* variables as dependent. I doubt, however, that the attempt to find a general balance between public and private expenditure is fruitful. I can conceive of situations where 70% of the national income might well be spent publicly even in peacetime and of others where 10% would be too much. So many variables are involved—*e.g.,* size and distribution of the national income, type of expenditure, tax structure—that I do not think a general rule can do justice to concrete situations unless it be interpreted as a warning to pay heed to the undesired and possibly self-defeating effects of very high general levels of taxation. Clark's attempt to weigh diminishing returns of taxation certainly has this merit.

II

Galbraith next offers a value judgment: consumers spend too much on trivialities. I share his judgment; but he misconceives the problem and pro-

---

[4] Incidentally, I am convinced our cities will be choked by automobiles if the present favored tax treatment continues.

[5] The general sales tax proposed by Galbraith in place of the excise taxes here suggested would have the opposite effect.

poses irrelevant and indefensible solutions likely to make matters worse.

Galbraith argues as though the problem were simply that there are not so good (*i.e.,* private) and good (*i.e.,* public) expenditures; and he calls on all right-thinking citizens to make sure that the good guys (government) get more money and the bad guys (consumers) less. This will do for a Western; but is it economic analysis? It replaces the all too real problem: what values are we to live by, or how can people be free *and* wise?, with a pseudo-problem: how can we keep people right-thinking and buying?, and then offers a pseudo-solution: by letting the government spend more of their income for them.

Thoughtful men have always agreed that consumers prefer trivialities and vulgarities to the satisfaction of their real needs; but they have never agreed on the real needs that ought to be satisfied; or on how to make consumers do what is good for them. This is not a new problem arising from affluence and advertising, as Galbraith suggests. Nor is Galbraith's solution new. It ignores what makes the problem problematic: neither an objective nor an agreed upon standard by which purchases could be judged more or less trivial in general is available.[6] Since Plato, those who in the past proposed what Galbraith proposes—let the government decide (and spend) more, consumers less—were more consistent than he: they did not believe in individual freedom; and they felt that right values could be objectively ascertained and collectively imposed. If Galbraith held these views, his theory would be consistent, however unacceptable, to me. But though they are

implied in much of *The Affluent Society,*[7] I think he would repudiate such views when stated explicitly.

Certainly trivialities and vulgarities are now a greater proportion of our total output than in the past, not because taste has deteriorated—it probably was always bad—but because it is satisfied more often. Affluence changes the ability to satisfy taste rather than the taste: whereas in the past only the rich had the privilege to indulge their taste, now the poor can too. I do not see why transferring expenditures to a government no wiser than the voters who elect it and less able to satisfy *individual* tastes would solve this problem. It would probably replace private folly with official silliness. *Si monumentum quaeris, circumspice.* And it would make harder satisfaction of the minority tastes, which are usually more interesting than those of the majority.

I see one advantage of democracy in making reasonably certain not that the government is better than the voters in general—but that it is not much worse; without democracy, this last happens quite easily. Still in a democracy, if the government is likely to be not worse than the average voter, it is also likely to be worse than some voters. Wherefore, the transfer of the power to decide from the individual to even a democratic government is justifiable only where the object is so indivisible, or indiscriminate, as to make collective decisions imperative.

The argument in favor of expansion of the public sector need not be based on the demerits of private expenditure alone. It can be based also on the merits of public expenditure. But these can never be general. Each expenditure must be considered on its own

---

[6] I am making a factual statement: such a standard is not *available*. Nothing is implied about its existence; and should it exist, its nature, applicability or imposition.

[7] One of the major defects of that book is that it disguises inchoate and chaotic philosophical ideas as economic analysis.

merits: will benefits exceed costs by more than the benefits of alternative expenditures, public or private, would? How are benefits and costs distributed? The admitted triviality of many private expenditures, as well as "imbalance"— whatever it means—are utterly irrelevant unless general superiority of public expenditures can be shown. By pointing to the triviality of private expenditures—which each consumer is likely to admit for all other consumers —Galbraith suggests that the government would restrain those other consumers; and that anyway it could not do worse. But it always can and usually does. (These two fallacies are perennial stand-bys of appeals for dictatorships: followers of would-be dictators usually think that matters can only improve; and that the dictator would frustrate the [trivial] wishes of others but not their own [untrivial] ones.)

III

Though lambasting consumers for their silliness, Galbraith does not hold them responsible for it: according to the principles of ritualistic liberalism, the people always have their heart (or is it their stomach?) in the right place; when they err, it is because they have misread their heart's prompting owing to some wicked seducer. This theory is popular all around: it enables people to eat their cake and profess that they didn't really want it; and it enables the theorist to have his cake (people are good) and eat it (people act bad). In the past, the seducers were devils, capitalists, or Jews. Madison Avenue is fast replacing them in the folklore of our society.[8]

---

[8] Certainly recent myths are less convenient than the ancient ones. Jews and capitalists suffer from them—whereas in the past the devils were the main sufferers. Let me

Galbraith argues that consumers no longer satisfy endogenous desires, but exogenous ones "contrived" by advertising. Industry thus first produces the desires it then satisfies—whereas before *The Affluent Society,* the needs satisfied arose independently. Now, to the extent to which we grant the truth and undesirability of this "dependence effect," it might argue against advertising. Surprisingly, Galbraith seems to think of it as an argument for reducing the purchasing power of consumers and increasing that of the government by means of a general sales tax. His not entirely explicit train of thought seems to be: consumers' purchases are trivial; they satisfy a demand "contrived" by advertising; therefore, we should transfer purchasing power from consumers to the government; public expenditures will be less contrived and less trivial. There is no logical connection among the various parts of this argument. Why should the government not do worse than consumers? Why are public expenditures less (rather than differently) contrived than private ones? Is the political process that spontaneous? Why is "contrived," *i.e.,* influenced, demand better or worse (more or less trivial) than uncontrived, *i.e.,* uninfluenced (if that is conceivable), demand? Is the "contrived" demand for education, books and soap

note that Galbraith's myth, though structurally analogous to those mentioned, if more urban, is functionally quite different: Galbraith does not urge liquidation of Jews, capitalists, or advertising men. His theoretical mountain gives birth to a quite modest, practical mouse: a general sales tax. But then mice can be quite voracious and they multiply fast. (The general sales tax may have technical merits as such. But Galbraith wants it because he believes it to be the best means to achieve his basic end of increasing the general level of taxation, of decreasing private and increasing public expenditure. I object to this end, rather than to a sales, as compared to an income tax.)

worse than uncontrived spontaneous dirt and ignorance? One may spontaneously desire trivial things—as any child knows and does. Culture is contrivance, *i.e.,* social *"influence";* and there is no society without it. There is no less contrivance in primitive, or for that matter, in Soviet, society than in ours. The problem is not that there is influence ("contrivance") but the quality, source and direction of such influence; above all, whether influence is monopolized or whether it comes from many competing sources. The high taxes Galbraith proposes obviously would not affect these problems except by reducing the power of individuals and adding to the power of the government.

Galbraith's argument is irrelevant then. Is it true? Are consumers hapless victims of Madison Avenue? One would expect that they bought Ford's Edsel car in droves and not small foreign cars; or that the political party that spends most on advertising always wins. Presidents Thomas Dewey and Richard Nixon, and the Republican Congressional majority would testify to these beliefs were they true. They aren't. But believers are unshaken by evidence.

Advertising is only one influence among others in political or purchasing decisions and is frequently offset by competing advertising. Yet, advertising men as well as their opponents (for different reasons) cherish the belief that advertising is always the decisive influence. Advertising agencies want to impress prospective clients with the importance of what they may do for them. The motivation of opponents is more complex though their faith is as strong. Some are looking for scapegoats; others are mildly paranoid; still others want to convince people that they lose nothing in getting government "protection" from their own use of freedom, since advertising mysteriously has deprived them of that freedom anyway.

Many consumers spend their money in ways many other consumers disapprove. The first group of consumers assumes that the second cannot possibly have freely decided to spend its money as it does. The disapproved expenditure pattern is taken for evidence of their lack of freedom—just as apologists for dictatorship have always presented election of a less than perfect democratic government or one they disapproved of, as evidence for lack of political freedom. If you don't "really" have it, what can you lose in giving it up? The moral connection between sumptuary and political freedom is anything but tenuous: if consumers are incapable of freely choosing among advertised products, why should they be deemed capable of freely choosing among propagandizing political parties? What is freedom if not the right to choose among competing influences? If these influences are considered coercion, or if people are deemed too incompetent to choose among them, freedom can never be more than sham, and we might just as well install a dictatorship.[9] But I like freedom because it allows me to make, and judge, my own choices, however foolish.

We might well oppose and seek to restrain seduction. But we cannot (unless it be practiced on the legally incompetent) treat it as though it were rape, precisely because it gives choice (and therewith part of the responsibility) to all parties concerned: it requires consent. Democracy does so not less than the "dependence effect": with freedom there always are competing influences. And advertisements for de-

---

[9] It would not follow that dictatorship will lead to better results; but there would be no reason to expect worse ones. We would give up something we never had, or were never able to use competently.

tergents no more hypnotize or coerce than advertisements for political candidates. If people are competent as citizens to choose among candidates, why should they not be competent as consumers to choose among goods? I find it hard to believe that those who confuse influence with coercion can be sincere, but I may overestimate both their intelligence and their malevolence.

Has the influence of advertising increased? The proportion of the population affected certainly has. Not, however, because Madison Avenue has discovered new tricks—there seems to have been little basic progress in propaganda techniques since Roman times —but because literacy and other communications media have spread; and because many people who did not in the past, do now have enough disposable income to follow fashions in purchasing. However, even the fixed purchasing patterns of the past were socially influenced. The peasant's dress, food and housing were no more individual creations than the wigs of noblemen, or their extravagant garments. Nor were these things less trivial than the things advertised in *Vogue* today. Versailles, a medieval cathedral, or Vanderbilt's yacht were neither more of a necessity nor more spontaneous than our tailfinned cars, or a copy of *The Affluent Society*—though perhaps of more lasting value. The actual change that has occurred is not any new "dependence effect" but a general change from a pre-industrial, tradition-directed to industrial, consumer-directed society with its concomitant mass culture. Which means that social influences are more changeable, that they come more often from below— with people more attuned to them (more other-directed)— rather than coming from nobility, king and church; or, having been internalized, they come from a greater variety of sources; the

advertising industry is among them, though it perhaps transmits more than it creates.

Characteristically, advertising agencies are not in the permanent service of a class, ideology, or church but of whoever hires them. Mostly private firms try to increase or maintain their profits by doing so. But firms are as interested in producing what people want as they are in making people want what they produce. The former is more profitable and more certain of success. In this sense, advertising probably is less engaged in "contriving" needs than the church was, or than Harvard University is when it raises funds. Indeed, the bad taste Mr. Galbraith deplores is indulged in largely because of the absence of the ancient contriving agencies—church and court. We are now catering to the taste of the masses, whereas before it could be ignored. There is no evidence to indicate that people would buy fewer or better things without advertising. They might buy slightly different things from slightly different people.

IV

The public expenditures Galbraith advocates to replace private expenditures—more public works, education, welfare services—are neither new nor supported by new arguments. This part of *The Affluent Society* amounts to tiresome exhortation. Yet a discussion of the specifics of public expenditures might have been fruitful. I am convinced that we do need public services not now undertaken; and that many public services presently offered at high cost to taxpayers are "contrived": they become necessary because the government prevents private industry from rendering them, or makes it excessively costly to do so, or, finally, because they offset noxious government activities elsewhere. What happens is classically illustrated in the case of farm subsidies.

The government raises farm prices, *i.e.,* the cost of living, mainly the price of food, but also of cotton, tobacco, etc., by means of price supports. The government spends more than $5 billion annually to give us the privilege of buying food at higher than free-market prices. This money is spent to buy supplies which would depress the market price, or to pay farmers for not producing them. No way to dispose of most of the supplies purchased has been found; they are stored at huge additional cost, until they spoil. Some are sold at a loss abroad or given away. The subsidy, of course, perpetuates the misallocation of resources between agriculture and the rest of the economy, which it is supposed to correct, and also within agriculture, so that more is produced of what is needed less, and less of what is needed more, *ad infinitum;* and subsidies are required *ad infinitum* to keep things that way.

There is no respectable argument known to economists for these subsidies. The argument usually heard is that without them the income of farmers would be lower than that of workers, or lower than it was in some past period. But most of the subsidy does not go to low-income farmers; their farms are so small and unproductive that higher prices, or payments for noncultivation of their property add little to their income. Most of the subsidy goes to big scale producers of unneeded farm products. (50% of our farmers produce less than 10% of the agricultural output.)

If we wanted to help low income farmers, it would be simple to do so without raising food prices, without fostering misallocation, and without subsidizing farmers whose income far exceeds the income of the taxpayers who must pay the subsidy. Without changing the whole complex structure of present legislation—a task that should not be neglected, but that requires time—we could do so by simply purchasing only from farmers whose net income from all sources in any given year does not exceed, say, $7000. (Surely farmers with higher incomes need no subsidies.) Any amount paid farmers whose income exceeds $7000 must be returned—and the government can return what it purchased from them. In time, the government might limit itself to purchases from progressively older farmers. This ultimately would solve the problem; only those would remain or go into farming who can make an income that satisfies them by selling their crops at unsubsidized market prices. This, of course, would correct the allocation of resources and make further subsidies unnecessary.

I have briefly outlined elsewhere how this proposal could be carried out and what the effects would be. I have received heartening letters from economists. But nothing else. The mood of our times is such that if a problem can be perpetuated and made worse by high subsidies and brought nearer solution by low ones, we prefer high subsidies. I deliberately speak of the mood of the times. For in terms of their economic interests, the farmers who would not lose under the proposal—let alone consumers—constitute an overwhelming majority. But our general tendency is to make individual incomes less and less dependent on individual efforts, on the value placed by the market on one's product, and more and more on political considerations, on the political power exercised by a group, or the power that can be gained by catering to it. Above all, the nature of the subsidy is carefully hidden. We speak of price supports when we make relief payments to some farmers who need them (and who should be trained for a different occupation rather than kept farming to receive relief) and to many who do not. This careful disguise helps persuade taxpayers.

By now the farm program has become a classical case. Many newer, equally dubious, programs seem more complicated. Thus, the government feels it necessary to subsidize low and middle-rent apartment-house building in many cities. It is contended that low and middle-income families, although more affluent than ever before, cannot afford the rent for unsubsidized housing. But if their income is too small, we should subsidize them, not housing. Why a subsidy in kind, which deprives them of choice? Is it feared that they would make a choice that appears wrong to the government? What evidence is there to show that they are wrong and the government right? Does not our system rest on the premise that the individual knows best what he needs—not the government? Why then should he be incompetent to decide whether he should spend additional money best on housing, clothing, or, say, education? If, finally, it is believed not that people's income requires supplementing but that the cost of housing has risen disproportionately, we must ask (1) why people should not make a greater proportionate outlay for housing than they used to; or, (2) why the cost of housing has risen dispropor-

tionately. Certainly there are measures the government could take to reduce it without paying out subsidies. What about taxes, obsolete building codes, and local laws and required briberies which unnecessarily raise the cost of building? What about the steadily rising labor costs of building—disproportionately high wage rates, featherbedding, deliberate inefficiency—caused in no small measure by labor unions, whose power to raise costs is due in the main to the governmental protection they enjoy? Does not the government first raise the cost of housing, then point out that it is high and proceed to subsidize housing? One may find similar situations throughout our economy: *e.g.,* in urban transportation, railroads, the merchant marine. . . .

As soon as we turn from vacuous generalizations about the affluent private and the starved public sector of our economy to an actual scrutiny of public expenditures, we find that, though it is true that some needed services are not performed, or not performed well, it is also true that many unneeded services are performed at immense cost, and that they serve as pretexts to perform still other services, or to pay subsidies to offset the effect they have. Increasing public expenditure is unlikely to remedy this state of affairs—on the contrary, it will make it worse.

50   COURAGE AND POLITICS

John F. Kennedy

President John F. Kennedy was United States Senator from Massachusetts when he wrote *Profiles in Courage.*

*   *   *

A nation which has forgotten the quality of courage which in the past has been brought to public life is not as likely to insist upon or reward that quality in its chosen leaders today— and in fact we have forgotten. We may remember how John Quincy Adams became President through the political schemes of Henry Clay, but we have forgotten how, as a young man, he gave up a promising Senatorial career to stand by the nation. We may remember Daniel Webster for his subservience to the National Bank throughout much of his career, but we have forgotten his sacrifice for the national good at the close of that career. We do not remember—and possibly we do not care.

"People don't give a damn," a syndicated columnist told millions of readers not so many years ago, "what the average Senator or Congressman says. The reason they don't care is that they know what you hear in Congress is 99% tripe, ignorance and demagoguery and not to be relied upon. . . ."

Earlier a member of the Cabinet had recorded in his diary:

While I am reluctant to believe in the total depravity of the Senate, I place but little dependence on the honesty and truthfulness of a large portion of the Senators. A majority of them are small lights, mentally weak, and wholly unfit to be Senators. Some are vulgar demagogues . . . some are men of wealth who have purchased their position . . . [some are] men of narrow intellect, limited comprehension, and low partisan prejudice. . . .

And still earlier a member of the Senate itself told his colleagues that "the confidence of the people is departing from us, owing to our unreasonable delays."

The Senate knows that many Americans today share these sentiments. Senators, we hear, must be politicians —and politicians must be concerned only with winning votes, not with statesmanship or courage. Mothers may still want their favorite sons to grow up to be President, but, according to a famous Gallop poll of some years ago, they do not want them to become politicians in the process.

Does this current rash of criticism and disrespect mean the quality of the Senate has declined? Certainly not. For of the three statements quoted above, the first was made in the twentieth century, the second in the nineteenth and the third in the eighteenth (when the first Senate, barely underway, was debating where the Capitol should be located).

Does it mean, then, that the Senate can no longer boast of men of courage?

Walter Lippmann, after nearly half a century of careful observation, rendered in his recent book a harsh judgment both on the politician and the electorate:

With exceptions so rare they are regarded as miracles of nature, successful democratic politicians are insecure and intimidated men. They advance politically only as they placate, appease, bribe,

---

"Courage and Politics," from *Profiles in Courage* by John F. Kennedy. Reprinted by permission of Harper & Row, Publishers.

seduce, bamboozle, or otherwise manage to manipulate the demanding threatening elements in their constituencies. The decisive consideration is not whether the proposition is good but whether it is popular—not whether it will work well and prove itself, but whether the active-talking constituents like it immediately.

I am not so sure, after nearly ten years of living and working in the midst of "successful democratic politicians," that they are all "insecure and intimidated men." I am convinced that the complication of public business and the competition for the public's attention have obscured innumerable acts of political courage—large and small—performed almost daily in the Senate Chamber. I am convinced that the decline—if there has been a decline—has been less in the Senate than in the public's appreciation of the art of politics, of the nature and necessity for compromise and balance, and of the nature of the Senate as a legislative chamber. And, finally, I am convinced that we have criticized those who have followed the crowd—and at the same time criticized those who have defied it—because we have not fully understood the responsibility of a Senator to his constituents or recognized the difficulty facing a politician conscientiously desiring, in Webster's words, "to push [his] skiff from the shore alone" into a hostile and turbulent sea. Perhaps if the American people more fully comprehended the terrible pressures which discourage acts of political courage, which drive a Senator to abandon or subdue his conscience, then they might be less critical of those who take the easier road—and more appreciative of those still able to follow the path of courage.

The *first pressure* to be mentioned is a form of pressure rarely recognized by the general public. Americans want to be liked—and Senators are no ex-

ception. They are by nature—and of necessity—social animals. We enjoy the comradeship and approval of our friends and colleagues. We prefer praise to abuse, popularity to contempt. Realizing that the path of the conscientious insurgent must frequently be a lonely one, we are anxious to get along with our fellow legislators, our fellow members of the club, to abide by the clubhouse rules and patterns, not to pursue a unique and independent course which would embarrass or irritate the other members. We realize, moreover, that our influence in the club—and the extent to which we can accomplish our objectives and those of our constituents—are dependent in some measure on the esteem with which we are regarded by other Senators. "The way to get along," I was told when I entered Congress, "is to go along."

Going along means more than just good fellowship—it includes the use of compromise, the sense of things possible. We should not be too hasty in condemning all compromise as bad morals. For politics and legislation are not matters for inflexible principles or unattainable ideals. Politics, as John Morley has acutely observed, "is a field where action is one long second best, and where the choice constantly lies between two blunders"; and legislation, under the democratic way of life and the Federal system of Government, requires compromise between the desires of each individual and group and those around them. Henry Clay, who should have known, said compromise was the cement that held the Union together:

All legislation . . . is founded upon the principle of mutual concession. . . . Let him who elevates himself above humanity, above its weaknesses, its infirmities, its wants, its necessities, say, if he pleases, "I never will compromise"; but but let no one who is not above the frailties of our common nature disdain compromise.

It is compromise that prevents each set of reformers—the wets and the drys, the one-worlders and the isolationists, the vivisectionists and the anti-vivisectionists—from crushing the group on the extreme opposite end of the political spectrum. The fanatics and extremists and even those conscientiously devoted to hard and fast principles are always disappointed at the failure of their Government to rush to implement all of their principles and to denounce those of their opponents. But the legislator has some responsibility to conciliate those opposing forces within his state and party and to represent them in the larger clash of interests on the national level; and he alone knows that there are few if any issues where all the truth and all the right and all the angels are on one side.

Some of my colleagues who are criticized today for lack of forthright principles—or who are looked upon with scornful eyes as compromising "politicians"—are simply engaged in the fine art of conciliating, balancing and interpreting the forces and factions of public opinion, an art essential to keeping our nation united and enabling our Government to function. Their consciences may direct them from time to time to take a more rigid stand for principle—but their intellects tell them that a fair or poor bill is better than no bill at all, and that only through the give-and-take of compromise will any bill receive the successive approval of the Senate, the House, the President and the nation.

But the question is how we will compromise and with whom. For it is easy to seize upon unnecessary concessions, not as means of legitimately resolving conflicts but as methods of "going along."

There were further implications in the warning that I should "go along" —implications of the rewards that would follow fulfillment of my obligation to follow the party leadership whom I had helped select. All of us in the Congress are made fully aware of the importance of party unity (what sins have been committed in that name!) and the adverse effect upon our party's chances in the next election which any rebellious conduct might bring. Moreover, in these days of Civil Service, the loaves and fishes of patronage available to the legislator—for distribution to those earnest campaigners whose efforts were inspired by something more than mere conviction —are comparatively few; and he who breaks the party's ranks may find that there are suddenly none at all. Even the success of legislation in which he is interested depends in part on the extent to which his support of his party's programs has won him the assistance of his party's leaders. Finally, the Senator who follows the independent course of conscience is likely to discover that he has earned the disdain not only of his colleagues in the Senate and his associates in his party but also that of the all-important contributors to his campaign fund.

It is thinking of that next campaign —the desire to be re-elected—that provides the *second* pressure on the conscientious Senator. It should not automatically be assumed that this is a wholly selfish motive—although it is not unnatural that those who have chosen politics as their profession should seek to continue their careers— for Senators who go down to defeat in a vain defense of a single principle will not be on hand to fight for that or any other principle in the future.

Defeat, moreover, is not only a setback for the Senator himself—he is also obligated to consider the effect upon the party he supports, upon the friends and supporters who have "gone out on a limb" for him or invested their savings in his career, and even upon the wife and children whose happiness and security—often depending at least in part upon his success in office—may mean more to him than anything else.

Where else, in a non-totalitarian country, but in the political profession is the individual expected to sacrifice all—including his own career—for the national good? In private life, as in industry, we expect the individual to advance his own enlightened self-interest—within the limitations of the law—in order to achieve over-all progress. But in public life we expect individuals to sacrifice their private interests to permit the national good to progress.

In no other occupation but politics is it expected that a man will sacrifice honors, prestige and his chosen career on a single issue. Lawyers, businessmen, teachers, doctors, all face difficult personal decisions involving their integrity—but few, if any, face them in the glare of the spotlight as do those in public office. Few, if any, face the same dread finality of decision that confronts a Senator facing an important call of the roll. He may want more time for his decision—he may believe there is something to be said for both sides—he may feel that a slight amendment could remove all difficulties—but when that roll is called he cannot hide, he cannot equivocate, he cannot delay—and he senses that his constituency, like the Raven in Poe's poem, is perched there on his Senate desk, croaking "Nevermore" as he casts the vote that stakes his political future.

Few Senators "retire to Pocatello" by choice. The virus of Potomac Fever, which rages everywhere in Washington, breeds nowhere in more virulent form than on the Senate floor. The

prospect of forced retirement from "the most exclusive club in the world," the possibilities of giving up the interesting work, the fascinating trappings and the impressive prerogatives of Congressional office, can cause even the most courageous politician serious loss of sleep. Thus, perhaps without realizing it, some Senators tend to take the easier, less troublesome path to harmonize or rationalize what at first appears to be a conflict between their conscience—or the result of their deliberations—and the majority opinion of their constituents. Such Senators are not political cowards—they have simply developed the habit of sincerely reaching conclusions inevitably in accordance with popular opinion.

Still other Senators have not developed that habit—they have neither conditioned nor subdued their consciences—but they feel, sincerely and without cynicism, that they must leave considerations of conscience aside if they are to be effective. The profession of politics, they would agree with political writer Frank Kent, is not immoral, simply nonmoral:

Probably the most important single accomplishment for the politically ambitious is the fine art of seeming to say something without doing so. . . . The important thing is not to be on the right side of the current issue but on the popular side . . . regardless of your own convictions or of the facts. This business of getting the votes is a severely practical one into which matters of morality, of right and wrong, should not be allowed to intrude.

And Kent quotes the advice allegedly given during the 1920 campaign by former Senator Ashurst of Arizona to his colleague Mark Smith:

Mark, the great trouble with you is that you refuse to be a demagogue. You will not submerge your principles in order to get yourself elected. *You must learn that there are times when a man in public life is compelled to rise above his principles.*

Not all Senators would agree—but few would deny that the desire to be re-elected exercises a strong brake on independent courage.

The *third* and most significant source of pressures which discourage political courage in the conscientious Senator or Congressman—and practically all of the problems described in this chapter apply equally to members of both Houses—is the pressure of his constituency, the interest groups, the organized letter writers, the economic blocs and even the average voter. To cope with such pressures, to defy them or even to satisfy them, is a formidable task. All of us occasionally have the urge to follow the example of Congressman John Steven McGroarty of California, who wrote a constituent in 1934:

One of the countless drawbacks of being in Congress is that I am compelled to receive impertinent letters from a jackass like you in which you say I promised to have the Sierra Madre mountains reforested and I have been in Congress two months and haven't done it. Will you please take two running jumps and go to hell.

Fortunately or unfortunately, few follow that urge—but the provocation is there—not only from unreasonable letters and impossible requests, but also from hopelessly inconsistent demands and endlessly unsatisfied grievances.

In my office today, for example, was a delegation representing New England textile mills, an industry essential to our prosperity. They want the tariff lowered on the imported wool they buy from Australia and they want the tariff raised on the finished woolen goods imported from England with which they must compete. One of my Southern colleagues told me that a similar group visited him not long ago with the same requests—but further urging that he take steps to (1) end the low-wage competition from Japan and (2) prevent the Congress from ending—through a higher minimum wage—the low-wage advantage they themselves enjoy to the dismay of my constituents. Only yesterday two groups called me off the Senate floor—the first was a group of businessmen seeking to have a local Government activity closed as unfair competition for private enterprise; and the other was a group representing the men who work in the Government installation and who are worried about their jobs.

All of us in the Senate meet endless examples of such conflicting pressures, which only reflect the inconsistencies inevitable in our complex economy. If we tell our constituents frankly that we can do nothing, they feel we are unsympathetic or inadequate. If we try and fail—usually meeting a counteraction from other Senators representing other interests—they say we are like all the rest of the politicians. All we can do is retreat into the Cloakroom and weep on the shoulder of a sympathetic colleague—or go home and snarl at our wives.

We may tell ourselves that these pressure groups and letter writers represent only a small percentage of the voters—and this is true. But they are the articulate few whose views cannot be ignored and who constitute the greater part of our contacts with the public at large, whose opinions we cannot know, whose vote we must obtain and yet who in all probability have a limited idea of what we are trying to do. (One Senator, since retired, said that he voted with the special interests on every issue, hoping that by election time all of them added together would constitute nearly a majority that would remember him favorably, while the other members of the public would never know about—much less remember—his vote against their welfare. It is reassuring to know that this seemingly unbeatable formula did not work in his case.)

These, then, are some of the pressures which confront a man of conscience. He cannot ignore the pressure groups, his constituents, his party, the comradeship of his colleagues, the needs of his family, his own pride in office, the necessity for compromise and the importance of remaining in office. He must judge for himself which path to chose, which step will most help or hinder the ideals to which he is committed. He realizes that once he begins to weigh each issue in terms of his chances for re-election, once he begins to compromise away his principles on one issue after another for fear that to do otherwise would halt his career and prevent future fights for principle, then he has lost the very freedom of conscience which justifies his continuance in office. But to decide at which point and on which issue he will risk his career is a difficult and soul-searching decision.

But this is no real problem, some will say. Always do what is right, regardless of whether it is popular. Ignore the pressures, the temptations, the false compromises.

That is an easy answer—but it is easy only for those who do not bear the responsibilities of elected office. For more is involved than pressure, politics and personal ambitions. Are we rightfully entitled to ignore the demands of our constituents even if we are able and willing to do so? We have noted the pressures that make political courage a difficult course—let us turn now to those Constitutional and more theoretical obligations which cast doubt

upon the propriety of such a course—obligations to our state and section, to our party, and above all, to our constituents.

The primary responsibility of a Senator, most people assume, is to represent the views of his state. Ours is a Federal system—a Union of relatively sovereign states whose needs differ greatly—and my Constitutional obligations as Senator would thus appear to require me to represent the interests of my state. Who will speak for Massachusetts if her own Senators do not? Her rights and even her identity become submerged. Her equal representation in Congress is lost. Her aspirations, however much they may from time to time be in the minority, are denied that equal opportunity to be heard to which all minority views are entitled.

Any Senator need not look very long to realize that his colleagues are representing *their* local interests. And if such interests are ever to be abandoned in favor of the national good, let the constituents—not the Senator—decide when and to what extent. For he is their agent in Washington, the protector of their rights, recognized by the Vice-President in the Senate Chamber as "the Senator from Massachusetts" or "the Senator from Texas."

But when all of this is said and admitted, we have not yet told the full story. For in Washington we are "United States Senators" and members of the Senate of the United States as well as Senators from Massachusetts and Texas. Our oath of office is administered by the Vice-President, not by the Governors of our respective states; and we come to Washington, to paraphrase Edmund Burke, not as hostile ambassadors or special pleaders for our state or section, in opposition to advocates and agents of other areas, but as members of the deliberative assembly of one nation with one interest. Of course, we should not ignore the needs of our area—nor could we easily as products of that area—but none could be found to look out for the national interest if local interests wholly dominated the role of each of us.

There are other obligations in addition to those of state and region—the obligations of the party whose pressures have already been described. Even if I can disregard those pressures, do I not have an obligation to go along with the party that placed me in office? We believe in this country in the principle of party responsibility, and we recognize the necessity of adhering to party platforms—if the party label is to mean anything to the voters. Only in this way can our basically two-party nation avoid the pitfalls of multiple splinter parties—whose purity and rigidity of principle, I might add—if I may suggest a sort of Gresham's Law of politics—increase inversely with the size of their membership.

And yet we cannot permit the pressures of party responsibility to submerge on every issue the call of personal responsibility. For the party which, in its drive for unity, discipline and success, ever decides to exclude new ideas, independent conduct or insurgent members, is in danger. In the words of Senator Albert Beveridge:

A party can live only by growing, intolerance of ideas brings its death. . . . An organization that depends upon reproduction only for its vote, son taking the place of father, is not a political party, but a Chinese tong; not citizens brought together by thought and conscience, but an Indian tribe held together by blood and prejudice.

The two-party system remains not because both are rigid but because both are flexible. The Republican party when I entered Congress was big enough to hold, for example, both

Robert Taft and Wayne Morse—and the Democratic side of the Senate in which I now serve can happily embrace, for example, both Harry Byrd and Wayne Morse.

Of course, both major parties today seek to serve the national interest. They would do so in order to obtain the broadest base of support, if for no nobler reason. But when party and officeholder differ as to how the national interest is to be served, we must place first the responsibility we owe not to our party or even to our constituents but to our individual consciences.

But it is a little easier to dismiss one's obligations to local interests and party ties than to face squarely the problem of one's responsibility to the will of his constituents. A Senator who avoids this responsibility would appear to be accountable to no one, and the basic safeguards of our democratic system would thus have vanished. He is no longer representative in the true sense, he has violated his public trust, he has betrayed the confidence demonstrated by those who voted for him to carry out their views. "Is the creature," as John Tyler asked the House of Representatives in his maiden speech, "to set himself in opposition to his Creator? Is the servant to disobey the wishes of his master?"

How can he be regarded as representing the people when he speaks, not their language, but his own? He ceases to be their representative when he does so, and represents himself alone.

In short, according to this school of thought, if I am to be properly responsive to the will of my constituents, it is my duty to place their principles, not mine, above all else. This may not always be easy, but it nevertheless is the essence of democracy, faith in the wisdom of the people and their views. To be sure, the people will make mistakes

—they will get no better government than they deserve—but that is far better than the representative of the people arrogating for himself the right to say he knows better than they what is good for them. Is he not chosen, the argument closes, to vote as they would vote were they in his place?

It is difficult to accept such a narrow view of the role of United States Senator—a view that assumes the people of Massachusetts sent me to Washington to serve merely as a seismograph to record shifts in popular opinion. I reject this view not because I lack faith in the "wisdom of the people," but because this concept of democracy actually puts too little faith in the people. Those who would deny the obligation of the representative to be bound by every impulse of the electorate—regardless of the conclusions his own deliberations direct—do trust in the wisdom of the people. They have faith in their ultimate sense of justice, faith in their ability to honor courage and respect judgment, and faith that in the long run they will act unselfishly for the good of the nation. It is that kind of faith on which democracy is based, not simply the often frustrated hope that public opinion will at all times under all circumstances promptly identify itself with the public interest.

The voters selected us, in short, because they had confidence in our judgment and our ability to exercise that judgment from a position where we could determine what were their own best interests, as a part of the nation's interests. This may mean that we must on occasion lead, inform, correct and sometimes even ignore constituent opinion, if we are to exercise fully that judgment for which we were elected. But acting without selfish motive or private bias, those who follow the dictates of an intelligent conscience are not aristocrats, demagogues, eccentrics

or callous politicians insensitive to the feelings of the public. They expect—and not without considerable trepidation—their constituents to be the final judges of the wisdom of their course; but they have faith that those constituents—today, tomorrow or even in another generation—will at least respect the principles that motivated their independent stand.

If their careers are temporarily or even permanently buried under an avalanche of abusive editorials, poison-pen letters, and opposition votes at the polls—as they sometimes are, for that is the risk they take—they await the future with hope and confidence, aware of the fact that the voting public frequently suffers from what ex-Congressman T. V. Smith called the lag "between our way of thought and our way of life." Smith compared it to the subject of the anonymous poem:

There was a dachshund, once so long
He hadn't any notion
How long it took to notify
His tail of his emotion;
And so it happened, while his eyes
Were filled with woe and sadness,
His little tail went wagging on
Because of previous gladness.

Moreover, I question whether any Senator, before we vote on a measure, can state with certainty exactly how the majority of his constituents feel on the issue as it is presented to the Senate. All of us in the Senate live in an iron lung—the iron lung of politics, and it is no easy task to emerge from that rarefied atmosphere in order to breathe the same fresh air our constituents breathe. It is difficult, too, to see in person an appreciable number of voters besides those professional hangers-on and vocal elements who gather about the politician on a trip home. In Washington I frequently find myself believing that forty or fifty letters, six visits from professional politicians and lobbyists, and three editorials in Massachusetts newspapers constitute public opinion on a given issue. Yet in truth I rarely know how the great majority of the voters feel, or even how much they know of the issues that seem so burning in Washington.

Today the challenge of political courage looms larger than ever before. For our everyday life is becoming so saturated with the tremendous power of mass communications that any unpopular or unorthodox course arouses a storm of protests such as John Quincy Adams—under attack in 1807 —could never have envisioned. Our political life is becoming so expensive, so mechanized and so dominated by professional politicians and public relations men that the idealist who dreams of independent statesmanship is rudely awakened by the necessities of election and accomplishment. And our public life is becoming so increasingly centered upon that seemingly unending war to which we have given the curious epithet "cold" that we tend to encourage rigid ideological unity and orthodox patterns of thought.

And thus, in the days ahead, only the very courageous will be able to take the hard and unpopular decisions necessary for our survival in the struggle with a powerful enemy—an enemy with leaders who need give little thought to the popularity of their course, who need pay little tribute to the public opinion they themselves manipulate, and who may force, without fear of retaliation at the polls, their citizens to sacrifice present laughter for future glory. And only the very courageous will be able to keep alive the spirit of individualism and dissent which gave birth to this nation, nourished it as an infant and carried it

through its severest tests upon the attainment of its maturity.

Of course, it would be much easier if we could all continue to think in traditional political patterns—of liberalism and conservatism, as Republicans and Democrats, from the viewpoint of North and South, management and labor, business and consumer or some equally narrow framework. It would be more comfortable to continue to move and vote in platoons, joining whomever of our colleagues are equally enslaved by some current fashion, raging prejudice or popular movement. But today this nation cannot tolerate the luxury of such lazy political habits. Only the strength and progress and peaceful change that come from independent judgment and individual ideas —and even from the unorthodox and the eccentric—can enable us to surpass that foreign ideology that fears free thought more than it fears hydrogen bombs.

We shall need compromises in the days ahead, to be sure. But these will be, or should be, compromises of issues, not of principles. We can compromise our political positions, but not ourselves. We can resolve the clash of interests without conceding our ideals. And even the necessity for the right kind of compromise does not eliminate the need for those idealists and reformers who keep our compromises moving ahead, who prevent all political situations from meeting the description supplied by Shaw: "smirched with compromise, rotted with opportunism, mildewed by expedience, stretched out of shape with wirepulling and putrefied with permeation." Compromise need not mean cowardice. Indeed it is frequently the compromisers and conciliators who are faced with the severest tests of political courage as they oppose the extremist views of their constituents. It was because Daniel Webster conscientiously favored compromise in 1850 that he earned a condemnation unsurpassed in the annals of political history.

His is a story worth remembering today. So, I believe, are the stories of other Senators of courage—men whose abiding loyalty to their nation triumphed over all personal and politi-

cal considerations, men who showed the real meaning of courage and a real faith in democracy, men who made the Senate of the United States something more than a mere collection of robots dutifully recording the views of their constituents, or a gathering of time-servers skilled only in predicting and following the tides of public sentiment.

*   *   *

51   FOR FASTEST GROWTH— WHAT KIND OF TAX?

Henry C. Wallich

Henry C. Wallich is Professor of Economics at Yale University.

More Americans pay a sales tax, and pay it more often, than any other kind of tax. Yet because so much of it is in pennies, the take from sales taxes is relatively modest. It does not begin to compare with the massive sums that some 40,000,000 income-tax payers annually turn over to the tax collector.

The present national argument about taxes—whether to cut them or to reform them, definitely not to abolish them—has brought out the interesting fact that Americans pay a higher proportion of their total taxes in the form of income taxes and other direct taxes than the citizens of almost any other industrial country. Conversely, they pay a lower proportion in the form of sales taxes and other indirect taxes.

The argument has also brought out that the industrial countries which have recently enjoyed the fastest economic growth are among those that rely much more on sales and similar taxes than on income taxes. This is strikingly true, for instance, as Prof.

William J. Fellner of Yale has shown, of the European top-growth countries (France, Italy and Germany) as well as of Japan. Other countries, relying more heavily on income taxes, have by and large grown less rapidly.

Findings like these do not prove anything conclusively, of course. The members of the "fast-growth club" may owe their success to some other factors, most likely to a variety of causes. And among the less developed countries of the world there are many that grow painfully slowly while relying exclusively on indirect taxes.

But in the cases of the successful countries of Europe, and of Japan, some logical connection between the tax system and growth does seem to emerge. No country can grow rapidly unless it plows back a high proportion of its output into productive investment. High income taxes probably tend to reduce the supply of savings that are needed, because they weigh most heavily on high-income earners who do the most saving. They may also undermine the incentive to invest, as well as the urge to work and make money.

The successful countries are all countries that save and invest a high proportion of their incomes. Recently, the rate of growth has slowed in some of them, for instance in Germany, though to a level still well above the growth of the United States. This has been accompanied by some slowing of investment. The Germans attribute this to overfull employment, shorter hours worked and a squeeze on profits through rising wages. The tax system, insofar as it has favored investment and growth in the past, still does so today.

The United States has been very successful throughout most of its history, but today it has become a low-investment country and our growth has slowed. These are grounds for suspicion, at least, that our tax system may have been one of the culprits in a complicated case.

Tax comparisons among countries are the most odious of comparisons, because in no two countries are tax laws ever exactly comparable. The variety of taxes is a monument to the ingenuity of governments. The simple distinction of income and sales taxes does not begin to do it justice. Even the economists' distinction of direct and indirect taxes, which covers roughly the same ground, does not really bring order into this chaos.

In the United States, the Federal Government levies no sales taxes proper at all. It manages, however, to raise about 13 per cent of its budgetary revenues from excises on gasoline, liquor and tobacco, on transportation, telephone calls and entertainment, and on a number of other articles and activities as well as from customs duties.

These are sales taxes in economic effect, if not in legal terminology. All the rest comes from taxes on income in one form or another. State and local governments do get a much larger share of their considerably smaller income from sales-type and property taxes.

The net result is that we hand over 62 per cent of our taxes in the form of income taxes and 38 per cent as sales and similar taxes. Only Sweden levies a slightly higher proportion of direct taxes. Meanwhile, France obtains only 26 per cent from income taxes, the rest as sales and similar imposts; Italy 30 per cent, including in all cases state and local revenues, but excluding social-security taxes which do not seem to fit properly into either category. It is quite possible that these figures contain some of the European growth secret for which President Kennedy told his advisers to go looking.

How did the United States get so far out of line with the tax policies of the most successful countries? The United States had its first brush with the income tax during the Civil War. The tax was dropped thereafter, and did not rear its head again until 1913, following the passage of the Sixteenth Amendment. Introduced just in time to help finance World War I at rates up to 77 per cent, it was cut back to a top rate of 24 per cent during the Nineteen Twenties by Secretary of the Treasury Andrew W. Melon. As a peace-time tax, it came to full flower (if that is the word) during the great depression. Its sponsors had in mind two principal purposes—to discourage people who want to save (their money is needed to finance growth), and to redistribute income. Politics aside, both purposes had their justification in the climate of the times.

Those were the days when it was believed, with some apparent basis in contemporary fact, that the United States economy had reached full maturity, that it offered few opportunities for new investment and could look forward to but little future growth. This meant that there was little need for new savings. Wealthy Mr. Smith, who saved a good part of his income, thereby merely cut down consumption and destroyed jobs. By taxing him and easing the tax burden on impecunious Mr. Jones, who spent most of what he earned, it was thought that a positive stimulus to the economy would be achieved. Redistribution of incomes, through taxes and public expenditures, seemed the only means of raising lower-bracket living standards in the absence of genuine growth.

Then came World War II, and with it tremendous financial needs and still higher taxes. In the different social climate of the post-World War II period, rates did not come down drastically as they did during the Twenties. Today, with a lowest bracket rate of 20 per cent and a top rate of 91 per cent, we are very close to all-time peak levels.

Income tax adherents rightly argue that the income tax is much more sophisticated than a tax on commodities. Taxes on the sale or transportation of commodities are easy to administer. Since the time immemorial, princes and potentates have levied them—at the city gate, at the harbor dock, at the places of primitive manufacture, or in the town market. The income tax is a tax on an abstract number which cannot be arrived at, for the larger taxpayers, without subtle accounting concepts like depreciation.

The income tax has been described as a fair tax because it demands more from the wealthy than from the poor. It also permits account to be taken of individual circumstances—such as the number of children, the age of the taxpayer, expense through illness, and the like—through appropriate exemptions and deductions. It is thought to encourage good citizenship because it is a clearly visible tax, allowing everyone to know exactly what the government costs him, in contrast to sales and excise taxes that can be concealed in the price.

Finally, the income tax seems attractive to many because it is flexible in recessions. When a taxpayer's income falls, the progressive feature of the tax, which makes the rate rise with the income bracket, goes into reverse. The taxpayer's liability falls faster than income and affords him relief.

But in the post-war years, the income tax has also revealed grave weaknesses. Tax rates designed to cope with supposedly permanent stagnation are out of place in an economy geared for growth. We can no longer afford to discourage saving—it is needed to finance growth. Even though, in the present state of the economy, there seem to be more savers than investors, that is largely a question of the business cycle and should not determine long-run tax policy.

We also have every reason not to discourage the willingness to work or invest. And we need no longer look to the redistribution of Smith's income to Jones as the principal means of raising Jones' living standards. Economic growth is a much more powerful lever than redistribution. If the two conflict, more is to be gained, for both Jones and Smith, if we go for growth than if we go for redistribution. All this suggests that a tax system relying less heavily on high income taxes may be more in tune with our times.

Practical experience with high tax rates has tarnished the glamour of the income tax in other ways. Tax avoidance and tax evasion have become familiar terms in the economic dictionary. Tax avoidance is the legitimate effort of the taxpayer to take advantage of all the facilities the law provides to hold his taxes down. A whole profession of tax specialists has been reared in the overheated tax climate of a 91 per cent top rate. In this strange world, a penny saved is ten pennies earned, and a penny of deductible expenditures is almost no cost at all. When a large part of a business man's time is devoted to tax problems, and a large part of his decisions governed by their tax consequences, little good can be expected for the economy.

Tax evasion is the name of illegitimate efforts to minimize taxes—tax cheating, for short. The United States taxpayer is probably one of the world's most honest—many other countries do not trust their taxpayers to assess themselves, as we do, but prepare returns for them. Yet high taxes put a strain on the honesty and raise the possibility that tax morale may soften and be neglected.

The tremendous pressure of the top rates has knocked some highly inequitable breaches in the wall separating pre-tax from post-tax income. Groups with strong political backing have molded the law to fit their interests. It is possible today to write off the same building several times over, to deduct depletion on an oil well long after the investment has been repaid, to charge off business expenses that are pure fun, and to stash away income for the future with a minimum of present tax.

Whatever the logic behind these devices, they make a mockery of the rate structure, and they create invidious distinctions between those who have oil wells, expense accounts or deductions and pension funds and those others with similar incomes who have not.

Even decisions regarding public expenditures are vitiated by high tax rates. When Mr. Jones, who has three children and pays a top rate of 20 per cent, looks at a proposal for Federal aid to higher education, he may feel that he would be sending his offspring to college rather cheaply at that price. Mr. Smith, who also has three children but pays a top rate of 70 per cent, figures that private education would cost him less.

Since in our taxable society there are more Joneses than Smiths, there is a chance that the Joneses may outvote the Smiths, and get the legislation passed. But the Smiths are apt to get more vocal about the matter, and perhaps they can pull the Congress their way. In any event, an arbitrary and irrational element is injected into national-expenditure decisions that distorts them one way or the other.

Even the ancient faith that income taxes cannot be shifted from seller to buyer has begun to wane. That many corporations can, in certain circumstances, pass along part or all of their income tax by raising prices has long been evident. Many corporate executives insist that this is precisely what they do. The personal income tax may be a little harder to shift. But the level of taxes certainly is a feature in wage negotiations. And would many corporate salaries be quite so high if executives could not point to the need to compensate for the tax bite?

The troubles of the income tax are beginning to make the sales tax intellectually respectable again. The new support comes from curiously ill-assorted elements. There are those who are concerned about economic growth and who believe that a little less income tax and a little more sales tax would be an improvement over the present mix. There are old-fashioned conservatives who are mainly concerned with getting their high rates down, and who see in a Federal sales tax a means of making that possible. And there are the liberals who want to raise public expenditures and who, feeling that the income tax has been milked almost dry, are trying to overcome their innate aversion to sales taxes.

For most liberals, to be sure, the sales tax still carries a stigma. But avant-garde thinkers like Harvard professors Alvin Hansen and John Kenneth Galbraith have given support to a Federal sales tax. Galbraith has argued, possibly to the chagrin of some of his disciples, that in an age of affluence a sales tax no longer means what a bread tax or a salt tax meant in ages gone by. Hansen has calculated that the income tax simply cannot yield the kind of money he believes the government should spend. Some former critics have sought to make their peace with the sales tax by suggesting that it be coupled with a special tax on luxuries. All in all, the sales tax seems to be coming up in the world. And there is work for it to do.

In trying to establish priorities among the various objectives of contemporary tax policy, the goal of faster growth strikes me as by far the most important. Faster growth will, in fact, give everybody pretty much what he wants. It will make the cost of big government easier to bear for the well-to-do. It will permit larger public expenditures to satisfy the proponents of social priorities. If we can speed up growth by cutting back the income tax and introducing a Federal sales tax, the effort would be worth while.

The evidence that the maneuver will succeed is not conclusive, to be sure.

In any case, no very striking result could be expected from such a reform alone. But there probably is enough sensible economics behind the case to justify moving in that direction.

We would have to move cautiously, however, because pitfalls are sure to beset the unwary sales tax enthusiast. Sales taxes have been the province of state and local authorities. A Federal sales tax would have to be designed so as not to interefere with this traditional source of revenue.

The question of coverage needs to be faced. Should the tax cover only goods, or also services? Should food be excluded? Should the rate be the same for all items? If a great many things were excluded, to which purpose tremendous political pressures are sure to be mobilized, and if the rate were severely fragmented, we might end up with little more than what we have now —a set of arbitrary Federal excise taxes.

I do not believe that in the near future there is much hope of reaching a national consensus on any of these questions, or even on the basic principle of a Federal sales tax. The experience of this year's tax bill, on its tortuous way through Congress, has made clear how very difficult it is to reach agreement even on relatively minor tax reforms. As a practical matter, the most likely way in which we might some day get a Federal sales tax is through a national emergency calling for large extra revenues. A sales tax might then be introduced instead of or along with the traditional income tax hike. Obviously that is not a consummation to be wished.

*   *   *

52 THE EFFECT OF HIGH TAX RATES ON EXECUTIVE INCENTIVE

Crawford H. Greenewalt

Crawford H. Greenewalt is Chairman of the Board of E. I. du Pont de Nemours & Co.

*   *   *

. . . The views I shall express are those of an executive who must face the very practical problems involved in the operation of a large corporation. These, of course, embrace the present, and the usual problems of customer, employee, and stockholder relations. In a much more important sense, however, they are problems of the future and comprise, insofar as possible, the development of policies and practices which will insure continuing effective performance well beyond present horizons.

*   *   *

As our country has developed and matured, we have become increasingly dependent on an active and dynamic industry for our economic growth and prosperity. Without minimizing in the slightest the important contributions to our national economy made by the farmers, the professions, the service trades, the fact is that our standard of living is firmly anchored to our industrial development.

Since this is so, it follows that how business and industry fare must be a matter of great importance to all Americans. Their standard of living, their future well-being, are vitally dependent upon an American industry that continues to be dynamic, resourceful, and progressive. This desirable state of affairs can continue only so long as industry can compete successfully for the limited supply of talented people. For an industrial corporation is not a machine that can be run by automation. It is a team of human beings that must have first-class direction by intelligent and able management. And if we have learned one fundamental truth in industry, it is that first-class performance can never come from second-class performers.

*   *   *

The point I make is that industry, if it is to keep abreast of its responsibilities to the Nation, must have a great number of first-class minds at its disposal. It must compete for them with all other phases of our society, for there are never enough to go around. The fields of government, education, the military, the arts, the professions, all are seeking to persuade able young men to cast their lot with them. Each has its own type of incentive to offer, and the demand for talent always exceeds the supply.

THE ESSENTIAL QUESTION OF INCENTIVE

*   *   *

Adequate incentives, of course, differ with different people. Some are attracted most strongly by the promise of prestige. Some are more interested in leisure time, to follow scholarly pur-

Reprinted from *Federal Tax Policy for Economic Growth and Stability*. Papers Submitted by Panelists Appearing before the Subcommittee on Tax Policy, Joint Economic Committee on the Economic Report, November 9, 1955, pp. 185–188.

suits or perhaps simply to meditate upon the ills of the world. To some people, public notice or outward signs of rank and importance are alluring goals. Some seek power. For most, however, the strongest and probably the most desirable incentive is financial reward. Furthermore, financial reward is not only an incentive in itself; it is the only fluid medium that can be used to balance the attractions of the more intangible compensations, such as prestige, power, or public notice.

There is another aspect of the monetary incentive that seems to me worthy of comment. It is the only reward that can be cut down on a basis of fixed percentages. We do not, for example, withhold 91 percent of an Oscar going to the best moving-picture actress of the year. The winner of a Nobel prize does not have to give the Government a certain percentage of the prestige accruing to him. A brilliant violinist does not have to share his applause with the collector of internal revenue. These illustrations may seem facetious, yet they are based on a serious foundation, for we do in fact make the recipient of monetary rewards, and him alone, give up significant percentages in taxes. We are, that is, penalizing only one manifestation of success, and this seems to me, frankly, not only unfair but, for the future, a dangerous practice.

*   *   *

Business, for the most part, is in a poor position to compete in these intangible areas. With few exceptions executives of great ability remain relatively unknown. A player of even minor roles in the films, a leader of a jazz orchestra, or a writer of only average accomplishment may be far better known than many leaders of industry. For businessmen there are few medals, prizes, degrees, uniforms, patriotic citations, or grandiose honorifics. There are few featured players on the industrial stage.

There is, of course, the satisfaction that comes from work well done. But this is peculiar to no special section of our society; it is common to all. For the purposes of this discussion, it simply cancels out.

And so industry must rely most importantly on financial compensation. As it becomes increasingly less able to do so, it will lose its capacity to induce qualified people to make their careers in industry, or to seek to advance to their maximum capacity.

THE EROSION OF THE MONEY INCENTIVE

It is here, as I see it, that our danger lies. I am certain that the effectiveness of the money incentive is being eroded by the tax rates that prevail in the upper brackets today. While many companies are experimenting with nonmonetary incentives, basically industry must rely upon the coin of compensation must suitable to its character. I am afraid the raw truth is that, in the long run, we shall begin to lose out and our proportion of the available candidates will fall unless some relief can be obtained.

I am necessarily talking in the future tense, because it is quite clear that the point of concern is not the executive of today, or even of the immediate future. I think, if we are to focus the picture, we must rule out consideration of the present management group. I doubt that high personal taxation has had substantial effect upon the performance of present-day management people, even though they may not be happy over the realization that at top levels each additional dollar of gross income nets its earner about 9 cents. I confess to some pain in this respect myself, but I cannot say that I am inclined as a result to work less diligently or to take my responsibilities less seriously.

Today's executives are, I think, reasonably immune. By the time a man has reached a position of eminence within his organization, he is influenced importantly by his sense of loyalty, his sense of obligation, a preoccupying interest in the work, or, as has been unkindly suggested, by conditioned reflex.

The same applies, I would guess, to those who may be regarded as the immediate successors, for they too have reached a point where the challenge and associations of the work present an incentive that will probably override reduced financial motivations. . . .

There are two major areas of concern. There is, first, the effect of high income-tax rates on long-range monetary incentives, which promises to make it more difficult than heretofore to persuade young men with real ability to enter the rank of business. Let me make it clear that I am not asking for an improvement in industry's competitive position opposite the other fields of endeavor. I merely want to maintain it.

There is, second, increased difficulty, also tracing to high tax rates, in persuading men of ability who have risen to the point where they are in sight of reaching their top capacity to keep on going rather than to rest on their oars.

*   *   *

53   WHO PAYS THE TAXES?

Richard A. Musgrave

Richard A. Musgrave is Professor of Economics at Princeton University.

The incidence of taxation and the effects of taxation on consumption are closely related. In order to appraise the latter, we must know something about the former. At the same time, they pose distinct policy problems. The determination of who should pay the taxes and the equitable distribution of the tax bill is one important consideration of tax policy. The choice between taxes which fall on consumption and taxes which do not is another consideration, involving a quite different set of factors. In some cases, the two will support each other, and in others they will conflict.

I begin with my first topic, who pays the taxes. We have prepared in this

connection a revision of our earlier estimates of tax burden distribution for the year 1948. While there have been no drastic changes in tax structure, the great increase in income since that time has rendered the earlier figures of little use for present purposes. The methods followed are more or less similar to those of the earlier study. While the calculations were made in less detail, some of the criticisms of the earlier study were taken into account.

From "The Incidence of the Tax Structure and Its Effects on Consumption," in *Federal Tax Policy for Economic Growth and Stability,* Papers Submitted by Panelists Appearing before the Subcommittee on Tax Policy, Joint Economic Committee on the Economic Report, November 9, 1955, pp. 96–102.

Table 1

ESTIMATED DISTRIBUTION OF TAX PAYMENTS FOR 1954

[Percent of total yield contributed by income brackets]

	Spending unit income brackets (thousands of dollars)							
	0– $2,000	$2,000– $3,000	$3,000– $4,000	$4,000– $5,000	$5,000– $7,500	$7,500– $10,000	Over $10,000	Total
FEDERAL TAXES								
(1) Personal income tax	1.6	3.7	8.0	10.2	28.3	13.9	34.3	100
(2) Estate and gift taxes	....	....	....	....	....	....	100.0	100
(3) Corporate profits tax	3.3	4.5	6.3	6.8	15.0	6.9	57.1	100
(4) Excises	8.2	9.8	14.4	14.8	28.2	10.3	14.3	100
(5) Customs	8.2	9.8	14.4	14.8	28.2	10.3	14.3	100
(6) Social-insurance contribution	6.8	10.3	17.9	18.5	28.6	8.6	9.1	100
(7) Total	3.7	5.6	9.7	10.9	24.4	10.7	35.0	100
(8) Without social-insurance contribution	3.2	4.9	8.5	9.8	23.9	11.0	38.7	100
STATE AND LOCAL TAXES								
(9) Personal income tax	.2	2.3	6.0	7.2	22.0	12.7	49.5	100
(10) Inheritance and gift taxes	....	....	....	....	....	....	100.0	100
(11) Corporate profits tax	3.3	4.6	6.4	6.8	15.0	6.9	56.9	100
(12) Excise and sales taxes	8.2	9.8	14.4	14.8	28.2	10.3	14.3	100
(13) Property	7.0	8.4	13.0	13.9	25.7	10.0	22.1	100
(14) Social-insurance contribution	4.7	8.8	13.2	18.8	30.8	11.5	12.1	100
(15) Total	6.9	8.5	13.0	13.9	26.3	10.1	21.3	100
(16) Without social-insurance contribution	7.0	8.5	12.9	13.6	26.0	10.0	21.9	100
ALL LEVELS OF GOVERNMENT								
(17) Total	4.6	6.4	10.6	11.8	25.0	10.5	31.2	100
(18) Without social-insurance contribution	4.3	6.0	9.8	10.9	24.5	10.7	33.8	100

RESULTS OF STUDY

1. Over-all Picture

A brief summary of the methods and the underlying data will be found in the appendix. The results are summarized in table 1 which shows the pertentage distribution of taxpayments by spending unit income brackets. The data are for 1954 and both the Federal and the State and local tax structures are covered. In table 2 we show the so-called effective rates of tax, that is, the ratio of taxpayments to income received for the various income brackets. It is this ratio which we look upon to determine whether the tax structure is regressive or progressive, and by how much.

The estimated incidence of the total tax structure, including all levels of government and all taxes, is shown in line (17). We find that the incidence is progressive throughout the scale, although the degree of progression appears to be quite moderate over the lower and middle income ranges. The picture for the Federal tax structure alone is more distinctly progressive as shown in line (7). That for State and local taxes is regressive as shown in line (15).

The general picture may be qualified in two ways. For one thing some people feel that social insurance contribu-

Table 2

ESTIMATED EFFECTIVE RATES OF TAX FOR 1954

[*Tax as percent of income*]

	Spending unit income brackets (thousands of dollars)							
	0– $2,000	$2,000– $3,000	$3,000– $4,000	$4,000– $5,000	$5,000– $7,500	$7,500– $10,000	Over $10,000	*Total*
FEDERAL TAXES								
(1) Personal income tax	3.1	5.3	7.1	8.4	11.5	14.2	14.6	10.7
(2) Estate and gift taxes	....	....	....	....	....	....	1.4	.3
(3) Corporate profits tax	3.7	3.8	3.3	3.2	3.6	4.1	14.1	6.2
(4) Excises	5.0	4.5	4.1	3.9	3.6	3.3	1.9	3.4
(5) Customs	2.3	.3	.2	.2	.2	.2	.1	.2
(6) Social-insurance con- tribution	3.6	4.1	4.4	4.2	3.2	2.4	1.1	3.0
(7) Total	15.7	17.9	19.1	20.0	22.2	24.2	33.2	23.8
(8) Without social-insur- ance contribution	12.1	13.8	14.7	15.8	19.0	21.8	32.1	20.9
STATE AND **LOCAL TAXES**								
(9) Personal income tax	.01	.1	.2	.2	.4	.5	.8	.4
(10) Inheritance and gift taxes	....	....	....	....	....	....	.4	.1
(11) Corporate profits tax	.2	.2	.1	.1	.2	.2	.6	.3
(12) Excise and sales taxes	5.7	5.1	4.6	4.4	4.2	3.8	2.2	3.9
(13) Property	4.8	4.3	4.1	4.1	3.8	3.6	3.4	3.8
(14) Social-insurance con- tribution	.5	.7	.7	.9	.7	.6	.3	5.9
(15) Total	11.2	10.4	9.8	9.8	9.1	8.8	7.7	9.1
(16) Without social-insur- ance contribution	10.7	9.7	9.1	8.9	8.4	8.1	7.4	8.5
ALL LEVELS OF **GOVERNMENT**								
(17) Total	26.9	28.3	28.9	29.8	31.3	33.0	40.9	32.9
(18) Without social-insur- ance contribution	22.8	23.5	23.8	24.7	27.4	29.9	39.5	29.4

tions (all or in part) ought not to be counted since they go to purchase special benefits which are not included in the picture. While I don't quite subscribe to this view, those who do will find the overall picture excluding social-security taxes in lines (8), (16), and (18). As shown in line (8) this makes for a more progressive picture, especially at the lower end of the scale.

A second qualification arises from the definition of income. It will be noted that the distribution of taxpayments shown in table 1 is essentially independent of the income concept used. But the pattern of effective rates shown in table 2 reflects both the distribution of taxpayments and the distribution of income; and the distribution of income in turn depends on the particular income concept that is used. The pattern of effective rates shown in table 2 is based on a concept of adjusted money income, including outright money income as defined by the Survey Research Center plus imputations for (a) capital gains and fiduciary incomes, and (b) retained earnings of corporations and the unshifted part of the corporation tax. The items under (b) must be included in the concept of income in order to permit a fair computation of effective rates because the entire unshifted part of the corporation tax is imputed to the shareholder. Now it might be argued that this is too narrow a concept, that allowance should be made also for other

Table 3

EFFECTIVE RATES USING BROADER INCOME CONCEPT

[*Tax as percent of income*]

	Spending unit income brackets (thousands of dollars)							
	0–$2,000	$2,000–$3,000	$3,000–$4,000	$4,000–$5,000	$5,000–$7,500	$7,500–$10,000	Over $10,000	Total
FEDERAL TAXES								
(1) Personal income tax	2.7	4.7	6.4	7.6	10.6	13.2	14.0	9.9
(2) Estate and gift taxes	....	....	....	....	....	....	1.3	.3
(3) Corporation profits tax	3.2	3.4	3.0	2.9	3.3	3.8	13.5	5.7
(4) Excises	4.4	4.0	3.7	3.5	3.4	3.1	1.9	3.1
(5) Customs	.3	.3	.2	.2	.2	.2	.1	.2
(6) Social-insurance contribution	3.1	3.7	4.0	3.8	3.0	2.3	1.0	2.7
(7) Total	13.7	16.1	17.3	18.0	20.5	22.6	31.8	22.0
(8) Without social-insurance contribution	10.5	12.4	13.3	14.2	17.5	20.3	30.8	19.3
STATE AND LOCAL TAXES								
(9) Personal income tax	.01	.1	.2	.2	.3	.5	.8	.4
(10) Inheritance and gift taxes	....	....	....	....	....	....	.4	.1
(11) Corporation profits tax	.1	.2	.1	.1	.1	.2	.6	.3
(12) Excise and sales taxes	5.0	4.6	4.2	4.0	3.9	3.5	2.1	3.6
(13) Property	4.2	3.9	3.8	3.7	3.5	3.4	3.2	3.5
(14) Social-insurance contribution	.4	.6	.6	.8	.6	.6	.3	.5
(15) Total	9.8	9.4	8.9	8.8	8.4	8.2	7.4	8.4
(16) Without social-insurance contribution	9.3	8.7	8.3	8.0	7.8	7.6	7.1	7.9
ALL LEVELS OF GOVERNMENT								
(17) Total	23.4	25.5	26.2	26.8	28.9	30.8	39.2	30.4
(18) Without social-insurance contribution	19.9	21.1	21.6	22.2	25.3	27.9	37.9	27.1

items of imputed income such as rental value of residences, food consumed on farms, employer contributions to pension funds, and so forth. In table 3 we repeat the results of table 2, using such a broader income concept. Since the imputed income thus added is distributed more equally than money income, a somewhat larger fraction of total income comes to be allocated to the lower groups. Since the distribution of taxpayments remains the same, the pattern of effective rates becomes slightly more progressive for the case of the Federal and slightly less regressive for the case of the State and local tax system.

In appraising the total picture, we are thus left with four patterns, shown in lines (17) and (18) of tables 2 and 3. Which of these is the most meaningful pattern is essentially a matter of judgment. While I see good reasons for thinking in terms of lines (17) and (18) of table 2, some readers may wish to operate with the broader income concept; and others may wish to use an even broader base including, say, an imputed income for the services performed by housewives.

2. Particular Taxes

We now turn to the role of particular taxes in bringing about this overall pattern of incidence.

Personal income tax.—Turning again to table 2, we find that the Federal personal income tax is the most distinctly progressive element in the tax structure. As shown in line (1), this feature does not only apply to the middle and higher income ranges but also at the lower end of the scale. This, I think, is a factor of paramount importance for Federal tax policy and a strong reason for placing primary emphasis on the personal income tax. The progressivity of State income taxes is more moderate, as shown in line (9). In estimating the incidence of these taxes, we assume in both cases that income-tax payments stay put with the taxpayer.

Estate and gift tax.—The estate and gift tax is a highly progressive part of the tax structure. If we assume that the tax falls on the donor, we will not be far off if we allocate the total amount to the top income bracket. If we assume it to fall on the recipient, some of the burden might accrue to the lower brackets, but the amount will be small. While the estate and gift tax is a highly progressive element in the tax structure, its weight in the total picture is very slight.

Corporation income tax.—The estimated incidence of the corporation income tax, as shown in lines (3) and (11), follows a ∪-shaped pattern. It is more or less proportional or even regressive over the lower to middle range of the income scale and becomes progressive only in the higher brackets. This somewhat surprising result reflects two factors which enter the analysis. One factor is the assumption that two-thirds of the corporation tax is borne by the shareholder while one-third is passed on to the consumer. Thus one-third of the corporation tax is in fact treated as a sales tax, with a correspondingly heavier burden on the lower income groups. While I am not in a

position to prove that this is the true ratio, I believe that theoretical reasoning as well as empirical observation renders this a much more defensible assumption than the standard textbook proposition that the corporation tax cannot be shifted except through its effects on capital formation. A second factor is that the ratio of dividend to other income is higher in the lower than in the middle income brackets, reflecting the importance of retirement income in the low brackets. To the extent that the corporation tax falls on the shareholder, the lower income brackets thus assume a proportionately larger burden than may be expected. Certain other methodological problems of the corporation tax case (in particular, the treatment of retained earnings and tax thereon) were discussed at length in the 1948 study and need not be repeated here.

These results as well as certain other considerations suggest that the corporation tax is not as progressive an element of the tax structure as some people believe it to be. Indeed, the popularity (insofar as taxes can be popular) of the corporation tax may well be due to the fact that its friends consider it to be highly progressive, while those who prefer it to the personal income tax suspect that in fact it is pretty much in the nature of a sales tax. Both can't be right at the same time. The incidence of the corporation tax, unnecessarily to say, is of crucial importance to tax policy. It has immediate bearing on the problem of integration and to me implies a strong argument in favor of the dividend credit (at the corporate level) approach. Also, it is of evident importance to the choice between taxes on consumption and taxes on investment.

Excises and customs.—The estimated incidence of excise and custom duties, shown in lines (4), (5), and

(12) of table 2, is distinctly regressive throughout the income scale. This result is based on the assumption that such taxes are paid for by the consumer and reflects the familiar fact that consumption expenditures decline as a percent of income when moving up the income scale. The assumption that such taxes are paid by the consumer is not beyond dispute, but I believe that it is a rather sensible one.

Property tax.—The estimated incidence of the property tax, shown in line (13), is again regressive, though less so at the upper end of the scale than that of excise and sales taxes. The general principle, in estimating the incidence of this tax is that the part assessed on owner-occupied residences rests on the owner, the part assessed on the improvement component in business property (including rental housing) rests on the consumer, and the part assessed on the rent component of business property rests on the owner. Farm real estate is treated as business property and a more detailed statement of our procedure is given in the appendix.

Social insurance contributions.— The estimated incidence of social insurance contributions, shown in lines (6) and (14) is progressive up to the $4,000 income range and becomes regressive thereafter. In arriving at this result, it was assumed that the employee contribution and one-half of the employer contribution fall upon the employee; and that one-half of the employer contribution is passed on to the consumer.

CONCLUSIONS

It goes without saying that the above estimates of tax incidence must be used with reservation. They do not constitute the results of laboratory experiments which unfortunately are not at the economist's disposal. Nor do they involve as exhaustive a statistical analysis as might be undertaken. All sorts of theoretical and methodological qualifications apply which were discussed in connection with the 1948 study and which need not be repeated here.

In spite of these reservations some such information is needed for intelligent policymaking, and the picture here presented should give a fair approximation to the distribution of tax-payments. The primary conclusion, as I read it, remains that the overall tax structure in the United States is but moderately progressive over the crucial range of middle incomes, extending from, say, $2,000 to $10,000 and including nearly three-quarters of all spending units. Whether this is good or bad from the point of view of equity is not for the economist to say, but it is a factor to be kept in mind in future tax legislation. Secondly, let me draw your attention to the sharp distinction in the incidence of the Federal and the State-local tax package, and what this implies for future trends in our fiscal structure. Finally, there is the distinction in the incidence pattern of particular taxes, and the somewhat surprising role of the corporation tax.

* * *

THE INTERNATIONAL ECONOMY

A.

INTERNATIONAL TRADE

54. U. S. Exports Provide Jobs

New York Times

The effects of international trade on domestic employment are not always easy to see. This article reports that in 1960, 3.1 million Americans had jobs which depended on our export trade.

55. Are We Exporting Jobs?

John Fayerweather

Many American firms have established manufacturing plants abroad to serve their overseas markets. Professor Fayerweather argues that these plants compete primarily with foreign producers and that they actually help home employment because they provide a market for American machinery and parts abroad.

56. Petition From the Manufacturers of Candles

Frederic Bastiat

Do we need a tariff to shut out the sunlight so as to create jobs for candle-makers? In a classic satire, Frederic Bastiat exposes the fallacies underlying the argument that we need tariffs to protect workers against "unfair" foreign competition.

57. A "Free Trade" Warning

Cleveland M. Bailey

Not everyone believes in freer international trade. Congressman Bailey of West Virginia argues that American coal miners have lost jobs because of the "unfair competition of an imported waste product" (residual fuel oil) which is used as a substitute for coal.

B.
TARIFF AND TRADE POLICIES

58.   High Tariff and World Trade: 1920–1932

Victor L. Albjerg

Following World War I, the United States embarked on a high-tariff policy which lasted for many years. Professor Albjerg describes the process of tariff making and analyzes the impact of this policy on our international trade and the attitudes of European nations.

59.   Common Market-Lesson in Trade Expansion

Irving B. Kravis

The European Common Market is the biggest international economic development of our generation. Professor Kravis analyzes its success to date, and contrasts and compares it with American experience and trade policy.

C.
INTERNATIONAL FINANCE

60.   International Financial Problems and Policies

Alfred Hayes

Mr. Hayes explains how the U. S. dollar has become an international "key currency" and the implications this development has for our domestic and international monetary policies. We are now "banker to the world," with new responsibilities and new problems, including proper management of our gold reserves.

61.   Requirements of an Effective International Monetary Mechanism

Subcommittee on International Exchange and Payments

Does the world have enough gold and other monetary reserves to prevent liquidity crises and deflationary pressures as national economies and world trade grow? A congressional committee analyzes alternative plans to assure adequate liquidity and a smoothly functioning international monetary mechanism.

62.   International Transmission of Business Cycles: Comment

Emile Despres

In this article Professor Despres argues that business cycles are no longer likely to be transmitted directly from one country to another through international monetary channels. But widely varying rates of technological advance may nevertheless create difficult balance of payments problems, which may require new adjustment processes and new international monetary arrangements.

A.

INTERNATIONAL TRADE

54   U. S. EXPORTS PROVIDE JOBS

The New York Times

About 3,100,000 workers in the United States owed their jobs to the nation's export trade in 1960, the Labor Department reported today.

They were employed in that year to produce, transport and market $20,-700,000,000 worth of merchandise sold overseas, according to a study prepared by the Bureau of Labor Statistics.

The total of 3,100,000 jobs represents about one-seventeenth of the jobs in the private sector of the economy. The over-all job total in the United States has been about 67,000,000 in recent months.

The study was released in conjunction with President Kennedy's message to Congress on foreign trade. Mr. Kennedy asked new authority to negotiate lower tariffs and to assist workers and industries affected by competing imports.

The bureau found that about 13 per cent of the total farm employment and 8 per cent of manufacturing employment was attributable to exports, with considerably higher percentages for such industries as chemicals and nonelectrical machinery.

"Study Shows Exports Provide Jobs for 3.1 Million in the U.S.," *The New York Times,* January 26, 1962; copyright by *The New York Times.* Reprinted by permission.

Jack Alterman, assistant chief of the bureau's division of productivity and technological developments, said there was no reliable figure on the post-war trend in export-generated employment. Exports have increased since 1945, but so has the amount produced by each worker.

"It is possible there has been relatively little change, or possibly a decline," he said.

Studies are under way dealing with the impact of imports on domestic job opportunities in 1960 and, for comparison purposes, on the export-import employment picture in 1953, Mr. Alterman said.

Of the 3,100,000 jobs created by exports in 1960, the report said, about 48 per cent were involved directly in the production, transportation and marketing of exported goods. The remainder came in supporting industries, as in making the steel contained in exported machinery, for example, or fabricating the tires and upholstery on an exported auto.

About 2,100,000 of the export-created jobs were in nonfarm occupations. The individual manufacturing groups that were most affected were chemicals, primary metals, machinery and automobiles and trucks.

In 1960, the report said, the United States, including Alaska and Hawaii, exported merchandise valued at about $20,700,000,000, including military and economic aid. With transportation, insurance, and Federal export payments for farm and food products added, it said, the total industrial output attributable to exports was $22,055,300,000.

The leading industries helped by exports were nonelectrical machinery, with 15.5 per cent of its employment attributable to exports; primary metals, including steel, 14.4 per cent; chemicals and allied products, 14.4 per cent; tobacco products, 12.8 per cent; scientific and control instruments, 10.2 per cent, and transportation equipment, 7.8 per cent.

The trade and service industries were affected least, with only 2.1 per cent work forces affected by exports.

"It should be noted," the report stated, "that the share of the machinery and primary metals industries in total export employment would be even higher if it were possible to distribute by industry the indirect employment attributable to military goods production and employment attributable to replacement of plant and equipment."

55   ARE WE EXPORTING JOBS?

John Fayerweather

John Fayerweather is Professor of International Business at New York University.

"Smith-Corona has announced that it is transferring its production of portable typewriters to a new European plant. The operations in Syracuse, N.Y. will be closed down and several hundred workers laid off."

If this news item reported an isolated incident, it would mean little to our economy. But the incident is not

Excerpted from *Challenge,* July, 1962, pp. 22–25. Reprinted by permission.

isolated. In recent years a multitude of companies have set up new plants abroad which have taken over production formerly handled by U.S. factories. The steady growth of foreign manufacture by U.S. companies adds up to a major revolution in the pattern of our industry.

Is this revolution progress? Or is it dangerous to our economic health? These are crucial questions that must be answered. They underlie major policy decisions in the areas of foreign trade and taxes which are presently confronting Congress.

         *   *   *

It is readily apparent that U.S. labor is displaced when a product is shifted from export to overseas production. For this reason it is easy to leap to the Senator's conclusion that American jobs would be saved if the process of foreign investment were checked. But the story is by no means as simple as that.

A few facts outlining the evolution of our overseas business in manufactured products will provide a good starting point for unraveling this story. First of all, our exports of finished manufactures have almost doubled since the end of World War II, rising from a 1946–50 average of $6.5 billion per year to $11.4 billion in 1960.

The output of U.S. overseas factories was not reported in government statistics until 1957, so we must judge the trend prior to that by investment figures. In the postwar era manufacturing investments abroad almost quadrupled, increasing from $2.8 billion in 1946 to $11.1 billion in 1960. In 1957 our manufacturing units overseas had a production volume of $18.3 billion. By 1960 their output had risen to $24 billion. In over-all terms, it is clear that while overseas manufacture has grown more rapidly and is now larger than exports, there has not been an absolute loss of exports in the postwar period.

Looking at specific industries, we find a more confused picture. The exports of some industries show a notable increase; exports of chemical specialties, for example, rose from an average of $155 million between 1946 and 1950 to $663 million in 1960. This growth represents the response to the demand created by industrial expansion abroad for a wide range of the products of advanced U.S. chemical research.

Similarly, industrial machinery exports increased from an average of $1.2 billion in the 1946–50 period to $2.5 billion in 1960. During 1961 foreign orders were accounting for about one-third of the total business of the U.S. machine tool industry. Industrialization in the underdeveloped countries and the European boom stimulated sales of a great assortment of machines, of which the United States is the dominant producer.

Exports in other industries have not fared so well. Shipments of passenger cars, for example, declined from 153,000 units in 1950 to 145,000 units in 1960, though the increase in prices raised the value of these exports from $179 million to $235 million. Data on output of all U.S. overseas auto plants is not available, but a good measure of the change is indicated by the increase in the number of General Motors cars and trucks manufactured abroad; whereas about 200,000 GM vehicles were produced abroad in 1951, in 1960 about 800,000 were produced. The rapidly growing market for automobiles overseas, especially in Europe, is being supplied for the most part by products made in foreign plants, and not by export.

Taken by themselves, the statistics for automobiles and other products whose exports have declined provide a solid base for the "exporting jobs" argument. Looking at the automobile situation, for example, one might readily agree with Sen. Gore's conclusion that, if General Motors had not expanded its plants abroad so rapidly, a large number of men would have been employed in Detroit making cars for export to the burgeoning foreign market.

Digging still deeper into the facts, however, we find that the switch to overseas manufacture has generally been a forced one and that in many cases it has actually preserved exports which might otherwise have been lost.

By and large, U.S. manufacturers would rather make products in the United States and export them abroad. This arrangement minimizes the economic and political risks which are substantial in many of the less developed countries and exist to some degree even in Europe or Canada. It simplifies operating control and utilizes capacity more effectively.

Each of Caterpillar Tractor Company's plants abroad is exposed to some risk. In Brazil political upheaval is a constant possibility and the country's financial condition is precarious. Australia, Britain and France are politically more stable, but each has had financial problems suggesting some risk for Caterpillar. And from a management control point of view, it would be much simpler to have all the operations in Peoria. Much duplication in production equipment and personnel could be eliminated and facilities could be utilized more efficiently.

For example, during the 1960–61 recession, tractor sales in the United States fell off, but they were booming abroad. With operations centralized in one plant, production volume could have been balanced better as sales rose in some areas of the world and fell in others. All in all, life would be much simpler and safer for the Caterpillar management, if they did not have plants scattered around the world.

Thus, the first instinct of most managements is to stick with exporting and the decision to manufacture abroad in order to meet the economic necessities of the current world situation is usually made with reluctance. A large portion of the foreign factories have been set up because of import restrictions which threatened to cut off export markets completely. In one extensive study of investment decisions, 48 per cent of the companies said they were "forced to invest to maintain markets." In the typical case, a country anxious to develop its local industry or to save foreign exchange imposes or threatens to impose import restrictions. The U.S. company has the simple choice of starting manufacture or losing the market.

In earlier years, U.S. businessmen often looked upon import restrictions as temporary checks and they were slow to move into manufacturing. In Australia for example, the H. J. Heinz Company had built up a good market for its soups when, in 1931, import restrictions were imposed suddenly, cutting off the market. Heinz did not decide to go into manufacturing in Australia until 1935. By then they found that the reputation they had built up for their brand name by years of promotion had largely been lost. It took 10 years of patient rebuilding to establish the company's market position again.

Made wiser by such experiences, most U.S. companies now accept the fact that import controls are likely to be a permanent barrier, and they realize that they must manufacture if they are to protect their business. To avoid having to start up production on a crash basis, managements try to get their manufacturing plans going somewhat before controls actually hit them. This is usually quite practical because most foreign governments give early warnings of import restrictions. For many months, and often years before imports are stopped, government officials will indicate their intentions by suggestions, threats and other signals designed to push the companies into local manufacture.

Often the future course of government policy is clearly set out in industrial development plans which state the areas in which local production will be promoted. The handwriting is then on the wall. To avoid a hasty decision under pressure, to get a jump on other manufacturers or to make a good impression on the government, the U.S. company starts manufacturing.

* * *

Besides these import restriction situations, there are a large number of manufacturing investment decisions which are responses to basic cost-profit economies. As sales abroad expand, large-scale production with cost savings is possible. The economies of production, combined with lower transportation costs and lower wages, have made the supplying of certain markets from overseas factories more profitable than exporting from the United States. The typewriter business is a notable case in point. In 1960 both Smith-Corona and Remington Rand switched their production of portable typewriters from plants in the United States to European factories where costs were lower.

Such profit-oriented decisions might seem to be exactly what Sen. Gore is inveighing against. The implication is that U.S. capital is deliberately cutting down U.S. exports, and thus jobs, solely for selfish profit motives. In the current rough world competition, however, it is more a decision for survival than for greater profit.

A company that sticks to export, when the economics of this situation favor overseas manufacture, runs a good chance of losing its market completely to competitors. The competition may come from another U.S. company, or from a German or perhaps a Japanese firm. But there are so many aggressive international companies today that it is safe to assume that any cost advantage from overseas manufacture will be quickly seized by someone. Thus, the company that does not capitalize on these cost advantages is not, in the long run, helping to save U.S. exports.

The decisions of Smith-Corona and Remington Rand seem, if anything, to have been dangerously slow. European firms like Olivetti were making deep inroads into the market for portable typewriters both in the United States and overseas. The U.S. companies had already lost a great deal of ground and were not operating profitably. Smith-Corona had a large loss in 1960. Underwood, after years of deficits, had been bought out by Olivetti. Thus the shift to European production wsa long overdue and essential to meet foreign competition.

* * *

In the principal Latin American countries, the U.S. companies have been under varying degrees of government pressure to increase the number of locally manufactured components used in cars. At first, the companies resisted this pressure strongly, arguing as in India that it was economically unsound. However, they have steadily come around to conformance with government wishes, prompted especially by the aggressive invasion of these markets by the German and Italian companies.

Fiat, Volkswagen and others have moved quickly and effectively into overseas manufacture, sometimes in partnership with the local governments. Despite belated efforts to make up for lost time, the U.S. companies have lost a substantial share of their markets, especially in Brazil and Mexico, to these competitors.

The evolution of the automobile industry in Europe is all too familiar to the American public. The little Volkswagens, Citroens, etc., which populate our highways are ample evidence of the economic competitiveness of European manufacturers. The market for cars in most European countries has now expanded to the point where a considerable degree of mass production is possible. This, combined with wages a half to a third of those in Detroit, gives European manufacture a strong cost and profit edge over products made here. Thus the U.S. companies have had no choice but to virtually abandon export to Europe, expanding their factories to produce there and even to import into the United States.

With minor variations, this story could be retold for most of our export industries: farm equipment, radios, drugs and so on down the line. It is not a "good" story in that export jobs have clearly been lost. But it is equally clear that the jobs would not have been saved if the company had insisted on sticking to exports. On the contrary, employment has been sustained through export of parts and machinery. This is the other major aspect of the subject overlooked by Sen. Gore.

When foreign manufacturers take over a part of our export market, our loss is usually complete because they draw all the imports they need from their home base. For example, when the Fiat automobile plant in Mexico needs tools, dies or parts, it buys them from Italy. But where we have held markets by establishing factories, we retain at least a position of our export volume. Sometimes the portion is large; the U.S. auto plants in Mexico, for example, still import a large percentage of their parts besides some specialized machinery. In other cases, such as soap manufacture, the exports are small, but even there the needs for machinery are significant.

The total benefit to our exports from this source is impressive. According to the 1957 government census, U.S. overseas operations purchased 10 per cent of their material requirements from the United States. Thus, approximately \$2 billion of our exports were sold to our overseas factories in the form of parts, basic chemicals, etc.

The census figures do not include purchases of plant equipment, but, according to a *Business Week* study, 40 per cent of the \$1.7 billion of new capital sent overseas for direct investments in 1960 was in the form of U.S. machinery and other exports. Setting these figures beside our total exports of around \$20 billion per year, it is evident that U.S. investments abroad have been a notable factor in sustaining our exports.

To sum up, the substitution of overseas manufacture is not desirable either for individual companies or for the country as a whole. But it is an inevitable adjustment to the growing and changing world economy. Far from being an avoidable form of "exporting jobs," it is the only way we can hold our share of world markets against foreign competition. Moreover, it permits us to keep a significant volume of exports in the form of machinery and materials, which otherwise would be completely lost.

56 PETITION FROM THE MANUFACTURERS OF CANDLES

Frederic Bastiat

"Petition from the Manufacturers of Candles, Wax-lights, Lamps, Chandeliers, Reflectors, Snuffers, Extinguishers; and From the Producers of Tallow, Oil, Resin, Alcohol, and Generally of Every Thing Used for Lights."

Frederic Bastiat was a noted French economist of the nineteenth century.

To the Honorable the Members of the Chamber of Deputies:

"GENTLEMEN,—You are in the right way: you reject abstract theories; abundance, cheapness, concerns you little. You are entirely occupied with the interest of the producer, whom you are anxious to free from foreign competition. In a word, you wish to secure the *national market* to *national labor*.

"We come now to offer you an admirable opportunity for the application of your —— what shall we say? your theory? no, nothing is more deceiving than theory;—your doctrine? your system? your principle? But you do not like doctrines; you hold systems in horror; and, as for principles, you declare that there are no such things in political economy. We will say then, your practice; your practice without theory, and without principle.

"We are subjected to the intolerable competition of a foreign rival, who enjoys, it would seem, such superior facilities for the production of light, that he is enabled to *inundate* our *national market* at so exceedingly reduced a price, that, the moment he makes his appearance, he draws off all custom from us; and thus an important branch of French industry, with all its innumerable ramifications, is suddenly reduced to a state of complete stagnation. This rival, who is no other than

the sun, carries on so bitter a war against us, that we have every reason to believe that he has been excited to this course by our prefidious neighbor England. (Good diplomacy this, for the present time!) In this belief we are confirmed by the fact that in all his transactions with this proud island, he is much more moderate and careful than with us.

"Our petition is, that it would please your honorable body to pass a law whereby shall be directed the shutting up of all windows, dormers, sky-lights, shutters, curtains, vasistas, œil-de-bœufs, in a word, all openings, holes, chinks and fissures through which the light of the sun is used to penetrate into our dwellings, to the prejudice of the profitable manufactures which we flatter ourselves we have been enabled to bestow upon the country; which country cannot, therefore, without ingratitude, leave us now to struggle unprotected through so unequal a contest.

"We pray your honorable body not to mistake our petition for a satire, nor to repulse us without at least hearing the reasons which we have to advance in its favor.

"And first, if, by shutting out as much as possible all access to natural light, you thus create the necessity for

_____

From *Sophisms of Protection* (New York: G. P. Putnam's Sons, 1874), pp. 73–80.

artificial light, is there in France an industrial pursuit which will not, through some connection with this important object, be benefited by it?

"If more tallow be consumed, there will arise a necessity for an increase of cattle and sheep. Thus artificial meadows must be in greater demand; and meat, wool, leather, and above all, manure, this basis of agricultural riches, must become more abundant.

"If more oil be consumed, it will cause an increase in the cultivation of the olive-tree. This plant, luxuriant and exhausting to the soil, will come in good time to profit by the increased fertility which the raising of cattle will have communicated to our fields.

"Our heaths will become covered with resinous trees. Numerous swarms of bees will gather upon our mountains the perfumed treasures, which are now cast upon the winds, useless as the blossoms from which they emanate. There is, in short, no branch of agriculture which would not be greatly developed by the granting of our petition.

"Navigation would equally profit. Thousands of vessels would soon be employed in the whale fisheries, and thence would arise a navy capable of sustaining the honor of France, and of responding to the patriotic sentiments of the undersigned petitioners, candle merchants, etc.

"But what words can express the magnificence which *Paris* will then exhibit! Cast an eye upon the future and behold the gildings, the bronzes, the magnificent crystal chandeliers, lamps, reflectors and candelabras, which will glitter in the spacious stores, compared with which the splendor of the present day will appear trifling and insignificant.

"There is none, not even the poor manufacturer of resin in the midst of his pine forests, nor the miserable miner in his dark dwelling, but who would enjoy an increase of salary and of comforts.

"Gentlemen, if you will be pleased to reflect, you cannot fail to be convinced that there is perhaps not one Frenchman, from the opulent stock holder of Anzin down to the poorest vender of matches, who is not interested in the success of our petition.

"We foresee your objections, gentlemen; but there is not one that you can oppose to us which you will not be obliged to gather from the works of the partisans of free trade. We dare challenge you to pronounce one word against our petition, which is not equally opposed to your own practice and the principle which guides your policy.

"Do you tell us, that if we gain by this protection, France will not gain, the consumer must pay the price of it?

"We answer you:

"You have no longer any right to cite the interest of the consumer. For whenever this has been found to compete with that of the producer, you have invariably sacrificed the first. You have done this to *encourage labor,* to *increase the demand for labor.* The same reason should now induce you to act in the same manner.

"You have yourselves already answered the objection. When you were told: The consumer is interested in the free introduction of iron, coal, corn, wheat, cloths, etc., your answer was: Yes, but the producer is interested in their exclusion. Thus, also, if the consumer is interested in the admission of light, we, the producers, pray for its interdiction.

"You have also said, the producer and the consumer are one. If the manufacturer gains by protection, he will cause the agriculturist to gain also; if agriculture prospers, it opens a market for manufactured goods. Thus we, if you confer upon us the monopoly of furnishing light during the day, will as a first consequence buy large quantities of tallow, coals, oil, resin, wax, alcohol, silver, iron, bronze, crystal, for the supply of our business; and then we and our numerous contractors having become rich, our consumption will be great, and will become a means of contributing to the comfort and competency of the workers in every branch of national labor.

"Will you say that the light of the sun is a gratuitous gift, and that to repulse gratuitous gifts, is to repulse riches under pretence of encouraging the means of obtaining them?

"Take care,—you carry the death-blow to your own policy. Remember that hitherto you have always repulsed foreign produce, *because* it was an approach to a gratuitous gift, and *the more in proportion* as this approach was more close. You have, in obeying the wishes of other monopolists, acted only from a *half-motive;* to grant our petition there is a much *fuller inducement.* To repulse us, precisely for the reason that our case is a more complete one than any which have preceded it, would be to lay down the following equation: $+ \times + = -$; in other words, it would be to accumulate absurdity upon absurdity.

"Labor and Nature concur in different proportions, according to country and climate, in every article of production. The portion of Nature is always gratuitous; that of labor alone regulates the price.

"If a Lisbon orange can be sold at half the price of a Parisian one, it is because a natural and gratuitous heat does for the one, what the other only obtains from an artificial and consequently expensive one.

"When, therefore, we purchase a Portuguese orange, we may say that we obtain it half gratuitously and half by the right of labor; in other words,

at *half price* compared to those of Paris.

"Now it is precisely on account of this *demi-gratuity* (excuse the word) that you argue in favor of exclusion. How, you say, could national labor sustain the competition of foreign labor, when the first has every thing to do, and the last is rid of half the trouble, the sun taking the rest of the business upon himself? If then the *demi-gratuity* can determine you to check competition, on what principle can the *entire gratuity* be alleged as a reason for admitting it? You are no logicians if, refusing the demi-gratuity as hurtful to human labor, you do not *à fortiori,* and with double zeal, reject the full gratuity.

"Again, when any article, as coal, iron, cheese, or cloth, comes to us from foreign countries with less labor than if we produced it ourselves, the difference in price is a *gratuitous gift* conferred upon us; and the gift is more or less considerable, according as the difference is greater or less. It is the quarter, the half, or the three-quarters of the value of the produce, in proportion as the foreign merchant requires the three-quarters, the half, or the quarter of the price. It is as complete as possible when the producer offers, as the sun does with light, the whole in free gift. The question is, and we put it formally, whether you wish for France the benefit of gratuitous consumption, or the supposed advantages of laborious production. Choose, but be consistent. And does it not argue the greatest inconsistency to check as you do the importation of coal, iron, cheese, and goods of foreign manufacture, merely because and even in proportion as their price approaches *zero,* while at the same time you freely admit, and without limitation, the light of the sun, whose price is during the whole day at *zero?*"

Cleveland M. Bailey

Cleveland M. Bailey is United States Congressman from West Virginia.

Rep. Cleveland M. Bailey (D., W. Va.), a staunch friend of the American coal industry and its workers, had some remarks to make in the House of Representatives recently that ought to be of interest to all American businessmen and working people in the light of the new Kennedy administration "free trade" bill.

Representative Bailey, who is running for reelection to the Congress, introduced his remarks by noting that the American coal industry "exemplifies better than any other industry in America, the value of the free-enterprise system." He pointed out that coal is an industry that in the past decade lost more than one-third of its total business to oil and natural gas. But, said Bailey, it "got off the floor and labor, management and capital all combined to fight back."

Bailey added:

Mr. John L. Lewis, the head of the *United Mine Workers,* recognized the fact that only through increased productivity could labor get higher wages. He advocated, on the one hand, increased mechanization and, on the other hand, he would not condone featherbedding. He wanted for his Union members only their share of the machine's profit, to which they are thoroughly entitled.

Over the years, productivity per man and daily wages have substantially increased.

AMERICAN COAL COSTS LESS

In spite of all this, and the depreciated dollar, the price of bituminous coal has not advanced in ten years and, in fact, it is slightly lower today than it was ten years ago. In addition, American bituminous coal can be sold in Germany, England, France, and Belgium—all producers of coal—at from $2 to $4 per ton less than those countries can produce it, and is of superior quality. Every one of these countries protects its home coal industry and either limits or entirely prevents the importation of American coal through quotas, tariffs, government licenses, et cetera. As an example, British steel mills recently petitioned their government to import American coking coal, as it was $2 to $3 a ton cheaper than British coal and of better quality, but were refused a license.

Now, with this magnificent record, what is this industry confronted with? A waste product left over from the processing of crude oil overseas—well named 'residual oil'—that is either thrown away or sold at whatever price it can get. This, of course, is noncompetitive in price, and it could be dumped in this country at less than the cost of producing coal at the mines. To give some protection against this waste product, the President in 1959 ordered a quota established on residual oil because the national security was threatened. Since 1959, however, the quantity of residual oil allowed to be imported under this quota has been increased almost 50 percent, including a recent 10-percent increase by the Secretary of the Interior. Thus the quota continues to be weakened until there is very little protection left in it for the American bituminous coal industry.

The latest 10-percent increase means

"A 'Free Trade' Warning by Bailey of West Virginia Based on Coal's Plight," reprinted by permission from *The United Mine Workers Journal,* July 1, 1962, p. 12.

another four million tons of coal lost to residual oil and another larger number of miners being put out of work, and for what purpose? To gain further favor with Venezuela, the principal source of residual oil, which is now exporting almost double the amount to this country that it did in 1957. But, of course, it will never be satisfied until it gets all the market. Who are the beneficiaries of these residual oil sales? The international oil companies, Venezuela, and a relatively few large buyers of fuel, principally utilities and others who are able to put in special equipment to burn this type of oil. The householders, of course, cannot burn this type of oil.

Now the administration hopes to retrain the miners who are out of work because of these increased imports of residual oil. It also proposed to retrain the railroad workers, more of whom will lose their jobs because bituminous coal is the best paying and the last of the bulk freight that is profitable to our hard-pressed railroads, and the skilled workers in the plants that make mining machinery. These American workers do not want retraining. They simply want their jobs, regardless of what our State Department, Venezuela or any other country in the world thinks.

Through the cooperation of labor, capital and management, the production of bituminous coal has been increased from 1½ tons per man per day to over 14 tons per man per day. Many new mines far exceed this, and some of the latest deep mines produce as high as 45 tons per man per day. Strip mines, of course, even exceed this high output. If this is not the free enterprise system, what is? After all, it is this system that made America great: the simple formula of paying higher wages to labor and increasing productivity so as to be able to compete in the world markets has paid off.

I think that this system is essential to our country, Mr. Speaker, and must be preserved at all costs. It is ironic, therefore, to see the coal industry limited in its exports, on the one hand, while on the other hand it is being destroyed in domestic markets by unfair competition of an imported waste product which is permitted to enter the country in almost unlimited quantities.

The same situation could, and likely has developed with other industries. It would seem only prudent and appropriate for our government to make certain that its actions do not endanger the soundness of our system by permitting uncontrolled competition from questionable sources.

B.

TARIFF AND TRADE POLICIES

58   HIGH TARIFF AND WORLD TRADE: 1920–1932

Victor L. Albjerg

Victor L. Albjerg is Professor of History at Purdue University.

The last casualty of World War I was idealism, and the first reflex of the ensuing peace was isolationism. Most Americans had entered the war in the mood of Paul en route to Damas-

cus; they had returned in the temper of Achilles sulking back to his tent. They

Reprinted by permission from *Current History,* June, 1962, pp. 344–348.

had had enough of Europe. Many of them rued our involvement in the war, and resolved never to enter their country in what they called a second saturnalia of blunders and humiliations. European statesmen, they believed, were diabolically clever and took a Mephistophelian pleasure in hoodwinking Americans.

While many Americans abhorred Europe and Europeans, they also exalted their own country and its people. With a self-anointed superiority they maintained a Pharisaic holier-than-thou attitude:

Clean-limbed American boys are not like others,
Only clean-limbed American boys have mothers.

Many Americans also assumed a policy of national aloofness. They thanked God for the Atlantic Ocean, and wished that He had made it wider. They felt about Americans as an old English noble viewed his class:

We are the chosen few,
All others will be damned.
There is no place in heaven for you
For heaven must not be crammed.

And to prevent human congestion in the United States Congress passed the Immigration Act of 1924 which admitted only the "chosen few."

The conviction of the majority was to exclude not merely foreigners, but also the products of foreign countries. The farmers were the first to be protected, because the end of the war also terminated their affluence. Farm income in the United States in 1913 stood at $6,336,000,000. It reached its peak in 1919 at $16,111,000,000, but in 1920 slumped to $11,467,000,-000. Worse followed. By 1920, in 15 corn and wheat states 8.5 per cent of the farmers had lost their farms through foreclosures or by surrendering them to their creditors.

To brief relief to the distressed country folks the Republicans who had just come to power passed the Emergency Tariff Act which imposed high duties on sugar, wool, wheat and meat. Since these commodities, with the exception of sugar, were the chief exports of American farmers a tariff on them would offer scant relief.

The Emergency Tariff Act did not bring agriculture back to "normalcy," for the plight of the farmer continued. Low prices on what he sold and high prices on what he bought confined him in the economic scissors; for many there was no escape except flight from the homestead, and in 1922 more than 2 million farmers abandoned their establishments for the cities. These evacuees were replaced by 880,000 people from the cities; but the shift still left a human deficit of 1.2 million farmers.

President Harding and his cabinet believed that "God intended the middle class to be rich," and that protective tariff was the legerdemain to effect that conjuration. This conviction should have startled no one, for President Harding's cabinet owned or controlled some $600 million. The most opulent of the team was Andrew Mellon, who was Secretary of the Treasury under three presidents; in that capacity, "three presidents served under him."

The Republican majority in the House of Representatives shared the cabinet's enthusiasm for tariff legislation. Nicholas Longworth, Speaker of the House, maintained that it would be preferable to forego the debt owed to the United States than to open the American market to foreign producers, while Joe Martin confessed that "If I had been Demosthenes I could not have reversed the powerful Republican sentiment in the House."

The response to this clamor was the Fordney-McCumber Tariff Act of

1922 which imposed the highest schedules until then in American history. The Administration, however, hoped that the Tariff Commission, which was authorized to recommend to the President the lowering or raising of the tariff rates not to exceed 50 per cent, would neutralize the bill's defects. It failed to effect improvements, for in the period from 1922 to 1929, on its recommendations, 32 schedules were increased, and only 5 were lowered.

The increase in the American tariff system generated vigorous protests from all over the world; by 1928 more than 60 countries had, in retaliation, raised their tariffs. There were some Americans who joined the ululation of protests. As European customers of American agricultural commodities imposed restrictions upon further imports, our farmers felt the pinch. Furthermore, when Europeans were handicapped in selling in the American market they were reluctant to buy from American producers. Likewise, American banks bulging with gold hesitated to lend money to European borrowers, who, because of loss of market, might not be able to repay. Some bankers, therefore, lacked enthusiasm for high tariff.

SMOOT-HAWLEY TARIFF

The disaffections did not disconcert tariff proponents. Shortly after President Hoover entered the White House the Smoot-Hawley Bill was introduced on April 15, 1929. After prolonged consideration it was passed on June 17, 1930, despite the fact that Professor Paul Douglas, president of the American Economics Association, drafted comprehensive criticism of the bill and sent it to the committee in charge of the bill with the signatures of 1,038 other economists. The strong

protests of more than 30 European countries were likewise ignored.

The Smoot-Hawley Bill hoisted American tariff schedules to new heights. It provided for higher duties on more than 800 commodities covering a wide variety of products in both industry and agriculture. It increased the tariff on dutiable goods on an average of from 39 to 59 per cent. From 61 to 63 per cent of our imports came in duty free.

Even before the passage of the Smoot-Hawley Bill, depression had descended on most of the world, and especially upon the United States, where its virulence was increased by retaliation of other countries. Very soon after the passage of the Smoot-Hawley Act France, Italy, Spain, Mexico, and Cuba raised their rates, and within a year China, Lithuania, Brazil, India and Peru enacted retaliatory measures. The decline in American exports from $4.013 billion in 1930 to $2.91 billion in 1931, though resulting mostly from the depression, was caused in part by these counter measures of our former customers.

These strictures were not confined to counter-tariff legislation, but embraced many other devices. The most widely practiced was the imposition of the quota system which imposes specific ceilings upon the quantity of any particular commodity which a country would accept.

Miscellaneous handicaps to the free flow of exports consisted in the interference with the importation in various countries of books in English protected by American copyright. Import restrictions were imposed upon drugs on the claim of protecting health; products manufactured by prison labor were excluded to shield industry.

Whatever may be said for or against the Smoot-Hawley Tariff, it did not prevent the United States from going deeper into the depression not recovering more slowly than other industrial countries.

VOLUME OF INDUSTRIAL PRODUCTION

Per Cent of 1929

	1929	1930	1931	1932	1933
France	100	100.7	89.2	69.1	77.4
Germany	100	88.3	71.7	59.8	66.8
England	100	92.4	83.8	83.8	86.1
U.S.S.R.	100	129.7	161.9	184.7	201.6
U.S.A.	100	80.7	68.1	53.8	64.9

Exporters from other countries protested that the high American tariff practically excluded their products from our markets. They contended, furthermore, that since they could not sell to us, they ultimately would be unable to buy from us, a situation which would be injurious to everyone. Therefore they urged a lower tariff.

Simultaneously Europeans insisted that our favorable balance of trade, especially since 1916, had given the United States a vast reserve of gold. Of the world's horde in 1929 of $10,-306,165,000, the United States had $3,900,160,000 or almost 40 per cent. France ranked second with $1,633,-402,000, England, third, with $709,-269,000, and Germany, fourth, with $543,838,000, while Japan was fifth with $411,770,000. This ratio was characteristic of the period from 1920 to 1932 excepting for the increasing horde in France where, it was claimed, there was a pot of gold under every manure pile. Our commercial and industrial competitors contended that the disproportionately large American gold reserve prevented them from making their fair share of purchases in the world market, a situation which also narrowed the American market.

INVISIBLE INCOME

This was by no means a full account of the ledger, for despite American tariffs all European countries profited from invisible incomes which ran into enormous sums. By 1930, England's foreign investments of $15 billion and France's of $2 billion yielded handsome dividends, which augmented their buying power.

Each year tourists with pockets full of travelers' checks, especially from the United States, converged upon Europe. From 1920 to 1929 American tourists spent $4.5 billion more abroad than foreign tourists spent in the United States.

The remittances of immigrants in the United States to relatives in their homelands constituted another balance of payments. In 1929, the Bureau of Foreign and Domestic Commerce estimated that remittances from 1919 to 1929 from American immigrants to their relatives in Europe amounted to $4 billion, twice as much as German reparations from 1925 to 1930.

Still another invisible income enjoyed by the maritime powers of Europe were the fees which shipping companies collected for freight and passenger services. In 1923, despite Britain's loss of more than 2,000 ships during World War I, it still had 18,-857,277 tons of shipping, France had 3,180,477, and Germany already had recouped to 2,434,555, while the United States had 12,238,195 tons. By 1929, these merchant fleets had been increased by approximately 8 per cent. The earnings of the British merchant marine in 1928 amounted to $1,314,900,000, those of the French came to $150,000,000 and Germany's, slightly less than the French.

During the period after World War I, London and Paris were still important financial centers, and insurance companies drew premiums from all over the world to add to their countries' purchasing power. London and Paris banks also collected commissions for

TARIFF RATES ON SELECTED ARTICLES IN THE ACTS OF 1913, 1922 AND 1930 [1]

Article	1913	1922	1930
Raw sugar			
96° centrifugals			
Full duty	1.26¢ per pound	2.21¢ per pound	2.50¢ per lb.
Cuban duty	1.005¢ per lb.	1.76¢ per lb.	2.00¢ per lb.
Cattle under 700 lbs.	Free	1.50¢ per	2.50¢ per lb.
Cattle over 700 lbs.	Free	1.50¢ per	3.00¢ per lb.
Milk	Free	2.50¢ per gal.	6.5¢ per gal.
Cream	Free	20¢ per gal.	56.6¢ per gal.
Butter	2½¢ per lb.	8¢ per lb.	14¢ per lb.
Wheat	Free	30¢ per bu. of 60 lbs. Later raised to 42¢ per bushel	42¢ per bu.
Oats	(6¢ per bu. of 32 lbs.)	15¢ per bu.	16¢ per bu.
Lemons	(½¢ per lb. in bulk or in pkgs. exceeding 5 cu. ft.)	2.0¢ per lb.	2.5¢ per lb.
Pig Iron	Free	(75¢ per ton. Later raised to $1.125 per ton)	$1.125 per ton
Manganese ore	Free	(1¢ per lb. of contained manganese in excess of 30%)	1¢ per lb. of contained manganese in excess of 10%
Tungsten-bearing ores	Free	(45¢ per lb. of contained tungsten)	(50¢ per lb. of contained tungsten)
Fir, spruce, hemlock, pine and larch lumber	Free	Free	$1.0 per M. feet
Long staple cotton	Free	Free	7¢ per lb.
Clothing wool, clean content	Free	31¢ per lb.	34¢ per lb.
Woolen blankets	25%	18¢ per lb. and 30% to 37¢ per lb. & 40%	40¢ per lb. and 40%
Woven silk fabrics	45%	55%	60%
(Silk clothing, not specially provided for)	50%	60%	65%
Brick	10%	Free	$1.25 per M.
Cement, hydraulic	Free	Free	6¢ per cwt.
Flax, straw	Free	$2 per ton	$3 per ton
Hemp and hemp tow	Free	1¢ per lb.	2¢ per lb.
Hides	Free	Free	10%
Sole leather	Free	Free	12½%
Shoes and boots	Free	Free	20%
Matches, not over 100 to a box	3¢ per gross	8¢ per gross	20¢ per gross
Olive oil	(20 to 30¢ per gal.)	7½¢ per lb.	9½¢ per lb.

[1] Abraham Berglund, "Tariff of 1930," *American Economic Review*, XX, 472.

the sale of foreign bills of exchange. While these rates were not high, the volume of transactions netted them tidy sums. Banks from many countries of the world also maintained deposits in these London and Paris banks the earnings of which yielded the latter financial institutions additional incomes, and bolstered French and British buying potential. Because of adverse trade balances experienced by many of the European powers, they remained solvent and maintained a high standard of living thanks to these hidden streams of income. They could continue to buy abroad even though their balances of payments were adverse.

But even with all this income, in addition to their other assets, Europeans complained that our tariff barred them from selling freely in our market. There was some substance to their charge, for our favorable trade balance from 1920 to 1932 amounted to $12,029,191,000. Europeans reiterated their contention that unless they could sell to us they would be unable to buy from us. But this logic did not induce Congress to lower the schedules. Other expedients promoted trade. Bankers with an eye for dividends, upon further reflection, and industrialists with a craving for an outlet for wares believed that they saw a business opportunity. American bankers would loan money at high interest rates to prospective buyers who would absorb American industrial production. Following that thesis United States lending institutions advanced $15 billion in credit from 1920 to 1932, and Europe's purchases contributed materially to our flourishing economy. It was like "children playing store," except that the currency wasn't bogus. (See Table, "Balance of Payments of the United States, 1920–1929" which follows.)

Although the United States had become the world's greatest creditor nation it pursued the policy of a debtor country, striving to acquire ever larger accumulations of gold or credit balances.

*   *   *

BALANCE OF PAYMENTS OF THE UNITED STATES, 1920–1929 [1]

(*Annual Average of Balances in Millions of Dollars*)

CREDITS		DEBITS	
Excess of commodity exports	1,062	Shipping and freight services	15
Interest and dividends	335	Tourist expenditures	433
War debt receipts	174	Immigration remittances, charity, etc.	474
Miscellaneous commodity and		Government transactions	44
service items	14	Gold imports	116
Short term capital movement	151	Currency imports	21
		Private long-term capital movement	576
		Errors and omissions in estimate	157

BALANCE OF PAYMENTS OF THE UNITED STATES, 1930–1933

(*Annual Average of Net Balances in Millions of Dollars*)

CREDITS		DEBITS	
Excess of commodity exports	408	Shipping and freight services	57
Interest and dividends	482	Tourist expenditures	414
War debt receipts	118	Immigration expenditures	178
Gold movement	15	Government transactions	76
Private long-term capital movements	55	Currency movements	40
Errors and omissions in estimates	184	Short-term capital movements	497

[1] Frank Whitson Fetter, "U.S. Balance of Payments," *Foreign Policy Reports,* May 15, 1936, pp. 59–60.

59 COMMON MARKET—LESSON IN TRADE EXPANSION

Irving B. Kravis

Irving B. Kravis is Professor of Economics at the University of Pennsylvania.

On November 28, 1961, the front page of the *New York Times* carried a remarkable statement by a high French official. He said that France had learned that she could do away with tariffs without harm to her industries. His statement—so remarkable because France had not long ago been one of the most protectionist countries in the Western world—was no idle boast.

In the previous three years, France had reduced tariffs by 30% in her trade with the five other members of the European Economic Community—or the Common Market as it is more commonly referred to. The result? No important segment of the French economy appears to have suffered. Nor does there seem to be any fear or objection from any part of French industry about the prospect of the complete elimination of intracommunity trade barriers within the next decade or so. The same statements can be made about the rest of "the Six"—Italy, West Germany, and the Benelux countries, Belgium, the Netherlands, and Luxembourg—who as members of the Common Market are, of course, making tariff reductions at the same pace as France, and none of their domestic industries appear to be endangered.

Is there a moral for United States tariff and trade policy to be drawn from this experience? Is trade expansion possible without injury to domestic industries? Or are there special circumstances that have made it possible for European countries to move safely toward freer trade, circumstances which do not apply to the United States?

The Contrast Between European and U.S. Trade Policy. Merely raising these questions calls attention to the great difference between tariff and trade policy in Western Europe and in the U.S. And this difference has to be made clear before any answers can be found.

European innovation—The Common Market's program for the elimination of trade barriers may be viewed as part of a more general movement toward freer trade in postwar Europe. The 18 members of OEEC, the Organization for European Economic Cooperation, succeeded during the late 1940's and in the 1950's in dismantling the great bulk of the quantitative restrictions on trade that had sprung up in depression and wartime. However, the OEEC was never successful in coping with tariff obstacles to trade, and these became more important as quotas were first expanded and then removed.

It was partly for this reason that the Six formed their Common Market. Earlier the Six had established free trade in coal and steel through the creation of the European Coal and Steel Community (ECSC). The countermovement, led by England and Sweden, of seven other countries into the European Free Trade Association (EFTA), while a less happy outcome than a

From *Harvard Business Review*, March–April, 1962, p. 6, ff. Reprinted by permission.

Europe-wide agreement to reduce trade barriers, represented a further attack on tariff and other obstacles to trade. The EFTA countries are reducing tariffs among themselves at about the same rate as the Common Market countries.

It would be wrong to think that these organizations favoring trade-barrier reduction were created in a blaze of idealism over European unity that blinded men to their short-run self-interests. While the ideal of European integration was a powerful motive force, there was hard bargaining. Terms were hammered out that would reconcile and protect the interests and aspirations of each country.

This reconciliation was no easy task, particularly in the close association that was involved in the establishment of the Common Market. For instance:

France wanted to be sure that her more generous scale for overtime pay and her more rigid adherence to the principle of equal pay for men and women would not handicap her industries in the free trade of the Common Market.

Italy wanted to be certain that her efforts to industrialize would not be swamped by the superior industrial machines of Germany and the other member countries.

West Germany had to be assured that her high-cost agriculture would not be inundated under a flood of low-cost Dutch and French products.

The Benelux countries wanted to maintain their ability to purchase raw materials and semifinished goods for their processing industries at low world market prices.

Furthermore, no country was willing to sacrifice any major domestic industry, or even any well-established minor industry, on the altar of the pan-European ideal. Indeed, it is hardly an exaggeration to say that there has been an almost unspoken "no injury" rule in the framing and application of the new European trade arrangements.

The significant point, however, is that the avoidance of injury was not allowed to interfere with the reduction of trade barriers and the expansion of trade. This required great ingenuity. Some day historians may compare the boldness and imagination with which the potential trade and other conflicts were resolved in forming the new European institutions with the similar qualities that contributed to the drafting of the United States Constitution.

American stagnation—Before examining the reasons for European success in expanding trade without injury, let us refresh our memories about American tariff and trade policy over the past dozen years. In the councils of nations, under both the Democratic and Republican administrations, we have been vigorous advocates of freer trade. Unfortunately, our own actions at home have fallen short of the principles we espouse to a sufficient extent to arouse cynicism abroad and to weaken our leadership.

Our policies with respect to imports are governed largely by the Reciprocal Trade Agreements Act of 1934 as amended. This law gave the President powers to reduce tariffs below the levels set in the Tariff Act of 1930, but renewals have been necessary since the powers were limited in time and extent. There have been seven extensions since 1948, the last of which is due to expire in June 1962. Each renewal has been the occasion for a political donnybrook between the supporters of freer trade and the advocates of protection.

*   *   *

How Europe Was Able to Expand Her Trade Without Injury. How can we explain our preoccupation in postwar years with staving off the effects of foreign competition at a time when

Europeans were reaching out for closer ties? In part, of course, the answer lies in the difference between the two situations. At the end of the war, Europe's trade barriers were higher and Europe's need to find ways to break out of these restrictions was greater and more urgent; i.e., the subdivision of the continent into small national units made "foreign" trade more essential.

Thus the Europeans were perhaps less fearful of foreign competition, or, since the gains of trade were more obvious and important to them, more willing to take risks. But, if this line of reasoning explains why Europe was willing to venture more, it does not explain why she succeeded in reducing barriers and expanding trade without injury to domestic industries. For there is little evidence that a decade of the OEEC program of trade liberalization and eight years of a common market in coal and steel have had seriously detrimental effects on any important industry in any country participating in either of these ventures.

While it is true that Belgian coal has been in trouble since 1958, its difficulties can hardly be ascribed to the functioning of the Common Market. In any case, safeguards were invoked and the operation of the Common Market was not allowed to worsen the position of Belgian coal. It is, of course, premature to evaluate the European Economic Community, but the record to date hardly seems inconsistent with a no-serious-injury rule.

Industries in the underdeveloped regions of Italy, agricultural processing industries in West Germany, and Benelux processing industries relying on low-cost imports from third countries have all been given special treatment to avoid injury.

Furthermore, not one of these forms of more or less intimate European co-operation shows substantial evidence of bringing about any significant shifts in the localization of European industry. Trade among the partners increased more than with third countries, but not as a result of the expansion of some industrial branches and the contraction of others in each of the countries. Nor does there appear to be an expectation in any responsible quarter that such shifts will occur in the future operation even of the Common Market, the closest of the forms of cooperation in Europe.

Favoring circumstances—How did Europe manage to avoid economic injury and yet get trade expansion? The European leaders and technicians who formulated the new institutions are human enough to say, "We planned it that way," and realistic enough to add, "We were also lucky." They are right on both counts. Let us take a closer look at the factors—both planned and fortuitous—which played important roles in Europe's success:

1. **Economic expansion** Perhaps the most important circumstantial factor has been the rapid rate of economic growth which characterized the Six both before and after the establishment of the Common Market. From 1953 to 1960 their total gross product increased by 45% (in constant prices) as compared to only 26% for the rest of Europe and 15% for the U.S. It is easy to make room for increased imports when domestic demand is booming. And in those sectors in which imports prove too competitive, it is not so difficult for businesses to find other lines which they can pursue with greater profit. Firm reciprocal demands for exports also help.

2. **Specialization in the fine** Economic expansion appears to have facilitated a form of specialization which differs from the usual textbook model. Most economics texts would lead us

to believe that the expansion of trade is likely to involve the disappearance of some branches of industry in one country and their expansion in another. Instead, specialization tended to develop in terms of particular designs, qualities, or types of product. This tendency, observed first in the operation of the Benelux customs union, has been widely commented on, but has not been satisfactorily explained. It may be related to the movement toward larger plant size that is produced when market horizons are extended by a customs union or common market. There has also tended to be a reduction in the number of varieties of a product turned out in a plant of a given size.

3. Business agreements   The development of product specialization and the avoidance of injury may be due also, to some degree, to agreements or combinations between producers in different countries. The European outlook on these matters is different from that of the United States. There is a closer working relationship in Europe between business and government, and the governments are more willing to rely on perhaps somewhat more highly organized trade and industrial associations to achieve governmentally desired ends. At the same time, business groups are more assured of a sympathetic and cooperative attitude on the part of the government in case difficulties are encountered, particularly if they arise from foreign competition.

Thus it is not surprising to find that European governments have sometimes called on business groups in the importing and exporting countries to negotiate solutions in cases where injury was caused or threatened. Perhaps the most extensive reliance on private business arrangements to cope with problems of international competition occurred in the Benelux customs union.

*   *   *

Good strategy—There is no denying that part of the success obtained by the Six in expanding trade without injury was due to a well-conceived strategy which had four essential points:

1. Gradualism   Industry was placed on notice that free trade would be established, but in gradual stages. Gradualism meant time for adaptation. Provision was made for relief to adversely affected industries; however, it was limited in duration and intended only to aid the industries to adapt themselves to the new situation.

2. Certainty   Thus it was made clear that the establishment of free trade could be expected with a high degree of certainty. As a result, the business community reached to the expectation of broadened markets and heightened competition by accelerating investment. High investment, in turn, played a significant part in creating and maintaining the prosperous conditions that made the adjustment to the Common Market easier. With less certainty —as there might have been if the escape clauses of the Treaty of Rome had not been so clearly phrased in terms of purely temporary exceptions —the possibility that trade barriers would not really come tumbling down or that they might be re-established might have encouraged businessmen to continue in their old paths rather than to seek new ones in preparation for increased foreign competition and opportunities.

3. Readaptation   Provisions for readaptation, or adjustment assistance to use the American term, helped to disarm the fears and suspicions of labor. The economic purposes of the readaptation clauses—that is, actually easing

the adjustments to changes in the location of industries—were probably
more in the minds of the framers of
the treaty establishing the coal and
steel community than in the minds of
the drafters of the Common Market
treaty. The passing of six prosperous
years had made readaptation seem less
urgent and also had made it clearer
that the national governments intended
to discharge this task themselves. Conceivably, the readaptation provisions
may still be called on to play a larger
economic role, but thus far there has
been little occasion to invoke them
and their importance has been largely
psychological and political.

4. Joint responsibility Again and
again the provisions of the treaties establishing the new European organizations make it clear that there is a
common concern for the difficulties
that any one member country encoun-
ters. Indeed, one can almost say that
the idea that the surplus country as
well as the deficit country has a responsibility for finding solutions to imbalance (a concept well accepted for
some years now in the field of international finance) is being extended to
the field of international trade. In the
trade area, the exporting and importing countries are concerned with the
disruption of particular markets in the
importing country rather than with
balance-of-payments problems. The
cooperation between the Dutch and
Belgian governments to curb Dutch
exports to Belgium, described above,
is an illustration of an application of the
principle of joint responsibility.

*   *   *

Relevant implications—Even after
admitting that [some] points favoring
European trade expansion do not apply to the U.S., the fact remains that
the bulk of what happened in Europe
has direct lessons for us, and therefore
is relevant.

Certainty—Making it absolutely certain that trade barriers are going to come
down is the keystone of the whole approach. It is the business of businessmen to make adjustment to changing
conditions, and this is, indeed, a main
reason for the high rewards paid for
successful business leadership. Once
it is clear that trade barriers are really
going to be eliminated, businessmen
may be expected to meet this change
as they do others—by making investment decisions that will minimize injury.

It cannot be presumed that American businessmen are less eager or less
adept at survival than their European
counterparts. Given the same certainty and the same degree of notice,
there is every reason to believe that
they will be just as successful in maintaining profitability by cutting costs or
by developing new lines. Our past
methods of advancing a half step
toward freer trade and then taking a
half step backward have created inducements for the avoidance of adjustment rather than for spontaneous
adjustment.

Security—Businessmen in vulnerable industries must be given confidence
that the government will not allow
catastrophic disaster to befall them.
The sudden disruption of markets for
individual commodities should be
avoided, if necessary by controls over
the rate of increase in imports. Businessmen should also understand that
the government will not be indifferent
to their long-run difficulties when the
trouble arises from increased imports.

Gradualism—Ample time must be
given for adaptation to the freer entry
of foreign competitors to the American market, and adjustment assistance
should be promised. Some industries

and firms will need more time than others. Where necessary, additional safeguards providing longer or even increased protection should be established, but only if linked to measures that will assure adaptation to the new conditions.

Adjustment   assistance—Provision should also be made to afford assistance to industries that have difficulty in adjusting to an upward trend of imports. Public funds should be available for resettlement and retraining of workers, for readaptation loans for affected enterprises, and perhaps also for new employment-creating investments in areas hit by import competition.

The purpose of this assistance should be to remove, as far as possible, the element of injury from the changes imposed by increased foreign competition. Of course, displacement itself— the need to shift out of old lines of work and away from the production of familiar products—is sometimes considered injurious in itself. However, if the adaptation to new lines and products can be brought about quickly or without loss of income either to capital or labor, real injury will be minimized.

Joint responsibility—The exporting as well as the importing country should assume responsibility for avoiding the disruption of markets for individual commodities. In the past, controls over sudden and large increases in imports have largely been exercised unilaterally by the importing country. Recently, a new element has begun to be introduced: quotas governing the size of shipments have been determined by agreements between the exporting and importing countries. The arrangements between the United States and Japan with respect to cotton textiles represent the first extensive use of this technique by the U.S. Last July, an international textile conference in Geneva agreed on the broader use of this method. The exercise of joint responsibility should minimize the possibility of a spiral of retaliatory restrictions on trade that might develop if import controls were unilaterally established. It should also make possible gradual adjustment to trade patterns that conform to market forces.

Economic expansion—In establishing the timing of trade barrier reductions, finally, we should bear in mind that adjustments to freer trade take place more easily during a period of rapid expansion. It would be unwise, however, to try to link the freeing of trade too closely to future cyclical conditions. The Common Market solution seems a good one here. A schedule could be established for the reduction of trade barriers which would include some flexibility for acceleration or retardation. Good economic conditions would then permit faster progress. If conditions were unfavorable, delays might be necessary.

A Revitalized Tariff and Trade Policy. These are the keys to Europe's success in expanding trade without injury. And they are available to us. We can, if we are determined and courageous enough, have free trade with no widespread injury to domestic industries. . . .

*   *   *

C.

INTERNATIONAL FINANCE

60 INTERNATIONAL FINANCIAL PROBLEMS AND POLICIES

Alfred Hayes

Alfred Hayes is President of the Federal Reserve Bank of New York.

For many years after World War II the United States economy was alone equipped to supply the goods and services so urgently required by a war-devastated world, and the resultant dollar shortage forced many foreign governments to impose severe controls over trade and capital transactions with this country. Today, the economies of Europe and Japan—assisted by generous United States aid—have not only fully recovered but have moved on into a new phase of dynamic expansion. Their resurgent economic strength has permitted the restoration of currency convertibility and the dismantling of most discriminatory exchange controls against the dollar. They have made major progress, as we have so often urged, toward a closer relationship of their commodity and financial markets with our own. But our very success in thus stimulating the recovery of Europe and Japan, and the liberalization of trade and payments among the nations of the Free World, has brought in its train a whole series of new problems.

From the experience of the past year, it has become abundantly clear that national economic and financial policies can no longer be based solely upon domestic considerations; they must also take into account potential repercussions in the exchange markets and the balance of payments. As the major foreign currencies have regained their strength and prestige, and facilities for capital transfers have become more readily available, we have now to face the problem of dealing with large-scale, and potentially disruptive, flows of short-term funds and other payments from one financial center to another. Further, the United States and, more recently, other developed countries, have undertaken to support massive programs of economic development in those vast areas of the world where an intolerably low standard of living still prevails. But unless the financial burden of this development effort is equitably shared among all countries capable of supplying capital and other assistance, the dollar, and indeed the entire international financial structure, could be subjected to excessive strain.

We thus face a wide range of new and perplexing problems to which there are no easy answers. The defense of the dollar is a job for all of us, since

Excerpted from a statement by Alfred Hayes in *Hearings Before the Subcommittee on International Exchange and Payments of the Joint Economic Committee,* Congress of the United States, June 2, 1961, pp. 83–92.

it depends basically on the maintenance of a sound and growing American economy. In the area of monetary policy, the Federal Reserve System must continue to seek to promote maximum sustainable economic growth. For the period immediately ahead, the System must continue to encourage the forces of recovery while at the same time guarding againt the re-emergence of inflationary forces as the recovery progresses. Proper fiscal and debt management policies are highly important; there is a danger that too great a burden will again be placed on monetary policy if budget deficits that were appropriate during a period of recession are allowed to persist during a phase of the business cycle in which such deficits would be inappropriate. Defense of the dollar equally requires the most serious efforts by both labor and management, and a growing awareness by the public generally that the American economy is not isolated from the rest of the world. The sellers' market of the early postwar period has become a part of history, and the vigorous competition of today serves as an additional warning that costs must be kept down and productivity increased if the United States is to retain its role as a leading exporter in world markets. These competitive forces have not been without a healthy influence on our domestic price structure, and there is hope—provided we keep our own house in order— that a period of sustained growth with reasonable price stability lies ahead for us and for the other leading countries of the world.

To some students of international finance the challenge appears so formidable as to require sweeping reforms in the international financial system itself. I do not agree. In my view, there is no reason to fear this new era of international competition and currency convertibility, nor to shrink from the challenge posed by the development needs of Latin America, Africa, and Asia. For me, the key to all these problems lies primarily in the formulation of appropriate policies and in their coordination through international consultations, rather than by radically transforming existing institutional arrangements. This is hardly intended to suggest that the present international financial system does not suffer from certain weaknesses, and I shall mention later some modifications which I think are needed.

The present international financial system is, of course, the result of gradual evolution over many years. The cornerstone of the whole structure is the link between gold and the United States dollar, with the dollar firmly anchored by its interconvertibility with gold at a fixed price of $35 per fine ounce. Most other governments in the Western World have established with the International Monetary Fund par values for their currencies in terms of either gold or the dollar, and monetary authorities generally are committed to maintaining these par values by buying or selling dollars in their exchange markets to maintain the rates for their currencies within a relatively narrow range. This network of fixed exchange rates has greatly facilitated the growth of international trade and capital movements, and has thereby contributed to the increasingly close integration of world trade and payments.

In this international system the United States plays the dual role of the most powerful trading nation and the foremost banker for the rest of the world.

The role of the United States as the world's leading trader is based upon many factors—the massive raw material requirements of our factories, the high consumption demands of our people, the competitive strength of many export industries, an abundant flow of private savings into investment abroad, and sizable governmental programs of foreign economic aid. The growth of our foreign trade has been further strongly stimulated by United States Government policy which has consistently sought to minimize artificial barriers to trade and payments between our domestic market and the rest of the world. Last year our total payments and receipts came to some $57 billion, with receipts falling short of the payments by $3.8 billion or, roughly, 13 per cent.

I am sure that many competent witnesses have already provided you with an exhaustive analysis of our balance-of-payments experience during recent years, and I shall try to highlight only a few points which, to me, seem particularly important.

As you know, the deficit position of 1960 was not something new. Indeed, such deficits have been a characteristic feature, except in 1957, of our balance of payments for more than a decade. Prior to 1958, however these deficits generally ran in the magnitude of $1.0 to $2.0 billion and served the highly useful purpose of reconstituting foreign dollar balances and securing a more appropriate distribution of gold stocks. Such deficits, in fact, were instrumental in helping to bring about the rapid expansion of international trade and investment, the dismantling of discriminatory controls abroad, and the restoration of currency convertibility by the leading Western European countries at the end of 1958. While some might be tempted to criticize what seemed a delayed awakening by the United States to its growing balance-of-payments problem, full recognition must be given to the changing nature of the problem during these transitional years.

By late 1959 it was reasonably clear that convertibility was a solid success

and that most of the leading trading nations had so reconstituted their international reserves that they had little need to build them up further. Moreover, there had been a very sizable increase in the dollar working balances in the hands of private foreign interests, and, with the restoration of confidence in European currencies, there was an increasing tendency for funds to flow to foreign financial centers where interest rates were most attractive. In this new context, and particularly with declining interest rates in the United States in 1960, the continuing balance-of-payments deficits of the United States took on a more ominous aspect. The storm signals had been raised.

I do not believe it is necessary to review with this group in any detail the various measures that were undertaken to defend the dollar. While I would reject the tying of United States foreign aid to the American market as a basic long-run principle of our aid program, I believe that the moves which have been taken in that direction since late 1959 are entirely appropriate under the circumstances. Subsequent measures and proposals designed to secure a more equitable sharing with our allies of economic and defense aid outlays, to stimulate exports, to economize on military expenditures abroad, to prohibit private United States ownership of gold abroad, and to reduce the duty-free allowances for returning tourists were all highly desirable. In addition, various official statements, especially President Kennedy's Message on Balance of Payments and Gold to the Congress in February of this year, had a highly beneficial effect, providing impressive reassurance to the world of our determination to defend the dollar. I have been particularly gratified that recourse to restrictive trade and other controls has had no part to play in this program. Continued efforts are still necessary to eliminate restrictions against United States exports and to encourage a number of countries to make their capital markets more freely accessible to foreign borrowers. We would only hurt ourselves by turning our backs on the principles of liberal trade and unrestricted international payments for which we have stood. Much still needs to be done to create a sufficient awareness of the need to expand our exports. It is encouraging, however, that there are indications of a more vigorous pursuit of foreign markets. I have full confidence in the ability of American labor and management to rise to the challenge, with benefits to all concerned.

I should now like to turn to the role of the United States as banker for the rest of the Free World. As a central banker, I am of course particularly concerned with this banking function of the United States and with the role of the dollar as an international reserve currency. The Federal Reserve Bank of New York now maintains accounts for 97 central banks and monetary authorities throughout the world, and this brings us into close day-by-day contact with the many complex problems facing the dollar as a reserve currency.

As of the end of 1948, foreign official holdings of gold and dollar reserves amounted to $8.8 billion and $2.8 billion, respectively. Since then, there has been an impressive rise in both types of reserve assets, with foreign official holdings of gold amounting as of the end of March 1961 to nearly $21 billion, while official dollar reserves had risen to somewhat more than $11 billion as of the same date. We hold earmarked in our vaults in New York $9.5 billion, or nearly one half, of total foreign official gold holdings, and also hold for foreign official account roughly $6.5 billion of dollar balances and other liquid dollar assets. In addition

to these official dollar holdings, foreign private and international holdings now amount to about $12 billion.

It is important to note that the $11 billion in official short-term balances is convertible into gold on demand. Balances held by foreign private interests, as well as those of domestic holders, acquire the convertibility privilege if they are shifted into foreign official accounts. Since the United States stands ready to convert, at a fixed price, foreign official dollar balances into gold on demand, these dollar balances are regarded by foreign countries as equivalent to gold itself and hence have been included in their official reserves. By thus serving as the banker for such a "gold exchange" or "dollar exchange" system, as it is sometimes called, the United States has made possible a massive reinforcement of international liquidity upon which the free flow of world trade so heavily depends.

There are many reasons why the dollar has acquired this status as a reserve or "key" currency and, of these, I would mention particularly its stability, its interconvertibility with gold, its widespread use in financing world trade, and the availability in New York of financial markets of unparalleled size and efficiency which permit dollar holdings to be readily put to work. These factors were instrumental in establishing the dollar equally with gold as the reference point for setting par values for other currencies with the International Monetary Fund. The emergence of the dollar as a "key" currency has been mainly a postwar phenomenon, although it had its beginnings in the prewar period when there was a massive inflow of capital from abroad in search of a safe haven.

It may be noted that the conditions which have made the dollar a reserve currency were not fostered solely, or even largely, for that purpose. Rather they are an integral part of our market economy and the result of our efforts to achieve much broader goals. The reserve currency status of the dollar thus ultimately flows from and depends upon the pre-eminent role of the United States in international trade and finance, a role which can be fulfilled only by continuing adherence to sound economic and financial policy. Any undermining of confidence in our ability to keep our financial house in order— any slackening of resolve in the pursuit of monetary stability or any weakening of fiscal responsibility—could result in a severe blow to the dollar as a reserve currency and, in fact, to the entire international financial system. This would be a development that would prejudice our economic well-being in the broadest sense by undermining the base on which so large a share of world trade and payments now depends. We, therefore, have a responsibility—and one not without advantages—which we have met, and should continue to meet, with a resolution equally as firm as that required for leadership in the security and economic progress of the Free World.

*   *   *

In conclusion, I should like to venture some comments on the question of the longer term problem of insuring an adequate growth of international liquidity over the years. It is sometimes contended that, if we succeed, as we must, in restoring balance-of-payments equilibrium, our very success will operate to the disadvantage of the rest of the world by limiting the amount of liquidity that will be added to the international financial system. I question seriously any such conclusion. Certainly there is at present a fully ample stock of world liquidity in the form of gold and foreign exchange balances and

other forms of credit. While the rate of new gold production over the years may slip somewhat behind the growth of world trade, there is no particular reason to assume that world liquidity needs will rise automatically and proportionately with trade and investment. Just as we have developed within our economy increasingly efficient uses of money and credit, so also similar possibilities are available internationally through cooperative arrangements which will not impair the individual responsibilities of each country. Moreover, while the United States must keep its balance of payments under firm control, this does not preclude moderate flows of dollars abroad when such movements would serve a constructive purpose. Furthermore, to the extent that the United States may find it desirable to accumulate foreign exchange balances, new sources of liquidity would be opened up. In this connection, it is important to recognize that liquidity should not be defined narrowly with reference solely to existing stocks of gold and foreign exchange but should also be taken to include private and governmental credits, the inter-central bank credit facilities I have discussed, and the resources of the Monetary Fund.

If, therefore, domestic policies are appropriate and fashioned with due regard to international realities, and if means to deal with short-term capital flows are available and adequate, there is no reason, in my judgment, why the international financial system cannot work satisfactorily for at least the foreseeable future. I would thus conclude that there is no present need for far-reaching reforms which would basically alter the present financial structure, practices, and institutions of the world.

61 REQUIREMENTS OF AN EFFECTIVE INTERNATIONAL MONETARY MECHANISM

Subcommittee on International
Exchange and Payments

*   *   *

On the basis of the foregoing analysis, it is now possible to state the requirements of an effective international monetary mechanism.

1. Adequate Supply of Supplementary Reserves

An effective international monetary mechanism would channel an assured, dependable, and truly adequate supply of supplementary reserves from surplus countries with sufficient or redundant reserves to deficit countries with insufficient reserves. This means, first, that supplementary reserves must be dependably available in sufficient amount to permit any sudden destabilizing, speculative outflows of short-term capital to be met without strain. Secondly, supplementary reserves must be available in sufficient amount to permit the adjustment of structural imbalances in the underlying balance of payments to be gradual and constructive rather than hasty and destructive. When deficits are structural in origin, swift adjustment can be achieved only by methods which would undermine free world economic growth and reverse the trend toward liberalization of trade and payments. Gradual adjustment can be achieved by means which promote both growth and closer economic integration. Within a single country structural imbalances in inter-regional payments are avoided chiefly through equalizing capital movements, involving large and continual shifts in ownership of financial assets from deficit to surplus regions. This occurs automatically and without attracting notice. At the international level, uncertainty regarding currency values and other institutional barriers prevent capital movements from automatically filling this role. Consequently, in an integrated free world economy this job must be done by reserves and supplementary credits.

2. Scope of Membership in Supplementary Reserve Arrangements

In the case of most underdeveloped countries, the demand for imports is too insistent, in relation to limited export earnings, to permit much accumulation of reserves. These countries live on a hand-to-mouth basis; their purchases abroad in excess of the amounts provided from export earnings are tied closely to the amount of aid which the economically advanced countries are willing to extend, supplemented by IMF drawings and special credits to meet temporary payments difficulties. Since long-term foreign aid, supplemented by IMF and other short-term credits, tends to supplant reserves in financing the balance of payments of underdeveloped countries, their prob-

---

Reprinted from *International Payments Imbalances and the Need For Strengthening International Financial Arrangements*. Report of the Subcommittee on International Exchange and Payments, 1961, pp. 11–20.

lems are rather sharply distinguishable from those of the economically advanced countries which accumulate sizable reserves and use them in meeting international payments. The IMF's resources in gold and key currencies are well adapted to the needs of underdeveloped countries; a new mechanism for providing needed supplementary reserves should be directed particularly toward fulfilling the mutual support needs of the economically advanced countries. This is particularly the case since any adequate supplementary reserve arrangement must be linked to close coordination of the economic policies of its members. The type of coordination needed is possible only among countries of similar institutions, similar stage of development, similar problems, and similar instruments of economic control.

3. Need for Coordination in Economic Policy

An effective mechanism for providing adequate supplementary reserves must be accompanied by much closer consultation and coordination of national economic policies than now exists. Such coordination would include (1) monetary and fiscal policies, (2) tariff and commercial policies, and (3) aid to underdeveloped countries and defense-burden sharing.

Coordination is necessary, in the first place, to provide assurance to the creditor countries that the supplementary reserve facilities are not being drawn upon by the debtors to enable them to sustain domestic inflationary policies. A country whose balance of payments deficit is the result of domestic inflation must be called upon to take prompt restrictive monetary and fiscal action instead of continuing to run a deficit. Second, through such a coordinating body, a country whose balance of payments is in surplus owing to cyclical deflation would be pressed by other members to adopt expansionary domestic policies. The effect would be to minimize the possibility, already slight, of long-sustained inflationary or deflationary tendencies in one or a few countries, although moderate and temporary cyclical divergencies are unavoidable.

Apart from inflation and deflation, international consultation and coordination should be developed for the purpose of concerting programs to adjust structural imbalances in international payments in ways which will accelerate economic growth. Such programs will cover the whole range of economic policies, rather than merely financial policy, and should include the principal industrial countries of the Atlantic Community plus Japan. Matters of commercial policy, including tariffs, export rebates, regional discrimination, and agricultural protection, would be involved. While reciprocal concessions by the United States are necessary for further trade liberalization, the special responsibility of the surplus countries to assume the leading role should be strongly pressed. Trade liberalization is a potent means of promoting structural adjustment, and tariff reductions by surplus countries are greatly preferable to upward revaluation of their currencies. A further objective of such policy coordination should be to reduce the present wide disparity among members of the Atlantic Community in the percentage of GNP contributed to common defense and foreign aid. Consultation and coordination among the leading industrial and trading countries with respect to economic policies bearing upon the balance of payments can be most appropriately organized under OECD, although the membership of the particular bodies dealing with these problems should include Japan and need not include certain of the smaller OECD members.

4. Restoration of Confidence in the Stability of Currencies and Exchange Rates

A basic factor accentuating present international payments difficulties is the atmosphere of uncertainty and skepticism regarding the stability of exchange rates. This is a consequence of our present system of quasi-fixed parities. If capital flowed to instead of away from countries whose payments were in deficit, present difficulties would be greatly eased.

The present speculative atmosphere cannot be cured merely by official declarations. Under today's conditions it is widely known that there may be no acceptable alternative, under some circumstances, to currency revaluation or devaluation as a means of correcting a large and persistent payments imbalance. Countries with deficits will not accept severe, prolonged deflation to achieve external balance, nor will surplus countries submit to sharp inflation. An adequate supplementary reserve arrangement, however, combined with appropriate coordination of national economic policies, would make it possible to reconcile the requirements of domestic stability and growth with balance of payments adjustment, without resorting to exchange rate adjustments. Domestic measures to combat recession would not need to be constrained by balance of payments difficulties.

A major policy objective should be to build up confidence in the permanence of the structure of exchange rates by avoiding any future changes in currency parities among the principal industrial and trading countries of the free world.

PROPOSALS FOR HANDLING PROBLEM OF RESERVES

If international reserves were as abundant as the plans that have been designed to deal with the problem, it would no longer be pressing. Ranging from an all-out return to gold coinage and no nonsense about paper money, to the development of claims on an international organization to replace gold in settling international payments, they at least attest to the sense of urgent need with which economists view the matter. It is not, however, the function of the subcommittee to choose one out of the many schemes that have been described, and recommend that the United States back it alone. Instead, with many of the schemes possessing attractive features, it seems wise to present our recommendations in terms of certain features which a number of the schemes possess. However, in order to provide a more concrete sense of some of these features, they will be presented in the context of short descriptions of some of the plans for reform.

1. Various Plans Described

The plans that are to be considered here range from a mere continuation of the present practice of making ad hoc central bank arangements to extend credit in order to meet particular "hot money" crises as they arise, to the creation of an international central bank.

(a) Ad Hoc Mutual Support Arrangements

Representatives of the major central banks or perhaps the various national treasuries could strengthen existing arrangements by providing for agreements for mutual support among the principal trading and financial countries. Such arrangements would deal primarily with short-term capital movements and in particular would protect the reserve centers (and their creditors) against the damaging effects of withdrawals of short-term funds. They might also be used, of course, to protect currencies against strains arising from other causes.

Such arrangements might take a wide variety of forms. Without going into detail, it will be enough to set out some of the dimensions of variations:

(a) Amount of support commitment.

(b) Duration of support.

(c) Conditions of support: Is there any dependable, advance commitment, or must the conditions be separately negotiated for each new situation, including satisfying lenders as to credit-worthiness of the borrower, satisfying them that the borrower is taking proper steps to rectify the basic cause of the strain, and so on?

(d) Intergovernmental or inter-central bank arrangements.

(e) Bilateral or multilateral arrangements.

(f) Form of support: Agreement to hold borrower's currency, or loan lender's currency (or possibly gold or a third currency).

(g) Exchange risk: If support takes form of holding borrower's currency, the currency holdings might be subject to a gold or exchange rate guarantee. Or a similar result could be accomplished by making the support take the form of a swap transaction; e.g., at a time of heavy pressure against the pound, the Swiss National Bank buys and holds sterling, but contracts to sell it 3 months forward to Bank of England at a specified rate of exchange.

It will be apparent that arrangements of this kind do not change the basic structure. Reserves would still consist of gold and reserve currencies. But particularly if the arrangements are intended to relieve a key-currency country, a commitment of this type is tantamount to a commitment to hold, and indeed to extend holdings of the reserve currency. From this standpoint, then, it could be regarded as a device for supplementing reserves at least temporarily.

(b) The Bernstein Plan

The Bernstein plan has earned strong support. Like the arrangements described above, it provides for no change in the form in which reserves are kept and the role of the key-currency countries would not be altered. It contains two elements:

(i) *The integration of Fund quotas with members' own reserves.*—Access to Fund resources would be entirely free, rather than restricted and discretionary, within the limits laid down in the articles of agreement: in the normal case, a member could draw 25 percent of its quota per year up to the point where total drawings were equal to 125 percent of its quota. Drawings in excess of 25 percent a year or 125 percent of quotas would require a waiver. Members would then treat their quotas as virtually an addition to their own reserves and would presumably meet deficits by drawing on the Fund pari passu with drawing on reserves.

(ii) *Increasing Fund resources in members' currencies.*—Free access to Fund resources on this basis would not be possible today. One of the weaknesses of the Fund is that its holdings of the currencies of some of its members are limited unduly and may easily be exhausted. The reserve currency countries have contributed disproportionately to the Fund's resources; other Western European countries not enough. Consequently, the Fund is poorly equipped to deal with a shift of funds from one of the reserve centers to continental European countries. For example, while at the end of 1960 the Fund held $3.4 billion of U.S. dollars (including $800 million of Treasury bills in its so-called gold investment account), and $1.5 billion worth of pounds sterling, it held only $500 million of deutsche marks and $600 million of French francs. It is ironical, indeed, that a large portion of the recent British drawing upon the Fund had to consist of dollars. If the United States should wish to make use of its drawing rights, it is difficult to know what currencies the Fund could provide.

One way of strengthening its position would be to increase all members' quotas. But while this would increase Fund holdings of all members' currencies (including many for which it has no use), it would also increase members' drawing facilities correspondingly. Moreover, the objection might be raised that such a step was taken as recently as 1959.

Bernstein (and others) have also suggested that certain of the Fund's members agree to lend the Fund additional amounts of their currencies should its holdings of these currencies fall too low. These standby credits need be negotiated only with the leading countries whose currencies are most likely to be in demand, though there is no reason why other Fund members with convertible currencies should not join. Currency borrowed in this way would be employed to meet needs caused by destabilizing short-term capital movements from one financial center to another, rather than to finance deficits in a member country's underlying balance of payments. In order to keep such transactions separate from ordinary Fund transactions, Bernstein proposes that they take place through a subsidiary reserve settlement account.

The Bernstein plan and the mutual support arrangements discussed above could be combined. For example, one witness suggested to the subcommittee that central bank mutual support operations might be the first line of defense, running for, say, 3-month periods. If support were needed beyond that period, the Fund would be brought in as a second line of defense to replace the central bank commitments for mutual support.

(c) The Zolotas Plan, and Others Like It

Similar proposals which would give the Fund standby borrowing facilities, but under article VII rather than through a separate subsidiary, have been made by Professor Zolotas, Governor of the Bank of Greece, by Maxwell Stamp, as an alternative plan B to his more ambitious and preferred plan (described below); and by Per Jacobsson in his annual report to ECOSOC, April 1961.

(d) The Franks-Radcliffe Committee Proposals

Sir Oliver Franks and the Radcliffe Committee have proposed that the International Monetary Fund be authorized to accept deposits from its members, which they would treat as reserves. These deposits could be created either by the Fund's lending operations, or by deposit with the Fund by its members of reserves now held in the form of dollars, sterling, or gold. Under this arrangement, the present reserve base would be supplemented by deposit balances with the Fund. Triffin, whose full proposals will be discussed below, has also urged this step as a desirable transition toward his full plan. His idea in proposing it is (*a*) that countries might be more willing to hold gold-guaranteed deposits with the Fund than unguaranteed sterling or dollars, and thus the structure of reserves would be rendered more stable, and (*b*) that the acceptance of voluntary deposits by the Fund would be a steppingstone toward the full Triffin plan.

(e) The Stamp Plan

Maxwell Stamp has proposed that the Fund issue certificates up to a specified amount in any period, e.g., $3 billion a year, to an international agency to aid economic development. This agency would allocate the certificates to developing countries, and the latter would spend them at will. No country, however, would be required to accept the certificates. Countries which did agree to accept them would find their exports stimulated.

(f) Payments Union for Developed Economies of Free World

The success of the operations of the European Payments Union has suggested still another series of proposals which, if implemented, would give rise to a new form of reserve to supplement gold and the reserve currencies. The members of the OECD (and Japan and possibly Australia and New Zealand) would form a clearing or payments union. Deficits and surpluses of the members on ordinary account would be settled at an agreed ratio (e.g., half or two-thirds) in gold or foreign exchange acceptable to the payee. The remainder would be settled in the form of debits and/or credits on the books of the clearing union. Destabilizing short-term capital movements, however, would be settled entirely in debits or credits in the union. Credit balances in the union would, of course, be a form of reserves. This scheme could be regarded as providing an automatic, though often only partial, credit offset for any deficit, thus reducing the amount of reserves needed.

(g) The Triffin Plan

Under the plan proposed by Triffin, claims against the International Monetary Fund, or other international institutions, are used as national reserves in place of the dollars and sterling now held as reserves. The essential elements are:

(a) Countries would agree to discontinue holding any reserves in the form of national currencies.

(b) Countries would agree to hold a minimum portion of their reserves in the form of deposits with the International Monetary Fund. (Triffin has suggested 20 percent as the initial percentage.)

(c) The International Monetary Fund would be authorized to expand its deposits by loans and "open market operations" subject to some appropriate limitation on the rate of expansion. Triffin has suggested that this expansion, together with the increase in monetary gold stocks, be limited to an annual increment in total reserves at some agreed rate, say 3 percent.

Thus the present International Monetary Fund would be converted into an international central bank, holding deposits and able to create credit. (The present IMF is a fund, not a bank. It can lend only the pool of currencies and gold represented by members' subscriptions.) The international central bank's deposit liabilities as well as its assets would be subject to a gold guarantee (or, strictly, a maintenance of gold value guarantee), as the present Fund's assets and liabilities are.

These are the bare essentials. There is room for considerable variation in their implementation. The point of prime importance is the transition from the present arrangement to the operation of the Triffin plan. Countries would initially acquire IMF deposits required to meet the minimum requirement by transferring to the IMF gold or foreign currencies they now hold as reserves, and by exchanging their present credit balances with the IMF for new deposits. To the extent that they do not choose to convert existing foreign exchange reserves into IMF deposits, they would liquidate them, by conversion into gold. (Triffin provides a minor exception for "working balances" in key currencies, and another exception for that portion of balances now held in sterling which is not convertible into gold.)

The transition from the present arrangements to the Triffin Fund-Bank would profoundly affect the international financial position of the reserve-currency countries. Their liabilities to other central banks and governments would be eliminated. In part, they would be replaced by liabilities to the Fund-Bank (maybe entirely in case of pounds). In part, they would be canceled against gold payments (perhaps only for the dollar).

Thus the Fund-Bank would acquire large amounts of dollars and sterling turned in by members. Triffin has calculated that if members who hold dollars and sterling prefer to retain their gold and deposit reserve currencies to meet their minimum deposit requirement (as of December 31, 1958), the

Fund-Bank would acquire about $5 billion worth of reserve currencies. In addition, if members chose to deposit the rest of their dollars and sterling, and thereby acquire Fund-Bank deposits in excess of their minimum requirements, the Fund-Bank would get an additional $10 billion worth of dollars and sterling. Triffin has proposed that these dollar and sterling holdings, which would amount to $5 to $15 billion, should be subject to amortization at some maximum agreed rate, say 5 percent a year. With the Fund's maximum holdings of dollars amounting to about $10 billion, at the 5 percent rate, the Fund-Bank's dollar holdings would be subject to liquidation at a rate of no more than $500 million a year. If instead only $4 billion were turned in to the Fund-Bank, the United States would have to pay off the remaining $6 billion of foreign official dollar balances in gold immediately.

Certain aspects of the Triffin plan are subject to modification. The Fund's "open market operations" might be directed to the purchase of Government obligations of advanced countries or instead to bonds issued by the International Bank for Reconstruction and Development. Likewise, the requirement for minimum deposits and the arrangements for the transfer and subsequent amortization of existing holdings of reserve currencies could of course be modified.

(h) Raising Price of Gold

Finally, it has been proposed that the problem could be handled most easily by means of a general increase in the price of gold. This would, of course, mean an increase in the monetary value of the existing reserves of the major gold-holding countries and it might, by increasing the ratio of gold reserves in the key-currency countries to their demand liabilities to foreigners, increase the readiness of these other countries to acquire dollars and sterling for reserve purposes.

Such a step would, however, have other effects which would have to be kept in mind. It would give a subsidy to the largest gold producers—South Africa and the Soviet Union. The incidence of windfall gains would be highly arbitrary, and it would "penalize" countries which had been willing to keep their reserves in the form of dollars and sterling, while favoring those which had insisted upon holding gold. Finally, it would provide a large windfall gain to private gold hoarders and probably stimulate speculative interest in gold. It might lead in the future to very large movements of funds out of the major currencies into gold in anticipation of further increases in its price, thereby vastly increasing the future need for reserves. In those Middle Eastern and Asian countries where gold hoarding has been endemic and has interfered with productive uses of saving, it would serve to enhance gold's prestige as a means of storing wealth.

2. Education of Proposals

Adequacy of reserves.—Supplementary reserves must be available in sufficient amounts to permit large outflows of short-term capital to be financed without strain, and to permit gradual and constructive adjustments to structural imbalances. Moreover, these reserves must be where they are needed and responsive in amount to growth in the need for them over time.

On this score most of the plans are reasonably satisfactory though with some it would be necessary to renegotiate the arrangements from time to time.

(1) The proposal for agreements among central banks for mutual support would not in itself provide any immediate increase in reserves. However, the increased borrowing facilities would permit an increase in liquidity for certain purposes. They would not provide for a steady future increase in reserves, except as countries might be more willing to add to their dollar (or sterling) holdings because these reserve currencies would be strengthened by the support arrangements.

(2) The Bernstein plan would provide for an immediate increase in reserves, through "integration" of Fund quotas with national reserves. However, it does not provide for an increasing level of reserves over time, although Bernstein is concerned about a future inadequacy of liquidity. In any case, since it secures a fairly large immediate increment, it could perhaps be counted on to meet the growth requirements for the next few years. Later, to quote the author, "it should be possible to have a more frequent review and revision of the quotas."

(3) The Zolotas plan would have similar effects.

(4) The Frank-Radcliffe suggestions would reduce the need for liquidity by limiting the use of the relatively unstable reserve currencies and bringing the new form of reserve under a gold guarantee. They would, however, do nothing to secure future relief.

(5) The Stamp plan does not bring about an increase in liquidity at once, though if it were put into effect reserves would be increased at a predetermined rate over the years. By providing for such an increase, it may be argued that the present "need" for liquidity would be reduced.

(6) The proposal to organize a Payments Union under the OECD would, if implemented, bring about an immediate increase in liquidity (or reduction in the need for it). In order to

secure further accommodations in the future, it would be necessary to reduce still further the fraction of payments to be made in gold. It might perhaps be possible to agree, at the time the plan was being negotiated, for a schedule of future changes in the ratio. Moreover, with membership limited to the advanced economies, it might be easier to get the changes required than it would be in a more inclusive organization.

(7) Finally, the Triffin plan would not provide at the outset for any sharp increase in reserves. Triffin regards the present level of reserves as "on the low side," but his concern is mainly with the adequacy of future increments. His plan would secure a more or less automatic annual increase in reserves within agreed limits.

Supply of reserves must be dependable.—In view of the great harm that a crisis can do to confidence even if it is successfully surmounted, it is desirable that the new arrangements be geared to avert crises by coming into operation early enough, rather than simply to counter them once they have developed. On this score, the strongest plans are the Triffin scheme, the Bernstein plan—provided that drawing rights on the Fund are automatic—and the plan for an OECD-sponsored Payments Union. But the others, which have a greater element of discretion about them, can also prove effective if those in authority are informed and concerned to act in time.

In this connection it is desirable to stress the point that any of these plans will prove more effective if it provides opportunity for frequent consultation.

As an additional aspect of the requirement for an adequate and dependable supply of reserves, special arrangements may be desirable to meet the needs of the reserve-currency countries. Certainly any plan worth consideration should reduce the instability inherent in the present mechanism, with its use of reserve currencies. In principle, this could be done either by strengthening the reserve currencies themselves, as for instance by introducing gold guarantees, or by supplying a substitute for reserve holdings of dollars and sterling. The various plans all contribute in some degree to these ends, with the standby arrangements for mutual support probably providing the most uncertain solution, mainly because they are likely to be held from view.

Finally, the amount of reserves needed can be reduced if the claims to finance "hot money" movements can be held down. Most of the plans make no special provision for the treatment of short-term capital flows, except as they modify the role of the key currencies, or strengthen them against speculative doubt. But perhaps the major destabilizing factor to be faced in the future will be outflows of short-term capital. The plan for an OECD Payments Union provides for an automatic and complete reverse flow of capital as an offset to such capital exports, and thus is likely to grapple most effectively with this danger.

Scope of the arrangements.—Some of the arrangements call for an extension of the role of the International Monetary Fund; others look to the OECD, or a group of the major economies, for their administration and operation. There are clearly arguments for both extremes. For simplicity, administrative ease, and the merit of grouping those countries whose problems are similar and which are already tackling other problems together, we see an advantage in a separate grouping of the economically advanced countries, whether it functions under the aegis of OECD or IMF. It would appear to be possible to implement the Triffin plan, or any of the others outlined above, on such a basis.

*   *   *

62 INTERNATIONAL TRANSMISSION OF BUSINESS CYCLES: COMMENT

Emile Despres

Emile Despres is Professor of Economics at Stanford University.

The papers of Mr. Gilbert and of Messrs. Polak and Rhomberg have provided further confirmation that short-term cyclical fluctuations—and their international propagation through the automatic operation of the foreign trade multiplier—are no longer problems of major importance for the industrially advanced countries. It is important to recognize, however, that we are by no means free of critical problems in this field.

The nature of the problem has changed. The chief present problem arises neither from short-term cyclical fluctuations nor from severe inflationary or deflationary developments in particular countries. It arises, rather, from rapid structural changes in the world economy within an international monetary and financial framework which is inadequate to accommodate the balance-of-payments consequences of these changes. This creates a serious danger of secular retardation of growth in countries suffering external deficits and its gradual propagation to other countries as well. Indeed, this process of secular retardation seems to have already begun.

The largest source of structural disturbance is the inevitable unevenness of improvements in productivity—unevenness from period to period, from industry to industry, and from country to country. Major structural changes are taking place today within a framework characterized by currency convertibility, relatively liberal commercial policies, and greatly constrained cyclical fluctuations. Within this framework, uneven rates of improvement in productivity tend to produce large shifts in trading patterns and large, prolonged swings in net current account balances which it would be undesirable to suppress. These swings are not short-term oscillations which cancel out in a few years; large imbalances in one direction or another should be expected to persist for a number of years. Although liberalized trading conditions widen the scope for eventual adaptation and adjustment of imbalances, this should not obscure the fact that, in the first instance, they allow such imbalances to become large and to persist for prolonged periods. Under the earlier regime of direct controls and inconvertibility, these imbalances could be quickly suppressed. Moreover, under our present system of quasi-fixed gold parities capital movements among the industrially advanced countries are more likely to reinforce than to neutralize the imbalances in current accounts.

Under today's conditions it is fatuous to expect balance-of-payments equilibrium, as conventionally defined, to be closely approximated from year to year or even over a period of several years. But the existing international monetary framework does not provide adequate facilities for financing the large and prolonged imbalances which, under liberalized trading con-

_____

From a symposium in *The American Economic Review*, pp. 93–126, in which Professor Despres comments on various papers. Reprinted by permission.

ditions, are the reflection of a dynamic international economy.

Our international monetary institutions simply do not fit our newly liberalized trading and payments arrangements. This creates a striking lack of symmetry between the reaction of deficit countries and that of surplus countries. As their reserves become deficient, deficit countries find themselves under increasingly urgent pressure to correct their deficits; the pressure on surplus countries to halt the accumulation of redundant reserves, either by increasing their domestic effective demand or by providing the external finance which would permit continued surpluses in their international accounts, is not so urgently felt. This asymmetry introduces a pervasive deflationary bias into the world economy, which first impinges on the deficit countries and then is transmitted by them to the surplus countries both directly and through underdeveloped countries as intermediaries.

The most likely consequence, unless adequate financial mechanisms are created, is international propagation of secular retardation; i.e., sluggish growth. There is no likelihood today that any country would accept sharp, cumulative deflation, deep depression, and massive unemployment as a means of eliminating a deficit in its international accounts. On the other hand, monetary and fiscal policies in the United States, in Britain, and perhaps also in Japan are being based today on a delicate and uneasy compromise between domestic growth objectives and balance-of-payments considerations. The difference over five or ten years between a close approach to full employment and an average level of unemployment of 5 to 7 per cent is much greater than the simpler calculations on this subject reveal. The difference between full employment and moderate unemployment is not chiefly that output is raised by increasing labor input, nor is it primarily that aggregate investment is higher when employment is full. The chief difference is that the climate of buoyant demand and active use of productive resources which full employment entails is one in which innovations and improvements come forward rapidly and resources gain mobility, moving readily from obsolete fields into newer fields of growing competitive strength. This is the main difference between full employment and "high-level stagnation"—5 to 7 per cent unemployment. Fundamental correction of underlying deficits in external payments of structural origin requires an acceleration of innovations, more rapid improvements in technology, and the transfer of resources to new industrial fields. But as Britain's experience since World War I has demonstrated, these conditions could not be realized when aggregate demand was constrained by policies which almost continually reflected a preoccupation with the balance of payments. The uneasy compromise between domestic economic objectives and the so-called "discipline" of the balance of payments serves to hamper economic growth and needed structural change, and thus to perpetuate the imbalance in external payments. When the source of payments imbalances is structural, a substantial increase in deficits in the short and intermediate run is likely to be indispensable for constructive long-run adjustment. The Marshall Plan, even after allowance for the special circumstances, was a vividly dramatic illustration of this principle. Until conditions are gradually created under which international captial movements on private account can perform an equalizing role, payments imbalances among advanced countries will require official compensatory financing on a much larger scale and for longer periods than has hitherto been customary.

It is wrong to think that such financing merely postpones necessary adjustments. On the contrary, it makes possible the structural changes and adaptations in both deficit and surplus countries necessary for removing the causes of unbalanced international payments, without handicapping growth. It would be ironical indeed if the advanced industrial countries, having proclaimed through OECD ambitious growth targets for the sixties, did not adopt the basically simple international financial measures without which these growth targets will have little chance of being realized.

SOME CURRENT ECONOMIC PROBLEMS AND APPROACHES

A.

AUTOMATION

63. Dead Horse and the Featherbird

Paul Jacobs

The fear of technological unemployment leads people to try to preserve jobs regardless of the need for the work. Mr. Jacobs examines the history of the Typographical Union's effort to preserve jobs, and discusses the social problems created by technological change.

64. Union Policies and Technological Change

George W. Taylor

Professor Taylor asserts that, in general, labor unions have accepted and cooperated with management in the introduction of technological change. He suggests that cooperation between unions and management offers the most promising road to solving this problem, and that not all apparently restrictive "work rules" are undesirable.

65. Bargaining Isn't Enough

Ralph Helstein

The members of Mr. Helstein's union (the Packinghouse Workers) have been hard hit by automation. He describes the discouraging results of their pioneering attempts to alleviate technological unemployment through collective bargaining, and urges that the problem be faced by the nation as a whole.

66. Automation and Joblessness

William Glazier

Mr. Glazier points out that automation elimi-
nates jobs and often diminishes skill requirements. Under these conditions, retraining cannot solve the unemployment problem, and the
price of faster technological advance may be
increased unemployment.

67. The Stupidity Problem

John Fischer

Mr. Fischer argues that technological change is
eliminating many of the jobs our labor force is
capable of performing, and that the I.Q. requirements for many of the new jobs are beyond the
capacity of the available labor force. He urges
that we must face the need to find useful jobs
for workers with low intelligence levels.

B.
DISARMAMENT

68. Economic Impacts of Disarmament

Panel on Economic Impacts of Disarmament,
Emile Benoit, Chairman

What if peace breaks out? Would disarmament
bring a depression in the United States? Who
would be hardest hit? This report analyzes the
complex economic implications of disarmament
and suggests a series of programs designed to
alleviate the impact of readjustment.

C.
SOCIAL INSURANCE

69. Pro and Con on Medicare

Abraham Ribicoff, former Secretary of
Health, Education, and Welfare;
Edward R. Annis, M. D.

The Kennedy Administration's proposal of
medical care for the aged within the framework of the federal social security system pro-
voked a storm of debate. Secretary Ribicoff and
Dr. Annis present the pros and cons for "Medicare," speaking, respectively, for the administration and the American Medical Association.

70. The Golden Years

Michael Harrington

It is easy to forget that social problems involve people, not just statistics. Mr. Harrington provides a graphic portrait of the eroding impact of dependence on the aged poor, and illustrates some problems faced in relief administration.

D.
ECONOMIC FORECASTING

71. Fortune's Forecast

Fortune

Economic prediction is a dangerous game, but business plans must be based on forecasts of the future. This *Fortune* report provides an example of economic forecasting which can be used as a basis for further analysis. How accurate were they, and why?

E.
THE UNDERDEVELOPED COUNTRIES

72. Why Are We Blessed?

Peggy and Pierre Streit

In the eyes of many of the world's poorer peoples America is rich beyond comprehension. Two reporters who have seen much of the world's misery ponder America's abundance and ask what can be done, beyond cold-war measures, to help the poor nations.

73. Economics For the Nuclear Age

W. W. Rostow

Using a broad brush, Professor Rostow generalizes from historical experience, and identifies five big stages of economic growth from economic backwardness to a mature, high-consumption society. He discusses the implications of his conclusions for the problems of underdeveloped areas, and examines the role of American government and business in aiding the growth process.

74.   Development Program in Afghanistan

United Nations Review

The very modest beginnings of a program designed to raise living standards in rural areas are described in this U.N. report. It shows how hard it is to introduce even the simplest changes in a backward society.

75.   Economic Development: Rival Systems and Comparative Advantage

John Kenneth Galbraith

The underdeveloped countries face a choice between Western democratic methods and the Marxist political and economic design. Dr. Galbraith compares the two approaches, and argues that a critical advantage of the Western model is its emphasis on liberty and constitutional process.

F.
COMPARATIVE ECONOMIC SYSTEMS

76.   The Drift of Modern Economic History

Robert L. Heilbroner

The capitalist market system remains today in only a few nations. Professor Heilbroner analyzes why different economic systems have developed in different nations, and compares other systems with the American market economy.

77.   Questions and Answers on Soviet Life

U.S.S.R.

What determines the standard of living of the Soviet citizen? The Soviet propaganda magazine, *U.S.S.R.*, provides an idealized description of how wages and consumption are distributed in the Communist world.

78. Soviet Union: How it Plans, Works, Grows

Business Week

In the absence of a market system, a communist society must devise an administrative process for the allocation and distribution of its resources. This article explains how the Soviets make and carry out their economic plans, and highlights some of the major problems that develop when a huge bureaucratic structure is required.

79. Lessons From the West German Miracle
Karl W. Roskamp

The author analyzes the rapid postwar economic growth in West Germany, and identifies the selective government policies which helped make it possible. He suggests that we consider similar policies for the American economy.

A.

AUTOMATION

63   DEAD HORSE AND THE FEATHERBIRD

Paul Jacobs

Paul Jacobs is director of the Fund for the Republic's study of American labor. He is also on the staff of the Institute of Industrial Relations at the University of California at Berkeley.

"DEAD HORSE" IS FOALED

The compositor who despises setting type for an ad that will end in the hellbox has an ancient lineage. Imprinters, men who put symbols or letters on bricks, were found in ancient Babylonia. Roman coins had letters on them; nobles used a form of printing when they pressed their seals into wax; and the Chinese had paper money printed from wood blocks before the tenth century. Typography was known in China as far back as 1041. In 1314 a Chinese printer used 60,000 separate wooden characters to publish a book on agriculture. But books in the Christian world were laboriously copied out by hand; only the Church and the

richest men could afford them. In the Middle Ages, books were chained to the lectern in the monastery or college fortunate enough to possess them. Charles V of France had a huge collection for the fourteenth century—910 volumes.

In the middle of the fifteenth century, Johann Gutenberg's invention for the cutting and casting of metal type created an enormous demand for books throughout Europe and England. To meet the new demand, printers were needed. In an age when most of the

---

Excerpted from *Dead Horse and the Featherbird,* A Report to the Center for the Study of Democratic Institutions (New York: Fund for the Republic, 1962). Reprinted by permission.

population was illiterate, a journeyman printer not only had to know how to read, spell, and write, but also had to possess an artistic sense, a flair for selecting the appropriate type and setting it in an attractive manner. Complicated measurements requiring a knowledge of mathematics were necessary to set up his forms. In addition, he had to be a skilled mechanic, capable not only of maintaining his equipment but of building new equipment.

How were these early craftsmen paid for their work? The first printers were paid in accordance with the amount of type they either set or produced. But as new type faces and sizes were introduced, more and more skill was required of the printer. Typography was becoming an art, and it was soon clear that the system of paying printers merely for the type they actually set would have to be changed.

How, for example, was a printer to be paid if some of the work he normally did in the shop was done outside and then brought into his workplace? How was he to make a living if an unlimited number of impressions could be made from the type he had set? And if the journeyman printer could not earn a living from one master, he might wander off to the next town in the hope that there would be more work for him there. A good printer was hard to find in those days; an employer, a master printer, had a big stake in keeping his skilled workers available even when work fell off. And so, in order to protect themselves, the master printers, not the journeymen workers, began developing restrictions on how many copies could be made from any one form of type.

During the sixteenth century, most English printing journeymen and masters lived in London where there were printing presses, each licensed and rigidly controlled under the tight guild system. Except for a press at Oxford and another at Cambridge, the London presses were the only ones in England. By 1557 the master printers of London had banded together as the London Stationers' Company and carried on their trade under a charter from the Crown. The Company, controlled by twenty-odd master printers, was among the most rigidly operated of guilds. By 1587, the work rules of the Company provided that type, once having been set and used, could not be used again without first being broken up and put back in the type box. Rule 1 decreed: "Ffyrst that no formes of letters be kept standinge to the prejudice of Woorkemen at any time." Rule 2 imposed a limit ranging from 1250 to 1500 on the number of impressions that might be made from any one form of type, except for "Grammars Accidences Prymers and Catechisms" when "3000 at the moste" were permitted. There were a few additional exemptions—"the statutes and proclamacons with all other bookes belonging to ye office of her maiesties printer which by reason of her maiesties affayres are to be limited to no numbers," "all Calendars printed Red and black," and finally, "all Almanaches and prognostications."

By 1635, the Stationers' Company had issued a new set of rules governing the operations of print shops and presses. An increase was granted in the number of impressions that might be drawn from a single form and the old rule that "no formes of letters be kept standinge" was modified to permit the use of the standing form, provided that if a compositor in the shop wanted work, he would be paid for the form that was used just as if he had composed it himself.

The most important of the new rules was Number 15, which prohibited the exchange or interchange of type material by journeymen. The rule, originally adopted for the benefit of the masters, "That noe work man lend Letter type without consent first obteyned of the Master on paine to loose the benefit of Hollydais and Copies," was the forerunner of the present law of the printers' union on "reproduction."

In the course of many years, another rule emerged: the printers in a shop or newspaper had a right to set all the type in that shop or be paid for any type or drawing that was actually used even if the master printer had borrowed it or purchased it already set up from another shop. There seemed to be no other way to handle the interchange of type and other materials, and the rule was accepted by both journeymen and masters.

WORK AND UNWORK MIGRATE TO AMERICA

"It may be safely presumed that America inherited its methods of working and trade customs from London, upon which it was always to some degree dependent on men, ideas and equipment," Benjamin Franklin wrote in 1754.

Like sailors, printers were internationalists, taking their craft with them all over the world. By 1638, there was a press established in colonial America —Stephen Day's at Cambridge, operated under the English practices brought to America from across the sea. But since most of the print shops of colonial America were one- or two-man operations, the labor customs common to England were unnecessary in colonial America. It was not until the middle of the eighteenth century that American printers began to worry about their own employment difficulties.

As early as 1815, the New York printers' union was issuing traveling cards to its members. Without such a card, the printer had a hard time finding work and a harder time keeping it. Lacking such a card, he was viewed suspiciously by other printers, who were fearful that he would work at wages less than those demanded by the union men. During the last years of the eighteenth century and the first part of the nineteenth, printers in New York, Albany, Boston, New Orleans, Washington, Philadelphia, and Baltimore made attempts to form unions or associations in their local communities to deal with employers. By 1831, the printers felt strong enough to demand a closed shop from their New York employers. Two years later they were insisting that any dispute between a printer and his employer would be finally resolved by the union members who were working at the place of employment, a practice still in effect today. In 1850, the scattered local unions of printers banded together to form the Journeymen Printers of the United States, the first national union of printers. It later became the International Typographical Union.

But up to the Civil War, in spite of their skills and the protection given them by their unions, American printers often lived as close to poverty as had their sixteenth century English cousins. They still set type by hand and worked under the old piecework system without any guaranteed minimum weekly wage. When a printer reported for work in one of the early newspaper offices, he never knew if there was to be any work for him and, if there was, how long it would last. If it was a slow day for news, he might set type for an hour; if war had broken out someplace, he might work steadily for fifteen hours. Sometimes, the printer arrived at the newspaper office to find an edition being printed from type that had been used earlier that day or even the day before.

Those were years of bitter rivalry between newspapers, and so there was very little interchange of type between them. Each paper had its own column width, which presented a formidable mechanical obstacle to the exchanging of type. Type out on loan was also unavailable for the publishers' own use. And there was an additional hazard— the type characters were made of heavy metal, not easily transportable through the crowded streets. Thus, in the formative years of the printers' union the exchange of type between employers was no great problem for the union's scattered locals. Instead, they concentrated on getting and maintaining the closed shop, enforcing the seniority rules by which men were hired and fired, trying to limit the number of low-paid apprentices, and setting piecework rates. By 1871, however, the exchange of type between publishers was becoming general enough to provoke a discussion at the union's convention. A newspaper publisher from New Albany, Indiana, appeared before the convention delegates to appeal a ruling against him made by the printers in his own plant.

Most American cities of the time had at least two daily newspapers, and the larger ones often more than a dozen. There were no nation-wide newspaper chains, all printing the same kind of paper throughout the country; instead, most papers were separately owned and competed bitterly with each other in circulation and advertising wars. That was how the papers in New Albany operated, too, until one of them began to borrow type, already set, from one of the newspapers in Louisville, just across the river. The printers' union in New Albany decided that the publisher there would have to pay for setting the borrowed type if he wanted

to use it. The local union's reasons were simple: the practice, if permitted, would have eliminated the jobs of the compositors who otherwise would have set the type that had been borrowed. But the union had another good reason to prohibit the practice—it had to protect the other publishers in the area. The use of borrowed type by one paper gave it an unfair competitive advantage over the other newspapers in New Albany because it could sell more pages without having had to pay the cost of producing them. Thus, the union was forced to use its economic power to police the industry, a policy since then often urged on it by employers anxious to reduce their competitors' economic advantage.

The New Albany publisher appealed the local union's decision to the national convention of the International Typographical Union, and lost. On June 7, 1872, the union, as part of its law, binding upon both members and employers, established "that the transfer of matter from one firm to another is detrimental to both proprietor and printer and should not be allowed."

For the next several years the "loaning and borrowing of matter" kept coming up at union conventions, until the prohibition extended to include even morning and evening newspapers printed in "separate and distinct establishments" by the same publisher. As yet, no union member was being paid to set type that had already been set and printed; rather, the union law was only that the type could not be used over again after it had been used once.

Meanwhile, technology was catching up with the printers. From the Civil War until 1890, the publishing industry in the United States was revolutionized by a series of inventions: the stereotype process, photo-engraving, the web press, and, finally, the one the printers believed threatened them most, the linotype machine.

When Otto Mergenthaler patented his linotype machine in 1885, type was still being set laboriously by hand. Two years later, fifty-five of the machines were manufactured. By 1891, the national union leaders had become convinced that the linotype represented a grave problem for their members. A committee investigated the machine's operations in New York and reported its findings to the union members. Linotype operators were doing three times the work of the hand compositors, the committee said, and seemed capable of increasing that amount to four times. The committee recommended that linotype operators be paid on a time basis instead of by the old piecework system and that the hours of work be cut. The union convention, held that same year, adopted both these principles, calling for a cut in the work day to a maximum of eight hours.

Linotypes were quickly put into use by newspapers all over the country. In 1894, 890 of them were produced; in 1895, more than a thousand; and by 1904, 7,500 linotype machines were in operation in the United States and Canada. The displacement of hand compositors by linotype operators grew as more and more of the machines were installed. Some of the younger men were able to learn the new skill; many of the older compositors became permanently unemployed.

But the introduction of the linotype did not have the long-run catastrophic consequences on their employment that printers had feared. Instead, the standardized, inexpensive papier-mâché stereotype mats and the photo-engraving process permitted manufacturers to advertise their products

nationally, without the great difficulties and expense involved in sending copy for advertisements to many different newspapers, all with different kinds of type and column sizes. Papers got bigger as the amount of advertising increased; there was more work for the printing trades. Because the linotype meant that printing could be done more cheaply, more printing was done; newspaper editors took to changing stories in later editions as changes in the news developed, since the cost of such changes was now a good deal less.

The eyes of the printers, however, were not focused on long-range, future developments. Even though the calamity they had been expecting did not take place, the immediate effect of the linotype was to disemploy the older hand compositors. In 1895, the secretary of the New York Typographical Union reported to the labor commissioner on the relationship between the linotype machine and printers' employment: 293 machines had displaced 544 hand compositors—just less than two men to each machine. The older compositors who were now reduced to loitering around the union office or doing odd jobs of substitute work were a constant reminder to employed printers that perhaps their own future was just as dismal.

The depression of that period reinforced these fears. Many members of the ITU roamed the streets. And so "unwork" in newspaper publishing was created from a constellation of circumstances: the difficulty of devising equitable standards for printers' pay, the desire of employers to have printers constantly available for work, the fears of publishers that their competitors might gain "unfair" economic advantages through new technological advances, the printers' apprehensions about being unemployed. In 1901, the national convention of the printers' union changed the flat prohibition against "loaning and borrowing matter" that had been enforced against the New Albany, Indiana, publisher. The union decided to allow the "interchanging, borrowing, lending or buying of matter previously used, either in the form of type, matrices or photoengraved plates" but under one condition—that it all be done over again. In the years since then, the original blanket insistence that *all* such "matter" be reproduced has been modified to cover only the advertisements inserted by local companies.

Thus it is that an ITU member can find himself sullenly and sloppily setting type, in August, for an ad that had run in the paper the previous Easter. The sullenness and sloppiness are the direct consequences of men who are tied to "unwork," which they despise. But without the "unwork," they fear, they might face permanent unemployment. And the fact that there is no unemployment in their industry at present does little to allay their apprehensions.

*   *   *

That machines do not, even at their first introduction, invariably throw human labor out of employment, must be admitted; and it has been maintained, by persons very competent to form an opinion on the subject, that they never produce that effect. The solution of this question depends on facts, which unfortunately, have not yet been collected.

—Charles Babbage, *Economy of Machinery and Manufacturers,* 1830

Who is to blame for the continued existence of "dead horse"? The responsibility must be distributed between the fearful printers who vote to retain reproduction even though most of them despise doing it and the newspaper publishers who publicly denounce reproduction but privately ask the union to force their competitors to set the never-printed type.

Who is to blame for the "featherbird" in the cockpit? Again, the responsibility must be shared. The Air Line Pilots Association has used its economic power, in the name of safety, to demand three pilots in the cockpit; the flight engineers have been equally adamant, again in the name of safety, that jets must have only two pilots and a mechanic-flight engineer; the managements of the seven airlines who bought themselves a little labor peace, also in the name of safety, cannot adopt the pose of innocent victims; and, finally, the government must assume its share of the responsibility because of the vagueness of its 1948 ruling.

More than anything else, however, the reason for "unwork" is the workers' fear of permanent job loss or temporary layoff. If an employee is given a choice between doing "unwork" or not working at all, he will choose the "unwork." Once having been trapped into doing something he hates, he seeks justification for it. He must rationalize that what he does is not only acceptable but necessary. If he does not do this, he cannot face himself or a society in which work is so important. Soon, his stake in "unwork" becomes as important to him as the economic benefits he may derive from it.

We seem not much better equipped now to find a "solution of this question" than was Babbage one hundred twenty-seven years ago, when he wrote that the facts "have not yet been collected." Economists are still arguing. The classical economists who justified the industrial revolution concentrated their attention on the effects the introduction of machinery had on wages, prices, and aggregate employment. There was a general assumption, then, that a neat, circular process took place: the price of a commodity produced in greater numbers by machine dropped, and the decrease in price caused an increase in demand for the product, thus eventually increasing the number of workers needed in the industry. If the process did not always operate perfectly and there was a reduction in the number of workers employed in an industry after new machinery was introduced, the loss of employment was not considered a serious problem. "A person trained to habits of industry and application can be easily moved from one employment to another," economist J. R. McCulloch wrote in 1830. "It is easy for a weaver of cottons to become a weaver of woolens or linen."

But nineteenth century economic theories have only a very limited application to twentieth century realities. The rapidly accelerating increase in the *rate* of technological change and the swift shifts in marketing patterns, public tastes, and styles made possible by the mass media have compounded a qualitatively different order of problem for society than existed in 1830. However "easy" it may have been then for a cotton weaver to shift over to work on wool or linen, it is extremely difficult for a displaced worker today to make such transitions. And despite the continuous rise in the size of the total work force, no one is certain whether the statistics of the jobs lost to technology are accurate, nor does anyone really know whether technology is creating an equal number of new jobs to replace the old ones.

New techniques have to be found for determining what percentage of our unemployed are not working because of a temporary recession and what percentage are not working because their jobs have disappeared without replacement. There are serious statistical difficulties in trying to decide whether the unemployed are

direct or indirect casualties of technology, but it should be possible to make a better evaluation of the data that do exist.

A new kind of industrial census might be in order, too: one that regularly samples not people but industries in order to discover whether new processes have been introduced and whether these processes have displaced workers.

The success or failure of the current retraining and relocation programs for unemployed workers needs to be carefully assessed. Some analyses of these programs show that the results have been far below expectations. If the comparatively small group of workers who have already gone through the retraining or relocation process either have not been able to find employment or can only work at a far lower skill and wage level, have we the right to assume that the same kind of program on a large scale will be anything more than a large-scale failure?

Even a successful program of this kind might prove to be too high a price to pay for too rapid a rate of technological change. The tensions that follow large-scale displacements of skill, the rupturing of family relationships involved in forced migrations, and the difficulties of adjustment faced by older jobless workers suddenly deprived of identity in a work-oriented society are still largely unknown. To all these unmeasured costs there must also be added the economic costs now being paid by the whole community.

All of the measures to relieve the burdens that come with unemployment are necessary because of an unchallenged assumption that management has an absolute right to automate its production system at all times. The newspapers attack union leaders who resist automation. "Management's right to manage must be preserved and as part of that right the unhindered, unqualified introduction of automation," a *New York Times* editorialist wrote. But who gave management its "right" to the "unhindered, unqualified introduction of automation"? If management's right to automate its property is an absolute one, then does not the union have an equally absolute right to resist automation in order to protect the workers' property—their jobs?

In fact, what fixed and absolute management or union rights are there outside newspaper editorials? Once, management insisted it had the "right" unilaterally to discharge an employee; now that right is considerably limited by public law and private contract. Once, management insisted it had the fixed and absolute right to move its plant where it pleased; now that right is becoming more and more limited by unions and the courts. Once, unions were free to keep out Negroes, but that kind of "freedom" is disappearing under the moral and legal pressures of the community. Ultimately, technology may force America to adopt a different set of axioms, based on an understanding that the acceptance of technology does not mean an unquestioning acceptance of its uses, products, and results.

We need new standards for assessing the effects of technology upon society. The total exploitation of oil fields made possible by technology is limited legally now whenever the interest of a stable price structure in the petroleum industry require it. Why then would it be improper to place limitations on those extensions of technology which *seriously* injure the human beings who work in oil refineries? Today, society must judge technology by not only what it brings in benefits of efficiency but also by the social costs,

both hidden and open, that inevitably must be paid.

The existence of these social costs is being recognized and society is accepting some responsibility for sharing them with their victims. Yet retraining programs and unemployment insurance, important as they are, are not enough. If the oil industry is permitted a 27½ per cent depletion tax allowance on the theory that oil extraction is a depletion of corporate assets, why, for example, should there not be a depletion allowance on jobs destroyed by technology? If corporations were given a technological tax allowance with the provision that the savings be used only for the development of new jobs, would not the community share more equitably in the benefits of technology and would not the corporation have a financial incentive for the creation of new jobs?

Until now, unions have led the attempts to ameliorate the effects of unemployment. They have restricted production, created "unwork," and even now are demanding a shorter work week. They have lobbied for increases in the amount of unemployment insurance. They have proposed guaranteed annual wages, supplementary unemployment insurance benefits, and improved pension plans. They have challenged the government to devise fiscal policies that will give greater impetus to the economy. But still, useful as these proposals may be, they are not enough.

Unions should take the lead in developing new standards for assessing the effects of technology. Their staffs are in a unique position to become the social ecologists of an industrialized society, the people who can best make judgments on the consequences of automation combined with feedback systems and computer controls. Once the consequences are assessed, even imperfectly, the increased efficiency gained through technology should be then weighed against other social values that may be important enough to justify limiting some uses of technology, just as the petroleum industry limits the amount of crude oil pumped from the fields. If we do not develop standards beyond the single one of efficiency for judging technological change, if we do not create new jobs by devising new economic instruments, and if we do not create new theories of industrial justice for the technological dilemmas of the twentieth century, only two alternatives may be open in the twenty-first century: either there will be so few jobs available that only an elite will be allowed to work while the remainder of society consumes, or the practice of "unwork" will need to spread. For the first alternative, a new social, cultural, and religious tradition will have to be substituted for the work-oriented one that we have now; for the second, many, many more "dead horses" and "featherbirds," with all of their unhappy, demeaning consequences.

64   UNION POLICIES AND TECHNOLOGICAL CHANGE

George W. Taylor

George W. Taylor is Professor of Economics at the University of Pennsylvania.

*   *   *

Within the limits imposed by their representational function, unions have generally accepted a form of "high wage—low labor cost" doctrine. This has long been, and still is, a notable characteristic of the American economic scene. Almost without exception, union leaders recognize that increased productivity per man hour, arising from mechanization, is the key to easier jobs and improved living standards for employees.

Reference to two instances in which this point of view has been made particularly explicit in labor agreements seems appropriate. The ground breaking 1948 and 1950 Agreements between General Motors Corporation and the United Automobile Workers of America provided for annual productivity wage increases. Article 101 (a) of the 1950 Agreement stated a principle important to the parties but rather lost sight of in the continuing argument about the soundness of this kind of employee sharing in productivity gains. It reads:

The annual improvement factor provided herein recognizes that a continuing improvement in the standard of living of employees depends upon technological progress, better tools, methods, processes and equipment and a cooperative attitude on the part of all parties in such progress. It further recognizes the principle that to produce more with the same amount of human effort is a sound economic and social objective.

On this basis, negotiations have been constructively carried out with a minimum of interruption to production and without governmental intervention.

Great interest has been aroused by

Excerpted from The American Assembly, *Automation and Technological Change;* copyright 1962. Reprinted by permission of Prentice-Hall, Inc., publisher.

a more recent undertaking. In the face of a drastic impairment of their members' job security, because of improved machinery and methods, the Amalgamated Meat Cutters and Butcher Workmen of North America and the United Packinghouse Workers of America agreed with Armour and Company on a policy toward technological change. This was enunciated in Appendix 1 of the August 31, 1959 Agreement. It reads:

. . . the meat packing industry is undergoing significant changes in methods of production, processing, marketing and distribution. Armours' moderization program is vital to its ability to compete and grow successfully, thus providing a reasonable return on capital invested in the enterprise and providing the assurance of continued employment for the employees under fair standards of wages, benefits and working conditions.

That Agreement went further. The company recognized that

. . . mechanization and new methods to promote operating and distributing efficiencies affect the number of employees required and the manner in which they perform their work . . . these problems require continued study to promote employment opportunities for employees affected by the introduction of more efficient methods and technological changes.

Novel steps were taken to carry out these general principles. Although the results fell considerably short of initial hopes, they afford invaluable experience for the guidance not only of the meat-packing industry but more generally for dealing with the displacement of semi-skilled workers.

There are other cases in which the salutary results of union cooperation in technological change is evident in the statistics. The bituminous coal industry is a notable example. The

United Mine Workers of America has, for many years, actively encouraged the modernization of mining operations. That made possible substantial gains in wage rates, hours, and working conditions for those who kept their jobs. Employment opportunities in the industry declined sharply but that brought advantages as well as disadvantages. From one point of view, the principal conservation of human values was in making it possible for the industry to meet society's demand for coal by exposing only 150,000 men instead of 500,000 to the harsh dangers of mining.

Substitution of machines for men is an old story in the bituminous coal industry. Since 1948, however, mechanization brought about an unprecedented transformation. It has been estimated that, in constant dollars, the net value of plant and equipment per worker in the industry increased at an annual rate of 10 per cent from 1948 to 1959. In consequence, within a decade, output per production worker man-hour increased by 85 per cent or at an annual rate of 6.4 per cent. Improvement rates were but slightly less for all employee man-hours including those worked in the offices. The number of production workers fell by three-fifths or to less than 150,000 employees while total production remained about the same. Only to a relatively limited extent, through industry welfare funds, did the displaced people share in the industry's technological gains. Their continued unemployment is essentially their own concern and the community's. It will be recalled that a combination of private and governmental programs was envisioned by the President's Advisory Committee on Labor-Management Policy as the most feasible way of treating technological displacement.

The record in coal epitomizes the

breath-taking promise of "automation." It also reveals the concomitant disruption of workers' lives and the serious social problems that are involved.

One of the great strengths of collective bargaining is in its capacity for devising practical solutions to meet particular problems of the private sector of the economy. Like the coal and the meat-packing arrangements, the much discussed West Coast Longshore Agreement could not have been created nor its mutual benefits realized except by agreement among the parties themselves.

After extended debate in 1958, representatives of the longshoremen "voted unanimously to explore with the employers the benefits to be gained if they were to adopt a cooperative policy for orderly introduction of new mechanical methods and changes in working rules." The Pacific Maritime Association decided that through cooperation with the Union, a free hand to mechanize could be realized effectively. In the collective agreement dated October 26, 1960, the union conceded management's right freely to mechanize and without regard to previously established work rules, including those regulating crew sizes. In return the companies agreed to contribute a sizable amount to an "automation fund" to protect the interests of affected employees. This reconciliation of diverse interests was brought about by an agreement, ratified by a majority of the workers, which met the circumstances of a particular case. As in the coal industry, workers have been displaced and there will be a marked shrinkage of job opportunities in longshoring. Costs to society are a part of technological advance if the interests of affected employees are to be taken into account.

The examples of collective bargaining agreements which accelerate and facilitate technological change would be incomplete without some reference to those under which the introduction of new machines and methods is synchronized with employee attrition rates in order to avoid displacement altogether. To the extent that attrition rates lag, cost savings will have to be deferred. In an increasing number of cases, however, companies are guaranteeing that "no regular employee shall lose his job in consequence of technological changes." This policy can be difficult to administer. A clear differentiation between job losses due to the specified cause and those occasioned by seasonal or cyclical variations of demand is often not possible. And, overtime work, even at premium rates of pay, will sometimes be scheduled as the alternative to engaging new employees. Nevertheless, particular circumstances sometimes make this approach feasible.

In point is the policy of the Transit Authority of the City of New York. As one part of the settlement of the labor agreement dispute with the Transport Workers of America in December, 1961, the Authority agreed to make explicit its established policy in this area. A letter, supplementary to the labor agreement, reads:

The Transit Authority in carrying out its managerial responsibilities for the safe and efficient operation of the transit facilities under its jurisdiction has introduced many efficiencies by automation and other means. In effecting these operating improvements, the Authority has consistently adhered to the policy of not laying off any permanent employees by assigning surplus employees to other productive work without any reduction in the employee's pay. . . .

That policy, more than any other single influence, seems to have made it possible for the Authority to introduce technological changes over the years. Its operations were conducted in 1961 with approximately 27,500 employees; a reduction of about 6,500 employees as compared to 1955.

There is, then, ample evidence of the widespread acceptance by unions of the high wage-low labor cost doctrine under which improved methods of production are encouraged as long as employee needs are also satisfied. In order to do this, a combination of private and government programs is the key.

It is now suggested that, in many ways, the collective bargaining approach has advantages over the making of technological changes by a company without the formal checks and balances of collective bargaining. One cannot assume that non-unionized operations, in themselves, provide a smooth road for management. Unorganized workers are as much concerned as everyone else in job security and a fair share of productivity gains.

As early as 1931, a publication appeared (by Stanley B. Mathewson) concerning the restriction of output by unorganized workers. Being unorganized, the employees studied were particularly vulnerable to the disciplinary action, heavily counted upon in earlier years, to induce a "fair day's work." Yet, restriction of production was found to be deeply entrenched and well-nigh universally practiced among virtually all employee groups. It was a response to the challenge of job insecurity and a reaction "on principle" to what were appraised as unfair terms of employment.

Restriction of production, as a form of employee self-protection, existed long before the 1931 Inquiry and has since continued as an active force. In 1949, Peter Drucker wrote about this matter (in *The New Society*) as follows:

. . . open restrictions on efficiency and productivity are only the part of the iceberg that is above water. Much more important are the invisible, unwritten, informal restrictions decreed by the custom and the common law of every plant . . . bosses have learned, however, that an attempt to break the production code of their department will bring nothing but serious trouble. They also sympathize as a rule with the men's attitude—they themselves may well share the workers' fear that increased productivity may cost them their job.

Neither employees nor foremen have an inherent conviction that they can freely contribute to production increases "without [according to Mathewson] incurring penalties in place of the rewards which usually accompany special attention to duty in other fields of endeavor." Yet, "most working people hate the whole messy business of restriction, and especially the complicated system of cunning devices they employ to cover it up."

The direct representation of employees by a union at least permits a facing up to and a direct dealing with those forces upon which the employee contribution to production is so dependent. Due process can supplant the often capricious unwritten laws and mores of the workplace. Many a management, unable to develop a satisfactory personnel policy, has attested in private conversation that dealing with a responsible union has improved the productive performance of employees. This is, of course, not a pre-ordained result, but neither does the absence of a union inevitably solve the problem.

On two counts, then, collective bargaining is a national asset in adjusting to the technological change which is under way. It provides an effective procedure for a practical reconciliation of conflicting objectives of management and the employees. To the extent that acquiescence of employees to the necessary adjustments is secured, a major contribution can be made to the effective utilization of new equipment and new methods.

WHAT ABOUT FEATHERBEDDING?

The wide degree of acceptance of technological change by unions can, thus, be demonstrated. Nevertheless, there is a gnawing general belief that the cost-saving benefits of such changes are, as a rule, dissipated by union adherence to capricious work rules which perpetuate unnecessary jobs and create unneeded hours of work. Extensive substantive evidence is at hand to provide a basis for the belief. Stand-by musicians and pilot truck drivers do secure choice job protection for themselves but at costs that can adversely affect prices and consumer demand. It should be possible to meet their demands for job security in more constructive ways. In one situation, the usefulness of a new machine was in grave doubt because of the employees' insistence upon production quotas, long established on older machines, which actually resulted in but six hours of actual work in an eight-hour day. The examples could be, but need not be, multiplied.

Such a high priority is presently being given to increased productivity, however, as to make popular the petulant dismissal of every inhibiting work rule as a simple case of "featherbedding" that should be eliminated forthwith. This has caused strikes. The trouble with the cavalier treatment is that "featherbedding" is not such a simple subject and can only be appraised on a case-by-case basis.

Some work rules unreasonably give preferential treatment to those who, in shop vernacular, "ride the gravy train." These rules are commonly though si-

lently resented by fellow workers. If they are specifically identified, their prompt elimination is usually feasible. On the other hand, many work rules, formal and informal, stem from an understandable desire of individuals to reduce their exposure to the economic risk inherent in a system of employment and of pay by the hour. In a part of the sugar refining industry it took the introduction of a kind of guaranteed annual wage to make a number of rigid work rules unprized by the employees. Under collective bargaining, the costs of work rules are formalized and on the table. For reasons already enunciated, it is a moot question whether collectively bargained work rules actually involve greater costs than the informal rules to which unorganized, as well as organized, workers adhere. This much is clear—work rules cannot be dealt with either as isolated phenomena or as "one ball of wax." A part of economic wisdom is to appreciate the depths that are plumbed in digging into work rules.

Some work rules are quite incomprehensible unless they are evaluated in terms of the individual's desire for personal status, so elusive in a workaday life embodying but little opportunity for personal triumphs. Rules in this area have odd manifestations. In one instance, the senior employees of a plant somehow gained a highly prized preference; their fellows allowed them to go first in punching out the time clock. The exit of the venerables from the parking lot was eased and they liked that. This particular informal rule, as it happened, also contributed to efficiency. Eliminated was another informal practice of everybody quitting work quite early in order to engage in what had been a sort of Oklahoma land rush to the time clocks.

Other work rules seem to represent a conscious choice of leisure over the greater productivity which could presumably make higher wages possible. The extended coffee break, provision for wash-up time and the like are examples. There are no more highly valued work rules in industrial relations and union leaders recommend a relinquishment at their peril. Along with provisions for longer vacations and more paid holidays such work rules can even be considered as one aspect of the longtime trend to shorter hours of work without a reduction in the weekly wage. Leisure is a normal personal goal.

The so-called featherbedding issue thus involves thousands of highly-particularized problems not amenable to understanding or treatment through broad generalization. A failure to recognize this fact can have disastrous consequences. No more sobering example can be referred to than the intensification of the 1959 steel strike by management's raising of the "2-B" issue in a way that was interpreted as a drive for unilateral management right to change work rules.

Work rules applicable to the utilization of labor cannot be summarily dismissed en masse as long as the conservation of those human values which individuals prize remains among the important goals. It is a sign of the times, perhaps, that the short-shrift treatment is so largely confined to those rules which benefit hourly paid workers while work rules prevalent in the professions, including college teaching with its tenure appointments, are more sympathetically viewed. Arrangements for balancing producers' interests with consumers' interests reflect a common desire to make one's working life more secure and more comfortable. Work rules are obviously neither an invention nor a monopoly of organized hourly workers. A defense of some forms of "featherbedding" is not difficult to mount.

*   *   *

65   BARGAINING ISN'T ENOUGH

Ralph Helstein

Ralph Helstein is President of the United Packinghouse, Food, and Allied Workers of America.

Automation is more than a narrow technical revolution, and is creating a situation which presents the central challenge to our economic well-being and to our social conscience.

Automation, as I use the term here, should be broadly defined. It is more than the introduction of new automatic equipment; it is a change in marketing of both raw material and finished product, in shipping, in plant location —in fact in the whole spectrum of the manufacturing process. Automation has led, among other things, to a serious loss of jobs for both production and white collar workers. The full impact of this development is just beginning to be felt.

The men and women of the meat packing industry have, in particular, been hard hit by these developments. As yet, we have found no satisfactory answers to our problem.

Between 1956 and 1960, employ-

From the *I.U.D. Digest* (Industrial Union Department, A.F.L.-C.I.O.), Summer, 1962, pp. 3–8. Reprinted by permission.

ment in our industry dropped from about 190,000 to 160,000— a drop of over 15 percent. During the same period, even with this loss of jobs, production has risen by about one percent.

Two years ago the United Packinghouse, Food & Allied Workers, together with a sister union, the Amalgamated Meat Cutters, raised the issue of job losses in its collective bargaining negotiations with the major companies. As a result of our discussions there was established a number of labor-management "automation fund committees" whose principal function was to inquire further into this problem that was creating widespread insecurity for the workers in the industry.

Armour Experiment

At Armour, the Automation Fund Committee had as its chairman Dr. Clark Kerr, president of the University of California, whose experience with the meat packing industry dated back to the days of the War Labor Board.

As a result of the committee's work we have more information about the impact of automation. It would be wrong, however, to say we are closer to a solution of the human problems created by automation.

We found, for example, that in a plant which had employed over a thousand people, far more than half of the people were unable, two years later, to find work anywhere, and they were still unemployed. Severance pay provisions in the contract, which had been a traditional way of meeting this problem, had provided some cushion, but offered no solution.

During the period the Automation Committee was in operation, a plant was closed in Oklahoma City. We made serious efforts to see if we could do something to assist approximately 350 people thrown out of work; we brought in a task force headed by a prominent economics professor to comb the entire area for job opportunities. Our search produced no jobs for the disemployed. We found that those over 35—and if Negroes, even younger— could not obtain interviews, let alone jobs. The committee went so far as to offer retraining of the former packinghouse workers for jobs at a new electrical manufacturing plant which was just opening in the same city. But the barriers of age and color could not be overcome.

Despite these discouragements, the Automation Fund Committee offered substantially subsidized retraining courses for the disemployed meat packing workers. Tests were given to determine their adaptability to training for new skills. Out of some 170 who showed up for the tests, all but 60 were told they could not be retrained for anything. Our last information concerning the 60 who did take retraining courses, was that only eight had been able to find employment.

Bargaining Limitations

These and other similar experiences have seriously raised the question whether the problem can be dealt with effectively through collective bargaining. Does a union fully discharge its responsibilities when it negotiates better pensions, better vacations, higher wages and other benefits that go into a collective bargaining agreement— for people who have no jobs? I think we do the whole concept of collective bargaining a wrong unless we realize its practical limitations.

This is a problem, in our view, that must be faced by the nation as a whole. It is difficult, if not wrong, to say to a particular company—or even to a particular industry—"this is a problem with which you have to deal and you alone must bear the whole cost." However, there may be no alternative unless we recognize, and quickly, that government must play an important role in meeting this problem. Government should be a coordinating force, bringing together the various components of our society to deal with the social dislocations resulting from automation.

No Easy Task

This is no easy task. The social cost is heavy and must be borne by the whole nation—not, as at present, by the unemployed worker. It is clear that in coming years, considering the people who are displaced as well as those now unemployed and those coming into the labor market, we are going to have to find an additional 2,500,000 jobs a year.

Yet, in the framework of these needs, engineers tell us that in 20 years or so, scarcely a single production worker will have to be employed in the process of making the necessities of American life.

A shorter workweek would, of course, provide relief for the period immediately ahead. I feel the concept voiced by the Administration that we need more production through more work, rather than leisure for workers, is really irrelevant. No such opportunity is at hand. It is not a labor shortage that acts as a damper on full use of the productive plant. The alternative is not one of increased leisure or less production.

The alternative is simply this: jobs or no jobs.

Basically, we have to abandon the easy, comfortable notion that every time we have an industrial revolution or a sharp change in our industrial system, new jobs are automatically created. We must put in proper perspective the kind of world that is being created as a result of recent scientific progress of major proportions. As we come to appreciate the full nature of the vast changes that are being produced we must also re-evaluate many of our traditional assumptions.

Such a critical examination will raise some fundamental questions. For example: Will we not have to change our ideas, because of the new technology, as to what constitutes work, and how income is provided? Over the centuries income for most of humanity has depended on work. Is there a necessary relationship between income and work? That is, without work can there be income? There are thousands of Americans whose current income is unrelated to work. There are other thousands whose current income reflects work done at some previous point in time, either by themselves or their forebears. This suggests that income and work are not tied together by inexorable laws—but rather by the traditional operations of our economic system. The problem is: how do we assure income for workers if work is not available?

Mr. W. H. Ferry, vice-president of *The Fund for the Republic,* has suggested that under these circumstances "we shall have to stop automatically regarding the unemployed as lazy, unlucky, indolent, and unworthy. We shall have to find means, public or private, of paying people to do no work."

Or, if we regard work as essential to man in keeping him attuned to reality, may we not have to broaden our conception of work to accord with Aristotle's—that is, as the creative process of learning and educating oneself to a greater understanding of the social and physical forces around us?

Transitional Stage

The shorter workweek will probably be a transitional stage on the road to the leisure society. The day must come when leisure on a broad scale is the accepted way of life. Before that day comes, the nature of our institutions will undergo great change. The nature and purpose of our corporations will, of necessity, be altered. Unions may evolve into different forms of service organizations for the people. All of that, however, lies in a yet uncharted future.

Meanwhile, there must be new concepts to give new meaning to full and creative living as leisure becomes more universal. This may be our chief problem, only a few decades hence. Far more attention must be paid both the problem of leisure itself and the creation of facilities we will need.

I am no sensationalist, but in all sobriety, I cannot help but view the onrush of automation with trepidation. The alternative to a society based upon creative leisure is one based upon misery for the many.

Daniel N. Michael, formerly of the Brookings Institute and presently director of the Peace Research Institute of Washington, has reported that automation will bring leisure surely enough —but the wrong way. In a report made for the Center for the Study of Democratic Institutions, Michael predicted that the new technology will wipe away white collar and service jobs as well as factory employment.

The report—entitled, "Cybernation: The Silent Conquest," foresaw an ever-growing "leisure" class of the unemployed living on a dole and having little to do that will be creative. It saw also an aimless low-income group working shorter hours, a well-paid group of professionals and semi-professionals able to rise to the problems of leisure, and a small, overworked group of "cyberneticians" and top managers who "may manage to get down to a 40-hour week" who will run our society.

Impact on Democracy

Automation, then, threatens the foundations of our democratic heritage since a society predicated upon a ruling elite will not long remain a government of the people. It is not enough to retrain a relative handful of displaced workers aimlessly, or even to better educate our youth toward a work-oriented society that is discernibly contracting.

There is a need now for those at the heights of American life to accept the idea of national long-range planning for the adjustments that must come in this society. We are fools if we deny the value of an over-all plan and program for the nation, or abdicate the field to the Communists.

Planning need not be totalitarian in nature. Democratic planning is consistent with the best traditions of freedom and is required to assure that automation will not create anarchy. It is indeed time to take the stigma out of planning and to create a National Planning Agency to plan for better cities, better education, better health, and widespread recreational facilities so that leisure will become increasingly meaningful.

Man has the capacity for great creative effort. The degree to which we make it possible for these creative motivations in man to be given expression—for his intelligence to turn to constructive and creative activity—to that degree work will be more meaningful, and our whole society will correspondingly benefit.

It is because the labor movement realizes in some broad form the nature of this challenge and of this scientific revolution that it presses so continually for a rational handling of the problems in this transitional period. The problems are of staggering proportions and will require the energy, the intelligence, and the understanding of all segments of American society.

Whether we like it or not, our social conscience will determine the future of our economic and political well-being.

66   AUTOMATION AND JOBLESSNESS

William Glazier

William Glazier is Assistant to the Director of the Salk Institute for Biological Studies, and for many years was associated with the International Longshoremen's and Warehousemen's Union.

There are few important economic issues in our nation which are not in some way attributed to automation. Whether it be joblessness, apprehension over the increased power and market influence of dominant corporations, major collective-bargaining conflicts, or the indifferent prospects for capital investment and economic growth, automation seems to be lurking somewhere in the background.

Ironically enough, the same lack of balance which ascribes too much blame to automation is equally responsible for expecting too many blessings from this advanced technology. Although a great deal of today's unemployment is correctly attributed to the displacement of men by machines, these same machines are also confidently expected to create higher-skill job opportunities, which the unemployed can presumably fill after retraining.

The present Administration, beset with a nationwide joblessness which refused to melt away in the 1961 business revival, and armed with soothing, projections demonstrating the higher-skill occupational requirements of an increasingly automated economy, has made a variety of proposals to facilitate the retraining of technologically displaced labor.

There is no denying the appeal of these proposals to retrain the unemployed. But, as so often is the case with complex economic problems, the simple solution is frequently either naïve or dangerously disingenuous.

Since World War II, unemployment in the troughs of each recession has averaged about 7.5 percent of the labor force, but when the recovery peaks were reached, it was discovered that not all of those who lost their jobs during the recession had been re-employed. In the peak year 1953, 2.9 percent of the labor force was jobless; in 1957 the proportion had climbed to 4.3 percent; and in 1960, the most recent peak year, 5.6 percent of the labor force was unable to find work.

Traditionally we have accepted the premise that the primary cause of joblessness is a temporary layoff during a business recession. With the help of

From *The Atlantic Monthly*, Vol. 210, No. 2, August, 1962, pp. 43–47. Reprinted by permission of the author.

unemployment compensation, the worker is tided over until economic conditions improve and he is called back to work. But how can we explain an economic recovery which does not reabsorb the unemployed? And what can be done about it?

One of the more facile explanations of this disturbing phenomenon is that the hard core of the unemployed is composed of individuals who cannot find employment primarily because they are not fitted for available job openings. They have either been technologically displaced or have reached working age without requisite industrial skills and training.

There is widespread agreement among congressmen of both parties that technological change is primarily responsible for displacing unskilled and semiskilled workers and for making old skills obsolete; but simultaneously, so the theory goes, this same technological change is responsible for opening up new jobs, of a higher skill content. The conclusion is neat and plausible: train and retrain the jobless, and fit the unemployed worker to the unfilled job.

Not only are most senators and congressmen sold on retraining as the answer to current hard-core unemployment and the technological displacement of labor, but the general public seems to share the same illusion. According to the Gallup Poll, of all the proposals specified by the President in his second State of the Union message, the proposal to train the unemployed was cited by 67 percent of those replying as one for which they were willing to make sacrifices. This was more than twice the support given any other recommendation.

The seriousness of the problem of persistent, hard-core unemployment cannot be exaggerated. When the National Planning Association studied the problem in early 1961, it found that the chronically unemployed had grown from fewer than 500,000 persons in late 1953 to about 1.5 million at the end of 1956 and to about 2 million at the beginning of 1960. The number has continued to grow since. Technological change, decline in some industries and growth in others, shifts in the geographical location of plants, and changes in consumer demand have caused these many millions of workers to be unemployed and have kept them that way. They are the victims of growth and progress in the American economy.

The consequential shifts in the structure of industry have left behind a growing pool of unskilled and semiskilled workers handicapped by the limits of a grade school education, equipped with years of routine production-work experience, and burdened with families to support. Many are members of minority groups. In addition, there are the young people under twenty-two years of age, who have the highest unemployment rate of any group in the nation today; half of them have still to get their first jobs. They are largely unskilled and untrained for employment.

Meanwhile, the paradox, as the advocates of training and retraining see it, is that all over the nation jobs go unfilled. In Detroit, with 12 to 14 percent of the labor force unemployed, employers are unable to fill openings for electronics technicians, computer operators, and bookkeeper system specialists. As the want ads demonstrate, there are nationwide shortages of draftsmen, technicians, and electronic, hydraulic, and pneumatic repairmen. There seems to be no lack of people on the one hand or unfilled jobs on the other; what appears to be lacking is people with sufficient training and the right skills. The jobless worker, in the wrong place with the wrong skills and aptitudes, has become the fall guy.

In most of the discussions about retraining, it is conveniently forgotten that the purpose of labor-saving technical improvements is to enable the same amount of product to be produced by fewer workers. Other things remaining equal, after a technological innovation has been applied in a factory or an office, some members of the work force will have lost their jobs. Moreover, technological progress as such is not going to reabsorb these workers. Only a sufficient increase in production, either in the plant or elsewhere, will provide alternative employment opportunities for the individuals whose labor and skills have been incorporated into a new piece of machinery. The nub of the problem is how to achieve this sufficiency of production.

Automation not only diminishes the number of workers employed in the factory, it also diminishes skill requirements. If this were not so, if the displacement of unskilled and semiskilled workers by machines necessitated the increased employment of higher-skilled, higher-paid workers, then obviously the whole evolution of production to a higher technological level would be economic foolishness.

Equally naïve is the expectation that as employment drops in the firms replacing men with machines, the displaced workers or their counterparts will find employment in building machines. If as many people were now employed in manufacturing the machines as had formerly been used in making the final product, there would be no point in substituting machines for people.

The immediate gains from rising productivity that result from the substitution of machines for men largely take the form of cost savings realized from the displacement of labor; this purpose would be frustrated if the labor savings at one point were contravened by increased labor costs elsewhere in the production cycle.

Of course, cases can be cited demonstrating that advanced technological innovations have come into a factory or office with few, if any, layoffs. For example, each of the dozen or so automation situations studied by the Bureau of Labor Statistics of the U.S. Department of Labor in 1960 and 1961 lends itself to the comforting conclusion that with proper preparation and planning, discharges can be virtually eliminated. But it would be unwise to generalize from these few instances in which technologically displaced workers were reabsorbed by their employers. The uniqueness of these particular experiences is demonstrated by the mounting number of technologically unemployed this same government agency reports each month.

Moreover, we cannot forget that the displacement of men by machines need not occur at the same time or even at the same place that the machine makes its appearance. When an auto manufacturer automates without layoffs, and in the process is able to manufacture a component formerly purchased from a supplier, the discharged employees of the supplier are as much the victims of automation as if they had been on the payroll of the automating firm. Or when workers who would have been hired by an automated firm no longer have job opportunities, they too are the victims of automation, of "silent firing."

In addition, the increase in the skill content of the work force in an automated factory is as elusive to pin down as the increase in new job opportunities.

As the studies made by Professor James Bright of the Harvard Business

School a few years ago show, the effect of automation is more than likely to reduce—or, at least, not to increase—the demand for skills and abilities on the part of the direct production workers. The same tendency holds for the indirect production workers, the men who service and maintain the machines, in contrast to those who operate or supervise them. The complaints about shortages of skilled engineers, technicians, and craftsmen are more likely to be heard from the builders of automatic machinery than from the users, who are profitably replacing human labor and human skills with automatic machines and control devices.

Professor Bright could find "little justification for the popular belief that present labor is employable in automated plants only with extensive retraining, or that there is a major shortage of new skills in the automated factories." His observations are persuasive in the light of what we know about the diminution of labor and the transfer of skills from men to machines in the evolution of automation.

As a social objective, training or retraining employed and unemployed persons is much to be desired. It would improve the employability of workers, open up more attractive and higher-paid job opportunities, and raise the productive level of the entire nation. The debatable issue is the appropriateness of retraining as a remedy for the current chronic unemployment. In the enthusiastic endorsement of the retraining proposals embodied in the Manpower Development and Training Act of 1961, a rather important consideration became obscured: there must be job opportunities in prospect for the trainees, or all such programs become exercises in futility. Retraining a skilled, unemployed West Virginia coal miner as an auto mechanic does not accomplish much if he cannot find a job as an auto mechanic.

Retraining and relocating displaced and unemployed labor, useful and necessary when economic growth and progress are giving rise to many new jobs in new places, become of dubious value when the economy is producing job seekers faster than job opportunities.

In late 1960, after the Oklahoma City plant of Armour and Company had shut down, the tripartite Armour Automation Committee offered to help finance retraining for any of the 431 former production workers who showed promise of benefiting from some form of vocational training. Of the 170 who responded and were tested, 60 were found capable of retraining; the balance were told that the best chance for re-employment would be in manual labor. About one year later, according to the AFL-CIO, 13 had completed the retraining courses and 7 had found employment in their new skills. This experience convinced the union members of the committee that to retrain under these circumstances was simply to raise the educational level of the unemployed.

In 1959, unemployed workers in the state of California who had exhausted their unemployment benefits and were found eligible for extended benefits for an additional thirteen weeks were offered retraining to improve their chances of finding jobs. Some 50,000 unemployed were eligible to take these courses. In the entire state 38 applied for retraining; 26 were approved and took courses.

It is not surprising that unemployed workers are so markedly unenthusiastic about retraining when they have so few reasonable expectations for reemployment, despite the want ads.

The Administration proposal for retraining unemployed workers in vocational schools will cost the federal government approximately $83 million the first year and reach $238 million the fourth year. This compares with total expenditures on vocational school training in the United States of $238.7 million in 1960, which represented $111 million on the local level, $82.4 on the state level, and $45.3 on the federal level.

The contention of the vocational school administators, who strongly endorsed the new legislation, that industrial skills are best learned in a vocational school is belied by the fact that three out of every five workers with special vocational skills have received their training on the job and through job progression. They worked up, step by step, to jobs of higher skills; training in most cases has been informal, and instruction and guidance have generally come from a foreman, supervisor, or more highly skilled fellow employee.

Training in new skills is much more practical and is likely to be more successful for both trainee and employer when the program is carried on within the plant and geared to specific job needs. An employer training or retraining his own employees knows whom he is retraining; he trains with specific job openings in view, and the program, no matter how informal, is tailored to the special needs of the plant or department.

On-the-job training is, of course, limited to workers already employed who have another job prospect at the same place. Unemployed persons, unless specifically hired for apprenticeship or training purposes, cannot be benefited. To recognize this is nevertheless no justification for arguing that vocational school training can be substituted with similar beneficial results for trainee and potential employer.

There is a good deal of confusion and exaggeration about just how much skill is included in a skilled or a semi-skilled job, and just how much training is required before a worker acquires employable and useful skills. A recent New York state study covering manpower needs and technological change in some of the most diversified industrial, commercial, and business areas in the nation points out that the skills required for the bulk of industrial jobs are relatively simple ones. Most can be taught on a full-time basis in a few days, a few weeks, or a few months. Approximately two thirds of all jobs in New York state at the present time fall into this category. The specific skills required by these jobs are typically taught by employers, on the job. If the jobs are there, the job seekers will learn the skills quickly enough once they are employed.

On the other hand, only about one third of all jobs are accounted for by the skilled crafts, the professions, and technical and managerial occupations. These occupations require complex skills and a wide range of knowledge which can only be gained in a matter of years, not weeks or months. They are far beyond the competence of most of the hard-core unemployed.

The lack of enthusiasm which unemployed workers display toward retraining when there is no assurance of employment is matched by management under these same circumstances. Management has never had any hesitancy about conducting on-the-job training programs when unfilled jobs were holding up production plans. During and immediately after World War II, for example, when American industry was desperately short of labor, many firms enlarged the scope of on-the-job training, not only to upgrade their employees but to equip newly hired unskilled and semiskilled workers for the tasks at hand. However, when business and employment are not expanding, when new employees are not being added, any businessmen would be imprudent not to curtail such programs.

Many large firms, according to reports, have found it advantageous in recent months to expand on-the-job training programs. And many unions, like the Auto Workers, Steelworkers, and Machinists, with large memberships in industries undergoing rapid technological change and labor displacement have made retraining a major collective-bargaining demand. In most cases the cost to the company is minimal, little more than the wages and salaries of instructors and trainees. And as some personnel managers have shrewdly recognized, employer-sponsored retraining programs minimize the usual resistance to change which exists in any work force facing the introduction of labor-displacing machines.

It would be unfair to imply that the Administration has altogether ignored the fact that human adjustments to technological improvements are relatively painless only in growing industries or in a rapidly growing economy with increasing job opportunities. But in the face of an economic recovery which has not reabsorbed the unemployed, the effectiveness of reducing joblessness by retraining has been repeatedly overstated. For, would not re-employment be achieved much more directly by policies which stimulate business activity, and thereby job opportunities? Under buoyant business conditions, retraining is not a critical matter. But, unfortunately, retraining is usually pressed by local and federal authorities when unemployment is high and job openings scarce.

Assuming that the present excessive unemployment has come about because output over the past decade has not

been sufficiently high to furnish employment to the young people seeking jobs and to the technologically displaced, it is no problem to determine arithmetically how much of an increase in the gross national product would be necessary to meet these job goals. But there is a dilemma here.

Economic growth will result in more, not less, technological progress and in more, not less, labor displacement. We have the pattern of the booms of the last ten years to remind us of this complication. The recent spurts in economic activity did not eliminate chronic unemployment or unused plant capacity.

When labor productivity has already reach a high level as a result of technological improvement, as is the case in the United States, then any given expansion in economic activity and production will induce a *slower* increase in job opportunities and total employment than would have been the case before the technological change. If we make increased output, and thereby more jobs, a first priority in the next decade, then we shall begin to find ourselves in the same predicament as the Red Queen—each successive increase in output will create fewer job opportunities. The more advanced we become in technological accomplishment, the faster we have to run to remain in the same place. If we were lower on the ladder of technological progress, it would be easier to maintain full employment.

Economic growth is a complex phenomenon in which the many factors that go into production are continually shifted about and recombined in new and more productive relationships. If it becomes more profitable to employ less human labor at some point, it is certainly fatuous to expect that training and retraining will automatically bring about labor's re-employment. Realistically, we cannot always expect to maximize output and employment by the same policies. Under certain circumstances these become mutually exclusive goals, whether in an underdeveloped country like India or a highly developed one like the United States.

If a national goal is to minimize technological displacement and unemployment without going back to horse-and-buggy production methods, then a variety of possible policies would appear to be appropriate to achieve optimum employment. For one, despite the objections of the Administration and most business leaders, we must move to a shorter work week or work year, combined, if desired, with multiple-shift operations; this would keep more people employed and would prevent expensive equipment from standing idle. For another, young people should be required to stay in school

longer. This requirement, combined with an earlier retirement age, would cut persons off from both ends of the labor force, thereby reducing the number of job seekers.

These policies would bring about a distribution of an increasing part of the fruits of advanced technology, through a higher standard of living made available in the form of less hard work, more leisure, earlier retirements, more education, and similar benefits. These benefits would not necessarily be confined exclusively to employed wage earners.

To suggest that technological change be regulated, directed, and harnessed is to call for a degree of economic planning few Americans are prepared to accept today. Yet how else can we ensure that our rising population of redundant labor will be able to share in an economy where the number of jobs is not growing fast enough?

67   THE STUPIDITY PROBLEM

John Fischer

John Fischer is Editor-in-Chief of *Harper's Magazine*.

*   *   *

It is perfectly clear, to me at least, why Mr. Kennedy hasn't been able to find jobs for our three or four million unemployed. The human race—or anyhow that sample of it located in North America—no longer fits the kind of society it has to live in. Our society just doesn't have any jobs for certain types of people. If it continues to develop along its present course, the number of such unemployables seems likely to grow rather rapidly. Meanwhile, at the other end of the scale, an increasing number of important jobs will remain

empty, because there aren't enough men and women able to fill them.

So the chief characteristic of The Overdeveloped Society (if that is the right label) will be a permanent surplus of some kinds of workers, together with a permanent shortage of others. For the assortment of jobs which need to be done is simply out of kilter with the natural distribution of brains.

A few figures show how this happened. According to the psychologists, intelligence seems to be parceled out among human beings in line with a fairly consistent pattern. If you should round up a hundred typical Americans off the street, getting a fair sample of our whole population, you would find that about 46 of them would have something close to "normal" intelligence—that is, Intelligence Quotients between 90 and 109. Another 29 would be quite bright, with IQs ranging from 110 to 139. And one or two would be really brilliant, with IQs of 140 or above.

On the other hand, 20 people in this group would have to be classed as fairly stupid, since their IQs would fall between 70 and 89. And two or three, with ratings below 70, would barely have enough sense to come in out of the rain.

From the beginning of history until fairly recently—say, a couple of generations ago—every society in the world had plenty of jobs for low IQ people. They could herd sheep, pick cotton, dig ditches (even the Erie Canal was made with spades), h'ist that bale and tote that load. Indeed, nearly all of the earth's work called for strong backs and weak minds—for drawers of water and hewers of wood. Jobs that demanded real intelligence, on the other hand, were strictly limited; most communities had room for only a few doctors, ministers, teachers, lawyers, and captains of industry. Scientists were practically unknown. (As Robert Oppenheimer once pointed out in these pages, quoting Professor Purcell of Harvard, 90 per cent of all the scientists that ever lived are living today.) Government administrators were almost as scarce; Alexander Hamilton could run the Treasury Department with five clerks. As a consequence, thousands of high IQ people lived in frustration, because they could find no work equal to their talents. In many parts of the world this is still true. Some of the brightest people I ever met—in Greece and Yugoslavia—are hauling nets, throwing the shuttle on hand looms, sweeping streets, and winnowing grain with a hand basket.

But in the industrialized countries, as we all know, human muscle has now become almost obsolete. Anything it can lift, a machine can lift better. Practically any task involving repetition of the same motions can be done faster and cheaper by a mechanical or electronic device. So the muscle-worker is out of luck. He can still find a few things to do—collecting garbage, for example, unloading trucks, replacing railway ties—but these are mostly in minor or backward industries which have not yet got around to complete mechanization. And the number of such low-IQ chores is dwindling every day.

Farming perhaps offers the most vivid illustration of what is happening. As recently as my grandfather's day, farming was a set of inherited motions, not very different from those used by the Babylonians. As a boy in Ohio, he sowed wheat by hand-broadcasting and harvested it with a scythe. Since neither of these operations strains the cerebral cortex, a youngster who was too dumb for anything else could always make a living on the farm; the demand for field hands was virtually unlimited.

Today, however, a successful farmer has to be a combination geneticist, mechanical engineer, chemist, cost accountant, agronomist, tax expert, and economist; in all likelihood he is a college graduate. While he may still hire some unskilled migrant labor for a few weeks a year to harvest certain fruit and vegetable crops, he can very frequently operate a big farm without any help outside the family. If he does take on a full-time hand, he looks for a smart one; no farmer wants to entrust $40,000 worth of complex agricultural machinery to a dope.

*   *   *

The youngsters who drop out of high school before graduation are a case in point. Most leave school, not because of economic problems, but because they can't keep up with the not-very-demanding work. The federal Bureau of Labor Statistics has reported that 80 per cent of the drop-outs are lagging by at least one grade; and Dr. Cronbach notes that "the very dull tend to drop out as soon as they reach age sixteen. . . . By the end of high school, almost no one with IQ below 85 is still in school." This is one reason why the unemployment rate for sixteen- to nineteen-year-olds is twice as high as for adults. A few get jobs as messengers, gas pump operators, or dishwashers. Many others drift straight from the classroom to the relief rolls, or to crime. For as our society is now organized, we can't find any use for most of these young dullards—a situation unjust and miserable to them, and to the rest of the community both costly and dangerous.

The counterpart of this situation is a severe and increasing shortage of people brainy enough to man the upper level jobs in our Overdeveloped Society. The design, supervision, and maintenance of automated equipment require a lot of smart, highly trained people—and even now industry can't find enough of them. Did you ever hear of a good computer-programmer who was out of work?

So too with the rest of our society. All the professions which demand better-than-average minds—medicine, law, journalism, teaching, the sciences, advertising, the military—are moaning about their difficulties in attracting enough competent recruits. And as the structure of society grows in both complexity and size, the need for able managers (in business and government alike) grows in almost geometric ratio. Our inability to locate enough first-rate managerial talent in many fields—from college presidents to corporate comptroller, from regional planner to operations analyst—may yet prove to be the breakdown point in our civilization.

For we have apparently built ourselves, unintentionally and without quite realizing it, a society which calls for a distribution of intelligence entirely different from that which God provided. It remains to be seen whether we can make it work.

*   *   *

We might also profit if we could change our national attitude toward certain kinds of employment.

From the earliest days of the Republic, most Americans have regarded personal service as somehow degrading. Hardly anybody wanted to be a housekeeper or cook, and those hapless widows who were forced into such work to avoid starvation usually did it bitterly and with little pride. Butlers and valets were legendary creatures who belonged in British country homes or Wodehouse novels, but had no place in democratic America. Waiting tables was, and is, so unpopular that many restaurants have to import their help from Europe or Puerto Rico.

These prejudices evidently are peculiar to America, not to democracies in general. In Switzerland, the oldest democracy in Euorpe, the profession of waiter is both honorable and much sought-after, while it is still possible to hire good-natured and efficient household help in Scandinavia, Ireland, and Greece. (In England, however, the Americanization of society has made the butler and the maid almost extinct; those few who still exist there are mostly imported from Sweden, Italy, and Eire.)

Whatever their origins, such attitudes are costly. Both the efficiency and the tone of American life would be vastly improved if personal service came to be regarded as an acceptable way to make a living. For we now have the curious spectacle of millions of people on relief, while at the same time millions of households are looking for desperately needed help—to care for elderly relatives, tend the children, and help with the heavier chores. If such help could be found, countless women —many of them highly educated— could be freed for teaching and other understaffed professsions . . . innumerable old people would not have to be condemned to nursing homes . . . any number of businessmen could save the energy now dissipated in shoveling snow, putting up storm windows, and tinkering with balky plumbing. It might even become possible to get prompt and courteous service in the average hotel and restaurant—but no, that is carrying fantasy too far.

Such work demands no great intelligence and only a minimum of training. Yet it is scorned by nearly all the people on the unemployment rolls. That isn't our kind of work, they say —and relief officials ordinarily will not require their clients to accept any job opening outside their customary trade.

I have no idea how such ingrained attitudes might be changed. Perhaps it could be done by professionalizing service work, and thus removing the stigma of the servant. Already this is being attempted, with some success, by a few companies which send out crews of trained men and women to do spring housecleaning, household repair, and the like. Their workers wear snappy uniforms, they work for the company instead of the householder, and they put in a regular eight-hour day; as a consequence they seem to feel more independence and self-respect.

No doubt there are many other and better ways to find useful work for the low IQs, and to persuade them to do it. My main point is that nobody seems to be thinking about such things, because nobody is yet willing to admit publicly that the Stupidity Problem needs coping with. The steps taken by the Kennedy Administration to fight unemployment—new factories for distressed areas, retraining for technologically displaced workers, general stimulus of the economy—may be fine for their own purposes; but they ignore the special problem of the dullard. This is not only expensive, but dangerous. When you condemn people indefinitely to idleness and public charity, you condemn them also to frustration and bitterness—to the kind of discontent which may have a lot to do with the crime rate, drug addiction, and political unrest.

It ought not to be beyond human ingenuity to create worthwhile jobs for these people, if we only set our minds to it. If we tended our forests, for example, as carefully as the Germans do, we would need millions of man-hours of not-very-skilled work— and we would increase enormously the value of a precious national asset. We could use a lot of muscle power in deferred maintenance of our dilapidated railways. We might even set a few hundred thousand men to work cleaning the litter off our streets and the beer cans out of our trash-clogged parks and streams. And we might start now to devise an educational system which will candidly train every youngster for a level of work that fits his intelligence, instead of pretending that each of them is potential college material.

B.

DISARMAMENT

68 ECONOMIC IMPACTS OF DISARMAMENT

Panel on Economic Impacts of Disarmament, Emile Benoit, Chairman

Emile Benoit is Professor of Economics in the Graduate School of Business at Columbia University.

THE PROBLEM

The chief public concern about the effects of disarmament is the possibility that it might create a sudden and severe decline in economic activity, i.e. a depression. Another danger, of a less dramatic but possibly more realistic character, is that a sustained decline in defense expeditures could impair the long-term stability and growth of our economy. Another obvious and unavoidable problem is that certain companies, industries, workers, and communities that are heavily involved in defense activities may face serious structural readjustment problems even if over-all demand can be kept high and no general decline occurs. Shifting people and resources to new uses takes time and may well create considerable hardship for the parts of the economy that have to make the shifts.

The reasons for concern can be set forth briefly. The defense program absorbs nearly a tenth of the total U.S. production of goods and services and employs, directly and indirectly, a like percentage of the labor force. (This is inclusive of personnel in the Armed Forces and in the Defense Department.)

In some industries the dependence on defense employment is especially high. Approximately 95 percent of the employment in aircraft and missiles, 60 percent in ship and boatbuilding, and 40 percent of the employment in radio and communications equipment is dependent on defense expenditures. On the other hand only 6 percent of employment in transportation, 2 percent in construction, and less than 1½ percent in trade and services is similarly dependent on the defense program; and much of this dependence is indirect. (See Table I.)

In some areas of the country the dependence on defense production is already very tangible and a serious source of concern. For example, in 1959 missile and aircraft production provided at least 82 percent of the manufacturing employment in San Diego, 72 percent in Wichita, 53 percent in Seattle, and 27 percent in the Los Angeles–Long Beach area. Certain States are clearly subject to disproportionately heavy economic impacts be-

Excerpted from *Economic Impacts of Disarmament,* A Report of the Panel on Economic Impacts of Disarmament, Emile Benoit, Chairman, submitted to the United States Arms Control and Disarmament Agency, January, 1962.

cause of the relatively heavy dependence of their manufacturing on major items of procurement. Table II shows 14 States with above-average dependence on major procurement for their employment, and 9 additional States with exceptionally heavy dependence on Department of Defense (DOD) payrolls to sustain their income. Kansas, Washington, New Mexico, California, and Connecticut appear as the cases of most severe relative dependence on defense manufacturing, with 20 to 30 percent of their manufacturing employment in major procurement; Alaska, Hawaii, District of Columbia, and Virginia have the heaviest dependence on DOD payrolls, with 10 to 26 percent of their income supplied by military pay and allowances or civilian wages and salaries. It is disquieting to note that several of the States with heavy dependence on major procurement for employment are also well above the average for dependence of income on Department of Defense payrolls. This is notably true for New Mexico and Utah, but it is also true to some extent for Kansas, Washington, and California.

Moreover, it appears that defense expenditures are particularly important in precisely those industries, notably the electronics and aerospace industries, that have shown the most rapid pattern of growth and technological innovation and provided a large share of the support for research and development. The defense program now finances about half of all industrial research and development and one-fourth of all pure research.

The projected earnings of firms heavily engaged in the defense program have been very highly capitalized in the stock market, and the present level of their common stock value would appear to be quite vulnerable in the event of any major reduction in defense expenditures.

Moreover, the industrial character of the defense program has been changing in ways that may intensify the problem of adjustment in major defense cutbacks. By contrast with the situation during World War II, and even the Korean War, a larger share of defense industry today is in the hands of highly specialized defense contractors whose products bear little resemblance to any civilian items, who have limited experience outside of defense production, who have never "converted" from civilian production, and for whom entry into production of civilian end-items would typically involve not so much "reconversion" as radical diversification. Their attempts to date to get into civilian lines of production have been frequently unprofitable.

*   *   *

DISARMAMENT ASSUMPTIONS

In attempting to project the economic impact of disarmament, it is first of all necessary to have a reasonably clear-cut set of assumptions about the nature and timing of the disarmament process. While these matters are and will continue to be the subject of negotiation, the ultimate outcome of which can hardly be predicted at this stage, it is nonetheless necessary to make assumptions about the general character of the disarmament process with respect at least to those factors that will have a decided economic impact.

The disarmament assumptions we used in making our projections are intended to be generally consistent with the major U.S. disarmament objectives and policies as set forth in the proposals presented by the President to the United Nations. . . .

With a different concept or model of disarmament, the economic implications might be considerably altered. For example, an arms control agreement involving a major change in the weapons mix might involve no reduction in defense expenditure and, because of the heavy new inspection costs, might even make for some net increase in military budgets—at least for a time. Similarly, a crash disarmament program, such as might arise out of a crisis situation . . . or a region-by-region sequential disarmament pattern as suggested by Louis Sohn, would considerably change the economic impact. Such more remote alternatives have been ignored here, to concentrate on the possible implications of more conventional conceptions of disarmament.

Even within such a conception, some of the elements are economically more strategic than others. Any important changes made with respect to these elements during the course of negotiation of a disarmament agreement could, in some degree, undermine the projections and analyses of this report.

One crucial assumption in this sense is with respect to the date of the cut-off in new production of delivery vehicles and nuclear warheads. Another is the pace of demobilization of personnel. Another is the magnitude and type of inspection, police, and deterrent forces established under an international control organization (or, as the September 25 plan calls it, I.D.O. —International Disarmament Organization) and responsible for administering and enforcing the disarmament agreement. The rate and timing of the buildup of such forces is likewise very important. . . . Another assumption of obvious importance is with respect to the total duration of the disarmament

program. Finally, the projected severity of the disarmament impact will also be affected by the assumptions with respect to the size of the national forces at the beginning of the program and after disarmament is completed.

*   *   *

The disarmament model adopted by the panel for the purposes of this report, and its implications for U.S. security expenditures—national and international—are shown in Table III. In approximate terms, it projects a decline in defense expenditure of $17 billion (1960 dollars) in the first 3 years, a further decline in national defense programs in the second stage of $12 billion partly offset by a $3.5 billion contribution to international inspection costs, and so forth (i.e., a net reduction of about $8.5 billion), and a further net reduction in the third (two-phase) stage of $13.5 billion in the last 6 years. The total net reduction in U.S. security expenditures (after allowance for the U.S. contribution to the costs of an international organization responsible for inspection, police, and deterrent functions) would thus be about $38.5 billion over a 12-year period, with roughly $6 billion a year in the initial 3-year period.

These cutbacks might be partly offset by a buildup in certain programs which have been closely associated with our defense effort in the past, such as the NASA and the civilian AEC programs. The projections with respect to these programs shown in Table III include an allowance for the NASA moon program recently announced, et cetera. If the revised projections prove realistic, the offsets provided by the expansion of both "associated programs" together would be close to a total of $2.5 billion over the initial 3-year period of maximum defense cutbacks. The total expansion of these programs over the whole disarmament program is estimated at $6.8 billion, based on existing plans. . . .

If we take account of the offset provided by the costs of inspection forces and the build up of the NASA and civilian AEC programs, we find a net reduction in U.S. security and associated expenditures of about $22 billion in the first 6 years, with only about $5 billion a year during the crucial introductory 3-year period of maximum impact.

THE FEAR OF DEPRESSION

The chief popular economic fear of disarmament is that it might suddenly lead to a severe depression. This seems to us a rather improbable contingency, assuming the relatively slow pace of the cuts as set forth herein and the strong likelihood of some offsetting policies. A net reduction of defense expenditures of only about $5 billion a year, or less than 1 percent of the gross national product, even in the initial period of maximum impact, would be a far smaller percentage of the GNP than was represented by the post World War II and post-Korean defense cuts, which for a time were, respectively, 30 percent and 3 percent of GNP.

It would, of course, be possible in the absence of further compensatory action for an initial deflationary net impact of even $5 billion a year to cause a serious slowdown, via the action of the multiplier. Under these conditions, the reduction in defense spending would be reflected in reduced incomes for employees of the defense industries and of the industries supplying, directly and indirectly, the defense contractors. Profits (after taxes) in these industries would also be reduced, and this almost certainly would

be reflected in some cutback in dividends. Declines in personal incomes would be mitigated by reduced taxes and increased transfer payments, but, given existing laws, a dollar reduction in defense spending would cause a fall in disposable income leading to about a dollar reduction in personal consumption. In addition, the decline in aggregate demand would lead to a reduction in capacity and inventory requirements and thus to some fall-off in investment. As a result, a $5 billion yearly cutback in defense spending might well generate a total decline of aggregate demand of between $10 billion and $12 billion a year, if compensating policies were not brought into play.

Yet it is hard to believe that we would stand by idly and let the multiplier have its full impact by failing to take some further compensatory action. Public pressures would be strong to reduce taxes and to permit the expansion of some high priority nondefense Government programs that are being kept on ice during the period of heavy defense budgets. It seems unlikely that we would repeat the mistake made in 1953–54 when Federal nondefense expenditures were cut by over $2 billion at the very time that heavy cuts were being made in defense. . . .

Perhaps the chief danger of a precipitant decline would be psychological. We would be facing an extended series of future defense cuts over more than a decade ahead. We have never had a situation exactly parallel to this in our history, and we cannot be sure just how this would affect business and consumer anticipations and expenditure plans. Pessimism might be heightened by a major break in stock market prices, which, as indicated above, would be likely to occur at such a time.

A great deal might depend on whether the Government could provide sufficient reassurance by demonstrating that a definite program of offsets had been readied and would be promptly implemented. In this connection, people's expectations would be considerably affected by their experience in the years prior to disarmament. If public policy had succeeded in reducing excessive unemployment and restoring a rapid rate of growth, the economy could more readily absorb deflationary impacts without serious hurt, and confidence in the Government's power to protect prosperity would be higher. On the whole, it is our judgment that a sharp letdown during disarmament remains unlikely and should be avoidable if the Government exercises a modicum of economic sense, foresight, and courageous leadership.

LONG-TERM ADEQUACY OF DEMAND

Dealing effectively with the year-by-year declines in defense expenditure may be much more difficult. It will be a problem to maintain sufficient aggregate demand to utilize the resources being released year after year by the defense program as well as the rapid expansion of our industrial potential. In particular, we appear to be in for a period of exceptionally rapid growth in the labor force, and some authorities believe we may also be on the threshold of a period of exceptionally rapid productivity advances. Yet failure to find constructive use for our growing resources might be especially dangerous in a postdisarmament situation because the international rivalry between the free and regimented societies might center to an even larger extent than at present on their respective economic performances and their ability to supply aid and leadership in international economic development. Certainly a continuing and growing burden of excess unemployment and a marked failure to restore a rapid growth of industrial output could gravely affect our international prestige as well as impair our domestic morale.

*   *   *

STRUCTURAL PROBLEMS

It seems entirely possible that some of the most stubborn and difficult problems connected with disarmament will be those arising from the concentration of persons and productive resources in particular industries, areas, or vocational groups and from the difficulties of making the necessary shifts in employment and resource utilization. To be sure, many of these shifts will be easily made through the spontaneous and unaided action of individuals responding to the pull of free market forces. The success of this type of adjustment process will be greatly facilitated if a high level of demand is maintained. There is less incentive to move or to retrain if unemployment is endemic and society derives little benefit from adjustment processes which provide jobs for some people only by taking jobs from others. Nevertheless, even under conditions of full employment opportunity some of the adjustment processes will be difficult for the individuals, companies, and communities concerned, and some Government measures to assist in this process may be morally justified, economically sound, and politically inevitable.

The employment phase of the readjustment may be complicated by the fact that the labor force will be expanding with exceptional rapidity and labor displacement through automation may also be advancing with great speed. It should be noted that the spread of automation may be accelerated as defense firms diversify their production and apply their advanced technology to more traditional industries.

Particular difficulty may be experienced in finding satisfactory reemployment for members of the permanent defense force, many of whom lack traditional civilian industrial skills, are in difficult age groups for placement, are accustomed to relatively high salary levels (taking into account the imputed values of living accommodations provided), or have personality orientations not well adapted to humdrum civilian employment. Certain cadres, on the other hand, may have outstanding civilian skills, plus a variety of attitudes and experiences which may be of special usefulness in civilian life— as e.g., leadership qualities, abilities to endure discomforts, and knowledge of foreign areas which might be particularly useful in international economic development work.

As for the rank and file workers in the defense industries, not enough is yet known about their skill and wage levels to make a reliable appraisal of the difficulties they may experience in reemployment. We expect, however, that a fair amount of retraining will be necessary, much of it of a fundamental sort involving elementary education. Policy decisions on the handling of such matters are rendered very difficult by the paucity of reliable research in this field. Some of the experiments in retraining, such as those by the Armour Company and in the Belgian coal mines, have been relatively unsuccessful in the sense of showing a relatively small number of workers willing and able to benefit from them and the requirement of a large investment in order to produce a rather small result. On the other hand, these conclusions have been criticized as premature and the experiments regarded as inconclusive by some qualified observers who believe that, by the use of improved teaching methods and measures to provide incentives, retraining programs may succeed better in the future.

In the solution of regional problems there is an important change of emphasis which has developed over the last quarter of a century. With the rapid rise in the cost of community facilities (housing, mass education and health facilities, and so on) relative to the cost of factories and equipment, with the lower proportionate costs of transportation and power, and with the increased rate of obsolescence in plant and equipment, the case becomes more and more persuasive for aiding new industry to enter areas where there is an existing skilled labor force, rather than seeking to move unemployed workers to where idle manufacturing facilities are. It seems to be no accident that most of the European programs have concentrated on bringing additional industry to structurally depressed areas, rather than helping the workers to go elsewhere. The new U.S. legislation on depressed areas takes the same approach, and experience gained under it should provide some useful guidelines for area readjustment policy under disarmament.

Because of the considerable concentration of defense industry in particular localities, the structural readjustment problems of the industries and the localities are almost inseparable, and in some respects the readjustment problems may better be handled in terms of the industries than of the areas. So far we have relatively little information about the distribution of defense industry by region except in relation to prime contracts and in regard to the West Coast. Our information about the distribution by industry is somewhat better and may be more illuminating.

An industrial breakdown of the employment impacts is provided in Table I. The big concentration of employment especially vulnerable to disarmament will likely be—in very round numbers—700,000 persons in aircraft, another quarter million each in ships and ordnance, and another 400,000 in radio and other electrical equipment and machinery, plus another 150,000 in nonelectrical machinery and in instruments. (Missile employment is chiefly in aircraft but also in ordnance and electronics.) While another million and a quarter persons in other industries are also likely to be dependent on defense demand, this dependence will be for the most part *indirect*. Also, the 90,000 or so who make the steel which enters directly or indirectly into defense uses could very well maintain their existing jobs after disarmament if alternative types of demand for quality and special steels could be quickly built up.

It is of interest to examine the extent to which different types of demand which might replace defense demand would provide employment opportunities for workers in those particular industries most likely to suffer from a loss of defense demand. This type of analysis has been pursued in the Leontief-Hoffenberg article, "Economic Consequences of Disarmament," in the April 1961 *Scientific American*. Essentially, this analysis proceeds by the use of what are called "trade-off matrices" which show the net change in demand for the output of particular industries if a given quantity of defense demand is replaced by an equal quantity of other final demand—personal consumption, investment, nondefense Government services, or exports. In general, the data presented suggest that

an expansion of investment or capital exports would more easily utilize the released resources than would other programs.

Considerations of this sort would supply a more relevant guide to policy in a crash disarmament program, where structural problems would be so severe as rightly to dominate adjustment policy, than in the case of a deliberate and moderately paced disarmament program of the sort here under consideration. Indeed, it should be the aim of policymakers, under these conditions, to resist the strong political pressures which will undoubtedly exist to provide particular opportunities which will reemploy released resources with the minimum amount of change in the existing industrial and geographic patterns. Rather, the opportunity should be taken to facilitate the movement of resources into those occupations, industries, and areas with the biggest expansion potential and which promise to make the largest long-run contribution to the achievement of our national goals.

A number of specific recommendations with respect to structural readjustment policies may be drawn from the foregoing analysis of the problems. It is clear first of all that a great deal of what may have to be done in the event of disarmament is along the same lines as would be highly desirable right now, since the economy is already suffering from various structural maladjustments arising from technical changes, population shifts, past changes in the composition of the defense program, et cetera. Among the particular programs upon which a start can well be made in the near future may be included:

(a) A strengthening of our system of employment offices so as to provide a more complete, accurate, and up-to-date central source of knowledge about job openings and job availabilities. (A leading obstacle—and one not easily overcome—is reluctance of industry to list job availabilities.)

(b) A strengthening of our unemployment insurance program with efforts to assure adequate minimum standards and a greater degree of uniformity between States.

(c) A stronger attempt to develop a workable retraining scheme, giving adequate recognition to the fact that such retraining will often require particular attention to elementary education and even such matters as literacy and elementary arithmetic.

(d) A more ambitious attempt to explore the potential value and costs of a relocation program which may possibly play a considerable role in highly specialized defense communities which either have no worthwhile potential for nondefense production or which will take some considerable time to develop alternative industrial opportunities.

(e) An open-minded consideration should be given to the possible helpfulness of encouraging defense industry to adopt more liberal provisions with respect to severance pay, even by making some allowance for such programs as a legitimate cost in defense contracts. (In fairness, the Government should then consider expending similar benefits to its own defense forces and civilian employees.)

(f) Similarly helpful would be Government attempts to influence industry to provide more liberal and flexible provisions permitting the vesting of pension rights, providing extended coverage with respect to group insurance, hospitalization, and similar prerequisites, and providing employees with company-wide rights of transfer. Measures of this sort would be valuable in removing existing constraints on worker mobility.

(g) Careful attention should be given to the possibility of encouraging defense contractors (possibly by subsidizing their research on these matters) to begin making studies as to their postdisarmament adjustments, including such things as the types of civilian items to the production of which they could convert with the least difficulty, the likely alternative employment availabilities in their immediate communities, grades of manpower and kinds of skill now on the staff which would probably be redundant in a civilian economy, the new type of research and development programs to which they might hopefully contribute, their financial requirements in the event of a sudden cancellation of defense contracts, and the types of financial assistance which they would find beneficial, and so forth.

(h) Knowledgeable people from defense industry have also suggested that financial provisions in defense contracts encouraging defense industry to begin exploratory work on research and development with respect to disarmament inspection requirements might be very helpful not only in developing advance planning and capabilities in this field (which could provide a useful type of offset program) but also in creating an atmosphere of greater realism about the whole subject of arms control and disarmament, indirectly encouraging other types of advance preparation for such a contingency. Last but not least, the search for technological breakthrough in the field of inspection is not necessarily a hopeless one, and any major achievements along this line could significantly add to the feasibility of disarmament.

C.

SOCIAL INSURANCE

69   PRO AND CON ON MEDICARE

BRIEF SUMMARY OF KING-ANDERSON BILL * (H.R. 4222)

Beneficiaries—

"Persons who have reached age 65 and are entitled to monthly benefits under the old age and survivors insurance program or under the railroad retirement system.

Benefits Provided—

"The services for which payment would be made under the proposal would be:

"1. Inpatient hospital services for up to 90 days. Hospital services would include those customarily furnished by a hospital for its patients, and would be subject to a deductible amount (paid by the patient) of $10 a day for up to 9 days, with a minimum of $20;

"2. Skilled nursing home services, after the patient is transferred from a hospital, for up to 180 days;

"3. Outpatient hospital diagnostic services, as required, subject to a $20 deductible amount for each diagnostic study;

"4. Home health services for up to 240 visits during a calendar year. Includes intermittent nursing care, therapy, and part-time homemaker services.

---

* Introduced in the House by Rep. Cecil King, Calif., D. Introduced in the Senate by Sen. Clinton Anderson, N. Mex., D.

"An individual could be eligible for up to 90 days of hospital services and 180 days of skilled nursing home services in each period of illness, but subject to a maximum of 150 'units of service.' A unit of service would be equal to: 1 day of inpatient hospital services or 2 days of skilled nursing home services. Thus, if during a period of illness a beneficiary transferred from a hospital to a skilled nursing home after 60 days, payment could be made for the 60 days of hospital care and for up to 180 days of his skilled nursing home care. If the beneficiary transferred after 95 days in the hospital, payment could be made for 90 days of hospital care and up to 120 days of his skilled nursing home care. A 'new period of illness' would not begin until 90 days had elapsed in which the patient was neither in a hospital or a skilled nursing home.

The Provider—

"Payments to the providers of service would be made on the basis of the reasonable cost incurred in providing care for beneficiaries. The amount paid under the program would be payment in full for covered services, except, of course, that the provider could charge the patient the amounts of the deductibles and extra charges for a private room or private duty nursing.

"The Secretary of Health, Education and Welfare would consult with appro-

442

priate State agencies and recognized national accrediting bodies in formulating the conditions of participation for providers of service. The Secretary would have the authority to utilize State agencies to perform the administrative functions of determining whether a provider meets the conditions for participation and to provide consultative services to providers.

"In order to be eligible to participate in the program, providers of service would have to meet specified conditions to assure the health and safety of the beneficiaries. If it desired, a State could recommend that more strict conditions be applied with respect to providers of service within that State.

Administrative Aspects—

"Responsibility for administration of the program for social security bene- ficiaries would rest with the Secretary of Health, Education and Welfare. Provisions would be made for the establishment of an Advisory Council which would advise the Secretary on policy matters in conection with administration.

Financing—

"The program would cost 0.6 per cent of covered payroll. In the early years of the program, benefit payments would amount to slightly more than 1 billion dollars a year. The social security contribution rates would be increased 1/4 of one per cent on employers and 1/4 of one per cent on employees and 3/8 of one per cent for the self-employed, effective in 1963. The taxable earnings base would be increased from $4,800 to $5,000 a year, beginning with 1962."

	Abraham Ribicoff, former Secretary of Health,
Pro †—Abraham Ribicoff	Education, and Welfare, is now U. S. Senator from Connecticut.

"Let me set forth my position clearly:

"1. The high costs of medical care for the aged are going to be paid for in this country. The issue is not whether to pay these costs. The only issue is how to pay them.

"2. The alternatives to health insurance that have been suggested are not adequate, not fair to the elderly who need the care, and not fair to the public which pays for it.

"Private insurance plus public assistance cannot do the complete job. If the medical assistance for the aged program, enacted by Congress last year, is expanded to cover a major share of the cost, the drain on State treasuries will be fantastic. If the issue is left to collective bargaining, the pressures on employers to absorb the total cost will be overwhelming. If hospitals have to collect from those who can pay the costs for those who cannot, the burden on middle-income hospital patients will be unconscionable.

"3. The facts will show that paying for hospital costs under the social security system is the conservative answer, the practical answer, the fair answer.

"Let me begin by discussing the need.

"The need for action: In his special

---

† From testimony before the Committee on Ways and Means, U. S. House of Representatives, July 24, 1961.

message to the Congress on health and hospital care, the President described the need of the aged for insurance against health care costs. You may recall that he said:

" 'Those among us who are over 65 —16 million today in the United States —go to the hospital more often and stay longer than their younger neighbors. Their physical activity is limited by six times as much disability as the rest of the population. Their annual medical bill is twice that of persons under 65—but their annual income is only half as high.'

"The President went on to say:

" 'Twenty-six years ago this Nation adopted the principle that every member of the labor force and his family should be insured against the haunting fear of loss of income caused by retirement, death, or unemployment. To that we have added insurance against the economic loss caused by disability. But there remains a significant gap that denies to all but those with the highest incomes a full measure of security— the high cost of ill health in old age.'

"The statistics to demonstrate the need are legion.

"Now a few facts that show the general situation of the aged.

"Nine out of ten of the people who live to be 65 go to the hospital at least once between age 65 and death.

"Among couples, in about half of the cases the husband and the wife will each have at least two hospital stays between age 65 and death—at least four hospital stays for half of the couples after age 65 .

"When an aged person goes to the hospital, he is likely to stay longer than a younger person because he is more likely to have serious and long-lasting disease. People over 65 are in hospitals, on the average, over 2½ times as much as younger people. The average cost per day in 1946 was $9.39; in 1950 the cost rose to $15.26; in 1955

the cost of hospital care per day was $23.12; and in 1960 the average hospital costs were $32.28 a day.

"The financial impact of repeated hospital stays becomes apparent when we consider that the median yearly income for a widow is about $1,000, and for an aged couple is less than $2,500. About one-third of the aged have no assets that can readily be turned into cash, and about half have less than $500. Much of the health insurance available to the aged provides very limited protection and that only at high cost to them, and less than half of the aged have any hospitalization insurance at all. This is not surprising, since it is impossible for most retired people to pay currently the high premiums that, considering the high incidence of illness among older people, would be necessary to provide adequate coverage.

"Is it not true, though, as some people are asking, that whether people can pay for it or not, everyone in this country gets the hospital care he ought to have? I doubt very much that this is true. I believe it is true that very few, if any, who are absolutely in need of urgent care are turned away from our hospitals because of inability to pay. But what about those who are too proud to accept what they look on as charity or going on relief, who will dangerously postpone seeking care because they fear cancellation of their insurance, or do not want to dip into their small savings or to burden the limited resources of their children? Who can say with confidence that needed hospital care has not been foregone, that terminal illness and premature death have not been caused by the unwillingness of our older people to seek the care they need?

"We know that hospital use by older people goes up when an assured source of financing is provided on terms that older people find acceptable. Insured older people do use more hospital care than the uninsured. Financial barriers do stand in the way of adequate care.

"The present role of Government: The need must be met. But by whom? In proposing that the Federal Government play a part, we are not suggesting anything new. The Government is already involved in meeting the cost of personal medical care, for the aged as well as for other groups, and on a large scale. We are simply proposing a more logical, a more equitable, a more efficient, and a more fiscally responsible approach to medical-care problems with which the Government is already involved and has been for quite some time.

"In 1959, total expenditures for personal health and medical care in this country amounted to $22.5 billion. Almost 22 per cent of this total—about $4.9 billion—was paid from public funds. Federal expenditures amounted to almost $2 billion, or about 40 per cent of the total public spending for personal health and medical care.

"The 1960 legislation providing for increased Federal grants for direct payments to providers of medical care under old-age assistance and for medical assistance for the aged will, of course, increase public expenditures for health care. If all States were to put into effect medical assistance programs for the aged comparable with the average program now in effect or under study in the States, and if health insurance for the aged is not provided under social security, the anual cost, Federal and State, for this category alone would be more than $650 million. If the State programs were to provide better benefits in the future than the average now provided, the cost of medical assistance for the aged, in the absence of a health insurance program for the aged under social security, could run to as much as $1 billion a year or even more, with the Federal Government paying

somewhat more than a half a billion dollars. Make no mistake about it; the Federal Government is already in medical care, and on a large scale.

"It is in this medical-care business because there were problems that had to be met. Action had to be taken. The program of medical assistance for the aged was and is urgently needed. In fact, we believe that still further action is needed: use of the social security approach to insure against the costs of hospital care for older people.

"The social insurance method: Provisions for health insurance benefits for the aged are a necessary part of income protection in retirement. Without such benefits the social security program cannot adequately provide basic security for the aged. For most older people old-age, survivors, and disability insurance cash benefits are barely large enough to keep them housed, clothed, and fed, and half of the beneficiaries do not have any significant additional regular income. The benefits are not large enough to meet the costs of expensive illnesses or to pay large health insurance premiums during retirement. The only way to remove the threat to the finanial independence of older people posed by the high cost of illness is through providing the aged with basic health insurance protection in addition to their monthly cash benefits. And this can be assured only through the social insurance methods.

"Basically the problem is that the larger medical-care needs of the aged as a group result in higher average costs than those incurred by younger people. To cover these costs higher premiums must be charged, and this at a time when, because they have retired, people's incomes are lower than in earlier years, and there is no employer to share the cost. We cannot expect them to finance the higher-than-average medical costs that they have at this time of their lives out of their lower-than-average financial resources. The best solution for a problem of this sort is an arrangement, like that for present social security benefits, under which people pay while they are working toward the cost of the protection that they will need to have in retirement, so that no further payment after retirement is required.

"The method of providing paid-up health insurance protection for retirement has not been followed on any large scale in private insurance, nor is it likely that it will be. The social insurance method, then, is the only practical way of enabling most people to pay during their working years toward meeting the health costs they will face in old age.

"Moreover, the social insurance approach affords the best assurance of keeping program costs under control, for there is a direct and known relationship between increases in benefits and increases in taxes, and the State and Federal Governments are relieved of a considerable burden on general revenues.

"I have mentioned that if we do not have health insurance for the aged under social security and if the State assistant programs were to provide better medical benefits than the ones in effect in the present initial programs, the cost of medical assistance for the aged could run as high as $1 billion a year or even more. With almost one-half of this coming from the States, the States would have to spend something like three times the $146 million they paid toward vendor payments for medical care under old-age assistance in 1960. Such a volume of expenditure, by some of the States, is almost impossible to envisage, but the need is there, and pressures to meet it will be great. Far better, surely, to look to meeting the major part of the costs through health insurance for the aged.

"The social insurance approach, on a national basis, makes possible provision of basic protection for the aged regardless of where they may happen to live. As you know, the State programs of medical assistance for the aged can, depending on State action, be very narrow, both in eligibility and in benefits, or on the other hand can provide virtually comprehensive medical care to a substantial portion of the aged. New York, for example, has enacted a comprehensive program, providing a broad range of medical services and a relatively liberal definition of 'medical indigence.' Unmarried aged people with annual incomes of $1,800 or less and couples with incomes totaling $2,600 or less are eligible. Kentucky's program, on the other hand, is limited to individuals with annual incomes of $1,200 or less and couples with annual incomes of $1,800 or less, and it provides payments only for 6 days of hospital care for acute emergency and life-endangering illness.

"Variations such as these and the fact that most States have no program at all raise the very serious question of whether this country can long tolerate a situation in which health care is available to many of its aged citizens in New York and Massachusetts but not to people similarly situated in Kentucky and North Carolina. There is nothing fair or equitable in a situation of this sort. The problem is nationwide, and it should be dealt with nationally.

"The social insurance approach would provide health insurance protection for the aged without limiting the patient's choice of doctor or hospital. In fact it makes possible greater freedom of choice than now exists, since the most important limitation for those who have not been able to pay—the financial barrier—would be removed. The only limitations on the patient's choice, for any beneficiary, would be what they are today for those who are able to pay: namely, that a hospital may be unable or unwilling to accept a patient and that one's physician may not happen to have hospital privileges at the hospital of one's choice. Thus, contrary to the argument of those who say that the plan would limit the patient's freedom of choice of doctor or hospital, it would in fact broaden freedom of choice for many and limit it for none.

"Finally, the social insurance approach means that those who qualify under it can be protected without having to undergo a means test. Requiring older people who have always been financially independent to undergo a means test, with its investigation of their personal circumstances, when serious illness strikes, denies them dignity and self-respect in their days of retirement.

"We have, then, in the social insurance approach these advantages: It is the only way in which people generally can pay during their working years toward meeting their health costs in retirement; it is sound and fiscally responsible; it makes possible provision of basic protection for the aged regardless of where they live; it preserves and increases freedom of choice of doctor and hospital; and it does all this in a way that is consistent with the dignity of the individual.

*   *   *

"To summarize, older people have low incomes and high health costs. We believe that many refrain from seeking care they need because they cannot pay for it or are unwilling to ask for help. Others, who do seek care, are made destitute by the cost of the care they get.

"With the cost of health care rising and the number of older persons increasing rapidly, the need for protection against the cost of health care for the aged is an urgent and pressing one. The only satisfactory way of providing the aged with adequate health insurance protection is through a system under which the cost of the health insurance will be paid by people during their working years, together with their employers. The social security program is the only practical mechanism which follows this approach and through which in the future practically everyone in every State in the United States can secure basic protection.

"A quarter of a century ago we faced a problem much like this one. We chose as our basic solution then, a system of social insurance under which the people, with their employers, would build their own old-age security. Now after 25 years, few would question the wisdom of that decision. I hope we will choose the social security approach again today as the answer to the problem of medical care for the aged."

Con ‡—Edward R. Annis, M.D.

Edward R. Annis writes here as an official representative of the American Medical Association.

"Although physicians have a vital stake in the action taken by Congress on H.R. 4222, our stake is minor by comparison with that of our patients. It is true that the freedom of the physician is involved in such decision; but

for our patients, action will affect the even more critical matters of pain and

‡ From testimony on behalf of the American Medical Association before the House Committee on Ways and Means, U. S. House of Representatives, August 2, 1961.

relief, illness and cure, life prolonged, and life concluded.

"On their behalf, as well as our own, we oppose this bill vigorously. We do so in the belief that as physicians we are better qualified to speak knowledgeably about health care than any other group. This is, after all, our full-time profession and our field of expertness. When we warn that H.R. 4222 would have disastrous effects on the quality of medical care our patients would receive, we know whereof we speak.

"It is necessary to recognize that we have experienced significant population changes. In 1900, only 1 in 25 Americans was age 65 or older. Today that ratio is about 1 in 11. In 1980 this ratio still is expected to be about 1 in 11. This means that although there may be more persons over age 65, the proportionate growth of the aged population is tapering off. Our problem is that we have not adjusted our thinking realistically to the increase in the aged population which has occurred since the turn of the century, but which, proportionately, is becoming stabilized.

"We Americans have arbitrarily established 65 as the age of obsolescence, but we have failed to compensate the hardships of economic discard with some degree of social appreciation. We can no more provide a statutory solution to this situation than we can legislate intolerance out of existence.

"Aging is not a new problem. People have always gotten older. However, the current problems in this field are related to increased numbers and the tendency toward the social and economic segregation of the aged. As to health, there is a limit to what doctors, nurses, and hospitals can accomplish. The rest is up to the society in which they function.

"We need a positive attitude concerning the aged. Medicine is proud of the role it has played in increasing the longevity of Americans. We are convinced that the years added to the lives of our citizens can be, should be, and must be treated as an asset to our society. We must revise our outlook and prepare to utilize the skills and talents of these older people. We must keep them gainfully employed and useful. We must not shunt them aside—as H.R. 4222 seeks to do—into a broad category of our population labeled: 'These are people who can't take care of themselves. These are people who must be cared for by the Federal Government at the expense of the rest of the population.'

"Before we tamper with a medical care system which has increased the longevity of our citizens, let us pause a moment for further consideration.

"By any standard, America's system of health care is unrivaled. The quality of medical education and the qualifications of physicians are unmatched anywhere. Our drugs, our facilities for treatment, our medical techniques are unexcelled. We treat, research, experiment, improvise—always moving ahead, always dissatisfied with the status quo.

"Quality care can be obtained only when the medical needs of the individual patient are placed first and financing is placed second. Under H.R. 4222, Government will decide for the patient what services should be provided and by whom and then assume the responsibility of paying for the services involved.

"When Government supplants the individual as the agent for payment, Government becomes an intruding third party, striving vainly to reconcile the demands of the patient for high quality care and the demand of the taxpayer for an efficient use of tax funds.

"Invariably, Government resolves

these conflicting demands, not on the basis of the patient's needs, but on the basis of the money available to pay for the program.

"Against this background let us examine H.R. 4222 in terms of its specific provisions.

"At first glance, the opening sections of the bill are reassuring. They disclaim control by any Federal officer or employee over the practice of medicine or the administration of hospitals, facilities, or agencies. They state that the patient may freely choose those who will provide the services covered.

"The following conflicting language occurs, however, when the power of the Secretary of Health, Education, and Welfare is described: '* * * Or, except as otherwise specifically provided, to exercise any supervision or control over the administration or operation of any such hospital, facility, or agency * * *.'

"Those five words, 'except as otherwise specifically provided,' are a blanket authorization for the Federal Government to control the providers of services. Include those words and the Secretary of HEW can exercise control over the administration or operation of a hospital, facility, physician, or agency. For the bill also states, as a requirement for participation by a hospital, that the Secretary would be empowered to set 'such other conditions of participation * * * as the Secretary may find it necessary in the interest of health and safety of individuals who are furnished services by or in such institution.'

"The permissive language of this proposal thus provides the means by which Federal officials can regiment and control all providers of the services covered.

"When H.R. 4222 disclaims its intention of interfering with the free practice of medicine, as is customary in all bills which seek to utilize the compulsory social security mechanism as a device for financing health care for the aged, it deceives no one. For if a single governmental agency is empowered to buy from 10 to 20 per cent of all care in the Nation's general hospitals, it is a foregone conclusion that this agency must have and would use the power to influence the operation and management of the hospitals.

"The beneficiary's alleged freedom of choice is also a worthless guarantee. What freedom of choice would a patient have if the hospital where his physician had privileges chose not to participate or was considered ineligible? What freedom of choice would a patient have if the only hospital in his area chose not to participate or was considered ineligible?

"The proponents of this measure have stated publicly and often that only a handful of physicians would be affected by the bill. In actuality, the bill entitles beneficiaries to the services supplied by pathologists, radiologists, physiatrists, anesthesiologists, and all interns and residents in training under an approved teaching program.

"Interns and residents are doctors in training. As such, they are agents of hospital staff physicians who are responsible for all the services these students render. Thus, H.R. 4222 involves the provision of services, and responsibility for the provision of services, of at least 50,000 physicians.

*   *   *

"In the process of giving the whip hand to the Secretary of HEW, the bill requires that the eligibility of hospitals to participate in the program be based on three conditions. These are: (1) adequate medical records; (2) by-laws in effect with respect to staff and physicians; and (3) such other conditions as the Secretary may find necessary in the interest of the health and safety of the individuals receiving the services provided.

"Here again H.R. 4222 provides a device for Federal control of hospitals and the medical services they furnish.

"We do not argue that the hospitals, like other institutions or business, should not maintain adequate records. But who is to say what records are adequate and what records are not? The bill is clear on this point. The arbiter of adequacy is to be the Secretary of HEW. If he so wishes, the Secretary could require records so adequate that compiling and maintaining them would require a doubling or tripling of hospital administrative staffs.

"The Secretary is further empowered to determine such other conditions of participation as he may find necessary in the interest of health and safety.

"What the Secretary and his successors might currently or eventually find necessary I do not know. I shall only point out that this section of the bill gives the Secretary enough authority to become the Nation's czar of hospital care.

"Very properly we fear unrestrained power in this country. It is all very well to say that our public officials are men of good will and that we can count upon that circumstance to safeguard us against misuse of the regulatory power. But an unrestrained license to regulate can become a license destructive to either a free nation or a free system of medical care. Even if we could be guaranteed of the good intentions of the Secretary and his successors, could we be guaranteed that all of them would be knowledgeable and wise in the exercise of this great authority?

"I suggest that we could not. Standards set by an appointed official, and regulations promulgated by him, may be responsive to the wishes of an administration. But would they be responsive to the needs of the patient? It is unlikely that the political expert would be equally expert in his control of a health system. Delegate these powers to the Federal Government and our free system of medical care—the world's best—would be placed in extreme jeopardy.

*   *   *

"Let me make a few more last points briefly:

"(1) H.R. 4222 would endanger the entire social security system.— The bill departs radically from the 'floor of protection' principle upon which the Social Security Act was based in that it provides a service, not a cash benefit. The precedent thus set would open the way for increased use of the social security mechanism to provide widely diversified, expensive benefits foreign to the system's experience, intent, or philosophy. The power to tax is the power to destroy; and the power to tax for the purposes of social security expansion would, if overused, destroy the system itself.

"(2) H.R. 4222 would undermine private health insurance and other prepayment mechanisms.—The measure would substitute a compulsory system of governmental health care financing for a private voluntary system that has shown phenomenal growth and an ability to provide a financial cushion against medical expenses for the vast majority of Americans. Those compelled by law to carry the cost of a national compulsory health plan would be neither able nor anxious to carry private health policies as well. The AMA is convinced that private health insurance and prepayment plans constitute the most effective device available to the elderly for the financing of health care. In our opinion, these mechanisms are versatile enough, available enough, and adequate enough to meet the needs of this Nation.

"(3) H.R. 422 would lead to the decline, if not the demise, of voluntary efforts at the community level.—Legislation of this sort would curb community incentive to support hospitals, nursing homes, health campaigns, and health centers; it would discourage freedom to experiment with new techniques, such as home care programs, homemaker services, progressive patient care, new concepts for treatment through outpatient departments, doctors' offices, and the like; it would usurp, albeit inadequately, the magnificent role played by our fraternal, civic, religious, and philanthropic groups in the care of the aged.

"(4) It would cover millions of people who neither need help in paying the costs of health care, nor want such help.—It should be pointed out that the proportionate growth of the aged population has tapered off and that the great bulk of the voting and tax-paying segment of the population will continue to be called on to support a costly old-age medical care program. But when costs increase even more, as they inevitably will, will it be fair to these younger people to have them shoulder the burden of this program? And, it may be asked, will they continue to support a program with unending increases in costs?

"(5) It would determine eligibility for medical aid on the basis of age rather than on the basis of need.— The AMA believes that those who need help should receive it. The medical profession's record in this country for making its services readily available to all, regardless of their ability to pay, confirms our commitment to this principle. We find it hard, therefore, to understand why age, instead of need, has been made the arbitrary basis upon which the financing of health care must be based. Under H.R. 4222 a person over 65 but still at work, and therefore collecting no benefits under social security, would be entitled to coverage for health purposes. Yet such a person has experienced no loss of income as a result of retirement and is presumably as capable as in former years of financing health care costs for himself. This particular provision of the measure demonstrates, in our opinion, the determination of the bill's supporters to initiate a program for program's sake—disregarding individual need on the false argument that need is universal at age 65.

"(6) H.R. 4222 would destroy the concepts of individual and familial responsibility.—It has been the tradition of Americans that independence and self-reliance are native virtues. We are still convinced that this is true. Accordingly, we believe that personal health care is primarily the responsibility of the individual. When he is unable to provide this care for himself, the responsibility should properly pass first to his family, then to the community, the State and, when all these others fail, to the Federal Government. It is now proposed that we reverse this chain of responsibility and give first priority to the Federal Government and last priority to individual responsibility. If we do so, we shall have lost more than the world's finest system of medical care; we shall have lost stature as individuals and stature as a nation.

"(7) The bill would eliminate the States' historical responsibility while further diminishing the States' authority in a vital area of government.— We are unwilling to believe that the separate States are willing to relinquish their rights and responsibilities in this field to the Federal Government or that this could be done without incalculable loss to our entire governmental system. Further, we do not believe that Federal programs are inherently superior to State programs, particularly in the welfare area.

"(8) Finally H.R. 4222 is unnecessary.—Most of the aged are in reasonably good financial circumstances, although some are not. Similarly, most of the aged are in relatively good health, although some are not. To the extent that the aged have a problem in financing the cost of their health care, the problem is diminishing as time goes on. Thus, a compulsory Federal program, permanent in nature, is not required for a solution of the problem."

*   *   *

70   THE GOLDEN YEARS

Michael Harrington

Michael Harrington was formerly editor of *New America*.

The aging woman in New York called her social worker on the telephone. She was in tears. Her check had not come from Welfare on the expected day, and she was terrified that she had been cut off, that now she would literally face starvation. Her life, like those of many in her situation, was suspended by a thread from the city's welfare system. The social worker was her symbol of hope.

The social worker: It is inevitable that this figure should emerge in a book on poverty. In every part of the other America there are social workers. Among the gangs of the city slums, it is even considered a mark of honor to have a full-time worker assigned to a particular group. It shows that the authorities are taking them seriously. In the Negro ghetto, once the social worker becomes known, he or she is the one person from the outside who can move with a certain ease down the streets.

But it is particularly fitting that the social worker appear in a chapter on the misery of age in contemporary America. For the millions of aging poor, and particularly for those who live alone, one of the main facts about life is that it becomes totally dependent. At best, they must count on the charity and love of a family; at worst, their fate belongs to the stranger from Welfare.

Much has been written against the social worker in the United States. The argument usually runs that callousness and cynicism are the inherent products of public charity. Unquestionably, social work has created some bureaucratic, unfeeling personalities, individuals who see only statistics and the mass, who never really look into the human face of poverty. There is a sort of welfare-state Lady Bountiful who subsists on a patronizing, routinized *noblesse oblige*. As time has gone on, the "clients" of these social workers have become wise. They adopt the jargon; they give the right answers; they become bureaucratically adept.

But this acid portrait is only part of the picture. To a considerable extent social workers are as they are because the funds with which they work are completely inadequate to solve the

Excerpts reprinted with permission of the Macmillan Company from *The Other America* by Michael Harrington; copyright 1962 by Michael Harrington.

problems that confront Welfare. The case load is usually overwhelming. Often, good, warm, and sincere people who genuinely want to help human beings are simply submerged in a routine that is not of their own making. (An irony: some years ago, a union of social workers in New York struck against the authorities by staying late on their own time and writing all of the money authorizations that were legally possible.) I remember a teacher in St. Louis who moved into the slum neighborhood of her school in order to be with the people all of the time. She is a symbol of the best in the social-work impulse.

If it is tragic that a bureaucratic impersonality is imposed on many social workers throughout the other America, that fact becomes most intolerable in relation to the aged poor. These are people whose plight is expressed in a torment of loneliness and isolation. They require, above all, individual and particular care. And no matter how passionately committed to humanity a social worker is, this requires a certain amount of money. America has not provided it.

In the fifties, a young woman social worker for aged at the Montgomery County Relief Area settled in Dayton, Ohio. What follows in the next few pages is a summation of her impressions of the reality of social work in that place.

In Ohio, relief programs are on the basis of county administration (or were in the mid-fifties, the period from which this description is taken). Standards were set for minimal payments required to give the people the basis of a subsistence existence. Then, as so often happens in the other America, each county would decide what percentage of the minimum it would provide. (Relief and welfare programs throughout the United States are com-

pletely uneven; it is much better to be poor in New York City than in Montgomery County, and better to be poor in almost any place than in Missisippi.) In Montgomery County the percentage of the minimum was 90 per cent—fairly high for the state.

The first thing that an older person would encounter when coming to the relief area was the necessity of documenting eligibility. In some cases proof of age was required, and there could be a long postponement, or even a rejection, if the proper papers were not produced. Some of the programs had a residency requirement that the individual had lived in the state for five out of the last nine years.

In this particular office, the young woman relates, the screening was carried on by people who were hostile to the applicants. They regarded most of those who came to them as "deadbeats" and "bums," and they were determined to keep freeloaders off the public rolls. As a result, they have achieved a rejection rate of 55 per cent, and they were quite proud of it and determined to keep it there.

To a person from the middle class, the fact that documents are required by a public agency seems to be obvious and rational. Yet this judgment misses a basic fact about the poor generally, and the aged poor in particular: that they are precisely the ones least equipped to deal with the bureaucracy of the welfare state. Some of the American poor have difficulty with the English language, and almost all of them are undereducated. There are those who develop their relations with welfare into a fine art, but there are many more who are literally terrified by the forms and the apparatus of a relief office.

This is doubly true for the aged. They are in failing health, and are completely and totally dependent upon the authorities. A trip to the relief office is a matter of life and death for them. And they tend to be bewildered by the routines of a world in which they did not grow up. The people described by the young social worker in Montgomery County were consciously hostile to those who came to them for help. But even those who are solicitous are forced to act in somewhat the same way. Money is limited, and in order to see that everyone gets something it is necessary to be brutal and probing.

In Montgomery County there were some who tried to steer the aged poor away from clinics. They felt that if a person went to a clinic where all kinds of complaints were treated, there would be a tendency to invent illness so as to get more out of the state. So they preferred to send them to individual doctors, and to certify treatment for a single ailment.

But within the present setup the single-doctor approach is not a simple evil. One of the standard indignities in the clinic is that the doctor is likely to change with each visit. This means that the old person has to recite symptoms anew each time. Because of such repetition, it seemed to some of the people that they were beginning treatment over and over and that nothing was really being done for them. (In New York, for instance, one old man I know goes to a clinic and an individual doctor through the Welfare Department. He feels that the doctor is really helping him, but the routine of the clinic has convinced him that nothing is being done for his condition.)

But again, all this is part of the poverty of public facilities in the affluent society. In Montgomery County, for example, there was a woman who would be confined to her bed unless she had a wheel chair. A relatively small expenditure of money would have

made her life infinitely more decent and dignified. When the social worker proposed that this be done, her superiors told her that there were hundreds of others who needed wheel chairs (to translate: hunderds of others who, by receiving a simple device, could have the horizons of their life broadened). The authorities granted that this particular case was a worthy one and that the benefits would be immediate and obvious, but they were afraid that it would start a run on wheel chairs. The woman stayed in bed.

In the incident of the wheel chair, the lack of public funds prolonged and made more miserable an already existing illness. In other cases, sickness and suffering are created by the squalor of the welfare services. Mrs. H——— was seventy-five. Her husband had suffered a stroke and a bad fall, and had lost control of his bowel and bladder functions. She tried to care for him, lift him, wash his sheets and underwear, and so on. There was enough government money to "live" on, but her life was near collapse and she had already been stricken by one siege of pneumonia.

Mrs. H——— was not an isolated individual. This is how the young social worker described the living conditions of her "clients": "They live in furnished rooms, as boarders with a family, in small furnished and unfurnished apartments, in homes of their own, in trailers and rest homes. Those in the furnished rooms are probably on the whole the most pitiable. Generally they are alone—single, widowed or widower, divorced—they live in complete seclusion, terribly lonely, yet deliberately cutting themselves off from their neighbors whose gossip they fear. They do not want it known that they are 'on relief.'

"If they are fortunate, they can find

one neighbor whom they can learn to trust. That neighbor will function as a companion and, equally important, as a responsible protector who will call the doctor or get the client into the hospital, or who will call the case worker if the client is too sick to do so. If this neighbor moves away they may never find another to rely on."

Another hard fact of this life comes from the bureaucratic demand that there be some *quid pro quo* for relief payments. In many areas, going on relief requires the signing of a lien on all property so that Welfare has the first claim against the estate. Usually, this is a technicality, since these people have no money and no assets in any case. But for those who have saved and skimped and bought a home during their middle years, this provision is a trauma, a sort of ultimate deprivation that puts an official stamp on society's rejection of them. And for almost all, whether there are assets or not, it is an emotional experience in which life itself is being signed away in a legal document. The individual is being made the property of the state in return for three inadequate meals a day, rent money, and some medical care.

There is a woman in New York who had been a vaudeville head-liner in the old days. When she was making money, she spent it foolishly, signing away rights and a fortune. Now she is on relief, and Welfare has demanded that she sign over her estate. There is a possibility that a movie may be made about her life. In her old age she has finally become crafty. Because she signed too much away when she was young, she is balking now. And perhaps she won't get care as a result.

At the end of the road, there is the county home. The staff people around Dayton are quite proud of this institution, the young woman relates. They regarded it as adequate to the needs of the people who were sent to them. But many of the aged themselves were terrified by the idea of the county home. In the popular feeling of America, there is something utterly degrading in the very name. (The popular feeling is partly right; the utter inadequacy of a good many of these places will be described shortly.)

How representative are these details of welfare administration in Ohio? As noted before, there is great variation in these programs from state to state, from city to city. But there are also the inescapable mathematics of the inadequacy of social security and other Federal programs and of the various local systems. As it is, the aged poor in America are condemned to deal with a bureaucratic, impersonal, frustrated setup.

D.
ECONOMIC FORECASTING

71 FORTUNE'S FORECAST

Fortune

It Adds Up

Against the backdrop of an economy that was producing $560 billion worth of goods and services while the stock market fell precipitously, men debated last month the possibilities of of continued growth, a slowdown, and even an outright recession. One task of the discipline of economic analysis and forecasting is to define some limits of the effects of swings in confidence such as the country is now experiencing.

In Roundup's judgment a real recession in the U.S. market economy—defined as a sharp turndown in production—is not in the cards during the next twelve months. As argued last month, the recent drop in the stock market in a period of monetary ease cannot be viewed as the harbinger of recession in the light of past experience. The condition of inventories, the structure of capital demands, the surge in government spending, the strength in housing, the incomes and savings of consumers, are all extraordinarily favorable and imply a large momentum. The worst immediate consequence Roundup can see issuing from today's loss of "confidence" would be that the economy would now simply level out for a time. It is barely conceivable that six months from now there could

be a mild dip on the order of 1960–61, but only if the economy had risen meanwhile with confidence still impaired. By then, however, it is far likelier that the fabric of confidence would be restored, given the stakes that both business and government have in economic growth.

The above are the outside pessimistic possibilities. In fact, Roundup's own forecast of the future remains basically optimistic. On this forecast G.N.P. will rise from its present $560 billion to around $593 billion next spring, in today's prices. This is as far as it appears sensible now to forecast specific sectors of the economy. . . . The logic of expansion, however, suggests that the economy will continue to rise, to $610 billion by the end of 1963, when it would be at full employment. For all of 1962, G.N.P. will be about $564 billion, a 7 per cent gain over 1961 but 2 per cent less than forecast last January. The range for 1963 would be near $600 billion.

The details behind these calculations are elaborated below, but behind them lie certain hard facts and more general assumptions. The foreground fact is that the economy is performing powerfully, not poorly. Total goods and services are moving to *final users* at precisely the rate Roundup forecast a year ago. Final demand has increased 8.5 per cent in five quarters, at once the best peacetime advance and yet the most belittled of the postwar. Total G.N.P. is running today some $10 billion below Roundup's forecast of January, but this is chiefly due to the early settlement of steel wage negotiations. Instead of a sharp buildup in inventories then assumed as likely, metal stocks are running down. This means, however, that inventory accumulation will rise in coming months, adding impetus to the unbroken advance of G.N.P.

Strength for the next six or twelve months is also notably plain in demand for apartments and houses, for cars and home goods, and in the increasing expenditures of government for roads as well as for armaments. Federal programs for depreciation revision and an investment tax credit, and for more public works and unemployment benefits will tend to offset some of the depressing effects recently emanating from Washington and Wall Street. The stability of U.S. prices, moreover, is quickening demand not only at home but also from abroad. While a feeling of boom is today lacking in the behavior of prices and unemployment, it is in one sense for the happiest of possible reasons. Productivity has performed sensationally, up 8 per cent in five quarters, better than in a dozen years or than anyone counted on. Nothing could be more salubrious for potential returns on investment or growth of output, and ordinarily the only question now would be how far beyond next year the economy's internal forces would carry its expansion.

These are, however, not ordinary times, owing to the steel crackdown and the market break, and Roundup has allowed for these dampeners on demand. As the result of the market break in particular, consumers will spend somewhat less than Roundup previously forecast. As for business investment, in January Roundup forecast a rise of $3.5 billion for the next two quarters, but now the rise may be on the order of only $1 billion per quarter till the end of this year. Thereafter, however, there should be an upturn, particularly marked in the second half of 1963. The growth of capital stock is now and has for some years been on the order of only 2.3 per cent per annum while total production has been advancing faster than that, and this rate is simply inadequate for a long-term growth of 4 per cent or more in the economy. The dampened rise in investment is presenting the nation with a due bill on the future. How and when this bill will be paid may depend, if only in part, on whether restraints on long-term growth implicit in the present tax system are lifted. It is a sign of hope, however, that such reforms are now being widely supported.

Even to attempt to look into 1963 may seem far off from present realities, but it serves to put present discussion of the state of the economy into broad perspective. Such perspective is today badly needed. The intangible of psychology is notoriously hard to judge and never more so than now after the stock-market decline and while the Administration's basic relation with the private economy is still not altogether clear. Of the two, the latter is wholly critical. The fact is that the business system of economy requires freedom on the part of entrepreneurs and managers to make their own market calculations about prices. Presumably everyone, including the Administration, knows this, and will work to clarify unnecessary uncertainties. If, as should be expected, men are thus reasonable, investor psychology might well shift, but in any case the economy would be free to fulfill its potential. In the meantime the economy's course in coming quarters may be no smoother than it was over the past eighteen months, when it ran strong and weak in successive periods, but on the whole registered a powerful advance. For practical operations, it has been less fruitful to bend to the breeze of each turn in psychology than to adhere to the inner logic of this expansion. That logic is further detailed in the following ten critical points.

Defense. Outlays have risen by $6 billion in the past year. But expenditures will go up about half as fast from now on: by a bit more than $3 billion per annum right through fiscal 1963 and well into 1964. These added expenditures include the swelling costs of the space program, small increases for the AEC and military aid overseas, and some increases for the Defense Department. The latter are going up across the board, for limited-war as well as Polaris equipment.

Budget. The regular federal budget will show a deficit of $7 billion for fiscal 1962 and will also be in deficit for fiscal 1963. More important for the economy is what happens to the so-called national income accounting of federal operations, which takes account of government trust funds, and treats corporate taxes on an accrual rather than a cash basis. Contrary to some published impressions the national accounts budget was in deficit by a rate of $1 billion this spring.

By next spring federal receipts will go up by at most $8.5 billion, and at a slower rate thereafter even if the economy is then moving toward full employment. Social-security tax rates, to be sure, will go up next January at a rate of over $2 billion a year. But the revision of depreciation rules will reduce revenues by $1 billion or so.

Meanwhile, federal outlays by next spring will have risen by $6.5 billion from a recent rate of $110 billion. This will include $3 billion more for national defense, and $3.5 billion more for a wide variety of nondefense purposes. The latter estimate assumes that Congress will vote a renewal of temporary unemployment insurance and special public works while compromising on proposed cuts in farm costs and a rise in postal rates.

Thus there would be only a small surplus of receipts over outlays twelve months from now on the national income accounting. Looking further ahead, there could be a small surplus in fiscal 1964 under full employment conditions, but not as big as is often assumed. This whole prospect of deficit now and only a small surplus in the future means that federal finances will not act as a drag on further economic recovery. But it also complicates the prospect for tax reform, which is badly needed to speed economic growth. There is relatively little margin for a tax program that involves a large loss of revenue.

Capital Spending. The rate of investment in plant and equipment has risen by $5 billion over the past year to $50 billion now. It may not better that rise in the next year, as the result of the steel imbroglio and the decline in stock prices. But the inherent strength in investment, which led Roundup in January to forecast a $7-billion annual advance, is still great. It precludes any real recession in capital goods, and on the contrary suggests a speedup some time in 1963.

As the economy entered the spring its over-all rate of utilization of capital stock was the highest since 1955. National output had grown 8 per cent since the 1960 peak, capital by only 5 per cent, and pressure on capacity was causing many businessmen to expand 1962 plans. In March the SEC-Commerce survey reported that plans called for an 8 per cent rise in capital spending in 1962 over 1961, and subsequent FORTUNE and McGraw-Hill surveys indicated that the rise would be larger than that. The SEC-Commerce survey taken in May, which reflected first reactions to the steel dispute, indicated expansion in some areas but cuts in spending plans for steel and automobiles, and soon balance plans were back to only an 8 per cent gain.

The break in stock-market prices introduced a new uncertainty. Initial reports indicated that a great majority of companies were holding fast to their plans—one factor being that they are not yet investing all their available cash flow. Nevertheless there have undoubtedly been scattered cutbacks by some companies, while others may now be holding back on new plans that otherwise would be in the making. While few have problems of financing, some may be worrying about the market as a harbinger.

But the probabilities favor a speedup in capital spending sometime in 1963, possibly by spring. It will be helped by revision of depreciation rules and the probable investment credit legislation. More important is the assumption that there will be a gradual lifting of uncertainty about pricing and some stabilization in the stock market. Pressure on capacity meanwhile will have increased as national output continues to grow faster than capital stock.

Such pressure is already leading electric utilities to budget more for 1963 and 1964 than for 1962. And the position today of the energy, metal, and transport industries, which account for about half of all capital investment, is enormously significant. Their out-lays were very high in 1957 and so accounted for most of the sharp 1958 drop. Thereupon their expansion was moderate and the 1960–61 dip in investment was small. Today their outlays are still below the best levels of 1960, despite an increase in replacement needs, and will remain so at the end of this year. In the "other half" of capital investment—i.e., nonmetal lines, communications, and commercial businesses—expansion has been accompanied by large increases in sales and output. In short, strength in the capital sector flows from the fact that spending has been comparatively moderate, or based on real market growth.

Inventories. The big point about inventories is that they are definitely on the low rather than the high side, and so is the rate of accumulation. In the second quarter of 1962 accumulation ran to only $3 billion per year, principally because steel users, who had accumulated inventories as a hedge against a possible midyear stoppage, were running off stocks. This runoff will soon stop, and Roundup expects that the rate of accumulation will increase in the third quarter and run at over $6 billion per year in 1963.

Dealer stocks of cars are the lowest in three years despite near-record sales, and stocks of other retail and wholesale merchants of hard goods are also low. Business has in the past year been pursuing the most conservative policy ever recorded by FORTUNE's quarterly surveys. Stocks have grown only half as much in the past two years as sales of goods to final users, which are up 8 per cent over mid-1960. All in all, inventories, which now come to more than $100 billion, should grow at least in pace with final sales of goods. Roundup projects this rate at a bit over 6 per cent a year through 1963.

Construction. Starts of nonfarm private houses should continue to run about their present 1,500,000 rate through the next twelve months. Contracts for apartment building this summer and fall swelled to a rate of 400,000 to 450,000 per year. Meanwhile builders of prefabricated and semifinished shell homes report increases in sales. Demand for one-family homes should strengthen since interest rates for both FHA and conventional mortgages are coming down. The whole market for housing is being expanded by an upturn in the marriage rate, and these young householders are not likely to be affected by the drop in the stock market. This drop may for a time adversely affect the market for alterations and additions to existing housing, which has been slow to respond to rising incomes. But there may be a catch-up in 1963 as more people come to understand the new home-repair credits legislated last year. Construction of dormitories, motels, and other nonhousekeeping units will continue to boom.

Public works will rise sharply with the start of the new fiscal year, which will open up large new allocations of highway trust funds, and end the lag in such construction. Also, Congress seems likely to vote an eighteen-month program for public works for depressed areas. Gains in housing and public works will interact upon one another and will also have effects on commercial and institutional building (a rising portion of capital investment).

Prices and Wages. The general price level keeps rising a bit over 1 per cent a year owing mainly to the slow, steady increase in the price of services. But commodity prices remain on even keel, and as unit labor costs have been stable for some years, this trend should continue. While manufacturing wage rates rose 2.7 per cent in the past year, productivity in manufacturing exceeded the postwar average gain of a bit over 3 per cent. Productivity in total nonfarm business has been going up spectacularly. After stalling from 1955 to 1957, and rising about normally thereafter from 1958 to 1961, gains in the past year have been unusually large and have restored the postwar trend of average gains of 2.9 per cent a year. Although cost pressures are naturally increasing a bit as productivity gains slow down to more normal rates, there appear to be no significant upward pressures on prices on the immediate horizon.

Income and Savings. Personal disposable income is running at a rate of about $385 billion. It is naturally expanding with rising employment, while benefit payments of all kinds will once again rise sharply in coming months, in part under new legislation (temporary unemployment insurance, manpower training, etc.). Real income per person has now climbed 6 per cent over five years ago (with the slowdown in wage rises balanced by slower price rises). It has gone up over 3 per cent in the past year and will do at least as well in the next.

It is quite possible that people who suffered outright or paper losses in the stock market will curtail some consumer expenditures in order to restore their assets. At the very most such savings could come to a rate of $10 billion. So Roundup expects that in the next several months the rate of savings may go up by $3 billion, and that the per cent of income saved will go back to over 7.

Consumer Spending. Consumer spending is now running at a rate of about $360 billion. Discounting for price increases, the volume of spending will be up about 4 per cent in the next year as against 5.5 per cent last year, and as compared to an average gain of about 3.5 per cent per annum since spring 1957.

The drop in the stock market may slow spending a little but more significant is the fact that incomes will continue to rise. Expenditures on food and services will continue to grow, but the big potential is in buying of goods, particularly as low-price lines have widened markets. Purchases of goods are up about 8 per cent over a year ago, and may rise by 5 per cent more. Home-goods sales particularly will expand a good deal with more new apartments and houses.

New cars have led the goods upswing, and 1962 sales (including imports) will crowd the 1955 records. This year's sales of cars will about match FORTUNE's projection of 7,200,-000, based on normal replacements and growth. An extra million jalopies of 1946–50 vintage, which should normally have been scrapped by now, are still on the road. Replacements generally will be speeded by the increasing appearance of compacts in the used-car market. All this suggests that another year could produce a rise in new-car sales from the 1962 volume.

Credit and Stocks. The stock market has hardly been acting according to Hoyle this spring. Bear markets are almost always preceded by a financial pinch that is reflected in banking figures (e.g., the debit-loan ratio). No such pinch has occurred, and indeed the debit-loan ratio is still rising, an anomaly with only two precedents in the past generation (in 1934 and in late 1938), and business did not follow the market down.

When business has followed the market down in the past, it has been after financial stringency, and not always then. Stocks fell 25 per cent in 1946, for example, but the financial pinch did not stop business from entering into the 1947–48 boom.

Industrial stock prices have fallen 26 per cent in six months as of the middle of last month, 15 per cent lower than at the writing of the June Round-up. At mid-June, Standard & Poor's 425 industrial stocks were selling at 13.5 times current annual earnings, as against nineteen times at the December highs and a range of twelve to sixteen times in 1955–57 (after eliminating inventory profits and extra depreciation charges).

Administration and Federal Reserve policy for nearly two years has attempted to keep credit easy (to spur domestic business) and yet to keep interest rates up (to avoid outflow of capital abroad). Hence rates have fluctuated relatively little, and instead of rising in pace with business this year, those at short term have been relatively steady and those on bonds and mortgages have actually declined a bit. The money supply is expanding (especially if the banks' soaring time deposits are included) and there is no present reason to expect any major change in these policies, though a continued outflow of capital is worrying the Treasury.

Exports. Foreign trade should act as a slight net stimulant to the U.S. economy over the next eighteen months. Imports will rise more gradually than they did over recent months. Exports should improve more rapidly, partly as the result of government programs to expand foreign aid, to tie it to U.S. goods, and to promote U.S. sales of commercial and military products. Equally important, business is improving among several major U.S. customers (e.g., Britain, Western Europe), and meanwhile prices are rising in most of the industrial nations.

This will tend to improve the over-all U.S. balance of payments. But capital movements are still a difficult problem since U.S. interest rates remain somewhat lower than abroad, and U.S. capital markets are open to all comers. The over-all rate of dollar deficit is now running at about half or less of the $3.8-billion average deficit of 1958–60. The Administration hopes to close the gap by the end of 1963. But this will not be easy to achieve.

E.

THE UNDERDEVELOPED COUNTRIES

72   WHY ARE WE BLESSED?

Peggy and Pierre Streit

Peggy and Pierre Streit are writers on Economic Affairs.

Shiraz, Iran

"Eighty-eight per cent of the people in America own television sets." There it is, the shortest of items in today's local English-language newspaper—there, amid the news about Iran, the cold war, and world crisis. "Eighty-eight per cent of the people in America own television sets"—the mere tick of a statistic, addressed, as it were, to whom it may concern. And our thoughts turn back to seven years of travel in the middle East and Asia.

We think of India and the daily drive we made to New Delhi from our home on the outskirts of the city. On the way there was a small refugee village and in it a dump heap. Each day, as we passed, we watched the village dogs and the village women, side by side, clawing through the refuse with unnerving intensity for scraps of food.

And we remember Kabul, Afghanistan, its newly paved streets dusted with a thin coat of sand blown in from the plains. Roaming those streets was a band of dirty, barefoot scavenger boys—all 7 or 8 years old, each with a square metal can strapped to his back. They followed the carriages, searching for horse droppings, and when they found some they scooped up the manure with their small hands and, with a deft practiced motion, tossed it over their shoulders into the cans, to be sold later to Afghan farmers.

We remember, a few winters ago, a little girl on the sleet-covered streets of South Teheran. Her head was bent into a wind that blew her cotton dress against her legs. She was barefoot. As she walked the flesh of her heels, cracked by the cold, left little arcs of blood in the snow.

And so, this morning, as we read that 88 per cent of all Americans own television sets, we ask ourselves, as we have so often before, what we and what our countrymen have done to merit the bounty and the comfort with which we live, and what so much of the world has done to warrant its destitution.

Why is it that we can look forward this evening to the quiet comfort of an ample meal while, not two miles away, thousands of drought-driven Iranian nomads are on their weary way south in search of food for themselves and their gaunt animals? Why is it that we can buy clothes—clothes we don't really need—while in Calcutta thousands of men, women and children who sleep under bridges and in doorways lack even a piece of cloth to put between themselves and the pavement?

Why are we permitted to look to tomorrow without fear of want, when for so many in this world, tomorrow may well bring flood, famine or disease to destroy all that they cherish? Why are we permitted to enjoy the blessings of freedom and security, knowing that well-established democratic institutions in the United States have peacefully elected a new President, while in most of the underdeveloped world there is no freedom, there are no democratic institutions—or even much understanding of them or hope that they may soon provide the blessings enjoyed in the West?

Why have we been so fortunate? It would be pleasant to believe we have earned our good fortune because we have worked harder than the millions of people we see toiling on barren land. But we know better.

We have seen too many Indian farmers trudging behind primitive, wooden plows under a searing sun; we have seen too many Nepalese women bent double in their rice fields, their legs covered with leeches; we have seen too many Iranian children hunched over their ill-lit carpet looms, to have

any such illusions. We know that never in our lives have we worked, one day, as hard as most of the people in the world work each day. We cannot lay claim to our comfortable lives because of diligence.

Perhaps we have been luckier than most because we are wiser, and wisdom brings its just rewards. But we are mindful of the many thoughtful, stimulating evenings spent under thatched roofs discussing the problems of the world with illiterate Indian or Afghan or Iranian farmers. It has been made abundantly clear to us that a man may be uneducated, but he may also be wise; he may be poor, but he may also have dignity; he may be hard-pressed but he may also maintain his pride. Thus, we cannot believe that we or our countrymen are more fortunate than others because we have a monopoly on intelligence.

Perhaps we are blessed above others because we are more generous, more honest or more dedicated. But this is not a point we would care to have to defend against the hungry peasants who have insisted on sharing their meals with us; against impoverished farmers who have gone to great lengths to return to us things we left in their villages; against the hundreds of young people we have met whose work for their young, struggling countries demands a kind of personal sacrifice we have never known.

We ask ourselves, then, if perhaps our good fortune is not due to our system of government, to our freedom and democracy, and if these are not our just inheritance from the men who won them in the United States—from George Washington, Thomas Jefferson and Abraham Lincoln. But this, too, we must reject. For, we ask, what have *we personally* ever done, more than most of the other people of the world, to earn or merit these blessings?

We can find no satisfactory reason, in short, to explain why, in a world that now has the capability of caring for *all* its people, there are so many poor and so few rich. And we feel very strongly that in this fact—in the very magnitude of the disparity of living standards, in the very number of people involved, in the very enormity of the injustice— a self-evident truth emerges: that apart from preserving the peace, the first, overriding, frighteningly pressing task of this year and this century is to feed, clothe and unleash from fear the millions who, through no fault of their own, live in such desolation.

This is a massive and urgent undertaking. It is no longer one for a few missionaries or teachers but one requiring the marshaling of the intellectual, material and spiritual resources of nations—nations rich enough to provide 88 per cent of their people with television sets. Whatever contributes to this mobilization, whatever speeds this process must be welcomed.

What *could* speed this process? To date, the greatest—one might almost say the only—impetus to this mobilization has been the cold war.

In the past fifteen years the tremendous job of bridging the gap between the affluence of the West and the poverty of the East has begun. In the seven years we have been travelling in this part of the world we have seen enormous accomplishment. Much of it has been due to Western aid. But a big part has also been played by the Russians.

Honesty compels us to admit, however, that the principal reason the United States has undertaken to help raise the world's standard of living is not that there are poor people who rightfully should be sharing more equally the good things of the earth, but that Americans are afraid that if they do not do something about their misery, the miserable will turn to the Communists in desperation. And undoubtedly the forces that motivate the Communists are very similar. The Soviets have undertaken a share of the burden, not because the welfare of the people is a primary concern, but because they want their ideology to prevail and aid is one means to that end.

It would be pleasant to believe that were East and West not embroiled in a cold war both the United States and the Soviet Union woud continue their help to the underdeveloped world. But, regretfully, we haven't that much faith. If the cold war ended tomorrow, so, we fear, would the bulk of the efforts being made to help the earth's unfortunates.

We wonder, actually, whether when the history of these days is written a century from now the cold war may not emerge as one of the greatest boons that mankind has ever known. Certainly, it seems to have been the one force powerful enough to marshal the intellectual and material resources of the United States on a national scale in behalf of the underprivileged, and to cause other countries to follow the American lead with aid programs of their own.

But we wonder if the cold war may not also emerge as a boon to the overprivileged—the 88 per centers. One can hope that it may prove to be a force that, carrying Americans to the far corners of the earth and opening their front pages, their eyes and their hearts to the needs around them, will finally transform a response based on fear and self-preservation into a true concern for justice and the welfare of all men.

73 ECONOMICS FOR THE NUCLEAR AGE

W. W. Rostow

W. W. Rostow is currently an official in the United States Department of State, on leave from his position as Professor of Economic History at Massachusetts Institute of Technology.

There are two important problems that must be solved before our nation can, in peace, fully enjoy the products and services which the continued growth of the American economy and the world's technology offer us and our children. One of these two problems, the arms race with Russia, is so immediately pressing, so serious in its implications, that we are tempted to ignore the other problem. The second issue is how to help underdeveloped nations maintain their independence and progress democratically from their present relative stagnation toward sustained growth and technological maturity. This second issue is no less important to the future security and prosperity of the United States than the first.

Even if we find the way to call a halt to the arms race with Russia, what happens if nations like India, Egypt, Argentina, Brazil, Venezuela, and the emergent states of Africa adopt forms of government that are inimical to democracy? Our problem with Communist China is a clear warning. How can we assist these nations to grow along lines that make it likely they will choose democratic rather than totalitarian forms of government? How can we reduce the temptations to military adventures of the type that so many of the now mature nations succumbed to during our century? In the end, how can both the United States *and* Russia make sure that any such temptations that do arise do not include those of nuclear warfare?

STAGES OF GROWTH

These two great issues of the second half of the century are illuminated by an understanding of how the process of growth has unfolded in the past. Certainly, the future will be full of surprises, of events and situations that no one can predict; but some of our problems and choices can be clarified by looking back as well as forward, and trying to generalize what we can learn of the past.

As a social scientist I have gradually come to the view that it is possible and useful to identify all societies as lying within one of five categories:

1. The traditional society.
2. The transitional society.
3. The society in the crucial process of take-off.
4. The society in the drive to technological maturity.
5. The society which has reached the age of mass consumption.

Based on a dynamic theory of production, the theory of these five stages of growth contains one key position: *at any period of time the momentum of an economy is maintained by the rapid rate of growth in a relatively few key, leading sectors.* Cotton textiles, for example, has been in some periods of growth a leading sector, as have rail-

From *Harvard Business Review,* January–February, 1960, p. 41 ff. Reprinted by permission.

ways, chemicals, electricity, and the automobile in others. As a consequence of their rapid expansion, the society experiences a direct demand for new inputs of capital to consolidate the new growth and to establish new growth industries. Some of the developments in this snowballing of the economy are indirect. For example, Sweden, because of a lack of coal, plunged into the electrification of its railways, and thus laid the basis indirectly for a first-class electrical engineering industry.

Each set of leading sectors slows down, as time passes; but, in successful societies, each is superseded by a new set, which carries the process of growth forward. An understanding of this principle may help to explain phenomena like the unique depression of the 1930's:

> This economic reversal, with its resultant unemployment, was due, not to long-run diminishing returns, but to (1) Western Europe's failure to create a setting for a prompt move into high mass consumption, and (2) America's failure to create, through public policy, a renewed setting for full employment permitting the new leading sectors—suburban housing, automobiles, durable consumer goods and services—to roll forward and beyond 1929.

> Today, however, modern democratic nations recognize the sensitivity of the political process even to small pockets of unemployment, and, to boom a flagging economy, would quickly institute policies to encourage new leading sectors.

More than the history of technology is involved, however. As growth proceeds, each stage of development is marked by certain characteristic ranges of per capita income. These, in turn, influence the kinds and amounts of goods consumers demand, and have important characteristic playback effects on production. To understand the stage of a society, we must look at both its technology and how it spends its income—at demand as well as at supply.

But a detailed discussion of all this would go beyond the intent of the present article. Those who are interested in a more technical discussion of these points may refer to my article in *The Economic History Review,*[1] and readers who seek a more popular version may turn to the presentation prepared by the editors of *The Economist.*[2] Here I shall summarize only briefly the stages of growth, and then consider some issues of possible special interest to the readers of this magazine.

Traditional Society

First comes the traditional society—one whose structure is developed within limited production functions, based on pre-Newtonian science and technology. Because this society is basically agrarian, with few technological innovations occurring in its limited industry, its productivity fluctuates with harvests, wars, plagues, discoveries of new crops, and so on. But the central fact about the traditional society is that a ceiling exists on the level of attainable output per head. This ceiling stems from the fact that the potentialities which flow from modern science and technology either are not available or are not applied in a regular flow.

---

[1] "The Stages of Economic Growth," August 1959, p. 1.

[2] "Rostow on Growth," August 15, 1959, p. 409, and August 22, 1959, p. 524, summarizing a set of lectures delivered at Cambridge University and shortly to be published by Cambridge University Press as a book, *The Stages of Economic Growth: A Non-Communist Manifesto.* At some points in this article, I have made use of *The Economist's* paraphrasing.

In terms of history, then, the phrase "traditional society" groups the whole pre-Newtonian world: the dynasties in China, the civilizations of the Middle East and the Mediterranean, the world of medieval Europe. To these we must add the post-Newtonian societies which, for a time, remained untouched or unmoved by man's new capability for regularly manipulating his environment to his economic advantage. Few of these still remain, except for certain regions in Africa.

Transitional Society

During the period when the preconditions for take-off are developed, a society may be said to be in transition. Usually in modern history this period has been initiated as a result of aggression by more advanced societies, an intrusion which mortally wounds the traditional society, although its death is a lingering one and it is superseded slowly and painfully. Gradually, there emerges a new consensus: that economic progress not only is possible but is, in fact, a necessary condition for some other good purpose—national dignity, private profit, general welfare, or a better life for the children.

Technically speaking, there are in the preconditions period three leading sectors whose transformation is a necessary condition for sustained industrial growth:

1. *Agriculture*—A productivity revolution in agriculture is required to feed the expanding population, especially the population of the cities which are likely to be growing at higher rates than the overall national average.

2. *The export sector*—The earliest stages of industrialization are likely to create an expanded bill for imports, which can only be met by quickly applying modern techniques to the extraction and processing of natural resources.

3. *Social overhead capital*—When growth becomes relatively automatic, large outlays on transport, education, sources of power, and the like, are required.

Once the transition has begun, new types of enterprising men come forward who, in both private and governmental finance, show a willingness to mobilize savings and take risks in pursuit of profit or modernization. As banks appear and investment increases, the scope of commerce broadens. Here and there, modern manufacturing enterprises spring up to utilize the new methods of production. But all this activity proceeds at a limited pace within an economy and a society still mainly characterized by traditional low-productivity methods, by the old social structure and values, and by the regionally based political institutions that developed in conjunction with them. One central task of the preconditions is to develop an effective, centralized national state, in opposition to the traditional landed interests of the regions or the colonial power, or both. The take-off can only begin, in most cases, when there exists an effective central government that means business as far as growth is concerned.

The Take-Off

During the interval when the old blocks and resistances to steady growth are finally overcome, the crucial process of take-off begins. The forces pressing for economic progress come to dominate the society; growth becomes its normal condition. Compound interest becomes built, as it were, into its structure.

In Great Britain, and the well-endowed parts of the world populated substantially from Great Britain (the United States and Canada), the proximate stimulus for take-off was mainly —but not wholly—technological. The original sector of primary growth in Great Britain was cotton textiles, but this is hardly a representative case. The substitution of a modern cotton textile industry for imports has more typically marked the pretake-off period. The most powerful single initiator of take-offs has been, as one would suspect, the introduction of railways.

During the take-off, some of the following conditions manifest themselves. The rate of effective investment and savings may rise from, say, 5% of the national income to 10% or more. New industries expand rapidly, yielding profits which are largely reinvested in new plants. As a result, a demand for industrial labor results, new urban areas develop around the factories, service industries and businesses spring up, and a new class of entrepreneurs is born to direct the enlarging flow of investment in the private sector.

To compensate for the diversion of manpower into industries (and to feed the cities), new methods of agriculture and of extracting natural resources must be developed. It is, therefore, one of the technical preconditions for take-off in the transitional areas that governments come to power which are prepared to channel a high proportion of their people's energies, talents, and resources into the tasks of economic growth as opposed to other possible objectives. One can approximate the take-off of Great Britain to the two decades after 1783; France and the United States to the several decades preceding 1860; Germany, the third quarter of the nineteenth century; Japan, the fourth quarter of the nineteenth century; Russia and Canada, the quarter century or so preceding 1914. Over the past five years India and China have, in quite different ways, launched their respective take-offs.

Technological Maturity

Some 60 years after a society begins take-off (or approximately 40 years after the end of the take-off), technological maturity is generally attained. On the road to this maturity, however, the make-up of the economy changes unceasingly as technology improves. New industries accelerate, older industries level off. The economy finds its place in the world of international trade. Goods formerly imported are produced at home; as a result, new import requirements develop, with new export commodities to match.

Once maturity has been reached, the economy has extended its range into more refined and often more complex technological processes. There may be, for example, a shift in focus from the coal, iron, and heavy engineering industries of the railway phase to machine tools, chemicals, and electrical equipment. This was the transition through which Germany, Great Britain, France, and the United States had passed by the end of the nineteenth century, or shortly thereafter.

Thus, we can formally define maturity as the stage in which an economy demonstrates its capacity to move beyond the original industries which powered its take-off and to absorb and apply efficiently, over virtually the whole range of its resources, the most advanced fruits of (then) modern technology. This is the stage in which an economy demonstrates that it has the technological and entrepreneurial skills to produce, perhaps not everything, but anything it chooses to produce.

Mass Consumption

We come now to a period in the growth of a nation in which mass consumption of durable consumers' goods and services becomes the central dynamic force in economic (and social) life. This is a phase from which Americans are beginning to emerge, whose not unequivocal joys Western Europe and Japan are beginning energetically to probe, and with which the Soviet regime uneasily flirts.

As societies achieved maturity in the twentieth century, two things happened:

(1) Real income per person rose to a point where a large number of people gained a command over consumption transcending basic food, shelter, and clothing.

(2) The structure of the working force changed in ways which increased not only the proportion of urban to total population, but also the proportion of the population in white- and blue-collar jobs, aware of and anxious to acquire the consumption fruits of a mature economy.

It is at this stage that, through the political process, Western societies have chosen to allocate increased resources to social welfare and security. The emergence of the welfare state is one manifestation of a society's moving beyond technological maturity. But it is also at this stage that resources tend increasingly to be directed to the production of consumers' durables and to the diffusion of services on a mass basis, if consumers' sovereignty reigns. The sewing machine, the bicycle, and then the various electric-powered household gadgets were gradually diffused. Historically, however, the decisive element, or leading sector, has been the cheap mass automobile with its quite revolutionary effects, social as well as economic, on the life and expectations of society.

For the United States, the turning point, perhaps, was Henry Ford's moving assembly line of 1913–1914. But it was in the 1920's, and again in the postwar decade of 1946–1956, that this stage of growth was pressed virtually to its logical conclusion. During the 1950's, Western Europe and Japan appear to have fully entered this phase, accounting substantially for a momentum in their economies quite unexpected in the immediate postwar years. The Soviet Union is technically ready for this stage and, by every sign, its citizens hunger for it. But communist leaders face some difficult political and social problems of adjustment if this stage is wholeheartedly launched. At the moment, they draw back from the mass-produced automobile and the single-family suburban house.

Future Development

Beyond this fifth stage of growth, it is impossible to predict, except, perhaps, to observe that Americans at least have behaved in the past decade as if diminishing relative marginal utility sets in, after a point, for durable consumers' goods; and they have chosen, at the margin, larger families. That is, Americans have behaved as if, having been born into a system that provided economic security and high mass consumption, they placed a lower valuation on acquiring additional increments of real income in the conventional form as opposed to the advantages and values of an enlarged family.

*   *   *

UNDERDEVELOPED AREAS

We come now to the problem of the underdeveloped areas. What light do the stages of growth analysis throw on their problems? What can and ought we as Americans do about them?

The first thing to be said about the underdeveloped areas is that, of course, they stand at various stages of the growth process. The phrase "underdeveloped" is inexact. Some of them are actually in the take-off: e.g., Mexico, Argentina, Brazil, Venezuela, and, above all, China and India. These societies face many vicissitudes; but I believe the bases have been laid for sustained growth.

Elsewhere there are societies in the late stages of the preconditions period: Iran, Iraq, Egypt, Morocco, for example, and several of the Latin American states. Indonesia, Pakistan, and Burma are only a little behind, if at all. I do not believe the beginnings of their take-offs are likely to be delayed more than a decade. But south of the Sahara in Africa there are societies close to the traditional stage which may have to pass through longer preconditioning processes before sustained growth can be undertaken.

The question now arises whether it is scientifically correct to use my concept of the stages of growth, derived from a generalization of the historical past, to analyze the contemporary problems of the underdeveloped areas.

In part, there is much that is familiar to the historian in the current scene. The technical problems of the preconditions still center about the three leading sectors of that stage—social overhead capital, the generation of increased exports, and a technological revolution in agriculture.

The social and psychological transformations that must occur are, again, broadly familiar from the past; they are the problem of siphoning off land rents into the modern sector, the changing of peasant attitudes, and the training of a new leadership—public, private, or both in various combinations —capable of bringing modern techniques to bear in the various sectors of the economy. And, above all, we can again see, as in the past, that a reactive nationalism, tempted to move in directions other than economic growth, lies close to the heart of the political process in many of these regions.

Two-Way Difference

There is a major technical difference, however. The pool of technology available to these underdeveloped nations is greater than ever before. Other latecomers have enjoyed this advantage to a degree—e.g., Germany, Russia, and Japan in the half century before World War I, coming a bit later than Great Britain and the United States. But in degree we must admit that there is a substantial difference between the present and the past, stemming from the size of the pool of unapplied technology.

This difference, however, cuts both ways: it not only offers the possibility of accelerating growth but complicates the problem of growth. The complication arises because the availability of modern techniques of medicine and public health leads to a radical fall in death rates, which yields much higher rates of population increase than those in most transitional societies in the past. Except for the United States and Russia, the population increase ratios in the precondition and take-off stages have been under 1.5%—generally about 1%. (The United States and Russia had reserves of good land that permitted high rates of population increase to be sustained—reserves which are not now available to the underdeveloped areas in most parts of the world.)

But these newer nations are trying to move forward with population increase rates of 2% and more. This means, in general, that higher rates of investment must be generated to achieve sustained growth; and, even more precisely, it means that the revolution in agricultural technique must be pressed forward with great vigor if the whole development process is not to be throttled for lack of food.

In these circumstances, how can the United States help? By taking all three of these steps, each one essential:

1. Offering the underdeveloped areas ample supplies of capital, to ease the general problem of capital formation under regimes of high rates of population increase.

2. Providing these nations special assistance which helps them achieve prompt and radical increases in agricultural output, including supplies of chemical fertilizers and aid in building irrigation facilities.

3. Developing policies which encourage the local politicians to concentrate their hopes and their energies on the task of economic development, and avoiding policies which tend to divert them from these objectives.

The Price

This is going to cost us money. Loans or grants in themselves cannot do the job. But there is a minimum price tag which the United States and the Free World generally must accept if we are to make a serious contribution to the problem of the underdeveloped areas.

How much? Estimates made independently by many different groups come out at about the same point: something like an extra $3 billion a year, for all the underdeveloped areas of Asia, the Middle East, Africa, and Latin America. Of this sum, half perhaps ought to be provided by the United States, half by Western Europe, Canada, and Japan. Arithmetic of this kind lay behind the proposal of the Senate Foreign Relations Committee to expand the Development Loan Fund to make $1.5 billion available from the United States for each of the next five years. This compares with an American GNP approaching $500 billion and with American military expenditures of over $40 billion annually.

Never, even under the Marshall Plan, have such large stakes hinged on so modest a sum.

Dramatic Question

The urgency and drama of the problem are illustrated by the question of India's Third Five Year Plan. Here is a nation of some 400 million people, representing about 40% of the population of the underdeveloped countries. It is committed in the next five years to attempt the take-off; that is, to move out of its present relative stagnation into sustained economic growth. It has accumulated considerable assets for this decisive effort: a government seeking to organize its resources and talents around the tasks of modernization, a competent civil service, and an expanding corps of private businessmen of competence, willing to accept new methods and to plough profits back into new capacity. Moreover, important capacity in steel and electric power has been developed in the past decade. The tasks of producing a sufficient increase in food to feed the expanding population and of getting enough foreign exchange in this decisive period to import what is needed are the two great remaining problems.

Of the total increase in loans I suggested as necessary, India needs about 40% or $1.2 billion for each year in the Third Plan. The food problems India must basically solve for itself, although our technical assistance and some food surpluses could be helpful.

If India demonstrates that a take-off under democratic auspices is possible with American and Western European help, then other nations of Asia, the Middle East, and Africa will take heart; and the most powerful single argument for communism will be weakened. If in India the present government fails, the breakdown of confidence in democracy and in association with the West may spread across the whole southern half of the globe, to our enormous cost.

This is a test which will now take place, whether we like it or not. Success or failure of India in the next five years will have immense consequences for ourselves and our children. Our choice is to ignore it, observe it, or participate in it with the vigor we once threw into the Marshall Plan.

What is true of India is only in degree less true and urgent in the other underdeveloped areas. Can noncommunist governments, in association with the West, create the preconditions for take-off and guide their societies through the precarious crucial take-off process? This is the question and the challenge.

THE BUSINESSMAN'S ROLE

What special bearing, if any, does this argument have on the life and profession of the American businessman?

Perhaps its greatest technical importance is to provide some insight into the peculiar problems of the underdeveloped areas with which the American businessman increasingly must deal. Some such analysis as this, properly developed, should permit us roughly to establish where, in the stages of growth, a particular region stands. Is it close to the traditional society, like many parts of Africa? Close to the take-off, like Egypt and Pakistan? Attempting the take-off, like India? Or in the early stages of the drive to technological maturity, like Mexico?

In this perspective, businessmen can have some notion of what the problems of doing business are likely to be and what to expect and what not to expect of a given society over a reasonable business-planning period. For example, businessmen should come to regard as normal a phase of nationalism focused against foreign business interests at times during the preconditioning process, for a reactive nationalism is typically the engine which uproots the traditional society and prepares it for modernization and growth.

Furthermore, businessmen should expect governments to play an important role in the economic process in the preconditioning and the take-off, when the build-up of social overhead capital constitutes so high a proportion of investment and the supply of energetic local businessmen is somewhat thin. On the other hand, this historical perspective might lead the American businessman to expect that, as the take-off proceeds and the new nation gains confidence and momentum, attitudes toward foreign business will become more temperate and sensible. Moreover, if communism does not seize these areas, we can expect the private business sector to grow and the role of government in economic affairs to diminish somewhat.

In a quite different dimension, the stages-of-growth analysis helps explain the nature of the boom in Western Europe and Japan, for those regions have entered the stage of high mass consumption, and are going through changes in their structure and momentum similar to those in the United States during the 1920's.

But ultimately, the relevance of this argument to the American businessman is its pertinence to him as an American citizen. It may be one way of helping us all to understand the inner meaning of this precarious stage of history which Mr. Khrushchev calls competitive coexistence. Whether the outcome of this stage is, as Mr. Khrushchev hopes, the isolation and defeat of the United States as a world power, as Asia, the Middle East, and Africa go communist—or whether it ends in earnest settlement, in which the Russians become convinced that their best option is to make a serious armaments control agreement and settle down within their present borders to enjoy the age of high mass consumption—either outcome depends on what we Americans do, both individually as citizens and nationally as leaders of the Free World alliance.

What we Americans do, finally, depends on the willingness of our citizens to lift their eyes from their own narrow concerns and to make their contribution in talent and in taxes to every dimension of this competition—from the deterrence of war to the provision of adequate assistance to the underdeveloped areas. In helping this country to accept Mr. Khrushchev's challenge, and in creating, over the next decade, a situation where peace—rather than world dominance—is the only realistic option available to Moscow, the American businessman has a decisive role to play, both as a citizen and as a community leader.

74 DEVELOPMENT PROGRAM IN AFGHANISTAN

United Nations Review

In Afghanistan, where 85 per cent of an estimated population of 13.8 million live in small villages, the first five-year community development program, aimed at raising the living standards in rural areas, has just been completed.

With the help of United Nations technical assistance advisers, eight comprehensive community development projects, covering almost all facets of rural life, were in operation by the end of 1961. Working cooperatively with the government's Rural Development Department, specialists from the United Nations and its specialized agencies are assisting some 420,000 people in more than 900 villages in such fields as education, agriculture, health and sanitation, industrial cooperatives, training, leather tanning and cottage industries, women's welfare, and planning and administration.

On duty in Afghanistan, as the community development program continues to expand, are technical advisers from the United Nations, the Food and Agriculture Organization, the World Health Organization, the United Nations Educational, Scientific, and Cultural Organization (UNESCO), the International Labor Organization, and the United Nations Children's Fund.

Now, according to Ch'un Wu, a Chinese community development adviser, a second five-year plan is under way and will be responsible for setting up 17 additional community development projects, each of which will affect some 50,000 rural inhabitants.

From *United Nations Review,* May, 1962, p. 29.

Mr. Wu, who recently returned to United Nations Headquarters after five years in Afghanistan, has described the program as "highly successful" and one in which the top government officials are "keenly interested because they now realize that it is most important to raise the living standards of the population living in rural areas."

"The essence of the program," he declared, "is to help the people help themselves."

By 1967, Mr. Wu estimates, the rural development program is likely to reach approximately one and a quarter million people, or one out of ten persons in the country. Within the next 15–20 years, if present plans materialize, the entire nation would be covered by about 250 projects.

The program is financed under the national budget, assisted by external aid and the contributions of the people themselves. Among the factors contributing to the rapid enlargement of the program is the administrative organization set up by the Government under the Rural Development Department, which acts as the central executing agency functions under the direction and supervision of the Office of the Prime Minister and the cooperation of the rural people themselves.

The basic operating unit of the program is the individual "project" which roughly would cover a 450 square mile area with a population of about 50,000. For each project there is a project officer in charge, under whom work a group of "subject-matter" specialists and village workers, an assistant project officer and administrative staff.

The village workers are "multi-purpose" in the sense that they have been trained to work with the villagers in a variety of fields corresponding to the special subjects recommended by the "subject-matter" specialists Each village worker covers one or several villages with a population ranging from 50–6,000. There are 101 village workers for the 913 villages included in the eight projects operating at present. Thus, each village worker is responsible for about nine villages.

Much of the success of the community development program in this rugged hill country is due to the importance attached to the training of project personnel. Among those trained under the existing programs were 45 "subject-matter" specialists; 10 project officers and supervisory staff; 177 village workers; 120 village leaders; and 209 fundamental education organizers, 11 of whom were trained in industrial cooperatives and 33 in carpentry.

In the field of *agriculture* there are now 40 demonstration farms in the program area, 20 of which were established in the past two years. As against 8,600 animals treated and vaccinated in 1956–57, almost 83,000 animals received such care in 1960–61.

As regards *education,* there was only one village boys' school in the program area in 1957. There are now 64 such schools; similarly the number of girls' schools has risen from one to 48 during the same period.

Health services are organized primarily through rural health units in each project area. Their major activities consist of surveying existing health needs and control of communicable diseases; maternal and child health; vital statistics; school health services; treatment and environmental sanitation. There are now in operation eight main health centres and 17 sub-centres which, together, have treated some 500,000 persons. More than 18,000 persons have been vaccinated against small-pox; and 42,000 have received inoculations against cholera, typhoid and paratyphoid.

The sanitation aspect of the program has made considerable headway.

In the field of *small-scale industries,* a fertilizer demonstration project has been set up to train local personnel in the use of locally-available waste material as a substitute for imported fertilizer. Larger units, operated on a commercial basis are to be installed shortly. A model tannery, utilizing modern machinery and equipment, has been established to train local tanners in finishing hides and skins.

Social Welfare: One centre and two sub-centres have been established for training women in home economics and handicrafts; there are 59 village development councils and five youth centres.

"The figures," said Mr. Wu, "speak for themselves." But much remains to be done, particularly in the construction of village roads. Roads, important in any country, are of special importance in a land-locked country such as Afghanistan where, Mr. Wu explained, there are no railroads or waterways of any kind. Thus, adequate village roads would not only promote solidarity within the community, Mr. Wu declared, they would also facilitate participation of villagers in community affairs and develop local leadership. A doctor can be brought to a village to visit a sick child; agricultural produce can be brought to market; and commercial activities introduced into the village.

75 ECONOMIC DEVELOPMENT: RIVAL SYSTEMS AND COMPARATIVE ADVANTAGE

John Kenneth Galbraith

John Kenneth Galbraith is United States Ambassador to India, on leave from his position as Professor of Economics at Harvard University.

One of the well-observed features of economic development in the 20th century is the need to choose between two broad political and economic designs. This choice, one from which developing nations of the 18th and 19th centuries were conveniently exempt, is between Western constitutional organization on the one hand and Marxian and neo-Marxian polity and economic organization on the other.

These are not, as everyone knows, homogeneous alternatives. Wide differences separate a state such as Poland, where the agriculture, and hence close to half the economy, remains in private hands and subject to market influences,

from the far more completely socialized economy of the Chinese mainland. There are similar distinctions between the non-Marxian economies, which, in this case, are enlarged by terminological preference and political semantics. In Scandinavia, the United Kingdom and modern India the word "socialism" is politically evocative. As a result politicians try to find as much of it as possible. In the United States, steps that would elsewhere be identified with

Address before the Commonwealth Club, San Francisco, California, on June 4, 1962, published in the *Department of State Bulletin,* July 2, 1962, pp. 13–17.

socialist enlightenment—social security, agricultural price guarantees, even the public development of public power sites—are firmly for the purpose of making private enterprise function better.

Also one must be cautious in speaking of a "choice" between the two designs. Geography and the proximity of military power have had much to do with the decision. Had Poland, to select a country not unaccustomed to movement, been radically relocated after World War II to approximately the position of Paraguay, her subsequent economic and political history would have been rather different. Individuals do commit themselves as a matter of free choice to a Marxian political and economic design. But nations have rarely done so in the normal course of unmanaged elections—a reluctance, incidentally, which was foreseen by both Marx and Lenin.

Nevertheless these broad alternatives exist. My purpose is to weigh their advantages and disadvantages from the standpoint of the developing country. I am aware that an American ambassador will not be considered by everyone a wholly impartial judge. And even in this liberal and sophisticated gathering there would doubtless be eyebrow-lifting if my evidence were to lead me to the wrong conclusion.

But the choice merits serious assessment. Much of the present literature consists of declarations of superiority by one side or the other. We share with the Communists a strong faith in the value of robust assertion. Were the advantage all on our side, we would have little reason to worry. But we do worry, and it might be well, accordingly, for us to have a moderately unemotional appraisal of what we have to offer the developing nations as compared with the Communists.

THE GOAL OF DEVELOPING COUNTRIES

The goal of the developing country can be quickly stated: It is to bring itself as rapidly as possible into the 20th century and with the apparatus of individual and group well-being—food, clothing, education, health services, housing, entertainment, and automobiles—which is associated in every mind, urban and rural, bourgeois and Bolshevist, with 20th-century existence. Here and there are some that demur. But in my observation the most monastic Christian, the most contemplative Buddhist, and the most devout Gandhian cannot be considered completely secure against the charms of the bicycle, motor scooter, or transistor radio.

The things associated with modern civilization are now denied by backwardness and poverty. The task of the two systems is to overcome this poverty. The causes of poverty, in turn, are not simple—although the problem has suffered prodigiously from oversimplification. One cause, clearly, is an oppressive social structure which channels return from the many to the few and which denies the individual the natural reward of his efforts at self-improvement. Another is a feeble, nonexistent, or corrupt apparatus of public administration which denies to the country the things—law and order, education, investment in roads, power, manufacturing—which are possible only where there is effective public authority. Or poverty may be itself a cause of poverty; it denies the country capital for investment, revenues for education, or purchasing power for consumer products which, in turn, are an incentive to effort. Thus poverty perpetuates itself. Such are the fundamentals that both systems must attack. It is unlikely that the same causes operate in the same form and with the same intensity in any two cases. An effective attack, therefore, requires not only efficient remedies but effective diagnosis of the condition to be cured.

Both systems agree on a number of important points. It is common ground that a shortage of capital is a likely cause of stagnation. Both agree on the need for a massive volume of investment to initiate and stimulate not only economic but social advance. There is agreement also that this investment should be in accordance with a carefully conceived plan. (Here we have paid the Soviets the compliment of appropriating an important idea.) There is increasing agreement that a principal object of this investment must be in the educational and cultural improvement of people themselves. The visitor to the more remote parts of Soviet Asia is immediately impressed by the volume of resources going into schools, colleges, adult education programs, and other forms of cultural extension as part of the attack on the traditional backwardness of these areas. If, in the years following World War II, we thought too much of investment in terms of physical capital and too little of the importance of a literate and educated populace, this is an error we are now correcting.

There are, however—and this will doubtless come as a relief—important differences between the two approaches, and these are vital. The first lies in the diagnosis of the causes of poverty and the related remedy. The second difference is in the way development is organized. The third is in the political and constitutional environment of development. Let me take up each of these differences in turn.

DIAGNOSING THE CAUSES OF POVERTY

In the Marxian view poverty is principally caused by institutions which chain the country to its past—which hold it in colonial subjection, which exploit and subjugate the masses and deny them the reward of their labor, which make government not the efficient servant of the many but the corrupt handmaiden of the few.

In the predominant Western view the poor are the victims of their poverty. All societies have capacity for growth; the poor society lacks the resources to invest in growth. Having less than enough for its current needs for food, clothing, and shelter, it has nothing for investment in education, improved agriculture, transportation, public utilities, or industrial enterprise.

Each of these views leads naturally to a prescription. If institutions hold a country to its past, the answer is the elimination of these institutions. If the problem is the self-perpetuating character of privation, the answer is to provide the catalyzing resources—specifically, economic aid and assistance in its use—which the country cannot supply to itself.

This is the first difference. The Marxian emphasis is on the institutions that inhibit progress and the need to eliminate them. Our emphasis is on the self-perpetuating character of poverty and the catalyzing role of aid. It will be noted that each system has a cause and remedy that is not without convenience to itself. The Soviets, at least until recently, were short of capital. They had a revolution which could be exported at moderate expense. Accordingly it was convenient to associate backwardness with colonialism, feudalism, and repressive capitalism, all of which could be eliminated by revolution. By contrast, we had capital. This we could export with greater ease than comprehensive social change.

The second difference is in the way development is organized. Although there is room for some national preference, and heresy cannot be entirely eliminated, the Marxian commitment is still to state ownership of the means of production—of land, capital plant, and natural resources. Private ownership of productive resources and their use for private gain is one of the retarding institutions. Its elimination leaves the state in possession and this continues. Incentives to individual and group effort are strongly supported. But incentives which use the device of property ownership to combine reward for individual effort with reward for management of property are excluded in principle and in large measure in practice.

The non-Marxian design for organizing development is not so easily characterized. In the past many countries—Japan, Germany, Canada, and to a remarkable degree also the United States—have made state ownership of canals, turnpikes, railroads, electric power and other utilities, and even steel mills the fulcrum of development policy. India, Egypt, and some South American countries are taking the same course today. However, the main and indeed overwhelming reliance in non-Marxian development, both in agriculture and industry, is on private ownership of productive plant. This is true of countries, such as India, which choose to describe themselves as socialist.

WESTERN ADVANTAGE IN PROVIDING CAPITAL

The foregoing differences are sufficiently sharp so that we can relate them to results. And in Eastern Europe and China, not to mention the much older case of the Soviet Union, there is now an ample experience of Marxian development on which to draw.

Two major advantages lie with the Western or non-Marxian alternatives. There is, we have anciently been advised, a certain physical difficulty in extracting blood from a stone. This, however, is comparatively easy as compared with getting savings out of a poor society. When people do not have enough to eat, they are loathe to forego any part of their meal in order to eat better in the future. Pleas on behalf of children and grandchildren leave the man of simple, uncomplicated intelligence unmoved; he reflects that starvation will prevent his having children and, *pro tanto,* grandchildren as well. But Marxian no less than non-Marxian societies must have savings; without them there can be no growth. Accordingly, the Western pattern of development, with its prospect of assistance from outside the country, eases one of the most painful problems of development. This is why economic aid has become such an important feature of Western foreign policy. It is the process by which savings are transferred from countries where saving is comparatively unpainful to those where it is very painful. It exploits one of the major advantages of our system.

The Communist countries are not without resources in this respect. The Soviet Union, though its capacity has been far less than ours, has spared some savings for other countries. Communist economic and political organization deals more effectively—or ruthlessly—with unproductive and excessively luxurious consumption, of which there is always some and may be much in the poor country. And Communist organization can, within limits, squeeze blood from its turnip. The penalty is the pain, and this cannot be avoided. The rioting in Poland in 1956 which brought Mr. Gomulka to power was occasioned in large measure by the enforcement of a rate of saving that was too grim for the people to bear. These last years on the Chinese mainland have evidently been ones of serious trouble and tension. Part of the problem is inherent in socialist organization of agriculture to which I will advert in a moment. But some has certainly been the consequence of squeezing a large volume of savings out of a very poor population.

The larger consequence is that Marxian development risks the alienation of the people as non-Marxian development does not. It seems doubtful if a majority of the Chinese people are very pleased with their government and would vote for it in an uninhibited poll. By contrast, in India, after a decade of development, there has been an overwhelming vote for the government that led the task. If the Indian Government had to subtract the $7.3 billions it has received from the West in overseas loans and grants since independence from the meager incomes—an average of about $70 per year—of its own people, its popularity might well have suffered. We see in India, in remarkably clear relief, the advantages of the Western design in providing capital.

WESTERN ADVANTAGE IN AGRICULTURE

The second and equally substantial advantage of Western development is in the matter of agriculture. Industry, on the record at least, is fairly tolerant as to forms of organization. American industry works well under private ownership. Even the most reluctant among us must agree that the Soviets have made considerable progress with socialism. So no decisive contrast can be registered here. But the underdeveloped country is, by definition, a pastoral or agrarian community. The agricultural policy is, accordingly, vital. And it is far from clear, as a practical matter, whether it is possible to socialize a small-scale, densely populated, peasant agriculture. Even in the Soviet Union the agricultural problem has not been wholly solved. And here, at least, there is no serious talk of catching up. Each year we insouciantly extend our advantage in manhour productivity without effort and somewhat to our regret. Outside the Soviet Union, agriculture has been even more of a problem. Poland and Yugoslavia have had to revert to private ownership. In China, by all external evidence, the effort to socialize agriculture has brought a serious crisis. Certainly it has forced her to turn to the West for the largest food imports in history.

There are good reasons for this failure. Farmers, when they are small and numerous, cannot be brought unwillingly into a state-run system of agriculture for they can defeat any system that is available for their control. The employees of a factory, like the men of an army, are subject to external discipline. Failure in performance can be detected, judged, and penalized. (The same rule holds for certain types of plantation agriculture.) A scattered peasantry, carrying on the diverse tasks of crop and especially of livestock husbandry cannot be so regimented. As a consequence, productivity falls off. Working for others, the farmer works at the minimum rather than the maximum, and the difference between the two is enormous. He can be made to work at the maximum by giving him land to work and rewarding him with the fruits of his labor or some substantial share to consume or exchange as he wishes. But this is to restore individual proprietorship—private capitalism—which its doctrine excludes.

One day the Marxian economies may succeed in socializing agriculture—no effort is being spared. And the ability of the small man in agriculture to sabotage a system he dislikes or which treats him badly is not confined to communism. It is the reason for the low productivity and backwardness of the latifundia of Latin America and the feudal domains of the Middle East. But the fact that it accepts independent agricultural proprietorship is the second clear advantage of Western development.

ELIMINATING RETARDING INSTITUTIONS

I come now to a disadvantage of Western development. The Marxian alternative, I have noted, emphasizes the destruction of the bonds that tie the economy to the past. Our emphasis is on capital, education, technical assistance, and the other instruments that allow change. Until recently, at least, we have been tempted to suppose that any society is a platform on which, given these missing elements, development can be built.

In fact, institutions do chain economies to the past, and the breaking of these chains is essential for progress. The promise that this will be done is a valid and an appealing part of the Marxian case. There is no chance of agricultural development in the underdeveloped and hence agricultural country under systems of absentee landlordism, with the workers or sharecroppers confined by law and tradition to a minor share of a meager product. And feudal systems of farming extend their corrupting influence to government, to the provision of public sinecures to those who lack a claim on the land, to

the milking of middle-class and industrial enterprise, and to the destruction of incentives and the morale of the society itself. "In our country," a South American guide once told me, "those who do the least get the most. I hear that in the United States it is the other way around. It's a better system." Progress does require the radical elimination of retarding institutions. If elimination can be had from no other source, the Marxian alternative will sooner or later be tried. The revolution they offer here, we should remind ourselves, is less the Russian Revolution than the French Revolution.

POLITICAL ENVIRONMENT

I come now to the final point of comparison—one, unfortunately, which has been much damaged by bad rhetoric. From the earliest days of their development, personal liberty, equal justice under law, and constitutional government have been important to Englishmen and to Americans. They haven't been the concern of everyone, but we have never supposed they were the fad of the esoteric and privileged minority.

And so it is in the undeveloped country today. The Andean Indian and the landless worker in the Indian village do have a preoccupying concern with keeping themselves fed. But the general yearning for the dignity of democratic and constitutional government is very great. No people who live under a dictatorship ever feel themselves to be first-class citizens.

There can be little question that most people believe that liberty and constitutional process are safer with the Western than with the Marxian alternative. We haven't, in my view, made as much of this advantage as we might. But the Communists are under the considerable handicap that their alternative involves a step into the dark. And while the details are obscure, most people know that it does not involve free selection of rulers by the governed, *habeas corpus,* equal justice under law, and a voluntary return to other economic arrangements should the experiment prove unpalatable.

MAKING USE OF THE ADVANTAGES

On first assessment, then, the advantage of the non-Marxian alternative for the developing country is considerable. It promises at least a partial avoidance of the pain that for the poor country is inherent in finding savings for investment and growth. It promises an acceptable and viable system of agriculture rather than a certain unpalatable and possibly unworkable one. And it offers personal liberty and constitutional process. Against this the Marxian alternative promises a more rigorous attack on the institutions—the unproductive claims on revenue and especially the feudal control of land—which exclude change.

But this is not a game where one can count the cards and decide the winner. Some cards count for more than others, and there is the unfortunate possibility that some good cards will not get played.

The Marxian promise can be decisive. That is because the things we offer are only effective and attractive after the retarding institutions are eliminated. In a country where land and other resources are held by and operated for the benefit of a slight minority and where the apparatus of government serves principally to reinforce such privilege, aid is not of much use. It will also benefit not the many but the few. Our promise of independent

proprietorship is obviously nullified so long as land remains in the hands of the few. And personal liberty and constitutional government have little meaning in countries where government is of the privileged for the rich.

We must, in short, meet the Marxian promise of reform of retarding institutions. We cannot organize revolution. We can place our influence solidly on the side of reform. Having done this, our cards give us a clear advantage. To be sure, we must play them. We must make good with aid on our promise of a less painful savings and investment process. We must give firm support to the small farmer. We must be clear in our commitment to constitutional process and personal liberty. We cannot suppose that these are wanted only by people of Anglo-Saxon origin of good income. And we must not excuse dictatorship on grounds of anticommunism or convenience in the absence of visible alternatives. The price of doing so, as we have so painfully learned, is disaster magnified by postponement.

These are highly practical matters. If there are no advantages in our alternative, it won't be chosen. The first resort to the Marxian alternative in this hemisphere was in a country where the concentration of wealth and land ownership was extreme, where these had extended a corrupting influence to other economic life and to government, and where dictatorship had been endemic. This being the experience with the Western alternative, it was not remarkable that so many were so little perturbed by the alternative. India, in face of formidable difficulties, is firmly committed to development on the Western model. That is because already in British India and over the whole country at the time of independence there was a strong attack on retarding institutions—especially on the feudal claims of princes, zamindars and great landlords, and government which was an extension of this landed power; because a substantial measure of peasant ownership had replaced the old system; because aid from outside eased the problem of supply capital;

and because people felt secure in the protection of constitutional guarantees and representative government.

The lesson is clear. The advantages are with us. We must, however, have confidence in them and exploit them to the full.

F.

COMPARATIVE ECONOMIC SYSTEMS

76   THE DRIFT OF MODERN ECONOMIC HISTORY

Robert L. Heilbroner

Robert L. Heilbroner is a member of the faculty at the New School for Social Research and a well-known free lance writer.

In our last chapters we have followed the broad development of American capitalism down to present times. Now, as we turn back from America to the continents of the East, West, and South an extraordinary fact strikes us immediately. When we left the European scene, in the early 1800's, capitalism was fast becoming the dominant form of economic society. England, as we saw, was the very cradle of industrial capitalism itself; France was rousing herself to follow in England's footsteps; elsewhere on the continent, if capitalism was not already established, it was clearly waiting in the wings for the last remnants of feudalism to disappear. Had we looked abroad from America at any time in the nineteenth century, our expectations would have been fully justified. By then all of Europe was unquestionably capitalist in orientation. And not only Europe —by the end of the nineteenth century, capitalism had reached out to touch

most of the other continents of the world. In Asia and Africa, the main European nations had established colonies or spheres of influence which projected the imprint of capitalism into societies, many of which had barely awakened from an age-long slumber of ancient ways. In South America, as well, capitalism was clearly the main fertilizing influence. Even in reactionary Russia—the last of the great European powers to abolish the legal fetters of feudalism—by the early 1900's, capitalism had succeeded in creating a small but active nucleus from which further growth seemed assured.

Yet what do we find today? To our astonishment, the seemingly unopposed evolution of the world into a capitalist market system has not taken place. In Europe, its original birthplace, capital-

From Robert L. Heilbroner, *The Making of Economic Society;* copyright 1962 by R. L. Heilbroner. Reprinted by permission of Prentice-Hall, Inc., publisher.

ism continues to be the dominant economic system; and, yet we find that socialist parties either hold power or constitute the main opposition in England, France, Belgium, Netherlands, Italy, Sweden, Norway, Denmark, Germany, and Austria. In Russia, the nucleus of capitalism has been entirely swept away by a communist society. In the huge continents of the East and South—in Asia and Africa and South America—we find that the original organizing impetus of capitalism has given way, in many of the most important nations, to a noncapitalist framework of economic organization. China is more communist than communist Russia. India proclaims herself a socialist state. So do Indonesia, Burma, Ceylon, Egypt, Ghana, Guinea. Only in South America do we find socialism absent from the official ideologies of political economy, and even there, the example of Cuba and the rumblings elsewhere hardly make it possible to anticipate the kind of capitalist society which we would have expected fifty years ago.

What happened outside America to abort the seemingly assured development of capitalism? A full answer to such a question would require much more than a book in itself, but we can begin to grasp the main picture of evolutionary trends if we follow, first, the factors which caused capitalism in Europe to take on a form different from that in America. From Europe it is not so long a jump, geographically or historically, to Russia; and from Russia we can turn with increased understanding to the so-called "underdeveloped" world.

European Capitalism: Feudal Heritage and National Rivalry

What are the reasons behind the turn of events in Europe? They must be sought, to begin with, not in the economic tendencies of European capitalism but in the social and political background whence those tendencies emerged.

Certainly the social background was significantly different from that of America. In the New World, capitalism developed with a population which had, to a large degree, spirtually and physically shed the feudal encumbrances of the Old World; but in that Old World, many of the social outlooks and habitudes of the past lingered on. An awareness of class position—and more than that, an explicit recognition of class hostility—was as conspicuous by its presence in Europe as by its absence in America. In Vienna, in 1847, writes one social historian:

> At the top were the nobles who considered themselves the only group worth noticing. The human race starts with barons, said one of them. Then there were the big businessmen who wanted to buy their way into the human race; the little businessmen; the proud but poor intellectuals; the students who were still poorer and still prouder; and the workers who were poor and had always been very, very humble.

The result was a totally different climate for the development of an economic society. In America, building on a new and vigorous foundation, capitalism was, from the beginning, a system of social consensus; in Europe, building on a feudal base, it was deeply tinged with class conflict. While capitalism in America managed without any effort to embrace the aspirations of its "lower orders," in Europe, already by the time of the revolutions of 1848, those lower orders had turned their backs on capitalism as a vehicle for their hopes and beliefs.

Second and no less important in explaining the divergence of American and European economic evolution was the profound difference between the political complexion of the two continents. In America, save only for the terrible crisis of the Civil War, a single national purpose fused the continent; in Europe, an historic division of languages, customs, and mutually suspicious nationalities again and again prevented just such a fusion.

Accordingly, American capitalism came of age in an environment in which political unity permitted the unhindered growth of an enormous unobstructed market, while in Europe a jigsaw puzzle of national boundaries forced industrial growth to take place in cramped quarters and in an atmosphere of continued national rivalry. It is curious to note that whereas Europe was considered "wealthier" than America all through the nineteenth century, in point of fact, American productivity in many fields began to outstrip that of Europe from at least the 1850's, and perhaps much earlier. For instance, at the Paris Exposition of 1854, an American threshing machine was twice as productive as its nearest (English) rival and eleven times as productive as its least (Belgian) competitive model.

These advantages of geographic space, richness of resources, and political unity were widened by subsequent developments in European industry. Not surprisingly, European producers, like those in America, sought to limit the destructive impact of industrial competition, and for this purpose they turned to *cartels*—contractual (rather than merely voluntary) agreements to share markets or fix prices. Unlike the case in America, however, this self-protective movement received the blessing, overt or tacit, of European governments. Although "anti-cartel" laws existed in many European countries, in fact, these laws were almost never enforced: by 1914 there were over 100 international cartels, representing the most varied industries, in which most European nations participated.*

Cartelization was undoubtedly good for the profit statements of the cartelized firms, but it was hardly conducive to growth—either for those firms or new ones. By establishing carefully delineated and protected "preserves," the cartel system rewarded unaggressive behavior rather than economic daring; and together with the everpresent problem of cramping national frontiers, it drove European producers into a typical high-cost, high profit-margin, low-volume pattern rather than into the American pattern of very large plants with very high efficiencies. The difference in economic scale is dramatically illustrated by steel. In 1885, Great Britain led the world in the production of steel; fourteen years later, her entire output was less than that of the Carnegie Steel Company alone.

As a result, by the early twentieth century, European productivity lagged very seriously behind American. A study by Professor Taussig in 1918 showed that the daily output of coal per underground worker was 4.68 tons in the United States, as contrasted with 1.9 tons in Great Britain, 1.4 tons in Prussia, and 0.91 tons in France. In 1905, the output of bricks per person was 141,000 in the United States and 40,000 in Germany; pig iron production was 84.5 tons per worker in 1909, compared with only 39 tons in Great Britain in 1907. As the twentieth century went on, United States production pulled steadily ahead.

The divergence was strikingly no-

---

* By 1939 an estimated 109 cartels also had American participation, since American companies were not prohibited by anti-trust laws from joining international restrictive agreements.

ticeable in per capita incomes. In 1911, for example, when per capita income in the United States was $368, the corresponding figure for Great Britain was $250, for Germany $178, for France $161, for Italy $108. By 1928, American per capita income was $541 (in unchanged dollar values), while that of the United Kingdom was only $293; of Germany, $199; of France, $188; and of Italy, $96. While American per capita incomes had grown by nearly 46 per cent, English and French per capita incomes had increased only a third as rapidly, German incomes rose only about a quarter as fast, and Italian per capita incomes had actually declined.*

The Breakdown of International Trade

Still another consequence followed from the division of European industry and agriculture into national compartments. To a far greater extent than in America, it made the development of European capitalism subject to the expansion of *international trade*.

It is significant that we have been able to describe the main lines of American economic growth without even mentioning international trade. American growth did depend, to a very important degree, on commodities and capital funds which it was able to obtain from other lands. In Colonial times, foreign trade was the very economic lifeline of the country; and even in 1850 it is estimated that 20 per cent of the goods we consumed were im-

* We must be wary of placing too much faith in the translation of one income—say £500—into its "equivalent"—$1400. Until we know the price levels, the living standards and customs of the nations we are comparing, we make such translations strictly at our own risk. But changes *within* a country, from year to year, are, of course, as meaningful in one currency as in another.

ported. By 1880, however, this was reduced to 10 per cent, and thereafter the trend was steadily downward. Imports as a per cent of GNP were never above 5 per cent in the twentieth century, and latterly, scarcely half of that. Similarly, exports, although of critical importance for certain industries (and for agriculture), never bulked as a major fraction of our total output. Thus international trade, taken as a whole, never dominated our economic picture.

In Europe, however, quite the contrary was the case. Here the division of the continent into many national units made international trade a continuous and critical preoccupation of economic life. For instance, a study has shown that in 1913, when manufactured imports provided but 3.6 per cent of United States' consumption of manufactured goods, they provided 9 per cent of Germany's, 14 per cent of England's, 21 per cent of Sweden's. Perhaps even more striking is the degree to which some nations in Europe depended on international trade for the foodstuffs on which they lived: in the five years preceding World War I, for instance, England produced less than 20 per cent of the wheat she consumed and barely over 55 per cent of the meat. We find the same dependence on foreign trade in the export side of the picture. Whereas the United States in 1913 exported a mere fifteenth of its national product, France and Germany exported a fifth, and Britain nearly a quarter of theirs.

To a far greater degree than America, Europe lived by foreign trade. The significance here needs underscoring, particularly for Americans. For we do not often appreciate that trade (with its semantic emphasis on "exchange") is, in fact, inextricably associated with production and *productivity*.

Why productivity? Because trade enables us to concentrate our effort and resources on the production of those things for which they are best suited. We could, for instance, at very considerable cost grow coffee in the United States. To do so, however, would use our land, labor, and capital in highly inefficient ways, instead of putting them to use where their productivity is high—say, in the production of cars. The fact that we can *trade* cars for coffee gives us the best of both worlds: we can have our coffee without sacrificing our productivity by producing a coffee crop. Ideally, the same advantages accrue to the coffee producer who would be sacrificing his productivity were he to devote his resources to the production of cars.* Trade makes possible a *division of labor* from which *all* gain.

Here we clearly see the advantage possessed by the enormous unbroken American market over the fragmented national markets of Europe. In America, the division of labor was permitted to attain whatever degree of efficiency technology made possible; for, in the end, virtually all products entered into a single vast market where they could be exchanged against one another. In Europe, where the need for, and the potential benefits of, a far-reaching division of labor were no less pressing, a tangle of national barriers prevented the optimal specialization of effort from taking place.

What was visible in Europe was a struggle between the need for international trade as a primary means for advancing productivity and the retarding hand of national suspicions, rival-

---

* As we shall later see, there are complications, with roots deep in history and politics, which prevent the full benefits of trade from manifesting themselves with many of the world's "coffee producers." The reasons for this will emerge in our discussion of the underdeveloped countries at the end of this chapter.

ries and distrusts. A striking example was provided as recently as the early 1950's by the great cluster of European steel and coal industry near the German-Belgian-Luxembourg borders. Here, in a triangle, 250 miles on a side, was gathered 90 per cent of European steel-making capacity in a kind of European "Pittsburgh." But this natural geographic division of labor had to contend with political barriers which largely vitiated its physical productivity. Typically, German coal mines in the Ruhr sold their output to French steelmakers at prices 30 per cent higher than to German plants; while, in turn, French iron-ore producers charged far higher prices in Germany than at home. As a result, while American steel production soared 300 per cent between 1913 and 1950, the output of Europe's steel triangle rose but 3 per cent during the same period.

Our example, itself, poses a question, however. Prior to 1913, as we have seen, something like a great international division of labor did, in fact, characterize the European market, albeit to nothing like the extent seen in America. By 1913, we will remember, a very considerable flow of international trade was enhancing European productivity, despite the hindrances of cartels and national divisiveness. It was only the beginning of a truly free and unhampered international market, but at least it *was* a beginning.

What brought this promising achievement to an end? Initially, it was the shock of the first World War, with its violent sundering of European trade channels and its no less destructive aftermath of punitive reparations, war debts, and monetary troubles. In a sense, Europe never recovered from its World War I experience. The slow drift toward national economic separatism, at the expense of international economic cooperation, now accelerated fatefully. Tariffs and quotas multiplied to place new handicaps before the growth of international trade. Then, the Depression of 1929 came as the final blow. As the Depression spread "contagiously," nation after nation sought to quarantine itself by erecting still further barriers against economic contacts with other countries. Starting in 1929, an ever-tightening contraction of trade began to strangle economic life on the continent.* Between the late 1920's and the mid-1930's, manufactured imports (in constant prices) fell by a third in Germany, by nearly 40 per cent in Italy, by almost 50 per cent in France. As international trade collapsed, so did Europe's chance for economic growth. For two long decades there followed a period of stagnation which earned for Europe the name of the "tired continent."

European Socialism

Against this background of economic malfunction it is easier to understand the growing insecurity which afflicted European capitalism. During the 1930's serious rumblings were already heard. In England, the Socialist Labour Party had clearly displaced the middle-class Liberals as the Opposition. In France, a mildly socialist "Popular Front" government came to the fore, as it did in Austria. Even in Italy and Germany, the fascist dictators repeatedly declared their sympathy with "socialist" objectives—and whereas their declarations may have been no more than a sop to the masses, it was certainly indicative of the sentiments the masses wanted to hear.

What was the aim of European socialism?

We can sum it up in two words: *equality* and *planning*. By equality, socialism meant first, of course, greater economic equality—higher wages for the working class and more stringent taxation for the upper class. But the meaning of the word did not confine itself to economic privilege. It stood also for social and political equality, for an end to the privileges of hierarchical status which, as we have seen, were deeply entrenched in the European heritage. Thus European socialism was a movement closely associated with *political democracy*, a fact which earned for it the enmity of not only the Right, but of the Communist Left as well.**

Socialism was concerned with removing more than the existing injustices of the European capitalist order; it sought as well to remove the economic malfunction of that order by replacing it with a planned economy. This objective did not imply, as with the Communists, the total state control of all enterprise and agriculture. To most socialists, planning meant only that the strategic centers of production would be nationalized, while the remainder of the economy would be regulated by indirect controls, not too much unlike those we have seen developed in America, reinforced by appropriate actions taken by the nationalized sector itself.

By the end of World War II, socialist ideas were clearly in the ascendant throughout most of Europe. Even before the war was concluded, the Labour Party swept into office in England and

* It was not only European trade which declined, but *world* trade. For 53 grim months following January 1929, the volume of world trade was lower each month than the preceding.

** Another very important difference between the Socialist and Communist movements was that the Socialists preached gradualism rather than revolution, and abhorred the use of violence.

rapidly nationalized the Bank of England, the coal and electricity industries, much of the transport and communications industry, and finally steel. As the first postwar governments were formed, it was evident that a socialist spectrum extended across Europe from Scandinavia through the Lowlands and France to Italy (where the communists came within an ace of gaining power). To many observers, it seemed as if capitalism in Europe had come to the end of its rope.

THE RECOVERY OF
EUROPEAN CAPITALISM

Yet, European capitalism did not come to an end. Instead, beginning in the late 1940's and early 1950's, it embarked on what is unquestionably its period of strongest economic growth. How could this have come about?

The first reason was that the postwar Socialist governments were not revolutionary but reform administrations. Once in power, they quickly instituted a number of welfare and social planning measures, such as public health facilities, family benefits and allowances, improved social security and the like, but they did not engage in changes of a sweeping order. When many of the socialist governments, facing the exigencies of the postwar period, were voted out again, they bequeathed to the conservatives the framework of a welfare state *which the conservatives accepted.* Consequently, we find today that in most European states, welfare expenditures form a considerably higher proportion of government expenditures than they do in the United States. We get some idea of this if we compare *non-defense* government expenditure among Western nations.

GOVERNMENT NONDEFENSE PURCHASES OF GOODS AND SERVICES AS A PROPORTION OF GNP

	Per cent
U.S. (1957)	9.7
West Germany (1953)	14.3
Belgium (1952)	11.0
United Kingdom (1953)	13.1
Sweden (1952)	13.6

SOURCES: Francis Bator, *The Question of Government Spending* (New York: Harper & Row, Publishers, 1960), Table 14, p. 157.

Harkening back to one of the traditional weaknesses of European capitalism, we can say that this represents an attempt to create a social service state which will mend the historic antagonism of the lower classes.

The second reason was even more important. This was the rise of a movement *within* the conservative ranks to overcome a still more dangerous heritage of the past—the national division of markets. This great step toward creating a full-scale continental market for European producers is called the European Community—or more usually, the Common Market.

To some extent, the Common Market was born out of the vital impetus given to European production by the Marshall Plan. Despite Marshall aid, it soon became apparent that Europe's upward climb would necessarily be limited if production were once again restrained by cartels and national protectionism. To forestall a return to the stagnation of the pre-war period, a few far-sighted and courageous statesmen, primary among them Jean Monnet and Robert Schuman, proposed a truly daring plan for the abolition of Europe's traditional economic barriers.

The plan as it took shape called for the creation of a *supranational* (not merely an inter-national) organization to integrate the steel and coal production of France, Germany, Italy, Belgium, Luxembourg, and the Netherlands. The new Iron and Steel Community, was to have a High Authority with power to eliminate all customs duties on coal and steel products among members of the Community, to outlaw all discriminatory pricing and trade practices, to approve or disapprove all mergers, to order the dissolution of cartels, and to provide social and welfare services for all Community miners and steelworkers. The Authority was to be given direct power to inspect books, levy fines, and enforce its decrees—and still more remarkable, it was to be responsible not to any single member government but to a multi-national Parliament and a multi-national Court, both to be created as part of the Community. A Council of Ministers was to act as a *national* advisory and permissory body, but even here action could be taken by majority vote, so that no single nation (or even two nations) could block a decision desired by the Community as a whole.

By the fall of 1952, the Coal and Steel Community was a reality, and it lost no time going about its business. At mid-1954, customs duties and discriminatory pricing within the coal and steel "triangle" had been virtually eliminated, and roughly 40 per cent more coal and steel was being shipped across national boundaries than had been shipped prior to the establishment of the Community.

The success of the Coal and Steel Community led, in 1956, to the next two organizations: Euratom, a supra-national atomic power agency, and the Common Market itself, an organization which was to do for commodities in general what the Coal and Steel Community had done for its products. Under the Common Market treaty, a definite schedule of tariff cuts was laid down, envisaging by 1969, at the latest, an entirely unimpeded continental market for Common Market members, with a single "external" tariff vis-à-vis the world. In addition, there were to be a single agricultural policy and, perhaps most imaginative, full freedom for the inter-member mobility of both capital and labor.

The Common Market is still in the process of achieving many of these goals, although it is well ahead of its timetable. Already, however, it has led to a remarkable increase in European production. By the early 1960's, industrial production has more than doubled, and agricultural output has risen by a third. Over the entire decade, western Europe's rate of growth has exceeded by 50 per cent that of the United States, and most important of all, for the first time the standard of living for the middle and working classes of Europe has begun to resemble that of America.

The Rise of Conservative Planning

It is not merely in these prosperous statistics that the European situation reminds us of the general course of affairs in the United States. Looking deeper, we can see a more profound resemblance. Abroad, as in America, the market system has had to turn toward what we might call "conservative planning" in order to survive.

In Europe, the direction of public intervention has perforce concerned itself with international trade more than is the case with the United States. The underlying problems and philosophy of conservative planning are much the same nonetheless. A need to keep the market process within bounds, to insure its continued smooth operation, to stabilize and, if need be, to stimulate its operation, has resulted in a strengthening of the role of government in both market societies. A growing agreement on the role of government as the active guardian of social welfare marks European as well as American capitalism, and a consensus on the use of monetary and tax and budgetary powers of adjustment again testifies to a common avenue of approach to the solution of common problems on both sides of the Atlantic.

This does not mean that the European situation is entirely comparable to America. Although the economy of Europe is today more dynamic, more hopeful, than perhaps ever in the past, its political problems have not yet been fully overcome. An undercurrent of political dissension continues to threaten the stability of many European countries, not only from the extreme Left but from the far Right, bringing about a certain tension in political life from which the United States has been mercifully spared. Then, too, the continued presence of a strong "socialist" movement, no matter how cooled its ardor or how watered-down its program, indicates that capitalism as an *ideology* is not yet without substantial opposition.

Thus European capitalism remains, to a certain extent, on political trial, despite its economic recovery. Yet, if history teaches us anything, it is that economic success tends to breed political success. If the trend of the past decade can be continued—and the purely economic auguries are reasonably favorable—there is surely reason to hope for a strengthening of the European social consensus and for a further healing of its historic political wounds.

NONMARKET ECONOMIES: THE SOVIET UNION

In the recovery of European capitalism through its development of a conservative planning structure, we have seen one aspect of the slow evolution of the modern economic history. Clearly, however, this is not the most significant change of the past half-century or so. For this we must look to the emergence of a *totally planned, nonmarket* society as the dominant economic pattern for at least a quarter of the globe. Here the guiding impetus of change has been the Soviet Union.

Early Soviet Planning

We cannot here recount in detail the history of Soviet socialism. Let us, rather, begin by noting the extraordinarily difficult problem that faced the revolutionary leaders who had secured the victory of "socialism" in Russia in 1917. In the first place, Russia was a semi-feudal society in which capitalism was restricted to a small industrial and commercial sector. Second, both production and distribution were highly disorganized in the chaotic situation following the civil war. Finally, there was little guidance in the official literature of the Communist movement as to how a socialist society should be run. Marx's *Das Kapital,* the great seminal work of communism, was entirely devoted to a study of capitalism; and in those few essays in which Marx looked to the future, his gaze rarely traveled beyond the watershed of the revolutionary act itself. With the achievement of the revolution, Marx thought, a temporary regime known as "the dictatorship of the proletariat" would take over the transition from capitalism to socialism, and thereafter a "planned socialist economy" would emerge as the first step towards a still less specified "communism." In the latter state —the final terminus of economic evolution according to Marx—there were hints that the necessary but humdrum tasks of production and distribution would take place by the voluntary cooperation of all citizens and that society would turn its serious attention to matters of cultural and humanistic importance.

In reality, the Revolution presented Lenin, Trotsky, and the other leaders of the new Soviet Union with problems far more complex than this utopian long-term design. Shortly after the initial success of the Revolution, Lenin nationalized the banks, the major factories, the railways, and canals. In the meantime, the peasants, themselves, had taken over the large landed estates on which they had been tenants and had carved them up into individual holdings. The central authorities then attempted for several years to run the economy by requisitioning food from the farms and allocating it to factory workers, while controlling the flow of output from the factories themselves by a system of direct controls from above.

This initial attempt to run the economy was a disastrous failure. Under inept management (and often cavalier disregard of "bourgeois" concerns with factory management), industrial output declined precipitously—by 1920 it had fallen to *14 per cent* of prewar levels. As goods available to the peasants became scarcer, the peasants, themselves, were less and less willing to acquiesce in giving up food to the cities. The result was a wild inflation followed by a degeneration into an economy of semi-barter. For a while, toward the end of 1920, the system threatened to break down completely.

To forestall the impending collapse, in 1921 Lenin instituted a New Economic Policy—the so-called NEP. This was a return toward a market system and a partial reconstitution of actual capitalism. Retail trade, for instance, was opened again to private ownership and operation. Small-scale industry also reverted to private direction. Most important, the farms were no longer

requisitioned but operated as profit-making units. Only the "commanding heights" of industry and finance were retained in government hands.

There ensued for several years a bitter debate as to the course of action to follow next. While the basic aim of the Soviet government was still to industrialize and to socialize (i.e., to replace the private ownership of the means of production by state ownership), the question was how fast to move ahead—and, indeed, *how* to move ahead. The pace of industrialization hinged critically on one highly uncertain factor—the willingness of the large, private peasant sector to make food deliveries with which the city workers could be sustained in their tasks. To what extent, therefore, should the need for additional capital-goods be sacrificed in order to turn out the consumption goods which could be used as an inducement for peasant cooperation?

The Drive to Total Planning

The student of Russian history—or, for that matter, of economic history—will find the record of that debate an engrossing subject. But the argument was never truly resolved. In 1927, Stalin moved into command, and the difficult question of how much to appease the unwilling peasant disappeared. Stalin simply made the ruthless decision to appease him not at all, but to *coerce* him by collectivizing his holdings.

The collectivization process solved in one swoop the problem of securing the essential transfer of food from the farm to the city, but it did so at frightful social (and economic) cost. Many peasants slaughtered their livestock rather than hand it over to the new collective farms; others waged outright war or practiced sabotage. In reprisal, the authorities acted with brutal force. An estimated five million "ku-laks" (rich peasants) were executed or put in labor camps, while in the cities an equally relentless policy showed it-self vis-à-vis labor. Workers were sum-marily ordered to the tasks required by the central authorities. The right to strike was forbidden, and the trade unions were reduced to impotence. Speed-ups were widely applied, and living conditions were allowed to de-teriorate to very low levels.

The history of this period of forced industrialization is ugly and repellent, and it has left abiding scars on Russian society. It is well for us, nonetheless, to attempt to view it with some objec-tivity. If the extremes to which the Stalinist authorities went were extra-ordinary, often unpardonable, and per-haps self-defeating, we must bear in mind that industrialization on the grand scale has always been wrenching, al-ways accompanied by economic sacri-fice, and always carried out by the more or less authoritarian use of power. We have already seen what happened in the West at the time of the Industrial Revolution, with the forced emigra-tion of the peasantry by enclosure and the heavy-handed exploitation of la-bor; and without "excusing" these acts, we have seen their function in paving the way for capital accumulation.

In much the same fashion, when the Soviet leaders deliberately held down consumption, regimented and trans-ferred their labor forces into the new raw industrial centers, and ruthlessly collected the foodstuffs to feed their

capital-building workers, they were, in fact, only enforcing the basic process of industrialization. What was new about the Soviet program was that to-talitarian control over the citizenry en-abled the planners to carry out this transformation at a much faster tempo than would have been possible had protests been permitted. Under Stalin's iron will, the planners did not scruple to exercise their industrializing power to the hilt.

Without seeking to justify the Rus-sian effort, it is worth pondering one last question. Can rapid industrializa-tion, with its inescapable price of low consumption, ever be a "popular" pol-icy? * Will poor people willingly vote for an economic transformation which will not "pay out" for twenty or forty years? Does rapid and large scale in-dustrialization *necessitate* a large de-gree of authoritorian political control? We will return to these problems when we turn to underdevelopment, but we might well begin to think about them now.

*   *   *

---

* We might note in passing that universal male suffrage was not gained in England un-til the late 1860's and 1870's. Aneurin Bevan has written: "It is highly doubtful whether the achievements of the Industrial Revolu-tion would have been permitted if the fran-chise had been universal. It is very doubtful because a great deal of the capital aggrega-tions that we are at present enjoying are the results of the wages that our fathers went without." (From Gunnar Myrdal, *Rich Lands and Poor,* New York: Harper & Row, Publishers, 1957, p. 46.)

U.S.S.R.

QUESTION: Can a Soviet worker quit his job of his own free will if he chooses to?
ANSWER: Certainly. The only requirement is that he give two weeks' notice. After the two weeks have expired, the management has no right to hold him if he wants to leave.

QUESTION: What is the old-age pension system in the Soviet Union?
ANSWER: Our pension system retires women at the age of 55 after 20 years of service and men at 60 after 25 years of service. Those working underground and in hot shops have more favorable retirement provisions.

The minimum payment is 30 rubles, and 120 rubles is the maximum. The amount is based on average earnings over a period of the last 12 months of employment or of any consecutive 5 years out of the last 10 employed. The pensioner may do two-months' paid work a year and still draw his full pension. Pensions are not taxable.

The pension granted to a worker who has reached retirement age but does not have the required 20 to 25 years of service is proportionate to his length of service, but in no case is it less than one-quarter of the full pension.

People on pension continue to get medical services and hospitalization free.

QUESTION: How is new housing distributed?
ANSWER: Every city in the USSR has a large-scale construction program. In 1961 some 119,000 Moscow families moved into new apartments. Available housing is distributed by the district Soviets strictly in order of need and without charge.

Every district Soviet has a housing committee composed of deputies and representatives of the trade unions and other public organizations. Anyone living in the district—even though he works in another district—may submit an application for a new apartment. Applications are reviewed by the housing committee and approved or disapproved by the executive committee of the district Soviet.

Preference is given to disabled war veterans, to families of men who were killed in the war, to large families, newlyweds and those suffering from tuberculosis or other chronic diseases. Rent averages about 5 per cent of earnings.

QUESTION: Do Soviet college students pay tuition?
ANSWER: They do not. Tuition is free in all colleges and professional schools. Moreover, students get maintenance scholarships ranging from 30 to 80 rubles a month, depending on years of study and grades. Out-of-town students pay very little for dormitory accommodations—one ruble a month for a room and 50 kopecks for linens.

QUESTION: Will you describe the system of distribution of material benefits in the Soviet Union?
ANSWER: Since all industrial enterprises and state farms are publicly owned, their income is public property. Add the income of the collective farms,

Excerpted from *U.S.S.R.*, January, 1962, and May, 1962.

and you have the total national income.

A quarter of the national income is spent to augment and develop the country's industry, transport and agriculture; to expand and modernize existing enterprises and build new ones. This is paid for out of the accumulation fund.

The remaining three-quarters of the national income makes up the consumption fund. It is spent for the material and cultural needs of the citizen.

The consumption fund is subdivided into the wage fund and the public consumption fund.

QUESTION: These, I gather, are two quite separate funds and go to pay for different things.

ANSWER: Yes, the wage fund, as the name implies, covers the wages of people working in factories and offices, in what we call the areas of material production.

QUESTION: How about the wages of workers in other spheres, say, in education, the arts, service industries, government?

ANSWER: Their wages come out of the public consumption fund since this fund pays for the development of science and culture as well as the maintenance of the educational and public health systems and the various social insurance benefits.

QUESTION: Does this mean that the public consumption fund is spent for a number of different things?

ANSWER: Yes. Besides the wages of those working in the non-material production areas I mentioned, the fund pays for pensions, student stipends, vacations, resort accommodations, temporary disability benefits, and the like. These are direct money payments to the individual citizen, direct additions to his income. There are also indirect additions to his income, the many necessary and valuable services provided by the kindergartens, schools, colleges, hospitals, research centers and health and holiday resorts, all of which are financed by the public consumption fund.

QUESTION: If you translate these various benefits and social services provided by the public consumption fund into monetary terms, how much would you say they increase the average Soviet worker's income?

ANSWER: By a third, over and above wages.

QUESTION: It would be helpful if you could show us how the public consumption fund affects the budget of a typical Soviet family.

ANSWER: Well, the Suslins are as typical as any. They live in Shchelkovo, a small town about 25 miles from Moscow. The family has two breadwinners—Alexei Suslin, who worked at a chemical plant, and his wife Valentina, an assembler. Their joint annual earnings, after taxes, come to 2,118 rubles.

Alexei's father does not work. He gets an old age pension of 493 rubles 20 kopecks a year. Alexei is in his fifth year at a specialized secondary school, where he studies after work. His tuition, textbooks and study aids are all free. He gets paid leave from his job—it amounts to 75 rubles 40 kopecks a year on the average—to take his school exams. That sum plus his father's pension adds up to 568 rubles 60 kopecks a year.

Alexei spent his regular summer vacation at a resort; 45 rubles 60 kopecks, or one third of the cost of his accommodations, was paid by his trade union. Add this to the sum above and you have 614 rubles 20 kopecks.

The youngest Suslin, two-year-old Valerik, goes to a kindergarten. The parents pay 10 rubles of the 34 rubles a month it cost the kindergarten to keep the child, so that in a year the state spends 288 rubles for this young citizen. Add this to the previous total of 614 rubles 20 kopecks and you have 902 rubles 20 kopecks.

In the shop where Alexei is employed, workers get a free lunch that would ordinarily cost 68 kopecks. This saves him about 200 rubles a year.

All told, the public consumption fund gives the Suslins 1,102 rubles 20 kopecks in the course of a year.

QUESTION: Since the public consumption fund serves as an indirect addition to wages, wouldn't it be simpler and better to raise wages directly?

ANSWER: Simpler perhaps, but not better. Our country operates on the principle of socialism—"From each according to his abilities, to each according to his work." This means that every able-bodied person receives equal pay for equal work, irrespective of sex, age, race or nationality. A person's earnings depend on the quantity and quality of work he does.

People vary in stamina and skill. Some workers are stronger, capable of greater effort and endurance, and can therefore do more. Workers with more skill do a better job. Consequently their earnings are higher and they have more cash income to spend to satisfy whatever personal needs they have. Besides that, there is the difference in size of families, number of wage earners and so on. All these things make for inequalities in material well-being which will be gradually ironed out as we move toward the communist principle of distibution—"From each according to his ability, to each according to his *needs.*"

When we come to the public consumption fund, this material inequality does not operate. Higher wages do not help a man to give his children a better education or to get more qualified medical attention, let us say. In West-

ern countries the quality of these services depends entirely on the amount the family earns and can afford to spend. Our approach is altogether different. The public consumption fund is distributed by the communist principle —according to needs. If you have children, they go to school. If you are ill, you get free medical attention, hospitalization, surgery or whatever else is indicated. When you grow old, you get an old age pension. The public consumption fund meets people's needs regardless of the quantity and quality of the work they do. It makes all Soviet citizens equal with regard to educational opportunity, medical care and

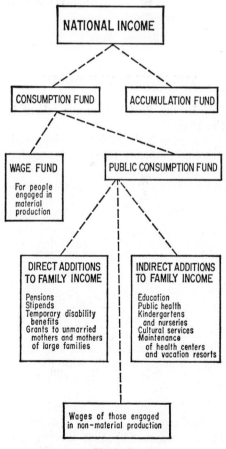

Figure 1.

the other services the public consumption fund supplies.

If you check back on the public consumption fund receipts of the Suslin family, you will see that they received, in monetary terms, a sum equal to more than half of their total earnings.

QUESTION: *Where does the money in the public consumption fund come from? Is the national budget its only source?*

ANSWER: The bulk of it is allocated in the national budget so that it can be distributed in a centralized fashion and with the interests of the whole society in mind.

The public consumption fund also includes enterprise funds—the money deducted from plant income and spent by management only with the approval of the trade union for the needs of its workers; and farm funds—cash or produce that collective farms allocate for the same purpose.

78   SOVIET UNION: HOW IT PLANS, WORKS, GROWS

Business Week

THE PLAN IS THE WORD

In the Soviet economy, there is the Plan.

The Plan is the Word, reaching with supreme authority from the leadership down to every factory, farm, and mine in the nation, to every worker and peasant, spelling out quotas and norms.

The Plan gives and the Plan takes away, assigning to enterprises their supplies and capital, specifying and allocating their output.

While the Plan comes down as a precise order, the process by which it evolves has little precision. Plan making, for one thing, entails a kind of nationwide bargaining session, with the directors of factories and other enterprises arguing annually with the allocators for minimum output targets and maximum inputs and with the allocators striving for just the opposite.

Dual miracles. The Plan is wondrous in two ways: (1) that it ever gets drawn up; (2) that it ever works.

Wassily Leontief, Harvard economist, compares the Russian technique of economic planning with a talking horse. "The remarkable thing is not what it says but that it speaks at all."

Yet, this is how the Soviet Union controls all economic activity in its 8.5-million square miles—one-seventh of the earth. American businessmen who remember World War II controls can imagine the confusion and frustration.

Chain of command. At the top is Gosplan-U.S.S.R., in Moscow. Gosplan is the State Planning Committee. Subordinate Gosplans in the 15 republics take orders from Moscow, pass them on in turn to the 105 regional economic councils under the republic Gosplans.

Annually, Moscow charts the Soviet Union's economic course for the next year by prescribing production targets,

From *Business Week,* October 28, 1962, p. 53 ff. Reprinted by permission.

capital investment, technical innovations, budgets, labor requirements, regional development.

This is done after consultation with the Soviet Union's highest leaders. Gosplan chief Vladimir Novikov sits on the Council of Ministers with the heads of all key ministries such as agriculture, defense, foreign affairs, atomic energy, finance, power station construction, transport. The council meets regularly through the year.

Khrushchev, of course, presides, setting general guidelines for planning with assistance from the Presidium of the Communist Party.

Operation dovetail. Gosplan's economists make up several interlocking plans in such areas as fiscal support and labor allocation, the most important of which is the key "supply" plan.

Work on the "supply" plan starts quietly six months preceding the plan year, with Gosplan-U.S.S.R. examining the nation's output results of the previous year and indications in the current year. Comparing these results with the Seven-Year Plan goals for 1965, Gosplan makes preliminary estimates of the supply to be needed of at least the 200 most important input materials.

Meanwhile, enterprises all over the nation are estimating their own output targets, to figure out how much of the various materials they will need, and filling out supply request forms.

The enterprises send the forms to their regional economic councils. The council correlates and reviews these supply estimates, cutting them down where possible. The enterprise director has the right to bargain. He even can appeal immediately to the republic Gosplan.

The regional councils forward their estimates of total supply needs to the republic Gosplan, where there is more bargaining. The republic Gosplan figures how much of its requirements can

be supplied from within the republic and how much must be brought in from other republics.

By Aug. 1, republic estimates must be sent into Gosplan-U.S.S.R., which then has until Sept. 15 to work out a balanced all-Union output and supply plan. Tentative plans are sent back down the line to the republic Gosplans, thence to the regional councils and finally to the enterprises. Deadline for complaints is Nov. 1.

Regional job. In Moscow, Gosplan-U.S.S.R. has faced the fact that it can't possibly keep its finger on the nation's myriad transactions, that there must be some autonomy on the periphery. Thus, retail consumer trade and considerable consumer goods manufacturing are left wholly in the hands of regional economic councils. And while all heavy industry stays under Gosplan-U.S.S.R., even enterprises in this economic sector are left to their own devices in obtaining simple materials like sand and gravel. For many other materials, republic Gosplans and regional economic councils handle details of supply in their own areas.

Rationing system. Gosplan-U.S.S.R. keeps tight control on all important or scarce materials, prohibiting an enterprise to buy on its own any steel, automation instruments, or any of about 1,000 "priority commodities" that require for purchase a "fond"—a specific allocation channeled down from Gosplan-U.S.S.R.

To keep tabs on its rationing system, Gosplan makes a balance sheet for each centrally allocated commodity. This lists the sources on one side and distribution on the other. Obviously, they should balance. For instance, a balance sheet for copper should show production from every mine and smelter in the Soviet Union, accumulated stocks, and foreign imports, plus all demand for copper—for wiring, power station equipment, instrument makers.

If supply doesn't equal demand, Gosplan tries not to lower demand through cutting goals but attempts to bring supply up by such means as increasing production through higher labor productivity or more economic use of materials.

Chain reaction. In this manner, Gosplan strives for plan tautness. Naturally, each time production of a particular item is increased or decreased, it sets off a chain reaction. Thus, a decision to manufacture one kind of tractor instead of another could result in changes for tires, engines, carburetors, plus raw material components such as certain types of steel, copper, cast iron, and paint.

SUPPLY SYSTEM BOGS DOWN

Despite its elaborate setup, the planning system has failed to get maximum results.

Shortages exceed even the worst days of the U.S. economy in World War II. At any given time, about one-fourth the Soviet Union's tractors and electric engines are idle for lack of spare parts. Many factories maintain machine shops just for making spare parts they can't buy.

The problem, of course, is not only with spares. Throughout the nation, basic materials run short. The Moscow City Economic Council, for instance, says it was allocated only half the amount of rolled pipe its factories needed to meet their quota last year. A combine plant in Taganrog stopped production of reapers for want of friction rings after an allocation of 37,000 rings failed to come through.

When supplies arrive, they often have the wrong specifications. Rather than return such deliveries, factories usually prefer to go ahead and use them if they can. Otherwise, they lose time—and may miss their quota. A typical case was the Novokakhovka Electrical Machinery Plant's use last year of oversized sheetsteel delivered by the Ukraine Metal Supply & Marketing Administration. The waste amounted to 23%.

Favoritism. Complicating already critical shortages is the growth of regionalism since Soviet industry's reorganization in 1957—a "decentralization" move that broke up many ministries and put 90% of Soviet industry under the command of regional economic councils.

Now, factories are showing favoritism toward their neighbors. The Ukraine's metallurgical plants, for instance, came through with all the deliveries for their Ukranian customers last year—but failed to meet their obligations to other republics.

When Bashkiria wildcatters found oil near their boundary with the neighboring Tatar region, they sought—but were refused—permission to cross and drill on the Tatar side. They thereupon slant-drilled into the pool from their own side, evoking Tatar cries of protest and an official rebuke from Moscow for throwing "millions of rubles to the winds" with such expensive drilling.

Parkinson's law. An outrageous application of Parkinson's law has come to plague the planners in the wake of the 1957 industrial reorganization. When the ministries were abolished (to streamline the economy), their supply agencies were transferred intact. Thus, the Russian Republic, for example, now has separate marketing agencies for ferrous metals, scrap, and nonferrous metals—and each has dozens of its own warehouses.

Where the abolished ministries had a total of 30 marketing agencies, there now are 15 under Gosplan-U.S.S.R., plus dozens more in the various republics. Personnel has more than doubled.

Now, 17 "major economic regions" have been set up to bring together officials of the regional economic councils included within each area, just for the purpose of getting the right hand to know what the left is doing.

Although these new regions won't constitute formally another level in planning between the republic Gosplan and the regional councils, their organization as a "monitor" requires still more personnel to be hired in the bureaucracy directing Soviet supply.

Ususally enough. Despite shortages, the Soviets seem to have enough of the right materials in the right places much of the time. Under their system, this is not easy. Unrealistic balances in a few key sectors can throw kinks into the whole economy. The Sixth Five-Year Plan, for instance, was scrapped for the current Seven-Year Plan simply because the planners bit off more than the nation could chew.

Computers are being used increasingly to help planners cope with the complexities of material balances. At best, however, this gives planners the results of just one prospective move.

What's really needed is a device to enable planners to choose the best solution among endless ways of doing things. When locating a plant, the Soviets have formidable difficulties selecting the most profitable site in terms of the availability and cost of power, raw materials, manpower, transportation, and so forth.

An obvious answer is linear programming, developed and used to a limited extent in the Soviet Union. Linear programming's equations, representing numerous alternatives and choosing among them, helps establish prices that are a reasonably accurate reflection of costs.

Inaccurate guide. But over-all, the Soviets acknowledge that prices are currently an inaccurate guide to costs for mathematical planning purposes. Since price is set by administrative decision (rather than by the market equilibrium, as in a capitalist supply-and-demand economy), the Soviets rarely know an item's true cost at any given time.

If you can't determine costs accurately, how do you determine what's a profitable investment? The Soviet system simply has not developed in practice a rational price system to guide efficiently the allocation of resources in accordance with changing demand, supply, and cost situations. A wholesale price reform is planned.

FILL THE QUOTA, OR HEADS ROLL

To meet these problems, the Soviet executive in charge of an ordinary enterprise has to live in a gray world of subterfuge.

By now, he certainly knows that his is not to wonder why at the Plan's oversights and failings, which loom up as full-blown crises for him to resolve. His job is to fill quotas.

A certain amount of the quota can be met legally. Chances are excellent that not all of it can be. Even if the plant has been allocated the necessary materials, the supplies may not show up. If they do, they may have the wrong specifications—or show up too late.

Legal recourse is none too effective. A factory manager may complain through channels. But Soviet bureaucrats have a way of turning a deaf ear —and looking for a new manager who may not fuss quite so much.

Soviet executives also may sue a supplier who violates his contract. But since any factory may only have one or two suppliers available, its director may look upon a lawsuit as bad public relations. There's the long term to think about. So, means other than strictly legal ones are sought.

For example. Let's take the hypothetical case of a rolling mill at Sverdlovsk.

At the end of the planning process, the plant director found his share of the nation's assigned production target higher than he had set in his preliminary estimates. At the same time, the supply of steel allocated to him was even less than he had requested.

The plant director then faces an ethical problem. His customers, the oil drilling trusts, have ordered small-diameter pipe for slim-hole drilling. If he somehow gets the steel and produces the specified quantity of small pipe, his total tonnage output almost certainly will fall short of the target set for him. He might exceed his quota —expressed in tons, not rubles—with production of heavier pipe, thus earning himself and his workers their bonus. So he goes ahead with the heavier pipe, knowing the oil drillers will be disappointed but hardly likely to turn down the shipment.

To get the steel, he resorts to a practice that has scandalized the Soviet Union for years, generated hundreds of "exposes" in the Communist press— and without which the Soviet Union's entire distribution system would grind to a virtual halt, if not fall apart completely. He sends a "tolkach."

Under-the-counter deals. The tolkachi are, literally, "pushers." Armed with funds for entertainment, gifts, or outright bribes, the rolling mill's tolkach visits steel mills to pry loose an extra supply for his chief. On the books, the tolkach is carried as, say, an engineer, his expenses as those for a visit to "study leading experience" in other cities.

Eventually, the tolkach finds a mill willing to sell part of its 5% throwaway reserve—the set amount of production that the planners allow most industries to write off as spoiled or waste. The steel mill director might give easier terms to an auto manufacturer's tolkach, in return for the promise of a car, or arrange a barter agreement with a factory manufacturing new equipment that his plant needs.

Because Soviet railroads are overloaded chronically, the rolling mill may not receive its under-the-counter steel for some time, and then at sporadic intervals. Sometimes, this requires the plant to operate at a slower tempo than usual. To compensate for this, the Soviet director then may ask his workers to stay after hours or work on days off to be sure the quota is fulfilled—and that they all get their bonuses. This practice, "storming," violates the labor input norm set by the regional economic council.

Desperate measures. The Soviet manager sometimes takes more desperate measures. He may cut back quality—or even ship unfinished products. One year, Kazakstan's collective farms received hundreds of tractors without carburetors. Turbines this year were delivered to power stations for "completion" on site.

The enterprise director often chooses not to install new equipment designed to increase labor productivity or produce better quality goods, even if the equipment has been allocated along with credit from the state bank. The reason is that time lost on installation might prevent the factory from fulfilling its quota in that period.

A rule adopted one year ago may be having some effect. It allows a greater portion of above-plan profits to be channeled into the enterprise fund, hence into bonuses, if the results are from technological improvement.

BUREAUCRATIC WATCHDOGS

Watching over the enterprise director's shoulders are several bureaucratic watchdogs. The most imposing is the State Control Commission, whose members perform a kind of inspector general function with periodic visits. The State Bank is another control; it keeps tabs on the legality of a company's transactions by controlling the enterprise's money and credit.

Inside the factory, the director works under the eyes of the Communist Party bureau chief and also the chief accountant, appointed to his job by higher authority. These controls are relatively ineffective, since these men, too, are judged by the plant's performance. In a kind of community relationship, they tend to look the other way when, say, a tolkach goes out on a mission.

The press gives the enterprises a bad time. Izvestia, the state newspaper, on occasion sends a team of reporters into a plant on a "raid," to sniff out irregularities and write them up in an expose. Other newspapers publish letters from workers complaining about factories.

Close supervision. One of the Soviet Union's more important enterprise directors is Grigori A. Surguchov. A heavyset, grayhaired man who peers genially from behind steelrim spectacles, Surguchov runs the large Krasni Proletari Machine Tool Plant in Moscow.

Surguchov says his work is "closely supervised." The Moscow Economic Council stays in "constant contact" with telephone calls and personal visits. In addition, Surguchov writes monthly reports that are channeled through the council up to Gosplan-U.S.S.R.

"The State Control Commission comes around only when things are going badly," Surguchov says. The last visit was four years ago.

His customers are only those enterprises with a "fond"—puchasing authorization—from Gosplan. These are handed down from Gosplan-U.S.S.R. to the republic-level Gosplans, and from there to the regional economic councils, which parcel them out among factories.

Only with the major "customers" does Surguchov handle details by telephone or telegraph. Most of the time he uses mail.

Pricing gauge. The plant manufactures close to 15,000 universal, or multipurpose, lathes a year, along with some special tools and individual components such as needle bearings. Since most of this production is considered of "All-Union" importance, Surguchov's prices are determined mainly by Gosplan-U.S.S.R. Items considered of "republic" importance are priced by the republic Gosplan. Commodities rated only locally important get their price from the Moscow Economic Council; at this level, customers are permitted to haggle over price.

If Surguchov's factory comes up with a new piece of equipment, the factory has a special committee to "nominate" a price. But the appropriate planning level must confirm it. In theory, the price is based on cost of materials and labor.

Major decisions. Although Surguchov can't make a major investment decision on his own, he proposes them to planning authorities for approval or disapproval. For very minor investments, such as alteration of a loading platform, Surguchov can dip into the enterprise fund.

Among other things, the enterprise fund is used for social services for the workers and their families. "I sent

2,000 children to summer camp this year," Surguchov says, "That makes me quite a father."

Surguchov's factory has a trade union any capitalist would enjoy working with. There's virtually no friction between "management" and "labor"; there's never a strike.

Like all Soviet trade unions, the one at Krasni Proletari Machine Tool Plant has the same goals as the manager—to increase production and efficiency. Together, workers and management are rewarded according to the plant's performance.

USING PEOPLE FOR MACHINES

Russians never tire of telling visitors—particularly those from underdeveloped countries—that the Communists have found the secret of moving from backwardness to industrialization in only a generation.

The Soviet's neglect to tell the rest of the story: that the Kremlin way, involving much pain and sacrifice for the people it is supposed to benefit, puts machines always ahead of men, sacrifices today's consumption for tomorrow's.

"Scarcity" economy. Basically, the Soviets have a scarcity economy, with a built-in seller's market.

To reach their present economic level, the Russians have depended to some degree on foreign capital. A little came in during the 1920s; World War II brought more, in the form of machinery, equipment, and other capital goods from the U.S. and other allies. Besides that, the Soviets helped offset their war losses with "reparations" and return of "property stolen from the U.S.S.R." in all the nations the Soviets occupied.

On balance, however, almost all capital for Soviet economic development has been obtained internally by restricting the consumption of the Soviet people and devoting an unusually large percentage of the national income to investment.

Bigger pie. Today, a larger percentage of national investment is going to heavy industry than ever before. To be sure, the Russians are enjoying a higher living standard today. But not because they are getting a bigger slice of the national income. The pie simply is bigger.

Before the Revolution, consumer goods accounted for two-thirds of Russia's industrial production. This share has dwindled until now it is only one-fourth. Capital goods production in the 30 years preceding the Seven-Year Plan increased by 50 times; output of consumer goods has risen only 11 times.

The same pattern will hold. The Plan calls for capital goods output to go up by 85%, while production of consumer goods is scheduled to rise only 62%.

Soviet peasants have borne the brunt. Until the agricultural reforms in the 1950s, collective farmers were assigned compulsory delivery quotas at artificially low prices that amounted to confiscation.

Much higher prices were allowed for deliveries in excess of quota in order to give farmers some incentive, but flagging production showed the system was not working well. So in 1953, 1956, and 1958, agricultural prices were raised, reducing to some extent the direct state reliance on agriculture for generation of capital.

Turnover tax. Since farmers are consumers—and almost half the population is still engaged in agriculture—they still are paying heavily for capital investment in industry through the so-called turnover tax, which amounts to an extremely stiff sales tax. Even in the decade 1931–40, this source is said to have accounted for between half and two-thirds of all Soviet government income annually.

This tax, together with profits from industry, currently supplies more than 90% of government revenue. The income tax, which doesn't amount to much but which is being abolished with much propaganda fanfare, accounts for the rest.

The turnover tax, besides raising revenue for investment, discourages consumption through the resulting high prices. It also channels consumption into socially "desirable" directions. For example, there's a high tax on vodka and private autos, a low one on children's clothing and airline fares (air transport is being encouraged for passenger travel).

Consumer goods prices. Just how high turnover taxes must be—they're rarely stated precisely—is evident from consumer goods prices in the Soviet Union. A refrigerator, small by American standards, costs 310 rubles (one ruble equals $1.11 at the official rate); a medium-size television set, 240 rubles; men's suits, 100 rubles; a woman's cloth coat, 140 rubles; women's hosiery, 3 to 5 rubles. Apparently, food has no turnover tax, but prices are so high that the government probably is making a good profit.

The average Soviet worker makes about 100 rubles a month, making the high prices more meaningful as a rationing mechanism. In virtually all Soviet consumer goods, of course, quality is low by Western standards.

The government, too, gets billions of rubles for its investment fund annually from sale of bonds and from deposits in savings banks.

FAVORITES GET THE NOD

The Soviet Union's rate of gross investment is usually estimated at 25%

to 30% of gross national product, compared with about 20% in the U.S. (American investment still is greater in absolute terms because of a larger base). This indicates that the whole answer to the Soviet Union's faster rate of industrial growth lies not in the total of investment outlays but in its structure.

While investment in consumer or service industries is minimized, investment is maximized in military and capital goods industries—which enhance national power.

Look at Soviet figures: In the 40 years preceding the Seven-Year Plan, 43% of Soviet capital investment went into heavy industry, and only 5.5% into consumer goods.

The Kremlin may be forced to give increasing attention to backward transportation and service enterprises. If so, the Soviets may run into trouble sustaining the investment rate for industrial expansion. Agriculture, too, needs capital.

Even now, funds are spread thin among too many projects, Khrushchev told the Party Congress last week. He suggested no more starts until some of the 100,000 projects now under way are completed.

Allocation by formula. Even within the huge investment fund earmarked for heavy industry, allocations are made under a formula that, in contrast to the U.S., singles out "leading sectors" of the economy for priority on men and materials. Stalin favored electric power, steel, machine building, and, to lesser degree, chemicals. As a corrective, Khrushchev has added petroleum and natural gas. The chemical industry— petrochemicals in particular—also has greater emphasis.

Exploiting workers. With labor traditionally more plentiful than capital, industry has exploited farm-to-city migration, and used workers instead of more efficient machines in many cases.

The Soviets preferred a lower capital outlay even when labor was not a major factor. Induction motors, for electric drive in industry were favored, for instance, simply because they were cheaper to build than synchronous motors.

Even during the Stalin era, exceptions had to be made to this policy, and approval was given to such capital intensive projects as the Dnieper Hydropower Project and the Gorki Auto Factory.

Coincident with the growing shortage of labor resulting from the low birthrate during World War II, some basic changes have been made since Khrushchev. The Soviets are preparing for wider scale automation throughout industry, with the hope that the high capital expenditure will be offset by savings on labor input and lower overall costs.

Priority system. The Soviet practice of giving priorities to certain industries has brought more rapid over-all economic growth than otherwise might have been possible.

But late development of the oil and gas industry is only one penalty paid for unbalanced growth. The Soviet Union is laggard, too, in such key industries as aluminum and plastics. Transportation and warehousing, all but neglected to this day, may yet prove to be a real Achilles heel in an increasingly complex industrial society.

Agriculture is way behind. So is construction of housing and school buildings. Most Soviet schools still operate on double or triple shifts.

To put it another way, the Soviet people have paid for rapid industrialization with a substandard diet and a generally short supply of the good things in life.

79   LESSONS FROM THE WEST GERMAN MIRACLE

Karl W. Roskamp

Karl W. Roskamp is a member of the Economics Faculty at Wayne State University.

What lessons does West Germany's remarkable postwar economic growth offer to the American economy today with its five million unemployed, gold outflow and "growth gap"? One comforting deduction is that a capitalist economy is still capable of achieving rates of growth comparable to the best that the socialist countries can offer.

But what type of capitalist economy has achieved these growth rates? Was the German "miracle" the result mainly of an orthodox monetary policy and the restoration of the free market that together galvanized private initiative?

This popular view is at best a half-truth. Some of the reasons for calling it a half-truth are reasonably obvious. West Germany had most of the basic ingredients for rapid growth. Its labor force was highly skilled and its physical plant was only partially demolished. Until 1955 it had a labor surplus (which stemmed largely from the

From *Challenge*, July 1, 1961, pp. 10–14. Reprinted by permission.

inflow of refugees from the east). Its trade unions were rather weak, partly because of this labor surplus. The cost to Germany of the Allied occupation was low; the U.S. provided special economic aid in the early postwar years, and the military burden has only in the past two or three years begun to approximate that of other European countries.

Less obvious, however, has been the major positive role of the government. It has fostered capital formation through large budgetary surpluses and has done much to influence the volume and direction of private investment. These actions, though little noted, shed a rather different light on the German "miracle" and on the mixed character of the postwar German economy. Far from being a paragon of McKinleyite rectitude, West Germany's economic policy is close enough to ours to provide us with some guidance on the effective use of selective fiscal measures to promote economic growth without inflation.

A few words of caution are, however, needed. In this article, I do not attempt to "explain" West Germany's growth. This was a complex process for which no simple explanation can be given. It was not solely due to a return to "free competition"—there is much oligopoly (domination of a market by a few firms) and monopoly in West Germany. Nor was the currency reform in 1948 the only cause. Likewise it cannot be attributed chiefly to general monetary and fiscal policy, trade union behavior or the influx of refugees.

Each of these factors had an important influence, but none of them, taken alone, can furnish an explanation of why the country progressed as fast as it did. The same is true of the important role of public authorities in this process; it is not *the* explanation of

why growth rates were high. Nevertheless, governmental influence was a very important ingredient, and it is certainly worthwhile to take a closer look at it.

PROPER PERSPECTIVE

To get the impact of governmental action upon the West German growth into the right perspective, and to understand its nature and extent, we must first outline the situation of the economy in 1948.

When Germany was divided after the war, West Germany was separated from agricultural districts in the east and highly developed light industries in central Germany. This forced severe readjustments on the West German economy. Its need for food imports increased and new light industry had to be constructed. Swept into a country devastated by the war were, between 1945 and 1948, about seven million refugees, many of them initially without employment. Through this influx the housing situation, which was already bad enough, became catastrophic. The lack of raw materials for industry handicapped production in early postwar years, but more important than this, perhaps, was the general lack of incentives.

There was a severe food shortage, which would have been disastrous if Allied supplies had not been available. There were black markets all over the country. Those who could still produce often preferred to hoard products rather than to sell them. In many cases, the reason for this was the fear that no new raw materials could be obtained except by barter.

An extremely severe inflation prevailed. The Allies excluded West Germany from direct international trade and limited its production of steel and other important items. In addition, they had raised income tax rates to such a high level that these alone would have probably been sufficient to strangle a good deal of all incentives.

The West German currency reform in 1948 marked a turning point in the country's history. This measure stimulated business strongly. But it also had many inequitable features. In brief, holders of old Reichsmarks were allowed to convert only a limited amount of them into Deutsche marks, the new currency. Most personal savings, certainly all small savings, the national debt and nearly all business cash reserves were thereby wiped out. But confidence that the new currency would retain its value caused businessmen to offer goods for sale that previously they had hoarded or bartered. Trade revived and the economy started on its upward course.

Accompanying the reform was the abolition of price controls over all but a few important commodities. Allied control of international trade was relaxed. The currency reform, however, discouraged saving by individuals for some time, since small savers had just had virtually all the fruit of their thrift confiscated.

At the time of the currency reform, there were industrial capacity, industrial skills and a powerful backlog of demand for all sorts of consumer goods—plus excess labor that kept wages down. As a result, profits were initially extremely high. In brief, the currency reform was a hard reform. It was an "efficiency" solution geared to create incentives rather than to promote social justice. It caused a lot of social hardship, but it got the economic machine started.

After 1950 the German "miracle" began; gross national product in constant 1954 prices rose from 113.1 billion DM in 1950 to 233.8 billion DM

in 1960. (Four Deutsche marks equalled $1 during this period.) In 1950 West Germany suffered from substantial unemployment and a large balance of payments deficit; today it has a serious labor shortage, rising prices and a large balance of payments surplus.

An outstanding feature of West Germany's economic growth was the astonishingly high rate of investment. That this was needed was recognized by many West Germans at an early date. Debates in the country's parliament in 1949 indicate that the government was keenly aware of this necessity.

West Germany needed new plants to meet domestic demand and to make its exports competitive in the world market. Big investments were also required to house and provide productive employment for the refugees. Thus the need for rapid capital formation was obvious to all. The problem was how to generate the necessary savings.

However, the Germans were disinclined to save; after both World Wars they had seen their savings wiped out by currency reforms. Thus, voluntary savings could be scarcely relied upon to supply enough funds for capital formation—at least not in the crucial years between 1950 and 1955. Even if interest rates had been extremely high, they would have scarcely induced a sufficient volume of savings, for incomes were rather low.

In these circumstances the government took a hand in the process of saving and investment. Had it not done so, and left saving and investment to the private decisions of a free market, what would have happened? There would have been too few funds seeking investment, and these would have flowed into sectors of the economy, such as trade, where high profits could be made quickly.

SOCIAL CONSIDERATIONS
AND GROWTH

Sectors of the economy vital to sustained growth would have been starved of funds. For instance, mining and basic industries such as steel could scarcely have attracted enough savings—dividends from investments in them would not have been high enough to do so. The fact that the remaining price controls applied largely to basic industries would have kept profit expectations down in this sector. Residential construction would also have been neglected as rent controls would have kept profits down. Not to supply cheap housing for destitute refugees was, however, socially unacceptable. Not to invest in sectors temporarily unprofitable but vital for future economic growth would have been shortsighted.

Therefore, for social reasons and to ensure future economic growth, the government intervened to supply and direct the flow of funds for investment. This government action was carried out on the federal, state and local level. A tight orthodox monetary policy kept interest rates high. With this was combined a complex and ingenious fiscal policy, largely implemented by tax exemptions. The often-heard argument that the high interest rates maintained by the Central Bank were the key to West Germany's growth is an oversimplification. It ignores the role of fiscal policy.

Thus, though West Germany had high *nominal* interest rates and high nominal tax rates, the selective tax measures softened their impact. One result of this was that for a long time bank rates were high but capital market rates were low. This was made possible by tax subsidies. Those sectors which were considered important for

the country's economic growth or in which investments were necessary for social reasons could obtain low-cost capital market funds. Other sectors had to pay stiff bank rates if they decided to finance investment externally.

How did it happen that the West Germans resorted to an extensive selective use of fiscal policy to further economic growth? The Allied occupational powers immediately after the war had substantially increased many tax rates, particularly on income, in the vain hope of stopping the mounting inflation. After the currency reform the West German government feared that the high tax rates would have a strong adverse effect on the economic incentives of capital and labor. The Allies, however, refused to allow a general tax cut, arguing that high tax revenues were essential to prevent inflation. In fact, they prohibited budget deficits by law.

As a result, the high tax rates, together with a broadening of the tax base due to rising incomes, generated large tax revenues. Moreover, "defense expenditures" (in the form of occupation costs) were relatively small, and as the national debt had been wiped off the slate in 1948, there were no interest charges on it. Thus, the public sector became an important supplier of funds for investment. If the West Germans did not save voluntarily, they certainly saved heavily through taxes.

Budgetary surpluses were used both for large direct government investments and for substantial loans and subsidies to private investors. What the precise criteria were for the allocation of these funds is not known, but the government clearly had a very effective means for selectively aiding various sectors of the economy and industries. In the period 1948–57, between 35 billion and 40 billion DM were used in this way. Residential construction, agriculture and industry all benefited from these public capital funds.

The tradition of public ownership in Germany facilitated this public capital formation. Government enterprises are much more numerous in West Germany than in the United States. Railroads and the telephone and telegraph systems are operated by the government, as are radio and TV stations. In addition, the government owns completely or in part numerous coal mines, power plants and manufacturing plants. For instance, the much discussed Volkswagen plant is partly public property. A recent study indicates that more than 14 per cent of all corporations are government-owned.

INFLUENCE ON INVESTMENT

But the role of government in supplying funds for investment went much beyond supporting public enterprises. Subsidies to housing under the "Social Residential Construction" program totaled about 21 billion DM between 1950 and 1957. Under the "Green Plan" low-cost credits were extended to agriculture. Under the "Investment Aid Law" in effect from 1952 to 1956 business in general was forced (not induced) to provide 1.1 billion DM for "bottleneck" sectors in industry. All of these programs provided low-cost funds for the private investments that helped to eliminate crucial shortages of capacity.

The influence of public authorities on investment was not limited to direct expenditures. After 1949 a large tax exemption program came into existence to promote investment. For, although West German tax authorities during the Allied occupation had no power to change the high personal and corporate income tax rates, they could grant tax exemptions. At a time when monetary policy was tight and tax rates

high, tax exemptions proved to be a very effective means of directing private investments into areas preferred by public authorities.

The tax exemptions granted under this program amounted to about 28 billion DM between 1949 and 1957. Below is a brief summary of the more important of these exemptions.

ACCELERATED DEPRECIATION

Under paragraph 7A of the income tax law introduced in 1948, capital goods (plant, equipment, etc.) acquired after January 1, 1949 could be depreciated up to 50 per cent in the first two years up to a limit of 100,000 DM per firm. Business made extensive use of this accelerated depreciation and applied tax savings to augment working capital. This measure probably cost the government about 1.3 billion DM between 1950 and 1957.

Paragraph 7B of the income tax law provided tax incentives for residential construction. In the first two years after the completion of a house, 20 per cent of its value could be deducted as depreciation. For subsequent years the annual depreciation allowance was three per cent. Thus in 12 years one could deduct 50 per cent as depreciation. The amounts deducted under this provision were substantial. They increased from 38 million DM during 1949 to an estimated 900 million DM in 1957.

Housing was favored not only by paragraph 7B but also by paragraph 7C. This provided that interest-free loans given for house building could be deducted as a business cost in the year in which the loan was granted. Later, when such loans were repaid in equal installments, the creditor had to report each repayment as taxable income. Between 1949 and 1957 about 3.5 billion DM were deducted in this way. This provision of the law was widely used to shift payment of taxes from years of extremely high profits to years with low profits or lower tax rates.

Under paragraph 7D, funds loaned for ship building could be declared as a business cost in the year in which they were granted. These loans were to be given free of interest and to be repaid after a stipulated time. After repayment the funds became taxable.

This provision seems to have provided a golden opportunity for corporations to avoid the tax collector and to establish an influence in shipping at the same time. A clever man could do a lot of things under this paragraph. West Germany was surprised in 1957 that a manufacturer of baking powder, through skillful use of this and other tax exemptions, had managed to build up a whole fleet of freighters. Probably 1.5 billion DM were made available under these provisions between 1949 and 1957. This helped, naturally, to rebuild West Germany's merchant marine.

Paragraph 10 of the German Income Tax Law had always allowed certain deductions for payments made to insurance, and building and loan associations. Contributions to these institutions were considered socially desirable and therefore tax-favored. Only individuals could receive these tax benefits. After 1949 the categories of personal savings which were considered socially desirable were considerably broadened. New forms of tax-exempt savings were introduced. Tax privileges were also granted if specific kinds of tax-exempt securities were bought. The provisions were complicated and changed from year to year. Banks would publish small booklets by tax experts that gave their customers advice on how to lower tax bills. Deductions made under these provisions constituted the largest budget losses. Between 1949 and 1957 they probably amounted to over 12 billion DM.

Finally, mention should be made of the "Investment Aid Law," the "Law to Favor Exports" and the "Capital Market Law." Deductions made under these laws between 1949 and 1957 probably amounted to 5.5 billion DM.

OVER-ALL PICTURE

Let us summarize the government influence on investment in order to get an over-all picture. Total West German net investment, domestic and foreign, between 1948 and 1957 was approximately 213.5 billion DM; of this, 92.8 billion DM, or 43.5 per cent, was directly supplied by the government. In addition, about 28 billion DM was "influenced" by government, through tax exemption. Thus, about 56 per cent of all net investment between 1948 and 1957 was influenced in one way or another by public preferences. This surely constituted a considerable interference with West Germany's alleged "competitive free market economy."

During the crucial first years of economic revival and growth, the necessary framework was re-established in which the market mechanism could function efficiently. The West Germans made sure that through public interference and guidance the allocation of resources into areas of shortage was facilitated. By 1955 the rapidly expanding West German economy was much nearer to a "free market economy" than it was in 1950.

But while government intervention rapidly increased the efficiency of the economy, the effects on income distribution were probably adverse. We have little precise information on personal income and property distribution during the postwar period. We do know, however, that profits were extremely high and that tax incentives benefited mainly those in the upper-income brackets.

There were, it is true, some factors making for a more equal distribution. The comprehensive West German Social Security System put a floor under low-income groups. In addition, a large program of partial compensation for war losses may have favored some of the low-income groups. There is good reason to assume that, on balance, the distribution became more unequal. Today, despite the general rise in incomes of all classes, income distribution in West Germany is probably more unequal than in Great Britain or the United States. If this is actually so— and it should be stressed that a lot of research is still necessary to throw more light on this subject—the social cost of the German "miracle" was not inconsiderable.

Of course, the West German economy, economic institutions and social environment are in many respects different from ours. Nevertheless, I believe that some of our problems have a marked family resemblance to West German ones. What lessons, then, can we learn from the West German experience?

Perhaps the most interesting lesson concerns the efficacy and use of *selective* economic policy measures. To the extent that many of our present economic troubles are of a structural nature which cannot be successfully tackled through general economic policy measures, this lesson has particular relevance for us.

Severe bottleneck problems exist or could come into existence here, as in West Germany—for instance, in education, research, housing, specific industries and urban redevelopment. Selective government expenditures or taxation measures may be the most effective means of eliminating them speedily. Their elimination through the working of the market mechanism may be too slow and may cause an undesirable degree of inflation.

The social cost of relying solely on the market mechanism could be forbidding. To illustrate, in West Germany the provision of housing for refugees was an essential first step toward rehabilitation. This could not be left to the market unless it was decided to exclude low-income receivers for a long time from decent housing. In addition providing housing in areas where labor was short facilitated the recruitment of a stable labor force. The problem was attacked and largely solved through selective government loans. (Between 1950 and 1957, 34 per cent of all funds used for residential construction were directly supplied by public authorities.)

To the extent that substantial shifts in the location of the U.S. labor force are necessary—and they may now be needed as a consequence of changes in the production or consumption pattern —they could be facilitated through selective government aid. This could take the form of providing retraining facilities, transportation and, if necessary, housing. (The Swedes, in their attempts to maintain a high level of employment, seem to have learned quite a bit from the West Germans in this respect.)

If we wish to increase capital formation to accelerate economic growth, we may think of using tax incentives for investments as the West Germans did. Accelerated depreciation and tax-exempt investment loans may be the answer. In West Germany these had a powerful boosting effect. However, if the U.S. granted such incentives, care should be taken that the right sectors of the economy get the benefits. (This problem seems to have caused the West

Germans some headaches.) Actually, it is difficult to be certain about the extent to which such selective tax measures could be applied in the U.S. Opposition to them could be quite strong on the ground that they were inequitable.

DESIRABLE BALANCE

If we wish to obtain a desirable balance between the needs of the public and the private sector, it may be necessary to increase public revenues by taxing less essential private expenditures. In West Germany there have been few complaints that the public sector has been neglected; rather the business community has complained that the public sector was too much favored and, in general, too large. Direct investments by public authorities have been very heavy and there is no sign that this sector is going to decline in importance. There is also no indication that the large public sector in West Germany retarded the country's growth.

Finally, to increase our exports, we may well consider the package of West German measures—discounting of bills for exports at low rates, tax rebates on exports and tax exemptions on investments in export industries. Some of these measures may be distasteful. Others may provide useful hints.

There is a growing consensus that many of our present economic problems require selective treatment. Such treatment was applied during the most crucial period of West Germany's economic growth. Further investigation of the selective measures employed by the government may throw some new light on the German "miracle"—which was, in fact, no miracle at all but the result of hard work, wise policy and a substantial amount of good luck. Moreover, such an investigation may provide us with new insights. There can be no doubt that the West Germans were and are strong believers in a free market system. But they were quick to recognize that there are many situations in which the free market forces must be aided and guided in order to facilitate structural adjustments and to generate a satisfactory rate of economic growth.